Collectanea De Rebus Hibernicis ...
- Primary Source Edition

Charles Vallencey

Vallancey, Charles.

COLLECTANEA

DE

REBUS HIBERNICIS.

VOL. III.

CONTAINING

WITH COPPER PLATES.

DUBLIN:

LUKE WHITE.

M,DCC,LXXXVI.

CONTENTS

OF VOL. III.

4. Kis

C O N T E N T S.

COLLECTANEA

DE

REBUS HIBERNICIS.

NUMBER X.

NUMBER X.

CONTAINING,

I. A Continuation of the BREHON LAWS; in the original IRISH, with a TRANSLATION into ENGLISH.

By LIEUT. COL. CHARLES VALLANCEY, L. L. D.
SOCIET. ANTIQ. HIB. ET SCOT. SOC.

II. The CHINESE LANGUAGE collated with the IRISH. By the Same.

III. The JAPONESE LANGUAGE collated with the IRISH. By the Same.

IV. On the ROUND TOWERS of IRELAND. By the Same.

V. An Account of the SHIP-TEMPLE near DUNDALK. By GOVERNOR POWNALL; in a Letter to LIEUT. COL. VALLANCEY, with some REMARKS. By the Same.

VI. Reflections on the HISTORY of IRELAND during the Times of HEATHENISM, with OBSERVATIONS on some late PUBLICATIONS on that Subject. By CHARLES O'CONOR, ESQ. SOCIET. ANTIQ. HIB. SOC.

VII. A LETTER from CURIO; with a further Explanation of the silver Instrument engraved and described in No. II. of the first Volume of this Collectanea.

ILLUSTRATED WITH A PLAN AND VIEWS OF THE SHIP-TEMPLE; AND A VIEW OF A ROUND TOWER.

DUBLIN:

PRINTED BY W. SPOTSWOOD,
PRINTER TO THE ANTIQUARIAN SOCIETY;
AND SOLD BY LUKE WHITE, DAME-STREET.

M DCC LXXXII.

TO

SIR JOHN SEBRIGHT, BART.

TO WHOSE MUNIFICENCE AND PUBLIC SPIRIT

THIS NATION IS INDEBTED

FOR

THE RESTORATION OF MANY OF ITS MOST VALUABLE

RECORDS OF ANTIQUITY;

THIS FIRST NUMBER OF THE THIRD VOLUME

OF THE

COLLECTANEA DE REBUS HIBERNICIS

IS DEDICATED,

BY

HIS MOST OBLIGED,

AND MOST HUMBLE SERVANT,

CHARLES VALLANCEY.

ERRATA.

Page 117, line 3d from bottom, *for* Canon *read* Saxon.
—— 120, law 81, *for* fluidhir *read* fuidhir.
—— 136, line 1, *for* Scythians *read* Scythias.
—— Do. —— 3, *for* Kamuc *read* Kalmuc.
—— 145, —— 19, *for* dupreme *read* supreme.
—— 159, —— 3 from bottom, *for* achon *read* cochon.
—— 168, —— 6, *for* Reim, Riogha *read* Reim-riogha.

FRAGMENTS

OF THE

BREHON LAWS

OF

IRELAND.

B

PREFACE.

I PRESUME not to think that I have given a proper tranſlation of the Laws of the ancient Iriſh. Ignorant of law terms in the Engliſh language, I have found it difficult in many places to expreſs the ſenſe of the original without circumlocution. A literal tranſlation has been attempted from the fragments, which conſiſt of ſingle ſheets of vellum, bound up without order, ſo that frequently a law, evidently ſome centuries more modern than the preceding, follows in this collection.

From theſe fragments it will appear, we have hitherto had no juſt idea of the ancient Iriſh. Some of their Laws ſeem to be a counterpart of thoſe of the *Goths* and *Vandals*, particularly what relates to the law of ſucceſſion called *Thaniſtry*. Some are evidently built on thoſe of the Germans, as recorded by Tacitus, and others reſemble thoſe of the Perſians, Gentoos, and the Oriental nations.

Mr. Richardſon, author of the Perſic and Arabic dictionary, and many other learned works, acknowledges that he was much aſtoniſhed to find *Arabic technically* uſed the code of *Gentoo Laws*.

My aſtoniſhment was much greater to find *Arab.* and *Perſic* terms in the *Iriſh laws:* and without the aſſiſtance of Mr. Richardſon's dictionary I could have made no progreſs in this work. The Iriſh and Walſh lexicons were of little uſe, as will

appear

appear by the *technical terms*, *titles* of *honour*, &c. &c. collated with the *Arabic* and *Perfic* in the following pages.

Pride of Blood, with the Irifh, contributed to the prefervation of writing and traditional hiftory: the word expreffing a code of laws, fignifies alfo genealogy, viz. Seanachas. Genealogy has therefore been cultivated with fingular attention, and is a ftudy fo intimately connected with hiftorical knowledge, that it is impoffible to arrive at any proficiency in the one, without being verfed in the other : Mr. Richardfon makes the fame obfervation of the Perfians.

The law terms of the Irifh correfpond furprifingly with the Arabic and Perfic; fuch among others are the following: *Soirceal* and *Saorgal* in Irifh is a feudal tenure in Perfic *Siyurghal*. *Bealac* a fief; the king's land, the king's high way; in Perfic *Beluk* is a fief; *Caithche*, lands given on condition of tribute; in Arabic *Ketiat*, receiving lands from a chief. *Aircineac* and *Athcharas* a fief; in Arabic *akahezet*. *Somaine* lands held on payment of tribute in cattle; in Arabic *Zaym* a feudal chief; *Ziyamet* a fief. Thefe and many other technical terms do not exift in the ancient Britifh language; from what people did the Irifh adopt them? From feveral of the lives of the Irifh faints, it appears they early vifited Afia; and their correfpondence with the Afiatick churches is further evident, not only from their following the Eaftern church, in the time of celebrating Eafter (and not the Roman, as may be feen in Bede and Ufher) but alfo from the names of the feftivals,

which

which are taken from the Eastern church. The antiquity of these laws is certainly prior to this, and it cannot be supposed these saints would introduce the Asiatick names for magick, sorcery, divination, &c. the practice of which was so common with the Heathen Irish.

The publication of such of the Breathamhan or Brehon laws of Ireland as have fallen into my hands, has been delayed in hopes of obtaining a sufficient number of manuscripts, so as to digest them under proper heads or chapters. *Sir John Sebright* has the greatest collection of these manuscripts; from the two first volumes I have transcribed the most part of what is in my possession. Sir John has generously bestowed this great collection of Irish manuscripts, containing 28 volumes to the college of Dublin; much time may yet elapse before they are deposited in the library of our University, and being pressed by my learned friends to communicate those laws, leisure has permitted me to translate, they are here offered to the publick.

As many technical terms contained in these laws, are not to be found in the printed Lexicons of the Irish language, it will not be improper to explain them in this preface, to which I have annexed such observations as have occurred to me in the perusal of other languages, particularly the *Oriental*.

By collating the technical terms in the Irish laws, with the Oriental dialects, I may be accused of yielding too much to the ancient historians of Ireland. It is now the general voice to condemn these writings as fabulous, and to deprive the Irish

of

of their *Fenius Farſi*, and their favourite *Aſiatick* origin. I ſhall beg the readers patience to liſten to what others have ſaid on the emigration of Eaſtern nations. Mr. Richardſon is a learned modern author, well ſkilled in Oriental hiſtories and languages; let his own words be my defence.

"The great *Officina gentium*, whence ſuch myriads of barbarians have at different periods poured into the more cultivated regions of the Earth, appears, with every probability, to have been *Tartary :* though our greateſt writers, following *Jornandez*, the Gothic, abridger of *Caſſiodorus*, have looked into *Scandinavia* and the northern parts of Germany for thoſe bodies of fierce warriors, who, in the early ages of Chriſtianity, overturned the government, and changed the manners of Europe. The Tartars, Scythians, or Turanians (under which general names the hiſtorians of different nations have comprehended the inhabitants of that immenſe tract, ſtretching from 53° to 130° Eaſt long.; and from about 39° to 80° North. lat.) have from the oldeſt times been remarked for a roving, irregular, martial life. People whoſe riches centered in cattle, who wandered for paſture from diſtrict to diſtrict, could in conſequence have no attachment to a ſpot. That *amor patriæ*, ſo conſpicuous in the Hottentot, in the Laplander, and in the wild inhabitant of every barren rock, has never been diſcovered in men of this deſcription. Attached to his tribe, and glorying in an extenſive line of anceſtors, the *natale ſolum* is to the Tartar an object of the moſt perfect indifference, and to abandon it in the company of his friends, a circumſtance cumftance rather of choice than regret. Thefe great outlines have accordingly marked the operations of this extraordinary people from the moft ancient times. Without thofe reftraints on matrimony, which are found in more civilized communities, their numbers had naturally a prodigious increafe; and as they defpifed the idea of cultivating the ground, the fame extent of country which could have maintained thoufands of hufbandmen, was found often infufficient for hundreds of roaming paftors. Emigrations alone could remedy this inconvenience. A celebrated warrior had only to proclaim, therefore, his intention of invading fome neighbouring ftate or more diftant country. He was immediately joined by the chiefs of many hords. Chance, oftener than defign, might fhape their courfe, to the South, to the North, to the Eaft, to the Weft, for every quarter of the globe has, at different times been the theatre of Tartar eftablifhment or plunder. The ancient annals of the Perfians are entirely employed in commemorating their numerous wars with the Turanians beyond the Gihon; China and Hindoftan have often felt their fury. Whilft Jengiz Khan, and Tamerlane, at the head of their bold and hardy fubjects, approached nearer to univerfal monarchy than any conquerors of ancient or modern times.

That the WEST muft have been the object of TARTAR invafion as well as the Eaft and South, there can be little ground to queftion; thefe people poffefs, as we may obferve, the whole interior almoft of the Afiatic and European continent. In

a con-

a conftant ftate of action and re-action, hiftory in—
forms us, that they have burft repeatedly upon
every adjacent country. Like fubterraneous va-
pours, when rarified beyond a certain degree, they
have at times acquired a great expanfive force, and
the violence of the explofion in one part, would
be generally in the ratio of the refiftance in others.
In the vigour of the Roman and Perfian powers,
they were often repulfed from their frontiers, but
they would not always return. Without fuccefs,
without plunder, that would have been an indelli-
ble difgrace. They might then have ftruck to the
Weft or to the North, where, finding countries
more thinly peopled; and the few inhabitants not
only ftrangers to the art of war, but unprotected
by fortified towns; the oppofition they might en-
counter, would in general be infufficient to check
their progrefs. Yet meeting with no rich fpoils in
thefe countries, which could give a fplendor to their
expedition among their countrymen, they would
often be induced rather to fettle in their conquefts
than to go back; and as there would be fufficient
territory for the invaders and the invaded, enmity
would foon give way to intermarriages and focial
intercourfe. The old inhabitants would adopt by
degrees fome of the manners and beliefs of the
eaftern ftrangers; and thefe, in return, falling in
with habits and ideas peculiar to the original people,
a few generations would naturally incorporate them,
and form in time thofe various nations, known by
the names of *Goths, Vandals, Lombards, Franks,*
whofe roaming, rapacious, Tartar genius, became
afterwards confpicuous, in the deftruction of the

Roman

Roman empire. No folid objection, it may here be obferved, againft thofe ancient Tartar invafions, can be built, upon the filence of hiftory; as this filence is the natural confequence of the unlettered manners both of the conquerors and the vanquifhed; and whilft the fhocks were too remote to be felt in the more civilized ftates of Europe, we cannot hope to find them in *their* annals. Tartary, China or Tonqueen, may poffibly, even in the prefent times, be the theatre of mighty revolutions unknown in Europe; and it is a moft undoubted fact, that Jengiz Khan, who fubdued almoft every country in the world to the eaftward of Euphrates, was dead many years before the accidental curiofity of Marco Paolo, who vifited the court of his grandfon Coblai Khan, in the year 1260, made Europe acquainted either with him or his dominions.

From the refearches and opinions of many northern antiquaries, the *Scandinavian Goths* are difcovered to have been early compofed of two diftinct bodies of people, the firft Aborigines; the other ftrangers; who are faid to have poffeffed a degree of refinement, civilization, and fcience, far fuperior to the older inhabitants. Frequent allufions are made to their ASIATIC ORIGIN. Their drefs, their manners, their language, being in general diftinguifhed by fome epithet defcriptive of fuperior elegance. It may poffibly be objected, that *Refinement* and a *Tartar* are ideas extremely repugnant, yet every thing of this kind is merely comparative, and the more favage inhabitant of the North, who never till then knew a luxury of

drefs

drefs higher than the fkin of an animal which he had killed, may eafily be fuppofed to have admired whatever was, even in a fmall degree, fuperior to his own. But, in fact, the drefs and equipage of the Tartar chiefs have ever been, in general, uncommonly fplendid, and few circumftances feem to have been lefs attended to by fome of our greateft writers, than a proper diftinction between the ruder and the more polifhed people who fill the immenfe extent of Tartary. Men totally diffimilar are grouped together, under one indifcriminate character, merely becaufe they are known in Europe by one general name; whilft, among their numerous nations, a difference of character may prevail, not inferior perhaps to that which marks an Englifhman from a Frenchman, a Hollander from a Portuguefe.

Every obfervation on the habits of thofe roving, daring people, ftrikingly difplays their love of liberty, and their fimilitude of character with the old *Gotbic nations*. Their averfion to culture, their paftoral life, their idlenefs, their eagernefs for plunder, and martial excurfion, with many *cuftoms* and *beliefs*, clearly *Eaftern*, form all together a chain of internal proofs, ftronger, perhaps, than direct hiftorical affertions. By many Northern writers they are actually diftinguifhed from the more ancient inhabitants of *Scandinavia*, by the epithet of *Orientals*; and nothing can furely approach nearer in refemblance than the original northern invaders of the Roman ftates, and thofe inundations, *immediately from Tartary*, who, under the names of *Alans*, and *Huns*, led by the famous

Attilla

Attilla and other bold chiefs, overwhelmed the Empire towards the close of the fourth century, and gave a final blow to the chains of Roman servitude.

The *Feudal* system (Mr. Richardson yet speaks) which was introduced and diffused over Europe by the *conquerors* of the Roman power, produced, in a civil light, an alteration in laws, government, and habits, no less important than the dismemberment of the empire by their arms. Our greatest lawyers, historians, and antiquaries, whose object has been less to trace its origin than to mark its influence, have uniformly attributed this great foundation of the jurisprudence of modern Europe, to the military policy of the northern nations; and seem in general, rather to have considered it as a consequence of their situation, after their conquests, than as existing, previous to their irruptions. It appears not only to have formed, however, their great system of policy before the grand invasion, but to have flourished in the *East*, with much vigour, in very early times.

In Persia, Tartary, India, and other eastern countries, the whole detail of government, from the most ancient accounts, down to the present hour, can hardly be defined by any other description. We observe, in general, one great king, to whom a number of subordinate princes pay *homage*, and *tribute:* all deviation from this system seeming merely temporary and accidental.

The rise and progress of the feudal system in Europe is marked, it was an *exotic* plant, and it has, of consequence, engaged the attention of our ablest antiquaries. But in the EAST it is indigenous,

nous, univerſal, and immemorial: and the eaſtern
hiſtorians have never dreamt of inveſtigating its
ſource, any more than the origin of regal government. Both have long been to them equally familiar, and the firſt extenſive monarchy gave probably a beginning to the firſt dependence of feudal
chiefs.

Every thing in the hiſtories of the Tartarian
princes, is indeed compleatly *feudal*. Before their
great expeditions, we find them iſſuing orders for
the attendance of their great vaſſals, with their
contingents of troops. And we alſo obſerve a *con-*
ſtitutional parliament or meeting of eſtates, who,
amongſt other privileges, claimed that of trying
great offenders. Diſſertation on the Languages, Literature, and Manners of Eaſtern Nations, p. 29, &c.

Mr. Richardſon publiſhed his Diſſertation in
1777; in the following year Monſ. Anquetil Duperron obliged the world with his *Legiſlation Orien-*
tale. Had theſe gentlemen ſtudied to have given
the picture of the Iriſh Brehon Laws, they could
not have done it to greater perfection; and the
pains they have taken to free the eaſtern nations
from *barbariſm* and *deſpotiſm*, by proving theſe
people to have had a written law, time immemorial, reflects honour on their humanity. At this
preſent time, that great luminary of eaſtern learning, Mr. *William Jones*, has in the preſs, *The Maho-*
metan law of ſucceſſion to the property of inteſtates, in
Arabick, taken from an ancient MS with a verbal
tranſlation and notes. This work will throw new
lights on the hiſtory of the eaſtern people.

Had the Iriſh received their feudal ſyſtem from
the northern nations, they would moſt certainly
have

have adopted the technical terms of the people from whom they received them. On the contrary we find every term flies up to the fountain head, viz. the Arabic or Perfic, which feems to indicate that fome colonies from the eaft, have fettled in Ireland, at a remote period; the ancient language of the people differing from all their neighbours, and having fo great an affinity with the Perfic and Arabic, ftrengthens this conjecture.

The Brehon laws of the ancient Irifh have been paffed over in fhameful filence by their hiftorians; they have been barely mentioned, but never tranflated or quoted. The late archbifhop Ufher fpeaks of them in his *Difcourfe fhewing when and how far the Imperial Laws were received by the old Irifh(a)*. The Irifh, fays he, never received the *Imperial Law*, but ufed ftill their own *Brehon-Law*, which confifted partly of the Ordinances enacted by their kings and chief governors, whereof there are *large volumes* yet extant in their own language. Yet the Brehons, in giving of judgment, were affifted by certain fcholars, who had learned many rules of the civil and canon law, rather by tradition than by reading; as by Sir John Davies is reported *(b)*. Although

(a) Printed in the Collectanea Curiofa, Oxford, 1781. Vol. i. p. 41.

(b) This report of Sir John Davies, arifes from this circumftance. Every *Filea* or royal poet, was obliged to learn by heart, the *Breatha neimh*, or Brehon law, in order to affift the memory of the judge. The *Filea* always attended the judge in court, and on being called on, was obliged to repeat the law referred to. In the *Seacht ngraidh Filea*, or academic rules

though for their ſkill in the canon law, Hannibal Roſſelli, the Calabrian, giveth unto them this teſtimony " *Olim homines illius Regionis plurimum intende-bant Juri Pontificio, erantque optimi Canoniſtæ (c)*."

At the head of one of the volumes in Sir John Sebright's collection is the following note.

As for old Iriſh Manuſcripts, I Thady Roddy, of Croſsfield, in the county of Leitrim, and province of Connaught, Eſq; have many Iriſh books of phyloſophy, law, romances, poetry, genealogies, phyſick, mathematicks, &c. and as ancient as any in Ireland. My honoured friend Roger O'Flaherty loſt a curious volume of mathematicks laſt war in Galway, which I lent him. Some of the ſaid books *were written Anno Chriſti* 15, in the reign of *Ferogh Fion Feaghtuagh*, who reigned then; ſome in the reign of *Cairbre Liffeachar*, who began his reign, Ann. Chr. 268; ſome in the reign of *Cormac mac Art*, Ann. Chr. 227.

As for Walſh manuſcripts, I ſaw none, except 18 letters in my cuſtody, before the war of 1688, being letters from the kings of Ireland to the princes of Wales, and from the ſaid princes to our kings and nobility, upon ſeveral occaſions. I have 30 books of our law, although my honoured friend
Sir

rules for the education of a *Filea*, it is expreſsly ſaid, that in the 4th year of his ſtudy, he ſhall repeat, in the preſence of the king and nobles, the *Breath neimh* or Brehon laws; and fifty poems of his own compoſition, or he ſhould not be entitled to the degree of *Cana*.——MSS vet.

(c) Roſſel. Comm. in Mercur. Herm. Iriſmegiſt, Pæmandr. & Aſcelp. tom. 5. p. 125. edit. colm.

Sir Richard Cox was once of opinion, that our law was arbitrary, and not fixed or written, till I satisfied him to the contrary, in summer 1699, by shewing him some of the old law books. We find some of our laws ordained by *Olim Fadig* or *Ollam Fadhla*, king of Ireland, who began his reign, A. M. 3883, before Christ, 1316, according to our calculation of 5199 from Adam to Christ, and so continued and augmented, as causes required, in the reigns of succeeding kings to the English invasion, Ann. Chr. 1169.

TECHNICAL TERMS EXPLAINED.

LAW. CODE OF LAWS.

Adh. agh. ach. ath.

This word is written either way, and implies the law human and divine: it is pronounced *Awe:* it is the root of the German *Ewa*, the Saxon *Ae*, and the Northern *Edda*: it is the root of the Latin *augeo, auctus, auctoritas: augeo, est etiam verbum sacrorum.* (Ainsworth.) Compounded with *eastoir* a defender, it formed the Latin *Augustus. Sanctius & reverentius est nomen Augusti.* Flor. l. 4. c. 12. *Augustus idem erat ac Sanctius.* Dio. Cass. l. 53. *Sanctum Augustumque. Constantius semper Augustus. Cic.* Compounded with the Celtic *reil*, i. e. established, it formed the Latin *Religio*, with *iodh*, i. e. worthy, meet, proper: it forms *Jodach, Judiach,* a Judge; *Judiacht, Juidicacht,*

Juidicacbt, Judgment; from whence the Latin *Judex*, *Judicium* (*Jodb* was also the insignia of office of a Judge, viz. a gold chain worn round the neck.)——It is the same as the Persic *agbasb*, recorded. *Yek* Persicè, and *yekk* or *iek* Arabicè, a law. *Iekyn*, Arab. the true faith. *Adbba* in the Turkish, the day of sacrifice at Mecca. *Ayac*, a Divan or Council in the Turkish.

In the Irish it forms *ban-acbt*, a blessing; *mal-acbt*, a curse. *Draoi-acbt*, *Druidism*, i. e. the religion or law of the Draoi or Magi: it is the Arabic *akudd*, a rule, mode, law; *abd*, a compact, contract, obligation, an oath, a vow, faith, security, a mandate, honour, respect, esteem, plighting faith; *abdet*, an obligation; *adet aad*, custom, mode, rite.——And lastly, it forms the English *awe*, *faith*, &c.

Airilleadh.

This word is derived from the Persic *Yerligb* or *Ierligb*, a royal mandate: it is the same in the Arabic and Tartar languages.

Adailgne.

The military law, compounded of *adb* and *ailgean* or *eilgne*, noble; Arabicè, *agblenta*, superior, conquering; Persicè, *alagb*, *ulugb*, great, powerful.

Bann.

Arab. *baia*, manifest; Perf. *Payendè*, a royal deploma; *band*, a code, a book.

Beterleach.

The old law, a name given also to the Lex Mosi, the Arabic *betarick*, i. e. Patriarchi.

Coir.

Coir.

The law human and divine, hence *Akoran*, or the great or holy law of the Mahometans.

Conradh, Coingiall.

Covenants between man and man.

Cadaigh, i. e. Cagaidh, i. e. Coir.

The law from the Oriental *Cadi*, a judge.

Arab. *Kydet*, a rule, regulation.

Coinreacta, Coindire, Coindleacht.

The law of Dogs, *Lex canum Venaticorum*, from *Con*, a hound or dog of sport.

Deachdadh.

From *deachd* or *diachd*, pious, holy, and *adb*, the law.

Dligheadh.

From *dligb*, perfect, excellent; and *adb* the law.

Deasad.

From *deasuim*, to correct. *Jasade*, with the ancient Indians, north of Indoftan, is a municipal law, (*un Code famille*,) which they say they received from Turk, fon of Japhet. See the learned work of Monf. Duperron, in his Legiflation Orientale, Amfterdam, 1778, 4to.

Perf. *Jasa*, a royal mandate.

Dinfheanacas

Of Din and Sheanacas.

Arab. *din*, faith, religion, cuftom, judgment, government, &c. See Seanacas.

Dior.

In the Arabic *derr*, a benefit, a good act.

Dual.

This word fignifies juft, meet, proper, duty, office; in Arabic, *delal* is a manifeftation, a herald,

C

rald, a public cryer; *delalet*, an Expofitor; **a**
guide; *delil*, a director, a demonftration; *dow-letlu*, in Perfic, moft illuftrious, happy.

Eigean.

Implies force, violence, compulfion; and alfo
lawful, rightful, juft; *igamet* in Arabic, is **to**
eftablifh; and *agawim*, tribes, nations.

Foras.

Signifies a law, age, and foundation; *foras-feafa*
is a hiftory; *foras-focal* an expofitor or etymologicon; in Arabic, *faryz* is aged, diftinct fpeech,
expofition.

Arab. *febris*, a canon, a rule, an index, fyllabus.

Fineacas.

This is the name of the moft ancient code of
laws, exifting in the Irifh; it has been explained
by fome Irifh writers by *fine-cuis*, the caufe of
the tribes, but כנקם *Finicas* in Chaldaic is *Tabula,
Codex*, a table or code of laws.

Leagh, i. e. al-agh.

The great law, hence the Latin *Lex*.

Irs. Iris.

Perfic and Tartar *iaza*, a law a code.

Naidhm. Naim.

Perficè, *namè*, a diploma, fpeculum, hiftory, as
Shah-namè, the mirror or hiftory of kings; *naam*,
Hebr. good; *naam*, the fame in Arabic; hence
the Irifh *naomh*, a faint.

Mòs.

Arab. *Muhazyr*. Pleading before a judge. *Mæs*,
important bufinefs.

Meis.

Meis.

Perſ. *muzd*, joyful tidings.

Arab. *meſnun*, a canon or rule ; *muſnud*, a king, an aſylum, a prop or ſupport ; *mes-rua*, preſcribed by law.

Ràn.

Perſ. *ran*, ſpeaking, explaining, pleading.

Riaghal, i. e. Ri-agh-al.

To govern by the holy law, a rule or government ; Latin, *Regula*.

Reachd. Reacht.

Compounded of *re* and *acht*, i. e. according to law ; Lat. *Rectum* ; or from the Arabic *rebk*, a good work ; *rebek*, tranſgreſſion of the law ; *reka*, eſtabliſhing peace.

Seanacas, Sanacas, Seanchus.

This ancient word for the laws of Ireland, has much perplexed the Iriſh Antiquaries and Etymologiſts. *Cormuc*, Archbiſhop of Caſhel, in the 10th century, thinks it a *Ceannfhochras*, or change of Letters, and that it ſhould be written *Fineacas*. I have ſhewn this laſt word to be Chaldaic, ſignifying a table or code of laws. A commentator of a fragment of theſe laws has thus explained *Seanacas*. " It implies, (ſays he) every " ancient cauſe ; *Seancas quaſi Senex cuſtodia*, i. e. " the regiſtry of ancient matters, i. e. *ſenſus* " *caſtigans*, the ſenſe of adjuſting every proper " thing in a proper manner : therefore *ſeancus* is " a term for every true ſcience, as for inſtance " *genealogies*, and *geneſis*, which is *ſeancus*, tho' a " book of laws. The prime laws of Ireland

C 2 " were

" were called *Feineacus*, perhaps from *Feine—*
" *chaoi—fhios*, i. e. the way of knowing the
" tribes of Ireland, for Irifhmen are called *Fenii*,
" from *Fenius Forfaidh*. The laws of Ireland
" always bore the names of *Fineacas* and *Seanacas*"
In the Cantabrian or Bafcuenza dialect, the name
of the old teftament is *Cinnacoa*, and the Lex Dei
is *jain-coaren*, (in Irifh *Shean-coiran*.) The old
Teftament in Irifh is named *Beterclach* and *Beter-
lach*, from the Arabic *Betarik*, i. e. Patriarchs.
In Arabic, *Seni* and *Sonna* is the law of *Mohamed*,
the *Alcoran*; *keza* is the decree, office and fentence of a judge; *kyfas* the law of retaliation;
kyft juftice, equity; confequently *feni-kyft* or *feni-
keza*, is of the fame fignification as the Irifh
Seanacas. *Senha* in Arabic, and *Sean* in Irifh,
fignify old, of long continuance; but feeing the
language of the ancient Irifh has fo great affinity
with the Arabic, I am of opinion that *Seancas*
is of the fame origin with the Arabic *Seni*. In
the Perfic *San* is law, right, cuftom—confequently
Seanacas and *Fineacas* are both proper names for
the ancient laws of Ireland.

Tora. Tara.

Chaldaicè *Thora*, a law; hence Tara, in Meath,
where the ancient Irifh held their triennial affemblies for the confideration and amendment of
their laws; it was alfo named *Teagh-mor*, *Tagh-
mar*, and *Tambar*, i. e. the great houfe, the palace, being the refidence of the kings. Arab.
Tekht, the Royal Refidence.

Tar.

Lex talionis. Arab. *tar*, *far*.

Tòic

Tòic Teaċta.

Per. *tocbra,* *fogbra,* royal diplomas.

Arab. *tawkyf,* appeal to the fovereign, as the fountain of the law ; *Towkia,* the royal fignet ; alfo judgment, opinion ; *Tek,* a diligent enquiry.

Per. *Taket,* cuftom, manner, &c.

A J U D G E.

Aighreire.

i. e. *Agb* the law, and *Aire* a chief.

Bearra, Beart, Breith, Breithamh, Breitheamhan, Barn, Buadhlann, Bualan.

Arabicè *barr,* beneficent, learned ; *bulend,* high, fupreme ; *belu,* to try, to examine ; *buliyan,* evidence, to call for evidence ; *barr,* juft, lawful ; Perficè, *berar,* a promoter of peace ; *berin,* high, fublime ; *bern, pern,* good, upright ; *barej.* moft worthy ; *perwanè,* a judge, the fentence of a judge ; Turcicè, *bailo.*

Buadhlan, Bualan.

Arab. *buu,* honour ; *lan,* full ; *Bub,* the fun, the fenfitive foul.

Ceada, Cadach.

Arabicè, *Cadi,* he judged ; *Kbudeck,* a judge.

Perficè, *Kbediou,* a benevolent man, a lord.

Bafc. *Cadoya,* a judge.

Turcicè, *Cadi, Cadbi,* a judge.

Deann.

Heb. *dan,* a judge.

Syr. *din,* he judged. Bafq. *din,* juft, right.

Arab.

Arab. *daian*, a judge.

Fragh.

Heb. *farag*. Arab. *afrag*.

Fithean.

i. e. *breitbeamb*, *vet. glofs. Cormuic*

Feighe.

Arab. *fekib*; Spanifh, *Alfagui*.

Arab. *fettab*, a judge.

Feitheadhoir.

Turcicè, *Fetfa*, the Mufti's affiftant; *Foujdar*, an officer of Indoftan, who takes cognizance of criminal matters.

Meifi

Arab. *mefbawer*, fenator; *mefbyeket*, feniors; *mufbir*, a fenator; *wezir*, a vizer; *wezi*, a guardian.

Ollamh re Lagh.

Sclavon. *Mifao*, a doctor of laws.

Arab. *ylm*, learned. The Arabic *Allam*, God, fignifies omnifcience.

Seift.

Arab. *Seis*, a governor, a public executioner.

Rachtaire, Reachtaire, Reachtmaor.

Compounded of *reacht*, law, and *aire*, a chief, and *maor*, a governor, director, &c.

German and Teuton, *rechter*, *richter*; Greek, *retor*.

Seift, Seifti.

Arab. *fais*, *feis*, a governor, a publick executioner.

Sclavon. *fuiteift*, the law.

Surathoir.

Surathoir.

> Compounded of *fur* or *faor*, which in all the Oriental tongues fignifies great, prince, &c. and of *atb* the law.

Tòcaire, Toictaire.

> From *toic*, law, judgment, and *aire*, a chief. See *toic*, *teacta*, under LAW.
> Arabicè, *Tekfit*, invefted with the robe.
>> *Tawkil*, a lieutenant, a deputy.
>> *Tawekkur*, refpected, honoured.
>> *Tawk*, power.

Bafcac.

> The judges Bailiff; Arab. *Bafgbak*, a governor, a præfect.

Riarai.

> Signifies a judge, any regulator of affairs.
> Arab. *raai*. judgment; *rai*, a rajah of the Eaft; *rai*, to judge, to determine; *rejrej*, a man without judgment.

SENTENCE. JUDGMENT.

Achd, acht, anacht.

> See *acht*.

Breath, Breith, Breithamhnas.

> See *Breith*, under the word JUDGE.

Breath-neamh.

> The code of laws; Perf. *Barnamè*, an edict, formula, canon, a bafis or foundation, a rule, regulation; *Peruanè*, fentence of a judge.

> > Bafal.

Bafal.

Perf. *bafb*, (fiat) be it fo ; *bafulcb*, an anfwer.

Arab. *befs*, publifhed, declared ; *baffbekb*, an anfwer ; *buzan*, judgment ; *bezul*, *bezla*, good coun-
fel ; *baz*, reftoration, exculpation ; *bezl*, ftudy,
care, clofe attention.

Càs, Cùis, Cios.

Arab. *kyfl*, juftice, a pair of fcales , *kyfas*, law
of retaliation ; *kefa*, the fentence of a judge,
fate, deftiny.

Codhaidh, cadhaigh, caghaidh.

See cada, a judge.

Dith.

Arab. *dyet*, the law of retaliation, an expiatory
mulct for murder, made by Mahomet's grandfather ; it was then fixed at ten camels.

Coigeart.

i. e. *coig-ceart*, *ceart*, juft ; *coig*, council; Lat.
Certus.

Dinn.

Perf. *dinunet*, judgment ; *dinur*, the day of judgment.

Eidirghleo.

I know not if *Eidir* here fignifies a ftate prifoner
on his tryal, or *eidir*, between ; as *eidir gbleo*,
would then fignify a complaint between two
perfons.

Arab. *gbelow*, a breach of the law, rebellion ;
gbelet, an error ; *gbell*, a crime ; *gela*, *kela*, guard-
ing, as God does man ; *kelou*, a tryal.

Perf *gelè*, a complaint brought before a judge ;
gbelij, an explanation.

Fiorfraighidh.

Fiorfraighidh.

From *fior*, truth, and *frag*, a judge.

Fughall, Fuigiall, Forroghall.

Arab. *farygh*, abſolved, diſcharged ; *fugham*, a a complaint ; *fukeba*, doctor of law ; *fukeh*, learned in the laws.

Meas.

From *Meiſl*, a judge ; *meas*, is alſo to tax.

Arab. *majlis*, a tribunal, in Iriſh meas-lis.

Riar, Riara.

See Riarai, a judge.

Arab. *reja*, an anſwer, reſtitution ; *rar*, diſcloſing.

Roſal.

Arab. *Riſalet*, the mandate of a judge, the gift of prophecy.

Reachtamhan.

See *Rachtaire*, a judge.

Reachdhaingneadh.

L E X   T A L I O N I S.

Camhad.

Arab. *Kawbed.*

C O U R T.   H A L L ᴏғ J U S T I C E.

Biolaid.   See Piolaid.

Cuirt Cheartais.

i. e. the Court of Juſtice.

Coindelgairt.

Coindelgairt.

From Coindealg, counfels.

Ceaduighe.　See Cada a Judge.

It implies alfo a feffion. Bafq. *Cadoi-teguia.* Irifh Cadai teagh, the Judges houfe.

Coifde.

Dr. O'Brien tranflates this word, a jury of 12 men to try according to Englifh law ;—it will appear by the following laws, that in cafes of difputed property, the ancient Irifh did alfo try by twelve men, whofe fentence muft be unanimous. *Coifde* is an original word implying a tryal by law, in many parts of Ireland it is ftill ufed in that fenfe as, *Cuirfidh me thu ar coifde.* I will bring you to tryal.

Sclavonicè, *Kuchja,* the hall of juftice.

Perficè, *Cucheri,* a code of laws (fee this word explained in Duperon's *Legiflation Orientale.)*

Moidhlis.

Arab. *Mejlis,* a tribunal.

Moid.

Arabicè, *Medaris,* a college.

Piolaid, Pioloid.

This word in old MSS. implies a royal palace, and a hall of juftice; it appears to be compounded of *Pill* and *ait,* i. e. the place or refidence of the pill.

Ara b. *bell, pil,* an elder, *bela* trying, examining, *pelus* poffeffed of general knowledge; *bili,* tryed, *bebelt,* a malediction, anathema.

Perf.

Perf. *belbar*, an ancient title of the Indian Princes, *pelbu*, warlike, *pelbuwan*, a hero; *peblèvi*, *peblaw*, an ancient Perſian, one of the Magi or Guebres.

Palàs,

Of the ſame derivation as the preceding.

Sclavonicè, *polaç od Sudac*; in Iriſh *Pàlas do Suidbtbe*, the court of ſeſſions.

Naàs.

Heb. *Naſia*. Præſes Senatorum The town of Naas in the County of Kildare took its name from the annual aſſembly of the nobles and judges of Leinſter to hear trials: it is remarkable that the ancient arms of the town are two Serpents, and that *Nabas* in Hebrew ſhould alſo be a ſerpent.

Nas now implies an anniverſary, noble, fame, an obligation, and alſo death.

Arab. *neſs*, appealing to the king; examination of evidence, manifeſto, the alcoran.

Perf. *Naſi*, empire, imperial dignity.

THE GENERAL ASSEMBLY OF THE STATES.

Tochomracc Tuaithe.

See *Toic*, under the word LAW.

Perf. *amrugb*, venerable, ſublime.

Arab. *amera*, princes, nobles; *amrag*, diſcourſing.

Tuaithe.

Of the nobles; *Tocbomracc* then implies a meeting of the nobles to deliberate on the Laws.

Cuireailte.

Cuireailte.

Compounded of *Cuire* a body of warriors, and *ail* noble.

Arab. *Kourlite*, a general meeting of the states.

S E S S I O N S.

Suidhthe.

Suidhe cuert, literally signifies a sitting, the court of seffions; hence the *Gorfedd* of the Walfh, i. e. *Coir-fuidhe*.

Sclavonicè, *Palac od Sudac*.

Flatha.

From *Flath* or *Flaith* a prince.

T R I B U T E. T A X. M U L C T. F I N E.

Bès.

Perf. *bazjb*, and *baj*, tribute, taxes, revenue; hence the Irifh *bafcac*, a bailiff, a collector of the revenue. See it under J U D G E.

Caraidhe, Caraghe.

Chald. *Caraga* tributum, cenfus capitalis.

Arab. *carga* exactio ; *kburaj* tributum.

Cain, Canach.

Chald. *chanona* ; Heb. *canas, cavit*, collegit.

Cios, Ciofcain.

Heb. *ces, kes, mekes*, an affeffed tribute ; Arab. *gizia, gaza* ; Perf. the royal treafure ; hence the French *accife*, and Englifh *excife* ; Arab. *kefas* lex talionis.

Cifte.

Cifte.

A royal treasury, pronounced *kifte*; *kifteoir* a treasurrer; hence *queftor* and *quæftor* the army treafurer of the Romans; Heb. *cefa, kefa,* a royal throne ; *kis* a purfe.

Cùs.

A corruption of Cios; Perf. *kuzit* a pole tax; *kuzied,* a tribute impofed by conquerors.

Cobhac.

Perf. *kebej.*

Caithce.

A tribute, and alfo a fine for trefpafs; Arab. *ketaa* price of ranfom ; *kawed* lex talionis.

Coir, Coire.

Arab. *kburaj,* tribute, tax, revenue; *kherj,* the fame ; *gbur,* the mulet for fhedding blood.

Ciontire, Cintire.

From *cain* and *tire,* the land, country, region, a tribute.

Cinemeas.

Of *cine,* a tribe, and *meas.* See *meas.*

Garama.

Arab. *gberam, gberamet,* a fine for bloodfhed.

Deachmad.

Implies a tenth part, a tythe.

Diofhochain.

A mulct paid for not marrying.

Eid.

Arab. *bedaya,* gifts, prefents; *bidd,* liberal; *buda,* an offering; *ada,* payment, fatisfaction; Perf. *idamal, idreri,* a tribute.

Farba.

Farba.

Chald. *farb.*

Earc, Eiric.

Perf. *arifb*, this word particulary means mulct for man flaughter, and fo does the Irifh *Eirce.* Perf. *iarè*, tax, revenue.
Sclav. *barac, barac çarrina*, tributum Zarinæ.
Turk. *burai*

Irifeat.

This rather means a free-will offering; Arab. *arzet.*

Meas.

Chald. *mas*; Syr. *mas*, contributio; Arab. *muh-effyl*, a collector of the revenue; *maas*, a debt fought after; Bafq. *gainte-maitza*, tributum familiæ; in Irifh *Cinte meafta.*

Millein.

The fevereft of fines.
Arab. *melun*, excommunicated; *melum*, accufed, guilty; *mawl*, giving away ones property; *meyelan*, refpect to fuperiors.

BE IT ENACTED.

Bla.

Arab. *bela.*

Blach.

Of *bla* and *ach*. See *ach* under LAW.

Blachard.

Of *bla, ach,* and *ard,* excellent; hence the Greek πλακι, the Spanifh *placarte,* and French *placard*; Sclav. *vlaft, oblaft.*

Deachta,

Deachta, Deachracht.

See thefe words under LAW; hence the *decretum* of the Latins.

Feithfa.

Turcice *fetfa*,—apply to the Mufti to have his *fetfa* or decree. Legiflation, Orientale, p. 59.

Olar, Oldas.

The fiat of the judge. See thefe words explained under *Secretay of ftate*.

PLEADINGS. TO PLEAD.

Aidhnim, aighnim, aghnaidhfam.

To plead.

Aghanidhe.

An advocate, a pleader; Perf. *aghayen*, learned men; great lords.

Aghnas, aighneas. Pleadings.

Perf. *agahaniden, agahiden*, to inform, to announce, to certify, to indicate; *ada* eloquence; Irifh *nim* to do, to make. Perf. *aghai*, notice, anunciation. Arab. *aghna*, fpeaking for another, fupplying his place.

HOMAGE. PROTECTION.

Eineac, Eineacus, Eineaclan.

A fine or tribute paid by the feud or vaffal for his protection, for permiffion to fettle under him. Arab. *anak, inak*, fafety, fecurity, protection.

Dire.

The fame as Eineac; Arab. *derb*, protection; Perf. *deri*, a fixed habitation.

Seath.

Seath.

Arab. *Sakai*, foreign; *fakin*, quiet, firm, fixed, an inhabitant; *Sukbur*, whatever is done from courtesy.

Miodhbhaidh.

Arab. *mubebbet*, friendſhip, benevolence.

Mac Faoſma.

Sons of Feudatifts under protection of the Fla. Arab. *feza*, taking refuge; Perſ. *fawz*, refuge, freedom, ſafety.

TITLES OF HONOUR.

KING, PRINCES, NOBLES.

Aire, airigh, aireach, arar.

Arab. *Arba*, noble tribes, chiefs; *Araknet, aras*; *Irak*, a chief, prince, foldier; *Herar*, of noble birth; *ayar*, a prince; *beri*, worthy; *erik*, a throne; *urek*, root, origin, ftock, moft worthy; *aryk*, of noble blood. Baſq. *Erregue*.

The Iriſh had nine degrees of nobles, viz.

 1 Aireac-foirgill,

 2 Aireac-treiſu,

 3 Aireac-ard,

 4 Aireac-deſa,

 5 Bo-aireac, this is the Boyard or noble of Walachia, ard and aireac are the ſame. See Ard.

 6 Oc-aireac,

 7 Triath,

 8 Airec Trithar,

 9 Ri.

Mr. Shaw,

Mr. Shaw has omitted the *Triath* and the *Aireac Triathar*. In an ancient glossary, it is said, Oenac n'Airc Treithar, 1. biadh, 7. edach loghmhur: cluimh, 7. coilceadh; brannuibh, 7. fithchealla; Eich 7 carbaid: miolcoin, 7. eisreachta, i. e. the magnificence of an Airec Triath, conconfists in good living and rich apparel, feather beds and quilts, chess boards and bagammon tables, horses and chariots, in hounds and in the number of orphans he maintains. Arab. *bink*, *bunk*, prosperity, wealth, munificence; *brannuibh*, rather means the men; *gon a brannaibh dead*, with his ivory Chess-men.

Atach.

Arab. *atik, atat*.

Aite.

Chinese *Aite*, the king or hero at Chess.

Agha, Oigh.

Heb. *agab*, mouere bellum. Perf. *agha*, a lord, a prince, a ruler; Kalm-mogal, *Aca*. Turc. *Aga*.

An, anach.

Arab. *anak*.

Adonnath.

Heb. *adoni*.

All, oll, ail, ull.

Heb. *el*, magnus, potens, Deus, *ull*, robur.
Arab. *all*-God, hence *alibet*, the sun; *illu*, lords.

Bar.

Perf. *Pir*; Arab. *Bebr*, Behrai, fit for the administration of publick affairs.

Ban-righean.

A queen; Perf. *banu*, a princefs.

Breas.

Perf. *beruiz*, *barviz*, i. e. victorious; *beras*, per-fection.

Breafach.

Perf. *Parfbek*, honourable, brave, bold.

Bruigh, Brui.

The *Brui* was the loweft rank of nobility; lands were affigned by the king for the fupport of the Bruigh's houfe, into which he was obliged to receive and entertain all travellers, as is fully expreffed in the laws.

Arab. *burj*, hofpitality, eating and drinking plen-tifully; *burji fberef*, the higheft degree of nobi-lity.

Perf. *berkb*, abundance, power, authority; alfo a low price put on provifion by edict of the ma-giftrate. *Burkendam*, a carnival.

Bal, Fal.

Perf. *Val*. Phœnicè, *Bal*.

Arab. *faal*, nobility, grace, excellence; *Wali*, the fame.

Borom, Boromh.

A king, monarch. This title was taken by the great *Brien*, monarch of Ireland, in the 11th cen-tury.

Perf. *Behram*, a king, a fword. The name of feveral kings of Perfia, and of other kingdoms in the Eaft; corrupted by the Greeks into that of *Varanes*. See Richardfon's Perfic Dictionary at Behram.

Caibhir,

Caibhir, Caith.

Perf. *Kabir* ; *Kebya*, a vicegerent.

Caidhni.

A Queen. Arab. *Kdyn.*

Car, Coraidh, Curadh.

Perf. *Gerr*, power ; *kurubè*, head, chief.

Arab. *Kir*, a lord. Greek κυριος.

Cuthadh.

Perf. *Kutbuda.*

Codaman.

Per. *Khudawend*, a king, a lord.

Cathal.

i. e. Charles, Warlike. Arab. *Kytal*, a battle ; *kettal*, a foldier.

Codhnac.

Arab. *Kenn*, a defender, *Kubun*, a prieft.

Perf. *Kundawer*, a hero ; *Kenek*, a cock.

Ceann, Keann, Conn.

Khan, the title of the Eaftern princes.

Donn.

Heb. *adon.* Arab. *din.*

Eile.

Signifies not only a king, a lord, but alfo his people, his country ; it is alfo a name of God, of adoration ; hence Eile ui Fhogurta, and Eile ui Chearabhail in the county of Tipperary ; Cnoc Eile the hill of adoration. Arab. *Ebl*, a lord, mafter, people, fpoufe, family, pious, God.

Fo.

Chinefe, *Fo.* Arab. *fowj*, a body of troops ; *fawk*, fuperiority ; *fatyb*, a conqueror.

Mal,

Mal, Malc.

Heb. *melk*.   Arab. *mulk*, a king.

Fal, Flath.

Arab. *wali*; noble; *felab*, victorious.

Mor.

Arab. *Mar*, a lord.

Neimh, Neimhid, Naomhid.

Nobles: it also signifies holy, bright, Heaven; and frequently occurs in the laws in these meanings; hence *Breith neimh*, the title of the Brehon Laws we are proceeding to.   Arab. *namus*, law, dignity; *naymma*, hail, excellent; *numan*, the name of the kings of Hyra, in Arabia, i. e. of blood royal.   Perf. *namè*, illustrious, *namebdud*, immense; *numud*, a guide, august; *namè*, a history, work, writing, mirror, speculum, hence *namè*, a title to most books in the Persic language, as *Shah namè*, the history or speculum of kings, &c.   *Nemaz*, prayers: it is also applied to the mass of the Christians in Persia. N. B. *Nemed* is the name of the Scythian leader, famous in Irish history, for colonizing this country, 630 years after the flood.

Ri, Righ, Rac.

King; Copticè, *Rys*.   Heb. *Rechus*, rich, powerful.

Arab. *Rik*, power; *Ray*, a protector; *Rajab*, title of honour of the Hindou princes; *Raas*, noble; *Rett*, a prince.

Ris.

A king; Heb. *Rosh*, a prince, a head.

Ruire,

Ruire, Ruidhre.

Perf. *Rad*, great, powerful.

Guaire.

Perf. *Gober* of a noble family ; *Al Gober*, the great Mogul, *Shab Allum*.

Raicneach.

A Queen.

Seaghlan, Seigh, Seighion, Seic.

Perf. *Sikender*, Alexander, two princes of this name are much celebrated in the Eaft. The conquefts of Alexander are celebrated in many Perfian, Arabic, and Turkifh hiftories, under the titles of *Sikender namè*, i. e. the book of Alexander ; *Aineb Ifkenderi*, i. e. the mirror of Alexander, &c. &c.

Arab. *Shekib*, a prince ; *fekba*, munificent, prince-ly.

Perf. *Sek*, terror, hence our Irifh *Seaghlan*, full of terror ; *Shebnè*, a viceroy ; *Yegbyr*, a king.

Schor, Sabh, Suidh.

Hence *Ufcor*, one of the ancient famous military heroes of Ireland, from whom the hill of Ufgar in the county of Limerick.

Arab. *Sharif*, noble.

Perf. *Shab*, a king, a fovereign, an emperor, a prince, a monarch. N. B. The king at the game of Chefs was called *Schor* in Irifh, and *Shab* in Perfic.

Arab. *Sabeb*, lord, governor, chief.

Perf. *Shabbaz*, royal, nòble, brave, *Shapour*, a king of Perfia, called by the Romans *Sapores* ; *Shebi*, a king ; *Seidi*, a lord ; *Yefir*, an emperor.

Saor.

Saor.

Arab. *Saur*, a prince.

Tonn.

Arab. *Tuwan*, power, valour.

Perf. *Tuwana*, omnipotent; hence the Peruvian *Tonus*, the fun; *Ton* the moon, which alfo implies fovereignty. See preface to the Japonefe language, in this number of the Collectanea.

Tor.

Perf. *Tar*, head, chief; *Tir*, magnificent, elevated.

Tuirighin.

Arab. *Turkhan*.

Tierna, Tighearna.

Heb. *Toran*, *Tironia*.

Torc, Torcan.

Arab. *Turkhan*.

Triatha, Triathar.

Perf. *Turaj*, conquering; *Teratur* noble; *Tra*, magnus.

Arab. *Turtur*, a king's officer; *Teref*, noble.

Armenicè, *Tir*, valdè. Græcè Σατϱ.

Tuis, Taofeac, Tuifeach.

This is a very ancient word.

Chin. *Tfu*, *Tchi*.

Kalmuc Mongul, *Taifhi*.

Tar. *Tfchaufchs*.

Moldav. Walach. *Chaufchs*.

Turc. *Tifchabi*, *Patifchabi*, or *Padifba*, king, emperor.

Arab. *Taafil*, noble.

Perf.

Perf. *Tajdar*, a king; hence *Tazi*, an Arabian'; hence the family of *Mac-an-Taois*, written Mac Intofh.

Tanaifte.

The prefumptive and apparent heir to the Prince. The word originally fignifies fecond, as in this example, *is giorra ro mbair an cèd tanaefte don ledradb fin, na an cèd toifinac,* i. e. the fecond hundred champions were fooner killed than the firft hundred. Chaldaicè, *Tanain*, Secundus.

Uais.

Noble. Arab. *Azz, Weza; Wazia,* a king, a prefect.

TITLES OF HONOURS.
CHIEFS, HEROES, WARRIOURS.

Amhra, Amhragh.

Arab *Amera, umera.*
Perf. *Emrugh—Yawer*, victorious.

Arufc.

A lord; Arab. *Arfb,* the royal throne; *aryz,* noble, rich.

Aghach, agfal.

Heb. *agaftes*, præfectus. See *Agba.*

Ainmeneach, aimneach.

Arab. *Hammami,* heroic.
Perf. *Humaiun,* royal, fortunate.

Ardamhan.

Of *ard,* and *bumaiun.* Perf. *ardavan,* the name of feveral princes of ancient *Perfia, Media, India,* fuppofed to be the *Artabanus* of the *Greeks.*

Ardachdach.

Ardachdach.

Of *ard*, and *achta*, or *achda*, victory.

Ard, art.

Heb. *ard*. Perf. *ard*, illuftrious, moft excellent, omnipotent; hence in Irifh *Art*, God; hence *Sagadbart*, *Sagart*, a prieft, from the Hebrew and chald, *Sagad*, to adore, to worfhip, and *art*, God: From this compound is formed the Greek and Latin *Sacerdos*. *Ird* and *Ard*, was the name of the angel fuppofed by the ancient Perfians to prefide over religion. Hyde Relig. Vet. Perf. p. 265.

Afcath, afcari.

Arab. *afkir* an army; *afkery* a foldier.

Afion, afin, ofin.

Arab. *Afin*, of illuftrious defcent, hence *afion* in Irifh a crown, a diadem. This is the title of the famous *Offian*.

Buadhaire, Buadharg.

A champion, a victorious hero, from *buaidh*, victory, and *aire* a chief, or *arg* plundering, &c. Perf. *behader*, a foldier, champion, hero, a chevalier, knight, horfeman. *Behader* forms part of the titles of honour conferred by the great Mogul, and other Eaftern potentates upon the Nabobs and other great men, bearing fome refemblance to the European title of military knighthood, as, *Omdatu' l'mumalik*, *eftenbaru' l'mulk*, *kumru'd' dowla Mohammed Khan*, *Behader*, i. e. the pillar of Empires, the glory of the kingdom, the full moon of the ftate, Mahommed Khan, the Brave.

Ballardach.

Ballardach. See Ball.

Barramhuil.

Of *barr*, and *ambuil*, i. e. fimilis. See Barr.

Beine.

Arab. *Behnes*, ſtrong, a lyon.

Perſ. *Bibin* excellent, *bin* the ſame, *ban* a lord; of good blood.

Bean-uaſal.

A gentlewoman; madam.

Bantierna.

A lady. Perſ. *Banu* a princeſs. See Tierna.

Brian, Briar.

Of *Bri* ſtrength, and *an*, *ar*, in him, on him; hence the Latin *Briarius*, and the family name *Brien* in the province of Munſter.

Perſ. *Bri*, *Bari*, God, omnipotent, true: *Berin*, high in dignity: *Barej*, beſt, moſt worthy.

Buarg, buadharg.

From *buadb* victorious. Arab. *Bahir*, victorious.

Berayar, nobles. Perſ. *pur*, *bur*, a king in Hindoſtan, whence the name of king *Porus*, who was defeated by Alexander.

Cadar.

Arab. *Kadyr*.

Cniocht.

A ſoldier, a knight. Arab. *Kiyanet* a protector. Sclav. *Knetz*. Perſ. *Nacht*.

Cing, king.

Arab. *Kingbal* a hero.

Dearſgaidh.

Perſ. *Dar* a lord, *Dara* a ſovereign. See *Scath*. *Dereje*, honourable.

Duine-

Duine-uafal.

    A Gentleman, fir. Arab. *uful*, a good man.

Dos.

    A gentleman, it is alfo a poet of the fifth clafs.

Ealg, ealc.

    Arab. *alc* high, *abil* an emperor, *balic* high, fub-
    lime, unde Helicon mons.

Eac-faor.

    A knight, a cavalier. Perf. *yekfewar*.

Earla, Iarla, Iarlamh.

    Perf. *Iar, yar*, a defender, protector; *lamb* the
    hand; this is the root of the Englifh title *Earl*.

Err, Irr.

    Perf. *Irr*, triumphant.

Farranta.

    Arab. *Furanis*, a chief, *Firend*, a fword.

    Perf. *Firawen* oppulent, *Faneften*, to excel.

Faris, farfa.

    Arab. *Faris* a horfeman, a cavalier.

Gaifce, gaifgidheach.

    Arab. *Gbazi* a hero, a conqueror, a general.

Guaire.

    Arab *Gberra*, noble.

    Perf. *Guwarè, Gober*; *Ali Gober* the title of the
    prefent prince or great Mogul, *Sbab Allum*.

Gnodh.

    Perf. *Gunda* learned, wife; *gundawer* a hero;
    gun, kun, a deftroyer.

Gorm.

    Perf. *Gbairm* invincible; *gburm* venerable.

    Arab. *Kurem*, honourable.

                                     Grata,

Grata, Gratan.

Arab. *Gburret* a lord, a chief of a people, maſter of a family, moſt excellent.

Graib, Angraibh.

A warrior, hero, conqueror; from this root are derived, *Graibbri*, titles of honour; *Graf* a battle; *Grafinn* a batalion, plur, *Graftuinn*, battalions; hence *Cnoc-Graffan*, one of the royal houſes of the ancient kings of Munſter, in the county of Tipperary.

Chald. *grab*, to lay waſte, to plunder.

Heb. *agraf*, a conflict.

Arab. *garfa*, a conflict.

Perſ. *giriften* to take, to ſeize, to overcome; *gurbur*, invincible, robuſt; *cherb*, *jerb*, a conqueror.

This is the root of the German *Grave*, *Graven*, *Landgrave*; titles of honour, ſignifying hero, Warrior, conqueror.

Irr. See Err.

Laoc.

Perſ. *Yeluk*, *ieluk*, a hero, a warrior, athletic.

Arab. *Laik*, worthy, able, qualified, deſerving honour; hence the Etruſcan *Lucu-mone*, Rex, Dux (in Iriſh *Laoc-moin*) the great hero.

Marcſcal.

A cavalier, *marc* a horſe. See *Scal*.

Mordha. See Mor.

Moralac. See Laoc.

Maſglac.

Arab. *Muzbek*, the deſtroyer, *mas* important; *maaſr*, illuſtrious; *muſlekym*, proud, haughty.

Nodh,

Nodh, Nothac, Nois, Nafadh, Neafa.

Arab. *Nafyb* a faithful minifter; *nafyr* a defender; *najib* profperous.

Perf. *Naz*, beneficent; *nafi* imperial dignity; *nadiret* incomparable.

Natha, Nathan.

Arab. *Neta*, noble, illuftrious.

Nuall, Nuallan, Naill, Neill.

Arab. *Niyu* warlike, *al* great; *nal* liberal, *neil* obtaining, conquering; *nalit* acquiring good.

Oirdheirc.

Arab. *Erakbinet*, princes, chiefs.

Perf. *Ardefbir*, the Artaxerxes of the Greeks.

Onòrac.

Seoid.

Arab. *jedd*, dignity, glory.

Seric.

Perf. *Serkar* a chief, a fuperintendant.

Scal, Sgal.

Arab. *Sykal*, horfemanfhip. See *Marcfcal*.

Sbawkel infantry; *Sbekbel* a youth, which is alfo the meaning of the Irifh *fcal*; *chebl* a chief.

Seitce.

A lady; Arab. *Seyidet*, a lady; Perf. *fitti*, my lady.

GENERALISSIMO of the ARMY.

Siphte, Sibhte.

Arab. *Zubte* Mahomet, the firft of men; *Sibat* lyons.

Perf.

Perf. *Sipab*, an army, cavalry; *fipabi*, military, chief of a town; *fipeban*, a king; *fipebbed*, emperor, general; *fipebdari*, commander of an army.

Moldavian and Valachian, *zaptzi*.

Tuarcnach-Catha.

Arab. *Turkban*, a prince; *catb* in Irifh, is a battle, a warrior; Arab. *Kaw* warlike.

P L E B S.

Brafgan.

Perf. *Berezgan* fervants, the common people.

Bodach.

Arab. *badi*.

Cudarman.

Perf. *kbydemetkar* a fervant.

Codromach.

Kburd-murd, trifles; *Kbud-rui*, ill-difpofed, rude.

Arab. *Kutret*, worthlefs.

Difgar.

Arab. *Dejaj, Dejr*.

Fleafgaigh.

Gramfgar, Gamfgar.

Perf. *Gumer*, a peafant; *Gbumkufar*, affociates, companions.

Pubal.

Tur, Tair, Tuirean.

Arab. *Turr*.

Treab.

A tribe: Arab. Perf. *Tebar*.

EMBAS-

EMBASSADOR.

Taibhligheoir.

> Arab. *Tebligh*, fending letters of compliments; *Tebjilet*, ceremonies, compliments.

SECRETARIES of STATE.

Eimide.

> Arab. *amadè*, made clear, refolved, prepared, difpatched.
>
> Turc. *Emini Phetva*, the truftee of Phetva has the keeping of the law papers given by the Mufti's clerk; thefe he firft collects, confiders them and fometimes advifes or fuggefts to the *Mufti* what ought to be anfwered, who at length decides the whole matter in one word *olur*, fo let it be; or *olmaz*, it muft not be; in Irifh *ol-ar*, *ol-das*. See the 30th Law in the following pages.

ROYAL SECRETARIES.

Foicljth.

> See *Fo*, under titles of honour.

Foidhbhcin.

Rùngraibhtheòr.

> From *Rùn*, and *Graibhim* to write.

Rùncleireach, Ruinreathoir.

> From *Rùn* a fervant, and *Cleireac* a clerk.
> Perf. *Ruywanè* veiling, hiding. Arab. *Rein* fealing up, concealing.

Urfoiclith.

Doctor O'Brien has miftaken the meaning of the word *Rùn* in Olaus Wormius *De literatura Runica.* According to the Doctor the *runæ* or writing of the Gothic Heathen priefts is derived from the Irifh Rùn, a fecret or myftery. Wormius certainly knew that *girunu* in the Saxon Tongue was myftery, Anglo-Sax *gervnze*, and Gothicè *runa*, myfterium; he certainly underftood his own language, and he would alfo have found it in the Gothic dictionary. But this did not fatisfy Wormius, and with great reafon, for there was no myftery or hieroglyphic intended by the priefts, who expofed their writings on monuments which ftill exift.

The Gothic *rùn*, a letter or character, is derived from the Arabic *runa* a found, becaufe fuch characters conveyed the found of the voice by naming them. The Arabic *rùn* implies more efpecially a mufical found, and *runum* is fongs, hymns; from whence the Irifh *ràn* and *oràn* a fong, and from this root is alfo the Irifh *ruine* a ftreak, a mark, or fignature, expreffive of a particular found or meaning.

Urfoiclith.

MARRIAGE. DOWER.

" Pofadh.

" Corrupted from *Bofadh*, fays Dr. O'Brien, in
" his Dictionary, is the only word in the Irifh
" language to fignify *marriage*. The Spaniards
" have no other word to fignify the conjugal con-
" tract but *cafamiento*, which literally means
" *houfing*,

" *houfing*, or taking a feparàte houfe to raife a
" family, *efta cafada*, fhe is houfed or married,
" from *cafa*, a houfe. But the Irifh word *bafadh*
" or *pofadh*, fignifying the conjugal contract, is
" borrowed in a more natural way from a mate-
" rial ceremony that is in the actual exhibition of
" the dowry, which confifted in nothing elfe but
" cattle, and more efpecially cows, *boues & fræna-*
" *tum equum*, as Tacitus fays of German portions;
" fo in Irifh, *bofadh* is to be endowed with cows,
" from *Bo*, a cow. The word *Sprè*, i. e. cattle,
" is the *only* word to fignify a woman's marriage
" portion. The men of quality amongft the old
" Irifh never required a marriage portion with their
" wives, but rather fettled fuch a dowry upon
" them, as was fufficient maintenance for life, in
" cafe of widowhood; and this was the cuftom
" of the German nobles and of the Franks.

" Pofda, Pofga.

" Married, joined in wedlock. Thus the Doc-
" tor."

It is not probable that a people, defcended in a
direct line from a nation which contefted its antiquity and knowledge with the Egyptians; a
people who fpeak the moft ancient language of
the Univerfe, replete with fcientific terms,
fhould adopt a name for a moft facred ceremony,
from a few cows given accidentally as a wife's
portion. I fay accidentally, for the Doctor allows
the rich required no portion with their wives;
then what was the name, fignifying marriage,
with the rich?

Whoever

Whoever reads Tacitus with care, or will turn to the learned Dr. Gilbert Stuart's *View of Society in Europe* (where he will find the fenfe of Tacitus more fully explained than in any other author) will be convinced that in remote times, no portion was given with the wife: And the following Laws of the ancient Irifh declare the fame. It is true, in later days, a portion was demanded and given; but fuch laws relating thereto, are evidently of modern date.

The name of the conjugal ceremony with the ancient Irifh was *Bod*, *Bad*, or *Bud*, a word which now indecently fignifies the *membrum Virile*; hence the Spanifh *Bodas*, *Boda*, a wedding; the etymology not known. See *Covarr*, and the Spanifh Lexicographer *Pinedas*. *Bad* was the name of the angel, fuppofed by the ancient Perfians to prefide over wedlock. "Viceffimus fecundus dies eft *Bad*, idem qui Indo—Perfis et Gilolenfibus vocatur *Ghuad*, fee *Gowad*, qui Famulus τῦ, *Churdad*. Cumque *Bad*, fignificet *Ventum*, hoc cenfetur nomen Angeli qui præeft *Ventis*, atque *Connubio et Matrimonio* et conductui omnium rerum quæ fiunt hoc die. Hyde Relig. Vet. Perf. p. 264." From the old Perfic *Ghuad* is derived the Irifh *Coidhe*, chaftity, and the vulgar *Coidèas*, the *pudendum muliebre*.

Pofadh and *Pofta* are derived from the Perfic *puyus*, a bride, derived from *puyweft*, joined together, attached, connected, from the verb *puyweften*, to bind. A wife in Perfic is *Sahybet*, *Sahye*, *Sahybet*, from whence the Irifh Seite, Seiteach, Seitche, a wife. Thus it is evident *Pofadh* (wedlock) has

E

no more to fay to *Cows* than to *Bears*. The Perfian *Pyk*, a bridegroom, has given the Irifh vulgar name *bioc* for the *membrum virile* : thefe tranfitions are common in all languages: from the Irifh *bri*, fortis, ftrong, and *bich* or *pos*, is formed the word *Priapus*.

Nuar or Nuathar is another Irifh word for marriage; Perfice, *newa*.

Doctor O'Brien has committed the fame miftake in the Spanifh language, here he is more excufable; Pinedas, the Spanifh Lexicographer, had deceived him by the following explanation : *Cafa*, a houfe, a family, and immediately follows *cafada*, a wife, *cafada*, the original or the rife of a family; *cafamentàr*, to marry; *cafamiento*, a wedding; which are all marked as of unknown etymology. *Cafada* and *Cafamiento* have here no more to fay to a *boufe*, than *pofda* had to *cows*. *Ceas* or *Keas* is an original word in the Irifh and Spanifh languages, fignifying Wedlock; the Doctor had tranflated *aithceas* or *aithkeas*, a harlot. I allow it is the modern vulgar fignification of the word, as *Ceis* or *Keis* is of the pudendum muliebre; Arab. *keza*, *kefs*, *keis* (coitus); but in the old dialect, and in the following laws, *aitceas* is explained to be a wife; *ait* is the prepofite article, the fame as the Arabic *att*, implying repetition; and *ceis*, *keis*, fignifying copulation, both in Irifh and Arabic, the Doctor and others have miftaken the word; but *ait* here is the inflexion of *atb* the law, and correfponds to the Spanifh *miento*, that is *cafa*, nuptials; *miento*, vowed or fworn at the *mon* or holy altar. *Ceas-*

ait or *ceaſt* in Iriſh, a wife (or woman attached to one man) is the root of the Latin *Caſtitas*; as *poſta* or *puſhti* in the Perſic is the name of *Ganymedes*, a Latin name, compoſed of two Iriſh or Celtic words, ſignifying the ſame, as *puſhti*, viz. profuſion of love.

The Iriſh *Keas* and the Spaniſh *Caſa* are of the like conſtruction and ſignification with the Arab. *Khaſeki*, a ſultana; the Perſic *cheſn*, nuptials, from the verb *cheſpiden*, to adhere, to ſow, to join together; but this word did not convey the ſame honourable idea as *puſhti* in the Oriental dialects; it ſometimes implied luſt, hence *Cheghz* is in Perſic a frog; *chuchu*, a ſparrow; from whence a very vulgar Iriſh word is derived, *ſhag* (i.e. coitus) Arab. *Zekhkh*; *Khejaa*, in Arabic, implying the enjoyment of a woman either in wedlock or not, it was neceſſary to diſtinguiſh the honourable and lawful ceremony of wedlock, from the reſult of paſſion. The Iriſh prefixed *aſh*, i. e. the law, the holy law. The Iberian Celts ſuffixed *mienta* or *manta*, derived from *man*, the altar at which the vow was made. *Man*, *mun*, or *mon*, is the tall upright ſtone always to be found on the outſide of, and near to the druidical circular Temples: it was the Juba or pulpit were the prieſts ſtood to explain the laws, human and divine. This ſtone was originally the altar of the almighty God; it was the *Eben Saged*, or lapis adorationis of the Hebrews; it was at firſt the *muna, amuna,* or *amna* of the Chaldeans, which, as Buxtorf rightly tranſlates, was *fides, religio, quis Deum colit, complectitur et reveretur*; it was alſo the *mana*;

Heb.

Heb. *mena*; Chald. *et manna*; Arab. the oblation or gift at the altar: at length it was the idolatrous *Cham-mim*, or Solaria, or images of the
Sun; and hence the idolatrous Jews worshipped
the material Heavens under the name *Mani*.
Man gives name to many places in this kingdom,
where druidical Temples are always to be found,
as Sleev-na-Man mountain; Mon na Veil or
Bheil or Mon na Bheil a mullac mountain; Mon-
uath or Monooth, Man-ava, Mangarton, &c. &c.
It is the origin of Mona or Anglesea; of the Isle
of Man; and of the *mon*, i. e. *Sanctus*, of the Japonese; and is probably the same as the *munnoo-
logue* of the Bramins; in Irish, *mann-lugbt*, i. e.
Druids. See Holwell's Indostan, Vol. 2. I propose
to treat this subject fully in a future number.

From the Irish *mitceas*, is derived the Bascuanza
Eztayac, wedlock; and from *posta*, the Sclavonic *pasjati*. *Notb*, *Nudb*, in Irish, is a contract, a
knot, a league,; hence *Nuadb-Cor* or *Nodbcor*,
(pronounced *Nuacor*) is a bride or bridegroom,
but *Nuac*, matrimony, is from the Arabic *nikab*;
nuaposta is a married couple, and this is the *nupiæ*
or *nuptiis* of the Latin, and not from *nubendo*, as
Vossius thinks. Causa appellationis ex eo, quod
sponsa, cum ad maritum deduceretur, *faciem flameo
nuberet, hoc est velaret.* Risum teneatis! Curiatius
is indeed nearer the sense of the origin of this word,
but equally distant from the letter; *nuptias a novum
et pactum;* Cornificius thought the word derived
from *novus et peto* quia *nova petantur conjugia.* How
absurd are all these Etymologists, proceeding from
their ignorance of that language which was the

mother

mother of the Greek and of the Latin. I fhall
not take up the reader's time in their whimfical
Etyma of the word *matrimonium*; *muin* or *muine* is
an original Irifh word fignifying *carnal copulation*;
it is fo ufed at this day with the prepofition *ar*,
for example, *cuadb fi ar muin*, or *dul fi ar muin*,
fhe went a whoring; and in the following laws,
the commentator explains *muine* by *ftriopac*, a harlot. *Muin* fignifying *copulation*, it was necefFary
to diftinguifh the lawful union of the man and
woman from the unlawful, and therefore as the
joining of hands at the altar was the principal
part of the ceremony, *matb* a hand, was prefixed to *ar muin*, which compound forms *matbar-
muin*, from whence the Latin *matrimonium*;
hence the Irifh word *muinteor*, *muinter*, a tribe,
a clan, a family; that is, fays the Royal Bifhop
Cormac Mc'Cullman in his ancient Gloffary now
before me, *muin tor*, i. e. *torrac muin*, the fruit
of wedlock. *Muinfiol* is another Irifh word for
a family, compounded of *muin*, and *fiol* feed,
iffue; fo likewife *lamb-nodb*, or *lamb-nuadb*, is a
married couple, from *lamb* the hand, &c. *nodb*
or *nuadb*, a compact, covenant, &c. &c.

Arab. *mun-yz*, libidine exardens, vir aut mulier,
      muni, fperma genitale,
      mun-berij, rem habens cum puella,
      munfil, generation, progeny,
      munfus, born,
      munkub, a lawful fpoufe,
      munakyd, marriage,
      munzem, joined, contracted, &c. &c.

                  Dr.

Dr. O'Brien forgot himſelf ſtrangely, in aſſert-
ing that *ſprè* is the *only* word in the Iriſh language
to ſignify a woman's marriage portion; the
reader is requeſted to turn to the word *crodb* in
his Iriſh dictionary, it is there explained, a *dowry*,
or *wife's portion, cattle, cows*; *crodb* ſignifies the
profit or produce of the cows, and not the animal; *ſprè* and *crodb* ſignify riches and wealth
of every kind. There are many other words to
expreſs a marriage portion, all which the Doctor
has inſerted in his dictionary, as,

Crodh, feartcrodh, lancrodh, bacrodh, croid-
heachd, coibhce, libheadhan, libhearn, diob-
hadh, tochra, ſprè, nual, nadhm.

Chald. *catbobab* implies a dowry, but it alſo ſignifies *inſtrumentum dotis, literæ contractus matrimo-
nialis*, from *catbab* ſcriptum.

Nadonia, Nadaz, are words alſo for a dowry.

Perſ. *Kabin*, a dowry, a portion; *ſepar* wealth,
houſehold furniture.

Arab. *Sebr, zebr*, a writing, a dowry, *zibrij* de-
coration of jewels; *ſebr* a form, mode, writing;
ſipebr fortune; *ſbebr* a gift, conjugal duty; *biba,
nibila, niama*, dos, a dowry.

From theſe words the above Iriſh compounds
are derived to expreſs a dowry or marriage portion.

M O N E Y. C O I N.

Soyez ſeul, et arriver par quelqu' accident chez
un peuple inconnu; ſi vous voyez une piece de
monnoye, comptez que vous etes arrivè chez un
peuple policè. *Eſprit des Loix*, lib. 18. *c.* 16.

The

The Irish had the use of money from the earliest accounts of their history. In the laws that have hitherto fallen into my poffeffion, money is defcribed by weight; the *fcreabal* of gold, and the *fcreabal* of filver is mentioned in feveral places; thefe were ftamped with certain marks to afcertain their value by weight. The religion of the Druids forbid the introduction of images into their ceremonies, and probably for this reafon their coin or money did not bear the heads of their kings; the golden and filver ornaments which have been found in our bogs, bear evident proof of the ability of the ancient Irish to have made fuch a coin; I can only attribute the want of it to the reafons above mentioned. Sir James Ware gives a plate of feveral coins, he thought might be Irish, but the epigraph was fo defaced it was conjecture only.

Screabal or *fgreabal*, fays O'Brien, was an annual tribute of three pence enjoined on every inhabitant of Munfter by their king *Aongus*, fon of *Nadfrey*, to be paid to faint Patrick; the word alfo fignifies a favour or prefent given by new married people. *Irish Dictionary*.

Screaball in a very ancient gloffary is thus defcribed: *puingene*, i. e. *fgreaball meidhe inbbiche: afe fin fgreaball nan Gaoidheal*, i. e. *oiffing*, i. e. Puingene or fcreaball, of fmall weight; this is the fgreaball of the Irish, i. e. an offing; *Puingene* is a penny in the modern dialect, and probably the oblation alludes to the tribute above mentioned; but *fcreabal* certainly implies a piece of money with a mark to notify its weight or value;

fcreabam,

fcreabam, or *fcribam*, is to fcratch, fcrape, or furrow, from whence *fcriob* a writing, and the Latin *fcribo*. See note to No. 2 in the laws.

Seid, *fèd*, & *feod*, are words frequently to be met with in the laws, expreffing the value of land, of apparel, and of mulcts and fines; the commentators have explained this word by *cows* and *fèd*, in the Irifh Lexicons is a milch-cow, or cow in profit, Arab. *we-jiet*. *Sed* & *feod* alfo fignify wealth, jewels, &c. therefore I conjecture that *fèd* was alfo a piece of money; in the Arabic *jedd* is riches, *jeyid* every thing excellent; *feidi* is brafs or copper, and *faidet* is an offering or oblation.

Fang or Faing was another name for the *fgreabal*, either of gold or filver, it was the fame as the *oiffing*. Fang (fays O'Brien) an ancient Irifh coin; *Fang*, *faing*, i. e. fgreaball oir no airgid, old glofs. Perf. *fanè* a wedge, *fenn* money, riches.

IRISH WORDS FOR MONEY.

Airgead.
    i. e. filver; hence the Latin argentum.
Boghe.
    i. e. ballan beg imbitis coic uingi oir; i. e. a fmall ball weighing five ounces of gold.
Cim, Kim.
    i. e. filver. Perf. *Sim* money, a dollar, an ingot.
Cis, Kis.
    i. e. tribute, rent, &c.
Cearb, Kearb.
    i. e. filver. Arab. *Ghereb*, filver.

Clodh-

Clodh-airgead.

i. e. ſtampt ſilver; *clodb* is ſtamped; hence *cur ar clodb* is to print a book or to mint money.

Or clodh bhuailte.

i. e. gold ſtamped, *buailte* is ſtruck; in Arabic *Kebil* is uncoined money, probably the root of the Iriſh *clod*, and the vulgar *kelter*, i. e. money.

Cron bhualte òr. Cron bhualte airged. Cron bhualte pràs.

That is, a ſign or mark *(cron)* ſtruck upon gold, ſilver, or braſs.

Lethe.

A word I know not the meaning of; in my old Gloſſary it is explained by *aſs*, probably the *as* of Pliny, a coin, ten of which made the *denarium*. Laithe is a balance or ſcales for weighing money, *meadb tbomais oir no airgid..*

Mona, Munadh, Munadan.

Heb. monah, mineh.

Munadhànaidh,

A coiner or maker of money.

Several of the Spaniſh names for particular coins are common in Ireland, at what time they adopted them I am ignorant, but it is worth remarking, that ſuch names are evidently of Iriſh derivation, and cannot be derived from the modern Spaniſh, as far as I can diſcover; ſuch are Piaſtre, Piaſtrin, a ſhilling, or two rials; Riali, ſixpence; Tuiſtùin, a groat; *Piaſtre* and *Piaſtarin*, appears to be derived from the Iriſh *Pioſa-tria*, or *triatb*, i. e. the king's piece; *Pioſa tierna* the ſame. Perſ. *peſbèz*, any ſmall money.

Patacùn

Patacùn a dollar, from the Flemiſh Patag.

Tuiſtùin, from tuis, the head, or tuis the jewel or precious value, and Tonn, the King.

Riali, from *Ri* king, and *ail* will pleaſure.

Piſtole will alſo imply *piòſa toll*, i. e. a piece with a head ſtampt on it.

Feorling is a farthing, and *cianog, kianog* was a *ſmall coin* as the word denotes, which paſſed for half a farthing.

Theſe are certainly modern names, and in the 9th century when the Danes obliged the Iriſh heads of families to pay the annual tribute, we find it expreſſed in the annals by the words *uinge oir*, i. e. ounces of gold ; this is the cruel tribute named by the Iriſh *Cios Sron*, or Noſe Tax, becauſe the Danes threatened to ſlit their noſes in caſe of non-payment.

I am therefore of opinion the ancient Iriſh had no minted or coined money, but pieces of gold and ſilver ſtamped or ſcratched with a mark, to denote the value and weight, ſuch as are current at this day in Spain and Portugal.

The Hebrew word *ſhekel* ſignified to weigh, and alſo a coin of gold or ſilver from its weight. The Iriſh *ſcreabal* was probably a weight alſo ; as we have the word *ſcruple* ſignifying a certain weight ; and I may be miſtaken in deriving this word from *ſcreabam* to ſcratch. It has been ſtrongly contended by *Conringius* and *Sperlingius* that the ancient Jews had no coined money, no *pecunia ſignata*. The Hebrew words *ſhekel* denotes weight ; *caſaph* denotes paleneſs of colour, and ſilver, like the Iriſh *airgid, cios, cearb* ; Caſaph

ſaph occurs frequently in the bible, Gen. 13. 2. 20. 16. 2 Kings, 12. 7. in the laſt it expreſsly ſays, " *Jehohaſh ſaid unto the prieſts, now therefore receive no more money of your acquaintance,*" which the vulgate tranſlates *pecunia argentum, ἀργύραν;* Sperlingius inſiſts this word *caſaph* muſt here likewiſe be underſtood *pro pondere ſolvendo,* and not *argento ſignato.*

That the ancient Iriſh had the art of *fuſing* metals is evident from the monuments of antiquity daily diſcovered, but more evident from the name *Breothina, Braithne,* or *Bruithneoir* a ſmelter, a refiner of metals, i. e. ſays my ancient Gloſſariſt, *fear bhios ag bearbhadh, no lag leaghadh no ar tineadh, oir, argid,* &c. i. e. a man who has the art of ſmelting, refining or diſſolving gold, ſilver, &c. &c. (let it here be noted that *tineadh* to fuſe, is the root of the Engliſh word *tin,* i. e. a metal eaſily fuſed) *breo* is a hot fire.

It will not be foreign to our ſubject in this place to mention another art of *fuſion,* well known to the ancient Iriſh, I mean the art of making glaſs. The Iriſh name for *glaſs* is *glaine,* or *gloine,* a word the author of the Gaelic antiquities wiſhes to derive from *gleo* and *tineadh,* i. e. to fuſe in a hot fire; in this caſe the compound would be written *gleothine* or *gloithine,* which certainly would pronounce nearly the ſame as *gloine;* but the word is always written *gloine.* Dr. Johnſon derives the word *glaſs* from the Saxon *glæs,* and the Dutch *glas,* as Pezron imagines from the Britiſh and Iriſh *glas,* which ſignifies green, clear; the Doctor obſerves, that in *Erſe klann* is glaſs, and alſo clean; true the word *glan*

in

in Erfe and Irifh fignifies clean, but not clear.
The Hebrew word *glas* to look fmooth and gloffy,
comes nearer the fenfe of our word glafs.
There is every reafon to think the Irifh word *glo-inne* is an original. Monfieur *Michael* has
proved that the ancient Jews had the art of mak-
ing glafs; and in the' third chapter of Ifai. and
23d verfe, the word *glinim* occurs, which Montanus tranflates looking glaffes, and the vulgate
glaffes; *glinim* is the plural number in the Hebrew, confequently *glin* is the fame word with
the Irifh *gloine*.

The word *porcelana* fignifying china or earthen
ware, was given to that manufacture by the
Portugueze; *porcelana*, fays Larramendi (in his
Bafcuence dictionary) is a word borrowed from
the Cantabrians or Bafc; called by them. *brocela-na*; which he explains by *brocela*, i. e. trabaxo,
i. e. work, and *lana*, i. e. *cario* a carriage; hence
fays he *porcelana* fignifies with the Spaniards and
Portugueze either china ware or a porringer.
This inconfiftent author (who frequently tells us
this, and this word is of my own invention) at
the word *vidrio*, i. e. glafs, gives a name in
the *Bafc*, fynonimous to the Irifh, viz. *beira-quia*,
that is, in the Irifh *breo-caoi*, fufed in the fire:
caoi-oir, *caoi-ariain*, is hot liquid gold or iron.
The Portugueze *porcelana* is evidently the Irifh
breo-gloine, or *breo-cloine*, i. e. glafs fufed by fire.
This art muft have been very early difcovered;
every fire made on the fea fhore with the fa-
line weeds dried and fcattered about, muft have
produced a vitrification; and to fuch an acci-

dent

dent Pliny attributes the difcovery of this art in the River *Belus*, or the *Rivus Pagida*. See Bochart's Hierozoic. p. 723. The *Bafc*, word *quia*, or *quiar*, very frequently occurs in the Irifh compounds, as in *caor-ghbeal*, red-hot, *caor-tbuin*, quickfilver, *caor-tbeine*, a firebrand, *caor-tintigbe*, a thunderbolt, &c. &c.

To return to our fubject. Sir James Ware and bifhop Nicolfon have treated on the coins and money of Ireland; Mr. Simon collected what they had written, and enlarged the work with the figures and defcriptions of many coins in his poffeffion †. From his Effay I fhall extract what he has faid on the ancient money of Ireland.

" Although we cannot trace out the firft in-
" vention of money in Ireland, yet it cannot
" be denied that it was in ufe here long before the
" arrival of the Danes, or Norwegians. The
" Irifh word *Monadh (a)*, as well as the other
" appellative words, ufed (with little variation in
. " the

---

† This valuable collection of coins, medals, foffils, &c. came into the poffeffion of Mr. Simon's fon, at prefent a merchant in this city; who not having the paffion of his father for antiquities, offered them for fale at a very low price—A purchafer could not be found in Ireland; they were fold to a foreigner and taken out of the country!

(a) *Monadh, Pecunia*, Money. Lluyd's Irifh Dictionary. The Irifh *Airgead*, ufed at prefent for the Englifh word money, originally and properly fignifies *Argentum*, filver; and was not probably made ufe of to defign money, until the ufe of filver coins was introduced into Ireland, when in all likelihood, fuch money was called by way of diftinction from iron or copper money, *Monadh na Argead*, and in procefs of time for brevity fake, *Airgead*, for money of filver.

" the pronunciation) in moſt of the ancient and
" modern languages to ſignify money, ſeem to
" be derived from one and the ſame origin, the
" Hebrew Monah, or Mineh *(b)*, the name both
" of a weight, and of a kind of money, worth a
" hundred *Denarii (c)*: the Mineh of gold be-
" ing worth a hundred ſhekels. Beſides this,
" we find in the Iriſh many mercantile and other
" words derived from the Hebrew, which, as
" they ſhew the antiquity of the Iriſh, and its
" affinity to that mother tongue, denote likewiſe
" the early uſe of trade, and of money in Ire-
" land; into which, no doubt, it was introduc-
" ed as ſoon as inhabited, or at leaſt frequented
" by other trading nations; the country afford-
" ing gold, ſilver, and other metals *(d)*, which
" perhaps were ſoon diſcovered by the firſt in-
" habitants.

A. M
3011.

" We find that in the reign of Tighernmhais
" Mac Fallamhuin *(e)*, the tenth monarch of
" the Mileſian race, gold ore was diſcovered,
" and refined at Fothart, near the river Liffey,
" in the county of Wicklow, where gold, ſilver,

(b) Mina eſt nomen ponderis et monetæ habentis centum
denarios, et centum ſiclos auri. Schindler's Lexicon-Pen-
taglot.

(c) The *Denarius* denier, according to Greaves and Ar-
buthnot, weighed 62 grains, and would be worth of our
preſent money, about 7 ¼ *d*.

(d) ———————— ſtannique fodinas
Et puri Argenti venas, quas terra refoſſis
Viſceribus manes imos viſura recludit.
Hadrianus Junius in Ware's Antiquit.

(e) O Flaherty's Ogygia, Lond. 1685. p. 195.

" ver, copper, lead and iron, have of late years
" been found out. And a mint is faid to have
" been erected, and filver money firft coined in
" Ireland, in the time of Eadna-Deargh, at   3482.
" Airgead-Rofs, (A. M. 3351) fo named from
" Airgid filver, or money (f). From this obfer-
" vation that filver-money was then firft ftruck,
" we may reafonably conclude that money of
" fome kind or other, whether of .iron or cop-
" per, was in ufe before that time; and indeed
" we find that in the reign of Sednæus-Innardh,   3453
" the foldiers wages were paid in money, wheat,
" and cloathes (g). 'Tis alfo very probable
" that this ifland was known to the Phœnicians,
" who ufed to refort to Britain for tin, which no
" doubt was likewife found in Ireland (b);
" though thofe mines feem to have been loft for
" fome ages paft. But moft certain it is, that
" this country was famous, in the beginning of
" the Roman empire; for Tacitus, fpeaking
                                     " com-

(f) Ogygia, p. 249.   (g) Ibid, p. 248.
(g) Ibid, p. 248.
(b) At a great council held at Drogheda on Friday before
the feaft of St. Andrew, (29 Hen. VI.) before James Earl
of Ormond, deputy to Richard duke of York lord lieutenant
of Ireland; it was enacted (cap. 14.); that licence be granted
to Sir Chriftopher St. Lawrence, lord of Howth, to fearch
for a mine within the feigniory of Howth, as well for tin as
lead ore, and to apply the profits thereof to his own ufe for
three years, yielding 6s. 8d. a year if the mine be found.
(cap. 17). As Richard Ingram miner and finer has at his
great charge found out divers mines of filver, lead, iron,
coal, &c. which would caufe great relief to the inhabitants
of Ireland if they were wrought; it is therefore enacted, &c.
—Rolls-office, Dublin.

" comparatively of Britain and Ireland, fays of
" the latter, that it was better known by its
" trade and commerce, by its eafy refort, and
" the goodnefs of its harbours, than the firft *(i)*.
" And when the Roman arms had reached Spain,
" Gaul, and Germany, abundance of people
" muft have retired out of thofe countries into
" this, and brought with them what riches they
" could fave, together with their trade, arts and
" fciences; for which reafon, the Romans had
" a coveting eye on Ireland, which, fays Ta-
" citus *(k)*, being fituated exactly between
" Spain and Britain, lies very convenient for
" the French fea, and would have united the
" ftrong members of the empire with great ad-
" vantage; and Agricola thought it could have
" been conquered, and kept in fubjection with
" one legion and fome few auxiliaries.

" There muft indeed have been a great deal
" of wealth and treafure in Ireland, to have al-
" lured the Oftmen and Nordmen to invade it
" fo often, and at laft to engage them to fettle in
" it. It was not for the fake of provifions, or of
" fome cattle, that they made fuch repeated at-
" tempts on this country; no, as thofe people
" enriched themfelves by their pyracies, money
" was what they moft fought for. For as the Bua-
" Saga expreffes it *(l)*, they ufed to enter into
partner-

(i) Melius aditus portufque per commercia et negotiatores
cogniti. Tacitus in Vita Agricolæ, p. 159. Edit. Elzev.
1649.
(k) Ut fupra.
(l) Societatem fub juramento inierunt, piraticam exercen-
tes,

" partnerships upon oath, to exercife their pyra-
" cies, whereby they honourably *(m)* acquired
" plenty of money. And Sturlefonius *(n)* fays
" that after their expeditions they ufed to bring
" home fo much money, which they had taken
" from the merchants and hufbandmen, that
" thofe who faw thefe riches, admired how fo
" much gold could be collected together in thofe
" northern countries.

" It appears from Saxo Grammaticus *(o)*, that
" thofe pyrates, under the conduct of Hacco
" and Starchater, having invaded Ireland, at-
" tacked and routed the Irifh, and killed their
" king Huglet, found in his treafury in Dublin
" fuch a vaft quantity of money, " that every
" man had as much as he could wifh or defire;
" fo as they needed not to fall out among them-
" felves for the partition, fince there was fo much
" for each Man's fhare, as he could conveniently
" carry away. *(p)*"

" The Prince, here called Huglet, was pro-
" bably Aodh VII. king or monarch of Ire-
                F   " land,

---

es, quâ pecuniam fibi honorificè quæfiverunt. Thomas Bar-
holinus, de Antiq. Dan. p. 457. Hafniæ 1689.

(m) Pyracy was then looked upon as honourable; the
:ing and lords of Denmark being often concerned in thofe
xpeditions. Ibid. cap. ii. & ix.

(n) Piraticam fufceperunt, deque prædonibns, qui agrico-
s et mercatores fpoliaverunt, magnas pecunias egerunt, et
mnes qui hæc videbant admirati funt, in feptentrionalibus
rris tantum auri collectum effe.—Ibid. p. 458.

(o) Saxo Grammat. Hift. Dan. lib. 6. Tho. Barthol. p,
5.

(p) Hollingfhed, vol. 2. p. 57.

" land, furnamed Finn-Liath; and of Aodh
" or Hugh and Liath, a foreigner fuch as our
" hiftorian was, might very well, inftead of
" Hugo-Liath, have called him Hugo-Leth, or
" Hughlet, in Latin '*Hugletus.* This admitted,
" the fact muft have happened in the year 879,
" which is the time affigned by O'Flaherty *(q)*
" for the death of this prince, though he doth
" not fay that he was either attacked or killed by
" the Danes; but that his fon and fucceffor Neil-
" Glundubh was by them killed in a battle near
" Dublin in 919, according to the annals of
" Dungalls *(r).* The fame author owns, that
" the Danes and Norwegians made feveral ir-
" ruptions into Ireland in the reign of Aodh V.
" furnamed Oirnigh, in the years 788, 807,
" 812, and 815 *(s).*

" We find, in feveral of our hiftorians, men-
" tion made of gold and filver being paid by the
" ounce. Thus in the annals of Ulfter *(t) ad*
" *An.* 1004, we find that Brian Boruma, king
" of Ireland, offered twenty ounces of gold on
" the altar of St. Patrick, in the cathedral church
" of Armagh. That Tirdelvac O'Conor, king
" of Ireland, *An.* 1152, having obtained a
" great victory over the people of Munfter, re-
" ceived for the ranfom of their leader fixty
" ounces of gold. That *An.* 1157, Maurice
" O'Loughlin,

(q) Ogygia, p. 433.
(r) Ibid. p. 434.   *(s)* Ibid. p. 433.
(t) Ware's Antiq. Edit. 1704, p. 70, and by Harris, p. 204.

" O'Loughlin, king of Ireland, upon the dedi-
" cation of the church of Mellifont, gave like-
" wife sixty ounces of gold to the monks of that
" house; to whom Donat O'Carrol, king of
" Ergal, founder of that church, gave also sixty
" ounces of gold; and Dervorgilla, wife of Tierna
" O'Ruark, as many (*u*). That *An.* 1161,
" Flahertach O'Brolcan, Comorban of Columb-
" kill, having visited the diocess of Offory, there
" were collected there for him among the peo-
" ple four hundred and twenty ounces of pure
" silver (*w*). And in a Latin manuscript copy of
" the Gospels (*x*), we find this marginal note,
" that Moriertagh O'Loughlin, king of Ireland,
" granted a parcel of land to the monastery of
" Ardbraccan in perpetuity, at a yearly rent of
" three ounces of gold. From all which, some
" have imagined, that there was no money
" struck in Ireland, before the arrival of the
" English. But probably these were particular
" cases; the gold and silver offered to churches
" might be for chalices, and other holy utensils
" or ornaments; and great payments were no
" doubt made by weight: So William the Con-
" queror allowed Edward Atheling a pound
" weight of silver every day (*y*). And by rea-
" son perhaps of the lightness of some of the

F 2   " then

(*u*) Ware's Antiq. p. 70.
(*w*) MS. annals of abby Boyle. Trin. Coll. Dublin.
(*x*) MSS. college library, Dublin.
(*y*) Speed's hist. of England, p. 504.

" then current money, people chofe to receive it
" *ad fcalam*, by weight (z). It appears for cer-
" tain from a letter of Lancfranc archbifhop of
" Canterbury to Tirlagh, king of Ireland, *An.*
" 1074, that money was then current in this
" kingdom, fince the bifhops ufed to confer holy
" orders for money, which evil cuftom he ad-
" jures him to reform (a.)

" I have, I fear, been too long in endeavouring
" to prove the early ufe of money and of mints
" in Ireland; I fhall therefore only add that Keat-
" ing (b) tells us, that mints were erected at Ar-
" magh and Cafhel about the time of St. Patrick's
" entering upon his apoftlefhip (in the fifth cen-
" tury) and that money was there coined for the
" fervice of the ftate. Another author (c) fays
" likewife, that Tirlagh O'Conor, king of Ire-
" land, erected a mint and had filver money
" ftruck at Clonmacnoife; and that he bequeath-
" ed to the clergy of that place five hundred and
" forty ounces of gold, and forty marks of
" filver.

" Whether the monarch of Ireland only, or
" each petty king in his province or territory,
" did

(z) Among many examples, I fhall give one : *An.* 1248,
Hen. III. the money was fo fhamefully clipped, that an order was iffued out, enjoining, that it fhould be taken only by
weight, and that no pieces fhould pafs, but fuch as were
round. Matt. Paris. Annales de Waverly.

(a) Ware ut fupra.
(b) Keating's Hift. p. 327.
(c) Cambrenfis Everfus, p. 85.

" did affume the power of ftriking money, doth
" not clearly appear from ancient hiftory : But
" if the coins in my firft plate, taken from Sir
" James Ware and Cambden, be Irifh, and
" Mr. Walker's notes on them admitted to be
" juft, we may well fuppofe that each prince in
" his kingdom, in imitation of the Anglo-
" Saxon kings in England, ftruck money of
" his own."

Addenda to page xx.

Seannacas is alfo an Oriental word, fignifying the
Law, as is fully explained by Millius in his differtation on Mohammedifm; *Sonna*, in Arabic, implies the Law or Alcoran in ufe among the ancient Arabs, Tartars and Moguls; it is yet in
great efteem with certain fects of the Mohamme-
dans, and is faid to contain fome religious tenets
omitted in the Alcoran. The word *Sonna* in Arabic,
like *Sean* in Irifh, fignifies alfo *converfation, talk,
preaching*; hence *Sean-mor* is a fermon, and *Seannacas*, the great Law; *Sean-focal* a proverb, or
wife fpeech, &c. &c. " Præter *Alcoranum* fumma
auctoritate apud Mohammedanos, liber eft, quem
(alfonna) *Sonnam* appellant, quo Mohammedis in-
ftituta et dicta in Alcorano non memorata conti-
nentur, orali traditione propagata olim, et tandem
in illum librum conjecta. Vocabulum *Sonna* præ-
cipuè fignificare *viam, converfationem*, docet Ebno'l
Athir; quoties autem in lege occurrat, omne id
denotare exiftimat, quod Propheta Mohammed vel

præ-

præceperit vel vetuerit in Alcorano omiffum, *(a)* ita quoque Ebno'l Kaffajus aliique. Turcæ in fummo pretio habent illum librum, Tartari itidem, Arabes et Indiani in Mogulis imperio, unde *Populus Sonnæ atque affenfus*, Sonnitæ vocantur: rejiciunt autem Perfæ, five *Alifchii*, a quibufdam *Karaei* vocati.

Millius de Mohammedifmo, p. 54.

(a) Radix (Sonna) five primaria hujus vocis fignificatio eft *via*, five *converfatio*. Verum fi ad LEGEM transfertur, ea denotatur *quicquid præcepit Propheta aut vetuit*, aut ad quod invitavit dicto vel facto, ex iis de quibus non locutus eft Alcoranus, adeoque, inter probationes legales numerantur liber et Sonna: id eft Alcoranus, et dicta factaque Mohammedis. Eb. Kaffaius; vide etiam Pocockii. Specim. Hift. Arab. p. 299.

BREITH NEMH;

O R,

BREHON LAWS

O F

IRELAND.

This Fragment is copied from an ancient MSS. in Trinity College, DUBLIN. Claſs E. Tab. 3. Nº. 5.

N. B. Comm. ſtands for Commentator; theſe fragments abound in comments of various readers.

☞ The firſt part of this Law is wanting.

ORIGINAL.	TRANSLATION.
leathcathach atairſci, odcathach macathach aidce ar ata andlig na feine buachaill oc cach ceatn fride ſceo aidce, as de ata cond bo a buachaill imban foillſe ambeith ambuailaid fo iadad anaidce; mad muca afeis afoil anaidce, madba bi imbo daingèan eich icuibreach techta nona ninde, cairig in a lias.	half fine in the day time, full fine (if treſpaſs) done in the night, for the cowherd muſt watch the cattle night and day; the owner of the cattle is to cauſe his cows to be bawned (i. e. incloſed) at nights, if there are ſwine they are to be ſtied at nights, if horſes they are to be fettered, if ſheep they are to be penned.

ORIGINAL.

Ata dono orcc con-
randa cinta fri tret 7 ag
conranda cindta fri heth,
oircc bis alis no afaithce,
lingeas eirlim an gort
faithce, fa di fa tri fa
ceathair anaen laithe ni
ling, im. in tret, s. ac-
neirlim conranad chinta
iarum inde, ag dono
conranna cinaid fri hed
forngid gealeas targeilt
nindric notar ime nin-
dric.

1. Caircaide inime in-
dric mad cora tri liag tri
traigte a leithead da dornn
deg dia hairde mad clas
tri traighthe a leithead
7 a doimne trigh a leithead
tis iar nichtar tri trighte
a leithead na maighne a
curtar in mur 7 tri trigh-
the anairde in muir, mad
nochtaile gebaidh fide fri
dam fcuithe, ni dicead
fcuithe ara dluithe 7 di
chet dam ara hairde 7 a
daingne da dornn X dia
hairde tri buncar indi

TRANSLATION.

Trefpaffes of fwine
are alike divided through
the whole herd or ftock
of cattle, and if petted
pigs leap into meadows
or corn fields twice,
thrice or four times a
day, either fingly or in
company, the trefpafs
fhall be levied each time,
equal to that of a whole
herd.

1. What are the dimen-
fions of the fences of a
(a) bawn by law? The
ditch muft be three feet
wide and three deep, the
wall three feet broad and
twelve hands high of
ftone work; and as it
will be then expofed, it
is to be raifed with fod
and brambles inter-
woven to the height of
twelve hands more, with
three fet-offs or retreats,
fo that at the top it fhall
be broad enough to re-

(a) The bawn was a fpace or area round the dwelling, inclofed with a fence, either to keep the cattle fafe by night
from moroders, or to milk them in by day.

ORIGINAL.

bunchor for a hichtar 7 araile indi air a medon 7 araile fair iar nuachtur co rugud cach cuaille iar nuachtur 7 lamcur doib conach urfaema in talam 7 tri beimeanna fair da archa trigh coruige deilnordaniīcā da cuaille tri duirnd fot in chuaille uafa anamain 7 cir draigain fair, diambe fair is dithfogail ar ceatⁿ ifamne cidh induirime iī airde 7 dluithe 7 indrueus.

TRANSLATION.

ceive a ftake, to be driven firmly into the fod; the ftakes are to rife three hands above all, and brambles to be woven between them, when done in this manner it is a daingean or ftrong hold for cattle.

2. Smacht peata chuirre 7 circe 7 peata ois, 7 peata mic tire, 7 peata feineoin, 7 peata findaigh,. tairgille nairib ite indfin a caithche.

2. Fines are to be levied for treffaffes committed by petted herns, petted fowls, petted deer, petted wolves, petted hawks, and petted foxes *(b)*.

(*b*) The commentator adds, two Screabal to be paid for every trefpafs committed by thefe animals. I am at a lofs to determine what this Screabal was; Mc'Curtin and O'Brien fay it was of the value of three pence, and was an annual tribute paid by each inhabitant to St. Patrick; *fcreabal bhathais* is alfo tranflated fees for baptifm; *fcreabal* alfo means a prefent given by new married people; in fome of the notes it is called *fcreabal dor*, and *fcreabal dairgid*, i. e. fcruples of gold and of filver. I find *fcreabal* was likewife a fmall meafure of corn, and *fcrupulus* in Du Cange is menfura agraria. See in the Technical Terms, COIN. MONEY.

ORIGINAL.

3. Car ciafa cathach fo fich cu fritir incoinicaid beirid chin conloin, cid fil afogain, buaine in con-luain ital 7 talam dara eife 7 a teora heimeide nich onluain a haimeid do im 7 a haimeid do gruth 7 a heimeid do taos ina dire toifcead ca-chaes drecht, conach inntaibh do neach faifead it dire 7 aithg.

4. Smachta comic-heafa caide coland acht la colaind afeich feritaib no airceand ite coland afeich.

5. Mbrugricht. cia ro neipidar racht mbroga fon ar na horr neach brog a comicaid, ar ni bia fidh a tire, ar nach orba ar nach ara ar nach aitre-aba ara tair gealla cach ara ceat^n for cach naile for cach tairfce for cach fuire.

TRANSLATION.

3. What are the fines on trefpaffes committed by dogs fuffered to wan-der over the country? They fhall pay fines e-qual to the damages done; and whoever fhall keep greyhounds, fhall pay for any wafte made by them on butter, curds, or dough; that is to fay, equal reftitution.

4. Fines fhall alfo be levied for wounds made by thefe animals, if they attack any perfon, whe-ther they are wounded in the body or the head.

5. Bruigh laws (c). whoever trefpaffes on the lands of Bruigh's, tho' the trefpaffer fhould have neither lands or dwelling, they fhall be obliged to give fatisfactory pledges for every trefpafs com-mitted by his cattle in breaking through his fences.

(c) N. B. The *Bruigh* was a public innholder fupported by the chief of every diftrict for the accommodation of tra-vellers,

ORIGINAL.

6. Caircaide tairſce. ta-
gacht tar ſeilb no tar adi
tairſce dona dul tar rod
dul tar abind na be ſnam
doib, tairſce tar fag ne-
iſcarta.

7. Os airm imbiad do
comarba treabar imeaſart
cid do gnitear fri heiſeart
gaibead imme conimcua
as muna be treabad in
forais lais, gaibtear a fine
comogas do, conimcua a
deire, no con tardad fer
dilſi, co ceann mbliadna
mad fer dilſe do bera a
fine, imfean ceachtair in
da comarba ognime 7 do
bād comaiream ind 7 do
airgealla cach diaraile as
iarum.

TRANSLATION.

6. What other treſ-
paſſes on fences? Croſſ-
ing out of the road,
clambering over ditches
into peoples lands,
ſwimming or fording
rivers into the ſame,
whereby contentions a-
riſe.

7. Where joint part-
ners in land are at vari-
ance, reſtitution ſhall be
made by the treſpaſſer,
unleſs he is the chief of
a clan, and then reſtitu-
tion ſhall be taken from
his tribe, if the treſpaſs
is not paid in the ſpace
of one year, either in hay,
graſs, &c. if the tribe be
compelled to pay the treſpaſs, the joint partners
ſhall number their cattle,
and each give ſufficient
ſecurity in proportion.

vellers, he was alſo a noble. See Brehon Laws, No. 4, of
the collectanea, p. 19. See alſo No. 35, of theſe laws.
Bruigh in the modern Iriſh denotes a wealthy farmer.
Bruighean formerly ſignified a palace or royal ſeat, from
Bruigh hoſpitality. See Titles of Honour, Kings, Princes,
Nobles.

ORIGINAL.

TRANSLATION.

8. Os ma do ti eiseart co treab lais anechtar, teid do chum a fine so longad co ceand mbl. 7 ni dia treabane so righ ina tir 7 is dileas douile.

8. If the chief of a tribe trespasses on that of another, the offender shall become a common tribesman to that tribe, and shall remain so for one year, and shall not be a chief for any king in the country, and shall take his property with him.

9. Ruiriud dona, rith ta teora sealba no ceitheora sealba od cathaig and sin, arus ág in follugh, ruirid raite dono rith tar tri haireann treora sealbha, is ruiriud 7 is follugh muna imge deithhe.

9. Ruiriud is the crime of breaking over the lands of three or four different proprietors; this is *Ruiriud* or great trespass unless some reasonable excuse can be shewn.

Comm. *Such as the absence of the Herdsman.*

10. Caircaide anairceand teora fairge. umcor flescaig is eiside bundsaighe acomfad and sin don tricht leath inindruic imme im rod im fean cach bes sui 7 anall im-

10. What are the laws relating to sea coasts ? The space of the cast of a dart shall be left from high water mark along the sea side for a road, which is to be inclosed

ORIGINAL.

TRANSLATION.

foilingead ime indruic atarru famĺ.

by two banks, one next the fea and one next the land.

> N. B. *This coaſt road is ſtill to be ſeen in many places, and is called Erien Boireamb's road.*

11. Cair cia meid ſmachta fil a comiceas. ado ſmacht ime 7 ceathra gen mo ta caithe, ca meid caithe fil a comicheas, teora caithe aile 7 caithe ceathra 7 düine caithe.

11. How many fines of this kind? two, one on men and one on cattle. How many kinds of treſpaſſes? three, viz. breaking of banks, waſte made by men, and waſte made by cattle.

12. Caircadiad duine caithe. 1. beim feda, eidir airẽ feada 7 aithar feada 7 fogla feada 7 loſa feada.

12. What are the timber treſpaſſes? cutting down trees and taking them away; as airigh timber, athar timber, fogla timber, and loſa timber.

13. Airigh feada. 1. dair, coll, cuileand, ibar, Jundus oghtach (*d*) a ball u. s. andire cach ae, bo

13. *Airigh timber*, are, oak, hazle, holly, yew, Indian pine, & apple; five cows penalty for cut-

(*d*) Jundus oghtach, i. e. Indian oghtach, the commentator explains by *crand giuis*, the pine tree, the word is not in our Lexicons: in the Indian language *oghneght* is a pine tree, a word very ſimilar to the Iriſh *oghtach*.

ORIGINAL.

buin beime, colpach ina ngablaib, dairt ina craebaib.

TRANSLATION.

ting down these trees; yearling cow calves for cutting the limbs; and heifers for cutting the branches.

> *The Commentator adds, that for the limbs 8 screaball may be taken, and for the branches 4 screaball.*

14. Athar feada. fernn fail, fceith, caertand, beithe, leamidha, boandire cach ae, dart ina craeba.

14. *Athar Wood*, are aldar, willow, hawthorn, quickbeam, birch, elm; a cow for each tree, a heifer for the branches.

15. Fogla feada. draigean, trom, feorus, fincoll crithach, caithne crandfir, dairt andire cachal.

15. *Fogla wood*, are black thorn, elder, spindle-tree, white hazel, aspen; these are the woods on which the law gives trespass, viz. a heifer for each.

> *The Commentator adds, 6 screabal shall be counted equal restitution.*

ORIGINAL.

16, Loſa feada. raith, rait, aiteand, dris, fraech, eideand gileach ſpin cura, andire cachal. (*e*)

17. Aurba tire dona, idu na caithe. dartaig atri cualli, cona nindteach. dart in cuic, colp ana uiii cuic, s. ana do X 7 aithḡ la cach na 7 beith fo cinaid na bernadh co ceand mbĺ.

TRANSLATION.

16. *Loſa wood* (or fire wood) ferne, furze, brier, heath, ivy, reeds, thornbuſh ; a fine on each.

The Commentator notices, the law does not declare this fine ; but he adds, it may be from 2 to 3 ſcreaball, in proportion to the quantity ſtolen.

17. Fines for breaking fences. For making a breach the breadth of 3 ſtakes, a young bull heifer ; for the breadth of 5 ſtakes, a full grown bull heifer ; for one of 8 ſtakes broad, a good heifer ; for that of 12 ſtakes, 5 cows ; this reſtitution to be paid within the ſpace of one year.

(*e*) In the *Uraceipt* or Primmer of the bards, by Cinſaela, one of the moſt ancient manuſcripts of the Iriſh, the trees are claſſed in the following manner.

Airigh wood.   Dair, Coll, Cuillin, Abhul, Uindſin, Ibhur, Gius.

Athaig wood.   Fearn, Sail, Beithe, Leomh, Sce, Crithach, Caorthaind.

ORIGINAL.

18. Ata orba nad
aclaidead, aurba neigne
ria flogh, ria lon lonaib,
ria flaitaib.

19. Ata aurba ceana
nad aclaidead, aurba
nimfeadna faire muilind
no durr thige no mein-
bra I faire duin rig ad
comarcar uile arus fean
fafach I no liancur gach
guidhe urba ria collaib
ria nailaicraib duntar cach
norba.

20. Comicheach don,
bis it da dir dlig lani-
mirce bid feifear umpu
triar o firtire 7 araile ofir
imirce, U feoit anain 7
atain madichmairc acht

TRANSLATION.

18. There are cer-
tain lands not to be in-
clofed; as lands for the
hofting of an army, and
for foraging the troops
of the Flaith or prince.

19. There are lands
left open for mill-wrights
to work on, or for car-
penters whilft conftruct-
ing a houfe; the royal
carpenters are priviledged
to dwell in the woods,
according to the Seana-
chas Law. Lands af-
figned and clofed for
burial places are not to
be opened, but by con-
fent of the proprietors.

20. Comicheach, i. e.
aliens defiring to emi-
grate, are to be attended
by fix perfons, three
from the owner of the
land, and three from the

Fodhla wood. Draighean, Trom, Feoruis, Crannfir, Feith-
lend, Fidhad, Findcholl.
Lofa wood. Aitten, Fraoch, Gilcach, Raid, Leacla, i. e.
Luachair.
And in a note is explained Ailm, i. e. Giuis, i. e. Ochtach.

ORIGINAL.

aineigne ni hacl‾ liactar
cricha ocomliachtaib feab
faerteaft modaig mairc
mbrugfaite coma comol
aitheam gaibeas tuinighe
madon teaft medon ach
ni firteaft tuinighe.

21. Teallach tararta.
c. teaft adh na techta tuinighe, teallach da dech-
mad cian ramar, ad do
coiflead tuinidhe.

22. Atait uii fealba
lā na gaibt‾ athḡ na beir
ceathra ina teaft it fir
indo loingad, toich do
boing atobach 7 a teaft
dun cen feilb. ceall gen
faitche, tir forfa mbai
fodlaig baifleach bo air
inuirmis mara ma beir
ceathra ura comol cis
Neimid tir daranda Flath
acleat‾ poll icurtar lia.

TRANSLATION.

tribe of the emigrator;
5 cows are to be paid
down if he emigrates by
his own defire, be he free
or bondman or bruigh;
if any fteal away pri-
vately, their chattels
may be feized on, as
they have no inhe-
ritance.

21. Teallach tararta,
is an inheritance or law-
ful poffeffion, which has
paid tythes (tenths) time
out of mind, the law
gives firm footing to
fuch poffeffion.

22. There are 7 pro-
perties pay no fine on
emigration; lands which
have been taken by force
in conqueft; families of
houfes without lands;
corban lands; lands of expelled moroders; where
there has been a mur-
rain amongft the cattle;
when the neimid or prince
has been fatisfied for the

ORIGINAL.

TRANSLATION.

rent of fuch lands divid-
ed between Flaiths after
conqueft; lands affigned
for dreffing victuals,
where holes are dug and
ftones fixed for that purpofe.

23. Tochomaig Cian-
nachat cian bruige. da ai
and fin famaigas, do
luidh tar feart a ced telt
bach for fine a forcomall
imana iarum ar feinea-
chas co hocht la iuidnige
fiadnaise ban a ceteall
nad reanad a. c. rufa
ceathrumad la atharach
ifead techta cach ban-
teallaig do luid iarum dia
ceandadaig condiablad
airme atharach lofad cria-
thar ceartfhuine cuairt
faigeas acomnaid la fear
f geall fiadnaife is iar
amathrach dian da freag^n
daig dlig ceath ruimthe
a. c. dlig aile amdon ach
tul fuigheall an deiga-
nach.

23. Ciannachat enact-
ed the cian bruige (*fine
to the houfe*) and or-
dained two fheep fhould
be paid for any perfon
trefpaffing on the lands
of a cedtellach (*firft inheritor*) and the tribe was
anfwerable for this fine.
She doubled the fine if
not paid in 8 days, fecu-
rity for which was to be
brought to the wife of
the cedteallach : if this
fine was not paid it was
doubled again, and fo
on to 8 fheep; and thefe
were the legal property
of the wife of a cedteal-
lach. This fine may be
exchanged for lofads,
fieves, kneading troughs,
or an entertainment at
the houfe. One man

TRANSLATION.

shall be pledged as secu-
rity of these fines (of 2,
4, and 8 sheep.)

    Comm. *Cinnachat was
    daughter of Conla
    mac Faidhg, son of
    Olioll Ollamh, he
    adds, one man or
    three women shall
    pledge themselves for
    the payment of these
    fines.*

Ced teallach and
ced muintir frequently
occur in these laws; the
Lexicons give no assist-
ance in the explanation
of these terms. Teallach
and muintir, signify fa-
mily; cedo in the Scla-
vonic tongue is a son,
filius, natus; I believe
ced teallach implies old
inheritors, i. e. born on
the land.

ORIGINAL.

24. Beartaid Senca cet-
brethach bantellach ar
ferteallach comdar ferba
fulachta f⁻ agruaide iar
cilbhrethaib.

Comm. *Cö ro im-*
fbuilngit⁻ nabolga for
a gruadib iar mbreitb
na claen breitb. i. iar
claen breithib.

25. Hic Saibrig a fi-
rinde a firbreathaib ifi
conmididar banteallach
comdar fearba falguide
for a gruaidaib iar fir-
breath⁻.

Comm. *Saibrig ingen*
Ifenca fin.

Da each alaim lea-
thaer dealba fi adnaife
indruic foircis dlig
cuice do dlig dianad
be Feineachas muna be
feineachais tellais iar fuidiu imidraind in dech-
maid iiii heich ailius
fcurtair faer fealba deige
fer fiad⁻ lat randta cof-
mailis treifi do dlig dianad be feineachas muna
be feineacas tellais iar

TRANSLATION.

24. When *Senca* form-
ed his code he diftin-
guifhed between male
and female property, left
he fhould fuffer that
judgment all Brehons
were punifhed with for
partiality; in having a
large wen grow out of
the cheek.

25. *Saibrig* eftablifhed
thefe fines in equity, and
thus faved her father
from this judgment of
the wen on his cheek.

Comm. *Saibrig was the*
daughter of this Senca.

Two horfes paid
down before witneffes
entitled to half freedom
of poffeffion. 5 were
formerly impofed, unlefs
it was a land inheritance
already under tythes. 4
horfes were afterwards
allowed, and two or three
witneffes required. Afterwards the law required
8 horfes from a tribe,
and three refponfible wit-

ORIGINAL.

fuidiu andigeand dech-
mad ocht neich aileas im
treib toruma treige fer
fiadan lat do gradaib
feine rannta cofmaifis tul
fuigheall uadaib diaad be
feineachas munad be fe-
ineach~ tectha tuinidhe
ilog do airgfean co feis co-
nodog co tein conaitreib
co toruime ceath~ acht tir
Cuind c. coraig no mitel-
gad mbruga noch is nei-
mead ifa fin telt fo do
bongar cach fealb.

TRANSLATION.

neffes. Thefe fines have
been impofed arbitrarily
and at pleafure, unlefs on
inheritances lawfully de-
fcending, then the *logb*
(fine) was fixed, except
in the country of *Conn*,
where he permitted
Bruighs to wafte fuch
lands as had been forced
from the poffeffor.

26. Crui tire do teal-
lach inaenan inain in-
oightear afetaib dorintar
mad la buar buir cumal
afe flandt~.munab fo feilb
techta tir gen cundgen
coibne dilfi buair b~ air.

26 Crui tire is the law
regulating that ruftics
fhall free themfelves by
giving cows; if they are
Boairec's their freedom
fhall be rated at 6 cows,
except the land be by
law exempted from tri-
bute.

27. Tuinide raitaigh a
triun fealba co dil no
derofc teilgead artreife
munab lais fobraid co-
tein conaitreib co flacha
faithche ite feich faithche

27. Such poffeffions
may be taxed to a third
of the ftock, if more, the
tax may be rejected; but
if they refift the lawful
tax by force, they fhall

ORIGINAL.

fir tellaig indligaig cli-
thear fet flaindte forgu
na nuile digu fet fomaine
la cofnam condeithbire
fir be fa haigrian.

28. Atait teora aimfea-
ra infeagaire itechta lā:
athgabhail eidechta tel-
lach indliḡ comrug gen
cura bel no gan elod
cundliḡ go tuaithe go
breitheaman nad beir fi-
acha cach ae.

29. Tofach befcna fo.

N. B. *This is in the margin.*

In ti do beir na techta
feilb afe doroñ co fiacaib
taige inti creanas centeol
gen taigi conglaine cuibfe
dileas dofuide o dia 7

TRANSLATION.

forfeit a milch cow ; Every chief has a right to a
dry cow from each, or at
leaft an heifer. The man
who owns the land may
legally defend the cattle
for the owner of them.

28. There are three
cafes where poffeffion is
illegal, retaking of land
without giving fureties ;
without application to
the chief or Brehon ;
without having fatisfied
the legal debts that were
upon it.

29. *The beginning of
peace :* it feems to denote
a diftinction between
thofe laws enacted in
time of paganifm, and
thofe eftablifhed fince
chriftianity.

Whoever poffeffes a
thing ftolen fhall pay the
fine of the thief from
whom he received it, if
the thief cannot be

ORIGINAL.

duine diam flan acubus
bid flan aanum.

30. Eimide dono dia-
nad forgeallt̄ ara feifear
coir comnadma ara ruice
fiream faigte faer faigaid
inmeafam cor comadais
cach anaicaidtear ara taeb
tanais ar ni feadar na-
darligtear lā do gres daig
fine 7 firgiallna na maith-
ri oiltreas ara atri ro fui-
gid do imfothaig cor.

Comm. *Eimide,* i. e.
the State Secretary.

31. Ni nais uma na
hairgead na hor acht
f̄ mal ni nais buarbach
india forneach lais na
biad ba ninais tir for im-
rum ach munas fotha
fealb ni nais edach for
nach nocht muna torma
tlacht ife greithe cento-
rad do gnid ro coubr̄ite
meafra ad gella acumung
do cach.

TRANSLATION.

found ; for whoever has
a clean confcience with
God and man will not be
guilty of fuch a crime.

30 The Eimide is to
clofe all matters on wit-
neffes having proved the
covenant. Surety of e-
qual value is not fufficient fecurity for a tanaift
according to old ftatutes;
tribefmen therefore fhall
give two witneffes or
fureties, and one of the
mother's fofterers, thefe
three fhall be deemed
proper fecurity.

31. No man is bound to
pay, brafs, filver or gold
but a king; cows are not
to be expected from a
man who has none, or
land from a man who has
no inheritance, or clothes
from a naked man ; a dif-
tinction of circumftances
muft be made in adjudg-
ing fines and penalties.

ORIGINAL.

TRANSLATION.

32. Ni mac bradas finntiga fine fri fodfrith ineafa munab neafa fircoibneas, mathair athair inorba.

32. A fon does not deprive the tribe of land unlefs he is the next eldeft of the mother, by the father who owned the land.

33. Horba mathair mur coirche a mic oflaithaib a ard thimna.

33. Mother's lands (dowries) are fecured for the fons by the will of the Flaith, as by Coir. *(See Coar explained at* N° 75).

34. Do aific aleath'im do cumfine fingrian aleath anaill afir brethaib. fil afeola fodlaigtear fine o cirt cobrainne. nis tic do ct comfocais acht ct orba in boaireach da vii cumal comarda orba biatach in boaireach orba for fet nim faebair as daranar leith dire.

34. One half of the inheritance is reftored to the tribe, and the other divided legally. The feed of his fleth (*baftards included*, fays the commentator) partake of this divifion with the tribe. 14 cumals (42 cows) entitles a Boairec to biatach lands; but lands that have been purchafed are not fubject to this divifion.

ORIGINAL.

35. Slan fairgſe inbrogad in bruidrechta. in graide tire comdidan coimitheach ni diſeanar iar mo bi bliadain acht beſaib fochruᵭta ar nach cnead be ſlan re meaſaib is dicaingean Ia.

36. Sir cach ſen dliḡ cacha criche condealg in tan is di coindelg cach crich is and berar cach digeand co Righ.

37. Ni Righ lais na biad geill inglaſaib dona tabarchis Flatha dona eirenedar feich cana in tan geibius in Righ in amama ſo is and doranar dire Righ gen gae gen eaſbrat gen eis indrucus fri thuatha.

TRANSLATION.

35. Bruighs being an order of men appointed for the entertainment of travellers, they ſhall not be taxed for the ſpace of one year; and as their lands are beſtowed them, the produce of his land is to be taxed after that time, by the old ſtatutes.

36. When an ancient inheritance is in diſpute, the caſe muſt be brought before the king.

Comm. *Unleſs it can be ſettled to the ſatisfaction of the parties by the Brehon or Judge.*

37. He is not a king who cannot demand hoſtages; who cannot command tributes from Flaiths; who cannot recover fines for treſpaſſes. When he can do theſe things without oppreſſing his nobles and plebeians, without doing injuſtice to his people, or ſuffering others to do the ſame, then he is truly a king.

ORIGINAL.   TRANSLATION.

38. Atait ʋɪɪ fiadnaife for gellad gaecach Righ. fenad do fodadh afa nairlifi cen fir cen dligˉ. dide aire. inge mad tar cert maidm catha fair nuna ina flaithius difce mblechta milˊead meafa feol neatha ite ʋɪɪ mbeo caindle and fo forofnad gae cach Righ.

38. Seven things bear witnefs of a king's improper conduct: an unlawful oppofition in the fenate; an overftraining of the law; an overthrow in battle; a dearth; barrenefs in cows; blight of fruit; blight of feed in the ground. Thefe are as 7 lighted candles to expofe the mifgovernment of a king.

N. B. *This is like the coronation oath of the emperor of Mexico, who, was required to fwear that duɪ ing his reign they fhould have feafonable rains; that no inundations of riveɪs, fterility of foil, or malignant influences of the fun fhould happen.* See De Solis's Hiftory of the Conqueft of Mexco, book 3, p. 94.

39. Ieora gua ata moam do fich dia for cach tuaith. fuilleam gu nadma forgeall gu fiadē gu breath ar fochraic.

39. Three capital crimes are adjudged the common people: breaking the earneft of fureties; breaking an oath

ORIGINAL.

TRANSLATION.

before witnesses; giving falfe evidence.

40. Atait iiii nadm nad feadad ciad roifcaidear mud for a flaith mac for a athair manach for a abaid ulach for araile mad anaenar ar fo fuaflaice flaith 7 fine 7 eaclas cach fochar 7 cach nocar fo cerdcar for ameamra acht ni for congrad ar ate ateora nadmand afpa innfin naifcaidtear lā cor for achaib fine ar do imtai flaith 7 fine 7 eaclas cach cor natoltnaigt ar dlegar doibfium na be lobtaigh cor ardiam bad lobtaigh feon cor ifand intinntatfom curu amemor.

40. There are four duties to be indifpenfably complied with, the ruftic to his flaith; the fon to his father; the monk to the abbot; to be amenable to the laws of the flaith, the tribe, and the Church. There are three covenants to be ftrictly obferved by the moft indigent, a covenant with the members of the church; a covenant of fervice to the flaith; a covenant of good behaviour to the tribe. Thefe covenants to the church, the flaith, and the tribe are indifpenfable.

41. Atait iii nadmanda lā nadroithead ni anaicaidf digaib do log eneach eireach no feagad naid forneach finntar f‾. urforcra, naid corufa gaide lagad aige gin ingada fa defin forcraid coibche fri eachlaid aratait da

41. There are three covenants which do not amount to a log-eineach, eiric or feagad; a covenant that has been made known by proclamation; a covenant for theft when the thief has been fuffered to efcape; a co-

ORIGINAL.

achlaid cor lā, bean fris
tabar coibche naidnai-
gead fer do beir coibche
mor fribaidfig fornafcara
dilfi ara ate cuir innfin
nad roithead co trian ro
fuidigeadh aniubartaib
cor lā. Acht urgartha
cor lā ni dileas ni gen
airillnidh ar nach craide
is eaflan iniaid acoibche
dliḡ flan craide a feir
breitheamnus acht uais
no urccairt no egmacht.

TRANSLATION.

venant of female dowry
when challenged; there
are two challenges of this
kind, when a woman
gives land to man for
adulterous communicati-
on, or when a man gives
land to the woman for
the fame, the fureties on
fuch occafion not extend-
ing to a third perfon, the
law juftly breaks them;
but thefe proclamations
muft be made in form,
and the man fhall be de-
clared to have been in-
firm, and not in a pro-
per ftate to have made a
grant of that kind.

42. Atait tri tond naiḋ
naifcaidt lⁿa, diceanglad
a feic eamna, bean fri
tabar coibche indichligh
feach a athair mad ar
dicheall anathair afath⁻
aendk̄n in coibche fin
cor fo cerdcor feach aga
fine ada cora do beith⁻
oga cor faefma fo cerdcor
feoch fine nurnaige ara

42. There are three
covenants not binding
by the old ftatutes, and
which are null and of no
effect: a covenant of
dowry made to a woman
without the father's con-
fent, for the dowry was
the father's property; a
covenant made with the
Flaith for his protection

te donadmand inn fo diceanglad a feicheamna nadad cora donadmaid˜.

without the confent of the whole tribe; a cove-nant exacted by the Flaith without confent of the tribe. Thefe co-venants are void in law.

43. Ataic uii˙ nurd-luide fine ar do longad cach fine ite uii nilaidte do laiead o fetaib 70 feal-baib, foirgeall o fiadaib arach for dagnadmaim tuinide for dagrathaib afdad lan log legad creice cenurgaire aitai diu fo taeb ecal˜ coingilt fri flaith.

43. There are feven fines to which the cattle and lands of each tribe are fubject; fureties be-fore proper witnefles; co-venants by fureties; pof-feffions held from fupe-rior Raths; detaining the logh or fine; fuffering moroding on the chief knowingly; moroding on church property; breaking covenants with the Flaith.

44. Ataic iii tire lˉı a-da dilfiu cin ni tardaidt˜ a logh ar indeall andilfe condate tri decmainge in domain adintud tir acam-bi flaith do dilfe tir a-cambi eaclais do dilfi tir ɪcambi connfine do dilfe.

44. There are three kinds of landed property that do not give the logh of their cattle: Land the real property of the Flaith; land immediate-ly belonging to the church; land properly and really belonging to the tribe.

ORIGINAL.

45. Atait iii. tire aile nadatuſa for feinaib na breithamnaib do tinntogh, tir dianairbiatar flaith, giatograid comharba do, munrodligtear ataiſeac co treabair, tir do ·berar do eaclais ar anmain nadfacaib eaſlan acraidhe, acht mad iartain la comarba, tir dia toirgtear ando ratar ina log do tindud na dentar ac neach 7 ata acuingid diubarta 7 tairgt aſeoid le afearaind fein 7 ni geib achuingid diubarta is dileas in f~ann do ticatha.

TRANSLATION.

45. There are three other landed properties neither the Tribes or Brehons can avert from their proper uſe: Lands aſſigned for the menſal of the chief, or can the ſucceſſor diſpenſe with this homage from the tribe ; lands aſſigned to the church for the ſoul's ſake, (Comm. *adds, the ſucceſſor may claim it, but not in the ſick man's life time*) ; lands given inſtead of a *logh* ſhall not be exchanged ; and if any one deſires to quit his holding, or is expelled, let the emigrator be offered his portion of property, but the expelled man has no right to any part of the landed property.

46. Ataìt iii. deirg mirinda nadetuſa ambelaib cacha Flatha na fadbad luibar na feine anaſtad bo cona timtach fri ſo-

46. There are three things difficult to be ſettled regarding the Flath which have been handed down by report only, and

ORIGINAL.

TRANSLATION.

maine naenaigh gabail aitidan tar duthracht, lan eric in ceile 7 ogh nairbid o comarbaib arus do fuidiu conameas lā nidofli uii cumala chumal as do Flaith ni dofli uii leathcumla leath cumal as do Flaith ni dofli iii. cumala iii. s. as do Flaith ni dofli cumal s. as do Flaith mad ni bes luga confoglaigtear ariaraibh feine arrogart Padric inna hindfa fo ar na conrabad la firu Eirind iflaith in Righ Laegaire Mac Neill do can 7 do cach eaclais arid tanfoltaig and fo uile.

are not to be found in the old ftatutes : Stopping cows of a poor peafant at fairs if he does not pay the duthrach or fairtax; in cafes of full Eiric for the murder of a wife or young ftudents, where the law demands 7 cumals, the Flath claims 1 cumal, where 3 cumals is the fine he demands half a cumal, when one cumal he claims a heifer, where the crime be lefs he obliges the tribe to compound. At Patrick's arrival in this Ifland, at the requeft of the men of Ireland, in the reign of king Laegaire Mc'Neill, he fhewed the evil tendency of all thefe to the people and to the church.

47. Cis lir tairgfin cacha fine, connar do labraidtar eaclais rofuigaidt⁰ Flaith for do tuigaid tear.

47. What was then offered to each tribe, that they fhould have a Flaith to fpeak for them in the church meetings. The

ORIGINAL.

.TRANSLATION.

Comm. *adds in* brei-theam *and in* eacl⁻, *in judgment and church af-femblies*, i. e. *in the civil and ecclefiaftic trials.*

48. Atait iii. cuir tind-tai mac beo ath⁻ ima a-thair nach airmead lui-bair na feine do airingaire a tindtog f⁻. go fetas tu-, ailing gill de fri bas, do fannad agrian techta do fannad ni rod imbi dibeo dil 7 marb dil do fannad connach bi ni fris nder-na a bethu.

48. There are three things required of a fon by all the books of the tribe laws, without varia-tion on the part of the fon : viz. at the death of a father to free his law-ful inheritance ; to fulfil the law and his father's will relating to his bre-thern ; to provide for each, that no one wants a maintenance.

49. Ni techta an fine dith ar fine arus cā moch-ta tuillean afeibe feadar imcaire feibe na feagar imtellach mboaireach ach iii haidche bede cora la thuaith 7 cenel cona nur-laind techta tuifeach cach fine ara nithead feib 7 befcna.

49. No ufurper fhall force himfelf on a tribe, on the election of a chief; but the chief of kin of every tribe fhall affemble at the houfe of a *Boair-each*, and remain three nights in the election of the proper chief, doing all things for the beft and peace of the people.

Comm. *In fl⁻ ro dib⁻ if̃ fun 7 ma ta bruigh is*

Comm. *On the death of a Flaith, or any*

ORIGINAL.

TRANSLATION.

tir 7 comadbuir imda
dul do lucht na tuaithe
uile go tech in bruigh
conna landaimh la ca
f. dib 7 ab 7 ≐ la 7
teora barvidchi an' ac
denamh comairle cia
gabait ifin fl's 7 gu-
rabe gabait inti dana
duch' in fimb̄nus 7
gural mac flatha 7
gurab ua air aile 7
go rabat na tri con-
taifme aige 7 gurab
indric gin gait cen
guin.

*fuch caufe the people
of that diftrict fhall
affemble at the houfe
of a Bruigh, and
fhall remain 3 days
and 3 nights, with
their attendants, in
confultation of the
election, and fhall
elect the proper heir,
whofe father and
grandfather has been
a Flaith, had three
royal palaces, and
governed himfelf
without injury or
hurt to his fub-
jects.*

50. Fallach cach fine
fris ambai micora ma da
feallas dar faer fairgfe ni
fanntar ni feacha fine
o becaib comoraib co-
ruige abad fine conarfaf-
tar doib fo lin fiadan ach
tall muire feth flatha 7
for comal chis flatha
icain aicillne no thorc
neochraide no boin gab-
hala no molt corufa fine

50. It is lawful to
plunder on the open fea,
but no tribe is to covet
the property of another,
from the loweft to the
higheft; on being accuf-
ed of plunder they fhall
produce witneffes that
they were taken at open
fea, out of the Flaith's
dominions. They fhall
pay the Flaiths rents and

H

ORIGINAL.

arus do ro dil fine fris
nangaibt athgabail na-
thai na giallna acht toir-
feat anatihga treifi cid be
imdi roib re dfinn fine
is do an fuiglib airechta
fuigeall impu.

TRANSLATION.

taxes, without oppofi-
tion, in fwine, horfes,
milch cows, or wethers,
and are forbidden to take
back pledges or cove-
nants; if thefe crimes
be committed by the *in-
fine* (Tribe) the Airech
fhall put the law in force
on them.

> N. B. *The different* fine
> *or tribes, are ex-*
> *plained in a fubfe-*
> *quent law, and the*
> *various tribes.*

51. Feab aindir be
carna, doranidhar fetaib
oige dia rubla fo fuiriftar
ach ro pennead anilpe-
acta cia rob iar nilar
comleachta.

Comm. *Do reir an-*
carat.

51. A woman con-
victed of obtaining
wealth from youth for
the crime of whoredom,
fhall be deprived of the
wealth fo obtained, and
do penance.

> Comm. *According*
> *to the heinoufnefs of*
> *her fins. Ancarat,*
> *in an ancient Glof-*
> *fary, is explained*
> *to fignify the rules*
> *of certain patron*
> *faints.*

52. Cifne iii leaca ro-
baid nad fuaflaici dlig
na fuigeall na fafach
na fir naicnig, ei-
birt nemda foraniada
comfcribeann deo da,
chis comdidean fri triar
fen dligead forrfaide
fine fen cuimne, co-
boirifc ui heatha adfui-
tear faire atarras.   .

53. Cifne iii haimfa
inad apail a torad ar cach
flaith combe dithle, ith,
(comm arbha) 7 blicht
(lacht) 7 meas (na cail-
leadh) taithmeach nud-
burta faerad fuidre fuaf-
lugad X mad fuaflucad
do mogaib.

54. Atait iii tedmanna
ada andfum tecaid in bith.
nuna do tiachtain. àr ci-
niuil do chur. duine ba
dia tiachtain.

52. What are the
three fundamental lef-
fons to be taught to all
ranks? The holy facri-
fice which has been writ-
ten by the will of God;
tribute, which the anti-
ent laws prefcribe, or
tradition has eftablifhed;
the regeneration of life
by water.

53. What are the
three feafonable offerings
from a Flaith? Corn,
milk, and fruit; the free
feuds redeem thefe offer-
ings by free gifts, the
flaves by tythes.

54. There are three
dreadful things happen
in this life: famine, civil
wars, death.

ORIGINAL.

55. Atait iii frither nodaicad f⁻. comed do breitheamnaib: ar na rugadh gubreath; almſ-ana o cach di cach, torad nemfoirgeall. gua no gu fiaꝺ ituaith.

56. Cain berad meirdreacha alanamnus imuine do ciallathar loghneineach incelad bainfeſa in taigi tairfine toranna mbruighe infaig orba lā mac doirche is brecht ceroithne mac muine anfaim cach ndoirche cach ina comfogail in manur coillead lanamnus incelad ruca cacha baitſaige ataige la fine mathar mac baitſide, do roig le imbreathaiô aicnigh 7 cuibſe 7 ſcrebtⁿ 7 la fine mathar mac baidſaide.

TRANSLATION.

55. There are three ſpecial things to be obſerved by Brehons; Not to give falſe judgment; to give alms without expeⷜation of requital; to rejeⷜ falſe witneſſes.

56. Married men guilty of whoredom ſhall pay the *logb eineacb* (mulⷜ); for baſtards are not to be ſtolen on the tribes, they are the ſons of darkneſs, and have no right to wreſt their landed property from them; every harlot ſtolen into a tribe, can only be the mother of a baſtard; and it is impoſſible for ſuch a woman to declare the real father of the child, for in the opinion of every Brehon and man of letters, ſhe can be only termed the mother of a baſtard.

ORIGINAL.

TRANSLATION.

57. Cis ne iii mic na gaibead urtechta mac cumaili mac mucfaide mac biride cid fo dera fon aris indfa mc cumaili i flaithius arid cutruma ado ailche fria in athair arus corarnac mucfaide fo chis ni hufa bach briathrach iflaithius.

57. What are the three defcendants not entitled to rank? The fons of women flaves, the fons of men flaves, the fons of idle brawling women; the fons of women flaves are excluded the rank of Flaith, let their claim be what what it may on the father's fide, for the fons of flaves fhould always be under tribute, and it is not proper the fons of harlots fhould ever be Flaiths.

58. Baidfeach cach lies taige no cach ben deairaig alanamnus cen deithbire ar nifaig atairfine fine cen to cuirid no cin log *faefma* no gin fir fo gerrta no *coimpta* noime.

58. Poor and naked women are to be avoided in marriage by the tribes-men; women not worthy of being endowed, not worthy of the fifc or protection; or of the comforts of life.

59. Guach cach brathum aenlus 7 taige it comfeich lā, ingad is taige ataige is merrlle

59. According to old ftatutes, theft and moroding are efteemed equal crimes, for mo-

ORIGINAL.

inmerlle itlan feich ar doran cach alaimnige ara laim 7 atheangid ara gnim 7 acubus dia fafar flan brethaib feancha lā it comarda an eiric aenlus 7 taige.

60. Atait iiii faba tuaithe no do des fruithidar imbecaib. Ri gu breathach; eafpoc tuis leadach; filid diubartach; airec eifindric; dlegar do cach Righ firinde, dleagar do cach eafpoc andgus; dleagar do cach Filid neamduib airtce aircedail; dleagar do cach aireach indrucus ar na doige amaā ni dlegar doibh dire.

61. Sruith fer finntiu, fen fer findthiu ni fuith muna fuafdar ni techta afinntiu fo da fith fo da clai foda derga foda tlean for do tuigaidt an fine 7 mi coraibh. Ni tuailing

TRANSLATION.

roding is theft, and a thief is to make reftitution; therefore theft and moroding, are equal crimes, and the *Eiric* equal.

60. There are four pefts to fociety, when they fo happen: A king given to falfe judgment; a bifhop inclined to vice; a falacious flattering poet; an unfaithful *airic*. Every king is bound to be juft; every bifhop to be pure; every poet to be fincere and open; every *aireach* to be faithful, and upright, and not expofed to the fines or punifhment of the law.

61. Proper tribefmen are diftinguifhed and known. Senior tribefmen are not to be expelled unlefs they have been guilty of great crimes, fuch as litigiouf-

ORIGINAL.

breitheamnacht lā na fiaſtar tellach ⁊ comicheas mbruigreachta co fiacaib cacha ceathra ⁊ duine caithib ⁊ duine chintaib a teatl fo techtughadh iſead doſli dilſi nairme ateall fo leadh toirſin iſead doſli tri ſeota fo imcumas naithḡ.

Comm. *Bo ⁊ ſam̄ ⁊ duirtad.*

62. Fer tailge aceath⁻ anathbothar, aceile no ar do aiceand do ſli leith fiach fri himcumus nathgabala aratha athgabala lā, do ſli, ſ. ina focſal no ina fuaſlocad athgabail fuaſlaicter ar toiriſean acomong lā firiſe do ſli leith fiacha.

TRANSLATION.

neſs, aſſaults on their neighbours, murder, and ſuch like crimes; they are not then entitled to the benefit of the law, unleſs they have conformed to the Bruigh law; have paid all treſpaſſes of men and cattle; they are forbidden to take up arms, or combine privately in reſiſtance under the penalty of three cows.

Comm. *A cow, a ſtripper, and a beifer.*

62. If men drive their cattle to treſpaſs on bare graſs (*in winter · ſeaſon* adds the Commentator) is half treſpaſs, and reſtitution accordingly by the Seanacas; and the redemption of the cattle ſhall be paid in *ſeads*, or cows.

<table>
<tr><td>ORIGINAL.</td><td>TRANSLATION.</td></tr>
</table>

63. Talgud do cea-
thra imbuailiug do ceile
do flifet ina muin, ar ni
mo dulc do gniat oldas
do maith, acht na maith
nach dich mairc.

63. If they drive cat-
tle into a bawn where
winter fodder is depofit-
ed, a cow is to be de-
manded for trefpafs; for
they do much mifchief
in wafting and confum-
ing hay.

64. Fer idaig ceathra
aceile ina fer diguin adre
iii feoto am bid aceath‾
fo defin adnagad ind.

64. If a man permits
his cattle to enter a
ftrange bawn with the
cattle of his neighbour,
he fhall forfeit 3 cows,
as if they had been
driven in by himfelf.

65. Fer do tleann a
ceathra a faithci indi-
guin a ceile as rean iii feota la·fer aithg‾ ataib no
airceand inti na bi fer
feraid a log a reir Breitheaman 7 afrean iii feota
ind a reir breithean‾.

65. If a man permits
his cattle to mix with his
neighbours, and enter
his meadows, where is
hay or grafs, he fhall forfeit 3 cows, or pay re-
ftitution; if he has no
hay, he fhall be fined by
the Brehon, not exceed-
ing 3 cows.

ORIGINAL.

66. Dileas fer foirfe i teall fealba na be dileas nac naen i teallach fealba acht fear foirfe caiti in fer do na gellaid feoit 7 faidbrige ifi faidbri caich i tellach fealba dilfi a airine.

67. Ini tochta imfir fear foichlide corab do noud nemdrong corofui-dis dar Padraeg fir fer n Eirind anofaib flatha a comcet fadaib eacal.

68. Tal no flifeam flancraid leafdar baduirnd tre lia inothar no fir nai-rifme fri haltoir, no fir

TRANSLATION.

66. Every man muft take poffeffion of land openly, and no property can be poffeffed but with the knowledge of all parties, and when he has paid his cattle or o-ther riches for land, it is then lawful for him to defend it by force of arms.

67. The rights of the church were eftablifhed in Ireland by Patrick, by the confent of the Flaiths or Princes.

Comm. *Laogaire, Corc & Daric, Patrick, Benin & Carmach* (a).

68. This was a chip of the old tree. 3 *lia* was the gift at the altar as a facrifice to Heaven. Pa-

(a) In the old book of Balymote, p. 167, is a catalogue of the more eminent Fileas, or authors of the early ages, which begins thus: " Nine perfons were concerned in the " *Seanacas-mor bearla Feine,* viz. 3 Kings, 3 learned Fileas, " and 3 holy men. The 3 Kings were Laogaire, Corc, " Daire. The 3 Fileas, Rofs, Dubthac, Fergus. The " 3 holy men, Patrick, Beneoin, and Cairfeac."

ORIGINAL.

fogearrta no compta naime, ate ind sin fira rosuidit Padraeg do gleod fer n'Erind islaith in righ Laegaire Mc'Neill inos fer n Eirind.

TRANSLATION.

trick ordained this on the Irish in the reign of *Laogaire mac Neill*, as he found it an established custom among the Irish *(b)*.

Comm. *Many good books explain this, such as the long book of Leighlin.* (Leabair fata Leglinde.)

69. Cislir dia ro suidighe comdire ła. Ged. corr. caitin. caileach canait comdire ła nihice nachae aithg̅ araile.

69. What was accepted from the vulgar: Geese, herns, kittens, cocks, whelps, were equally offered according to the *Seanacas*, or old law.

70. Crim feam fiadubull dia ro techtaidt̅ greas for nideoin admad acerdca tirad anaith (1. gradh flatha) bleith amuilleand bleith alamhbroin dichmairc bleith for libroin deanam cleib denam cleithe lascad luise loscad guaile t̅obā tire claide mianna tochar puirt imirt

70. Flaiths of their generosity bestow wild apple-trees to smiths for anvil-blocks; and to millwrights for cogs and handles to querns; for making baskets and wattles; for burning weeds and lighting coals; for toghers to houses (*i. e. hurdles over bogs*) for the game

(b) Lia, in Arabic *leyah*, is a white bull; the Commentator here explains this word a speckled calf.

ORIGINAL.

glaith for rot epe cacha feada acht fid neimead no degfidh im feadain in damaib fo imrim nac t leafdair imrim eich ach tri heocha conoifcead dire each righ each eapfcoib each fuadh no nae co lin feafa iffide condaile comdire friu dul tar chill dul tar dun urba int na fert airech glanad raite cofcradh aile cain dorn cliath corus aeaig urclaide tairis.

. 71. Corus indbir. atu forgain forcraid fomelta for eoin fuafclucad athgabala a forrgabail aga-

TRANSLATION.

of (c) gliath on the roads; thefe are cut out of every wood except holy woods. The horfes of kings and bifhops make good all damages for breaking through the fences of a church or dun, or deftroying the tomb of an *Airech*, to be determined by an Umpire, and they muft afterwards be fettered.

71. River Laws. It is forbidden to fifh in rivers, or to deftroy birds on them, without leave

(c) *gliath*—This word is now obfolete. I believe it fignifies the game of *hurly*, now called camánt; in Perfic *ghaluk* is a play ball and *ghulte* a round ftick, a rolling pin; gliath may therefore fignify a *hurling bat* or a goff club — gliath in Irifh is fkirmifh, fighting hand to hand; *ghelis* in Arabic the fame. All the puerile games and manly exercifes mentioned by Nieuhbur in his voyages into Arabia, are common with the Irifh; fuch as the games of five ftones, pitching the ftone, the bar, &c. &c. the *Quern* or hand mill for grinding corn, of which he gives a plate and defcription as of great curiofity, is in ufe in Ireland at this day in many places. In Perfic Kemanè is any thing arched, as the bow of a fiddle, &c. in Irifh camàn, is the batt or hurling club, which is alfo arched.

ORIGINAL.

bail edechta a focfal afaichthe afcoir dia didean fuaflucad coimdeadh farcuibreach for eocha derged comraig nadfornaſt cuibreach fir na do turguid imeaforgain oca teilgtar fuili nadligead othrus urgabail mnacen amcablugad forcraid nimana for ceath is aire conaimeas na comdire feo icuic fetaib ar na hernigt inar imbec 7 ar na beth ni gen eiric 7 arnhimirba neach na be hai. Ar do imarna Padraeg na tiafdais na comdire feo tara ni doruirmifeam afiir naicnid 7 coibfe 7 fcrebtir andul gan ni is mo arate comdire and fo ro fuigeaftir Padraeg anos fer nerinn iar creideam cuig *fed* conaimeas in cach dire do fund la haithgin.

72. Cis lir cain iꞇ na bi imaclaid la cona do ro dilfib do cach dib cedna friaraile. Cia himirba cach dib friaraile ni

TRANSLATION.

firſt obtained, whoever is caught in this trefpafs, ſhall reſtore what they have taken ; and if their horfes ſhall break into meadows, they ſhall be detained until redeemed. All horfes let loofe in open grounds ſhall be long-fettered to prevent difputes, and if any quarrel ſhall arife to the fpilling of blood, in this caufe Eiric ſhall be demanded. At the coming of Patrick thefe fines were fettled in true wifdom; and Patrick agreed to them, as he found they had been before eftablifhed in Ireland; five cows he allowed to be the full reftitution for each of thefe trefpaffes.

72. What are the degrees of confanguinity or ties, between perfons, where reftitution is made by fafting only, or fub-

ORIGINAL.

tuille acht aithḡ cotrofcad
no himcim iar trofcad na
hapad. Mac 7 a athair.
Ingean 7 a Mathair.
Dalta 7 aide. Ingean
7 a buime. Mac 7 a
maithre. mad oige ma-
magaire Flaith 7 aceile.
Eacʈ 7 a manaig. fuaidre
bith comaideadan cis 7
afli Righ 7 anathig orr-
tha, cumal (1. daera) 7
aflaithe, techta adaltra-
cha iar na hurnaïd no
aidite dia finaib fria firu
oedmuindter acus a ceile
do rair ngairead intan do
nic fatna him aclaide feo.
is and do nic fad na du-
ba digeanna cenail gen
fafach cen dicetal na
berrdar afiraicnaid na
fcrbeῖ na fafaigh ar ro
fuigideadh na cana fo
otofach domain co diaig
cen imaclaid.

73. Cis lir ro fuidi-
gead ro dilfe cacha tu-
aithe ada comdilfe da
cach 7 recht hae aite

TRANSLATION.

mitting to the chaftife-
ment of the Abbot after
fafting. This kind of
reftitution fubfifts according to the Seanacas or
old law, between the fon
and the father; the
daughter and her mo-
ther; the daughters and
fons of a Flaith and his
wife; between the church
and its monks; the feuds
and the Flaith; the king
and his chief warriors;
the bond families and the
Flaith, except in cafes of
adultery which extend
to the tribes of the firft
families and their wives,
which law muft be fub-
mitted to without re-
ferve; the moft learned
men and writers and all
holy men have ordained
thefe fines from the be-
ginning of the world to
this day, and for ever.

73. What are the pri-
vileges allowed to native
Ruftics? To cut wild
crab trees for handles of

ORIGINAL.

Crim allda mainandach
cach uifce biath foibirt
cacha frotha lortudh
aidche do crinach cach
fid gen trenugud ful-
acht cacha chaille cnuas
cach feada arad cacha
fedna crand fedna collna
cranngill atharguib luith-
each laime da achlais bi-
rer and treige nurcomail
damna fondffa damna
looinida fiad cacha feda
adaig eadarba condeith-
bire feam cacha trachta
dulifg cacha cairge torad
cach trethain ala cairrge
cach fid cen criniughad
imbleith forlig aenach
naiditan dul aneathar
imirt fithcille tige aireach
faland tige briugad dirind
uas cach flabrad forch-
imig adaig eatarba in-
glas.

74. Fuaflaice each ru-
grad for fna heatha ai-
ditiu as ingaib fir fithiu
fuaflaict go comlabra fir

TRANSLATION.

fifhing fpears, for river
fifhing; to burn brufh-
wood in the night for
drefling of fifh; to cut
fmall branches of white
hazels for yokes or fuch
tackle as will twift for
the plough, and for
hoops and churnftaves;
they are free to the pro-
duce of woods border-
ing on the fea, to fea-
wreck, dulifk, and to
every eatable thrown up
by the fea on the fhore
and rocks, but in col-
lecting thefe, they muft
go quietly and peaceably
from place to place by
fea. They are alfo al-
lowed to play the game
of chefs in the houfe of
an Aireach, and to have
falt in the houfe of a
Bruigh: On leaving the
fhore, the boats muft
be chained and locked.

74. It is noble and ge-
nerous to forgive little
trefpaffes committed by
humble ruftics; the

ORIGINAL.	TRANSLATION.
fealba feoit indilfigar airgfe na haiti diu eudail na tranlide neirt.	ftrong fhould not fhew their ftrength over the weak.

End of the Fragment of the Brehon 'Laws in the MSS. of Trinity College.

The following are from the MSS. in the poffeffion of Sir John Sebright, Bart.

At the beginning of this Fragment is the following remark, part of which I have inferted in the Preface relating to the Brehon Laws:

As for the Forts called Danes Forts, it is a vulgar error, for thofe Forts called Raths, were entrenchments made by the Irifh about their houfes, for we had no ftone houfes in Ireland till after St. Patrick's coming, A. Chrifti 432, the 5th of the Reign of Laogary Mc.Neill, and then we began to build churches of ftone; fo that all our kings, gentry, &c. had fuch Raths about their houfes, witnefs Tara Raths, where the Kings of Ireland lived, Rath Crogan, &c. &c. &c.

THADEUS RODDY.

☞ The Reader will find Mr. Roddy's affertion of the Raths confirmed in the following Laws,

FRAGMENT.

ORIGINAL.

75.. Cis ſ fala foriadat dilſe cā aſelba, as na tintuither cidiupart.

Fal fine hicas a caithche coronicchar fa cā ſet ronicca conaſumuine natet inairmidi fer gleth names naith intire cid maith acht ni rocclanna a lam fa deiſſin fir aſacathach.

Fal fir chrenas imbecc luaig do forcid arro fera arro fertar fris na cetar.

TRANSLATION.

75. What is Fal, granted to landed property; on taking poſſeſſion or on quitting the concerns *(d)* ?

Fal granted to a man to become one of a tribe, ſubjects him to pay tribute of all his property, of cattle grazing, of fruit, of corn, &c. and all increaſe of ſtock is from thenceforth ſubject to tribute.

Fal is granted to the man who purchaſes land, and offers the value agreed on, but cannot get poſſeſſion.

(d) Fal implies a king or chief, but here ſignifies certain royal privileges conditionally granted the Tenant, on his ſettling under a Flaith or Chief. *Pal* and *Phal* in the Perſian and Turkiſh language is a guardian, and the word is often joined with *Schal*, which ſignifies a king: it is ſometimes corruptly written *Pad*, *Phad*, and forms *Padiſchal*, a title given to the great kings of the eaſt. See the Turkiſh Lexicon, at the word *Pad.*

ORIGINAL.

Comm. a cafe. *Ferand
do recaftar duine and
fo, ๅ ata acacra a di-
ubarta and ๅ do aircend
in duine ro cendaig in
ferand afberand fein
do aris ๅ afeoit do-
fum ๅ ni bail leiffuim
acbt adiubairt ma ta
trebaire a dilfi uili ar
iiii. buairib* xx[t] *meni-
uil dilfi atrian ar iiii.
buarib* xxet ๅ *ada trin
a x maid* ๅ *is fal fein.*

TRANSLATION.

Com. *Here it is fup-
pofed that land is
fold to a man
by agreement, and
the holder will not
give poffeffion, but
offers to return the
value and keep his
land; if the pur-
chafer has paid down
the value he may
force the other to quit,
if not* $\frac{1}{3}$ *muft be depofited in* 24 *hours,
and the remaining* $\frac{2}{3}$ *in
ten more, which en-
titles him to Fal, i. e.
he is to claim the in-
terpofition of the
chief.*

Fal naud barta imbelu
uafal nemed, fal do tire
ranne do flaith iar ne-
ludh.

Fal given verbally by
an Uafalnemed or Flaith,
muft be obferved when
any Ruftics quit his ter-
ritories (e).

Fal fir fofuiditar dag
nadinand coforathaib ๅ
foidh fiadnaib aris ann

Fal is granted to a
man who fettles under a
Rath, for fervice and la-

(e) A verbal *fal*, is the protection which a noble gives to a ruftic on fettling under him; and when about to quit his chief, he fays, I demand my liberty and the cattle I gave for my protection; and he fhall not leave the chief's land until he is fatisfied; this is alfo called *Fal.*

I

ORIGINAL.

do tcet fual fo trebuire
in tan dona thongaiter
cuir dar enech fer.

Fal anfuitchiffa iffe
fede tintaite aiter iar tain
arin dilfide.

75. Aĩ iii tire fris na
contobir ṁc na Rath ua
fiadhnaife la. na dilfe is
go airechta anaftud di-
gaib dilogainech aireach
no dofegat.

Tir fomaicc dona ta-
bair log cia do bĩ fine
ar nitechta conn na ciall
foṁc intan nafcair inn
inan ifin ecnaircc.

TRANSLATION.

bour; and has given
furety for his orderly behaviour, in conforming
to the laws of the Tribe,
and for payment of
Enech (f).

Fal is granted to mi-
nors who have property,
until they are of age.

75. There are three ca-
fes of lands under the
protection of Raths or
tribes, to be reftored to
the proper male line ac-
cording to Seanchas or
Old Law, where the lo-
gheineach has been ex-
acted contrary to law.

Lands of minors
feized for the payment of
the Logh, which is con-
trary to the law till the
minors are of proper
age to govern their own
affairs.

(f) The Enech or Logh eineach as explained hereafter,
is a tribute given by the tenants to the chief for settling under his protection; *Enach, emenda, Scotis, vel fatisfactio quæ
datur alicui pro aliquo delicto feu injuriâ;*—occurrit in Regiam
Majeftatem, L. 2. C. 12. This is called *Eineclann* in thefe
Laws, and is the fame as *Eiric* or reftitution for murder,
theft, &c. in many places.

ORIGINAL.	TRANSLATION.
Tir do beir icoibchi mna nad bi maith na-duidnaidet afolta coire.	Land given in dowry to women which has been alienated from the male line by effect of the Coir (g).
Tir do beir dar braigit fine aratreufu inda tengaid dec diathintud oldas intoen tenga do aftud.	Land unlawfully wrefted by force from another of the fame Tribe, this fhall be reftored by the judgment of 12 tongues (voices) but one diffentient tongue (voice) fhall retain it.
Comm. *Totbchus is meffu ifenchas and fo tochus duiri 7 dochraite.*	Comm. *This was a cruel and unjuft law of the ancients, and rendered property precarious.*

(g) The Coir exifted in the time of Sir Hen. Piers: it is explained in his hiftory of the county of Weftmeath. pp. 117. 118. See Collectanea de Rebus Hibernicis, No. 1. Vol. I. " Every town land is grazed in common ; fo one who is not acquainted with them, would think, that they plowed in common too ; for it is ufual with them to have 10 or 12 plows at once going in one fmall field ; neverthelefs every one hath tillage diftinct. He then defcribes the method of dividing the land to be plowed in lots, and proceeds when the fquabble about dividing is over, they as often fall by the ears again about joining together or coupling to the plow, for fometimes two, three or more will join together to plow. This they call Coir or Coar, which may import an *equal man, fuch another as myfelf,* and with little alteration of the found

I 2

ORIGINAL.

76. Cach fuidir *(h)* conatothcus techta ni icca cinaid a meic nachai

TRANSLATION.

76. Every Feud, or Feudift, that has no legal poffeffion, no wealth

may fignify help, right or juftice."—In this they are alfo often very litigious—but in cafe of difagreement, their cuftoms hath provided for them, that with confidence they may come before their landlord and demand from him their *Coar* or equal man, or helper to plow, which they count the landlord bound to provide for them, and if he cannot, he is obliged to affift him himfelf.—This, fays Sir Hen. is called Bearded Owen's law ; he was one of their Brehons. If Sir Henry had not preferved this word and its explanation, in the 17th century, I fhould have been at a lofs. It is evident that when the Irifh feudift had no property in land, but held from the Chief, that a Das or Dowr, at the death of the widow, might have been confounded and loft in the *Coir* or divifion of the ground ; but this law obliges the tribes to watch over this part of the chief's land. There is a Caftle on the banks of the Suire called Tighe gan Coir, and vulgarly Ticancur, i. e. the houfe not fubject to the Coar. Tacitus defcribes this Law among the Germans. De Mor. Germ. C. 26. Agri pro numero cultorum, &c. The members of a German nation, fays Tacitus, cultivate, by turns, for its ufe, an extent of land, correfponding to their number, which is then parcelled out to individuals, in proportion to their dignity. Thefe divifions are the more eafily afcertained, as the plains of Germany are extenfive ; and though they annually occupy

a new

(*h*) Fuidhir in the Irifh Lexicons is tranflated a hireling or attendant ; it appears to be the radix of the Englifh *Feud* or *Feudift* a vaffal or villain, and to be derived from the Hiberno-Celtic *fod*, glebe, foil, from whence the Latin *fodio* to turn up the earth, to dig ; French *fouir*. In an ancient gloffary in my poffeffion, it is derived from *fo* under, *daer* protection ; Arabicè derh. I find the words *foer, fuidir* and *daer-fuidir* in the laws, which exprefsly means the free feud and the bond feud.

ORIGINAL.

nachai armui nach ain-
dui nacha comoccus fine
nach a cinaid fadeifin
flaith idmbiatha ife ic-
cais acinaid air nilais dire
a feoit acht colauin aith-

TRANSLATION.

nor ftock of his own,
pays no trefpaffes of his
fon or of his neareft akin.
The Flaith who victuals
or fupports him, pays
all fines for his thefts, in

a new piece of ground, they are not exhaufted in territory.
This paffage, fays the learned Dr. Stuart, abounds in inftruction the moft important. It informs us, that the German had no private property in land, and that it was his
tribe which allowed him annually for his fupport a proportion of territory. That the property of the land was invefted in the tribe, and that the lands dealt out to individuals returned to the public, after they had reaped the fruits
of them; that to be entitled to a partition of land from his
nation, was the diftinction of a citizen, and that in confequence of this partition he became bound to attend to its
defence and to its glory; with thefe ideas and with
this practice, the Germans made conquefts. In conformity therefore, with their ancient manners, when a
fettlement was made in a province of the empire, the property of the land belonged to the victorious nation, and the
brave laid claim to their poffeffions. A tract of ground was
marked out for the Sovereign; and to the inferior orders of
men, divifions correfponding to their importance were allotted. View of Society in Europe, p. 24.
   The word Coir or Coar, or Carr, fignifies lot, chance,
fortune; and Cranncar, is a lot drawn by fticks of different
lengths, in the manner the Arabs pretend to divine at this
day: And this was the method followed by the Irifh in the
divifions of the ground; thus the longeft ftick had fuch a lot
(which had been previoufly marked out) the next longeft
another lot, and fo on.——A number of thefe Coirr's or
Carr's made a *Cir* or Circle, which perhaps gave name to
the prefent *Circles* of Germany, and to the Canon *Cire* and
Englifh *Shire*, unlefs we may derive the word from the *Cir*
or Circle round the altar ftone, of which in another place.

ORIGINAL.

gena nama ni gaib dire
aṁc nai naca dibad na
ceraicc nacha inathar
flaith arambiatha iili nod
beir 7 iccas achinaid 7
folloing acinta.

Fuidir laiis mbiat. u.
treba dia ceniul fadeilin
is tualaing ionicca a
chinta 7 araruib iatha a
Flaith is lafuide dire a feoit acht trian do flaith.

Fuidir iuð cin comfo-
gois manib. u..treba aigi
da thoirithin. i. u. Raith-
chedach 7 manib aigen
flaith beid.

Comm. *Is iad na u.
treba* 1. *teachmor,*
7 *bothach* 7 *foilmucc,*
7 *has cereach,* 7 *has
laegh.*

77. Log *(i)* enech
fuidre ma doer fuitiir can
mittir ainchaib a Flatha

TRANSLATION.

an equal reftitution on-
ly.   He fhall not receive
Eiric for his fon, or bo-
dily Eiric for his mother.
The Flaith who fupports
him pays all fines and
trefpaffes.

A Feud having . five
treba (or that has pro-
perty) fhall pay fines and
trefpaffes, and fhall give
one third of his profits
towards victualing the
Flaith.

A Feud is not liable to
fines and trefpaffes for
his next of kin, unlefs
he has thefe 5 treba, i. e.
a Rathchedach, and vic-
tuals his Flaith.

Thefe are the five treba,
i. e. 1. *a great houfe,*
2. *an Ox-ftall,* 3. *a
Hog-ftye,* 4. *a Sheep-
houfe,* 5. *a Calf-
houfe.*

77. The Logh tribute
of a Feud, if a bond feud
is one fourth of his ftock

(*i*) Enech is a tribute, fine, mulct, &c. I take logh
encch to be the fame as the Locatio of our ancient tenures,
i. e. a contract by which land is let or demifed.

ORIGINAL.

cethramthu a dire ales alethfaide diamnai, ar cacht recht ta acht oentriar is leth log aenech diamnai, ferfon cenfelb cen thothchus las mbi ban comarba ainchuib amna dire narfide 7 fer inetet tom amna tarcrich direnar ainchuib amna 7 cuglas direnarfi de ainchauib amna 7 ifi iccas a cinta madiarnu urnadmaim no aititen dia finib.

78. Is tualaing na teora ranna fo imoicheda cora cele connatatmeife recce nacrecce fech amna acht ni forcongrat.

79. Log nainech cach fuidire acht doerfuidir direnar afalethothchus alleth naill is na Flatha 7 nech iccas a cinta.

TRANSLATION.

to the Flaith, and one eighth to the Flaith's wife; if he has no Flaith but a Dowager, the ufual tribute muft be paid to her; and if any man fettles under a dowager, he fhall pay the ufual tributes, and alfo all feafaring men under her, not having a Flaith over them; and if they were nurfed or brought up by the tribe, fhe fhall pay all their fines and trefpaffes.

78. Thefe three claffes of men may make covenants with the tribes, for they are not under the immediate controul of the Dowager.

79. The tribute of every Feud, the bondfeud excepted, is half of his ftock to the Flaith, but he is not to pay the feuds, fines, and trefpaffes.

ORIGINAL.

80. Atait teacht fuidi-
ła fuidir fofcuil a aithrib
fuidir dedlaid frifine co-
nail fuire cach fuidir acht
teora fuidre adadurem
dib. 1.

Fuidhir goible, no fuid-
hir crui.
Fuidhir gola.

Fuidhir flàn.
Fuidhir faer.

Fuidhir cinad a muir.
Fuidhir accu fed.
Fuidhir griain.

81. Is meifi fuidhir
griain imfcartha fri flatha
acht do airfena a felba
do flā acht ni forgaba
cinaid for flatha do aif-
bena an gaibes o flatha
met laiget bis eitir fod 7
indngnam beirid aen tri-
an facaib da trian la flatha ol cena.

TRANSLATION.

80. According to old
Law there are 7 kinds of
feuds who quit their na-
tive tribes to feek pro-
tection of a Flaith, and
thefe may be mixed with
the free tribes as conve-
nient, viz.

Who have been guilty
of blood-fhed.
Who have loft their land
by wars.
Who have fled for debt.
Who have forfeited co-
venants.
Pirates.
Who have wealth.
Who have land.

N. B. *Thefe explanati-
ons are by the Com-
mentator.*

81. The *fluidhir griain*
may feparate from his
Flaith when he pleafes,
but muft pay the proper
fine, by producing his
ftock, one third of
which he fhall take with
him, and the remaining
two thirds are the pro-
perty of the Flaith.

ORIGINAL.

82. Do eftethar meth cacha fuidre for cuic fetataib 7 iffed dā do doɓr do ar a auccu ar a chain arachairde ar arechtnge ar a dire acethra ar a dond 7 ar a meifce.

83. Cair ciflear fini tuaithe 7 cid inet arfcarat ite fine cacha tuaithe, Geilfine, Deirfine, Jarfine, Indfine, Deirgfine, Dubfine, Fine taccuir, Glasfine, Ingenar meraib, Duafine; ifam diba finntedaib.

Geilfine coccuicer ifi aide gaibes dibad cach cind comacuis dineoch diba uaid.

Deirfine cononbor ni daba huaide cobraind folin cenn comocas.

Iarfine cotriferraib dec ni beride acht cethram thain dichin na fomane diorbu nafaetur.

TRANSLATION.

82. The fine or mulct of a Feud is five cows, and thefe fhall be given for his fettlement, for his tribute, for his protection, for his law-fuits, for his cattle trefpaffes, for his venery, and for drunkennefs.

83. Of the names of *fine* or tribes in every diftrict, viz. Geilfine, Deirfine, Iarfine, Indfine, Deirgfine, Dubfine, Fine taccuir, Glaffine, Ingenar meraib, Duafine; thefe are the *Fines* or tribes.

Geilfine are thofe who have no inheritance, and accept of a portion from the next of kin; this tribe may confift of five men.

Deirfine are next of kin to the lawful heirs; their nnmber is limitted to nine.

Iarfine may confift of 13 men, they are to give one fourth of cattle and fervice.

ORIGINAL.	TRANSLATION.

Infine co feacht firu dec conranna cadeifin finteda dineoch diba uaide amal befchoir duthaig duine otha feniffan fcarait finntetha.

Infine confift of 17 men; when any of thefe die, the property may be divided as if native tribes; all above this number to be fcattered through the Tribes.

Deirgfine iffede crueis nidiba huaide ni cobrannaide finntea iffeach comoccuis.

Deirgfine are fuch as have been guilty of murder, they fhall not be admitted till the mulct or reftitution has been made.

Dubfine iffede dombeair fir noilleg na fintar imbi fir foanfir ni cobranaide finthea condatuice fir caire no cranncuir is iarum conranna cethraimthain fri indfine.

Dubfine are fuch as have been guilty of theft, they fhall not be received whilft accufation lies againft them, or entitled to cor or cranchur (fee Law 75) thefe may be divided through the Indfine.

Fine taccuir iffede tomberat cuir bel afoeifam ni cobrannaide dā finnteda acht ni ifuifedar cuir bel.

Fine taccuir are thofe who fettle under condition of the *coir bel* (i. e. coir o bealaib.) They forfeit protection if they do not comply with the *coir bel.*

ORIGINAL.

TRANSLATION.

Comm. *These are* mac-faefma *settling under a verbal promife of the Flath (k).*

Glasfine mic mna dit-fini bearas do Albanach ni gaibfaide acht orba mad no duthrachta ded-laid fri fine.

Glasfine are the fons of women of Scotch defcent; they fhall have land only, and may be divided through the tribes.

Comm.   *Gabair tar glas no fairge—bearas bean don fine d'albanach.*

Comm.   *Thefe are brought from beyond fea, born of women of a Scotch tribe.*

Ingen ar meruib ifu-ide dodindnaig cluais do cluais do comceniuil ded-laid fri fine connranna-fide finnteda on med ad-daimther ifine.

Ingen ar meruib, are brawling, idle, tattling women, related to the tribes; they muft be divided through the tribes.

Comm.   *Gelfbis indfir feo do ghlefbis ind-fhir ele.*

Comm.   *Flying from one man to another.*

Duthagfine ni cobran-naide eitir iffan diba fin-tedaib finte fuidir cota fille fodail fon enmuin moigethar mac fri a a-thair 7 ni ren intathair

Duthagfine do not di-vide their property on the death of any of the tribe, but it afcends to fuch feud next in blood as have raifed themfelves

(*k*) In a hand writing different from the Commentator's, is the following remark: The writer of this note is Aodhgan and he is repairing this very old MS. at the mill of Duna-daighne, the place of his abode, and making very unfkilful remarks on thefe old Laws, in the year of our Lord 1575.

ORIGINAL.

ni fech michu fech ua
fech iarmu fech indue.

84. Forgu cach fine foſ-
cuchuad fallſcuichte cen-
trom cach muin arailid
cach rath aſomuine co-
feoit ernnair do fognam-
thaidib.

Ahui chuinn cofaelas
turanau taſcuru nimcho-
maid Airech madiarma-
mad mbrogthair dinaro-
fat ramatu tabar doib
ditchus fodling foſagud
fele furired co failte cen-
duine dicill ditreib taraſ-
tar diamiar naurfocru
techta dlegait ſiur foeru
manip centola tinſcgra
riam ruirter.

85. Cia lin Raith do
cuiſſin. fine rath. me-
rath; iar rath; foer rath;
rath doboing; comracc
rath; naicille rathirraith;
rathicuit find chorach;

TRANSLATION.

from a ruſtic ſtate, and
defcends from father to
fon, and ſo on to the
grandfon, and great-
grandfon.

84. The Forgu (*fir tho-
ga*) or chofen head or chief
of every tribe or fine,
may leave the tribe when
he pleafes, and is enti-
tled to fuch ſtock of the
Rath as ſhall be adjudg-
ed him for his fervices.

The Aireach or chief of
a country when he aſ-
fembles the *Fine* in bo-
dies for his own defence,
ſhall give them recom-
pence for their trouble;
each head of a *fine* ſhall
provide fufficient for his
maintenance, and after
a victory or routing it is
forbidden to plunder, un-
lefs it be previoufly or-
dered, as a reward.

85. Of the number
of Raths; they are thus
named, Fine rath; Me-
rath; Yarrath; Soer rath;
Rath doboing: Comracc
rath; Naicille rath-irr-

ORIGINAL.	TRANSLATION.
forgurath; airifs mefe cach a athcuir no roigthi laime dia rath.	aith; Rathicuit tind chorach; Forgu rath: the ftock given to thefe raths may be retaken (by the chief) at pleafure.

Thefe Names are thus explained by the Commentator.

Finne rath,	belonging to eftablifhed tribes.
Merath,	new fettlers.
Yar rath,	compofed of the followers of a Flath.
Saer rath,	made free by the Flath *(l)*.
Rath doboing,	have forced themfelves on a Flath and overwhelmed the native inhabitants.
Comracc rath,	who have withftood an affault and defended the Rath.
Naicille rath-irraith,	fettled under a Flaith and paid fines and fureties.
Rath icuitrid chorach,	entertain the Flaith and enlarge their holdings by new covenants.
Forgu rath faer rath,	chofen by the Flath to be free Raths.

(l) Rath is pronounced *Rah*. In Arabic *Reha* is an independant tribe; it is alfo an area of ground with a rifing in the center.—This is much the figure of the Irifh Raths or Forts.

ORIGINAL.

86. Nach Rath fris nafcar iar neccaib flatha ni tormaig log nenach manitairce fomuine.

87. Iren cāngaeth. maith cach beannad bidruth genmnaide : cach macc beifgor diathair : cach manach befgor dia eclas nindar banar uaide. cia dofnecmai forcofnam arni tuidmenat cuir nemed ar infamlaiter nemed fri befu carpait nach tuidme tonuidmenar do is uathfuaflucud uad.

TRANSLATION.

86. No Rath fhall have the fine of location increafed at the death of a Flath, unlefs the ftock is increafed in proportion.

87. Hear the words of wifdom; good is the woman who loves without luft; good is the fon who is amenable to his father; and the monk to his church, he will not be expelled with fhame. Who ever refufes to make fatisfaction for his fins increafes his guilt againft Heaven, for Heaven is like a chariot on wheels, the more the refiftance, the farther it flies from you.

(To be continued in a future Number.)

THE

CHINESE LANGUAGE

COLLATED WITH THE

I R I S H.

BY

LIEUT. COL. VALLANCEY.

THE

CHINESE LANGUAGE

COLLATED WITH THE

I R I S H.

THE Chinese, it is said, began to improve letters from the earliest times of their Monarchy, at least from the reigns of Yao and Chum, who lived upwards of 2200 years before Christ. It is a common opinion, and universally received by those who have investigated the origin of a people of such unquestionable antiquity, that the sons of Noah were dispersed over the Eastern parts of Asia, and that there were some of them who penetrated into China, a few ages after the deluge, and there laid the first foundation of the oldest monarchy we know in the world.

It is not to be denied, that these first founders, instructed from a tradition not very remote from its source, in the greatness and power of the *first being*, taught their posterity to honour this sovereign Lord of the Universe, and to live agreeably to the principles of that Law of Nature

he

he had engraven on their hearts. Their claffical books, fome of them written even in the time of the two Emperors juft named, leave no room to doubt of it. Among thefe books there are five that they call the Kink, and for which they have an extreme veneration. Though thefe books contain only the fundamental Laws of the ftate, and do not directly meddle with religion, their authors intention having been to fecure the peace and tranquility of the Empire; yet they are very proper to inform us what was the religion of that ancient people, fince we are told in every page that in order to compafs that peace and tranquility, two things were neceffary to be obferved, the duties of religion and the rules of a good government. It appears through the whole, that the firft object of their worfhip was one *Being*, the fupreme *Lord* and *Sovereign Principle* of all things, whom they honoured under the name of *Chang-ti*, that is, Supreme Emperor, or *Tien*, which in their language is of the fame import. *Tien*, fay the interpreters of thefe books, is the *Spirit who prefides over Heaven*; it is true, the fame word often fignifies among the Chinefe, the material Heavens; and now fince Atheifm has been for fome ages introduced among their literati, it is reftricted to that fenfe; but in their ancient books they underftood by it the *Lord of Heaven*, the *Sovereign of the World*. In them there is mention upon all occafions of the providence of *Tien*, of the chaftifements he inflicts upon the bad Emperors, and of the rewards he difpenfes to the good. They likewife reprefent him as one who is flexible to vows and prayers, appeafed by facrifices, and who

diverts

diverts those calamities that threaten the Empire; with a thousand other things which can agree to none but an intelligent being. The reader is referred to the Extracts which Father Du Halde has taken from these ancient books, in the second volume of his History of China, and what he farther says in the beginning of the third, & to Banier's Mythology, Tom. I. p. 130.

There is not only a great conformity between this *Kink* of the Chinese and the Brehon Laws of the ancient Irish, but the name of the supreme Being is also the same. Ti, is the appellation of the great God in all the old Irish writings, and *Ti mor*, i. e. *Ti*, God, spirit, will, design, intention, and *mor* great, is the modern name of the supreme Deity. See Shaw's Lexicon. *Tiarna* is the name for a prince, a lord, and also of God. *Teinn, Teann* is strength, power, and also fire. *Eampal* and *eampaid* was the altar stone, and tieampal formed the word Teampal a church, and the Latin Templum. It is certain, that in these antient books, proofs are to be found of the knowledge the *Chinese* had of the supreme Being, and of the religious worship they have paid him for a long series of ages; it is no less certain that no footsteps are there to be seen of an idolatrous worship. But this will appear less surprising when we consider; 1st. That Idolatry spread itself through the world but slowly, and step by step; and that having probably taken its rise in Assyria, as Eusebius alledges, where there was not even the appearance of an Idol till long after *Belus*, or according to others in *Phœnicia* or in *Egypt*, it could not have made its way so soon

K 2　　　　　　　　　　into

into China, a nation that has ever been fequeftered from others, and feparated by the great Indies from the center of Idolatry.

2dly, That there was always in China a fupreme Court, or Court of Rites to take care of the affairs of Religion, which with the utmoft exactnefs kept a watchful eye over the principal object. Thus it was no eafy matter to introduce new laws and new ceremonies among a people fo much attached to their antient traditions. Befides, as the Chinefe have always been accuftomed to write their Hiftory with great care, and have hiftorians cotemporary with all the facts they relate ; they would never have failed to take notice of what innovations had happened in religion, as they have done at great length, when the idol *Fo* and his worfhip were in-troduced.

Such was the eftablifhed religion of China, and fuch nearly was the eftablifhed religion of the an-cient Irifh Druids : like the ancient Chinefe, they never worfhipped any animal ; like them they had no carved or engraven images ; like them they be-lieved in the *Metempfychofis*, as a proof of the foul's exiftence after death ; and in this religion the Chi-nefe continued till the time of *Confucius*, who hav-ing often repeated, *that it was in the Weft they would find the Holy One*, they fent ambaffadors into the Indies in queft of him ; thefe tranfported into *China* the idol *Fo*, together with the fuperftitions and Atheifm of that fect.

The

The learned and ingenious author of *Recherches Philofophiques fur les Egyptiens et les Chinois*, *(a)* has very clearly demonftrated from the worfhip, cuftoms and ceremonies of the Chinefe, that they did not proceed from the Egyptians, but from the Scythians. The collation of the Chinefe language with the Irifh or *Iberno-Celto Scythian* dialect, will confirm Monf. Paw's affertions. And with this author, I am of opinion that they had not the ufe of Letters fo early as is pretended, for they feem to have loft their ancient Orthography; from the perifhable materials their ancient books were compofed of, it is impoffible, they could exift many years as Monf. Paw has proved, and to this lofs I attribute, the prefent defect of the Chinefe language, viz. the omiffion of the letter R, and the termination of almoft every word with a vowel. The Irifh lofe the force of moft terminating confonants, but ftill preferve them in the writing, and that thefe confonants were in the roots of the words originally, is evident by comparing the Irifh Radices with the Hebrew.

The prefervation of thefe confonants not founded in the Irifh dialect, appears to be the ftrongeft argument for the early ufe of letters among the Irifh. The fimilitude of the Irifh language with all the Oriental dialects is aftonifhing; but particularly with the Arabic, Perfic and Tartarian : and if the *old British* was once the fame language, the Britains muft have loft their dialect, becaufe fuch words are

not

(a) Monf. Paw, 2 Tom. 8vo. a Berlin, 1773. He is the author alfo of Recherches fur les Amèricains ; a work replete with knowledge, learning and difcernment.

not to be found in their Lexicons; but the more probable reason of this similitude is, that the Irish language has been enriched with colonies of *Oriental* nations, from *Spain* and *Africa*, agreeable to the traditions of their most ancient *Seanachies* or historians.

The following vocables of the Chinese Language are extracted from the Lexicons of Bayer and Fourmont; the roots or keys as they call them are only 214 in number; but the language as spoken, they say consists of 1500 words, and the characters are 80,000 in number, to which they are daily making additions, as they improve in knowledge; for Monf. P. has plainly proved they are as yet but a very ignorant people, notwithstanding the pompous accounts given of them by the Missionaries; and that the best of the manufactures brought from China to Europe, are made in Japan, and exported from thence to China.

The manner of writing used by this people must at length become so obscure, that if ever arts and sciences are brought to perfection among them, it will be impossible to continue the use of it, or for posterity to read it. For example, if they would write *some men have killed a wild beast*; they make the character which expresses *plural*, to this they add the character expressing *a man*; then that of the verb to *kill*; and, lastly, that of a *wild beast*, all which are united in one figure, without any other distinction.

The authors of the Universal History thus express themselves concerning the Chinese.

That the descendants of *Japhet* peopled China as well as *Tartary*, we see no reason to doubt, tho'

when

when they firſt arrived in that Country, we cannot pretend to ſay. That a conſiderable part of it muſt have been uncultivated, even in the year 637 preceding Chriſt, when the *Scythians*, under the conduct of *Maydes* firſt made an irruption into upper Aſia, has been clearly evinced *(b)*. That the language of the *Chineſe* was pretty nearly related to the *Hebrew*, and the other tongues which the learned conſider as dialects of it, notwithſtanding what has been advanced to the contrary, we own ourſelves inclined to believe. *Thomaſſinus, Maſſonius, Rudbeckius,* and *Pfelfferus,* ſeem to have proved this almoſt to demonſtration; though Mr. *Bayer* does not come ſo readily into their opinion.

It is true a great number of words in the preſent *Chineſe* ſeem not deducible either from the *Hebrew* or any other language; but then theſe may be conſidered as an acceſſion to the primæval terms uſed in *China,* which were exceeding few, and undoubtedly favoured of the primitive tongue. Theſe authors then proceed to examine *ſeven* roots, which, they ſay, the Chineſe conſider as the firſt and moſt ſimple of any in their language. Seven Roots in a language! Univerſal Hiſtory, 8vo. London, 1748, vol. 20.

Treating of the origin of the Tartars and Moguls, theſe learned authors obſerve, that the progeny of *Magog, Meſhech* and *Tubal,* planted both

the

(*b*) Monſ. Paw proves that moſt of the interior parts are uncultivated and uninhabited at this day, except the borders of the Rivers and of the great Canals. *Recherches Philoſ.*

the *Scythians*, and confequently the country of the ancient *Moguls* and *Tartars*. I have fhewn the fimilarity of the *Kamuc-Mongul* language with the *Irifh*, in an Effay on the Celtic Language prefixed to the fecond edition of the Irifh Grammar, and fhall in this place take notice, that the Irifh name for a bow or crofs-bow, is *crann-tubhail*, i. e. the bough or ftick of *Tubal*. See all the Irifh Lexicons.

Thefe obfervations will lead me to difcufs this fubject further, in a future work. I fhall now proceed to the collation of the Chinefe and Japonefe Languages with the Irifh, which I flatter myfelf will confirm what I have frequently advanced, viz. that the purity and antiquity of the Irifh Language is ineftimable in the refearches into the Hiftory and antiquity of nations, and merits the attention of the learned, as Leibnitz, Lhuyd and many others, have obferved.

Collation of the Irifh with the Chinefe and Japonefe Languages.

It muft be obferved that the Chinefe from a vicious pronunciation, have rejected the found of the letters B, D, R, X, Z, and have changed thefe into P, T, L, S, S. The commutations of thefe letters is common in many European dialects, yet none have abfolutely rejected them. See Lhuyd's Compar. Vocab.

The Orthography of the Chinefe words, in the Roman letter, varies much according to the national dialect of the tranfcriber; for example, fuch words as Bayer writes with ç, Ludovicus writes with *th*; *ch* with *tch*; Fourmont with *tfch*.

I fhall

I ſhall here follow Bayer.

Non inutile erit ſcire, quem in modum Luſitani et Hiſpani hæc pronunciant. Luſitanicum et Hiſpanicum ſcribendi modum utcumque ſequamur.

An, *on* efferuntur pronunciatione inter utramque vocalem media, ſic etiam ao et au, ut ſit ſonus aliquis medius.

ç Hiſpanico more effertur. Ludovicus ſcripſit *tba*, pro ça.

C ante *e* et *i* ut apud Germanos et pleroſque alios, exceptis Italis.

cb ut apud Italos c ante e et i, et apud Germanos fere ut tſch. Ludovicus ſcripſit *tcba* pro *cba*.

g ante *e* et *i* ut *dſcb*, adſpiratione in gutture formata, in fine g eſt durum.

y et i ante conſonantem et vocalem aliam, eodem fere modo ut de g· diximus, efferuntur: ſed ore magis clauſo et ſibilante, ſic *yue* fere ut *gue*.

ku et qu non differunt.

n ante g tamquam unica litera pronunciatur.

m in fine ut *ng* ore aperto, ut g liquidus exprimatur.

ie cum puncto ut gallicum ụ ſed ut ſibbilum anſeris.

x ut *ſcb* Germanicum.

h fortiter effertur dura aſpiratione ut proxime abſit a k.

Signa quinque tonorum in hoc exemplo dari ſolent.

	LATIN.	IRISH.
Yȃ,	ſtupor,	gaige, gair, gairige, gean.
Yà,	excellens,	gar, gaoine, gur, gaiſge.
Yă, yă,	anſer,	gè.
Yā,	mutus,	gaoi, taoi, to.
Yȃ,	dens,	feag, fia-cul, kia-cul.

The

The Reader muſt obſerve, that in the Iriſh, the terminating conſonants are not ſounded, when aſpirated with the letter *b*; which makes the ſound of many words the ſame as in the Chineſe; theſe terminating conſonants being *Radices* in the Hebrew, Arabic and Iriſh, give great room to conjecture that the uſe of letters among the Chineſe, is not of ſo ancient a date as they have aſſerted, I mean of the letters or characters now in uſe in China; for according to *Cuper* and *Wiltzen*, they had a different character a thouſand years ago; a mirror of ſteel was dug up at Vergatur in Siberia, with an inſcription round the margin in Chineſe characters as it was ſuppoſed, which none of the Chineſe Litterati could read; they pretended to give a tranſlation, but it was conjecture only; and ſaid the mirror was written in a character uſed in China about 1800 years ago. See the account and figures in *Lettres de Monſ. Cuper*, p. 20. The characters reſemble the Iriſh *Ogham*, given in the laſt Edition of the Iriſh grammar, and are probably the antient Scythian.

The Chineſe language collated with the Iriſh, or Iberno-Celto-Scythic Dialect.

CHINESE.	IRISH.
que, a houſe,	cai.
que, a hedge,	cuana.
oirt, a tree,	gort, ceirt, (coirt, bark).
te, a houſe of recreation,	ti; teach.
qnia, to walk,	cuadh.
tung, a large houſe,	Dun, dunadh; daingean.
tung, a billow,	tonn.
toa, a hot coal,	teo, warm; doig, fire.
lang, a man,	lonn, ſtrong; luinn, a hero.

CHINESE.   IRISH.

tay ku. Thefe words or characters, fays Menzelius, are not the name of an emperor but of his title, i. e. principium rerum. Tai or Taidhe ku in Irish, will exprefs principium Heroum.

bonze, a monk, a hermit, who keeps open houfe for travellers.

bainze, entertainment, feafting.

kuen, quen, refpect,

conoidh.

kive, connection,

comh.

foe, (this root betokens wet, moifture.)

foi and fo, the fame in Irifh as in foal, fual, water.

fola, blood.

foid, wet turf.

foinfi, wells, fprings.

foarge, fairge, the fea, &c. &c.

chu, the character betokening command.

fùidh, fùi, caith, cu, as in cu-cullam, cu-connor, &c.

xen, the hand, greeting, falutation.

fonnas, greeting, fhaking by the hand.

fu, learned; it is alfo a mandarine.

fuidh, faoi, noble, learned.

Status et dignitas mandarini : nefcio cur in monumento Sinico explicetur. Plebs, vir vulgaris (fays Bayer) ut apud Menzeluim in Lexico.

by the following Irifh word, we may fuppofe Menzelius is right, for fuithean, fuihean, plebs, the vulgar.

CHINESE.	IRISH.
ço, a foldier,	fuoithreac, i. e. fuoai-reach, a foldier.
çai, it is, he is,	fe; ife.
hia, under, behind,	iar, ria.
xi, a temple, church, pa-lace,	fith, the old name of the church of Cafhel was Sith-drum; fithbhe, a city.
fan, expiation,	fan-leac, the ftone of Expiation, the name of the Druidical altars in Ireland, with a top ftone in an inclined pofition; hence probably the Irifh fan and the Latin fanum, a church; *fan-leac* and *crom-leac*, are fynonimous words for this altar; hence Phanephorus, i. e. folis facerdos, quia φάνης *fol.* See *Saccheus*, ch. 69, *de expiationis altaris ritu.* Arab. Perf. *fanus,* a Pharos.
guei, fear, dread,	agh, fear. guidhe, prayer, entreaty, gubha, bemoaning, a fuffering.

CHINESE.	IRISH.
tu, country, land,	tuath.
yo, cruel,	dora.
ngan, fortune, profpe-rity,	gaoine.
yeu, yeus, the right hand,	deas, yas, deafuith.
ço, çi, the left hand,	cli, fo, awkward (gauchè).
dzy, the fouth,	deas.
fy, the weft,	fiar, iar.
tum, the eaft,	tam, tùaim, oir.
pe, the north,	teth, badhbh.
nan, the fouth,	noin.

There cannot be a ftronger fimilitude in any two languages than in thefe names of the cardinal points of the compafs. The Irifh, after the manner of the Hebrews and all oriental nations, name thefe points, with refpect to the fituation of the perfon looking to the Eaft; thus *Oir*, is before or in front; *tuaim* is the fame; it fignifies alfo the face or front; (*tuàim*, i. e. *èdan*, i. e. *agbaidb*, (old-glofs. of the *Irifh language*) tuachioll moving round againft the fun; *deas* is the right hand, and the South; *fiar*, behind, in rear, and the Weft; *tuag*, is the left hand, and the North; *tetb (te)* and *badbbb*, or *bav*, are alfo names for the North. Hence the northern Chinefe, to fignify they were the firft inhabitants of China, call the Southern Chinefe *man-dzy*, Barbarians, or South-men. See *Quef-tiones Petropolitanæ de nominibus Imperii Sinarum, p.* 35. Gottingæ, 1770.

It

It has been obferved by fome Irifh writers that Eirin, the name of Ireland could not be derived from *fiar* or *iar* the Weft. Thefe authors did not know that *aeron* or *ieroun* in Hebrew implies *Weft-ward*, the fame as the Phœnician *Iber-nae*, or Weftern Ifland.

CHINESE.	IRISH.
tim, a key,	ting, the clafp of a lock, tongue of a buckle, &c.
hu, a wolf,	faoil-chu (faoil, treacherous.)
yum, glory,	daimh, dia-yaimh, the glory of God.
chum, menfura,	tomadh, to meafure; cumha, a veffel.
guei, honoured majefty,	gùr, guimh.
min, to engrave,	minn, mann.
	mindreach, an engraved image.
	dreac, an image, is the root of the word man-dreac, or man-drake.
	miun, a letter of the alphabet, becaufe engraved in the bark of the ancients.
lie, feries, order,	lai, laine, laidhne.
kin, a commander, a chief,	cionn, ceann.

CHINESE.	IRISH.
kin, to inhabit, dwell,	conaidh.
teu, the head,	*tuaim*, the face, *tait*, *tuis*, *tuas*, the head, the top; hence *tua*, a noble, and *ta*, i. e. *mulean*, an owl or the great headed bird.
mien, foundation of a house,	mein to dig; hence mine, oar.
niu, a woman,	nae, a woman, naing, a mother.
yven, hiven, a deep abyfs; the material heavens for *tien* fignifies excellent.	*duvaighin, dovain,* an abyfs; *neav,* heaven; *fla-eavnus,* heaven, i. e. flaitheamhnus, fla, noble, great, fupreme.
van, dead,	bann, bano, death,
van, without (fine)	fan, gan.
kam, great, drynefs,	cam-lofithe, burnt up, parched with heat; cuime, hard, probably this is the root of the Irifh *cuimin,* the murrain among cattle, proceeding from great droughts.
yen, fpeech,	caint, hean-mor, i. e. fhean-mor, great talk.
kien, a crime, a fault,	cionn, cionta.

CHINESE. | IRISH.

kuon, a mitre, a crown, — cean-beirt, a helmet, a crown.

chu, reft, eafe, — fùa, fuamh; hence, fùan, found fleep.

kiùn, a foldier, — cuathan, kethrain, foldiers.

kua, qua, a certain divination by lots, — cuar, i. e. draoidheacht, (*old glofs.*) Sorcery or Druidic knowledge.

cùig, a fecret art.

cuar cumaifgna draoithe, the magical circle of the Druids.

cu-ard-thofaigh, the great Druidical myftery.

crann-cuir, a divination by twiggs or fticks.

cuivrionn, forcery; rainn is alfo forcery.

fum, breath, wind, — feidhm, a figh.

fu, to die, — fab, death.

çiam, chief leader of armies, — fithbhe, fithmhe.

kua, the penalty of man-flaughter, — cumal; the common word is *Eiric*, which rather implies a tribute; in Sclavonian *barac*; in Turkifh *barai*.

guei, a circle, about, round about, — cuar, cuairt.

CHINESE.	IRISH.
ge, the fun, the day,	grith, the fun; cè, the night; gerait, the heavens, i. e. ait (the place of) ger, (the fun.)
yre, **the moon,**	gabhar (gavar) i. e. folus, gan timdhi-bhe, i. e. gan loigh-diughadh, a light without a blaze, (*old glofs.*)
kin, a hat, bonnet, &c.	ceann-afg, ceann-bheirt.
cum, to reverence, to worfhip,	cam.
ken, weaknefs, decay of ftrength,	leon.
xam, dupreme, a man-darine, a bonza,	faimh, rich, honourable, learned in the law; faimh-feler, a coun-fellor.
cum, a palace,	fambh, i.e. teagh maith, (*old glofs.*) ciom, a ftone building.
gin, a man, mankind,	gein, duine.
bo, fire,	aoth, doigh.
yum, eternity,	gomhnuighe.
yu, monumentum tem-poris,	uibhal; *Quære?*
lim, to teach,	lamas, learned; luam, an abbot, an in-ftructor.
gin, pious, charity,	caoin, kin-ealta.

L

CHINESE.	IRISH.
fo, to overcome.	fo, a prince, a conqueror; faoi, fubjugated.
tay, an age; fæculum, a fpace of time.	taidhe, taiteog, a moment; taithmhead, a record, a monument or memorial.
fu, ço, to make,	faor, a workman, operarius.
ye, night,	cè, gè, oidhche (e *pronounced.*)
çien, a great man, a man to be refpected.	feine, facinh, fan, i. e. ri frigheadh, (*old glofs.*)
xia, goodnefs,	fo, faine, fián, firfan.
fu, fummus regni fenator,	fuidh, faoi.
che, him, that,	fe.
kiu, to go about, to encompafs,	cuadh, cuairt.
leao, a cabin, a hovel,	laithreach, leath-taice, a houfe proped up.
kim, to bend, to bow one's felf; cem, a prieft,	cam, to worfhip, to adore.
kivèn, a dog,	cuib, cuivin, cuan.
ngao, proud,	guag, gotha.
fum, wages, hire,	fath, fathan, fonnfa, hired foldiers.
fu, a mafter,	fo.
chuen, to promulgate,	cuadhan, i. e. innifinn, (*old glofs.*)

CHINESE.	IRISH.
fiam, an image or likeness,	famh, famhlachd.
chuen, a torrent, a river,	cuan, a river's mouth, a port; fummaine, roaring waves; fcheineadh, a torrent.
xu, a tree,	fuibh, the fap of a tree. cubhas, a tree.
nge, the countenance, the forehead,	an aghaidh.
lin, full, collected.	lion.
teu, fighting, quarrelling among friends.	tàth.
yn, a found, a voice.	caoine, finging.
xui, water,	fuir.
ciam, a fpear,	famhag, a fharp pointed inftrument. feamfa, a nail. fceimhle, fgeimhle, a fkirmifh with fpear-men.
lo, joy,	lua, luath-gair.
tum, winter,	gam.
chi, ftirps familiæ,	fiol.
fui, flow, late,	fear.
tao, a knife, a hatchet,	tuagh.
kim, integer, opus totum,	cim, kim.
lie, the law,	dligh.
xao, virtue, fuperior,	faoi.

L 2

CHINESE.

IRISH.

cum, a bow, et arma ad arcum pertinentia,

cuim, a femicircle; cum, a combat with bows and arrows; cumè, a coat of mail.

nie, dead,

nas, death.

ki, invited,

cuir.

chi, qui, quæ, quod.

ci, cià.

çu, a fon,

lao, old age, to reverence, to worfhip,

liath, grey-headed; lith, of old; lith, a folemn feftival.

can, oppofite, againft,

a ceann, ceanntradha.

cuon, to fell or buy,

cannaidhe.

çai, learning,

fui, faoi.

yun, in the fingular number,

aon, ceann.

nieu, an ox, bull or cow,

lan, noir.

nao, to be angry,

ainine, anger.

kie, felicity,

kaomh.

kieu, a mountain, cacumen,

coice.

u, five,

cuig.

chi, quiet, peace, reft,

fith.

chuan, quen, a river, a harbour,

cuan.

tien, land, country,

tàn.

ki, a hog, or fow,

keis.

tam, an altar,

taim, a fepulchre.

fa, a great city,

fo-lis; lis, a fort.

tam, pride,

time.

quon, a mandarine,

keann, keann cuire, an officer over a band of foldiers.

CHINESE.	IRISH.
ke, a trader, a merchant,	keardai.
kia, a houfe,	cai.
me, wheat,	man.
cheu, a fmall city,	cathair, caer.
chu, a moufe,	luchu, *fuiridh*, nimble, active; hence the French *fouris*.
mu, mother,	ma, mathair, mother; athair, father. N. B. *Athar* is to cleave to, to embrace, to twine about, as atharlus, ground-ivy; i. e. the twining plant.
hiun, the elder brother,	aidhne, achne, aine.
ço, the foot,	cos.
kia, a cup,	cuac.
xeu, good,	fuidhe.
geu, a vomit,	fgea.
keu, all,	cach.
vo, a houfe,	both.
fu, a man,	fear.
gin-fen, the root ginfen, quafi homini fimilis radix, eft enim mandragoræ forma,	gein-fin i fear fean, i. e. homini fimilis.
tun, chaos,	tonn.
lieu, to flow, to promulgate,	lia, a flood; liah, promulgated, news, &c.

hai, the fea,

ai-gein; hence ocean; aithbhe, the ebb of the fea.

kiam, an arm of the fea,

camus.

fun, any fhining matter,

foinionn.

min, a river,

mein, a harbour; aman, a river.

muen, full,

muadhan.

chi, tfchi, ftirps familiæ,

aofac, tuis, tuifcac.

lu, a road, a way, journey,

lua, the foot, the action of walking, haftening along.

heu, after, afterwards,

hiai, i. e. an dhiagh.

kie, and,

keo.

fan, contrarius,

fan.

chuen, arms, warlike,

cùa, martial; funn, fortified; funn caiflean, a fortified caftle.

gin, the point or edge of a plow-fhare,

ginn.

chin, piety,

cineal.

çai, a wound, a thruft,

faith.

ko, arms,

co, co-croth, a target; co-drum, arms, weapons.

chai, fafting,

caith-cachta, hunger. cacht, a faft. cargus, Lent, the fafting feafon.

hoi, a fortified city,

choi.

çien, a fheepfold,

fion, fiona, a confinement.

CHINESE.	IRISH.
kiven, parents, kindred,	cine, kine, kaovneas, fociety.
çu, a fon,	fo, a youth; foi-fior, the youngeft fon; fearr, a colt; fcoth, a fon.
pai, falutation, either in fpeech or writing,	baigh, love, friendfhip; phailte, failte, the Irifh falutation.
chen, weak, infirm,	feang.
hiao, to worfhip, adore, to obey,	iodh, a facrifice; iodhbeirt, the fame; altori iodhan, holy altar; aora aodhra, to worfhip, to adore; aodhradh don Righ, obedience to the king.
çieu, autumn,	futh, fine weather; faoth, the harveft feafon.
kien, to elevate,	cionn, elevation.
guei, becaufe, although,	gur, ge, gè-go.
ye, ad regionum nomina adhibetur,	ibh.
chu, to divide,	cuid, divifion.
xim, promotio doctorum ad aulicorum,	ceim.
yu, the top or fummit,	udh, uas, uan.
tien, true hiftory,	teann, truth; tiomna, the gofpel.
fo, a fon,	foth, of the fame womb.
xoa, a broom, a comb,	fcuab, a broom; cir, a comb.

CHINESE.	IRISH.
çiao, to cook, to boil,	fath, cooked victuals.
puen, fundamentum, principale,	bunn.
mi, rice,	min, meal, flour.
lin, a collection of trees,	lion, a gathering or collection.
lui, a harrow,	kliath, a harrow; lui, branches of trees, to harrow with.
cha, a fork,	fath, a thruft with any inftrument.
cim, war,	cime, captives; famhadh, affembling troops.
bieu, corruption, putrid,	buireadh, corrupt matter; buidhe, a plague; buinne, an ulcer.
fem, life, youth,	famh, active, lively.
teu, a meafure,	tomhas, a meafure.
kin, diligently,	kintac.
xue, prophet,	fuaitheantais, a prophecy; fùr, inveftigation.
uc, a fwine,	rucht, muc.
	tonn, a king.
tien, ti, an emperor, a lord,	tiarna, a lord; ti, God.
tien, heaven, that is, the fpirit who prefides over heaven; hence the *ti-ampai-oll*, the great altar of	ti-mor, the great ti, or the fupreme being, God; this is the *Beil-ti-mor*, or great fpirit of Baal, whofe

CHINESE.

Ti; from whence the Celtic *tiampul*, and the Latin, *templum*. *Ampai*, *eampai* or • *eampaidb*, was the ftone altar of facrifice to *Ti*. Thefe altars being always *in excelfis*, the Greeks from thence formed their *omphi-el* and *al-omphi* or *Olympus*. See Mr. Bryant's learned obfervations on this word. Antient Mythology, Vol. I. p. 235,

tan, a region,

lum, a dragon, a ferpent,

kieu, a flower,

li, precious, valuable,

fum, honorari a Rege primum involuerum epiftolæ.

çuon, color papaveris rubri,

mo, the end or extremity,

mo, fruit,

yen, foft, fweet,

to, univerfal,

IRISH.

greàt altar was at the town of Baltimore, in the county of Cork; fo alfo Beil-ti-an-gleas or the pure undefiled fpirit of Baal, from whence Baltinglafs, in the county of Wicklow.

tan.

leoman, a lyon, a dragon.

cuac.

lua, lith.

fo, fom, honour, efteem; follam, a cover.

fùgh, fùghan, purple.

mòid.

meas, muadh, ripe.

gean.

tot.

CHINESE.	IRISH.
tuen, to judge, to condemn,	tuinigh, a judge; tuinneamh, death; tuinge, an oath administered before a judge.
	modh, luc.
mau lao, savages, i. e. rat-men,	cèana, behold.
ken, evident,	
kan, the trunk of a tree,	connas, connadh.
çan, to shine,	soin.
su, dominus,	fo.
chu, a hero,	suadh, cua, caith.
kiun, a prince,	cionn, ceann.
gu, understanding,	guth, speech.
	gùag, a fellow of no sense.
sie, a purging medicine,	scè, a purge or vomit.
chu, dominus,	suadh.
vam, to die,	bea-vam.
him, happy, favour,	amhra, aimheann, iomradh.
li, ceremony,	li, lil, lith.
cho, to pray to beseech,	soir, soirim.
fo, fortuna,	fo.
fo, the first letter in fokien,	fo, the head.
cyam, felicity,	samh.
keu, a dog,	cu.
leu, a prop,	leath, leathtaice.
lo, food,	lon.
su, a sacrifice,	suth.
su, a senator,	s uadh.
chi, quiet, rest,	suidh, suadhnas.

CHINESE.	IRISH.
lao, to worſhip,	laomhdha, proſtrated.
che, paſticula, termi- nativa,	ch.
kiao, learning, wiſdom,	keadal, keadhſadh.
chi, to deſiſt,	ſith, ſioth, ſit-ſit, leave off.
guei, to join together,	guth, a vowel, quaſi junxit in unum.
xan, a mountain,	ſion.
ſui, a year,	ſaoghal, an age, a cer- tain ſpace of time.
lam, domicilium,	lamhdheacus.
ki, the air,	ceo.
ngai, to love,	gean, love.
lin, covetous,	lionn, leann.
vom, finis,	bonn.
tan, reddiſh,	donn.
cheu, a ſhip,	ſùd, ſchùd.
co, a bone,	coth, fleſh.
chao, early in the morning,	moch, i. e. am ocaidh, the time for work, (*old gloſs.*)
hoei, the time of new moon, obſcurity, darkneſs,	oidhche, the night.
kien, I ſee,	kim.
lo, a rib,	lo ſeems to be the root of all words ex- preſſing the parts of the body, as long, the breaſt; lorg, the thigh;

CHINESE.	IRISH.
	lois, the hand ; lo-thac, finews, veins, &c. &c.
fien fem, firft born,	fionfior, feine.
xui, water,	fuir, uifce.
çhao, a multitude,	faith.
kù, a caufe, a reafon,	cùs.
kia, a burthen, a load,	kial, kual,
kim, cim, I afk or pray,	gim, guidhim,
yam, a fheep,	uan, a lamb.
gìn, to recollect, to re-member,	cinim, cuimhnighim.
cim ço, I pray you be feated,	guidhim fuidhthe.
kai, oportebat,	kaithear,
kàn, to drink,	kanac, water, liquid.
pai, proftration.	baic. 1. crom.
çheu ye, dies et nox una fimul,	cè-dhia.
çhin, to prognofticate weather,	fine, weather. cinneam huin, ominous prognoftications of the weather.
to, fecret,	to, dumb, filent.
fiun, to vifit,	fiona, to idle away time. fon, to chat, to talk to-gether.
han, the foul,	anm.
pu, beans, peafe,	pòn, poneine.
gao, to laugh,	gaire.
miao, fupreme, excel-lent,	muadh, maor.

CHINESE.	IRISH.
ma, a horfe,	marc.
tu, a hare,	pa-tu.
çie, a concubine,	fi, femininè, fiteog, the fame; nua-coinfeac, fiurtach, a concubine.
mo, moft high,	mo, monn.
çeu, I go, I run,	fuibhal, cuadh.
nien, a year,	eang, 'neang.
chu, a jewel,	fheòd.
cheg, tcheg, a houfe,	teag,
kua, a melon,	kuamar, mor great.
guei, honourable, to govern,	guaire, this was the name of feveral Irifh princes; the termination aire is a chief; gubearnidhim, to govern, i. e. nidhim, to act; gu bearr, the part of an honourable judge.
to, the helm of a fhip,	ftiur.
niao, ki, hvan, avis, modus volandi,	namham, fnamham, to fwim; èn, ean, èon, a bird; ci, cè, a goofe; fciathan, a wing.
ki, a hen,	kearki.
min, a command, a manifeftation,	mann.
ku, a goat,	ku, a dog, a hound; gour, i. e. gabhar, a goat.

CHINESE.	IRISH.
fay, colours,	fai, dyed ſtuff, as ſilk, &c. ſalt, colour.
leam, rice,	leam, taſteleſs, inſipid, (*Quære.*)
tay, a bench, theatre, throne, a ſeat of dignity,	ti, teach, taidhleac, as in *Eoghan taidhleac,* Owen the glorious and honourable.
poi, precious things; poi-çu, fine ornaments,	poincnae, gold foil, plate gold, gold leaf, precious ornaments.
yen, the eye,	aedhan, aedh, (*Quære*) is the bird named èn, from quickneſs of ſight.
cheu, to invite to a potation,	cuairt, ſuithinge, chearful over a glaſs.
mien, the head,	mionn.
çan, praiſe, commendation,	ſean, ſann.
che hum, red,	ſainne, purple.
	ſanarc, red orpiment.
hoa, to write, pingue literas,	odh, the point of the ſtylus with which the ancients wrote; odh, muſick and muſical notes.
tao ye, legum domine,	taich, judex.
	a ye, O Domine.
ngan, an encloſure,	ganar.
lao, an old woman,	liath, old.

CHINESE.	IRISH.
yuèn, longevity,	cian, gian.
miao, the maufoleum of a king,	mias, an altar, a tumulus.

The ancient Chinefe begun their reckoning of time from the night ; the ancient Irifh and Scythians did the fame.

The ancient Chinefe divided the year into four quarters or feafons, and named the months from the beginning, middle and end of each quarter ; the ancient Irifh did the fame. See thefe explained in the firft Edition of the Irifh Grammar.

The Chinefe named the 12 months of the year from certain animals ; the ancient Irifh did the fame, and from the operations of the feafon in agriculture.

The Chinefe name the Zodiac, *kum ge*, the houfe of the Sun ; the Irifh name is *Grian-ftadt*, the ftopping places of the Sun : they call it alfo *Grian-crios*, and *Grian-beacht* ; i. e. the belt or ring of the fun.

The Chinefe facrificed horfes, oxen, fheep, dogs, fowl and hogs *(c)* ; the ancient Irifh did the fame, as appears by the preceding laws.

The Chinefe mode of burying their princes, was fimilar to that of the ancient Irifh. Du Halde gives an exaggerated defcription of the monument of Schi-chuan-di, erected on the top of the mountain

(c) Les differentes fêtes de l' année conftituent fix genres nommès vulgairement *Pao-chi*, cèft a dire le beuf, le cheval, la brebis, le chien, la poule & enfin le achon, dont le fang coule a grand flots on l'honneur de tous les Dieux Chinoife. Recherches Philof. tom. i. p. 220.

tain called Ly, which corresponds exactly with our Irish Carns, excepting the lake of quickfilver, and the golden birds floating thereon, which he says was in the subterraneous part—but father Du Halde has exaggerated in many other parts of his History of China.

The Chinese divide their Mandarines or Nobles into 9 classes ; the ancient Irish divided their Nobles or Aireachs into 9 classes.

The Chinese observe the Equinoxes and Solstices, as religious solemnities, at which time they offer sacrifices, AND the ancient Irish did the same.

THE

THE

JAPONESE LANGUAGE

COLLATED WITH THE

I R I S H.

M

THE

JAPONESE LANGUAGE

COLLATED WITH THE

I R I S H.

THE Ifland of Japon was probably firft peopled from China; but the Japonefe having traded with the Manchou Tartars, and fettled thefe people in the ifland, they are now a diftinct nation from the Chinefe, and have a language peculiar to themfelves. This language is probably for the moft part that of the Manchou Tartars, who were of Scythian origin, as were alfo the tribes of the Huns, Alans, Avares, Turks, Moguls and Parians *(a)*. The authors of the Univerfal Hiftory, place a branch of the Huns alfo, in the fartheft part of Afia, under the name of *Cunadani* or *Canadani*, fo called from *Conad*, their habitation near the city. Hence fay they we find a city in upper Hungary, built by their defcendants, denominated *Chonad*, the inhabitants of which, and thofe of the neighbouring diftrict, ftill retain the name of *Chonadi* or *Cunadi*. From thefe *Hornius* believes the natives of

M 2   *Canada,*

(a) Univ. Hift. vol. 20, p. 168.

Canada, in North America, to have deduced their origin and denomination.

This is no certain evidence of the migration of the Huns into the new world, for *Conaid* is an original word for a fettled abode or dwelling, and is the only word now ufed by the Irifh.   They write it *Combnaidbe* and *Conaidb*, and thefe words exprefs both a dwelling, and to be at quiet, or to reft.   In Arabic, *Canè* or *Kanè*, is alfo a houfe ; and *Conaidb-duine* and *Conaidb-dae*, in the Irifh, implies men fettled or dwelling in one place, a diftinction properly made between them and the *Nomades* or wanderers.

When the Europeans firft came among the Canadians of North America, they were told that Chinefe and Japonefe fhips had been there before them : And *Acofta* fays, that Chinefe fhips had been wrecked in the *Mare del Nord*, above Florida.

To prove the Japonefe fettlements in America, the authors of the Univerfal Hiftory, felect a few words common to both people, viz.

Chiapa, a river, province and lake in Mexico.

Ke, japan, in the ifland of Trinidada.

Tonus, in Japonefe, the fun, moon, ftars, governors, kings, princes.

Tona, the moon.

Thefe words are not thus written by Father *D. Cullado*, who publifhed the Japonefe Lexicon in 1632, from which the following collection is made ; *Tien*, is the Heavens, but it is explained in a very different manner, namely the dwelling of the great Spirit or God *Ti*, as has been defcribed

in

in the Chinefe. *Tona*, the moon, may be derived from the Iberno-Scythic *tonnadh*, glittering; but *Tonn* was a common title given to Irifh princes. See Titles of Honour in the preceding pages. *Motezume*, or *Motazaiuma*, is the common appellation or title of the emperors of Mexico and of Japon; but *Taoife*, *Tuife*, *Taoifeac* and *Tavifeamb*, are words in all the old languages, as well as the Irifh, to exprefs a chief or prince; it is alfo written *Tuis*, and in the Chinefe contracted to *Tfi*; *Mo* is great; thus *Motazuma*, is the great chief or emperor; thus in Irifh *Ruire* is a champion; and *Ruirmefam*, a degree of nobility.

The learned author of the *Recherches Philofophiques fur les Americains* thinks he has made a difcovery in the Hiftory of Japon *(b)*. " I fuppofe, fays he, the Tartar *Lamas* or the *Mongals*, have in a very remote time, conquered Japon, and carried their manners and religion to thefe iflands, having eftablifhed a Grand Prieft, fubject to the *Dala Lama* of *Thibet*. The ecclefiaftic fovereign of Japon, which our travellers name fometimes *Fo*, and fometimes *Dari*, has under him many bifhops, who are called *Kuches*, and by fome modern authors *Cubo*; the Portugueze write the name Dairi and Dairo. The Priefthood is much humbled by the preponderating faction of the Japonefe tyrants, and is now become an empty title without power.

This fettlement of the Tartar Lamas in Japon will appear in a ftronger light, if we confider that *Xaca* is the principal divinity of the modern Japonefe and of the Lama. I do not recollect any

hiftorian

(b) Tom. 2d. p. 363.

hiſtorian who has made theſe obſervations before, which may ſerve to illuſtrate the hiſtory of Japon."

With ſubmiſſion to this learned author, the authors of the Univerſal Hiſtory had eſtabliſhed the fact before.

Strahlenberg has given another name for the principal Deity of the Monguls, viz. *Borr-cheann*, which is an old word in Iriſh and Welch, ſignifying Lord, maſter *(c)*, *Xaca*, or *Saca* was alſo the name of the great God with the Scythians, it is now written by the Iriſh *Seatbar*.

Dairi is a proper name with the Iriſh, ſignifying *great, excellent, learned*; *dru*, or *daru* in the Perſic, is a good man, and is the root of the Iriſh *Draoi*, or *Drui*, a Druid or Magus; it was alſo the name of a Celtic King, as *Covarrurias* the Spaniſh Hiſtorian informs us, in his *Teſoro*, or repoſitory of ancient cuſtoms. "Druidas, ciertos ſacerdotes de " Francia antiguos eſtimados en mucho, y dichos " aſſi ſegun la opinion de algunas del nombro del " quarto Rey de los Celtos dicha *Druy*." *Cobas*, *Cuibais*, *Cutb*, do alſo betoken the Head, Supreme, or Holy, in the Iriſh Language.

From the affinity of words in ancient languages no ſolid baſis can be formed, for the conſtruction of hiſtory. The language of Japhet and his deſcendants was the univerſal tongue; it is moſt wonderfully preſerved in the Iriſh, and with the aſſiſtance of this language, the hiſtorian will be enabled

to

(c) See the Mongul language collated with the Iriſh, in the Eſſay on the Celtic language, in the preface of my Iriſh Grammar, 2d. edition, and Boxhornius de Lingua Gallica, at the word *mil*.

to unfold the origin of people, and the settlement of colonies in the various parts of the old world. The explanation of the Thibetan medal by the Irish language, has been treated in a ridiculous light; in a future number, this subject shall be more fully explained, and the religion of the Lamas will be shewn to have much connection with that of the antient Irish.

The authors of the Universal History, very justly observe, that the doctrine of the Brachmins or Brahmins, is related by different authors, with a variety, not easy to be reconciled; the occasion of which has been more owing to the relator's want of skill in the language, than to the reservedness of the Brahmins. The same may be said in general of all the works of the missionaries; who for a series of years have imposed upon the world by their publications.

Monsieur *Paw* has very learnedly confuted many romantic stories of these travelling pedants, in his *Recherches Philosophiques.* Their writings are so various, and so voluminous, that it will require many years to purge the whole of their egregious blunders.

In none of their works have they exposed themselves more than in the History of Peru; they tell us, the Peruvians celebrate the summer solstice, with a grand feast called *Raymi*; the principal part of the ceremony consists in eating bread, which they call *cancou* or *cancu.* This *Cancu* is made by virgins devoted to the worship of *Pancha Camac*, or the *Sun*; and Acosta tells us, by their accounts

he

he could not make the age of the world more than
400 years!   Now the ancient Irish named the fummer folftice, *Ream, Reim, Reiman*; that is a beginning, as they conceived the Sun then began his
annual courfe; *Reim* alfo fignified a feries; hence
Reim, Riogha, the chronology of Kings.   They
named the day of the Solftice *Can-cir*, or *Ceann-
kir*, that is, *can* head, *kir* circle, to fignify the
Sun was then at the head, or beginning of the circle; a day they celebrated with fires in honour of
Baal or *Panga Saenbas*, that is, the *globular fun*;
fires are ftill made all over Ireland, in honour of St. John, whofe feftival falls on this
day.   *Rimmin*, was the Irifh folemn feftival of all
the heavenly hoft, probably on this day.   See this
word explained in the Effay on the Antiquity of
the Irifh Language.   Colleétanea, No. 8, vol. ii.

The crab being a remarkable animal for walking backward, none could more properly defcribe
that place in the Heavens at which, as one of the
barriers of the Sun's courfe, when he was arrived,
he began to go backward, and to defcend obliquely;
hence the Latin name *Cancer* for a crab.   The Irifh
named this fifh *portain*, that is, the door of the
ring; as they did the year *bliadhain*, corrupted,
from *Beil-ain*, or the ring of *Belus*; *Trogh-ain*,
the rifing of the Sun, &c. &c.   The Chinefe name
the Zodiac *kum ge*, i. e. the houfe of the Sun, a
name fimilar to *portain*, the firft fign in it, viz. the
crab.

What will philofophers fay to this identity of
names and cuftoms between the ancient Irifh and the
Peruvians?   Will the modern hiftorians ftill confine

fine the peopling of this Ifland to the third century? Let them recollect what *Varenius* faith, "*Verisimilius est septentrionalis* AMERICÆ *partem olim adhæsisse* HIBERNIÆ." He guessed it to be more likely that the northern part of *America* should in old times have joined, or come near to Ireland. Within the space of these last ten years, a bank of sand has been discovered which extends from the West of Ireland to the banks of Newfoundland; this gives great reason to think Varenius had good grounds for his conjecture. I cannot avoid noticing in this place that in the Irish Language *Du-Caledoni*, or *Dur-Caledoni*, expresses the flood or waters of Caledonia, or the Scotch Sea; hence *Bertius* in his *Breviarium* speaks as a certain truth that *Deu Caledonia* or the flood said to have been in *Thessaly*, should have been placed in the Scotch fea.

Mr. Astle of London, a very diligent enquirer into remote antiquity, has obligingly furnished me with an ancient MS. in Irish, on Astronomy; I propose at leisure to favour the public with a translation and observations on this MS. it is the Ptolemaic system explained. The Irish call the solstices by another name, viz. *Grianstad*, that is the stopping place of the Sun; the Zodiac is named *Grian-crios*, the belt or circle of the Sun. The learned reader will recollect the *Grannus Apollo*, and the city of *Gryneum* of the ancients; and that the Latin *Solstitium* is of the same construction as *Grian-stat*.

Doctor O'Brien at the word *Ratha*, or as it is pronounced *Raha*, a quarter of a year or three months, makes the following observation;—" This word carries all the appearance of being corrupted and
changed

changed from its true radical formation, in the fame manner that the word *Bliadbain*, a year, hath been corrupted from *Bel-ain*, i. e. the circle of *Bel* or of the Sun; Lat. *Annus*; I am therefore inclined to think that this word *Raba* is only a corrupt writing of *Archa* or *Arc*; Lat. Arcus. Becaufe in the fpace of three calendar months, the Sun runs over an arch, which makes the fourth part of the entire folar circle. We find an affinity between the Irifh appellatives of all other parts of time, and the Latin or Greek or fome other ancient language; thus *dia* or *de* the Irifh for *day*, has a very near affinity with the Latin *dies*; and *la* or *lo*, plur. *laiona* and *laethe* or *laoithe*, another Irifh word fignifying the day, has a plain affinity with *lion*, in the Greek compound *geneth-lion*, natalis dies, and *la* or *lo*, bears alfo an analogy with the Latin *Lux*, &c. It follows then that the word *Ratha* fhould, in its proper writing, find an affinity in the Latin or Greek, which I do not fee how it could, without regarding it as a corruption of the Irifh word *archa*, Latin *arcus*.

In this manner have the modern Lexicographers, and advocates for their mother tongue, depreciated the very ancient language of Ireland, by attempting to derive every Irifh word from the *Greek* or *Latin*; not confidering that this was a language replete and full, before the Greeks or Romans had a name.

Ratho, or *Raha* is the Arabic *Raja*, a quarter of the Heavens. *La* or *lo* a day, may be derived from the Hebrew *Laor*, the accufative of *aor* a day, as in Genefis, *vocabat laor diem*; or from the Coptic *la*, plur. *lathaith*.

O'Brien

O'Brien is right in his derivation of *Bel-ain*, a year; but he passes over another very ancient word for that space of time, viz. *iomthoincadh*, evidently compounded of the Hebrew *icm* a day, and *toinead*, numeration, i. e. the numbering of the days. *La, lo, laoi*, all express a day, but not the space of time comprehended in the day which composed the ancient calculation, for they counted from the sun set, or the night; hence *laoi* means the light; in Arabic *layib* bright, splendid; *elyaum* to day. *Litb-laitb*, in Irish is solemn festivals; this word occurs often in the Old Laws; the Commentators have explained it by *Caifc agus nodhlag*, i. e. *Easter* and *Christmas*; but it was the Druidical name for all solemn fasts and feasts, and is the same as the Arabic Leta beating on the breast, *Lebit* anointing with oil, *Labut* divinity. In the Arabic we find *lidat* the plur. of *lida*, birth days; but this is certainly from *lidet* generation, bringing forth; the same as the Irish *lida*, or *laide*; the Anglo-Saxon month called *lida*, has led the learned Monf. Gibelin astray. See Essay on the Celtic language, p. 149.

The Irish termination *ain* in *Bliadbain* a year, or as we translate it, the ring of *Belus*, is from the Arabic *ana*, circles or tracts of the Heavenly bodies.

I shall conclude this short preface with the words of Dr. Huchinfon, late Bishop of Down and Connor; " to prove that Ireland was peopled from very ancient times, whether its history be known or not, we need only refer to the *language*, the many *customs*, the *alphabet*, &c. &c. of the inhabitants."

tants. "And bifhop *Lloyd*, in the preface to his Hiftorical account of Church Government in Great
Britain and Ireland, ‗ fays; " I do not fpeak here
of the ancient *Scots* that live in *Ireland*, who, no
doubt, have fome remains of *very antient true biftory*; our bufinefs is with them that live in the ifle
of Britain, the *Albanian Scots*".

The Japonefe Language collated with the Irifh.

JAPONESE.	IRISH.
aicanai, to agree, to hold together,	kaomhnaidhe.
cùmi, affeċtion,	cuma, cumanach.
cùmi no xù, brotherly love	cuma na foth.
voyàco, of one family,	fo-aice.
camuri foquam, a crown,	camurra, wreathed, twifted, the fame as *atar*, from whence the Tiara.
	fo-caràn, fo-cuanna, a royal diadem.
cava, càfa; back of a tree,	càs, cafadh, binding round.
caràfu, a crane, a crow,	corr, any bird of the crane kind.
	corr-afaidh, would imply a bird that does not migrate.
	corr-afhar, a cormorant; the Englifh

	name is from the Celtic *corr-muirean*, i. e. a fea-corr.
mionichi, to-morrow,	noidhiche, the night. mi-noidhiche, after this night.
ari, thick,	ramhar.
curuxime, to crucify, to torment,	crocham.
furùdona, morofe,	fearrdhan.
qendon, foit, injuftice, diftrefs,	ceandon, donás, fot.
fuxeri, fuxi, to lie down, to reft,	fois, foifite, reft.
cùri, a kitchen,	cocuire, a cook.
quàntai, nan, tçumi, a fault, a crime, a fin,	cionta, a fault, a crime; nionadh, plundering, robbing.
ton-iòcu yocu, earneft defire,	tonn-eochair. diochur. deoigh.
faxiri, to run, to haften,	feachfaithear, they fhall haften.
curuma, a cart, a carriage,	carr, carbad. curac, a boat.
cagami, crooked, curved,	cafama, camoga.
daiju, decimum capitalum,	deachaidh.
jigo nigo, deinceps,	doigh go doigh.
faga, teeth,	feag, fiacal.
go, qinen, inòri, intreating, befeeching, praying,	cinim, to pray, to intreat.

JAPONESE.	IRISH.
	cin, or caon-duthract, devotion; ora, praying; anora, reverencing.
jùzu, tjuzu, a kind of beads ufed at devotion,	tuis is tranflated in the Irifh Lexicons, a jewel; it is alfo a beginning; incenfe, frankincenfe : But the mafs-book is called *pur-tuis*, the derivation of which feems to be in this word *tuis*, meaning beads, or certain marks for the repetition of prayers. In the Arabic, *ufnun* is a form of prayer. In the Perfic, *bezar* fignifies beads for faying prayers, on counting of which they repeat the attributes of God.
cùrai, dignity, power, taixo, a chief, dux, tera, a church,	cur, curaidh, champions, taoifeac. toir, of or belonging to a church. toir, confecrated ground.
taca funda, a public edict,	toic, fanearad, a proclaimed law.

JAPONESE.	IRISH.
	deachta bannadha, the same.
cai, to buy, to obtain,	ciuram.
taixut, yieqi, to go,	teacham, to go, teachta, a meſſenger; (tecchi in the Sclavonic, to run).
riacu, an epilogue,	rachaire.
sàn, an epitaph,	ſanas, greeting, know-ledge, (old gloſs.)
zoyàcu, a mare,	eac, a horſe.
	ſegh-eac, the female horſe.
guiu-ba, horſes and cows,	gavar-ba.
ſito-nari, an hermaphro-dite,	phita-naire; this is a very extraordinary compound; the two words expreſs in Iriſh, the privities of both ſexes.
to, and,	ceeo, neo.
ivare, etymology,	ferbhaire.
nanbàn, Europe,	
ſoca, on the outſide,	amoch, amach.
mane, a bean,	meann, wheat, food.
baccun, abundance,	beacht, a multitude; beacan, a muſh-room, from its quick and plentiful growth; bacthinas,

JAPONESE.	IRISH.
	a furfeit, and in many other compounds.
tçuqi, to approach,	tucham, tudhcham.
tàca, a hawk,	tacan, a fea hawk or martin, from tacair, fighting.
gai, bun, accurately,	go, bun ; go bonn,
tçumi, to apply, to adhere,	coimeas.
fu, fuyùi, fharp, four,	fuibh, fearv.
fa, the edge of a fword,	faov.
fari, a needle, a fpit, &c.	biora.
qiyona, intelligent, acutus,	cuini, cionnadh, kùn.
coieta, abura, fat, greafy,	caiteog, butter ; buireadh, flime, gore, matter.
facari coto, adinventio,	faghaidh cotadh ; hence faigh, a prophet ; faigha-draochd, divination ; codach, invention.
tàchi foi, approach,	teach an fo.
camàye, to adorn,	caomham.
faixi, to worfhip,	feacam, to proftrate ; feis, a folemnity.
vaqi maie, to confider well,	machtadh maith.
còriu xi, to erect, to build,	cuir fuas (literally to put up) is the vulgar expreffion ; but cò-

JAPONESE.	IRISH.
	ra did antiently imply a building or palace, as Ceann-cora, i. e. the palace of Brian Boireamh; Cora finn, Finn's palace; Innis-cora, and many others.
xicu, equal in number,	feach, alternately.
doy, equal in dignity,	doch, an indigene.
	dothchamhuil, of a good family.
	doigh, a man of confidence.
caje, air,	ceo, mift, vapour; caocan, an eddy of air; gao, wind.
fora, the atmofphere,	an tfathar.
cane, cana mono, metal,	cron, min.
dai, irai, age, a man's life,	deo, deilm; irr, iris, an æra.
dengi, a field, an inclofure,	daingean, but now applied to a ftrong hold, a fort.
tçucuri, to do, to act,	cuirim, tofughadh, action; tafgaire, a fervant.
xiroi, white,	cearb, filver; caorthuin, quick lime.
uzzu tacai, moft high,	uas tiocfa.
tacafa, altitude,	tiocfa, diocfa.
aruqi, ariqi, to walk, to go,	racadh, ruaig.

N

JAPONESE.

IRISH.

gurui, mono, a foolish fellow,

goirrige, man full of tricks.

xita, ximi, chun, a friend,

feitche, a wife.

coinne, a wife.

caoin (keen) mild, gentle, friendly.

cinid, a relation.

fion, an union.

gàn, a duck,

gaǹra, a goofe.

guefu, guerro, a maidfervant, a hand-maid,

gearait, gerais.

gairfe, guirfeach; the laſt is uſed in the Armoric for the Virgin Mary.—See the collation of the Lord's prayer in the eſſay on the Celtic language, prefixed to the laſt edition of the Iriſh grammar.

icari, an anchor,

accaire.

cuchi nava, a ſerpent,

nimh or niv, a ſerpent;

guaſachd niv, the dangerous ſerpent;

cucht nimh, the painted or variegated ſerpent.

baho, breath, life,

beatha.

chicuxo, a beaſt, an animal,

feac, as in feacbo, a heifer.

feacloc, a park.

JAPONESE.	IRISH.
	ſeighdhe, wild beaſts;
	ceiſeog, young of any beaſts.
●	
toxi, a year,	tocht, tucht, a meaſured ſpace of time.
yubigune, a ring,	badhgan, badhg.
afiru, a gooſe,	faire, watchful, *Quære*.
cono ami mucaxi, of old,	ciana-am. moch-aos.
fachi, a bee,	beach.
niji, the rainbow,	naſg, a ring. naſcaire, a ſurety, a covenant. *Quære*.
guſocu, yoroi, to arm, to be in arms,	gas, gaſogac, armed heroes; gaſra, a band of troops; gaiſce, a hero, a warrior; this is the radix of the Geſſi, and Geſſitæ, of the Germans and Gauls.
	gaias, Heb. ⎫
	gaiſa, Syr. ⎬ an army.
	gais, Arab. ⎭
	aire, a chief a warrior; oireagha, the ſame; go aire, ſpear-men.
tage, a prop, ſupport,	taca, taic.
xirà, a top, peek, or ridge,	cirin; hence cirain the creſt, or comb of a bird.

JAPONESE.	IRISH.
aqi, autumn,	earrac, ſpring, earr the end.
guai bun, good fame,	guth bonn.
mioga, good fortune,	mio-aghor, bad fortune.
	mo-aghor, good fortune.
qafo, felicity,	cufar.
moja, xigai, a carcaſs,	mudhughadh.
	ſeacadh, decayed, parched up ;
	ſeghuinidh, dead men, mortally wounded.
ten, heaven,	this word has been explained in the Chineſe.
banſui, a feaſt, a meal,	bainſe.
yumexi, a ſet meal,	itheadh mithiſi, meal time.
cami, hair,	ciamh.
fumi, to be hot, to warm,	fuineadham, to boil.
	fomoſac, auguſt, the hot month.
	fomhar, the harveſt.
fibarri, a calendar, an almanack,	barr, in Iriſh, is the calendar of the Romans; hence *ceann-barr*, January, &c. from whence the Latin October, November. See this fully explained in

JAPONESE.	IRISH.
	the Effay on the Celtic, p. 142, 143, &c.
cutçu, fhoes, flippers,	gufeir, hofe, foirtchi, a fhoe.
ata, tacana, warm, hot,	teith, teagham, to warm. teith tan, the fun.
qincan, bald,	kinnfhionn, kiam can.
raffocu, a candle,	rufòg, the candle ufed by the peafants, made by dipping a rufh into tallow. rufg, is alfo light, the eye, &c.
yo, night,	eo, dark. oiche, night. ceo, a fog.
yaguiu, a goat,	gour, gabhar.
inu, a dog,	gione, gibhne, cùn.
cobe, the head,	cab, cob.
torio, a prince,	tor, airi.
nicu, flefh,	cua.
xifai, a caufe or motive,	cùis.
fofo, quick, active,	fuiri, fothaire, an active fellow.
cagui, a key,	eocar, a key. cugaire, rugaire, the bar of a door.
guxi, a chief, a leader,	gaifce, gùs, as in gufm-har, valiant, power-] ful.

JAPONESE.	IRISH.
coraxi, to chaftife,	curugham.
mono, a family,	muin-tir.
cutan, grief, raging mad with grief,	cuthach.
nari, a figure, a refemblance,	nearnaim, to liken.
foxi, yonger fons,	foifior, fofar.
foreo, elder fons,	finnfior, rearai.
moqe, a fon,	mac.
fino, a blaze,	faithin, faith, heat; fàn-leac, the altar of the fun, φαης.
fana, a flower,	fionn fgoch.
co, co chi, here,	fo, go fo, co fo.
fatto, the law,	faite, knowledge; featarlach, the old law; feite, taking care of, keeping in order.
minori, the holy law,	
daimio, nobility, magnates,	daimh, a learned man. daimheach, a companion of equal rank. righ damhna, prefumpive heir to the crown.
zaimòcu, timber for building,	fail-modh.
cuji, ftrife,	cogadh.
fava, a mother,	fadhbh, a widow.
caca, a matron,	cè.
fan, the centre.	fonnfa, the circumference.

JAPONESE.	IRISH.
ixa, a phyſician.	ic, a cure, a remedy; hence uile-ica, all-heal; miſsletoe, *ℨ⊕*. ixos, in the Greek.
maſaxi, xizai, xiqio, fo-guio, death,	madhas, a trance. bas, death; nas, etſeach, fugha.
bioxi, dead,	baſadh.
ca, mouldy, hoary,	ceo, tachd.
fefe, muliebria,	feidhbhfe.
nhotai, female,	naoithi, bearing children.
vonna, a woman, michi vonna, a virgin, }	bean, vean.
me gia, my wife,	mo cè.
tçubonè, a harlot,	teiſebean, feiſebean. druiſebean.
fai, a fly,	faithirleog, a ſwallow. faoilean, the gull. feidhan, flight. fithean, a bird's quill. from theſe and many other compounds, it appears that *fai* was an original word for flying.
jaco, moſs,	moin-teac, caoineac.
fiqi mòno, a certain muſical inſtrument,.	feat, and feacht, is muſick, harmony; fonn, a tune.
qire, a part, a fragment,	ciara, this is in the compound ciaraidhe, i. e. the county of

JAPONESE.	IRISH.

Kerry; in Ceirt, arag; ceirt-mhèòd-han, the centre, or middle part; cuir-tir, and Eunuch, &c. &c.

JAPONESE.	IRISH.
denqoraiden, lightening and thunder,	teinteac ceo toran.
ixizuye, the bottom,	iachdar, ifiofal.
faico, foundation,	toifeach, tus.
qezzune, the fpur of a cock,	greafucha.
qeavaxe, a cock-fight,	comraoh caoilleach.
qemaru, a cock-fighter,	comhra,
cori, ice, froft,	oighre.
guefai, men of infamous characters,	guthfir.
ninguen, mankind,	naoidh-gein.
catàna, a fword,	gathan, a fmall fpear.
dan, a degree in literature,	dana.
qoinin, a woman with child,	coinne, coint, coinin.
qeda mono, a herd,	cèad, treud; caidean, caibhdan; iomain, a drove.
gacu monjo, gymnafia,	coicht mùineadh. cochar mùineadh.
giunin, an inhabitant,	conaidh.
tàte, a fpear a halbard,	tath, flaughter; gath, a fpear.

JAPONESE.	IRISH.
rei, a little bell,	reataire, the clerk, the ringer of the bell. *Quare.*
fânya, a field, a plain,	feannaidhe, ground wherein corn may be fown.
gio, a head,	cuth.
ro, a prifon,	ronn.
ivare, a caufe or matter,	adhbhar, avar.
feya, a cellar or under-ground,	faoi, below.
xocubut, food,	fath coth beatha.
iqe, a ciftern,	aicean, a cauldron.
to, quick, foon,	tonn.
zaixo, a city,	feife, a fettlement.
cobai, red,	curbh, 1. buidh agus dearg,
yen, love, friendfhip,	gean, love.
nen rài, no of old,	nunn rè.
ino, a wild boar,	near.
notamai, a term ufed in fpeaking of the Gods, the king, &c.	nodh, noble. nodhac, nobility.
chacùgan xi, to call to you,	tar, cugin, fo, come here to us.
fûqi, a plough,	foc.
uru, moie-uru, to burn,	ura.
go bun, well,	go bonn.
nomi, to drink,	nim, a fmall quantity of liquor.
qiffo, a teller of good news,	cifire, a ftory teller, a romancer.

JAPONESE.	IRISH.
fucùro, burſa,	fo-coire.
xigai, a carcaſs,	ſigh, a goblin; ſeich, a ſkeleton.
mecura, momocu, blind,	muca, dark, gloomy.
ſaccazuqi, a jug, chalice, &c.	ſoidheac.
coſa cazzuqi, a little jug,	coſa ſoidheac.
xuſòcu, a foot,	cos, a foot, feaſadh to ſtand on the feet.
caſhicara, feet,	coiſithe.
monriu monpa, religion,	monn, as will be hereafter explained; it is the *amuna* of the Chaldeans. See Buxtorf.
vo teivo, a king,	fo, triath.
cùni, a kingdom,	conaidh, a permanent ſettlement or dwelling.
	cuing, a king.
còie, fun, dung,	càc, cornicè, kauh. fanc.
uxi, a cow,	agh, an ox.
tcu, foque, vapour,	ceo.
gòqe, a widow,	goice, ſcoffed at, *Quære.* coibhce, a dowry.
qan, a ſepulchre,	tuama, uagh, uaghan.
fori, to dig, to plow,	fuireadh, to prepare; air, plowed.
nhonin, a woman,	nae, a man or woman; nian, a daughter; naoi-nin, man's image.

JAPONESE.	IRISH.
ani, the eldeſt brother,	aine, aged, honourable. tanaiſt, the heir apparent to a prince.
taro, the youngeſt brother,	taire, obſcure, baſe.
fitai, the front, in front,	fiathnaiſe, in preſence; hence fiathnaiſeadh, bearing witneſs.
cùmo, a cloud,	dluim, gruam. kummul (Welſh).
curume, a nut,	comhthra, cuauinne, crauen (Armorice).
fon, primitive, original,	bun, bun-aidheac.
daigi, the earth, the world,	domhan, domhghan. daig, is fire.
figaxi, the Eaſt,	feige, feici, 1. follus (old gloſs.) light; feic, ſight, light; 1. radharc. feaſcor, the Weſt.
cùchi, the mouth,	guiſeac, an aperture.
cùchi, the face,	gnùis, eaccoſg.
manaco, an eye,	roſg, roſgan.
riogan eyes,	
qirai, to hate,	grain, hatred, creachra, to ſtigmatize; còiri, to deſpiſe, to teize, to vex.
icon, hatred,	eacconn, rage, fury; eccnac, reproof; eicean, violence.
mòro, many,	mòr.

JAPONESE.	IRISH.
mòro mòro, all,	mòr mhòr.
tamàgo, an egg,	ugh, an egg; tam, round, lumpy, &c.
tachi, a palace, a houſe,	teach, a houſe.
yacata, a nobleman's houſe,	teach, athach, (*Quære*).
jùr acu, cuden rocacu, a royal palace,	toir-theach.
mixe, a tavern or tipling houſe,	meiſce, miſce, is drunkeneſs in the modern Iriſh; meſkir in Arabic, and meiſte in Perſic; the root is certainly in the Hebrew; it occurs in Eſther, ch. 7. v. 1, 2. The king (Ahaſuerus) ſaid to Eſther, on the ſecond day of *meiſhti jin*, which *Montanus* has properly tranſlated *convivium vini*.
gitai, care, diligence,	gaoth, 1. glic (*old gloſs.*)
biocu, infirm,	bacuidhe.
bioja, lame,	
taibio, very infirm, weak,	taim.
xita, downwards,	ſitheadh, inclining; ſios, downwards.
tèqi, an enemy,	taichre, a battle.

JAPONESE.	IRISH.
tocuxin, I underſtand,	tuicſin, underſtanding.
fùqi, to blow,	fogaoth, a blaſt, a gentle gale.
ſui, to ſuck,	ſùgh, from ſuth, juice.
ixi, a ſtone,	oiceas, free-ſtone.
bin, a lagena, a flagon,	bian, the old name of the hide of an animal made to hold liquor in; bian is a pelt or ſkin.
fogue, a hole,	paigear, faigear.
ari, an ant,	aire, care, attention, ingenuity. *Quære.*
bireina, beautiful, comely,	bredha (eirean Welſh.)

SOME

REMARKS

ON THE

ROUND TOWERS

OF

IRELAND,

BY

LIEUT. COL. VALLANCEY.

ON THE

ROUND TOWERS

OF

IRELAND.

THE reverend Mr. Ledwich, in his differtation on the round towers, has collected much matter concerning them and their ufe fince the times of chriftianity; but I am of opinion, that thefe towers are of a more ancient date than he allows, and that they are of Scythian origin, and I am confirmed in this opinion from the difcoveries of fome modern travellers, who have defcribed thefe extraordinary buildings. In the *Hiftoire de decouvertes dans la Ruffie et la Perfe*, in two volumes, 8vo. printed at Berlin, 1779, there is an account of many of thefe towers ftill remaining on the continent, and defcribed by the inhabitants as the work of very remote times, and like the Irifh towers applied to the ufe of public worfhip.

I fhall here tranfcribe the paffage, containing a defcription of one of thefe towers, to which is added a drawing, alfo copied from the Berlin edition.

" The

" The village of Bulgari was the famous city
" of Brjæchinof, the ancient capital of Bulgaria ;
" as no defcription had been given of the ruins of
" this place, Meffrs. Pallas and Lepechin were
" induced to vifit it.

" The village of Bulgari is built on the ruins of
" the ancient city; it is fituated on an eminence,
" bordering on a marfhy ground overgrown with
" bufhes and thickets. It is furprifing that fo con-
" fiderable and well peopled city as this muft once
" have been, fhould be conftructed in a fituation,
" which could not be fupplied with water ; they
" are now obliged to fink wells or pits in the
" marfh, and this is their only refource.

" The river Wolga is 9 werfts diftant in a right
" line, and as the ground flopes from the village
" to the river, it is not probable the features of na-
" ture could be fo changed, as to have once al-
" lowed its courfe to have run by the city.

" The village contains about 100 good houfes ;
" it was feized by the crown with other church-
" lands. On the fouth is a plain, furrounded
" with refinous trees, or evergreens, interfperfed
" with birch ; this plain at prefent covered with
" fertile fields, was once the efplanade of the ci-
" ty; it is yet furrounded with a rampart and
" ditch, which once formed an irregular half oval,
" at leaft fix werfts in circumference."

" Moft of the veftiges of the ancient buildings
" are within the rampart ; among others are the
" ruins of a convent with an inclofed area, which
" at prefent contains a handfome ftone-built
" church, and fome wooden houfes.

                                          " The

" The moft remarkable of thefe ancient build-
" ings is a tower, *Mifgir* or *Midfgir*, conftructed
" of cut ftone, extremely well wrought; it is a
" little more than twelve toifes high (about 75
" feet.) Its proportions are nearly reprefented in
" the figure annexed; it is well preferved, and is
" afcended by a circular ftair-cafe of 72 fteps,
" each meafuring exactly 12 inches, French mea-
" fure in the rife; the ftair-cafe is in perfect re-
" pair, and the roof is covered with wood;
" withinfide is an infcription in modern Ara-
" bic.

" The tower ftands in the north-eaft angle of a
" wall of an irregular fquare form, which appears
" by its great thicknefs to have been part of a
" fortrefs, or probably of a grand mofque. On
" the weft fide of the tower is the ruins of a Tarta-
" rian oratory which is entirely vaulted; it has
" been repaired, and is now a chapel dedicated
" to Saint Nicholas."

' From this defcription, and from the drawing,
it is evident the oratory is in the foundation of the
tower, and that the entrance to the upper part of
the tower muft be over the vault of the oratory,
which makes the likenefs to our towers much
ftronger; it is to be wifhed thefe curious travellers had copied the Arabic infcription.

It is to be obferved the name given to thefe
towers is *mifgir* or *midfgir*; a word I tranflate *fire-
circle* or *fire-tower*, hence the Perfian word *mudfkir*,
one who continually praifes God; *muzki*, making
the holy fire burn bright; in Arabic *medkyn* is
fmoaking incenfe; perfuming with burning

odours;

odours; and *mudakis*, is the dance of the *Magi* round the holy fire.

The ancient hiftorians of Ireland, relate, that *Nemedius* the *Scythian*, brought with him to Ireland a chief druid named *Midghe*, who taught the inhabitants the ufe of *fire;* I beg leave to put another conftruction on this paffage : I think it denotes that *Midghe* taught them the worfhip of the *divinity* by fire. *Midhe* and *Midhghe* in Irifh implies *fight*, afpect, and confequently *light*, *fire*. It is faid in Irifh hiftory, that it was the facred fire which was worfhipped on their altars that gave the name to *Midhe* now the county of *Meath*, which from its centrical fituation, was the union of their religion and the feat of judgment. But *Midhe* and *Meath* are two different words. *Meath* in the oriental languages means a plain country, fuch is *Meath* compared to moft other counties in *Ireland. Incolæ olim Maiatas & Caledoneos diftincti erant*, i. e. *Campeftres & Montanos.* *Mauth* in Arabic is *terra expanfa*, in Hebrew *Maes*, from whence probably our *Dun-na-Maes* in the Queen's County; that is a hill ftanding in a plain country.

A N

AN ACCOUNT

OF THE

SHIP-TEMPLE,

NEAR

DUNDALK in IRELAND.

IN A LETTER

FROM

GOVERNOR POWNALL,

TO

LIEUT. COL. VALLANCEY.

TO WHICH ARE ADDED

SOME REMARKS,

BY

LIEUT. COL. VALLANCEY.

A N

A C C O U N T

O F   T H E

SHIP-TEMPLE.

SIR,

Richmond-Hill, Surrey,
June 22d, 1781.

FROM the firſt time ţhàt I ſaw the drawing,
which Mr. Wright gives in his Louthiana of the
ruin calleḑ by him, *Faghs na ain eighe, or the one
night's work*, and read his account, I have always
conſidered " this moſt *uncommon of all buildings*"
as he calls it, as one of the moſt ſingular and
curious pieces of antiquity which remain in any
part of Europe, being, what it is repreſénted, a
temple in the ſhape of a ſhip's hulk, it may be
ſaid to be unique.

Mr. Wright's account is but tranſient and
general ; but the account which, by your obliging
means, I have obtained from Mr. Beranger is
accurate, comprehending and diſcerning with
great judgment, all the ſpecifick particulars with
the idea of it, he has alſo accompanied and explained this by three maſterly drawings, the firſt a
ground plan, the ſecond a ſide view, and the
other a portrait view of the end.

A breach

A   a breach 15 feet level with the ground.

B   a breach 11 feet, two or three feet high.

C   a large stone shewing the ancient form.

See the plate.

From this account I am enabled to form, and take the liberty to present through your hands to the antiquarian society of Dublin my conjectures on the subject of this curious antiquity.

The commerce, occupancy, and various inhabitancy, which the ancient state of Ireland has been under and experienced, leaves to conjecture two lines of investigation which it may pursue in examination of the many remnants of antiquity that are every day newly discovered in it.

The one leads to those circumstances and state of things which may be supposed to exist in it, while the *Phœnicians and Carthaginians* had their intercourse there; the other to those, which accompanied the occupancy and inhabitancy of the *Guhds*, *Guths*, or (as they called themselves) *Vikandres*, the sea rovers and pirates who in the earliest times came to Ireland from the Baltic and the coasts of the North Sea.

If the antiquary is inclined to suppose this curious ruin to have been one of the *Arkite-Temples*, which the people of the east, perhaps the navigators in particular, were supposed to have built in the form of a ship, I should wish to persuade Mr. Bryant to give to your society his opinion upon it.   He is deep in these Arkite mysteries, as he is in every point of ancient literature; and I will try to tempt him by sending the drawings and description to him.

In

In the mean time, I will purfue the other line as more confonant to my own opinion.

I have in another place and on another occafion, proved that thefe *Victs*, or *Ficts* as the Welfh called them, or *Picti*, *Pictones*, *Vicingi*, & *Victo-nes*, as the Romans in different fituations pronounced the name ; or *Vikanders*, and *Vikengers*, as the word is written in their own runic monuments ; made very early incurfions to, and even invafions of Ireland, and were found in Scotland as having been fettled there in a ftate of government and eftablifhment. They governed part of this country, then called Calidonia, as they did various other parts where they made eftablifh-ments by reguli, or vice-roys, or fuffered them to be governed by their own kings as fubfidiary, and called them therefore Scots-konung. Thefe Victs or Picts were the firft people who checked the career of the Roman Eagle, fo far as even to oblige the Romans to build works of defénce againft the recoil of this northern valour.

Thefe people came from a country and were of a race, who paid divine honors to the form of a fhip as the fimbol, idol, or rather as the temple of the divinity whom they worfhipped. Tacitus is willing to fuppofe this divinity to be Ifis, and the fimbol to reprefent *the fhip of Ifis :* yet he cannot but exprefs his doubt at the fame time in thefe words, " *Unde Caufa & Origo perigrino Sacro* " *parum comperi, nifi lignum ipfum, in modum* " *LIBURNÆ figuratum, docet advectam religia-* " *nem.*"

Upon

Upon this paſſage Monſieur l'Abbé de Tontenu in his two learned diſcourſes, by ſeveral very ingenious conjeĉtures, endeavours to prove how and in what way this *Religio* was brought from Ægypt to theſe northern parts of Germany. Being taught by Cæſar in his *(a)* Commentaries, that theſe people knew not *even by hearſay* of any other Gods than their own (to which however according to the Roman cuſtom, he is pleaſed to give the Roman names Sol, Vulcanus, Luna,) I cannot ſubſcribe to theſe far-fetched myſteries. Theſe people had metaphyſical religious fables of their own reſpeĉting the various manifeſtations of the divine powers, amongſt other inventions they ſuppoſed the gods called ASES to have a ſhip, which the *Nani* made for them, in which they ſailed—to this ſhip they gave the name *(b)* SKIDBLADNER. *(c)* " Nani fecerunt Skidblad-
" nerum & dederunt Frejero, hæc adeo magna
" eſt ut par ſit omnibus Aſis, & quidem armatis,
" ferandis; veliſque explicatis ſtatim ventum
" nanſciſcitur ſecundum, quocunque ſit abitura :
" cum vero navigandum non ſit, adeo multis
" conſtat partibus, ut complicata in perâ includi
" poſſit". In like manner when Tor or Thor is
deſcribed

(*a*) Deorum numero eos ſolos ducunt quos cernunt, & quorum opibus apertè juvantur; Solum, Vulcanum, & Lunam. Reliquos *nè famâ quidem acciperunt*. Bell: Gall. l. 6. § 21.

(*b*) Skidbladner cavitas cochlearis.
         John Ihre's Diĉt.

(*c*) Edda.
     Operâ & ſtudio Johannis Goranſon.

defcribed as going a fifhing for the great ferpent *Midgard*, he borrowed *the fkiff* of the giant *Eymer*. Reading this we need not go in fearch of the vanities of foreign idol-fervice, we need go no further than thefe peoples own notions for this fimbolic and myfterious fhip. If their religious faith taught them to believe, that the gods themfelves chofe this kind of vehicle, and that the miniftring gods, or priefts of the intellectual world, prepared fuch for them; *what form of temple* could be more conform to thefe divine myfteries, or become a more proper fimbol of the dwelling of the gods, to which their prefence might be invoked, *than that of a fhip?* I believe this to be the original and genuine meaning of the *idol* or *temple*, the fimbol of the prefence, under which Tacitus found the Suevi adoring their divinity, which finding to be in the form of a fhip, he fuppofed to be, as I faid, the fhip of Ifis. My conjecture therefore (and which with all diffidence I fubmit to the learning of your fociety,) is *that this Ship-Temple is the Simbol of the facred Skidbladner, built by the Nani,* and which therefore I fhould call a *Nanic-T mple* founded and built on the inftitution of thofe myfteries in Ireland, when firft thefe northern people eftablifhed themfelves there. The traditional name (corrupted as the pronunciation, and nonfenfical as the tranflator's name feems to me) confirms me in this opinion. Mr. Wright gives the name as follows, *Faghs na ain eighe*; Mr. Beranger *Fas nabion eidhche.* One of thefe muft be wrong,

and

and the laſt has various readings, as *Fas nabin doidhche* and *Faas na hane eughe.* The ſuppoſed real pronunciation which Mr. Beranger had from the Iriſh teacher, I ſuſpect to be a tranſlation back into Iriſh, of the nonſenſical name—*The one night's work*, to be the reformed correction of this teacher as uſual with other great claſſical criticks. I take the whole to be a corruption of ſomething which has reference to very high antiquity, to the *Nanic inſtitution of theſe Ship-Temples*, expreſſive of (as Tacitus under another idea expreſſes it) *advectæ religionis.* If I knew enough of the ancient Celtic language to enable me to analyſe this corruption, I ſhould be led to a ſecond conjecture, and read the name as follows.

The $\left\{\begin{array}{c}\text{Strength}\\\text{or}\\\text{Power}\end{array}\right\}$ of the Nani founded this.

With great reſpect, which I beg to preſent, to your ſociety, I have the honor to be,

Sir, Your moſt Obedient and

Humble Servant,

T. POWNALL.

SOME

SOME

REMARKS

on

Mr. POWNALL's LETTER,

by

LIEUT. COL. VALLANCEY.

THE Irish historians do not allow that the Picts
had any footing in this island, at their first emigration from Scythia; they assert, that the Irish
expelled them forthwith, to Scotland. Beda and
Florilegus agree in this part of the Irish history.
It is true, Fordun brings the Picts back to Ireland,
being driven from Britain, but this is contradicted
by the learned Usher, " in Norvegiam, Daniamque,
" non ut Fordunus scripsit in Hiberniam concess-
" isse."—A considerable space of time elapsed from
the first appearance of the Picts, to the arrival of
the Danes and Norwegians. If the Picts, (mixed
with these nations) preserved the tenets of their
ancient religion at the time of the invasion of
Ireland.

Ireland by the Danes, Mr. Pownall's conjecture may be right ; and if they built one ship-temple in this island, they certainly did many others. Let us hear what Beda and Florilegus have said on the arrival of the Picts.

Contigit gentem Pictorum de Scythiâ, ut perhibent, longis navibus non multis Oceanum ingreſſam, circumagente flatu ventorum extra fines omnes Britanniæ Hiberniam perveniſſe, ejuſque ſeptentrionales oras intraſſe ; atque inventâ ibi gente Scotorum, ſibi quoque in partibus illius ſedes petiſſe, nec impetrare potuiſſe.——Ad hanc ergo uſque pervenientes navigio Picti (ut diximus) petierunt in eâ ſibi quoque ſedes & habitationem donari. Reſpondebant Scoti, quia non ambos eos caperet inſula, ſed poſſumus (inquiunt) ſalubre vobis dare conſilium, quid agere valeatis. Novimus inſulam eſſe aliam non procul a noſtrâ contra ortum ſolis, quam ſæpè lucidioribus diebus de longè aſpicere ſolemus. Hanc adire ſi vultis, habitabilem vobis facere valeatis ; vel ſi qui reſtiterint, nobis auxiliariis utimini. Itaque petentes Brittaniam Picti, habitare per ſeptentrionales inſula partes cæperunt. Nam auſtrina Britones occupaverant. Cumque uxores Picti non habentes peterunt a Scotis ; eâ ſolùm conditione dare conſenſerunt, ut ubi res veniret in dubium, magis de fæmineâ regum profapiâ quàm de maſculinâ Regem ſibi eligerent ; quod uſque hodie apud Pictos conſtat eſſe ſervatum.

Britannia

Britannia post Britons & Pictos tertiam Scotorum nationem in Pictorum parte recepit; quia Duce Reudâ de Hibernia progressi, vel amicitiâ vel ferro sibimet inter eas sedes, quas hactenùs habent, vindicârunt. A quo videlicèt duce usque hodie Dal-Reudini vocantur; nam linguâ eorum *dal* partem significat. *(a)*

Florilegus says,

Contigit tempore Vespasiani gentem Pictorum de Scythiâ navigasse: & flatu ventorum oras boreales Hiberniæ ingressi sunt; ubi in multitudine copiosâ Scottos invenerunt. Nam cùm terra illa ambas gentes sustinere non potuit, miserunt Scotti Pictos ad septentrionalem partem Brittanniæ, opem contra adversarios promittentes. Tempore Vespasiani Cæsaris, apud Britones regnante Mario filio Arviragi, Rodericus rex Pictorum cœpit Albaniam devastare.

Britanniæ Chronicus anonym. in *Primordia Usberi.* Tempore Vespasiani, gens Pictorum de Scythiâ per Oceanum Britanniam ingressa, regnante apud Britannos Mario filio Arviragi: cujus rex Rodericus Albaniam devastavit: quem Marius rex Britonum prœlio interfecit juxta Lugubaliam, quæ est nunc Karliol: & populo devicto qui cum Roderico

(a) Beda, lib. I. cap. I.

venerat

venerat borealem partem Albaniæ quæ Kathenefia dicitur ad habitandum dedit. Illi vero uxoribus carentes, cùm de natione Britonum habere non poffent, transfretantes Hiberniam fibi Hibernienfium filias copulârunt; eo tamen pacto, ut fanguis maternies in fucceffionibus præferatur.

From the plan of this building, named by Mr. Wright, the Ship-Temple, (from its refemblance to the hulk of a fhip) it is evident the ftructure was not intended for a dwelling; there are no crofs walls, fire-places, or chimneys. The inhabitants call it *fàs na heun oidhche* or the growth of one night; it is the name for a mufhroom: the Irifh language is not fo fterile to apply a term of vegetation to a building. Fàs fignifies the growth of trees, roots, &c. *Faghs na ain eighe*, given by Mr. Wright, has no meaning: and as we have not yet met with the true orthography, all our explanations muft be conjectural. *Naoi* is a fhip, and *faghas na héun Naoi*, by a forced conftruction, may imply the remains of the *only fhip*. *Faghcas* or *Faighcas* is an obfelete word, explained in an ancient gloffary, by *faighleann*, i. e. *alcaing*, i. e. *ait accuirthear fciatha acus airm an gaifgidh*, i. e. an armoury, or place where the warriors depofited their fhields and arms. *Faighcas na Niadh* would fignify the armoury of the nobles. *Foghcas* is an inn, or houfe of entertainment, and *Foghcas na Naoidh*, would imply the caravanfera or houfe of entertainment of the *Naoids*. Thefe were an order of monks

monks belonging to the Druids; they were divided into *Saor-Naoidh*, and *Daor-Naoidh*, or free Naoid and bond Naoid. The firſt were of noble deſcent, and kept open houſe for the accommodation of ſtrangers and travellers, like the *Bonzes* of China; hence, *Naoidh* in the modern Iriſh, ſignifies an hoſpitable man, and *Teach-Naoidh*, a houſe of hoſpitality. The *Daor-Naoidh* were plebeians, who had been guilty of ſome tranſgreſſion of the law, and not being able to pay the mulct or *ciric*, were conſigned in bondage to the Druids; they were taught to fabricate taliſmans, vaſes, beads of glaſs, &c. hence the *gloinne-naoidr*, or *glonne-naidr* of the Welſh; *Naoidr* ſignifying alſo a ſerpent, gave riſe to the fable of the ſerpent's egg; a ſtory impoſed on Pliny.

All theſe names read nearly the ſame, and to the modern vulgar Iriſh, may readily be corrupted to *fàs na heun oidhche*, or the growth of one night.

C. V.

REFLECTIONS

ON THE

HISTORY of IRELAND

DURING THE

TIMES of HEATHENISM;

WITH OBSERVATIONS ON SOME LATE
PUBLICATIONS ON THAT SUBJECT.

ADDRESSED TO

LIEUT. COL. CHARLES VALLANCEY,

BY

CHARLES O'CONOR, Esq. SOC. ANTIQ. HIB. SOC.

ADVERTISEMENT.

THE facts expofed in the following effay, have been taken chiefly from the Leabhar Gabhala, or Book of Conquefts; the Compilations of Balimote; Extracts from the Pfalter of Cafhel, and Book of Glendaloch in the fame Work; the Annals of Tigernach, of Innis Fallen and of the four Mafters; with Extracts from the Lecan records: The author has alfo availed himfelf of fome antient documents collected by the late Mr. O'Flaherty. This general notice is given at once, to fave the trouble of frequeut marginal references to manufcripts, which are very feldom confulted, and are very difficult to be come at.

REFLECTIONS

ON THE

HISTORY of IRELAND.

SIR,

I HAVE ventured to throw together the following ſtrictures on a ſubject much agitated in ſome
late publications; I make no apology for addreſſing
them to you, as you formed the plan, and have
taken the lead, in a body of *Collectanea*, for
throwing a fuller light than has hitherto appeared
on the antient ſtate of this country, heathen and
chriſtian; this you have done with the laudable
view of adding to the ſtock of knowledge ob-
tainable from hiſtory; and of diſcovering, whether any part of ſuch knowledge could be
augmented from the polity and manners of a
people ſequeſtered here in Ireland for many ages,
and cut off from any ſcientific commerce with
the more enlightened nations of Greece and
Rome. A circumſtance ſo apparently negative
of any civilization in this iſland, till introduced
with the goſpel, did not diſcourage you, or
induce you, as it has others, to pronounce arbitrarily, that all hiſtorical notices from the native

Senachies

Senachies, anterior to the fifth century, have been little better than crude inventions, committed to writing on the reception of chriftianity, when the mind fhould be rather prepared for rejecting the errors of antient time, and for adopting every truth, that could be made fubfervient to the caufe of true religion; and when, in fact, the miffionary who had moft fuccefs in propagating that religion, had himfelf affifted in clearing the antient hiftory of this ifland from the fables in which it was enveloped.——Unfatisfied with mere opinion, you confidered, philofophically, that this retired nation of Ireland might, probably, in its heathen ftate, receive the elements of knowledge from a fource different from that, which fooner or later, poured the ftreams of fcience through the other Celtic regions of the North. You made the trial, and you fucceeded happily. You collected, and confronted, the evidences foreign and domeftic, which regarded this fubject, and found *one* which depofed fo effectually, for the early cultivation of literature in Ireland, as to overturn, at once, the minute accounts of foreign writers, who receiving all their informations on truft, or drawing conclufions from conjecture, have in general terms reprefented the inhabitants, as the moft ignorant of barbarians, and a difgrace to humanity. In your learned refearches on our antient language, you have exhibited proofs more authentic than the oldeft infcriptions on marble or metal, that it had been formed among a cultivated people. Copious and energetic, regu-

lar

lar and harmonious, it muft take a confiderable time, as all languages have taken, to arrive at the grammatical degree of perfection it clofed with. Its terms for thofe abftract ideas and mixed modes, which a civilized people only can invent, and which barbarians neither want nor ufe, demonftrate that this language arrived at its claffical ftandard before the introduction of chriftianity, when Grecian and Roman terms, were firft taught in Ireland by the chriftian miffionaries. Rich in their own ftores, the natives borrowed but few figns of compound ideas from the learned languages; a fingular circumftance in the hiftory of this country, while the continental nations of the North, were indebted to the Greeks and Romans for thofe technical terms, which mark the change from barbarifm to civilization.

On the difperfion from the plains of *Shinaar*, the miraculous confufion of tongues, did not produce as you have well obferved, an oblivion of the figns of ideas formerly in ufe, but a change in their fyntaxes only. Thofe figns were few in number, and confined to the few wants of the primæval fpeakers: They became the ground on which all antient languages have been conftructed, before the invention of new terms, or the corruption of the old, in a long courfe of time; in *one* inftance, the improvement of arts, required new figns, in the *other*, dialects were multiplied, and every tongue remained long in a flux and anomalous ftate. It is only through the

ufe

ufe of letters, and long ftudy, that any language can be brought to the grammatical perfection it is nearly capable of; for heteroclites are unavoidable, even in the beft. To attain energy and copioufnefs, much muft depend on the form of civil government, and on the manners of the people, the fecurity of the one from foreign conqueft, and the tendency of the other, to bring men forward by popular arts, and in particular by that *of fpeaking*. Under fuch circumftances has the language of Ireland been formed, and evidently it could not in early times, be formed under any other. By comparing fome compofitions of the fifth century, with others down to the feventeenth, we found, the fame fyntax retained through all, with little variation, except fuch as muft unavoidably happen in a courfe of fo many revolutions, and in a feries of fo many ages.

How the Heathen inhabitants of Ireland could obtain the elements of literature, and improve them into knowledge earlier than other northern people can be accounted for: Thofe elements were imported from Spain, a country whofe Celtic inhabitants were initiated in arts and letters, by the Phœnicians who fettled among them. Whether over-crowded by numbers, or otherwife made uneafy at home, a colony of Scytho-Celts, failed from that country to Ireland, and eftablifhed themfelves in it. Among other appellations, they gave themfelves the name of *Phenii*, and very probably a tribe of Phenians,

or

or Phœnicians joined in their expedition. We now call them Milefians, and that people have invariably, from age to age, recorded themselves to be of Spanish extraction. No fact of remote antiquity comes attended with better proofs than *this*, and you, fir, have produced one of the ftrongeft. The great number of Phœnician or Punic terms you difcovered in the Iberno-Celtic, or Irifh language, lead us directly to the fource from whence they were derived; They fhew an intimate communication with the Phœnicians, and the knowledge of letters—confequently, in the countries where that people made lafting eftablifh- ments. It was from the Phœnicians that the Ionians learned the art of writing, and in this art the Grecians and antient Spaniards had the fame mafters, their letters were originally but fixteen in all; and it is remarkable that the Milefian Irifh had no greater number, till the chriftian Miffionaries made known to them the additional cyphers.

Though thefe evidences fupport the fact, that a colony from Spain eftablifhed itfelf in Ireland, yet the time of its arrival cannot be fixed by any exact chronology. The antiquaries who make it coeval with the age of Cyrus the great, (*a*) are probably neareft to the truth. It anfwers beft to the period when the Celtic dialects of the weftern countries of Europe, varied fo little as to be ftill intelligible to the feveral tribes who inhabited them; for we find it recorded, that thofe new

comers

(*a*) About 540 years before the birth of CHRIST.

comers from Spain could converfe with the Belgians and Danans they found in Ireland, without the help of interpreters. It was only after quitting the roving ftate, for fixed abodes, and in the progrefs of civilization, that thofe dialects were gradually converted into diftinct tongues, intelligible only in the countries of their formation, and this facility of converfing without interpreters, has very probably continued in the weft, till between three or four hundred years anterior to the Chriftian æra. The Milefians, the introducers of the Phœnician letters into Ireland, gave the law in fpeech, as well as in civil government, to its old inhabitants, and the Iberno-Celtic or Irifh language, was probably formed in the courfe of three or four centuries; it muft have been, doubtlefs, in proportion to the improvements made in literature, and the poetic art; for all our earlieft compofitions were delivered in verfe, and nothing contributes more to the perfection of a language, than the treating every fubject in the harmony of numbers.

Falfe chronology, doth not affect facts. Whether the commerce of the antient Phænicians, with the Britifh ifles, commenced five hundred years before our vulgar æra, or in a later period; certain it is, that fuch a commerce had for a confiderable time fubfifted; and we may be affured, that thofe Phœnicians, availed themfelves of the Celtes of Spain, as interpreters between them and thofe of Britain, for carrying it on. In the courfe of this traffic, we difcover, that a tribe of the Spanifh Celtes actually fettled in Britain, by the name of *Brigans* or *Brigantes*:

But

But though initiated in Phœnician literature, they were not sufficiently powerful for giving the law in language in the greater isle, as their brethern the Milesians did, in the lesser. In forming the Gymraeg, the present language of Wales, the old British dialects prevailed over any imported by strangers; in time, a regular and vigorous tongue was formed; but it differs entirely in Syntax, from the Iberno-Celtic or Irish tongue: both, indeed, may be easily traced to the same original; to the primæval language of Europe, first splitting into dialects, and lastly ending in two tongues, as different in construction, as the modern English is from the modern German; two languages which may with equal facility be traced to the antient Teutonic. These facts, have not been sufficiently attended to by antiquaries.—An identity of terms in two tongues, of different construction, doth not infer the descent of one from the other.

Ignorance of our language, and of the documents still preserved in it, induced some modern antiquaries in their researches to consider both as useless; disgusted also with some late publications on this subject, (either defective in matter, or injudicious in the selection) these moderns have rejected as crude fables, whatever we have recorded of the times antecedent to Christianity. In this idea, (which excludes any useful knowledge of our country in its heathen state,) one should think, that they would leave the great blank as they found it; but that was not the case. The *supposed* void, they have laboured to fill up with hypotheses of their own, grafted on a few scraps

from

from antient authors, and explained in the fenfe that each hypothefis required. In fo extenfive a field to range in, imagination has been very pro-ductive; ridiculous etymologies have ftept in to its aid, and in the variety of fchemes, not one agrees with the other, except in the neceffary pofition, that no colony from *Spain* ever fettled in Ireland, and that in confequence, no letters were known to the inhabitants during their heathen ftate : but arbitrary pofitions are eafily laid down, and like the hypothefes which they generate, are fatisfactory only to thofe who frame them, or to carelefs readers who perufe them without exami-nation.

Certain it is, that without the notices left us in the antient language of Ireland, we fhould know nothing, or next to nothing, of its heathen hiftory. Our earlieft accounts, like thofe of the Grecians, are mixed with fables, but fome of thofe fables are grounded on facts; and difficult as it is, to ftrip off the fanciful garb which Poetry has thrown over the earlieft events in Europe, yet fome critics have attempted it, and fome have had good fuccefs in the attempt. The more antient traditions of Ire-land, fhould undergo a like inveftigation, for the feparation of the true from the falfe, as far as it can be done ; and fome facts preferved in the fables of Ireland, would probably have remained in their native obfcurity, had not the chronological refearches of Sir Ifaac Newton, affifted us, (though unintentionally to that great man) in fhewing, that fome of the earlieft reports of our Irifh bards, are not groundlefs. They are facts, indeed, which

relate

relate to continental, not to our infular antiquities, and are the more remarkable on that account. Our *Niul, Sru, Afru, Tat,* and *Ogaman,* correfpond exactly, with the *Nil, Sihor, Ofihor, Thoth* and *Ogmius* of Sir Ifaac. In the Irifh traditions, as in thofe of Greece, they are celebrated as heroes who performed mighty exploits in Egypt, Spain and other countries ; and whether thofe names belonged to a fingle prince, who multiplied his appellations with his conquefts (as the great author judges,) or referred to different conquerors, is not material to our prefent purpofe : but it is highly obfervable, that this correfpondence in names and facts, this coincidence in the traditions of remote nations, who held no communication with each other, could not happen by mere accident. To Newton, who ftripped off the Poetic veil, we owe the difcovery, and the light he has caft on our oldeft reports, is remarkably reflected back on his own fyftem.

Thefe traces of things, which paffed on the great theatres of the continent, fhew that the people who retained them, were a colony from that continent ; and the Punic terms, which you have difcovered in their language, fhew that Spain was the country they arrived from, and fo their own accounts affirm invariably. They were Iberian Scytho-Celtes, who once mixed with the Phœnicians, or their Carthaginian pofterity. In Ireland they took various denominations : they called themfelves Gædhil, or (as we pronounce it) Gæil, very properly, in memory of their Celtic origin. With equal propriety, they took the name of

Scuit

Scuit or Scots, to commemorate their Scythian extraction; Celts and Scythians having intermixed with each other in Spain, as in Gaul and other Celtic regions. They also had the name of Clan-Breogain (which we Latinize Brigantes) as the descendants of a celebrated Breogan, who they say, held the government of Brigantia, or Brigantium, in Spain. They mention likewise among their ancestors, a celebrated *Phenius*, who first instructed mankind in the knowledge of letters; a fable, which has its use, in shewing that the colony which arrived in Ireland from the continent, had their rudiments of literature from the Phœnicians. Such notices, combined with several others, which I here omit, demonstrate the settlement of a Spanish or Celtiberian people in Ireland, and that in an early period of time. The descent of the Romans or antient Latins, from a colony of fugitive Trojans, cannot be so well ascertained.

At the period of the Milesian expedition into Ireland, arts were yet in their infancy. The new comers were employed chiefly in making room for themselves, in an island covered with immense forests. The cultivation of the land was prior to that of the mind, and it took some time before a monarch, emphatically surnamed * *Ollam Fodhla*, established a College in Teamor for the education of the principal families of the kingdom, under the direction of an order of men called *Ollamhs* and *Fileas*. Of that monarch's regulations, both in his legislative and literary capacities, we have but a
slender

* *i. e.* The Instructor of Ireland.

flender account. It doth not appear, that his infti-
tutes had much influence, through the diforderly
reigns of his fucceffors, down to the elevation of
Kimbaoth (a prince of his pofterity) to the throne
of Ireland; this Kimbaoth flourifhed fix generations before the Chriftian æra. He is celebrated for
his buildings in Eamania, and the fchools he
eftablifhed for educating the principal families of
his kingdom in arts, arms and literature. From
his time, Tigernach with other antiquaries, date
our more exact hiftorical notices, pronouncing the
former to be uncertain. A reform in the civil
government, fucceeded to the regulations made
in Eamania. In a convention of the ftates, Hugony
furnamed the Great, (an Heremonian prince educated under Kimbaoth, and Macha his queen)
was raifed to the throne; and by a folemn law,
it was enacted, that the regal fucceffion fhould
for the future, be continued by hereditary right
in his family. Pretenders from the other royal
families, were by the fame law excluded; but no
regard being paid to primogeniture in this conftitution, it was of fhort duration. The excluded
families forced their way to the throne by bloody
contefts with the Hugonians, and with one another,
till a new reform was made in the beginning of
the firft century under *Eochy Feyloch*. But the
radical defects of an elective government, ftill
remained. The Belgian tribes, difcontented with
their Milefian mafters, rebelled againft them, and
fet up a monarch of their own. In a fecond rebellion, they banifhed the royal Hugonian race
into North Britain, and the kingdom laid in
ruins,

ruins, was expofed to all the miferies of civil war and famine.

Thus ended the fecond period of Irifh hiftory, commencing with the legal elevation of Hugony the Great, to regal power, and ending with the ufurpation of Elim the fon of Conra; the whole time, marks a robuft, but fickly conftitution, in the treatment of which, remedies proved but too often, new difeafes; fome kings were rather introduced by factions, than elected by the national voice; their titles were difputed, their power was limited, and their end was tragical; others proved able princes, and gave the nation repofe during their adminiftration. In the confufion of the times, and frequency of revolutions, we are not to wonder that the reigns of kings were ill regiftered; or that contenders for royalty, who were faluted kings by their feveral parties, fhould by future fenachies be enrolled in the lift of legitimate monarchs. In a word, it is from the fucceffion of Feradach the Juft, and the great revolution foon after under Tuathal the acceptable, that we can date exactnefs in our Heathen hiftory. Undoubtedly, fome events of antecedent times bear ftrong marks of authenticity; fome princes appear with luftre, but they appear like ftars of magnitude in a clouded night.

Thus it was, Sir, in our ifland, as in all other Pagan countries; our earlieft tranfactions were delivered in the fongs of the bards, and in our firft written accounts, the heroic and marvellous prevailed; yet fome truths have been preferved, even in that ftate of things. The lights of genuine

biftory

hiftory came on gradually, in proportion to the progrefs made in civilization and literature. In the northern countries of Europe this progrefs was extremely flow, and it is highly remarkable that in Ireland, and in Ireland alone, we firft meet with Celtic hiftory in Celtic language; and that, long before the natives had any acquaintance with the learning of Greece or Rome.

The Tuathalian era, the moft exact in our heathen annals, commenced with the year of Chrift 130. In a full convention of the ftates the old Hugonian conftitution was renewed with great improvements; the fine province of Meath, extending from the Shannon to the eaftern fea, was taken from the other provinces, and erected into a domain for every future monarch of the ifle; as a fupport to the regal dignity, independent of the provincial tribute formerly ill paid and often withheld, in the tumults of civil contention. In the fame convention, the regal fucceffion was eftablifhed in the family of Tuathal Soley, fanctioned by the moft binding teft that the Druids could frame, or that their religion could afford; conformably to this law, *ten* monarchs of Tuathal's line, from father to fon, mounted the throne of Ireland, and the interruptions which ambition or difcontent gave to this conftitution, were but of fhort continuance. During the whole period, which takes in three hundred years, a right of fucceffion by primogeniture, appears to have been eftablifhed, as none but elder fons affumed the reins of government; it muft be obferved however, that during two

Q   minorities,

minorities, the Tuathalian law was difpenfed with
in the fucceffion of Conary II. A. D. 212, and of
Crimhan in 366. Such fucceffions were not confidered as violations of the Tuathalian conftitution,
and on the demife of each of thofe princes, the
legitimate inheritor immediately afcended the
throne of his anceftors.

It was during this period of three hundred
years, antecedent to chriftianity, that the regulations antiently begun in Teamor and Eamania
were re-eftablifhed and extended. Foreign alliances were renewed, and in particular with the
Cruthenians of North-Britain, among whom our
Carbry-Riada (the fon of Conary II.) found an
eftablifhment for his colony of Scots, the firft that
migrated from Ireland to Britain. Both nations
(Scots and Picts united) warred againft the
Romans, and the Scots of the mother country
entered into alliances with the Saxons, before the
latter had obtained any footing in Britain.

Should thefe outlines be filled up hereafter by
the pencil of ability, the hiftory of Ireland, even
in its heathen ftate, will afford matter for inftruction ; the national manners excited to the employment, and the form of government required
the full exercife of the mental faculties. It was
however a ftate of things attended with difadvan-
tages, as well as benefits; A conftitution wherein
the three orders of legiflation were never fufficiently poized, concealed maladies of fatal operation. The executive power was weak, and our
ableft monarchs, feldom had authority enough to
controul, or power fufficient to fubdue the oppo-
                                        fi ti on

fition of provincial princes, who took the lead in the ariftocratical order, and often fet themfelves up, rather as rivals than fubjects to the firft magiftrate of the ftate.

Affairs affumed a better afpect under the cele-brated monarch Corbmac O'Cuinn, and moft of his fucceffors. The court of Teamor appeared in all the fplendor that could be derived from the local manners, and local regulations of a fequef-tered people. Science was improved; the fuper-ftitions of Druidifm were examined and expofed; the truths of natural religion were ftudied and propagated; new laws were promulgated, and the increafe of knowledge, proved an increafe of power to every wife adminiftration. In this ftate the nation flourifhed and profpered, and the people became known and celebrated in Europe, by the name of SCOTS, an appellation they *always* bore at home. At this period, they meafured their arms with thofe of Rome, firft in Britain and afterwards in Gaul. At length they embraced the true religion, and in no country did the gofpel make a more rapid progrefs than in theirs; a circumftance, which alone points them out to us a thinking and rational people, and confirms the obfervation of ecclefiaftical hiftorians, that chriftianity made its quicker and more lafting eftablifhments among cultivated nations.

You fee, Sir, that I have reduced the forego-ing obfervations on our heathen hiftory under three heads; Firft, The expedition of the Mile-fians from Spain to Ireland; Secondly, The building of Eamania, and the Hugonian civil

Q 2   reform,

reform, about two hundred years before the chriſtian era; and Thirdly, The new conſtitution under Tuathal the *acceptable*, A. D. 130.—The commencement and duration of the firſt period, cannot be fixed with any exactneſs; the regal and genealogical liſts can be but little depended upon, and the accounts tranſmitted by the bards in that infancy of hiſtory, are by Tigernach with other antiquaries, pronounced uncertain. Under the ſecond period from the reign of Hugony the great, facts were recorded with a greater attention to truth; the monarch Eochy Feyloch made a change in the form of civil government; laws were committed to writing under Corcovar Mac Neſſa, king of Ulſter; and other incidents, coeval with the firſt chriſtian century, are evidences of the gradual improvement made in government and literature. The third period commencing with the political regulations under Tuathal the *acceptable*, continued for three hundred years. The documents ſtill preſerved of thoſe three heathen ages, bear all the ſignatures of authentic hiſtory; they accurately mark the ſeveral invaſions of the civil conſtitution, and the ſpeedy puniſhment of the invaders.

My troubling you, Sir, in particular, with theſe hints, in the looſe form of a letter, can be juſtified for a reaſon already aſſigned; but I confeſs that they are thrown out chiefly, with the view of recalling others from ſome groſs miſtakes on this ſubject, which no wrong information can excuſe, while better can be procured, from a critical examination of the antient facts, ſtill almoſt

buried

buried in our old language. Such miftakes publifhed in the *Collectanea*, muft in a high degree
fruftrate your defign of extracting as much as can
be extracted from thefe fources.

It pains me that a gentleman, I much efteem,
fhould reject thefe fources of intelligence for any
modern hypothefis. In the hiftory of Kilkenny,
publifhed in the ninth number of the *Collectanea*,
the reverend author adopts the fyftem of the
learned Mr. Whitaker of Manchefter, who affirms, that " about three hundred and fifty years
" before the chriftian era, the Britons invaded
" and difpoffeffed by the Belgæ, from the conti-
" nent, fled hither and firft inhabited this ifland.
" That in two hundred and fifty years after, a
" fecond migration, and from the fame caufes,
" happened; the latter incorporated with the
" former, and both people were called by their
" countrymen (their brethern) who remained in
" Britain, Scuites and Scots, that is, wanderers
" or refugees." Here, Sir, are feveral affertions
crowded into a few lines, and as they ftand in
contradiction to all the hiftorical documents of
the nation, they refer to, they fhould come fupported, at leaft, with fome plaufible proofs; but
the fhadow of a proof is not offered.

Indeed none was offered by the inventor of the
tale; the whole is an arbitrary fcheme of an
obfcure monk of a dark age, a retailer of
Geoffry of Monmouth's fables, and a writer
flighted by Camden, Ufher, and our beft antiquaries of the feventeenth century. How fo excellent an antiquary, as Mr. Whitaker, fhould in

our

our own time give any credit to the unauthorized affertions of the monk of Cirencefter, is amazing; and it is equally fo, that he who fo ably detected the falfities, and expofed the inconfiftencies, of a late declaimer on this fubject fhould adopt for authentic facts feveral relations in the poems attributed to OSSIAN. In other parts of his hiftory Mr. Whitaker has acquitted himfelf admirably; a mafter of elegant compofition, happy in his refearches and judicious in his reflections, he has thrown lights, which have not appeared before, on the earlier periods of Britifh antiquities; but affuredly, any detached part of his hiftorical fabric reared on the foundations of monk Richard and Mr. Mac Pherfon's Offian, cannot ftand.

Conducted by his monaftic guide, Mr. Whitaker is led aftray in his topography of Ireland; and on this fubject I muft obferve, that foreign writers knew but little of the internal ftate of this ifland, till after the reception of chriftianity among its inhabitants. The Egyptian geographer, Ptolemy, could know but little of it certainly, and that little from hearfay or from feafaring men who made fome ftay on our coafts; and what kind of informers fuch men were, we may judge from the erroneous accounts of our firft European voyagers to India and other remote regions of Afia. In fact, Ptolemy gives us but few genuine names of tribes and diftricts, and he omits fuch as were moft celebrated at the time of his writing; other names thrown in arbitrarily, I fuppofe, by interpolators, have not the common roots of the Celtic language to countenance their infertion.

For

For the antient topography of Ireland it is but reasonable that we should refer to the materials furnished by our native documents; in the compilations of Lecan, in those of Balymote, and in the book of Glendaloch, we have an accurate recital of most of the tribes, who inhabited Ireland in the geographer Ptolemy's own time; a copy of it (in the hand-writing of the celebrated antiquary Duald Mac Firbis) is now in the choice collection of a worthy nobleman, the earl of Roden, and another is in my hands.

In the parts of Ireland described by Mr. Ledwich, Mr. Whitaker's mistakes from the monk Richard are acquiesced in, as good information. The central regions are assigned to the Scots, and the other districts are supposed to be occupied by swarms of British Belgæ with the Durotriges and Damnonii, who fled hither from the Roman power in the reign of Vespasian. Of this emigration from Britain to Ireland not a syllable is offered in proof; and indeed none can be offered. All our native Senachies have been unanimous in asserting, that the Scots had extensive territories, in Munster, Leinster, Meath and Ulster, not only in Vespasian's time, but for many ages before; they were the leading people, and their princes had by long prescription, the civil government of the whole island under their power, in the form of monarchy.

The Belgians from South Britain, and the Danans from the northern parts of that island, were in possession of Ireland, long before the arrival of the Scots or Milesians from Spain.

the

the time of Vespasian, the remains of those old inhabitants were the more numerous part of the nation, and their successful rebellion at the close of the first century, appears to have been provoked by hard treatment from their Milesian masters. But their second rebellion, A. D. 126, was ruinous, and yet had the consequences of ending in a better constitution of government, than the people had before enjoyed.

From the elevation of Tuathal *the acceptable*, to the throne of Teamor A. D. 130, the chief power of the Belgians was confined to the province of Connaught, under some celebrated provincial kings of their own race; but their civil œconomy was utterly dissolved in the fourth century, by the Irish monarch *Muriach Tireach*, who seized on that province, and left the government of it to his posterity, who held it in an uninterrupted succession, through a period of more than nine hundred years. Such accounts, transmitted invariably from age to age, deserve credit; those of the monk of Cirencester deserve none.

The capital towns of the Scots are said to be Rheba and Ibernia; but in no antient document of Ireland, are any such towns mentioned, and undoubtedly, no towns under these denominations, ever existed. Those of chief note in Vespasian's time were Teamor, the royal seat of the Irish monarch's in Meath, and Eamhain or Eamania, the capital of the provincial king's of Ulster. These indeed, were towns of great celebrity; and yet Ptolemy makes no mention of them.

Thefe

These preliminary mistakes in the history of Kilkenny lead to others. Mr. Ledwich thinks, that *Baile-Gaedhlach* (not Bally-Gael-loch) or Irishtown of Kilkenny, was the Ibernia of monk Richard. But it is well known, that the Latin name of Ibernia was imposed on the whole island by foreign writers, and did not belong to any village in it; and the term *Gaedhalach*, is not a compound but an adjective from Gaedhal, or Gaeal as we pronounce it, to avoid the consonantal harshness, or radical letters in this and many other words in our Iberno-Celtic. Thus we derive Hibernicus from Hibernia, and Scoticus from Scotia.

This learned gentleman derives Kilkenny from a supposed compound, *Coil*, or *Kyle-ken-ui, the wooded head or hill near the river!*——Never was etymology put more on the rack, yet no torture can wring from it the intelligence required. The *original* and *translation*, are equally groundless, and the more inexcusable, as the learned writer had, or might have, true and incontrovertible information on this subject from our antient annals.

The Irish name of Kilkenny is *Cill-Chainnigh*, and it means *literally*, the cell or oratory of *Cainneach*, the first abbot of Achabo in the sixth century; as an ecclesiastic revered for the holiness of his life, several other Kills, beside this of Offory, were dedicated to his name and memory, and particularly, that of Kilkenny in Westmeath, now distinguished by the appellation of Kilkenny West. This is the fact. In asserting it, Primate Usher

Uſher has followed the current of all our antient annals, and the charge made to that great antiquary, as adopting herein a vulgar and groundleſs notion, is not juſt.

" We have numberleſs inſtances of the Monks " in dark ages (ſays Mr. Ledwich) perſonifying " rivers and places, like the heathen mythologiſts." A charge of this nature conveying a contemptuous idea of the Iriſh clergy in the earlier ages of the Iriſh church, ſhould ſurely come ſupported with the proper proofs ; certain I am, that thoſe produced, are moſt unhappily ſelected ; they ſtand in contradiction to hiſtory and chronology.

Notwithſtanding the authority of all our antient documents, we are told that the Iriſh monks have made of the river Shannon or Senus, St. Senanus, and of Down or Dunum St. Dunus, and of Kilkenny St. Kenny! Senan a celebrated abbot of the ſixth century, undoubtedly fixed his monaſtery in the iſland of Cathay (now Scattery) ſurrounded by the Shannon ; but that great river bore the name of Shannon or Senus many ages before the Abbot *Senan* was born ; even Ptolemy himſelf, who flouriſhed in the ſecond century, ſets it down in his map. —That Down or Down-Patrick is made of St. Dunus, is a notion equally fanciful, as no ſuch perſon as a St. Dunus can be found either in our kalendars or annals ; in fact, the names of Kilkenny, Kill-Senan and Down-Patrick were impoſed in the firſt ages of the Iriſh church.

The ſtate of Chriſtianity in Ireland from the fifth to the ninth century, is of all inquiries into the hiſtory of this country, the moſt important,

not

not only from the nature of the subject, but from its effects, through the labours of Irish ecclesiastics in foreign countries as well as in their native land. At home, they supported and instructed Christian princes and youths, who fled hither from persecution ; and abroad, they had success in converting the persecutors, I mean the Pagan barbarians, who seized on the western provinces of the Roman empire. Amidst the fiercest domestic hostilities, the districts of the Irish monks were free from any violation, and under that security Ireland, as Dean Prideaux has observed, became the prime seat of learning in Christendom. In no age, even the darkest, can a single instance be produced, that Irish monks have personified rivers and places, like the heathen mythologists. '

To point out the mistakes of my reverend friend on the subject of our antiquities, will, I trust, give him no pain, as I am confident that right information must be acceptable to every philosophic mind. now return to the more pleasing office, that of joining the public in approbation of the other and far greater parts of his history of Kilkenny; his matter is well selected, and many of his observations are highly judicious.

Before I conclude, I request your attention to a few remarks on the learned Mr. Beauford's tracts (in the seventh number of the *Collectanea*) on the theology, origin and language of the heathen Irish.

On the general subject of Celtic druidism, he writes judiciously from Greek and Roman documents. Like other modes of religion, it undoubt-

edly

edly took various forms in various countries and ages, but of thofe which it received from time to time, in our own ifland, we have now but few notices. It certainly had its fource in the religion of nature and patriarchal worfhip; but the ftream corrupted as it flowed.

In your profound inveftigations relative to our Irifh Ogham, and our antient characters literal and fymbolical, you have opened a path, and a fecure one, for further difcoveries on the ftate of learning in Ireland, antecedent to the intro-duction of Greek and Roman literature in the fifth century. In that path, Mr. Beauford trod with fuccefs, and brought additional proofs to yours, that the elements of our heathen literature were derived from the Phœnicians, or their Car-thaginian pofterity.

Initiated thus in the rudiments of knowledge, it might well be expected that a people long fe-queftered in a remote ifland, and long undifturbed by foreign conqueft, might make fome confi-derable progrefs in intellectual improvements, and leave pofterity fome fatisfactory account of themfelves. But according to Mr. Beauford, this was not the cafe; of the infignificancy of their literature to any hiftorical purpofe, he is far from fpeaking doubtfully; he affirms pofitively, that " little dependance can be had on any tranfactions " relative to the affairs of Ireland, prior to the fixth " century; and adds, " The moft antient and re-fpected hiftorians, as Cormac, king and archbifhop of Cafhel in the beginning of the tenth century, and Tigernach who wrote the Irifh annals in the eleventh,

venth, begin their hiftories, in the fifth age, without taking *the leaft notice* of any tranfactions prior to that period!—Thefe are great miftakes, and they involve greater.

Some extracts from the pfalter of Cafhel, I have perufed in the compilations of Balimote. The learned archbifhop begins with the fettlement of the Scots in Ireland under Heremon and Heber; he does not indeed point out the precife time of their arrival from Spain; but from the number of generations fet down by him in the genealogy of his own family, he fhews that they muft have arrived feveral ages before the Chriftian era.

Through your indulgence, Sir, I had the ufe of the annals of Tigernach for fome months. Far from rejecting the tranfactions prior to the Chriftian period, as Mr. Beauford afferts, he commences with the building of Eamania fix generations before the incarnation of our Saviour; he gives us the fucceffion of the Eamanian kings to Concovar Mac Neffa, under whofe patronage Irifh laws were firft committed to writing. The learned abbot alfo makes mention of fuch Heathen monarchs and princes, as made the moft confpicuous figure in hiftory during this early period, as well as in the times which fucceeded. His acounts, it is true, are fhort, and appear to be a chronological index to a larger work, compiled by himfelf, or fome others who went before him.

You have laid me under equal obligations by putting the annals of Inisfallen (erroneoufly called thofe of Inisfail) into my hands. They commence with the time of *Qliol Olom*, the celebrated heathen
king

king of the two Munfters, who died a hundred and
feventy-two years before the arrival of St. Patrick.

Angus, the learned Culdee, wrote his Pfalter-na-
rann two hundred years before king Cormac began
the Pfalter of Cafhel. That writer alfo mentions
the fettlement under the fons of Milefius ; places
the Heberian Scots in the fouth, and the Heremonian Scots in the north, and relates that
Heremon was the firft of the Scottifh monarchs.
Writing about the year 800, he doubtlefs had
good documents before him, but they have not
reached our times ; of all Angus's works, I have
met with no part except the abftract I have here
quoted from Sir James Ware.

In the long continuance of the wars with the
Norman ravagers in this ifland, our larger works
on civil and ecclefiaftical fubjects have been deftroyed, with the monaftries wherein they were depofited. It is, undoubtedly, a lofs to literature,
which can never be repaired. But fome remains
of our hiftorical wreck have been preferved, which
are fufficient to fhew us diftinctly the more
eminent characters in church and ftate. They unfold the political vices which arofe from the form
of government under the *Hy-Niall* race, through
a period of fix hundred years ; the domeftic virtues, public and private, which counteracted
thofe vices ; the cultivation of fcience before the
commencement of the Norman devaftations ; the
edifying conduct of the clergy, the freedom
enjoyed within their diftricts ; the immunities and
endowments of the Fileas and Orfidies ; the conftant attention to the arts of poetry and mufic ;

arts

arts of political ufe, in foftening the mind to worthy feelings, and in checking its ferocity, amidft the
fierceft rage of party contentions. For cafting light,
I fay, on that ftate of things, we ftill have fome
good materials, though poffibly, moft may not out-
live the prefent generation, through a difguft to
examine them, or to learn the language in which
they are conveyed.

On thefe documents Mr. Beauford has pronounced a very fevere fentence, without any fair trial,
or indeed without any trial at all, and an incon-
fiftency which he charges on our old writers, are
not theirs, but his own. The Irifh chronologers
(as he advances) put a long diftance of time between Olamh-Fodhla and Conar Mac Neffan [Con-
covar Mac Neffa] yet in the following page he reprefents the Irifh Hiftorians, as making that monarch and Concovar Mac Neffa one and the fame
perfon; and he charges them further with identi-
fying thofe princes with Fedlimidh the legiflator,
who died A. D. 174.—How unfair, and how
carelefs! The Irifh fenachies are unanimous in
recording that the names mentioned, belonged to
three diftinct princes, and not to one alone;
Concovar Mac Neffa, king of Ulfter died A. D.
48, and Fedlimidh the legiflator, monarch of the
whole ifland, died one hundred and twenty fix
years after him.

The rejection of our domeftic accounts, without
perufing them, cannot be well excufed, and the
lefs fo, as the internal ftate of this remote ifland
in ancient times, could be but very partially
known to foreign writers, who had all their information

mation from hear-fay evidence. It is a ftate
which certainly was known hardly in any meafure
to a late writer, who in the name of Offian, gave
us fome well fabricated novels, raifed on the tales,
which to this day amufe the common people in
Ireland and in the highlands of Scotland, and re-.
late chiefly, to Fin Mac Cumhal and his Fenian
heroes, who acted under the great monarch Cormac o'Cuinn, to whom that Fin was a fon-in-law.
The antient ftate of Ireland, I fay, could be but
little known to this novelift, and doubtlefs the obfcure monk of Cirencefter was equally ignorant;
yet fuch are the authors preferred by Mr. Beauford to all our old documents, and hence many
miftakes of his, which at prefent I forbear noticing.
I will only in his own words give you the fum of
his affirmations on this fubject; ift. That little
dependance is to be had on any tranfactions relative
to the affairs of Ireland prior to the fixth century."
2d. "That the ancient inhabitants of Ireland obtained the name of Scots during the middle ages, from
their (wandering) occupation, and mode of life which
they retained until agriculture, the arts of civil life
and encreafe of population about the tenth century,
had in fome meafure, confined their refidence to particular fpots." Surely, Sir, there is nothing in
this defcription of an ancient nation, to claim attention, or invite curiofity; it creates difguft, it
can convey no inftruction.

But the defcription, I dare affirm, is not juft,
and I hope that in the foregoing pages I have afforded fome proofs of a different ftate of things,
and particularly from the commencement of the

Tua-

Tuathalian conftitution, and end of the Belgic and
Attacotic wars in the fecond century.

Before that time we find the Scots long ftationary in fixed fettlements; the Heberians in Munfter, the Heremonians in Leinfter, and the Rudricians in Ulfter. In the perufal of what we
have left of that people in their own language,
and particularly from the Tuathalian æra to the
deceafe of Malachy II. (a period of near nine
hundred years) we find a body politic, robuft and
vigorous, in the care of men who often refifted,
and too often fed, the diftempers to which it was
incident. It was a government of freemen, who
never were happy enough to fet proper limits to
freedom, they therefore were deftitute of proper
fecurity. In that ftate, we meet with examples
of political virtues and vices, which, by turns,
adorn and difgrace this people, till the feeds of
diffolution fowed in the infancy of their conftitution, came to full maturity in the tenth century,
at the very period when, according to Mr. Beauford, they ceafed to be ftragling barbarians and,
in fome meafure, confined their refidence to particular fpots.

I do not deny, but am ever ready to acknowledge Mr. Beauford's merit in his ingenious
explications of our antient infcriptions, literal
and fymbolical. They conftituted a part of our
local learning in heathen times; but of their ufe
or improvement to hiftorical or intellectual purpofes, he appears entirely diffident.

Before I conclude a letter which I fear you may
think already too long, I muft obferve that how-

R

ever

ever foreigners have been miftaken, relative to the hiftory of Ireland in its heathen ftate, yet that our own native writers of the laft and prefent century (Ware excepted) have fallen into miftakes alfo, by giving full credit to Gilla-Coeman and other old compilers, who no way cautious in regard to the uncertainties of hiftory in the infant ftate of government and arts, have put the reports of our earlier bards on an equal foot of credibility with the more authenticated accounts, which have fucceeded to the Eamanian æra. Fond of an high antiquity, they have put more than a thoufand years between the expedition of the Scots from Spain and the chriftian æra; and (as I have obferved before) the great void they made in time, they were neceffitated to fill up with fictitious generations in their genealogies, and in confequence, to infert a number of monarchs of whom nothing is recorded, but that each killed his predeceffor in battle. True and falfe reigns thus intermixed, we fhould have no rule for diftinguifhing between them, had not fome remarkable revolutions in government enabled us, to difcover a few who were monarchs in fact.

The learned Mr. O'Flaherty has employed much labour to fupport the authenticity of Gilla-Coeman's lift of heathen monarchs. He could not difmifs the notion, that the commencement of the Milefian monarchy, was coincident with the reign of Solomon in the eaft; and hence his curtailing the number of years or reigns affigned by Gilla-Coeman to Irifh monarchs, and hence his amputa-

tions

tions of genealogical generations, to make the
whole correfpondent with his own fyftem; for they
by no means correfpond with the courfe of nature,
notwithftanding all his care that they fhould. His
dates, however, from the reign of Feradach the
Juft, A. D. 95, are exact, and thence to the preaching of the gofpel, his chronology is moft accurate.

It was, Sir, in this, as in all other European countries; hiftory had its night of darknefs,
but in fome, it was a darknefs vifible. In ours,
fome objects are feen diftinctly even in that ftate;
the dawn of light comes on gradually from the
time of Kimbaoth; and full day opens on the
elevation of Tuathal the acceptable to the throne
of Teamor.

In fuch a courfe of things, it is no wonder that
Gilla-Coeman and many other of our old antiquaries have fallen into miftakes and anachronifms;
to their earlieft reports Mr. O'Flaherty gave too
much credit, and to their later accounts, fir James
Ware gave too little. That learned gentleman
did not underftand our language, nor had he any
good interpreter to explain the documents it contained, till a few months before his death, when
he called in the celebrated antiquary Duald Mac
Firbifs to his affiftance.

In fome effays of mine on this fubject, I have
fallen into miftakes; fome you have kindly pointed
out to me, and I have retracted. On perufing
the annals of Tigernach and other documents in
the compilations of Balimote, I have retracted

more, and on the detection of any miſtake in this
preſent eſſay, I ſhall retract again ; *Nil enim poſſumus contra veritatem.* You, Sir, have done great
ſervice in this walk of learning ; and by ſhewing,
though indirectly, how far ſome writers have ſtray-
ed out of it, you not only guard others from
treading in their paths, but open to them ſuch as
they may ſecurely follow. You began with tracing
our old language to its Celtic ſource ; You marked the terms, and diſcovered the conſtruction, it
partly received, through an early commerce with
the Phœnicians ; and it being compoſed from fewer Celtic dialects than any other tongue among the
continental Celts, it involves at this day the pu-
reſt remains of the primæval language of Europe.
From its copiouſneſs and energy you have found
it amply fitted for the purpoſes of a thinking people, who were long at leiſure for the cultivation of
their intellectual powers : and poſſeſſed of that
fact, you have ſet on foot the enquiry whether the
ſpeakers of that language left any uſeful memorials
in it, relative to their arts, their manners, their
civil inſtitutes and the revolutions all muſt have
undergone, through the viciſſitudes of improvement
and decline, in a ſucceſſion of ages. Your plan
was rational, and the acquiſition of knowledge
was the end you propoſed to yourſelf in forming
it, and ſome knowledge it is hoped will be gained
from your own labour, and that of others on this
ſubject. — Man, to know him well, ſhould be viewed on every ſtage of life, not ſo much indeed
through the uniform habits of barbariſm, as
                                        through

through the diverfities of action in civil affociation, under the direction of local religions, local manners, and local fituations. The hiftory of this ifland is that of a people who remained many ages in a fecluded ftate ; it expofes to our view, a free and warlike nation, generally divided by parties and exhibiting many examples of the abufe of liberty, as well under the Tuathalian conftitution, as in that which followed in the times of chriftianity under the Hy-Niall race. In too many inftances we find the people preyed upon, and employed to fupport parties ; tyrannical themfelves when at the fummit of power, and when ftripped of that power, juftly punifhed by opponents equally tyrannical. Such examples exhibit falutary leffons to nations ftill free, but yet tardy in removing exceffes, which fooner or later muft end unhappily. The cure of evils arifing out of liberty itfelf is, no doubt, difficult ; it can hardly, however, continue fo in times enlightened by philofophy, and inftructed by former as well as recent fufferings. In Ireland this cure has been applied, and has fucceeded happily. Under the aufpices of our prefent Moft Gracious Sovereign, we have obtained civil, religious and commercial liberty in full meafure ; and England, your native country, Sir, affifted us in obtaining IT. A glorious epocha ! commencing with unanimity in one creed of politics and in a profeffion of civil faith abundantly fufficient for every purpofe of political falvation. —With a revolution fo happy, fo operative on the minds, as well as the conditions of *all* our people, I fhall conclude my remarks.

Pardon,

Pardon, Sir, my detaining you, fo long, on the ſubjeʒt of antient times ; you will ever find me

Your very grateful,

Belinagar,
Sept. 3d, 1782.
and obedient ſervant,

CHARLES O'CONOR.

A LETTER from CURIO;

With a further Explanation of the ſilver Inſtrument engraved and deſcribed in No. II. of the firſt Volume of this Colleʒtanea.

To Lieut. Col. VALLANCEY.

S I R,

THE within are two drawings of the ſilver in-ſtrument deſcribed in the IId. No. of your Colleʒtanea de Rebus Hibernicis, fig. 2. and in return to the queries therein propoſed to CURIO, I have the honor to make the following anſwers.

It weighs 4oz. 12dwt. * The ſpear (or tongue which is wanting) had been ſoldered into the ſock-et of the moveable globe II. (See your plate.)

* By the drawings which the writer of this letter has obligingly incloſed, it appears that the longeſt diameter of the oval is about three inches and half, and that the boſſes are ornamented exaʒtly in the manner of thoſe given in fig. 1. of plate 1. p. 207 of No. 2, of this Colleʒtanea.

And

And now, Sir, give me leave to offer you some conjectures with regard to the use of these instruments, as they are called, in that description.

It is by all our antiquaries allowed, that the habits of our ancient kings, princes and nobles of Ireland, were a close vest, long trows or breeches down to the ankle, and a long loose robe over all, that reached to the ground, which was brought over the shoulders and fastened on the breast by a clasp, a buckle or broche. For example of which I may refer to many ancient monuments of our Irish princes, still extant, but particularly to that of the Mac Grane's, in the ruined abbey of Sligo ; a family long extinct, but heretofore princes of Bannagh in Lower Donegall. On the front of the tomb are several sculptures, amongst which is a king habited as before, his robe fastened with a broche of the same form as in the drawings. An eminent goldsmith in Dublin informed me that he has seen several of those instruments of pure gold, and some of them of fine brass; which might lead one to suppose that these different metals were affixt by sumptuary laws for the use or wear of the different classes or ranks of nobles.

This hint pursued further might tend to prove, what has been by some imagined, from a perfect similarity in several customs, that the Irish are a branch of the Hebrew nation ; and for this one to the present purpose, I must refer you to an old book from whence may be had great information—I mean the Bible. See the first book of Maccabees, chap. 14th

and

and verfe 44th.

" And that it fhould be lawful for none of the
" people or priefts to break any of thefe things or
" to gainfay his (Simon's) words, or to gather an
" affembly of the people without him, or to be
" cloathed in purple, or wear *a buckle of gold.*"

It is highly probable, that this inftrument, or
broche, was made about the time of the introduction of chriftianity into this ifland, from the very
rude croffes on the nobs; which nobs on the other
fide are intended (by the artift) to reprefent acorns
(or the cones of pines) which were druidic fym-
bols; by this duplicity the temporifing wearer
might attend the inftructions of the faint, or affift
at the myftick rites in the facred grove, as would
beft fuit his purpofe.

I am, SIR,

With great efteem for your learned labours,

Your moft obedient, humble,

(tho' unknown) fervant,

December 17th,
1781.

W. M.

I. G.

☞ The further correfpondence of the learned writer of the
above letter, will be efteemed a particular favour.

Collectanea de Rebus Hibernicis.

NUMBER XI.

CONTAINING THE

ANTIENT TOPOGRAPHY

OF

IRELAND.

WITH A PRELIMINARY DISCOURSE.

ILLUSTRATED WITH A MAP OF ANTIENT IRELAND:

BY WILLIAM BEAUFORD, A. M.
SOCIET. ANTIQ. HIB. SOC.

TO WHICH IS ADDED,

SOME OBSERVATIONS ON IRISH ANTIQUITIES;

WITH A

PARTICULAR APPLICATION OF THEM

TO THE

SHIP TEMPLE NEAR DUNDALK.

In a Letter to THOMAS POWNAL, Efq; F. S. A. Lond.
from EDWARD LEDWICH, L. L. B. Vicar of Aghaboe,
in the Queen's County, Societ. Antiq. Hib. & Scot. Soc.

DUBLIN:

PRINTED BY W. SPOTSWOOD,
PRINTER TO THE ANTIQUARIAN SOCIETY:

AND SOLD BY LUKE WHITE, DAME-STREET.

M DCC LXXXIII.

TO

THE RIGHT HONOURABLE

WILLIAM CONYNGHAM,

PRESIDENT

OF THE

HIBERNIAN ANTIQUARIAN SOCIETY;

A

GENEROUS PATRON OF THE LEARNED,

AND A

WARM FRIEND TO THE PROSPERITY OF IRELAND;

THIS NUMBER

OF THE

COLLECTANEA,

IS,

WITH GRATITUDE AND RESPECT,

INSCRIBED,

BY HIS

OBLIGED AND MOST OBEDIENT,
HUMBLE SERVANT,

WILLIAM BEAUFORD.

PRELIMINARY DISCOURSE.

Innumerable and almoſt unſurmountable difficulties attend the elucidation of the ancient Topography of Ireland; little or no information relative to this ſubject is to be obtained from our foreign and not much from our domeſtic writers. Ptolemy, in the beginning of the ſecond century, is the only writer of antiquity who treats with any degree of preciſion on the Geography of ancient Ireland; but even his information, drawn principally from Marinus Tyrius, doth not extend beyond the maritime regions, the internal diviſion being in a great meaſure unknown to the Romans in his time; though from their reſidence in Britain for near 300 years, they muſt in the end have obtained a competent knowledge of its internal ſtate; and Richard of Cirenceſter, from them, has collected ſeveral notices, which have thrown much light on this dark and intricate ſubject, though the projection of his map is extremely erroneous. As to Marinus Tyrius, from whom Ptolemy received his informations relative to the Britiſh iſles, it is not certain in what period he wrote, or from whom he obtained his information; though from ſeveral circumſtances there is the greateſt probability that he derived it from either the Britiſh or Roman navigators, as the names given by Ptolemy to the people and places are evidently of the Cimbric dialect of the Celtic tongue, and not the Gaëlic; and though much mutilated by paſſing through the Greek and Latin languages, they yet retain convincing proofs of their Celtic origin.

If we conſider the infant ſtate of Geography not only in the time of Ptolemy but in much later periods, and the imperfect inſtruments uſed in taking obſervations; the almoſt total ignorance of longitude, with the want of the magnetic needle, without which there is no poſſibility of taking the bearings and directions at ſea with any degree of truth; we ſhall have much greater reaſon to be ſurprized, that they were able to make any geographical charts, than to wonder at the imperfect ones they have left us. It was not until towards the cloſe of the 15th century, that the ſcience of Geography received any conſiderable improvements and a proper method of delineating maps was diſcovered; Richard of Cirenceſter therefore, who wrote towards the cloſe of the 14th century, has committed great errors in his map of the Britiſh iſles, eſpecially in that of Ireland.

IRELAND,

IRELAND, by reafon of its fituation at fome diſtance from the weſtern confines of Europe, remained unknown to the Greeks and Romans until a very late period; there is fome probability, that the Phœnicians during their trade to Britain were not ignorant either of its fituation or internal ſtate; but theſe people, fo far from acquainting the world with the diſcoveries obtained by means of their extenſive commerce, took all poſſible care to conceal them. Whence the commerce of the ancients, weſt of the Streights of Gibraltar, centered intirely in the hands of the Phœnicians and Tyrians and their colonies on the coaſts of Iberia,* whilſt the reſt of the world was excluded not only from the benefits accruing therefrom, but alſo in a great meaſure from the knowledge of thoſe countries which ſupplied thoſe merchants of antiquity with ſeveral articles of lucrative traffic. From theſe circumſtances we ought not to be ſurprized that the relations given by the writers of antiquity relative to the ancient ſtate of Ireland ſhould, in ſeveral inſtances, be not only imperfect but contradictory.

DURING the middle ages, foreign writers appear to be extremely ignorant of the internal ſtate of this iſland. Even the natives have, in all periods, been very remiſs in tranſmitting to poſterity the ſeveral

* Strabo, L. 3. c. 175.

diviſions

divifions of their country. They do indeed, in different parts of their ancient hiftory and antiquities, mention a number of names relative to the ancient Topography, but feldom fpecify the fituation of the diftricts to which they belonged. To enter fully into this bufinefs it will be neceffary to confider, in fome meafure, the fpecies of government and the nature of the tenures in ufe among the Iberno Celtic tribes, from the remoteft periods.

WE have, in another place,[*] obferved, that the original inhabitants of Ireland in general derived their origin from Britain and were of the Celtic race, confequently their laws and government were radically the fame as the other aborigines of Europe.

WHEN mankind for their mutual fupport and protection were obliged to affociate together, they found it neceffary for the welfare of fociety, to eftablifh fome regular form of government. Whence we find that not only the ancient inhabitants of Ireland, but all the Celtes from the remoteft periods, in every part of their dominions, were divided into a number of fmall communities or clans, each governed by its proper chief and, in a great meafure, independent of each other. In thefe communities, every individual was free and independent, there being a ftate of equa-

* Collectanea, No. 7.

lity

lity through the whole, and the authority which a chief had over his fellows was delegated to him by election, and was not derived as has been erroneously supposed from hereditary succession. For hereditary possession and sanguinary right, did not take place among the Celtic and Scythic clans until, by the introduction of commerce, the arts of civil life had made some progress; but each sept had rather perambulated than inhabited their respective districts, subsisting intirely on the chace and the fruits of the forest. On the increase of population and the introduction of agriculture, these wandering tribes were under the necessity of confining themselves to certain permanent districts: which districts were generally denominated either from their situation or quality of the soil, and from which also the inhabitants obtained their collective appellation. Whence in the most ancient Irish poems and histories, we frequently find *Clan* and *Slioght* added to the name of a country, to signify the inhabitants; as *Clan Cuilean*, *Slioght Breoghain* and *Slioght Gae*; wherefore the children and race of any division were the invariable names by which the ancient Hibernian septs were distinguished from the remotest antiquity, and not as frequently asserted, the children and descendants of their respective leaders. On the establishment of any colony, the entire district was divided among the principal warriors according-

ing

ing to their feniority, each having abfolute authority in his refpective diftrict, paying only a certain tribute or acknowledgement to the eldeft
captain of the race, as king or governor of the
whole colony. The divifions appertaining to the
feveral captains, called in the Irifh tongue, *Connair Airech-ard*, and by the Latin writers Dynaft,
were generally denominated ceantreds, or chief
divifions, at prefent diftinguifhed by the name of
baronies. Each cantred was again divided into a
number of fmaller portions from 500 to 1500
acres; each called *Ballebetaghs*, or townlands,
and were the inheritance of the family of the
dynafts devolving to them by the laws of gavel-
kind: * that is, the inheritance appertaining to
any dynaft was unalienable, and on his demife,
was equally divided among his fons, both legitimate and illegitimate, to the intire exclufion of
the daughters; thefe again were fubdivided in
like manner on the demife of their proprietors,
fo that it frequently happened, that a dynaft who
by his feniority had a right to be elected chief
of his diftrict, was in poffeffion of a very fmall
patrimony. When a dynaft died without iffue, his property was divided amongft his neareft
relations; on which account not only the magnitude and boundaries of the *Ballebetaghs* were

---

* Collectanea, No. 3, and 1. Ware's Ant.

changed

changed, but alſo the leſſer diviſions denominated *Taghs*, or habitations, containing from 40 to 100 acres, and cultivated in common by a certain number of peaſants reſiding thereon, were changed alſo.*

THE chiefs of every diſtrict were elected from the elder branch of the dynaſts; and the kings of the principalities from the ſenior chief of the ſubordinate diſtricts, who, on their advancement to the dignity, obtained the name of the diſtrict or clan over which they preſided; it being an univerſal cuſtom amongſt all the Celtic tribes, to denominate the nobleſſe, with their other appellations, from the place of their reſidence; a cuſtom in ſome meaſure yet retained in the Highlands of Scotland. The variety of names uſed by the ancient Iriſh have occaſioned great confuſion in their hiſtory; for before the 10th century, ſirnames were not hereditary, and prior to the eſtabliſhment of the Chriſtian religion in this country no Perſon was diſtinguiſhed by one permanent nomination. It is true, during their Pagan ſtate, every child at his birth received a name generally from ſome imaginary divinity under whoſe protection it was ſuppoſed to be; but this name was ſeldom retained longer than the ſtate of infancy, from which period it was ge-

* Collectanea, No. 2 and 3.

nerally

nerally changed for others, arifing from fome perfection or imperfection of the body, the difpofition and qualities of the mind, atchievements in
war, or the chace, the place of birth, refidence,
&c. fo that it frequently happened, that the fame
perfon was diftinguifhed by feveral appellations:
our ancient hiftorians, not properly attending
to this, have committed great errors in relating
the tranfactions of early periods, by afferting the fame
action to be performed by feveral different people
which in reality was performed by one only, thereby throwing their hiftory and antiquities into too diftant a period. A fimilar error has alfo been committed by not fully confidering the dignitary names
of the chiefs, who, on their election to the government, conftantly obtained the name appertaining to the clan over whom they prefided,
or rather that of the diftrict. Thefe dignitary
names becoming in the 10th century hereditary
and family diftinctions, created new difficulties to
the genealogifts of the latter ages: for diftricts
having the fame denomination whofe chiefs in
confequence bare the like names, have conftantly
been derived from the fame family, though in
reality, they had not the leaft affinity; thus the
O'Kelleys of Caelan in the county of Kildare,
thofe of Coulan in the County of Wicklow, and
thofe of Caëllagh in the County of Gallway, are
fuppofed to be different branches of the fame
family;

family; whereas they evidently obtained their respective names from ancient chiefs of the above districts, independent of every other consideration. The O'Conors also, though descended from the ancient chiefs of different septs, are universally considered as of the same race. It is true, from the different departments of government being held in the senior line, it was necessary to keep exact genealogical accounts, which during the latter ages, have been greatly mutilated and misrepresented.

THE number of kingdoms, or principalities, whose chiefs obtained the name of *Riogh* or king, were frequently variable, depending on the number of subordinate septs which any chief held in vassallage; though the ancient kingdoms, were generally regulated by the number of the original colonies.

MARCIANUSHERACLEOTA, speaking of Ireland, says it contained the provinces or principalities, governed by their respective kings, comprehending 184 canthreds, each under the dominion of its proper dynast or subordinate chief.[*] Whether this number be correct or not, is uncertain, the names and situation of the respective districts

* Ware's Antiquities.

being

being not fpecified. However in the middle ages, we find the ifland divided into the following kingdoms or principalities.

1 Midhne	12 Cafiol
2 Hy Faillia	13 Ara or Ormond
3 Breffiny	14 Decies
4 Angallia	15 Limrick
5 Orgall or Tyrone	16 Cierighe
6 Eirgall or Tyrconnal	17 Thomond
7 Dalriada	18 Conaght
8 Ulladh	19 Cork
9 Ele	20 Caëllagh
10 Hy Cinfillagh	21 Gaëllen or Caëllan.
11 Offery	

Thefe, according to our antiquaries, were in a very early period united in a kind of pentarchy, comprehending the five monarchies of Meath, Leinfter, Munfter, Conaght and Ulfter. Though the Irifh hiftorians have been circumftantial on this form of government, yet they have given us very imperfect ideas relative to its origin and conftitution. In order therefore to place this fubject in a confpicuous point of view, it will be neceffary in fome meafure to confider the original colonization of the ifland; as the monarchs derived their dignity from being the chiefs of the eldeft fepts of the refpective monarchies.

We

We have in a former place obferved that the ancient inhabitants of Ireland in general derived their origin from the Celtic tribes of Britain.* The Nemethæ, as Aborigines, having from thence taken poffeffion of the ifland about 700 years before the Chriftian Æra, gave place to the Bolgæ, who towards the middle of the 4th century before Chrift, fettled in the county of Meath under the conduct of Hugony or Learmon; from whence, in procefs of time, they inhabited every part of the prefent province of Leinfter, diftinguifhed by them by the name of *Heremon*, or weftern country; and themfelves, in confequence thereof, *Heremonii*, or weftern people.† This diftrict was, for feveral ages, governed by the chief of the eldeft fept or tribe of the Bolgæ inhabiting the prefent county of Eaft Meath; in confequence of his feniority, he was not only denominated king of the *Heremonii*, but monarch of the whole ifland, and from him all the fubfequent kings of Meath and Monarchs of All Ireland were obliged to derive their origin to obtain the dignity. *Heremon*, the ancient and original feat of the *Bolgæ* in Ireland, remained under the government of its paternal kings, defcendants of Hugony or Learmon, until the beginning of the fecond century, when it was

* Collectanea, No. 7.

† See the Words Bolgæ and Nemethæ in this Effay.

divided

divided into two diftinct provinces by *Tuathal Teachtmar*, under the denomination of northern and fouthern *Heremon*. The northern was diftinguifhed by the name of *Tuathal Teachtmor*, or the northern divifion of the great diftrict; comprehending the prefent counties of Eaft and Weft Meath; the fouthern divifion comprehending, in the early ages the prefent counties of Kildare, Kilkenny, Carlow and the King and Queen's counties, was for fome ages under the government of the chiefs of Hy Fallia, but afterwards was ufurped by the Chieftains of Hy Laoighis, and towards the clofe of the middle ages, by the chiefs of Moragh, (the prefent county of Wexford) who were denominated kings of Leinfter at the arrival of the Englifh.* On the firft migration of the Bolgæ, numbers of the *Nemethæ* were conftrained to retire into the fouthern parts of the ifland, where they were joined by fubfequent colonies of the Bolgæ from Britain, who frequently denominated themfelves *Iberii* or *Hiberii*, that is, the moft weftern people; the fenior chiefs of whom were the M'c Carthys, hereditary chieftains of *Corcahigibe*, and kings of the *Dergtenii*, or South Munfter; thefe chieftains from their feniority, were in the early ages, denominated monarchs of all Munfter though that dignity

---

* See under the Words Heremonii, Hy Laoighis and Morragh.

was frequently obtained by the chiefs of the diftrict about Cafhel, and towards the clofe of the middle ages by the kings of Thomond, the prefent county of Clare. Which chiefs, in the perfon of Brien Boromh, by their military abilities, obtained not only the monarchy of Munfter, but that of the whole ifland.

Though the Bolgæ, under the denomination of *Iberii*, had obtained the government of the fouthern divifion of Ireland, yet the *Nemethæ* or *Momonii*, the Aboriginal inhabitants, invariably denominated it *Momon*, or the Maternal Country, by reafon of it being principally inhabited by the *Momonii* or Aborigines: whence by all the Irifh writers we find this diftrict is called *Mumban*, or Aboriginal Country, from which is derived its prefent name of *Munfter*, that is the land of the *Momonii*. On the arrival of the Caledonian colonies, fome few years before the birth of Chrift, *Eoghagh Failogh*, or *O'Faly*, chieftain or king of the ancient *Hy Fallia*, retired acrofs the Shannon with numbers of his people, and eftablifhed a government in the prefent county of Rofcommon, which afterwards was extended into the counties of Gallway, Mayo and Sligoe, under the general denomination of *Olnemacht* or *Conmachtne*, viz. the chief tribe, and *Hy Coneir*, or the diftrict of the principal weftern inhabitants; whence the defcendants of *O'Faly*,

as

as monarchs of this part of the island, obtained the name of O'Conor, and their country that of *Connaght*, which it retains to this day.[*]

THE northern parts of the island, comprehending the present province of Ulster, anciently denominated *Thuath allad*, or the northern habitation of the Bolgæ, was erected into several governments in a very early period; the senior of which was that of *Cinel Eoghan*, comprehending the present county of Tyrone, established soon after the first arrival of the Bolgæ. The chiefs of Cinel Eoghan were esteemed monarchs of Ulster, until the 4th century, when one of the sons of O'Niall, the king of the ancient Hy Fallia or the northern part of Hermonia, having conquered the Rudricians the ancient inhabitants of Cinel Eoghan, established a government in that district, which, in process of time, extended over all the northern tribes; whence the O'Nialls were during the latter ages denominated Monarchs of Ulster; a dignity which they maintained to the 15th century.[†]

THUS was ancient Ireland, agreeable to the assertions of its antiquaries and historians, divided by the Bolgæ into five monarchies, which monarchs

[*] O'Conor's Dissert.
[†] O'Conor's Dissert. Keating.

derived

derived their dignity from being chiefs of the elder tribes in each diſtrict. However, this dignity, appears in a number of inſtances to have been rather a title of honour than power, for the monarchs had little authority beyond the limits of their own ſepts; and the tribute which they frequently demanded from the ſeveral kings of the principalities was ſeldom paid. Even the ſepts, appertaining to their reſpective provinces, frequently rebelled or joined the parties in open war againſt them; ſo little authority had theſe nominal monarchs, at all times, to reſtrain their ſubjects within the limits of their duty. The truth is, there was never any provincial king elected and formally inſtituted; from their ſeniority, the chiefs or kings of the oldeſt ſept of each province had a right to the upper place at the aſſembly of the ſtates; and when his abilities were conſpicuous, he was frequently elected general of the armies in time of imminent danger; and alſo to be in ſome meaſure a check on the depredations frequently committed by one ſept on another; as well as to aſſemble the ſtates of the province, in order to enact ſuch laws and ordinances as might be neceſſary for the public welfare. In other reſpects he ſeems not to have had much authority, except ſuch as was delegated to him from time to time by the people.

IN

In the fame manner, the hereditary Chieftains of Meath, as kings of the eldeft tribe of the original colony of the Bolgæ, were denominated monarchs of the whole ifland; but whatever authority they might have had in the early periods as fuch, their power during the middle ages, was much confined, being reduced within the limits of their own diftricts, except when their martial or mental abilities called them to the confidence of the other kings, and they in confequence thereof were elected commanders of the armies, or prefidents of the general affembly of the ftates.

The only dignity hereditary among the ancient Irifh, and alfo with all the Celtic tribes, was the kings of the feveral principalities; they were elected from the eldeft dynafts or chiefs of the cantreds, and were folemnly inaugurated according to the cuftom of the tribe. On their advancement to the kingly dignity or captainfhip of the fept, they immediately adopted the general name of the tribe or people over whom they reigned, in the fame manner as the dynafts did that of their feveral diftricts.

An account of the different principalities and their fubordinate diftricts, with feveral other fubjects relative to the antiquities of Ireland; will be given in the enfuing pages; and their etymology deduced

from

from pure celtic roots; but innumerable difficulties occur in the explanation of the ancient Topography, arising principally from the fluctuating state of the orthography of the Irish tongue, and the various significations, which the same word frequently admits. A, ao, oi, ei, and o are often used in the Irish language for each other; also i, ui, and u. Bh, th, mh, gh, and ch, frequently exprefs the same found, and when placed in the middle of words, between vowels, have not any found of their own, but only lengthen the syllable, and were introduced by the poets for the greater harmony of their verfification. Thus O, *Hy*, *Y*, I, *Eochadh*, *Eogha*, and *Ibb*, have the fame found, being like the English O, open; *Eoghan* is pronounced *Owen* and *Eamhania Ownia*. G and C are frequently written for each other, and C invariably has the power of the English K. M and N are fometimes ufed for each other, as *Maistean* for *Nausteaghan*, and *Nemetha* for *Moma*. Alfo ch, gh and dh, at the end of words. In order therefore to obtain the true etymology of Irish words it is neceffary to attend to the found and not to the orthography, for the words *Con*, *Can*, *Gan*, *Eien*, *Caen* and *Cin*, have nearly the fame found, and fignify a head or chief; alfo *Boe*, *Bheith* and *Baith* are pronounced *Bo* and are the appellations for a beaft or ox in the Irish language. A number of words have different fignifications, and fome of them diametrically oppofite to each other;

thus *Cu* a greyhound, signifies also a wolf, chief, or commander. *Cullan* signifies either a chief or headland, whence *Cucullan* is either the chief commander, principal promontory, or wolf's headland. *Itb* pronounced ü, signifies either a district, tribe, or good, and originally was an appellation for water. *Cas*, the sea, signifies likewise strong or valiant; and, *Dal*, a country, signifies a tribe or clan, whence *Dal Cas*, is either the valiant tribe, or maritime country. *Druim* or *Drom*, a ridge or dome, signifies also a house, and a pig's back. *Neach*, a horse signifies also any thing noble, grand or beautifull. *Leim*, a strand, wharf, or port, signifies in general, any bare or naked place, whence *Leimneach*, is either the great port or a place bare for horses. Several words are curruptly written for each other; as *Cullan* for *Caëllan* and *Coullan*, *Car* for *Gar*, &c. The want of a proper attention to these circumstances have caused innumerable errors in the explanation of the names, relative to the ancient divisions of Ireland, and indeed most of the other mistakes committed in the genealogy of the Irish noblesse and historical transactions by the poets and antiquaries of the latter ages. In the ensuing pages, all possible care has been taken to guard against such errors, where the roots of the several denominations have been sought by a comparison of the different orthography of the words, and their signification ascertained by a collation with the situation

and

and quality of the refpective diſtricts; and where ſeveral interpretations were admitted that which was moſt conſonant to the nature, qualities and ſituation of the diviſions was given for the true one. The intricacy of the ſubject, the difficulty of obtaining the real root and ſignification from a vicious orthography, have, probably, cauſed ſome errors in the tranſlation of a few names, but we hope they are not numerous; the ſubject however has not been treated in the ample manner it is capable of, the ſeveral cantreds and leſſer diſtricts have in general been omitted through want of proper information, ſo that this eſſay can only be conſidered as the outlines of a plan to be finiſhed by a more able hand.

T H E

THE
ANTIENT TOPOGRAPHY
OF
IRELAND.

—————————

A

ABHAN-MORE, or the great river. A small river rifing in the upper lake of Glendaloch in the county of Wicklow; from whence taking a S. E. courfe through a glen, formerly covered with wood, it falls into the fea at Arklow. The river Black-water, or Broad-water in the county of Waterford, is named by Ptolemy Daurona, but by Necham Abhan-more.

ACHAD-BHOE, Agabhoe, or Aghavoe, that is the field of Oxen,* formerly an open plain or favannah in Offory, and in the Queen's county. In this place St. Canice, the fon of Laidec, an eminent poet, towards the clofe of the 6th century, founded a monaftery, in which he died on the 11th of October 599 or 600. Near the fcite of this monaftery about the year 1052 a church was built, and the fhrine of St. Canice placed therein. On

* From Achad or Aghad, a field or open place and Bhoe an ox.

which the epifcopal See of Offory was tranflated
from Saigre in Ely O'Carrol to this place; where
it continued until about the end of the reign of
Henry the II. when by Felix O'Dullany, bifhop
of Offory. it was tranflated to Kilkenny.   From a
plain in the center of dark and thick woods,
Achad-bhoe on account of its ecclefiaftical foundations became a city and was endowed with feveral
privileges, and even was no inconfiderable town at
the clofe of the laft century; but the only remains
now vifible are the church and the ruins of a Domi-
nican abby founded by one of the Mac-Gilla Pa-
druics, ancient chiefs and anceftors of the prefent
earl of Offory.   There is here alfo an old fquare
fort, which feems to have been erected about the
14th century.*

ACHAD-CHAON, or Achad-Conair, that is,
the principal field or place, now known by the
name of Achonry, from *Achad-chon-re,*† that is the
chief place of the king or bifhop.   St. Finian bifhop of Clonard, founded a church here about the
year 530, the fcite was granted by a dynaft of the
ancient diftrict of Luigny, the barony of Leney, in
the county of Sligo.   This church and monaftery
were afterwards given by the founder to St. Cruim-
thir Nathy, who was made bifhop thereof and of
the neighbouring diftrict of Luigny ; whence the
bifhops of Achonry, in the ancient Irifh annals, are
generally called bifhops of Luigny.   This bifhop-

---

* Harris' Ware.

† *Achad, Aga,* a field or place, and *Chaon, Con, Cain,* and
Cin, a head or chief, *Re, Rhi* or *Rhoigh,* a king, prince or
bifhop.

ric remained a diftrict diocefe until the year 1607, when it was united to that of Killala.*

ACHAD-FOBHAIR, now Aghagower, a plain near Mount Aichle in the ancient Hy-Malia, comprehending the prefent barony of Morifk in the county of Mayo. In this place St. Patrick founded a church and placed St. Senach one of his difciples over it, in confequence of which it continued an epifcopal fee for feveral years, but was at length united to that of Tuam and is now only a parifh church, and the head of a rural deanery.†

ACHIL-INSULAE, i. e. Eagles iflands, two iflands in Clew bay on the weftern coaft of the county of Mayo; they are not mentioned by either Ptolemy or Richard, and appear to have obtained their names from the great refort of eagles thither.

ACHONRY, near the river Owenmore, and fifteen miles S. W. of Sligo. See Achad-Chaon.

ADROS, an ifland in the Irifh fea mentioned by Ptolemy, and called by him *Adri Deferta*: ‡ by Pliny corruptly written Andros; by others Edri, and by Richard of Cirencefter Edria. Ware takes it for Beg-eri, one of the Saltees on the coaft of Wexford. *Adros* feems a corruption from the Britifh word *Adar*, which fignifies birds; whence Inis-Adar, Birds Ifland in old Saxon, Birds Eye, or the Ifle of Birds. It is now vulgarly denominated Ireland's Eye, and is fituated north of the hill of Hoath, the Ben-Hadar of the ancients.

AIGHLE, fee Aileach.

---

* Harris' Ware, vol. 1. p. 658.
† Harris' Ware, vol. 1. p. 17.
‡ Ἄδρου ἔρημος. Ptolomy.

AILEACH, or Ailich Neid, Oileach Neid and Aighle, that is, the Eagle's Neft. A rath or caftle of the O'Neill's in the barony of Inifowen, three miles north of Derry, the royal palace of Tyrconnal. This rath, which is yet remaining, is afferted to have been erected by the great Hy Fallia or Hy Nailia ancient chief of Hy Fallia, on his fettlement in the north of Ireland in the fourth century. This ancient palace which probably obtained the appellation of Eagle's Neft from the height of its ramparts, is of the fame conftruction as thofe monuments of antiquity commonly called Danifh forts, and was laid in ruins by Mortogh mor O'Brien in 1101.* See Tura.

AILICH NEID, fee Cromla.

AINE CLIACH, or Eoganacht Aine Cliach, that is the diftrict of the country on the river of fifhing wiers. This diftrict was fituated on the Shannon, and contained the prefent county of Limerick. The chief of which was Hy Ciaruigh, or O'Kiarwick, defcended from Feidhlem, fon of Nadfry king of Munfter.† See Cliach.

AIRTHER, fee Oirther.

ALNECMACHT, fee Olnegmacht.

ANDRUIM, fee Dalnaruidhe.

ANGALIA, or Annaly, corrupted from An Gadhilagh, or the woody country, a diftrict comprehending the ancient north Teffia and the prefent county of Longford. The chiefs of this diftrict were formerly denominated Hy Ferghaël or

* Harris' Ware. vol. 1. p. 18. O'Conor's Differtations. Collectanea, No. 4. p. 552.
† Collectanea, No. 3. p. 377.

the prince of the men of Ghaël, by corruption O'Feral. The defcendants of this ancient family was in poffeffion of the north, weft and fouth parts of the county of Longford on the commencement of the laft century, but were difpoffeffed of the eaftern parts by the Englifh fettlers the Tuites and Delameres.[*] Annaly was alfo called Conmacne.

AOIBH CAISIN, or the territory of Little Cas in Thomond. See Dal-Cas.

AOIBH LIATHAIN, or the diftrict of the level watry country,[†] called alfo Cinealtalmhuin, or the chief diftrict of the country on the water; [‡] being part of the ancient diftrict called by the Irifh antiquaries *Dergtenach* and *Corcaduibbne*, and by Ptolemy *Vodie*; all of which have nearly the fame fignification as Aoibh Liathain, which fee under the refpective names. The chiefs of this diftrict from Aiobh Liathain obtained the name of Hy Lehane, or chief of the watry plain, from whence O'Lehane, a branch of which family obtained the appellation of O'Anamhchadha. They were difpoffeffed by the Barries; whence their country was denominated Barrymore, now a barony in the county of Cork.[§]

AONACH, a word derived from *Shamhana*, a heathen goddefs of Ireland, and pronounced formerly Aona, but now corruptly Aina. On the feftivals of this divinity the fairs of the ancient

---

[*] Harris' Ware. vol. 1. p. 13. O'Conor's Ortelius.

[†] *Aoibh*, *ui*, *by*, a diftrict and liathain, or lean, from lea, a plain and *ain* water.

[‡] *Cin* a head or chief, *ea* or *ou* water, and *talmhuin* earth or land.

[§] Collectanea, No. 3. p. 372. O'Conor's Ortelius.

Irish were held ; from whence *Aonach* or *Aina* came to signify in the modern Irish language, a fair or place of traffic.

AONACH, or the Mart or place of traffic, an ancient town in lower Ormond, and capital of the ancient district of Eoganacht Aine Cliach. Near this town, now Nainagh or Nenagh in the county of Tippeaary, Brien son of Mahon Menevy O'Brien in 1370 obtained a complete victory over his uncle Turlogh, assisted by the English forces under the command of the earl of Desmond. From which battle he obtained the firname of Brien Catha an Aonaig, or Brien of the battle of Nenagh.*

ARD, an ancient district in the N. W. part of the county of Tipperary, comprehending originally both upper and lower Ormond, being generally denominated *Eogan Ara*, or the district of Ara ; whose ancient chiefs were called from thence Egan Ara or Qwen Ara, and sometimes Mac Egan, whose descendants were in possession of the northern parts of lower Ormond in the beginning of the last century ; but the southern or upper Ormond, in an early period appertained to another branch of the same family, called *Hy Dun Eogan* or the chief of the hilly or upper district, by corruption O'Donnegan. In the same manner the chiefs of lower Ormond were called *Hy Magh Eogan* or chief of the plain district, by corruption Mac Eagan. O'Donnegan was dispossessed of his territory in 1318, by the descendants of Brien Rua, king of Thomond ; who from thence were called O'Briens of Ara, and who remained in possession of the greater part of it in the beginning of the last century.

---

* Collectanea, No. 4. p. 622.

Ara feems to be a corruption from Airther, Oirther or Artha, and Ar which fignifies the eaft or eaftern. Whence this diftrict, in confequence of its eaftern fituation on the Shannon, was frequently denominated Eoganacht Ara Mhumhan, or the eaftern diftrict of Munfter, and by corruption Ormond.* See Dalnaruidhe.

ARDAGH, one of the moft ancient churches in Ireland, fituated in the ancient Angalia and county of Longford. St. Mæll, a difciple of St. Patrick and his fifters fon, is faid to have been placed over this church before the year 454, as bifhop and abbot. From which time this fee was governed by its own bifhops until 1692, when it was united to that of Kilmore, from which it is now disjointed, and held in commendam by the archbifhops of Tuam. Ardagh, fo denominated from its elevated fituation, has at prefent neither chapter nor prebendary, and the only remains of the cathedral is part of a wall built with large ftones, which from its prefent appearance muft have been when entire a very fmall building.

ARDFERT, or Hy-ferte, that is the height or place of miracles. An ancient epifcopal fee, in the barony of Clanmaurice, not far from Tralee and county of Kerry. This bifhoprick is faid to have been founded by St. Ert, about the middle of the fixth century, and was fucceffively governed by its own bifhops to the year 1663, when it was united to the fee of Limerick.

ARDMAGH, now Armagh; an ancient ecclefiaftical city and the metropolitan fee of all Ireland. It

---

* Collectanea, No. 3. p. 375. O'Conor's map.

was founded by St. Patrick about the year 444 or
445, on a hill or rifing ground, granted by Daire,
a chief of the adjacent country. This like moft
other of the primitive Hibernian churches, being
couftructed of wattles, obtained at the firft the
name of Druim-failec, or the cell or church
of willows.* Though in after ages, on account of its elevated fituation it has been denominated Ardmagh, or the great high-place or field.
On the eftablifhment of the chriftian religion in this
country, Ardmagh, from the eminent learning and
fanctity of its prelates and abbots, became a confiderable city, and a celebrated fchool or univerfity,
which during the middle ages was not only much
reforted to by the natives, but alfo by the Anglo-
Saxon youths from Britain. In confequence of
which it was greatly augmented, enriched, and a
number of ample privileges granted to it for the
better fupport of its ecclefiaftical Dignity. But in
the year 670 and 687, it was nearly confumed by
fire ; and on the arrival of the Danes was frequently plundered by thefe pirates, its inhabitants
put to the fword, and the greater part of its books
and records taken away and deftroyed ; an irrepa-
rable lofs to the ecclefiaftical and civil hiftory and
antiquities of Ireland. During thefe calamities
the cathedral church being alfo often deftroyed,
and as frequently repaired, was in the year 1262
or 1263, rebuilt nearly in its prefent form by Patrick O'Scanlan, then archbifhop, whofe fucceffor,
Nicholas Mac Moliffa added to it feveral rich gifts

---

* From *Drum* or *Druim* a cave or cell and *Saileog* a willow,
though Druim Saileog has been falfely interpreted the height of
willows. Druim properly fignifies a hollow hill or dome.

and emoluments. Since whofe time Ardmagh has maintained its dignity as the metropolitan fee of all Ireland, but never regained its antient honour as a feat of the mufes. It is much to be wifhed however that an univerfity or academy was eftablifhed in that part of the kingdom, as it could not fail of being of the greateft public utility.

ARDMORE, or the great height; an ancient Epifcopal See, in the barony of the Decies and county of Waterford on the eaft fide of the bay of Youghall, now a fmall village. †

ARDSRATH, now Ardftragh, in the barony of Strabane, or the high rath, called alfo Rathlure or the rath on the water. A rath or fort on the river Derg, near which was founded the primitive church of the epifcopal See of Derry, dedicated to St. Luroch, from this place it was tranflated to Maghere and from thence to Derry. St. Eugene is faid to have founded the church of Ardfrath in the 6th. century, and died the 3d. of Auguft 618. There is no Catalogue extent of the bifhops of Ardfrath. *

ARGETROSS, or Argiodrofs, i. e. the filver mine on the water. An ancient copper mine in mountains near the river Nore, whence filver was extracted; and according to. antiquaries, money was firft coined in Ireland by Enius Ruber. Argiodrofs was in Lower Offory,‡ on the river Nore, and is fuppofed to be the modern village of Rathbeagh, within five miles of Kilkenny, and three of Ballyragget.

† Harris's Ware, vol. 1. p. 21.
* Harris's Ware, vol. 1. p. 286.
‡ Harris's Ware, vol. 2. p. 204.

ARGITA, the ancient name of a river or lough in the North of Ireland mentioned by Ptolemy, and thought by some to be Lough Swilly; by others the river Ban, which proceeds from Lough Neagh. The word seems to be a corruption from the British *Ergid*, or *Ergit*, which signifies an æstuarium or projection of water into the land; litterally the mouth or opening of the land; and and therefore may be any bay. § But Richard of Cirencester thinks it is Lough Swilly, which is by no means improbable, as the form of that bay agrees perfectly with the signification of the word.

ARMAGH; see Ardmagh.

ARRAN, the North isle of; see Venisnia.

ARRAN-MORE, the largest of the south isles of Arran on the coast of Galway. Here several of the antient Irish saints were buried, whence the island obtained the name of Arrannanoim. The inhabitants are still persuaded, that in a clear day they can see from this coast Hy Brasail, or the inchanted island, the paradise of the pagan Irish; and concerning which they relate a number of romantic stories.

ATHA, an ancient city in Connaght; *Atha* signifies an habitation near a broad shallow water or ford, and is called by the Irish antiquaries *Atha:b* and Attathach or Attabhach, that is the great habitation near the shallow water. It was also denominated Cromchin and Croghan, antiently called Drum-Druid, at present Rath-Crayhan, and is situated near Elphin in the county of Roscommon. The Irish annals mention a rath or fort being erected here by Eochy Feylogh, or Eoghagh Feghlogh, in the time of Augustus

Cæsar. Atha was also by the Irish called *Croghan*, from its situation near a hill, and *Cromcbin* in consequence of a sacred druidic cave in the adjacent mountain dedicated to fate or providence, which in old Irish and British was called *Crom*. Whence we find Cairbar in the Irish annals denominated Cairbre Cromchin, or chief of Cromchin, and his son who was born here, from the place of his birth is named Luig Attathach, that is the lake of the habitation on the shallow water. ‖ The only remains of this famous ancient city, where once Cathmor, the friend of strangers exercised his unbounded hospitality, are the celebrated Rath, before spoken of, the Naasteaghan where the states of Connaght assembled, and the sacred cave. See Croghan, Drum Druid, and Moma.

ATH CLIATH NA MEARUIDHE; see Legh con.

ATHENRY; see Bealatha.

ATH MAIGHNE, or the plain or the shallow water; a place in the county West-Meath but where uncertain. It is however distinguished by a bloody battle fought there between Turlough O'Brien king of Munster and Turlogh O'Conor king of Connaght in 1152; when O'Conor was entirely defeated with the loss of nine chiefs and 900 common men. Ath Maighne was probably a little to the north of Lough Derrevarragh, in the parish of Maina, and half barony of Fore.

ATHSCULL; see Coalan.

ATTATHACH; see Atha.

AUSOBA, the antient name of a river in the west of Connaght mentioned by Ptolemy, and supposed by Ware to be the river Galvia, in Gal-

‖ O Conor's Diff. p. 180.   Colle&t. No. 4. p. 416.

way; but by Camden and Baxter Lough Corbes. It is indeed extremely difficult to afcertain its exact fituation, the word Aufoba fignifies an Oeftuarium, being derived from the Britifh *Auifc aba*, or in ancient Irifh *Aufc obba*, a projection of water, confequently a bay or gulph. Richard of Cirencefter makes it Clew Bay in the county of Mayo, but as it was a place frequented by foreign merchants, the bay of Galway feems the moft probable place.

AUSONA, the fame as Aufoba, fo called by Ware and fome others.

AUSTRINUM, a Promontory in the weft of Ireland, mentioned by Richard of Cirencefter; it fignifies a head projecting in the water, it is the fame as the Notium of Ptolemy which fee.

AUTERÆ, an ancient city mentioned by Ptolemy as the capital of the Auterii; and by Richard of Cirencefter corruptly written Anterum. The domeftic writers do not make the leaft mention of fuch a city; but as the word fignifies an habitation on the weftern water, there is the greateft probability, that it was a place fomewhere on the bay of Galway, which the natives, during their commerce with the Gallic, Iberian and Roman merchants, reforted for the benefit of traffic; if it was not the ancient town of Galway itfelf.

AUTERII, a people of ancient Ireland mentioned by Ptolemy and thought by fome to be the inhabitants of the counties of Galway and Rofcommon; but Ptolemy doth not appear to have been in the leaft acquainted with the internal parts of this ifland; the Auterii therefore moft probably inhabited the fea coafts. The word Auterii is evidently a corruption from the Celtic *Aubb* or *Aub*

Water, and *Eireigh* western people, signifying therefore the western people on the water, under this consideration the Auteirij must have been the ancient inhabitants of the western coasts of the counties of Galway and Mayo, that is from the north of the bay of Galway to Dunfine Head, comprehending the ancient district of Muriag, called frequently Hy Moruisge or the district on the waters of the sea, yet retained in the barony of Morisk in the county of Mayo. The ancient Murisg or Moruisg, the Auterij of Ptolemy, we find in the commencement of the middle ages containing the districts of *Tir-Amalgaid*, *Hy Malia* and *Jar* or *Eir-Conmacne*. Which see under the respective names. This description agrees with the account which Mr. Whitaker gives in his history of Manchester.

B

BALLY-EO; Bally, a town and eo a grave; an ancient name for Slane. * See Ferta-fir-feic.

BALLY-LEAN-CLIATH, see Lean-cliath.

BALTIMORE, see Bealtimor.

BARRAGH, see Breba.

BARROW river, see Breba.

BEALLAGH-MORE, or the great rath or habitation. A rath on a lake in the county of West-Meath, the same as Bregmuin, which see.

BEALATHA, or the place of Beal on the water; now Athenry in the county of Galway, destroyed in 1133 by Conor O'Brien. †

* Annal. annon. MS.   † Collect. No. 4. p. 566.

BEALLAGH-MORE, Vide fupra.

BEALTIMORE, or the great habitation of
Beal, a fanctuary of the Druids in the ancient diftrict of Leim Con in the weft of Carbury, and
county of Cork, now Baltimore.

BEAL-TINNE, or Beal's Fire; the facred fires
that were lighted on rocks, mountains, cairns of
ftone and altars in honour of Beal or the fun, on
the vernal equinox, firft of May, fummer folftice,
firft of Auguft and the eve of the firft of November, by the Arch Druids in their feveral diftricts.
Alfo a fpecies of altars compofed of a large flat ftone
placed horizontally on feveral upright rock ftones,
on which fires were burned on the above mentioned days by the feveral orders of Druids; which
fires were taken from the facred eternal fires preferved by the veftal virgins. A number of thefe
altars are ftill remaining in different parts of Ireland, fituated either on hills or plains, and during
the time of facrifice were encompaffed three feveral
times by the votaries adorned with garlands, finging hymns in honour of Apollo or Beal, and throwing into the fire, at proper intervals, flefh, fruits,
flowers and aromatic herbs; from the colour of
the flame and fmoak arifing therefrom the Druid,
who prefided over the ceremony, drew prefages
relative to the fubject enquired into by the votaries. Some of the Beal-tinnes confift only of immenfe rock ftones raifed about fix inches above
the ground by others placed under them. Hiftoire
des Celtes, Jurieu's critical hift. of the church
vol. ii. Collectanea, No. 5.

BEAL-TINNE-GLAS, or the fire of Beal's
myfteries, the hill of Baltinglafs in the county of

Wicklow whereon fires were lighted, on the firft
of May and firft of Auguft, in honour of the fun
by the Druids; it was the grand Beal-tinne of the
fouthern ftates of Leinfter; there are ftill remaining
in its neighbourhood a number of Druidic altars
and other monuments of heathen fuperftition.

BEARLA FENE, or the noble of learned language, the polite and learned dialect of the ancient Irifh tongue, being that fpoken by the no-
bleffe and Druids, and diftinguifhed by its foftnefs
from the Caëlic, or that fpoken by the common
people, which was remarkable for its harfhnefs and
gutteral founds. The pronunciation of the *Bearla
Fene* depended principally on the power of the
vowels, whilft the *Bearla Caëlic* retained the gutteral founds of the confonants for which the principal dialects of the Celtic tongue were remarkable. This reformation in the Hiberno-Celtic language was owing to the bards in their poetical
compofitions in order to harmonize the verfification, and fince the extirpation of the bards and
difcontinuance of the language is nearly loft, the
Irifh language fpoken at this day by the common
people is the Caëlic dialect and retains all its original harfhnefs.

The claffic dialect of the ancient Irifh language
being denominated by the bards *Bearla Fene*, feveral modern antiquaries have thought it fignified
the Phœnician language, introduced by thofe people during their commerce with the Britifh ifles.
The ancient Celtic, Hebrew, Phœnician and Punic languages had undoubtedly a great affinity with
and were only different dialects of the fame ori-

ginal tongue fpoken by the whole world before
the confufion of Babel, as has been fully evinced
by A learned antiquary in his effay on the antiquity of the Irifh language ; but Bearla Fene
cannot fignify the Phœnician language as has been
fhewn under the words Fene and Phœnician.

BEGERI, or the little land in the water, an ifl-
land on the coaft of Wexford, where St. Ibarus
had a monaftery and fchool.*

BELA-FEARSAD, from *Beallagh*, a town, and
Farfad the mouth of a river or harbour, the ancient name of the harbour and town of Belfaft; Bea-
la is the fine rath at Drumboe, being 2526
feet in circumference, called the Giant's Ring †

BEN-GOLBAN, or Ben-Cael-ban, that is, the
head or hill of the woody country ; a famous
mountain in the barony of Carbry and county of
Sligo, near which the Nagnata of Ptolemy is fuppofed to be fituated ‡ It is now called Benvoliben,
and is four miles N. of Sligo, and two from the
ocean.

BEN-HEDAR, or Ben-Adar, that is, the birds
promontory ; from *Ben* a head or promontory, and
Hedar or Adar birds ; the prefent Hill of Hoath.
Celebrated for having Dun-criomthan erected on
it, the royal palace or rath of Criomthan, chief or
king of that diftrict ; and who made feveral fuc-
cefsful defcents on the coafts of Britain againft the
Romans, in the time of Agricola.§

BENVOLIBEN, fee Ben Golban.

BERVA, fee Breba.

---

* Ware.   † Collect. No. 5.   ‡ O'Conor's Diff. p. 177.
§ O'Conor's Diff. Intr. p. 13.

BHURRIN, see Burrin.

BLADHMA SLIABH, a range of mountains between the King and Queen's Counties, and which in ancient times was one of the boundaries of Munster on the Leinster side. *Bladhma* is evidently corrupted from *Beal-di-mai* whence Sliabh Beal di mai is the mountain of the worship, or necromancy of Beal's day. There is still remaining in these mountains a large pyramid of white stones, the true simulacre of the sun-fire among all the Celtic nations.

BOAND, see Buvinda.

BOIRCE, or the magnificent Place; the palace of the kings of Ullagh or Down, and probably the Rath of Dunum or Down-patrick.

BOLGÆ, or Fir Bolgæ, a people mentioned in the Irish annals to have been the most ancient inhabitants of this country, and who are supposed to have transmigrated from Britain in a very early period. As these people are in the most ancient Irish poems and chronicles universally distinguished by the name of Fir Bolgæ, Siol mBolgæ, and Slioght mBealidh; the learned have been much divided respecting the derivation of the word Bolga, a name, by which the aboriginal inhabitants of Ireland, have ever been distinguished. Some think they were Belgians, who setled here about the time that their brethern made their first descent on Britain; others assert, they were denominated Bolgæ, or Archers, from Bolg a quiver; whilst others maintain, they were so called, from Bol a poet, whence Bolgæ a race of poets or learned people. There is the greatest probability they were Belgians, and derived their name from the object of their faith. The principal object of adoration amongst all the ancient inhabitants

of Europe, was the Sun, which they denominated Baal, Beal, Bal or Bol, viz. the great Lord ;
and All, Oll, Uu, Ual or Haul, that is the all
powerful Being, on which account all the Celtic
tribes denominated themfelves Balga, Bolga, Bea-
logh or Ollabh, Ullagh and Haullin ; according
to their feveral dialects ; words which literally
fignify Belgians or the worfhippers of Beal.
Whence in the moft ancient Irifh poems we find
them diftinguifhed by *Siol mBolga*, and Slioght
mBealidh, or Slioght Mileadh, that is the race of
the worfhippers of Beal. An appellation that as
univerfally diftinguifhed the ancient inhabitants
of Europe, as that of Chriftians doth the prefent.
The Belgians or Bolgæ thereof, who firft replenifh-
ed this ifland with inhabitants after the deluge,
were ancient Britons of Celtic origin, and Beal-
gian faith.

There appears to have been two grand migrations
from Britain under this denomination. The firft,
from the Irifh poems yet preferved in the Leabhar Leacan, feem to have arrived under the conduct of Hugony, about 330 years before the
chriftian æra, on the firft Belgic invafion of Britain.
This colony perhaps was by no means numerous
until joined by fubfequent ones from the fame
ifland ; which though continually arriving, were
not of any confiderable magnitude, until that
under the conduct of Dela Mac Loich, or the
prince of the mariners. This adventurous leader
was chief of Lumon, the Luentum of Ptolemy
now Lhannio in fouth Wales, and of the race of
the ancient Silures, who originally inhabited the
northern and fouthern banks of the Severn, and
who had retired from the more fouthern parts, on

the firft arrival of the Belgæ from the continent.
They probably tranfmigrated to Ireland, about the
time of the arrival of Diviaticus in Britain, or 100
years before the birth of Chrift; though it is poffible, they might have arrived fomewhat earlier,
or 150 years prior to the Chriftian æra. They
appear to have eftablifhed their original fettlement
on the fouthern banks of the Shannon; from
whence, in procefs of time, in conjunction with fubfequent colonies, they extended their fettlements
over the fouth of Ireland, forming one people with
the Aborigines; who had before this period taken
poffeffion of the middle and northern parts of the
ifland. We muft not however fuppofe, that the
Belgic inhabitants of Ireland, thus augmented
were very numerous; it is evident from the fragments of feveral Irifh poems ftill remaining, that,
though the entire ifland was divided among their
different tribes, yet they rather perambulated, than
inhabited their feveral diftricts; until the arrival
of other Celtic colonies from the north of Britain,
under the denomination of Ullagh and Tuath de
Danans; which fee*.

Though all the ancient inhabitants of Ireland may
juftly be denominated Fir Bolga or Belgians, yet during the middle ages, the word Bolga by the poets
and hiftorians was ufed to fignify the inhabitants of
Conaught fo denominated from Ollne maght, or
the tribe of *Beal* or *Oll*, whence *Fir Bolgagh* that
is the men of Ollnemaght. Wherefore when any
of the ancient chiefs of this diftrict obtained the
title of monarchs of the whole ifland, the hiftorians have afferted that they were of the race of

---

* Richard of Cirencefter, p. 50. Keating. O'Conor's
Differt. & Baxter's Gloff. Brit. in Belgæ.

the Fir Bolgs, to diftinguifh them from thofe of the Heremonii, Heberii and Ernai. But when the Bolgæ is mentioned in the Irifh poems and hiftories in contradiction to the Milefians, they fignify the plebeians or herdfmen, from Bol horned cattle, whence *Bolg* or *Bolga* a herdfman or keeper of horned cattle, by reafon, that this fpecies of animals was dedicated to Beal or Bol.

For further particulars of the Bolgæ, fee MOMONII, MUMHAN, OLNEACHT and COIGIDUGA-REAN.

BOREUM, a promontory in the north of Ireland mentioned by Ptolemy. Boreum fignifies northern, whence Boreum Promontorium is the northern Promontory; it is now called the North Cape or Horn-head, and is fituated in the north of the county of Donegall.

BOYNE river; fee Buvinda.

BREAGH, Bhreagh, Breg, Brigh, Brugh, Bruigh and Berg, an habitation of a noblefſe, and fignifies either a rath or laos.

BREBA, from Breogh-Abha, or the forked river; the northern branch of the Abhan Breoghan, called alfo Berva the ancient name of the river Barrow. In the latter ages it obtained the name of Bárragh, or boundary river; being for fome centuries the boundary between the Englifh pale and the Irifh fepts.

BREDAGH, or Bredagh Abhan, that is, the hilly or mountaneous river, a fmall river that rifes in a mountain between Lough Foyle and Lough Swilly in the barony of Inis Owen and county of Donegall. After a fhort S. E. courfe it falls into Lough Foyle; near this, St. Patrick founded the church of Domnach Bile in the middle of the fifth century.

BREFINE, Brefne or Breghane, that is, the country of the little hills; called also Hy Re Leigh, or the diftrict of the country of the king; the chiefs of which were the O'Reilyes. The fubordinate diftricts of this country were Hy Flath ean eoghan, or the diftrict of the chief of the country on the water; the Dynaft of which was O'Flanegan; with Hy Ru-arc, Hy Bredagh, Hy Coreigh, Hy Cabhan or Hy Re-leigh, Magh Ciernan, Magh Gauroll, and Hy Ser-ui-don, each governed by their refpective chiefs, O'Ruarc, O'Brady, O'Corry, O'Sheridan, Mc. Kiernan and Mc. Gauroll, moft of whom were in poffeffion of their eftates at the beginning of the laft century. Brefine is now called the county of Cavan, though formerly it took in Leitrim, and part of Annaly.

BREGIA or Bregmuin, that is, the place or plain of the habitation. A plain extending round the royal palace of Tara, called alfo Magh Bregh; it extended as far as Trim and Duleek.

BREOGHAIN, an ancient diftrict containing the intire county of Waterford, fo denominated from lying on the river Braghan or Brigus; the inhabitants of this diftrict were frequently called Slioght Breoghain or the race dwelling on the forked river, and were the Brigantes of Ptolemy, their country was bounded on the eaft by Abhan Braghan, on the north by the Sure, on the weft by the Black-water, and on the fouth by the fea. Their moft ancient chiefs were denominated Hy Breoghan and O'Breoghan, whence by corruption O'Brain, which the genealogifts of the latter ages have made defcend from the O'Briens of Thomond, whereby they have confounded one race with the other. The Hy Breoghans were difpof-feffed of the fouth parts of their country by Aon-gus at the head of the clan of the Defii; who had been expelled the county of Meath by Cormac mac Art in 278. From that time the fouthern parts of this ancient diftrict was in the poffeffion of the chiefs of the Defii. But the northern remained under the government of its native princes until the arrival of the Englifh, when the greater part of the country was divided among the Boyles, Sherlocks, Poors, Aylwards, Daltons, Waddings, &c. feudatory tenants to Henry II. who, after the general diftribution of the kingdom among his followers, referved to himfelf all the Country from Cork to Waterford. The ancient princes however ftill retained a part which they held by grant from the Englifh monarchs; and we find an O'Brien in the tenure of a confiderable landed property in this county at the commencement of the laft cen-tury; but whether defcended from the Hy Bre-oghans or O'Briens of Thomond, is not certain. The Slioght Breoghan was called alfo by the ancient Irifh writers Slioght Lugach, or the race on the water which feem to be the fame as the *Luceni* of Ptolemy, * though others place the Luceni or Lucenii along Dingle bay in the county of Kerry.

BREOGHAIN-ABHAIN, fee Brigus.
BRIGANTES, fee Brigus and Breoghain.
BRIGANTIA, a town mentioned by Richard of Cirencefter, and fuppofed the capital of the Bri-

* Smith's co. Waterford. O'Conor's Differt. p. 178. Ware.

gantes of Ptolemy. Probably a place somewhere near the mouth of the Brigus, where the natives affembled to traffic with foreigners ; perhaps the prefent city of Waterford.

BRIGH-THAIGH, or Brigh Mac Thaidghe, that is the habitation of Mc Thaigh, in Meath. Here Gelafius bifhop of Ardmagh held a Synod in 1153.

BRIGUS, the ancient name of a river mentioned by Ptolemy in the fouth of Ireland, and generally thought to be the Barrow, but here feems to be a fmall error ; the Brigus of Ptolemy did not properly belong to the Barrow, but to the main-channel of the three rivers, the Barrow, Nore and Sure, which uniting near Rofs and Waterford, were from thence to the fea diftinguifhed by the ancient Irifh by the general name of Breoghan Abhan or forked river, and from whence Ptolemy, undoubtedly obtained his name of Brigus. The three branches Barrow, Nore and Sure, anciently the Sure, Feorus and Breba were equally unknown to this ancient geographer, who obtained his information from the foreign merchants, who only vifited the fea coafts. The people inhabiting near the mouth and fouthern branch of this river, were by the natives denominated as we have before obferved, Slioght Breoghan or the race on the forked river ; whence Ptolemy calls them by corruption, Brigantes. The real fignification of the word, Brigantes, not being known to the writers of the middle and latter ages have caufed innumerable conjectures ; Richard of Cirencefter thinks they were Britons who fled from the terror of the Roman arms about 50 years after the birth of Chrift.

That they were colonies from Britain is evident, but they certainly arrived much earlier than the time specified, at least the major part.

BRIGUS, mistaken by Camden, Ware and some others for Brigantia, and thought to be Leighlin on the Barrow in the county of Carlow; but no such place existed in the early ages.

BRUGHNA-BOYNE, a Cemetery of the ancient kings of Ireland, now Trim.

BRUGHRIGH, that is the habitation of the king; the seat of the kings of Cairbre Aobhdha, now Kenry in the county of Limerick; and appears to be the Regia Altera of Ptolemy. Here Auliff-mor O'Donaghue king of Cairbre Aobhdha was slain by Mortogh O'Brien in 1165; now called Brury.

BRUIGHEN DA DARG, or the habitation of the two caves, called also *Teach n'aoi droma Raithe*, that is the house of the chief or elder, in the Rath of the hollow mount. This Rath contained the royal palace of Taragh, so much spoken of by the Irish poets and antiquaries; and was situated in view, and not far from the Hill of Taragh, whereon the States assembled. Conar the son of Trenmor, called by the Irish historians Conar-mor, and chief of a colony of Caledonians, who settled in this country about the birth of Christ, originally built the palace of Taragh; called the habitation or Rath of the caves, from containing several caves under the platform. By some accident the royal palace situated in the rath, was burned to the ground, in the first year of its erection; but was immediately repaired and improved, by Conar, who resided in it several years. This king how-

ever having expelled Ankle, one of his Caledonian
captains into the Ifle of Man, made him fo much
his enemy, that fome time after, he returned with
an army, took Tara by furprize and fet fire to
the palace; in the flames of which Conar perifhed.
From this time it remained in ruins for feveral
years, during the conteft between the Caledonian
and Belgian fepts. It was however at length rebuilt in great fplendor, and fo continued for a
number of years after; during the frequent wars it
fuffered feveral conflagrations, and was finally deftroyed by Brien Boromh, in 995, near a thoufand
years after its firft erection. The rath of this celebrated palace, is yet remaining, under which,
tradition fays, there are a number of caves. The
royal apartments and other buildings, fituated
within the ramparts, were conftructed of wattles
or wicker work, fupported by whited pillars formed of the trunks of trees, and whofe walls were li-
ned with mats, made of fine rufhes. The number and dimenfions of the principal buildings com-
pofing the palace of Teamor or Taragh, during
the middle ages, have been given by the Irifh antiquaries; but who have in general confounded them
with the Naoifteaghan on the hill of Taragh where
the States affembled. The buildings of the palace, confifted of the Teach Miodhcuharta, or
chief court, where the princes were entertained,
and four other large houfes, for the lodging of the
nobles and royal family; all fituated round the foot
of the rampart after the manner of the ancient
Greeks, in the conftruction of their villas. Keating has given a pompous defcription of the great
court, apparently much exaggerated; according
to him, it was 300 feet long, 40 feet high, and

60 feet broad. If fuch were the dimenfions, it muft have been an open court furrounded with the royal apartments; a circumftance indeed extremely probable, as we know open courts were cuftomary among the ancient Greeks. In the middle of the court was erected the throne, whereon the monarch fat; the kings of Munfter with the provincial deputies on his left hand, thofe of Ulfter on the right, the king of Leinfter in front, and the king of Conaught behind; they being after the manner of the Pagan times, feated circularly round the throne †.

BURRIN, Bhurrin or Bhorrin, that is, the diftant or external country; a barony in the County of Clare, on the fouth of the bay of Galway, denominated alfo formerly Hy Loch-lean, or the diftrict on the waters of the fea; the chiefs whereof were called O'Loghlin, or O'Laghlin; fome of whom remained in poffeffion, at the commencement of the laft century.—In this diftrict were the Canganij of Ptolemy.

BUVINDA, or Bubinda, the ancient name of a river mentioned by Ptolemy, and thought to be the Boyne. The word *Burvinda* feems to be derived from the Cimbric-Britifh words, *Bu-tien-dau*, that is the clear rapid water; whence called by the Irifh *Boand* or *Boüind*, by corruption the Boyne.

C

CAELANI or Galeni, the ancient inhabitants of Caëlan. They were a branch of the Scotii;

---

† O'Conor's Differt. p. 129. 135. and Introduction p. 12. Collectanea No. 3. p. 377. No. 4. p. 518. 585.

but during the middle ages were tributary either to the chiefs of Cuolan or Hy Falgia. See Oalan.

CAIRBRE-AOBHDHA, or the diſtrict on the water; from *Cairbre* a diſtrict, and *Aobhdha* waters; the preſent barony of Kenry in the county of Limerick. This country was alſo denominated Hy Dun na bhan, or the hilly diſtrict on the river; the ancient chiefs whereof were called Hy Dunnavan, or O'Donovan, that is the chiefs of the hilly country on the river [*]. The principal place was Brughrigh, the Rigia altera of Ptolemy. See Brughrigh and Rigia.

CAIRN, or a heap of ſtones; large mounds of ſtones found in different parts of Ireland, and indeed in moſt countries of Europe. They were the ſepulchres of the ancient Celtic heroes, eſpecially of celebrated commanders of armies, and founders of colonies. On theſe mounds ſacrifices were offered in honour of the Earth or univerſal Nature on the eve of the firſt of November, from whence they were denominated *Flachgo*, or temples of Veſta by the Iriſh, but *Andate* by the ancient Britons. Spoils and priſoners taken in war were alſo frequently ſacrificed on them in order to appeaſe the manes of the departed worthies, after the manner of the ancient Mexicans. Here was exerciſed a ſpecies of divination denominated, the *Ob*, in order to conſult the ſpirits of ancient times relative to future events.

As repoſitaries of the dead, they were frequently called *Mogh ad air*, or *Mogh air cair nagh*, that is temples, ſanctuaries, or cairns of *Mogh* or *Sodorn*, the genius who preſided over human affairs, and

[*] Collect. No. 3, p. 377.

and the manes of the dead; whence the Romans called them temples of Mercury and sanctuaries of Saturn, on which fires were occasionally lighted in honour of the sun and earth.

According to the Irish antiquaries, these Cairns were the most ancient sepulchres of the old Irish, the principal person was interred or his urn placed in a cave or dome in the centre of the mount, and in the early ages was accompanied by his wife and nearest friends, who were inclosed alive with him in the tomb; for which reason we frequently find in opening these tumuli, human bones uncovered on the floor of the vault, whilst the urn containing the ashes of the hero lies interred under the tabernacle.

This barbarous custom, however, was at length abolished, and the friends, relations and descendants of the deceased chief were interred under the upright stones encircling the base of the monument. A number of these Tumuli are still remaining in Ireland, particularly Cairn Ængus at *New Grange* in the county of East Meath, *Cairn ban* near Newry, *Cairn Dare* near Kildare, Cairn Cluin.—And a fine one on the banks of the Liffey, about ten miles from Dublin.—See Tlachgo, and Mogh-adair. *

CANCORA, or the chief residence; a rath or castle near Killaloe, the palace of the ancient kings of Thomond, built by Brien Boromh. It was destroyed by O'Neill and his Ultonians in 1101. The only remains now visible of this ancient royal palace are the ramparts and fosse of the rath.

* Mc. Curtin's Antiq. Histoire des Celtes. Jurieu's Critical Hist. of the Church, and Collectanea No. 5 and 6.

CANGANÆ INSULÆ, mentioned by Richard of Cirencester, the prefent fouth ifles of Arran on the coafts of Burrin ; the Canganij of Ptolemy.

CANGANIJ, or Ganganii, a people inhabiting the weftern parts of the county of Clare, mentioned by Ptolemy. Canganij or Ceanganij are evidently deried from Cean a head or promontory, and Gan external ; whence Canganij the people of the external promontory ; They were the ancient inhabitants of the prefent barony of Burrin, in the county of Clare ; Burrin having nearly the fame fignification as Canganij, which fee.

CARAN, fee Coran.

CARMEN, or the inclofed place, from *car* a round enclofure and *men* a place ; whence Cathermen the place of the city. This place was the capital of the ancient Coulan, and the Naafteighan where the ftates of the fouthern parts of Leinfter met. It was fituated on a gentle floping hill about five miles eaft of Athy in the county of Kildare, now diftinguifhed by the moat of Mullamaft, or the moat of decapitation ; from the murder of a number of Irifh gentlemen by feveral Englifh adventurers in the fixteenth century. The hill of Carmen exactly refembles that of Tara in the county of Meath ; iffuing originally from the bofom of a thick wood, of an oblate, conical figure, about a mile in diameter at the bafe ; from the fummit, which is nearly three quarters of a mile in length, the feveral counties of fouth Leinfter may be feen ; there are yet remaining on it the Rath and Laois in which the chiefs encamped ; alfo the Labereigh or Areopagus, confifting of fixteen conical mounds of earth in a circle of 68 feet in diameter, on which the chiefs fat in council. Near this place was fought the celebrated battle of Carmen towards the clofe of the third century, between the people of fouth Leinfter, and Carmac Cas king of Munfter*. The field where this battle was fought is about three miles from Carmen, and two from Athy; at this day numbers of the bodies of the flain are frequently dug up about a foot below the prefent furface, and in the feveral directions in which they fell.

CARRAN-FEARAIDHE, or the hill or rock of the men of the water, now Knock-Aine, in the county of Limerick. At or near this place, a bloody battle was fought between the princes of Conaught and Dioma king of Munfter; in which the former were entirely defeated, and five chiefs and four thoufand officers and foldiers left dead on the field †.

CARRICKASTICKEN, fee Cierric-naoiteaghan.

CARRICKFERGUS, fee Dunfobarky.

CARRIGOGINNIOL, or Carric ui cinniol, that is the rock of the diftrict of the chief tribe, called alfo Pobal Brien, or the people of Brien. Donogh Cairbreach O'Brien in 1211 received from John king of England patents for the eftate of Carrigoginniol, in the county of Limerick, at the yearly rent of fixty marks. The earls of Defmond afterwards became lords of this diftrict ‡.

CARSIOL, or the habitation on the rock, from *car* or *carric* a rock, and *fiol* a race or habitation;

---

* Collect. No. 4. p. 427. O'Conor's Diff. p. 177.
† Collect. No. 4. p. 444.
‡ Collect. No. 4. p. 624.

now Cashel. The rock of Cashel was originally a dun or castle of the ancient chiefs of Eoganacht-Caisil, or Magh-Feimen, called from their habitation on this isolated rock, *Hy Dun na moi*, or chief of the hill of the plain, by corruption O'Donnohue; in later ages they were distinguished by the name of Cartheigh, or inhabitants of the rock, whence descended the Mac Carthies hereditary chiefs of this district. However, some years before the establishment of christianity in this country, Cashel became the royal seat of the monarchs of Munster, in which state it appears to have continued until the commencement of the tenth century; when Cormac Mac Culinan, being king of Cashel and bishop of Emly, erected on the scite of the old palace an elegant chapel, and removed thither the episcopal see from Emly, making it the metropolitan see of all Munster; Which chapel of of Cormac was repaired, and a synod held in it in the year 1134. But Donald O'Brien in the reign of Henry II. built a new church from the .foundation, and converted Cormac's chapel into a chapter-house, and made considerable grants of land to the see; which his son Donat augmented with other benefactions; King John also adding something to the revenue, confirmed the donations of Donat in 1215. About the year 1415 the church built by Cormac and Donald O'Brien and dedicated to St. Patrick, being through age, in a ruinous state, was repaired by Richard O'Hedian, archbishop of Cashel, who also built a hall for the vicars choral, and endowed it with lands. From this time the cathedral of Cashel was made use of as the metropolitan church of Munster, until about the year 1750, when it was shamefully given up to ruin,—and in which ſtate it now lies; doctor Arthur Price was then archbiſhop *.

CAS, ſee Ga.

CASIOL IRRA, or weſt Caſhel, ſix miles ſouth of Sligo, where a biſhoprick was erected by St. Bron in the begining of the ſixth century†.

CATHAIGH INIS, or Inis-cathay, denominated alſo Inis Gatha, or Inis Ga; that is the iſland in the ſea, it being ſituated in the mouth of the Shannon, between the counties of Clare and Kerry. St. Patrick founded a monaſtery here and placed over it St. Senan; It became afterwards a biſhoprick, and was united to that of Limerick in 1188 or 1190. The monaſtery was frequently plundered by the Danes. It is now called Inis-Scattery ‡.

CATHERLOCH, or the city on the lake; now the town of Carlow. Here king John erected a caſtle for the protection of the Engliſh colonies, the ruins of which are yet viſible. It was taken by one of the Cavanaghs, named Donald Mc. Art who ſtiled himſelf Mc. Murrough, king of Leinſter in the twentieth year of Richard II. in his poſſeſſion it remained ſome time §.

CATHERLOUGH county, or the county of Carlow, comprehending the ancient diſtricts of Hy Cabhanagh and Hy Drone, being the northern part of the principality of Hy Cinſiolagh. It was made a county by king John about 1210.

* Collect. No. 3. p. 375 Harris's Ware, v. p. 1. 464.
† Harris's Ware v. 1. p. 464.
‡ Uſher p. 454. Harris's Ware vol. 1. p. 502.
§ Ware's Annals.

CAUCIJ, an ancient people of Ireland, placed by Richard of Cirencefter in the county of Dublin, on the banks of the Liffey, and in the northern parts of the county of. Wicklow. The word, Caucij, is evidently derived from the ancient Britifh, *Caüc Iü*, that is the high diftrict between the rivers; whence the ancient Germans, inhabiting the country betwen the Elb and Wefer, are called by Ptolemy Chaucii Majores, and thofe dwelling between the Wefer and the Emfe, were denominated *Chaucii Minores.* The Caucij of Ireland therefor undoubtedly were the ancient inhabitants of the mountainous country lying between the rivers Barrow and Nore, called by the ancient Irifh *Hy Breoghain Gabbran,* or the diftrict of the high country between the forks. The chiefs of which were denominated Hy Breghnan, by corruption O'Brenan, fome of whom were in poffeffion of that country at the commencement of the laft century*.

CERRIGIA, or the rocky country, the prefent county of Kerry, from Cerrig or Carric a rock.

CHILL, fee Cill and Kil.

CIARUIDHE, or the rocky diftrict on the water, from ciar or cer, a rock, and *uidhe* or *ui dha*, a diftrict on the water; the prefent barony of Iraght in the county of Kerry, on the fouthern banks of the Shannon, and from which is derived Cerrigia and Kerry. The chiefs of this country were called Hy Cain air Ciaruidhe, that is the chief of the weftern diftrict of the rocky country; by contraction O'Conor Kerry; whofe defcendants were in poffeffion of their ancient patrimony in the beginning of the laft century. This dif-

* O'Conor's Ortelius.

trict was sometimes denominated *Ciaruidhe Luachra*, or the rocky district on the great lake or water, and *Feor na Floinn*, that is the people of the chief or leader *.

CIERRIENAOITEAGHAN, now corruptly called Carrickasticken, that is the rock or hill of the assembly of the elders; the Maistean of the ancient inhabitants of the county of Louth, the Voluntii of Ptolemy. It is situated near Dundalk, in several hills or mounds composing the Leaberagh or Areopagus, urns containing the ashes of the old chiefs have been found; but the principal rath has been in part destroyed.†

CILL-AICE, that is the full grown wood, or strong church. A place in the county of Meath destroyed by Callaghan, a king of south Munster in 939 ‡.

CILL MAC DUAGH, or the church of Mc. Duagh; a church and bishoprick in the county of Galway, founded in the middle of the sixth century by St. Colman, son of Duagh, descended from the ancient chiefs of Tir-malgaid. The bishoprick of Cillmacduagh was united to that of Clonfert in 1602 §.

CINEAL EOGHEAN, or *Cean all Eaghain*, from *Cean thuath oll Eagh an*, prononunced *Connal Owen* or the principal division of the northern county of the Oll or Bolga; an ancient district in the province of Ulster comprehending originally the present counties of Tyrone, Armagh, Donegall, and part of the county of Derry, being

* Collect. No. 3. p. 379.
† Wright's Louthiana.
‡ Collect. No. 4. p. 462.
§ Harris's Ware, v. 1. p. 634, and 648.

the ancient divifions of *Eirgall* and *Orgall*. It was
the firft fettlement of the Bolga in the North a-
bout 300 years before Chrift, the chiefs of which
were denominated Connel or Connar, until the
fourth century, when one of the fons of O'Nial
the great principal king of Hy Faillia took poffeffion of the eaftern part, or *Orgall*; whilft the weftern or *Eirgall* remained under the dominion of
its native princes, which from them was called
in the latter ages *Tir Connal*, or the country of Connal, comprehending the prefent county of Donegall.
Cinel Eogbean being thus confined to the counties of
Derry, Tyrone and Armagh, continued un-
der the dominion of the O'Nials fome time after
the arrival of the Englifh, but at length was
reduced to the prefent county of Tyrone, being
called *Tir Owen*, or the land of Owen, from whence
Tyrone is derived *.

CINEALFEARMAIC, or the chief diftrict of
the fons of men; a country in the ancient Thomond and county of Clare; the ancient chiefs
thereof were the O'Deas.

CINEALTALMHUIM, fee Aoibh Liathain.

CINNEICH, or the chief place, the refidence of
Dermod Mc. Carthy, near Bandon, deftroyed in
1150 by Mortogh O'Brien.

CLANN-CUILEAN, or the race or children
of the corner on the water; called alfo *Hy na
Mor*, or the diftrict of the fea; the chiefs of which
were denominated *Mac na Mor aois*, or the fon of
the elders of the fea, by contraction Mac Nama-
ras; fome of whom were in poffeffion of this
country, fituated in the S. E. part of the county

* Keating. O'Conor's Diff. Harris's Ware, vol. 1.

of Clare on the Shannon, at the commencement of the laſt century. It was alſo part of Dail Gais, which ſee *.

CLANRICARD, ſee Hy Fiacria aidne.

CLOGHADH, or *Clogha*, the Hiberno-celtic name of thoſe ſlender round towers at this day found in ſeveral parts of Ireland. The word is derived from the old Iriſh *Tlachgo* from *Tlacht* the earth or univerſe. The Druidic temples of Veſta in which were kept the ſacred or eternal fire, were called *Tlachgo* or temples of Cybele, being of the ſame conſtruction with the *Pyrathea* of the ancient Perſians, and the *Chammia* of the Phœnicians and Carthaginians, ſome of which are ſtill remaining in Perſia and Bulgaria. The Hibernian Druids erected theſe temples in their ſanctuaries, as is evident from the ruins of ſeveral ſtill remaining in different parts of the kingdom, particularly at Ballynaſliebh in the county of Kilkenny, Navan near Armagh, &c. They were conſtructed of rock ſtone without cement, and were of the ſame diameter with thoſe towers now remaining, but to what altitude they were carried is not certain ; little more than the foundations being now viſible. After the eſtabliſhment of chriſtianity in Ireland, among a number of Druic ſuperſtitions, the ſacred or eternal fires were preſerved for ſeveral centuries, and the *Tlachgo* by the chriſtian clergy removed from the ſanctuaries of paganiſm to thoſe of the true faith, and became appurtenances to churches and monaſteries, though ſtill retaining their ancient denomination of *Tlachgo* or temples of Veſta. On the abolition of theſe fires, about the twelfth cen-

* Collect. No. 4. p. 602.

tury, and the introduction of bells, the *Tlachgo* were in general converted into belfries, whence the modern name for a bell in Irish is *clogh*, from being placed in the *Tlachgo* or vestal temples. As these round towers are neither found in Britain or the European continent, they were most probably introduced into this island by the Persian Magi or Gaürs, who in the time of Constantine the Great ran over the world, carrying in their hands *censors* containing the holy fire; asserting their God should destroy all other Gods, which in some measure they effected by lighting fires under them, thereby burning those of wood and melting those of metal. In this period the christian religion had made considerable progress in the southern and western parts of Europe, but in Ireland druidic superstition remaining in its original purity, whose tenets not being widely different from those of the Gaürs, these pagan philosophers found a ready assent to their doctrines; whence Pyratheias or vestal towers became universal throughout the island, in the place of the ancient *Tlachgo*, which we have shewn under that word were mounts of stone containing the remains of their ancient heroes, and on which fires were occasionally lighted from the sacred vaults at the times of sacrifice. The *Cloghadh* now remaining in Ireland were all erected by the christian clergy, and are none of them older probably than the beginning of the seventh century, nor none of a later date than the close of the eleventh, though evidently derived from structures of a similar nature used by the pagan priests; they were however continued as belfries to the close of the fourteenth century, for which reason a belfry in the Irish language is termed *Clogbadh*, from being originally temples of *Tlacht*. (See Tlachgo and Gadalians.) *

CLOGHER, or the place of the ftone; fituated on the river Launy in the county of Tyrone. This place during the times of paganifm was a druidic fanctuary; in which was kept a ftone of divination called the golden ftone; and which according to the regifter of Clogher, the Devil pronounced jugling anfwers, like the oracles of Apollo Pythius.   Several antiquaries have thought the ftone of Clogher to have been the fame with the celebrated Lec Fail, fo much fpoken of by the ancient Irifh writers.   But from being denominated the golden ftone, it appears to have been a gem of a yellow colour, and probably was of the fame fpecies as that mentioned by Pliny, and called Ananchites; by which the Greeks, Romans and all the Aborigines of Europe divined; refembling the Urim and Thummin of the Hebrews †.   Here alfo was fituated the royal feat of the ancient kings of Ergal, near which St. Macartin, in 490, by order of St. Patrick, founded a monaftery and bifhoprick.   In 1041 the church of Clogher was rebuilt and dedicated to the memory of St. Macartin; fince which time it has received feveral alterations and improvements by fucceeding bifhops, efpecially by Mathew Mc. Catafaid, who in 1295, rebuilt the cathedral, erected other buildings, and granted feveral valuable donations to it.   The fee of Louth was united to this bifhoprick about the middle of the eleventh century ‡, together with

* Ware Ant. Dufrene's Gloff. tom. 3. Jurieu's critical Hift. of the Church. vol. 2.
† Pliny, l. 37. 11.   ‡ Harris's Ware, v. 1. p. 175.

the deaneries of Drogheda, Athirdee and Dundalk. See Regia.

CLONARD, an ancient monaſtery and biſhoprick near the river Boyne in the county of Meath, founded by St. Finian in 520, who eſtabliſhed a ſchool in his monaſtery of Clonard, celebrated for producing ſeveral learned men. The biſhoprick of Clonard, with thoſe of Trim, Ardbraccan, Donſhaghlin, Slane and Foure, were conſolidated before the year ·1152, and united to that of Meath about the beginning of the thirteenth century*. Clonard ſeems to be the ſame place as Cluainiaraid, which ſee.

CLONFERT, that is the holy retirement; ſituated near the Shannon. An abbey, church and biſhoprick was founded here in 558, by St. Brendan, who was interred in his own church in May 577. During the middle ages this church was celebrated for its ſeven altars, and the weſt front ſuppoſed to have been erected by John biſhop of Clonfert, about 1270, is ſtill beautiful. The biſhoprick of Chillmacduagh was united to this ſee in 1602 †.

CLONMACNOIS, or Cluainmacnois, that is the retirement or reſting place of the ſons of the chiefs, on account of its being the cemitery or burying place of a number of the ancient Iriſh chriſtian kings; it is ſituated on a riſing ground on the eaſtern bank of the Shannon, between the confines of the King's county and the county of Weſt Meath, and was anciently denominated Druim Tipraid or Druim Tipraic, that · is the

---

* Harris's Ware, v. 1. p. 135.
† Harris's Ware, v. 1. p. 637. 648.

church of the nobles, or the church in the centre,
it being fuppofed to ftand in the centre of Ireland.
An abbey was founded here in 548 by St. Ki-
aran, which abbey church was converted into a
cathedral, and to which in procefs of time nine
other churches were added by the kings and petty
princes of the country, as places of fepulture;
all erected in one inclofure of about two Irifh
acres. The bifhoprick of Clonmac.iois v. united
to that of Meath in 1568, by authority of parliament. Since which time the churches, epifcopal
palace and other buildings have been fuffered to
decay, being at prefent little better than a heap
of ruins, entombing a number of the fepulchres of the nobility and bifhops, containing infcriptions in the Latin, Hebrew and Irifh languages *.

CLOPOKE, fee Dun-cluin-poiic.

CLOYNE, fee Cluain-vamah.

CLUAINAINEACH, or the bountiful retirement, a church or monaftery in the Queen's
county deftroyed in 939 by Callaghan king of
fouth Munfter. The word is derived from *Cluain, Cloan, Chin* or *Clone*, a fequeftered place, and
aineach or *eineach*, bountiful or liberal †. It was
called alfo Cluain-ednach.

CLUAINIRAIRD, or the retirement on the
weftern height, a religious houfe, deftroyed by
Callaghan in 939. See Clonard.

CLUAINRAMHAD, or the retirement of the
royal heir; near Ennis, built by Donogh Cair-

* Harris's Ware, v. p. 165.
† Collect. No. 4. p. 462.

breach O'Brien prince of Thomond, on being expelled Limerick by the Englifh in 1236 *.

CLUAIN-VAMAH, now Cloyne in the county of Cork. Here a church was erected and a bifhoprick founded by St. Colman, who died on the 4th of November, 604. The bifhoprick of Cluain-vamah, which fignifies the fequeftered cave or habitation, was united to that of Cork in 1430, which union continued until the 11th of November 1638, when George Synge, D. D. was confecrated bifhop of Cloyne. From that time Cloyne has been governed by its own prelates; it is fituated about fifteen miles from Cork †, in the barony of Imokilly.

CLUNES, fee Kilmore.

CNAMHCHOILL, or the eminent wood, now called Knawhill between Cafhell and Sulchoid, and celebrated on account of a victory obtained over the Danes by Brien Boromh in 968 ‡.

COALAN, Caëlan, or Galen, an ancient diftrict in Leinfter, containing the county of Kildare with part of Wicklow and Carlow, being bounded on the eaft by the Wiclow mountains; on the fouth and weft by the river Barrow; and on the north by the Liffey, and part of the bog of Allen. It was called Caëlan or Galen, that is the woody country, being in the early ages almoft one continued wood. The name is yet retained in Kilcullan, corrupted from Kill-coalan or Kill-caëlan. The chiefs of this country were Hy Caëlan or Mc. Kelly, whofe principal refidence was at Rath-aois-Caël, now corruptly called Rathafcul, or the

* Collect. No. 4. p. 593. † Harris's Ware, v. 1. p. 547. ‡ Collect. No. 4. p. 481.

moat of Afcul, about three miles N. E. of Athy. This family of the O'Kelly's is now extinct, at leaſt they are reduced to a very low condition, being in an early period difpoſſeſſed of their property by the Fitz-Geralds, Fitz-Henrys and Keatings.

COENDRUIN, ſee Fiodh-aongufa.

COIGIDUGARIAN, or *Coitidh u ga rian*, that is the kingdom of the woody country in the ſea; the moſt ancient Celtic name of Ireland, but in particular applied to the counties of Fermanagh, Leitrim, Meath, Dublin, Kildare, and the King and Queen's counties, from being in the early ages almoſt covered with immenſe foreſts.

COITEIGH, Scoiteigh, or Scottii, that is woodlanders, from *coit* a wood, whence Scoiteigh or Scottii in the plural, a race dwelling in a woody country. They were the moſt ancient inhabitants of the middle, northern and weſtern parts of Leinſter, aud the Scotti of Richard of Cirenceſter, who thinks they were Britiſh colonies, who retired into this country on the firſt arrival of the Belgic tribes in Britain about 350 years before the Chriſtian æra; for ſome years they rather perambulated than inhabited this iſland; that is until the arrival of ſubſequent colonies, when they were confined to the interior parts and denominated Scots[*]. The Iriſh writers frequently called them Heremonii, and aſſert that the Scots were the deſcendants of Heremon the eldeſt ſon of Mileſius, who ſettled in this country. It is true in the moſt ancient Iriſh poems they are called, *Scottagh ſlioght Heremoneigh clann Melidh*, which the Monks and Bards of the middle and latter ages, not underſtanding the

[*] Richard of Cirenceſter, p. 50.

ancient Celtic tongue, have tranflated the Scots of the race of Heremon one of the fons of Milefius; whereas the true fignification is, *the inhabitants of the woody country of the race of the weftern people.* Bhealgagh was the principal tribe of the Scots in the middle ages, and their country, comprehending the prefent King's County and County of Weft-Meath, has ever born the appellation of Hy Bhealgeigh, Hy Failgii, or Hy Fallan, that is, the country of the Bealgians, or worfhippers of Beal. It appears from O'Flaherty's Ogygia, that Hugony the great was the firft who reigned over the Heremonii in Ireland, about 330 years before Chrift, and from whom all the kings and nobles of Leinfter endeavoured to derive their origin. A circumftance which nearly coincides with the affertion of Richard before fpoken of, relative to the arrival of the Scots in Ireland about the middle of the fourth century before the Chriftian æra. Some years prior to the arrival of St. Patrick, we find the Scots, the ancient inhabitants of Leinfter and firft of the Fir Bolg in Ireland extending their fettlements over all Leinfter, divided into a number of clans or petty ftates, each governed by its own paternal chief, but fubordinate, in fome refpects, to the chief of the head clan refiding at Tara in the county of Meath. Thefe were the Falgii, the Colmanii or Cäelmanii, the Fearmorii, the Teffii, the Slanii, the Debleanii, the Galenii or Caëlenii, the Moedinii, and the Elii fubjecting to their dominion the Cuolanii or Menapii of Ptolemy, and the Morii, the Coriondii of Ptolemy, which fee under their refpective names. They alfo from the middle of the fecond to the beginning of the fifth century made feveral eftablifhments in the other provinces of Munfter, Conaught and Ulfter, among the Momonii, Olnegmachts and Ultonians, and thereby claiming the fovereignty of the whole ifland, which about the fourth century obtained the name of Scotia, and the inhabitants Scots. But the ancient inhabitants of Ireland were principally known to foreigners by the name of Scoti from their pyratical depredations during the middle ages. See Scotii, Heremonii, Bolgæ, Milefians, Falgii, &c. *

COITIDH-U-GA-RIAN, fee Coigidugarian.

COLBDI, or Coulbhdui, that is the projecting corner in the water; now Colp at the mouth of the Boyne. Here St. Patrick landed on his miffion to the ftates of Ireland affembled at Tara. †

COLERAINE, fee Cuilrathen.

COLMAN, an ancient name of Weft Meath; fee Mediolanum.

CONAL-EACHLUATH; fee Ibh Torna Eigeas.

CONAL-GABHRA, or Ua Caonnuill Gabhra, that is the upper divifion of the chief diftrict, now Upper Conello in the fouthern part of the county of Limerick. It was alfo called En Eiragh, or the weftern country; the chiefs of which were the Mac Eneirys, who were difpoffeffed of their country by the earls of Defmond. ‡

CONG, or the chief place, an ancient city and capital of the province of Conaught, fituated between Lough Mafk and Lough Corrib, in the

* Baxter's Gloff. Brit. O'Conor's Differt. Richard of Cirencefter. O'Flaherty. Collectanea, No. 7.
† Harris's Ware, vol. I, p. 13.   ‡ Collect. No. 3, p. 37.

County of Mayo, and Barony of Kilmaine; now an inconfiderable place.

CONMACNE, or the chief race, clan or tribe. A number of the ancient Irifh Septs took this denomination; as the

CONMACNE, a diftrict in the county of Leitrim on the Shannon, called alfo Magh-ra-n'all, or Magh-ra-nBhall, that is the plain of the great or royal worfhippers of Beal; the chiefs of which were corruptly called Magrannals, or Mac Rannals; fome of whom were in the poffeffion of the country in the beginning of the laft century.

CONMACNE-CUILT-OLA, or the chief race of the noble warriors. This diftrict comprehended part of the prefent county of Mayo, the principal refidence of the Olnegmachts, alfo Magh-Nay, the prefent county of Rofcommon. The hereditary chiefs of this diftrict were the Conairs, kings of all Conaught, and whofe principal feat was at Croghan. From Conmacne is derived Conaught the prefent name of the weftern province of Ireland. See Olnegmacht and Magh-Nay.

CONMACNE DE CINEL DUBHAIN, or Conmacne de Dunmore, the chief tribe of the principal diftrict of the dark or woody country, comprehending the north and eaftern parts of the county of Galway, the ancient Galehgh or Hy Caëllagh, the chiefs of which were the Hy Cellaghs or O'Kellys, a number of whom were in poffeffion of the country at the beginning of the laft century; though a great part was occupied by the Englifh fettlers the Birminghams, Burks, and others of that nation *.

CONMACNE DE MOYREIN, or Conmacne de magh rian, that is, the chief tribe of the plain of the kings, fituated in the county of Longford near Lough Ree; the fame as Angalia which fee.

CONMACNE IRA, fee Conmacne-mara.

CONMACNE-MARA, or the chief tribe on the great fea, comprehending the weftern parts of the county of Galway on the fea coaft; it was alfo called Conmacne-Ira or the chief tribe in the weft, and Jar Conaught, that is weft Conaught, likewife Hy Jartagh, or the weftern country; the chiefs of which were denominated Hy Flaherty, or O'Flaherty, that is the chief of the nobles of the weftern country; and contained the prefent baronies of Morogh, Moycullen and Ballinahinch.

CONNAIR, or Connor, that is the chief-place, in the diftrict of Lann-ela or the enclofed plain, an ancient bifhoprick in the county of Down, founded by St. Macnifius in the beginning of the fixth century, and united to that of Down in 1442.

CONNALLA, or lower Connal, in the county of Limerick; it was alfo called Thyhan or the north country; the chiefs of which were the Hy Thyhans or O'Thyhans, called Hy Cinealagh or O'Kinealy and O'Collins; difpoffeffed by the Fitz-Geralds.

CORAN, or Caran, that is, the place of the city; the refidence of the chiefs of Luigney in the county of Sligo.

---

* See Harris's Ware, v. 1. p. 167, for all the Conmacnes.

CORCABHAISCIN, or the morafs of the harbour or bay, from *Corcagh* a morafs, and *Bhaiſin*, a harbour narrow at the entrance; an antient diſtrict round the harbour of Cork, and from whence the preſent city has obtained its name. The Engliſh families ſettled in this country were the Boyles and Barrys *.

CORCAC, a wet plain, marſh or morafs; now the city of Cork.

CORCADUIBHNE, or the marſh near the water, the ſame as Aoibh Liathain, which ſee.

CORCALUIGHE, or *Corc-cael luigh*, that is the woody morafs on the water or lake; an ancient diſtrict in the ſouth part of the county of Cork on the ſea, containing the preſent barony of Carbury, the ancient chiefs of which were called, Magh Cor Teagh, or the chief of the habitation of the morafs, by corruption Mac Carty, by which means they have been confounded with the Mc. Carty's of Kerry. The leſſer diſtricts of this country were Hy Leareigh, Hy Maghoneigh and Hy Driſcuil, under the dominion of their reſpective chiefs, O'Leary, O'Mahony and O'Driſcol, all dynaſts and ſubordinate chiefs to Mac Carty, king of Corcaluighe, who in proceſs of time became the ſovereign of all the petty ſtates in the preſent county of Cork, and was therefore denominated *Mac Carty reagh*, or Mac Carty the king. Some of whoſe deſcendants were in poſſeſſion at the commencement of the laſt century; though the Engliſh families of the Courcies and Barries had eſtates therein †.

---

* Collect. No. 3. p. 378. O'Conor's Ortelius.
† Collect. No. 3. p. 372. O'Conor's Ortelius.

CORCUMRUADH, Corcumroe or Corcumruah, derived from Cor cuim radh, or the marſh on the great Harbour; a diſtrict ſituated on the weſtern coaſt of the county of Clare, in which is the ancient biſhoprick of Fenebore or Kilfenoragh. In 1317 a battle was fought here in which were ſlain Mortogh Garbh, and Teige O'Briens*.

CORIONDIJ, an ancient people of Ireland mentioned by Ptolemy, and thought to be the ancient inhabitants of the preſent county of Wexford. The word is evidently derived from the ancient Britiſh *Corcach* ſhips and *ondii* waves; whence Coriondiü or Coriondos, navigators; the ancient Iriſh frequently called them Corthagh or boatmen, and their country Hy Moragh or the diſtrict of the ſea; and Feſtus Avienus in his deſcription of the Scilly iſles takes notice of the inhabitants of the Britiſh iſles navigating the channel in corraghs or wicker boats covered with ſkins. The antient chiefs of this diſtrict were denominated Hy Morroghs, or O'Morroghs, and in the latter ages Mac Morroghs. They were the chiefs of Hy Kinſelagh, a large diſtrict containing the greater part of ſouth Leinſter, being an union of the ancient Septs of Hy Morragh, Hy Cabhanagh, Hy-Drone Cuala, Hy Moradh, Oſſeraigii and Hy Breoghain Gabhran; conſiſting of the preſent counties of Wexford, Wicklow and Carlow, with the north part of the county of Kilkenny and Tipperary and the ſouth of the Queen's county. In the Iriſh hiſtory we find the Mc. Morroghs frequently ſtiled kings of Leinſter; and to them the Engliſh are indebted for

---

* Collect. No. 4. Ware.

their firſt eſtabliſhment in this country. A branch of them alſo ſettled in Hy Cabhanagh, (the barony of Idrone in the county of Carlow,) and who took the name of that diſtrict, ſome of whom are yet remaining and poſſeſſed of conſiderable property in that country. *

CORTHÆ, the capital of the Coriandii, or Morogh, now Innis-Corthy in the county of Wexford. This place has been miſtaken for Carmen in the county of Kildare.

CRIOCH-CUOLAN, ſee Cuolan.

CRIOCH-FUINIDH, ſee Eirion.

CROAGH-PATRICK, ſee Cruachan-Achuil.

CROGHAN, or the place of the hill. A royal reſidence, and the capital of Conaught : the ſame as Atha, which ſee

CROIGHAN, ſee Hy Falgia.

CROM, an ancient diſtrict in the County of Kildare, and part of the County of Dublin, being ſituated in the bend of the river Liffey, from whence it was called Magh Labhia, and *Ibb crom abb*, or the diſtrict on the crooked water, and the hereditary chiefs were denominated, *Crom abb Ibb* or chief of the diſtrict on the crooked water, corruptly written *Crom a bboe*. In the early ages this diſtrict extended over the greater part of Hy Allain, and after the arrival of the Engliſh, fell to the ſhare of Hugh de Lacey and Gilbert de Borard : but ſome time after came into the poſſeſſion of the noble family of the Fitzgeralds, in whoſe hands it ſtill remains. This family on obtaining the above property, obtained among the native inhabitants

* Baxter's Gloſſ. Brit,

the original title of *Crom a bboe*, or chiefs of the diſtrict on the crooked water; a title ſtill retained as
a motto to their arms, and in former ages was the
war-cry of the Sept, according to the cuſtom of the
old Iriſh clans.*

CROMLA or Crommal, a mountain or hill between Lough Foyle and Lough Swilly. From
the eaſtern ſide of this mountain proceeded the
river Lubar, called by the Iriſh Bredagh; and from
the weſtern, the Lavath, near the ſource of which
on the declivity of the mountain was the cave of
Cluna, where reſided Ferad Artho, and the bard
Condan, after the murder of Cormac Mc. Art, his
nephew. During the middle ages, we find it denominated Cruachan Achuil, or Mount Eagle. It
ſeems to have obtained the name of Mount Cromla
or Crommal, that is the mountain of Fate or
Deſtiny, from having an altar or cave, dedicated to
Fate or Providence, called by the ancient inhabitants
of theſe iſlands, *Crom*; whence *Cromla*, a place of
worſhip, and *Crommal* a place of deſtiny. In the
neighbourhood of Cromla, ſtood the rath or fortreſs
of Tura, called by the Iriſh writers Ailich Neid,
celebrated by all the ancient Iriſh hiſtories, as the
principal reſidence of the northern kings of Ulſter.
See Tura, Moilena, Leana Loch and Aileach. †

CROMLA SLIABH, a mountain in the diſtrict
of Crom, now the hill of Allain in the county of
Kildare.

CROM-LECH, or the ſtone of devotion, from
Crom to bow down or worſhip, and *Lech* a ſtone.
A name given at this day to a ſpecies of Druidic

* Ware's Ant. Lodge's Peerage, vol. 1.
† O'Conor's Diſſert. p. 96.

altars, ftill remaining in different parts of the kingdom, confifting generally of an inclined rock ftone,
fupported by feveral upright ones, thereby forming
a room or apartment, in which the Druids attending
the fervice of the altar, generally refided ; on which
account they were alfo denominated *Both-all*, or *houfe*
of *God*, and were nearly of the fame conftruction with
thofe erected by Abraham and the patriarchs mentioned by Mofes, and called *Bethel*, which in the Hebrew language is of the fame fignification as *Bothal* in
Irifh.   Thefe altars were dedicated to the fupreme
Being or firft caufe, called frequently *Crom-al*, or the
all-powerful Being ; and erected either on plains, or
on eminences in the centre of dark and thick woods.
The victims facrificed on them were deer and oxen,
whence on many of them canals are cut in the
ftone into which the blood flowed at the time of
facrifice, in order that divinations might be taken
therefrom.   There was no ftated period for the
facrifice offered to Crom ; but when any perfon
was willing to confult Fate or Providence relative
to the future events of his own affairs, either in war
or the chace, he brought the victim to the Druid,
who from the ftate of the entrails and flowing of
the blood, drew prefages relative to the fuccefs or
failure of the enterprize.   After the eftablifhment
of Polytheifm among the Celtic nations, little adoration was paid to the fupreme Being.   Confucius
is faid to have been the firft who reftored it amongft
the eaftern people, and according to the Irifh antiquaries, it was introduced into this ifland by Tighernas about 260 years before the Chriftian æra ; but
was violently oppofed by the Druids, who favoured
the doctrine of Polytheifm ; whence Tighernas and

his followers and reported to have been deftroyed during the time of facrifice at *Magh Sleuchta* in the county of Leitrim. The worfhip of the true God however from this period gained ground in Ireland, but was not univerfal until about the middle of the third century, when Cormac king of north Leinfter openly declared in favour of the unity of the Deity and condemned all degrees of Polytheifm. A circumftance which greatly contributed to the introduction of Chriftianity fome ages after.

Several of the altars of Crom are yet remaining, nearly intire, in feveral parts of the kingdom, particularly at Tobin and Brown's towns in the county of Carlow, and near Dundalk in the county of Louth *.

CRUACHAN, the fame as Croghan and Atha.

CRUACHAN-ACHUIL, or Mount Eagle, an high mountain in the barony of Morifk and and county of Mayo. Here St. Patrick in imitation of Chrift fafted during lent; from whence this mountain has obtained the name of Croagh Patrick.

CUAN-LEARGI, or the port on the fea, from Cuan a port or harbour, and Lear the fea; the ancient name of the city of Waterford, the Brigantia of Richard; corruptly called by feveral modern writers, Port Largi †.

CUILRATHEN, now Colerain, a town fituated on the river Bann in the county of Antrim. Cuilrathen has been tranflated the corner of ferns,

* Keating, Collectanea, No. 5.
† Baxter's Glof. Brit. O'Halloran's introd.

but it is evidently derived from *Cuil rath ean*, that is, the *corner of the fort on the water*, or rather according to the Irish idiom, the *fort on the corner of the water*. It probably was the fame as Rath-mor-muighe-line, the royal feat of the kings of Dalnaruidhe, and the Rhobogdii of Ptolemy [*].

CUOLAN, or Crioch Cuolan, that is the diftrict of the corner, being that narrow plain in the county of Wicklow contained between the mountains and the fea; the people were the Evoleni of Probus, the Menapij of Ptolemy. This country was under the dominion of the Mac Mhthuils, or O'Tools, and is frequently confounded by antiquaries with Coalan or Caëlan; it is true thefe two countries were often governed by the fame chief, that is, either the O'Tools or Mc. Kellys; which probably occafioned the error.

D.

DAIBRE, or Daobh-eragh, or Ibheragh, that is the weftern country on the water; the prefent barony of Iveragh in the county of Kerry, and the fame as Ciaruidhe, which fee [†].

DAIMLEAGH, fee Domleagh.

DAIR-CALGAIC, or Dair Coilleagh, that is the woody country of Oaks, comprehending the prefent town and county of Derry, and part of the county of Donegal, being fituated on both fides of Lough Foyle; it was the Darnij of Ptolemy. The ancient chieftains of this diftrict were called Hy Daher-teagh, that is the chief of the habitation

[*] Harris's Ware, v. 1. p. 19. Collect. No. 4. 522.
[†] Collect. No. 4.

of oaks, by corruption O'Dogherty. They were difpoffeffed of the fouthern parts of their country in an early period by the O'Donalls, chiefs of Duneir Gall, and the O'Conars.

DAIRINNE, the fame as Corcaluighe and Dergtenij, which fee.

DAL, a word evidently derived from Ttalamh, pronounced Dalla, the earth; whence Dal a divifion of the earth, a diftrict. Wherefore this word added to a name of a country fignifies a diftrict; but before the proper name of a perfon it is to be underftood a race or tribe, efpecially when fuch names have been derived from a country.

DALARADIA, or the diftrict of the eaftern country next the fea. From *Dal ar adbui*, that is *Dal*, a diftrict, *ar*, *oir*, eaftern and *abb üi* the watery country. This diftrict coprehended the fouth and S. E. parts of the county of Antrim, and all the county of Down, during the middle ages; called alfo frequently Magh Genuifge, or the diftrict of the bays, or heads of lakes; having the bays of Carlingford and Dundrum on the fouth; Strangford and Carricfergus on the eaft, and Lough Neach on the N. W. The principal chiefs of which were the Mac Gennis, fome of whom were in poffeffion of this country, the Damonij of Ptolemy, in the beginning of the laft century, but a branch of the O'Neils had taken poffeffion of the northern parts in a very early period. It was divided into the leffer diftricts of Ibh Each, or Ullagh, Dal dichu, Dal arida, and Hy huanan; which fee under the refpective words *.

---

* Harris's Ware, v. 1. p. 8. O'Conor's Ortelius.

DAL-ARIDA, from Dal-ardobha, or Dal ard-aubha, that is the high diſtrict on the water, now the Ards or highlands in the county of Down, between the bay of Strangford and the ſea. The ancient chiefs of this diſtrict were called Magh Ardan, by corruption Mac Artan, that is, the chief of the high country; and were diſpoſſeſſed by the Savages; Some of them remained in poſſeſſion of the weſtern parts at the commencement of the laſt century *.

DAL-CAS, or Dal Gaes, that is the diſtrict on the ſea. An ancient diſtrict, containing all Thomond, the preſent county of Clare. The principal chiefs of this diſtrict were called Magh Gaes, or Mac Cas. A ſon of Olliol Olim about the beginning of the third century was elected chief of this diſtrict, on which he took the name of Cormac Cas, and greatly diſtinguiſhed himſelf by his military abilities. From him the ſucceeding chiefs of Dal-Cas endeavoured to derive their origin. However this may be, it appears from the Iriſh annals, that the chiefs of the ſubordinate diſtricts, were frequently choſen kings of Dal-cas, until the ſovereignty came into the hands of Brien Boromh, hereditary chief of Hy Loch-lean, now Burrin; whoſe deſcendants enjoyed that dignity, until the arrival of the Engliſh, when the de Clares obtained a grant of the entire country; which from them, has ſince obtained the denomination of Clare. Dal-cas was originally inhabited by a colony of the ſecond migration of the Fir Bolgæ, called Momonii, whence it obtained the name of Tuath

---

* Harris's Ware, v. 1.

Mumhan or north Munſter, by corruption Thomond. See Mumhan, Thomond and Clare *.

DAL-DICHU, or Dal-decha, that is, the diſtrict between the mouth of the waters or bays;
from *Dech* or *Tech* an opening, and *ui* waters; being ſituated in the plain and peninſula between
the bays of Dundrum and Strangford, called alſo
Magh-innis or the iſland of the plain, and more
anciently Leth-Cathel, or the plain of the wood;
now the barony of Lecale in the county of Down.
The chiefs or dynaſts of this diſtrict were called
Dal-dichu, or Cathel, ſubject to the Magh Gen-
nuiſge. This country is remarkable from its chief
Dichu, being the firſt convert St. Patrick made to
the chriſtian faith in the north of Ireland †.

DAL-GAES, ſee Dal-cas.

DAL-LEAGH-NUI, ſee Eile-ui-chearbhuil.

DALMACHSCOEB, from Dal machſc oabh, or
the diſtrict of the race on the water; containing
all the country on the eaſtern coaſt of the counties
of Wicklow and Wexford between the mountains
and the ſea ‡.

DAL-MOGRUITH, ſee Fermuighe.

DAL-NARUIDHE, or the diſtrict of the country
on the water; containing the north part of the
county of Antrim and the Robogdij of Ptolemy.
It has been corruptly called Dalriadia, and ſometimes Ara or the eaſtern country. During the latter ages it frequently went by the denomination of
An-druim, or Ean-druim that is the habitation on
the waters; from whence the preſent name of
Antrim. It was divided into ſeveral ſubordinate

* Collect. No. 4, † Harris's Ware, v. 1. p. 12. ‡ Ware.

divifions, the principal of which were Magh-cuilan, Hy-ara, Magh-dun-el and Hy-fiol, whofe refpective chiefs were Magh-cuillan, O'Hara, O'Don-
nal and O'Shiel, feveral of whom were in poffeffion of the country in the laft century. From this
part feveral great colonies tranfmigrated to Caledonia about the year 503. They were principally
of the race of the Scots from Hy Failgia who fettled
in the northern parts of this country, about the
commencement of the fifth century, under the
conduct of Hy nFail or O'Neal the great. In confequence of which they were denominated Scots,
and have thereby communicated their name to
the entire north diftrict of Britain*. See Rhobogdii.

DALRIADIA, fee Dalnaruidhe.

DAM-LECH, that is the houfe of ftone, a general name amongft the old chriftian Irifh for their
churches when conftructed of lime and ftone, to
diftinguifh them from thofe of timber and wattles, efpecially thofe with ftone roofs. For the
ancient churches of Ireland, particularly thofe erected from the beginning of the eighth to the clofe of
the eleventh century, are in a different ftile of architecture from any at this day to be found either
in Britain or the weftern parts of Europe; and are
evidently built in imitation of the original chriftian
churches, in the fouthern countries, taken from the
ancient heathen temples of the Greeks and Romans; and probably were introduced into this
ifland by the Greek and Roman clergy who retired
from their native countries on the arrival of the

* Collect. No. 4. O'Flaherty. O'Conor's Differt. Baxter's
Gloff. Brit. Harris's Ware, v. 1.

Goths and Vandals into the Roman empire. Thefe churches now remaining in Ireland, fuch as Cormac's chapel, the churches of Glendalogh, St. Dulach's church, and the monaftery of Monainfheigh, are all remarkably fmall, feldom exceeding forty feet in length and twenty in breadth, being covered with circular ftone arches under ftone pediment roofs of the true Gothic pitch; and the walls and arches frequently ornamented with columns and pilafters in rude imitation of the Corinthian and Doric orders. They are however in refpect to tafte far fuperior to any erected during the beginning of the latter ages, when the Gothic method of building was introduced from Britain. See Domleagh.

DAMNIJ, an ancient people of Ireland, mentioned by Ptolemy, the inhabitants of the prefent county of Down. The word is evidently derived from the ancient Britifh, Davon or Daun, a river or bay, whence Daunij, Dunij, &c. the country of rivers or lakes, &c. In which fenfe it anfwers to the Irifh denomination of that country Magh Gennuifg. This word being corruptly written in fome of the copies of Ptolemy, Damnonioi, has given rife to the conjectures that the Damnij of Ptolemy was derived from Dunum the prefent city of Down.

DAMNONIJ, or Damhnonij of the Irifh writers, a people inhabiting the ancient diftrict of Hy-moruifge, now the barony of Morifk in the county of Mayo. The word feems to be a corruption from the old Celtic and Cimbric Britifh *Dyvneint* or *Duvnon*, deep water; whence Duvnonij, Dabhnonij or Damhnonij, by corruption Damnonij, a people living on the deep water or fea. See Hy-moruifge, and Auterij *.

DAR, fee Darg.

DARABONIS, a bay or river in the north of Ireland mentioned by Richard of Cirencefter, and placed by him in Lough Foyle. Darabonis is evidently derived from *Dair abbon üis*, that is the lympid river of the oaken grove. It was the Lugbheabhail of the ancient Irifh, now Lough Foyle.

DARG, Dar, Dare, a dark place, a hollow cave or habitation.

DARINIS, an ifland at the mouth of the bay of Youghall, it fignifies the habitation in the ifland; a monaftery was founded here by St. Molanfid, in the fixth century †.

DARINIS, another ifland near Wexford; a monaftery was founded here by St. Nemamb, about the middle of the feventh century.

DARNIJ, the ancient inhabitants of the county. of Derry, mentioned by Ptolemy, the word fignifies the inhabitants of the oaken groves, from Dair an oak, and is of the fame import as Dair-calgaic, which fee.

DEALBHNA, the prefent barony of Delvin, in the county of Weftmeath ‡. There were feven territories of this name in Ireland.

DEALBNA-MOR, the country of the O'Finallans, afterwards of the Nugents.

DEALBNA-BEG, the country of the O'Maelchallains, contiguous to the former, thefe two

---

* Q'Conor's Differt. p. 179. † Harris's Ware, v. 1. p. 176. ‡ Colleft. N°. 4.

make the prefent barony of Delvin in the county of Weftmeath.

DEALBNA-EATHRA, Mc. Coghlan's country, the barony of Garrycaftle in the King's county.

DEALBHNA-IARTHAR, alfo called Dealbhna-teanmoy, O'Scoluigh's country, in the antient territory of Meath.

DEALBHNA-NUADHAT, the prefent baronies of Athlone and Moycarne in the County Rofcommon.

DEALBHNA DE CUILFEABHAIR, in the County of Galway.

DEALBHNA-FEADHA, between Lough Curb and Lough Lurgan in Tirdaloch; the prefent barony of Moycullen in the County of Galway; it was divided into two diftricts, Gno-more and Gno-beag; the O'Conrys were chiefs of Gno-beg until they were partly difpoffed and partly made tributaries by the O'Flahertys.

DEAS MUMHAN, fee Defmond.

DEASSIES, or fouthern people, a territory containing the greater part of the county of Waterford, and is the prefent barony of the Decies. According to fome Irifh chronicles, the Deaffies were a colony from a people of that name inhabiting the fouth parts of the county of Meath, near the county of Dublin; and were expelled that country by Cormac Ulfadha, or Cormac Mc. Art, about the year 278.*

DEASSII, or fouthern people, a people inhabiting in ancient times, a diftrict in the fouthern parts of the county of Eaft Meath, on the northern

* Harris's Ware, vol. 1. p. 490.

banks of the Liffey and Rye rivers, called Ean, or Magh-ean, that is the country on the water; the chieftains of which were called Magh-ean, or Ean-gus, that is, the chief or commander of the diftrict of Ean; corruptly written Æengus. A chief of this diftrict, about the year 278, having rebelled againft Cormac Mc. Art king of Meath and Ta- ragh, entered the royal palace, and flew the king's fon Kellach. On which Cormac raifed an army, fuppreffed the rebellion, aud drove Eangus out of Meath, who with feveral of the Deafii fettled in the county of Waterford, which bears their name to this day.*

DEGADES, a colony of the Scots of Leinfter, who fettled in the weft of the county of Kerry fome years before the eftablifhment of Chriftianity. The word feems to be derived from *De ga deas*, that is the diftrict on the fouth fea. †

DERG, or Derg-abhan, that is the river of the woody morafs; a river rifing out of a lake of that name in the barony of Tyrhugh in the county of Donegal, from whence joining feveral other rivers, as the Mourne and Finny, it falls into Lough Foyle at Derry. The lake from whence this river rifes, is famous for having in it the ifland that con- tains St. Patrick's purgatory. ‡

DERGTENII, or *Derg-teachneagh*, that is the habitation of the woody morafs; a diftrict com- prehending all the fouthern coafts of the county of Cork, including the ancient diftricts of Corca- duibhne, Corcabhaifin and Corcaluighne, being the Vodie of Ptolemy.§

*. Smith's Waterford.   † O'Conor's Differt.
‡ Harris's Ware, vol. 1. p. 286.   § O'Conor's Differt.

DESMOND, or Deaf-mumhan, that is South Munster; a diftrict which during the latter ages contained the counties of Cork and Kerry. After the arrival of the Englifh, it gave title of earl to the family of the Fitzgeralds. Its ancient kings were the Mac Cairthachs, or Mac Carthys, hereditary chiefs of Corcaluighe.

DEVA, a river mentioned by Richard to be in the eaftern parts of Ireland. Deva is derived from the Britifh *Dubb-ui*, deep or black water, and is the bay of Carlingford.

DIN, fee Dun.

DINROY, or rather Dun-riogh, that is the Dun or Fort of the king; a royal refidence of the chiefs of Corcaluighe near Rofs Carbury. *

DOMLEAGH, or Daimleag and Damleag, that is the houfe of ftone, now called Duleek in the county of Eaft Meath. This place is celebrated for having in it the firft ftone church in Ireland, built by St. Kenan, in the fourth century. Which church the head of a bifhoprick for feveral ages, was frequently plundered by the Danes, efpecially in 830, 878, 1023, 1037, 1149 and 1171, and twice burned, that is in 1059 and 1169. The bifhoprick of Domleagh was united to that of Meath in the thirteenth century †. See Damlech.

DOMNACH-BILE, or the church of Bile, fituated in Magh-bile in Inis-owen on the N. W. of Lough Foyle. This church was founded by Saint Patrick, where in after ages was erected a monaftery.

---

* O'Conor's Differt. p. 179.   † Harris's Ware, vol. 1. p. 138.

DOMNACH MOR MAGH EAN, or the great church of the plain of the water. A church founded by Saint Patrick, in a plain on the north of Lough Ern.*

DONUM, or Dunum, an ancient city mentioned by Ptolemy, and thought by Cambden and some others to be the present city of Down, from the dun or fort near it, and formerly the residence of the chieftains of that country; but a number of the ancient Irish raths or castles were named Dons, Duns and Dins. See Dunum.

DRIM, see Druim.

DROM, see Druim.

DROMORE, or as it was anciently denominated Dromarragh, that is, the church or habitation in the maritime country. A bishoprick in the barony of Iveagh and county of Down, founded in the sixth century by St. Colman, in the ancient district called Mochmarragh. †

DRUIM, Drum, Drom, Drim, Truim and Trim, in the ancient Irish signifies a conical hill with a cave, a hollow dome, a house or habitation; figuratively a church or any building the sides and roof of which slope in the manner of a dome.

DRUIM-CLIABH, or the church of Hurdles, on account of being constructed of wicker work, and at present called Drumclive. In this place St. Patrick founded a church and bishoprick, though it is now only a village in the barony of Carbury, and county of Sligo, about three miles north of the town of Sligo. ‡

---

* Harris's Ware, vol. 1. p. 18.   † Ibid. vol. 1.
‡ Ibid. vol. 1. p. 18.

DRUIM-SAILEC, or the church built with willows. The ancient name of the cathedral of Ardmagh, being originally, as moſt of the primitive churches of Ireland were, conſtructed with wattles or willows wrought in the manner of wicker-work *.

DRUM, ſee Druim.

DRUM-DRUID, a ſacred cave of the Druids near the royal rath of Croghan, dedicated to Crom or Providence ‡.

DUBANA, a river in the ſouth of Ireland mentioned by Richard of Cirenceſter. The word is evidently a corruption of *Dubb-eana*, or the black or deep water. It is the river Lee which falls into Cork harbour.

DUBH, black, and when applied to water, as rivers, lakes and bays, generally ſignifies deep; by reaſon that deep waters are in general of a dark colour. Dubh was alſo frequently applied to ſuch rivers as ran through bogs and moraſſes; and to the waters of the ſea.

DUBH-ULA, or Duth-ula, that is the dark ruſhing water. A river in Conaught.

DUBLANA, one of the ancient names of Dublin, called by Ptolemy, *Eblana*. Dublana, whence Dublinum and Dublin, is evidently derived from *Dubb-leana*, or the place of the black harbour or lake, or rather the lake of the ſea, the bay of Dublin being frequently ſo called. (See Bally-Lean-Cliath or Lean-Cliath)

DUBRONA, a river in the ſouth of Ireland, mentioned by Richard, and called by Ptolemy *Dabrona*. *Dubrona*, corruptly Dabrona, is evident-

---

* Harris's Ware, v. 1. p. 1.　‡ O'Conor's Diſſert. p. 179

ly derived from *Dubb ro æna*, or the great black water, called by the Irish Dubh-abhan-mor, and by the English at this day the Black water; it falls into the bay of Youghall. It was also called frequently *Nemb Abban* or the divine River and Süidifman or the river of fouth Munster.

DULEEK, fee Domleagh.

DUN, *Don, Din*. An ifolated hill or rock, an artificial mount or hill furrounded by a ditch, whereon the ancient chiefs erected their habitations. An elevated place, or any habitation on a hill or mount.

DUN-CLUIN-POIIC, or the Dun in the fequeftered corner, now vulgarly called the dun of Clopoke, in the Queen's County about four miles fouth of Stradbally. It was a fort or caftle of a branch of the family of O'More's, ancient chieftains of Leix. It confifts of an ifolated rock in which are fome natural caves; on the top is a plain formerly furrounded by a wall compofed of rock ftones without cement, with a grand entrance from the fouth. There doth not appear ever to have been any building of lime and ftone erected on this dun, but the feveral edifices were conftructed intirely in the ancient Irish ftile. That it was an habitation fome years before the eftablifhment of chriftianity in this ifle is extremely probable, as in an adjacent field is an ancient tomb with an infcription in Druidic characters, fignifying Hy Mordha, the great king.

DUN-CRUTHAIN, or *Dun-Croich-ean*, that is the caftle of the diftrict of the water, and the refidence of O'Gahan chief of *Hy-gahan*, or the diftrict of the fea, containing the northern part of the barony of Colerain in the county of Derry. Here St. Patrick founded a church *.

DUN-DALEATHGLASS, or the dun or fortress of the separated district of the sacred place, a rath near Bangor in the county of Down, where during the middle ages a school or university was kept, but it was destroyed by the Danes in 837. The ruins of this university are still visible in the rath of Donaghadee †.

DUN-KERMNA, or the dun of the rock. A fortress of the chiefs of Corcaluidhe §, where Kinfale now stands.

DUN-MOGHDHAIRNE, or the fortress of the pleasant plain, destroyed by Conor O'Brien, 1133 ‡.

DUN-MORE, that is the shady hill or fortress. It was the residence of the ancient chiefs of Galeng or Conmacne de Cinel-dudhain, and a royal seat of the O'Kelly's. It was destroyed in 1133 by Conor O'Brien ‖.

DUN-NA-MAES, or the fort or dun of the plain. An isolated rock near Maryborough in the Queen's county, originally the royal residence of Laoisach Hy Moradh, or the honourable O'More, hereditary chieftain of the ancient district of *Ibb Laoishheach ni Mordha,* or *Eli by Mora,* in the latter ages denominated Léix in the Queen's county. Dunnamaes is said to have been made a fortress by Laigseach about the beginning of the third century, from which time it not only continued the paternal residence of the chiefs of this district,

---

* Harris's Ware, v. 1. p. 18.   † Keating.
§ O'Conor's Dissertat.   ‡ Collect. No. 4. p. 566.
‖ O'Conor's Dissertat.

but on their connection with the Mc. Morroghs
chieftains of Hy Morragh, was esteemed one of
the royal fortresses of Hy Kinselagh, and frequently was one of the seats of the kings of Leinster.
On the arrival of the English it was in the possession of Dermot Mac Morrogh maol Mordha,
chief of Hy Kinselagh and king of Leinster. This
prince marrying his daughter Eva to Strongbow
earl of Pembroke, it fell into the possession of that
nobleman; whose only daughter Isabel, espousing
William Marshal earl of Pembroke, Dunnamaes
with the adjacent territory came into the possession
of the said earl who erected it into a county palatine and built on the Dun about the year 1216 an
elegant castle. In 1325 it was taken by Lysagh
O'More, the ancient proprietor of this country,
from which time it was alternately in the possession
of the Irish and English families until the year
1650, when it was taken from the O'Mores by
the colonels Heuson and Reynolds, and blown up
and effectually destroyed. The only remains of
this ancient castle and Fortress are some of the
walls and gates which are yet venerable in their
ruins *.

DUN-RIOGH, see Dinroy.

DUN-SGINNE, see Lismore.

DUN-SHAGHLIN, see Domach Schachlin.

DUN-SOBARKY, or *Dun sobharchiegh*, that is
the impregnable fortress, from *Dun* a fortress, and
sobhar strong or powerful. It is now called Carricfergus or Knockfergus, that is the rock, hill or
fort of the general, to which also its ancient name

* Ware. Collect. No. 6. p. 147.

may be tranflated, *fofar* or *obbar*, fignifying valiant.

DUNUM, an ancient city or fortrefs in the north of Ireland, mentioned by Ptolemy, and called by the Irifh writers *Dunedb* and *Rath-keltar*; it was fituated near Downpatrick. See Donum and Rath-keltar.

DUNUM, a city and capital of the Menapii mentioned by Ptolemy; it was the feat of the chiefs of Cuolan, and called by the Irifh Rath-druim. It is ftill remaining and gives name to the adjacent town of Rathdrum in the county of Wicklow.

DUR, or the water, an ancient river in the S. W. of Ireland mentioned by Ptolemy, and thought, by Ware and Camden, to be the bay of Dingle.

DUTHULA, fee Dubh-ula.

E.

EADHNA, or *Eoghna* from *Adh anagh*, pronounced oona, viz. the divinity of the country. One of the principal deities of the pagan inhabitants of Ireland, being the fame as *Tlachgo* or the earth and univerfal nature, whofe fanctuaries were the fepulchres of the ancient heroes. The affemblies appertaining to this mode of worfhip were frequently denominated *Teaghan Eadbna*, or the affemblies of the paternal divinity, whence *Eadbna* now pronounced *Eana* came in the modern Irifh to fignify an affembly or fair in general. The word became likewife a proper name, and was ufed by the ancient noblefle as an honourable mark of diſtinction, eſpecially when applied to the fair ſex, it was of the ſame import as *my lady* in Engliſh ; it being cuſtomary amongſt the old Iriſh to adopt the names of their divinities as honourable titles. Even at this day it is retained for a chriſtian name amongſt the country women, and is generally tranſlated into Engliſh by the word Honour. *Eadbna* when uſed as the name of the genius of the earth, was conſtantly of the feminine gender, and the ſame as the Greek *Ceres, Cybele, Pallas* and *Diana,* the Italian *Ops,* the Egyptian *Iſis,* the Syrian *Aſtarte,* the Phœnician *Mogbum,* the Britiſh *Adraſte* or *Andate,* and the Saxon *Eoſter* ; ſhe was alſo denominated by the Iriſh *Tlacbt, Momo* and *Mbumban.* See the words Tlachgo and Mhumhan.

EAMHAIN, or Eamania, derived from *aembuim ui,* that is, the potent or noble place or city ; an ancient royal reſidence, and capital of Ulſter, ſituated near Ardmagh. It is ſaid to have been originally founded by one of the Scotiſh chiefs near two hundred years before the Chriſtian æra, and was deſtroyed by Caibre Liffecar a prince of Conaught, at the beginning of the fourth century. Colgan ſays there were ſome ruins of it remaining in his time, probably the rath in which the royal palace called Croave-roigh, was erected [*].

EAN, ſee Deaſſii.

EANDRUIM, ſee Dalnaruidhe.

EASROA, anciently *Eaſaodruaid,* or the noble cataract, a great waterfall on the river Ern famous for Salmon [†].

EBLANA, ſee Deblana,

---

[*] O'Conor's Diſſert. p. 176.   [†] Harris's Ware, v. p. 18.

EBLANIJ, a people in the eaſt of Ireland, mentioned by Ptolemy, and written in ſome copies of that ancient geographer Blanii. The word is evidently derived from *Aobb* or *Ebb*, a diſtrict, and *Lean*, the bay of the ſea, whence the diſtrict on the bay of the ſea. The ancient inhabitants of the county of Dublin, near the bay of that name.

EBLINII, from Aobh, or Ebhleaneigh, the inhabitants on the waters of the ſea; mentioned by ſeveral of the Iriſh antiquaries as being in Munſter, probably the preſent county of Limerick. Though the word may alſo be derived from *Ebblùin*, or the diſtrict of the inland country *.

EDRI, the ſame with Adros, which ſee.

EILE, or Hy-Leagh, that is the diſtrict of the level county. Comprehending the ſouth part of the King's county, the weſtern part of the Queen's county, and the northern part of the county of Tipperary; divided into three principalities, each governed by its paternal chief; as:

EILE UI BHOG AR TEAGH, or the level diſtrict of the race of the boggy country, compehending the plain and moraſſes north of Caſhel; the chiefs of which were called Hy Bhogarteagh, by corruption O'Fogarty. The Engliſh families of Butler, Purcel and Mathew were ſettled in this country before the beginning of the laſt century.

EILE UI CHEARBHUIL, ſituated in the ſouth of the King's county, and weſt of Sliabh-Bladhma mountains; whence it obtained the name of Ele ui Chearbhuil, or the plain diſtrict near the

* O'Conor's Diſſert.

rock. The chiefs of this diftrict were called O'Carrol, under whom was a fubordinate Dynaft named
O'Delany, prefiding over a diftrict in the fouth
denominated *Dal Leagh n'ui*, or the diftrict of the
flat country *.

EILE UI MORDHA, or Eile ui Mora, that is
the diftrict of the plain in the fhady or woody
country; comprehending the greater part of the
prefent Queen's county, and diftinguifhed in the
latter ages by the name of Leix. It was bounded
on the north and eaft by the river Barrow; on the
weft by Sliabh-Bladhma mountains, and on the
fouth by the river Nore and Sliabh-marragagh
mountains. The hereditary chiefs were called Hy
Mordha, or O'More, and fometimes Moal Mordha.
They were the chief tribe of all the Eilys, and
defcended from the Laighfeachs, ancient chieftains
of Hy Leagh, which fee under that name. In confequence of this feniority, they were frequently
ftiled king's of Leinfter. The O'Mores remained
in the poffeffion of the greater part of their country until the commencement of the laft century,
when being in rebellion, the lands were forfeited
and diftributed amongft the Englifh adventurers †.

EIRCAEL, or Eargal, that is the weftern
Caël or woodlanders; a large diftrict in the weft
of Ulfter, comprehending the prefent counties of
Fermanagh and Donegal ‡.

EIROIN, or Erin, that is weftern ifland.
The invariable name of Ireland amongft the original inhabitants from the remoteft periods. The

* Collect. No. 3. p. 376.
† Collect. No. 3, 4, and 6. Harris's Ware v. 1.
‡ Harris's Ware, v. 1.

poets and hiftorians indeed frequently made ufe of feveral other appellations, arifing from latent circumftances ; as *Ere* and *Crioch-fuinidh*, or weftern country ; *Fiodh-Innis*, or the woody ifland ; *Innis-Elga*, or the noble ifland ; *Teach-Tuathail*, or the dark habitation ; arifing from its thick and immenfe forefts. *Inis Banba*, or the ifland of the herds of fwine ; this country in the early periods being ever celebrated for containing great herds of thofe animals ; and *Innis Bheal*, or *Innis Fail*, that is the ifland of Beal. But the body of the people conftantly denominated it Eiroin, or the weftern ifland, and themfelves *Erenach*, or weftern people. The Britons called Ireland *Ydberdan*, or the country beyond the weftern water ; the Greeks called it *Overnia*, or the moft weftern country ; whence the Latins *Hibernia* of the fame import, from *Bernia*, and *Hypper-ernia*, or the moft weftern Ifland. It was alfo denominated *Irelond*, or weftern land by the Anglo-Saxons *.

EISGIR-RIADA, fee Legh Mogh.

ELI HY MORA, now called Leix, fee Eile ui Mordha.

EMLEY, fee Imleach-jobhuir.

ENACHDUNE, or *Eoghnach-dun*, that is the dun or fortrefs of the diftrict, or the chief fortrefs. A royal refidence near Tuam, the fame as *Dun-more*, which fee.

EN-EIRAGH, fee Conal-Gabhra.

EOGANACHT AINE CLIACH, fee Aine Cliach.

ERDINIJ, a people inhabiting the weftern parts of Ulfter ; mentioned by Ptolemy, and called by

* Q'Conor's. Differt.

Richard of Cirencefter Hardinij. Erdinij is deriv-ed from *Eir dunedb*, that is, the inhabitants of the weftern hilly country, comprehending the fouth parts of the county of Donegall and county of Fer-managh. See Ernai and Rheba.

ERE, fee Eiroin.

ERENACH, fee Eiroin.

ERGAL, fee Eircael and alfo Vennicnii.

ERIN, fee Eiroin.

ERNAI, or weftern People, a name given by the Irifh Antiquaries to the ancient inhabitants of the county of Fermanagh near Lough Ern, they were the Erdinii of Ptolemy *.

EUGENIANS, or the maritime people; the ancient inhabitants of the S. W. of Ireland on the coafts of the counties of Cork and Kerry; and fometimes taken in an enlarged fenfe to fignify the inhabitants of all Defmond or fouth Munfter.

EVOLENI, derived from *Aobh leaneigh*, or the diftrict of the waters of the fea, an ancient diftrict mentioned by Probus, fituated on the eaftern coaft of the county of Wicklow; the Coulan of the Irifh, which fee.

EURRUS, a people mentioned by Irifh antiqua-ries to inhabit the weftern parts of Conaught. The word is evidently a corruption from *Eir-uïs*, or the weftern diftrict on the water, and was pro-bably the weftern parts of the county of Mayo.

* O'Conor's Differt.

F.

FANE, Fene, Feine, Fion, Fin, or Vain, as
it is differently written in the feveral dialects of the
Celtic tongue, fignified originally moft excellent,
eminent and diftinguifhed. Figuratively a mark,
boundary, end, or any thing confpicuous or elevated. When joined to matters of religion, it fignified facred, as Ollavain, the facred high prieft;
and as white was univerfally, throughout the pagan
world, appropriated to the divinity, Fin, Fion
and Feine frequently fignifies in the Irifh language,
that colour; When joined to perfons, it fignified
either that they were of the facred or druidic order,
or eminent for their learning and abilities in war;
whence Feineigh or Fenius, a wife or learned perfon, and Mileadh-feine, a learned nobleman;
When applied to places, it either fignified that they
were places of worfhip, or appertained to the
Druids, as Fanus a temple or place of worfhip
among the Romans, and Magh Feine or the facred
plain, in Ireland; When applied to waters, it either
fignified that they were on eminences, clear, pure
or dedicated to religion. Thefe words frequently
occurring in the ancient Irifh poems and chronicles,
have given rife to the opinion, relative to the eftablifhment of a colony of Phœnicians in this ifland,
in an early period. But where ever thofe words,
Fene, Feine, &c. are found in the Irifh language,
they muft be confidered under fome of the above
defcriptions.

FEARMUIGHE, corrupted from Fear-magh,
now the barony of Fermoy in the county of Cork.
This diftrict was formerly the country of the Clan

Gibbons, Condons and Roches. It was alfo in ancient times, denominated *Glean na Mbain* or *Magb na Feine*, that is the facred plain, or plain of the learned. About the year 254, Fiach Muillethan provincial king of Munfter, beftowed the greateft part of this country on the Druid Mogruth, from whom it obtained the name of Dal-Mogruith. The Druid on coming into the poffeffion of the country, converted it into a kind of fanctuary, and on the high land which bounds it, erected a number of altars and places of worfhip; feveral of which are remaining to this day. From this circumftance, Dal-Mogruith obtained the name of Magh Feine, or the facred plain, which before bore that of Magh Neirce. In the latter ages the inhabitants of Magh Feine were called Fear Magh Feine, or the men of the facred plain, or Fear Magh, and by corruption Fer-moy *. See Magh Neirce

FEINE, fee Fane.

FENABORE, fee Kilfenoragh.

FENE, fee Fane.

FENIUSA FARSA, or Pheniufa Farfa, a Perfon mentioned in the old Irifh poems and Chronicles, and fuppofed to be the firft who introduced letters into Ireland. From the fimilarity of the word Pheniufa to Phæni, it has been frequently afferted, that Feniufa Farfa was either a Phœnician or Carthaginian who arrived in this country in a very early period. But as the real fignification of Feniufa Farfa, is the moft wife or learned perfon, it is moft probable that he was the fame with Forchern, who is faid to have written the firft Irifh uraiceact

---

* Harris's Ware, v. 1. p. 53. Collect. No. 5. p. 69, 70, & No. 4.

or primer, fome few years before the birth of
Chrift. Feniufa Farfa or Forchern therefore, feems
to have been a British Druid, who had obtained
the ufe of letters from the Punic or Iberian traders, about the beginning of the laft century preceding the Chriftian æra. According to the Irifh
annals, Eochadh Aireamh firft introduced burying
in this country, inftead of burning or inclofing the
body in urns; over the grave, a flat or inclined
ftone was to be placed with the name of the perfon written thereon. This tranfaction is generally placed in the year of the world 3952, or according to the computation of Jofephus, before
Chrift 240; and according to the prefent only 46
years; but according to the computation of St.
Hierom, which was generally followed during the
middle ages by the ancient Irifh Clergy, A. D. 11;
about which time a number of the Britifh Druids
fled into Ireland from the terror of the Roman
arms. A number of thefe tombs are yet remaining in different parts of Ireland; feveral of which
are infcribed with Druidic characters, and at this day
are called by the natives, *Leaba na Feine*, that is
the bed or grave of the learned or noble people.
From thefe circumftances there is the greateft probability, that the celebrated Fenulfa Farfa or Forchern was a Britifh Druid who retired into this
country about the time of the arrival of the Romans
in Britain under Cæfar. In fifty years from which
time, or about the beginning of the firft century,
the knowledge of letters had become univerfal
among the Hibernian heathen priefts, and the celebrated convention of Tara was in confequence

thereof inftituted towards the middle of the firft age.*

FEOR NA FLOINN, fee Ciariudhe.

FEORUS, the ancient name of the river Nore; which rifes near the Devil's Bit, in the county of Tipperary, and falls into the Barrow. Feorus is evidently derived from *Abhan nFeor uis*, or the river of the rapid ftream, whence it was frequently called Abhan nFeor, and by the Englifh the Nore; this river in time of floods being exceedingly rapid.†

FERMANAGH, or the people of the diftrict on the water, a people inhabiting the country round Lough Ern, the Erdinii of Ptolemy; this country called alfo Magh Guhuir, or the plain of the water, was made a county in the reign of Queen Elizabeth; the ancient chiefs of which were called Magh Guhuir or Mac Guire, who remained in the intire poffeffion of their country until the beginning of the laft century.‡

FERMOY, fee Fearmuighe.

FERNUS, or Ferna, evidently derived from *Fear nd uis*, or men of the diftrict on the water; as the ancient inhabitants of Hy Morragh, the prefent county of Wexford, frequently were called; Ferna was the principal refidence of the ancient chiefs of this diftrict, and is mentioned by Ptolemy. A mo- naftery and bifhoprick were founded here by St. Edan, about 598, and united to that of Leighlin in 1600. The church of Ferns was in the middle ages frequently efteemed the metropolitan church of Leinfter. §

* Collect. No. 5. O'Conor's Differt. M'Curtin. Keating. Tighernac. † O'Conor's Differt. ‡ O'Conor's Differt. § Harris's Ware, vol. 1. p. 435.

FERTA FIR FEIC, derived from Fertagh fir bheitheach, or the graves of the herdfmen, from a number of thefe people being flain here in battle, and buried in this place. It is now called Slane, and is fituated in the county of Meath, on the northern bank of the river Boyne. Here Saint Patrick pitched his tent the night before his arrival at the court of Taragh; at which, early in the morning he lighted up that fire, which gave fo much aftonifhment to the Druids and affembly of the ftates. A monaftery and bifhoprick were afterwards founded in this place by St. Erc*.

FIODH AONGUSA, or the wood or country of Aongus, a diftrict in the county of Weft Meath and barony of Rathconrath. It was in the early ages called *Coen druim*, or the diftrict of the hill or dome, from containing the hill of Ufneach, famous for being the place where the ancient fynods and publick affemblies were frequently held; efpecially that in 1112, or 1111, under Celfus archbifhop of Ardmagh†. See Ufneach.

FIODHA RHEHE, pronounced fairy, that is Sylvan divinities, from *Fiodba* woods, and *Rbebe* divinities. The *Fiodba Rbebe*, in the ancient Celtic mythology were fubordinate genii who prefided over the vegetable productions of nature, and the animals of the foreft. They were the fatyrs and elves of the Greeks and Romans; the chief of whom was Pan or Pallas, called by the ancient Irifh Mogh, Magh or Mabh. The notion of fairies fo prevalent amongft the country people at this day, is the remains of this heathen fuperftition. See Mogh, Mogh-adair and Satarn.

* Harris's Ware, vol. 1. p. 13.   † Ibid. vol. 1. p. 53.

FIODH-INIS, fee Eirion.

FIRBOLGÆ, fee Bolgæ.

FIRCRABII, or Fir-na-crabii, that is the men
or inhabitants of the diftrict, called alfo Hy Maghneigh, now the county of Monaghan and part of
the ancient Oirgaël, the chiefs of which were the
Mac Mahons*. See Hy Maghneigh and Oirgaël.

FIRTHUATHAL, or Fortuatha, that is the
men of the dark or gloomy region; an ancient diftrict comprehending the mountainous tract of country on the weft of the county of Wicklow, called
Hy Tuathal, or the gloomy region; being compofed
of barren mountains and dark vallies. The
ancient chiefs were called Hy Tuathal, and Mac
Mhthuil, by corruption O'Tool, they were alfo
hereditary chiefs of Guolan, during the middle
ages, and often brought under their fubjection the
chiefs of Caëlan or Galen. This rocky diftrict was
likewife denominated Ciarmen or Ciermen, that is
the place or country of rocks, corruptly written
Carmen, whence the mountains next the bay of
Dublin, are frequently in the Irifh writings called
Sliebh Ciermen, or the rocky mountains. As the
O'Tools were either by defcent or marriage of the
fame family with the Mac Moroghs, O'Moras and
O'Kellys of Caëlan, they were frequently denominated kings of Leinfter, according to their fe-
niority†.

FOCHMUINE-ABHAN, or the river of the low
country; a river rifing in the barony of Tirekerin,
and county of Derry; from whence taking a
N. N. W. courfe, it falls into Lough Foyle. Saint

---

* O'Conor's Differt.   † Harris's Ware.

Patrick refided fome time * on the banks of this river.

FOCLUT, an ancient foreft on the weftern bank of the river Mayo, and diftrict of Tir-malgaid; famous for being the fubject of the celebrated dream of Saint Patrick, before he entered on his miffion to Ireland. †

FOMHORAICC, or *Formoragh*, that is feamen or pyrates. A people mentioned in the ancient Irifh poems, and faid to have infefted the fouthern coafts of Ireland during the time that the ifland was in poffeffion of the *Nemethæ*. They were undoubtedly the Punic traders, who firft arrived on the coafts of the Britifh ifles about 440 or 500 years before the Chriftian æra, under the conduct of Midacritus, and difcovered the valuable tin mines of Cornwall, and which they kept for feveral years a fecret from the reft of the world. During the voyages frequently made to that part of Britain, we may reafonably conclude thofe ancient navigators, occafionally vifited the coafts of Ireland, and traded with the barbarous natives, for fkins and fuch other commodities as the country then produced; but it doth not appear that they made any fettlement therein, indeed the country in thefe early periods, producing little, except wood, fkins and fifh, could never be an object of colonization; whilft Britain, on account of its tin mines, moft probably was the place of general rendezvous, and where factories were eftablifhed. As to the affertions of feveral of the ancient poems and chronicles, relative to letters, laws and commerce being introduced by the Milefians, who are fuppofed to be

* Harris's Ware, vol. 1, p. 18.   † Ibid. vol. 1. p. 9.

Phœnicians and Carthaginians, they belong to a much later period. For it is by no means evident, that the Phœnicians during their commerce with the Britiſh iſles, either eſtabliſhed colonies or introduced their learning among the natives ; theſe things being reſerved for the Iberian and Gallic merchants, about one hundred years before Chriſt. Beſides, if the Phœnicians or Carthaginians had made ſettlements in Ireland, the old Iriſh bards could not have diſtinguiſhed them by the name of Pœni ; it is true theſe people were generally called by the Greeks Θοινικις, and by the Latins *Pænos* and *Punicos*, yet they always denominated themſelves *Canaim* or merchants, the Iriſh therefore in their own language, muſt either have called them *Canuithe* merchants, or *Fomboraicc* ſeamen, and we find them actually called Fomhoraicc, in all the old Iriſh poems. Their arrival, however, as mentioned by the ancient hiſtorians, and compared with the traditions in the Iriſh poems, ſerve in a great meaſure to aſcertain the time in which Ireland received her firſt people ; for allowing the *Nemetha* to have been in poſſeſſion of this iſland 200 years before the arrival of the Fomhoraicc, we ſhall obtain 640 or 700 years prior to the Chriſtian æra, for the firſt colonization of Ireland by the Aborigines of Britain. An event which agrees perfectly with ancient foreign hiſtory, and the natural circumſtances of things.*

The firſt arrival of the aboriginal Britons on the Hibernian coaſts being about 350 years after the eſtabliſhment of the Celtic tribes in that iſland,

---

* Keating. O'Conor's Diſſert. Plin. l. 7. c. 56. Herodot, p. 254. Strabo, p. 265. Collect. No. 8. Hiſt. of Manchester,

whence the periods in which the feveral grand migrations from Britain to Ireland were effected, will be as follows:

		bef. Chrift.
Nemethæ as Aboriginals,	-	640
Bolgæ or Belgians, the Heremonii of the poets,	}	350
Heberii, or Britifh Silures,	—	100
Britons who fled from the terror of the Roman arms,	} after Chrift.	50
Britons who fled from the Saxons,		500

Wherefore in the fpace of 1140 years the colonization from Britain was compleated.

See Nemethæ, Momonii, Fomorii, Bolgæ, Heberii, Heremonii, Phœnicians and Scotii.

FOMORII, or Fomorians, that is the fea men, or mariners; a people mentioned in the moft ancient Irifh poems to have arrived in this ifland in a very early period; even before the eftablifhment of the fecond colony of the Bolgæ. They undoubtedly were foreign merchants, and perhaps the Punic or Iberian traders who frequently vifited the coafts of Ireland, during their commerce with the Britons for tin, &c. It is remarkable, though the foreigners who traded to Ireland from the firft century before to the fixth after the Chriftian æra, are frequently mentioned in the poems of the moft ancient bards, under the names of Fomoreigh, Learmonii, Lathmonii, Lochmanii, &c. yet there is not the leaft hint given from what country they came, nor the nature of their commerce. From feveral antient Irifh poems it appears, that in the fecond century, feveral of the arms and utenfils ufed by the ancient Irifh chiefs, were of foreign manufacture; yet we have not the leaft account, from whence they obtained them. Circumstances which prove in a great measure, that though the Carthaginians, Iberians, Gauls and Romans carried on a considerable commerce with Ireland during the period before specified, yet not any of them established factories or colonies in the country, but only visited occasionally the ports, and bartered with the natives for such commodities as they had occasion for*. See Phœnicians, Lochmanii, Fomhoraice, &c.

FORTUATHA, see Firthuathal.

G.

GA, GAES, CAS, and Gha,. Gaes or Ghae, signify the sea, or a large extended piece of water; whence Morghai, corruptly Fearghe, the ocean.

GABHRAN, from *Gabh re an*, the high habitation of the king, the capital and royal residence of the kings of Ossory. The rath of this ancient palace is yet remaining situated in upper Ossory and the Queen's County †.

GADALIANS, *Gadelii* or *Gaoidhal*, a people mentioned in several of the ancient Irish poems and chronicles, and by the writers of the latter ages and supposed to be the ancestors of the Milesians who are asserted to have travelled into different parts of the world, prior to their establishment in Ireland. The names *Gadelij* and *Gaoidbel*, though taken for the same, are probably of different significa-

---

* O'Conor's Differt. p. 163. Leabhar Lecan. † Colled. No. 3.

tions. *Gaoidbel* is evidently the fame as *Gaël* or Caël, and were the iflandic or marititime Celtic tribes eftablifhed on the weftern confines of Europe before their migration to this ifland. Whence the *Melidh fene fliogbt Gaoidbel* of the poets fignifies the learned nobles of the Celtic race, and were none other than the Britifh, Gallic 'and Iberian druids who arrived in this country in different periods, either with the feveral colonies, or by means of commerce. But *Gadelii* moft probably is not of Celtic origin, this word in the old Perfic or Median Language fignifies a tower, whence *Melidh fene fliogbt Gadelagh*, fignifies the learned nobles of the tower race, and are afferted by the ancient bards to have introduced into Ireland the art of building with lime and ftone, and other improvements not before known to the ancient inhabitants of this ifland. There is the greateft probablity that thefe people were the Gaurs or Perfian magi; amongft thofe who received them they erected fchools or academies, in which they taught the tenets of their faith, and the feveral fublime fciences at that time cultivated by the orientals. The greater part of the fouthern and weftern countries having in this period received the chriftian faith, the Gaurs found little encouragement in thefe parts of the continent. But in Ireland, where the Pagan religion remained almoft in its original purity and its tenets not being widely different from that of the ancient Perfians, thefe itinerant philofophers found a ready affent to their doctrines among the Hibernian druids. To them we may attribute the origin of thofe flender round towers at this day remaining in feveral parts of Ireland, they being exactly of the fame conftruction with the Perfian pyrathiēa of the middle ages, called by the Phœnicians *Chammia*, and by the magi *Gadele*, or temples of God, but by the ancient Irish *Tlachgo* or temples of the univerſe, whence their preſent name in the Irish language *Cloghadh* *. (See Cloghadh.)

GALEN, ſee Coalan.

GALENG, or the woody diſtrict, the ancient name of the preſent county of Galway; called alſo, Hy Caëllagh and Conmacne Dubhain, which ſee †.

GALENI, ſee Caelani.

GALIAN, from Caëlian, or the woody country, an ancient diſtrict in Leinſter, ʼcomprehending the greater part of the counties of Kildare, Carlow and Queen's county, containing the ancient diſtricts of Eli ui Mordha and Caolan. In the early ages this diſtrict was almoſt one continued foreſt ‡. (See Eli ui Mordha and Caëlan.)

GAMANRADII, or the government of the diſtrict on the ſea, comprehending the northern part of the county of Mayo, between the river Moy and the ſea. See Tirmalgaid.

GANGANII, ſee Canganii.

GARMEN, or Gaermen, that is, the place or habitation on the ſea; it was the principal place of Hy Morragh, (which ſee) the Coriondii of Ptolemy. It has frequently been confounded with Carmen in Caelan, though ſeveral miles diſtant. It was either the preſent town of Wexford or Enniſcorthy, though probably the former.

---

* Jurieu's Crit. Hiſtory of the Church, vol. 2. Vallancey's Eſſay on the Celtic Tongue. Keating. M'Curtin's Ant.
† O'Conor's Diſſert. ‡ O'Conor's Diſſert.

GESHIL, from Gaël fiol, or the habitation of the race of the wood. An ancient refidence of fome of the chiefs of Hy Falgia; fituated in the diftrict of the O'Malloys and King's county.

GLEANNAMHUIM, or Glennamhuin, that is, the dark or horrid valley, now Glanworth in the county of Cork. See Fearmuighe.

GLENDALOCH, or the valley of the two lakes. A valley fituated in the mountaineous parts of the antient territory of Firtuathal in the county of Wicklow; it was fo denominated from containing two lakes. In this valley, furrounded by high and almoft inacceffible mountains, St. Cavan, called alfo St. Coemgene, about the middle of the fixth century, founded a monaftery, which in a fhort time from the fanctity of its founder was much reforted to, and at length became a bifhoprick and a religious city. During the middle ages, the city of Glendaloch, called by Hovedon Epifcopatus Biftagnienfis was held in great efteem and received feveral valuable donations and priviledges; its epifcopal jurifdiction extending to the walls of Dublin. About the middle of the twelfth century, on fome account or other, Glendaloch was much neglected by the clergy, and became inftead of a holy city a den of thieves, wherefore cardinal Papiro in 1214, united it to the fee of Dublin, which union was confirmed by king John. The O'Tools, chiefs of Firtuathal, however by the affiftance of the Pope, continued long after this period to elect bifhops and abbots to Glendaloch, though they had neither revenues nor authority beyond the diftrict of Tuathal; in confequence of which, the city was neglected and fuffered to decay, and was nearly a defert in 1497, when

Dennis White, the laſt titular biſhop, ſurrendered his right in the cathedral church of St. Patrick's Dublin. From the ruins of this ancient city, ſtill remaining, it appears to have been a place of conſequence ; and to have contained ſeven churches and religious Houſes, ſmall indeed, but built in a neat elegant ſtile in imitation of the Greek archi‑ tecture. The cathedral, the walls of which are yet ſtanding, was dedicated to the ſaints Peter and Paul. South from the cathedral, ſtands a ſmall church roofed with ſtone, nearly entire, and in ſeveral parts of the valley are a number of ſtone croſſes, ſome of which are curiouſly carved but without any inſcriptions. In the N. W. corner of the cemetery belonging to the cathedral, ſtands a round tower, 95 feet high, and 15 in diameter ; and in the cemetery of a ſmall church, on the ſouth ſide of the river near the great lake, called the Rhefeart church, are ſome tombs, inſcribed with Iriſh inſcriptions, belonging to the O'Tools ancient chiefs of this diſtrict. In a perpendicular project‑ ing rock on the ſouth ſide of the great lake, thirty yards above the ſurface of the water, is the cele‑ brated bed of St. Coemgene, hewn out of the rock, capable of containing three perſons : exceed‑ ing difficult of acceſs and terrible in proſpect. Amongſt the ruins have been diſcovered a number of ſtones, curiouſly carved, and containing inſcrip‑ tions in the Latin, Greek and Iriſh languages. As this city was in a valley ſurrounded on all ſides, except the eaſt, by high, barren and inacceſſible mountains, the artificial roads leading thereto are by no means the leaſt curious part of the remains ; the principal is that leading from the market place into the county of Kildare, through Glendaſon.

This road for near two miles is yet perfect, compoſed of ſtones placed on their edges, making a
firm and durable pavement of the breadth of about
ten feet. Another road, reſembling this, appears
to have been intended to be carried over the
mountains from Holy-Wood ; it is marked out,
and in ſeveral places the materials were collected,
but the execution, from ſome circumſtances, was
neglected. From the ſtyle of the buildings diſcovered in the ruins of Glendaloch, they appear to
have been erected about the middle of the tenth
century, and were deſigned by foreign architects
on the Greek and Roman models, but the execution falls ſhort of the deſign*.

GRENARD, from Grian-ard, or the height of
the Sun ; a town in the county of Longford, and
formerly the reſidence of the chiefs of north Teffia.

H.

HARDINII, ſee Erdinii,

HEBERII, or Hiberians, that is the moſt weſtern people, the ancient inhabitants of the county
of Kerry and part of the county of Clare. The
poets have fabled that this part of the iſland was
peopled by Heber, elder brother of Heremon and
ſons of Meleſius, in which they have confounded
the Heberii with the *Mhumhans*, or aboriginal inhabitants. Richard of Cirenceſter thinks they were
the Britiſh Silures, the ancient inhabitants of Cornwall, who retired into this iſland on the arrival of
Divitiacus about one hundred years before Chriſt ;

* Harris's Ware, v. 1. p. 371,

and who, according to Keating, landed at *Inbber Sceine* now the mouth of the Shannon, from whence advancing into the country were oppofed by the Mhumhams, the original inhabitants under the conduct of their queen Eire, but that heroine being defeated at the battle of Magh Greine near Tralee bay, the Heberii eftablifhed themfelves in the country, and probably were the firft who opened the mines of Ireland; as Eadhna Dearg a king of this diftrict is faid to have coined the firft money at Airgiod Rofs, about thirty years before the chriftian æra*.

HEREMONII, an ancient people inhabiting the eaftern and middle parts of Ireland, comprehending the prefent province of Leinfter; they are faid by the fabulifts to have defcended from Heremon, a fon of Milefius the Spaniard. *Heremon* fignifies the weftern country; and *Heremonii*, the inhabitants of the weftern country. They appear to have been Belgians, who arrived from Britain under the conduct of Hugony, about the middle of the fourth century before the Chriftian æra; and were afterwards diftinguifhed by the name of Scots, from dwelling in woods. The Heremonii comprehended the ancient tribes of the Falgii, Elii, Caëlenii and Morii. See Hy Falgia, Scotii, Coitii and Coigedugarian.

HIBERNIA, or the moft weftern ifland; the name given to Ireland by the Greeks and Romans.

HY, UI, or O, in the ancient Irifh and Celtic tongues, fignified a country, diftrict and tribe.

---

* Keating. Richard of Cirencefter.

When annexed to the names of perfons, they frequently fignified a chief or lord.

HY ALLAIN, or *Hy al Lain*, that is, the diftrict of the great plain country, containing the eaftern part of the Magh Leana, at prefent diftinguifhed under the denomination of the ifle of Allin in the county of Kildare, in which ftands the hill of Allin, the mount Cromla of the ancient bards. The chiefs of this diftrict were denominated *Hy Allain*.

HY ANLAN, fee Oirthir.

HY ARA, fee Dalnaruidhe.

HY BHEALGEIGH, fee Coiteagh.

HY BREDAGH, fee Brefine.

HY BREOGHAIN GABHRAIN, fee Caucii.

HY CABHAN, fee Brefine.

HY CABHANAGH, fee Coriandii.

HY CAELLAGH, or the woody diftrict, containing the prefent county of Galway, fee Galeng and Conmacne dubhain.

HY CHEARBHUIL, fee Eli ui Chearbhuil.

HY CONAR, fee Hy Falgia.

HY COAREIGH, fee Brefine.

HY DA LEIGH,
HY DAM SEIGH, } fee Hy Falgia.

HY DINGLE, fee Vellabori.

HY DRISCUIL, fee Corcaluighe.

HY DUNNABHAN, fee Cairbre aobhdha.

HY FALGIA, or ui Faillia, derived from Hy Bhealgia, that is the country of the worfhippers of Beal. This diftrict formerly comprehended the counties of Eaft and Weft Meath, Dublin, part of the county of Kildare, and all the King's county.

The inhabitants appear to have been descended from the most ancient colony of the Belgians, whose hereditary chiefs were denominated Hy nFaillia, by corruption O'Neal; and in whose line, as descendants of Hugony the great, of the race of the Heremonii, the monarchs of Ireland were to be elected. Some few years before the christian æra, on the arrival of several Caledonian colonies under the domination of Ullagh, a number of the ancient Fallgii, under the conduct of Eoghagh Bhealogh, or Eoghagh Failoch, retired across the Shannon and established a colony at Croighan; others with their chief retired southward into the district of Coiteigh, now the King's county. From which period, Hy Falgia was confined principally to the King's county and part of the county of Kildare, distinguished, during the latter ages, by the name of the kingdom of Offaly. About the beginning of the fifth century, a colony from this district settled in the north of Ireland, where for several ages, it was distinguished by the name of Hy Failia, and Tir hy nFail, by corruption Tironel, and Tirone, that is, the land of the district of the Fail. A circumstance that gave rise to the north and south Hy Failia so much spoken of by the Irish historians of the middle ages. South Hy Falia contained the subordinate districts of Hy Magh-loneigh, Hy Da-Leigh, Hy Mul-loigh, Hy Con-ar, Hy Dam-feigh, Magh-coit-lan, Magh-coit-eoghan, Mach-all-leigh and Hy Faliegh, whose respective dynasts during the latter ages were denominated O'Malone, O'Daly, O'Muloy, O'Connor, O'Demfy, Macoghlan, Mageoghagan, Macawley and O'Faley; all of whom were in possession of their ancient patrimonies at the commence-

ment of the laft century, and feveral of their def
fcendants retain confiderable landed properties in the
King's county to this day. All thefe Dynafts derived their origin from Hugony the great of the
Heremonian race, and accordingly were elected
chieftains of Hy Fallia and monarchs of all Ireland
in confequence of the feniority of their tribe to
others of the Belgian race *.

HY-FALLIA, fee Hy-Falgia.

HY-FERTE, fee Ardfert.

HY-FIACRIA AIDNE, an ancient diftrict in
the county of Galway, afterwards called Clanriccard.

HY-FIACRIJ, or Hy-Fiachria, an ancient diftrict in the county of Tyrone, on the River Derg ‡.

HY-FLATH-EAN-EOGHAN, fee Brefine.

HY-GAIRA, fee Luighne.

HY-HANLAN, fee Oirther.

HY-HUANAN, fee Dalaradia.

HY-JARTAGH, fee Conmacne-Mara.

HY-KINSELAGH, or the diftrict of the chief
tribe, a large ancient diftrict comprehending the
greater part of fouth Leinfter; being an union of
the Septs of Hy-Moragh, Coulan, Hy-Tuathal,
Hy-Breoghan Gabhran, Eli-ui-Mora, and fometimes Offory, containing the prefent counties of
Wexford, Wicklow, Kilkenny and the fouth part
of the Queen's County; the principal chief of which
was generally O'Morragh, hereditary chief of Hy-
Moragh, and in confequence denominated king of
Leinfter, though from the ancient Irifh hiftory it

* O'Conor's Differt. Harris's Ware, v. 1.
‡ Harris's Ware, v. 1. p. 182.

appears, that the chiefs of Eli-ui-Mora, Coulan and Tuathal according to their feniority were elected chiefs of Kinfelagh, and kings of Leinfter.

HY-LAOIGHIS, or Hy-Leagh, that is, the diftrict of the level country ; a large ancient territory comprehending the ancient Hy-Fallia, the prefent King's County, Eli-ui-Moradh or Leix in the Queen's County, and Eli-ui-Chearbhuil with part of the counties of Dublin and Kildare, containing the ancient Septs of ui-Moradh, ui-Chearbhuil, ui-Dal-leaneigh, ui-Mul-Laoigh, ui-Don, ui-Deamfeigh, magh-Coitlan, magh-Coiteoghan, magh-Caëllagh and ui-magh-Louinie. The fovereignity of which generally was invefted in the chief of the eldeft Sept of ui-Moradh, who on this occafion affumed the title of Hy-Laoighfeach, or Hy-Laighfeach, whofe principal place of refidence was at the fortrefs of Dun-na-mais, in the Queen's County, and capital of Eli-ui-Moradh. The inhabitants of this diftrict were frequently denominated Laoighaneigh, Loinfeach or Leagenians, that is the inhabitants of the level country, and make a confiderable figure in the ancient Irifh hiftory, from whom the prefent name of Leinfter is derived. The fouthern parts of this diftrict, during the latter part of the middle ages, became tributary to the chieftain of Hy Morragh, who took upon him the title of chief of Kinfelagh and king of Leinfter. However from the Irifh annals it appears, that the chiefs of the other Septs, according to their feniority, were elected to the regal dignity of Leinfter, that is, Mac Coghlan chieftain of Mac Coitlan, Mac Kellagh chieftain of Mac Caëllagh, O'Tool chieftain of Ui-Tuathal and O'Guar chieftain of Dal

Machſcoeb, all of whom deemed themſelves Scots of the Heremonian race. See Coitæ, Scotii, Heremonii, Bolgæ, Coriondii and Coigidugarian.

HY-LEAREIGH, ſee Corcaluighe.

HY-LOCHLEAN, ſee Brefine and Burrin.

HY-MAGH-LOCKLIN, the antient name of Weſtmeath, ſee Mediolanum.

HY-MAGH-LONEIGH, ſee Hy-Falgia.

HY-MAHONEIGH, ſee Corcaluighe.

HY-MALIA, or Umalia, that is, the diſtrict near the great watery plain; an ancient diviſion in the weſt of the county of Mayo, comprehending the preſent barony of Moriſk, and half the barony of Roſs in the county of Galway, containing the ſouth part of the ancient Hy-Muriſg, the Auterij of Ptolemy. The hereditary chiefs of this diſtrict were denominated Hy-Malia, or O'Maly, ſome of whom were in poſſeſſion of the ſouthern parts at the beginning of the laſt century. In this country Saint Patrick founded the church of Achad Fobhair, afterwards a biſhoprick *. See Auterij, Moriſk and Achad Fobhair.

HY-MORAGH, or the diſtrict on the ſea, an ancient diſtrict comprehending the preſent county of Wexford, the Coriondij of Ptolemy. See Coriondij.

HY-MULLOIGH, ſee Hy-Falgia.

HY-MURISG, ſee Hy-Malia.

HY-NA-MOR, ſee Clan Cuilean.

HY-PAUDRUIG, ſee Oſragii.

HY-RELEIGH, ſee Brefine.

HY-ROARE, ſee Brefine.

---

* Harris's Ware, v. I. p. 17.

HY-SERUIDON, fee Brefine.

HY-SIOL, fee Dalnaruidhe.

HY-SIOL-ABHAN, fee Iberia.

HY-TIRMALGAID, or the diftrict of the land
on the great fea; the prefent barony of Tirawley
in the county of Mayo; in this diftrict the wood
Foclut ftood, celebrated for being the fcene of the
vifion of Saint Patrick before he undertook the miffion of Ireland. Hy-Tirmalgaid contained the
north part of the ancient Hy-Moruifg, the Auterij
of Ptolemy *.

HY-TUATH, fee Inis-ocn.

HY-TUATHAL, fee Firthuathal.

I.

I, IBH, or IVE, fignifies a diftrict or territory
on the water, and frequently water only, being
the fame as Aobh or Abh the old Celtic word for
any fluid fubftance; we alfo find that Aobh frequently in the old Irifh fignifies fire.

IAR-CONAUGHT, fee Conmacne-mara.

IAR-MUMHAN or weft Munfter, comprehending the prefent county of Kerry.

IBERI, or the weftern people of the water, they
are mentioned by Ptolemy and were inhabitants of
Iberia, and the fouth coafts of the county of Kerry,
(fee Ibh-eochach.) There were other Iberi mentioned by the Irifh writers who inhabited the north of
Ireland, in the county of Derry, between Lough.
Foyle and the river Ban †.

---

* Harris's Ware, v. 1. p. 9.   † O'Conor's Differt.

IBERIA, or the western country on the water; an ancient district mentioned by Richard of Ciren-cester, situated round Bear-Haven, and was deno-minated by the ancient Irish *Hy-Siol-Aban*, or the district of the race on the river, the chiefs of which were called Hy-Sulabhan, by corruption O'Sullivan.

IBERNII, see Uternii.

IBH, see I.

IBH EACH, see Dalaradia.

IBH EOCHACH, or the district on the water, in the S. W. part of the county of Cork, the Iberii of Ptolemy.

IBH-GAISAN, see Ive-Caisin.

IBH-LAOISHEACH, now Leix, see Eile-ui-Mordha.

IBH-TORNA-EIGEAS, or the district of the mountains near the sea; the barony of Clán-mor-ris in the county of Kerry, it was in the early ages distinguished by the name of Conal Eachluath, or the Captain-ship of the country on the lake.

IMLEACH-JOBHUIR, or Imelaca Ibair, deri-ved from *Bim lach a Ib er*, that is the land of the lake of the western district; an ancient ecclesiastical city situated about fourteen miles west of Cashel on the borders of a lake, formerly containing upwards of two hundred acres, though now dry cultivated ground. Here a church and bishoprick was found-ed by St. Ailbe towards the close of the fourth century, some years before the arrival of St. Patrick. On the arrival of St. Patrick and the conversion of Ængus Mac Nafrick, king of Cashel, the church of Imelaca Ibair was declared the metropolitan church of Munster, in which dignity it continued several centuries, until translated to Cashel where it now remains. The city of Imelaca Ibair, now Emly, was plundered by robbers in 1125, and the mitre of St. Ailbe burned. It was also deftroyed by fire in 1192, but was afterwards re-built and continued a confiderable town for feveral ages, even to the time of Henry the eighth, in whofe reign Thomas Hurly, bifhop of Emly, erected a college for fecular priefts, but the only remains, at prefent, of this ancient and perhaps firft ecclefiaftical city in Ireland, are the ruins of a church, fome walls, a large unhewn ftone crofs, and an holy well. The fee of Emly was united to that of Cafhel in 1568 *.

INCHINEMEO, fee Moin-na-infeigh.

INIS BANBA, fee Eiroin.

INIS BHEAL, fee Eiroin.

INIS BOFIN, or the ifland of the white Oxen; an ifland on the weftern coaft of the county of Mayo, where St. Colman, bifhop of Lindisfern, with a number of Scots, and thirty Saxons founded a monaftery in 676, and refided there nine years §.

INIS CATHAY, fee Cathaigh Inis.

INIS CLIARE, fee Inis Turk.

INIS CLOGHRAN, or the ftony ifland; an ifland in Lough Ree, in the Shannon; where, about the beginning of the fixth century, a monaftery was founded by St. Dermod.

INIS CORTHY, fee Corthæ.

INIS EGHEN, fee Inis Oen.

INIS ELGA, fee Eiroin.

INIS ENDAIMB, or the ifland of the habitation in the water, an ifland in Lough Ree.

* Harris's Ware, v, 1. p. 490.   § Ware.

INIS FAIL, derived from Inis Bheal, that is the ifland of Beal; one of the ancient names of Ireland, fo denominated from Beal, the principal object of adoration among the ancient inhabitants of the Britifh ifles. Inis Fail has been erroneoufly tranflated the Ifland of Deftiny, as Beal was fometimes taken for Fate or Providence.

INIS GATHAY, fee Cathaig Inis.

INIS OEN, or Inis Eoghen, that is the diftrict of the ifle, comprehending the peninfula between Lough Swilly and Lough Foyle. It was alfo called *Hy Tuath ar teagh*, or the diftrict of the country of the northern habitation; the dynaft of which was denominated *Hy Tuath ar teagh*, or *Hy Duath erteagh*, by corruption O'Dogherty; fome of whom were in poffeffion at the commencement of the laft century †.

INIS SCATTERY, fee Cathaigh Inis.

INIS TORRE, or high ifland, an ifland eight miles from the N. W. coaft of the county of Donegall.

INIS TURK and INIS CLIARE, two iflands at the entrance of Clew bay, on the coaft of the county of Mayo, where ftood a cell of the abbey of Knockmoy.

IRELOND, fee Eiroin.

INSOVENACH, or the habitation on the mouth of the bay or harbour, an ancient port in the fouth of Ireland, much frequented about the time of the arrival of the Englifh; it appears to be the prefent Bear, fituated at the entrance of Kenmair river.

IRAGHT, fee Ciaruidhe.

† Ware. O'Conor's Differt. and his Ortellus.

ISAMNUM Promontory, Portaferry cape at the entrance of the bay of Strangford, mentioned by Richard of Cirencester.

IVEAGH, a barony in the county of Down, see Dalaradia.

IVE BLOID, the same as Ara and Ormond, which see.

IVE CAISIN, or IBH GAIS AN, that is the district of the maritime country; an ancient district in Thomond, and the eastern part of the county of Clare *.

IVE FIOINTE, the same as Cairbre Aodhbhe, which see.

IVERNIS, or the habitation on the western water; an ancient city and capital of the Scots, as mentioned by Richard of Cirencester; who asserts, that it was situated on the eastern banks of the Shannon, but where is not very certain; though most probably it was the present town of Banagher in the King's county; as Banagher signifies also, the western habitation on the water, and is situated in the ancient *Coitidugarian*, the *Scotii* of Richard.

K.

KENANUS, from *Cean an uis*, that is the principal country of the water, an ancient district in the county of Westmeath, situated near the lakes.

* Collect. No. 4. p. 569.

KENRY, fee Brughrigh.

KILDALUA, fee Loania.

KILDARE, or *Chille-dair*, that is the wood of oaks. A large ancient foreft, comprehending the middle part of the prefent county of Kildare. In the center of this wood was a large plain, facred to heathen fuperftition, and at prefent called the Curragh of Kildare. At the extremity of this plain, about the commencement of the fixth century, St. Brigid, one of the heathen veftals, on her converfion to the Chriftian faith, founded with the affiftance of St. Conlæth, a church and monaftery, near which, after the manner of the Pagans, St. Brigid kept the facred fire in a cell, the ruins of which are ftill vifible. The church of Kildare was in a fhort time erected into a cathedral, with epifcopal jurifdiction, which dignity it retains to this day; the cathedral, however, has been for feveral years neglected, and at prefent lies in ruins, little remaining befides the walls and a round tower.

KILALOE, fee Loania.

KILMACDUAGH, fee Chillmacduagh.

KILMANTAN, from *Chille man tan*, that is the wood of the narrow country; an ancient wood in the diftrict of Cuolan, in which, on the fea coaft, ftood the Menapia of Ptolemy, now Wicklow.

KILMORE, or the great church; called in former ages Clunes or Cluain, that is the fequeftered place; fituated near Lough Ern. Here a church and bifhoprick were founded in the fixth century by St. Fedlimid, which was afterwards removed to an obfcure village called Triburna, where it continued until the year 1454, when Andrew mac Brady, bifhop of Triburna, erected a church on the

fite of that founded by St. Fedlimid to whofe me‑
mory it was dedicated, and denominated Kilmore.
At prefent there are neither cathedral, chapter, nor
canons belonging to this fee; the fmall parifh
church of Kilmore, contiguous to the epifcopal
houfe, ferving for the purpofe of a cathedral.[*]

KINEL‑EOGHAIN, or the principal diftrict; an
ancient territory, comprehending the prefent coun‑
ty of Tyrone.

KNOCK‑AINE, fee Carran‑fearaidhe.

L.

LABERUS, or *Laberos*, an ancient city men‑
tioned by Ptolemy, and placed by him near the
river Boyne. Richard of Cirencefter makes it the
capital of the Voluntii. Laberus is evidently derived
from the ancient Britifh *Lbavar*, whence *Labbereigh*,
a fpeaking place in the ancient Irifh language, figu‑
ratively, a place of parliament where the ftates
affembled. The Laberus of Ptolemy was the hill
of Taragh, celebrated in the Irifh annals for being
the place where fat the convention of Taragh,
during the pagan times. This celebrated convention
appears to have been originally inftituted by the
Heremonian Belgians, on their firft fettlement in
Ireland, about 350 years before the Chriftian æra.
During the contefts between the feveral Belgian
and Caledonian fettlers, the ftates feldom had the
opportunity of affembling at ftated periods, until
about the beginning of the firft century, when
Cormar mor, called by feveral of the Irifh antiqua‑

[*] Harris's Ware, vol. 1. p. 225.

ries, *Concobar mac Neſſan*, by the advice of the arch-druid Cathbad, called in ſome of the ancient poems Ollam Fodla, or the learned High Prieſt, revived the inſtitution. From which period the monarchs of Ireland were conſtantly inaugurated on the ſtone of Deſtiny, erected on the hill near the Labhereigh, until the reign of Dermod mac Keruail, in 560; when the Chriſtian clergy anathematized the place. From that time the ſtates aſſembled in the court of the palace of Taragh, until the final deſtruction of that fortreſs by Brien Boromh, in 995. The Naaſ-teighan and Labhereigh, where the ſtates aſſembled, are ſtill viſible on the hill of Taragh. See Taragh.*

LABIUS, from *abh uis*, or the diſtrict of the river. A river mentioned by Richard of Cirenceſter; at preſent denominated the Liffey, being a corruption from Labheigh, the watery diſtrict.

LACHMANII, ſee Luchmanii.

LAGEAN, or the level country, the ſame as Hy Laoighis, which ſee.

LAMBAY, ſee Lumni.

LAVATH, from *Labh ath*, the ſhallow water; a river which iſſues from the weſtern declivity of Mount Cremmal, and falls into Lough Swilly. See Cromla.

LEA, or the plain; a diſtrict on the river Ban in the county of Antrim.

LEABA-FEINE, that is the beds or graves of the nobles. A name given by the preſent inhabit-ants to a ſpecies of tombs appertaining to the Mileſians, or ancient Iriſh nobleſſe; they conſiſt in general, of immenſe rock ſtones, placed on others,

---

* O'Conor's Diſſert. p. 13. 138. Baxter's Gloſſ. Ware.

either upright, or laid flat, the covering ftone being placed fome horizontal, others inclined, and often circumfcribed by a wall of loofe ftones. On feveral of thefe tombs, efpecially on thofe belonging to the Druids or Bards, are found infcriptions in fymbolic and alphabetic characters, fpecifying the name and quality of the perfon interred. According to the Irifh antiquaries, this fpecies of tombs were introduced about the beginning of the third century, burning the dead having then been univerfally difcontinued throughout the ifland. *

LEACHT-MHAGHTHAMHNA, fee Mufgruidhe.

LEANA, or Lena, a lake in the north of Ireland; Leana or Lena fignifies the place of the waters, and was moft probably Lough Foyle.

LEAN CLIATH, or the Fifhing Harbour; The prefent harbour of Dublin. Lean Cliath, or Leam Cliath, is derived from Lean or Leam, a harbour, and *Cliath* or *Cliabh*, which literally fignifies a hurdle, or any thing made of wicker work; it alfo fignified certain wiers made of hurdles and placed in rivers and bays by the ancient Irifh, for the purpofe of taking fifh. Whence any river or bay having thefe wiers placed in them, generally had the name of Cliath or Cliabh, added to them to fignify the eftablifhment of a fifhery. Dublin, therefore, being originally built on, or near one of thefe harbours, was anciently called *Bally lean Cliath*, that is the town on the fifhing harbour, and not as frequently tranflated, the town built on hurdles †.

* Mc. Curtin's Antiquities. Collectanea, No. 5.
† Baxter's Gloff. Harris's Ware, vol. 1.

LEAN CORRADH, or the harbour for boats; an ancient port on the Shannon near Killaloe.

LEGH MOGH and **LEGH CON**, otherwife written Leath Mogh and Leath Cuinn; two ancient grand divifions of Ireland made towards the clofe of the fecond century between Eogan More, furnamed Mogh Nuagad, king of Munfter, and Con, furnamed Ceadchathach, king of Taragh, dividing the ifland into two parts by a line drawn from Atchliath na Mearuidhe, now called Clarin's bridge, near Galway, to the ridge of mountains denominated Eifgir Riada, on which Cluainmacnois and Cluainirard are fituated, and from thence to Dublin. The fouthern divifion was called *Leagh Mogh*, or Mogh's part, and the northern Leagh Cuin or Conn's part. The intire country by this divifion was divided into two governments; which by the continual contentions of the feveral chiefs fubfifted only fifteen years, though the names were retained for feveral ages after, the fouthern part of Ireland being frequently called Legh Mogh and the northern Legh Conn, down to the fourteenth century.

LEGO, or the lake, fituated either in the county of Rofcommon or Sligo. Lego appears alfo to fignify a country of lakes, and was one of the ancient names of the prefent county of Rofcommon.

LEIM CON, or the harbour of the Cape, now Miffen Head.

LEIM CUCHULLAN, or *Leim na Con*, that is the harbour of the principal cape or headland, or the harbour of the cape; it is now called Loop

Head or Cape Lean, at the mouth of the Shannon *.

LEIX, fee Eile ui Mordha.

LENA, fee Moi Lena.

LESSMORE, or Lios-mor, that is the great inclofure or habitation; an ancient city and univerfity fituated on the banks of the Black water in the barony of the Decies, and county of Waterford. St. Carthagh, or Mochudu, in the beginning of the feventh century, founded an abbey and fchool in this place, which in a fhort time was much reforted to, not only by the natives, but alfo by the Britons and Saxons during the middle ages. According to an ancient writer of the life of St. Carthagh, Leffmor was in general inhabited by monks, half of it being an afylum into which no woman dare enter; confifting intirely of cells and monafteries, the ruins of which with feven churches are yet vifible; a caftle was built here by king John. The fite of Leffmor was in the early ages denominated *Magh Sgiath*, or the chofen field; being the fituation of a dun or fort of the ancient chieftains of the Decies, one of whom granted it to St. Carthagh on his expulfion from the abbey of Ratheny in Weftmeath. On becoming a univerfity, Magh Sgiath obtained the name of Dunfginne, or the fort of the Saxons, from the number of Saxons which reforted thereto, but foon after that of Lios-mor, or Leffmore. The bifhoprick of Leffmore was united to that of Waterford in 1363, feven hundred and thirty years after its foundation †.

* Collect. No. 4.
† Harris's Ware, v. 1. p. 589.

LETH CATHEL, from Lea Caël, that is the wood of the plain; the prefent barony of Lecale in the county of Down. See Dal Dichu.

LETHMANNICC, fee Luchmanii.

LIBINUS, from the old Britifh *Livn ui*, the clear water; a river in the weft of Ireland mentioned by Ptolemy, and thought by Cambden to be Sligo river, called by the Irifh *Slegach*, and by Cambrenfis *Slicbney*. But Richard of Cirencefter makes it to be Clew Bay *.

LIMNUS, fee Lumni.

LIOSMORE, fee Leffmore.

LOANIA, or the habitation on the wave, the prefent Kilaloe, or as it was anciently written *Kill da Lua*, that is the church of Lua, from *Lua* or *Molua*, who about the beginning of the fixth century founded an abbey in this place. St. Molua appears to have derived his name from Loania, the place of his refidence, as was cuftomary amongft the ancient Irifh. On the death of St. Molua, St. Flannan, his difciple and fon of the chieftain of the diftrict, was confecrated bifhop of Kill da Lua at Rome about the year 639; and the church endowed with confiderable eftates by his father Theodorick. Towards the clofe of the twelfth century, the ancient fee of Rofcrea was united to that of Kilaloe. From which period thefe united bifhopricks have been governed by the fame bifhops †.

LOCH, LOC, LUCH, Luigh, Loich, Lough, words in the ancient Hiberno-Celtic tongue, fig-

* Baxter's Gloff. Camden. Ware.
† Harris's Ware, v. p. 589.

nify a lake or a large piece of water, and sometimes the fea.

LOCH CUAN, or the lake of the harbour; the
prefent bay of Strangford.

LOCH EACHA, or *Loch Neach*, fo called from
Loch a lake, and *Neach* wonderful, divine, eminent or heavenly, is by far the largeft undivided
piece of water in Ireland, and fituated in the
county of Antrim. Its petrifying powers are not
inftantaneous, as feveral of the ancients have
fuppofed, but require a long feries of ages to bring
them to perfection, and appear to be occafioned
by a fine mud or fand which infinuates itfelf into
the pores of the wood, and which in procefs of
time, becomes hard like ftone. *Neach* has been
afferted by feveral modern antiquaries to fignify
a horfe, whence Loch Neach has been elegantly
tranflated a horfe-pond; but Neach in the old Irifh
tongue never fignified a horfe; it has been frequently indeed ufed in that fenfe by feveral of
the latter bards, as a metaphor, though the original fignification was *any thing noble, excellent or
eminent.*

LOCH ERE, or the weftern lake; an ancient
lake, where the city of Cork now ftands.

LOCH FEBHAIL, derived from *Loch Bheal,*
that is the lake of Beal; being facred in the times
of Heathenifm to pagan fuperftition; it is at prefent called Lough Foyle, being a corruption from
Febhail or Bheal, and is fituated in the county of
Derry.

LOCHLANIC, fee Luchmanii.

LOCH LEAN, or the enclofed lake, from being
furrounded by high mountains; the prefent lakes

of Killarney in the county of Kerry. Nennius fays that thefe lakes were encompaffed by four circles of mines; the firft was of tin, the fecond of lead, the third of iron, and the fourth of copper. In the feveral mountains, adjacent to the lakes, are ftill to be feen the veftiges of the ancient mines of iron, lead and copper, but tin has not as yet been difcovered here. Silver and gold are faid by the Irifh antiquaries to have been found in the early ages, but this is fomewhat doubtful, efpecially in any confiderable quantity, though fome filver probably was extracted from the lead ore, and fmall quantities of gold might have been obtained from the yellow copper ore of Mucrufs. However in the neighbourhood of thofe lakes were found in the early ages as well as at prefent, pebbles of feveral colours, which taking a beautiful polifh, the ancient Irifh wore in their ears, girdles and in other articles of their drefs and furniture *.

LOCH NAIR, a lake in Meath, in which Turgefius was drowned †.

LOCH NEACH, fee Loch eacha.

LOGIA, from the ancient Britifh *Lug ui*, or lake of the flowing waters; figuratively, any river, bay, or harbour where the 'tide flows; an ancient river in the north of Ireland mentioned by Ptolemy; thought by Baxter to be Lough Foyle, but by Ptolemy's and Richard's charts, it is evidently the bay of Carrigfergus.

LUBAR, a river in the north of Ireland. See Cromla.

---

* Nennii Hift. Britan. Ware.   † Collect. No. 4. p. 461.

LUCANIJ, or the people of the maritime country, from *Luch*, a lake or the fea, and *aneigh*, the
inhabitants of a country; an ancient people of Ireland, mentioned by Richard of Cirencefter, and
placed by him in the county of Kerry near Dingle
bay. But Ptolemy calls them *Luceni*, and they appear to be the Lugadii of the Irifh writers; which
in a general fenfe comprehended all the inhabitants
on the fouthern coafts, from the harbour of Waterford
to the mouth of the Shannon; though fometimes
confined to thofe of the county of Waterford. See
Breoghain and Lugadii.

LUCENI, fee Breoghain.

LUCHMANII, Lochlanicc, Loch-lannach, Lachmanii, and Leth-mannicc, names that frequently
occur in the Irifh hiftories during the middle ages,
as a foreign people who arrived in different periods
in this ifland. Who they were, and from what
country they came, have, for fome time, been a
fubject of enquiry among the learned in antiquities. But, without involving ourfelves in a cloud
of ufelefs erudition, it will be fufficient to obferve,
that *Luchmanii, Lachmanii, Lethmannicc, Lochlannicc,*
and *Lochlannach* fignify, in the old Irifh and Celtic
tongues, feamen or mariners; and are of
the fame import as the *Formorians* and *Ferloich* mentioned in the old Irifh Poems. They derived
their origin in reality from no particular country,
but were the merchants and feamen who vifited the
coafts of Ireland from the fecond century to the
clofe of the ninth after the chriftian æra, and whom
the feveral Irifh chiefs frequently engaged to affift
them againft their enemies during their ftay in the

ifland. Thefe Luchmanii were of the feveral countries of Iberia, Gaul, Britain, Belgia and Scandinavia, all of which in different periods held occafional commerce with Ireland *.

LUENTUM, an ancient town or city in Britain, mentioned by Ptolemy. Luentum or Luentinum is evidently from *Luen*, a harbour or bay, and *dunum*, *din*, a caftle or fortrefs; whence *Luentum* for *Luendum*, the habitation on the bay. It is now called *Lbannis*, or the place near the water, and Caér Keftylh or Caftle-town, and is fituated in fouth Wales †.

LUGADII, or Sliocht Lugach mac Ithy, that is, the maritime race defcendants of the inhabitants on the water; the ancient inhabitants of the prefent county of Waterford, called by Ptolemy Brigantes, and by the Irifh writers, Slioght Breoghain. (See Breoghain.)

LUG BHEATHAIL, fee Darabonis.

LUIGHNE, or the country of the lakes; an ancient diftrict in the fouth of the county of Sligo; part of which is ftill retained in the prefent barony of *Leyney*. It was alfo denominated *Hy Gaira*, or the diftrict of the land of waters, from containing feveral lakes. The ancient chieftains were called Hy Yara, or O'Gara; and the fubordinate dynafts were O'Donogh and O'Hara, all of whom remained in poffeffion of their ancient territories at the beginning of the laft century.

LUMNEACH, the moft ancient name of the prefent city of Limerick. The word is derived

---

* Collect. No. 4. Tacitus. Whitaker's Manchefter. O'Conor's Differt. † Baxter's Glofſ.

from *Luam* or *Liem*, a ftrand or port, and *Neach* eminent, whence Lumneach, by corruption Limerick, the eminent port. Ptolemy calls it *Macolicum*, which in the Cambric dialect of the Celtic tongue has nearly the fame fignification as Lumneach. Lumneach during the firft ages of chriftianity was much frequented by foreign merchants, and after the arrival of the Danes was a place of confiderable commerce until the twelfth century. It was plundered by Mahon, brother of Brien Boromh, after the battle of Sulchoid in 970; and Brien, in a future period, is faid to have exacted from the Danes of this city three hundred and fixty-five tuns of wine, as a tribute: which, if true, fhews the extenfive traffic carried on by thofe people in that article. About the middle of · the fixth century, St. Munchin erected a church and founded a bifhoprick at Lumneach, which however was deftroyed by the Danes on their taking poffeffion of this port in 853, and remained in ruins until their converfion to the chriftian faith in the tenth century; at which period the church of St. Munchin was rebuilt and the bifhoprick reftablifhed. Donald O'Brien, about the time of the arrival of the Englifh, founded and endowed the cathedral; and Donat O'Brien bifhop of Limerick in the thirteenth century contributed much to the opulence of the fee. About the clofe of the twelfth century, the bifhoprick of Inis-cathay was united to that of Limerick [*]

LUMNI, an ifland on the eaftern coaft of Ireland; mentioned by Ptolemy, and called by Pliny *Limnus*; *Lumni* or *Limnus* is evidently a cor-

[*] Collect. No. 4. Harris's Ware, v. 1. p. 50.

K 2

ruption from the ancient Britifh *Lan n'ùi*, or intirely in the water; being at fome diftance from the coaft. It is at prefent called Lambay, on the coaft of the county of Dublin *.

M.

MACOLICUM, an ancient Irifh city mentioned by Ptolemy, and placed by him and Richard of Cirencefter on the banks of the Shannon. The word appears to be a corruption from *Magh-Ol i cand*, that is the place of the principal wharf or port, and was evidently therefore the city of Limerick, the ancient *Lumneach*; though Baxter endeavours to derive it from *Magh Coille can*, or the place of the principal wood; whence he thinks it may be the prefent city of Kilkenny. But Ptolemy was intirely ignorant of the [internal parts of this ifland, and none of our domeftic writers mention Kilkenny before the tenth century under any denomination whatever.

MAGH, Moy, Moi, Ma and Mogh, in the old Irifh, fignified a plain in general, and fometimes a field or open place free from wood; in which fenfe it was of the fame import as Savannah or lawn; and was by no means fynonimous to *La-oighis* and *Moan*, the firft fignifying a flat or level country, and the latter a bog or wet plain.

MAGH-ADHAIR, or the field beyond the weftern water; A place in Thomond where the kings of north Munfter were inaugurated †.

MAGH-ALL-LEIGH, fee Hy-Falgia.

---

* Baxter's Gloff.   † Colleæ. No. 4.

MAGH-BREG, or the field of the caftles, or fortrefs; a plain round Taragh, in which was fituated the raths or palaces of the monarchs of Ireland, and of feveral of the princes and chiefs. See Bregia.

MAGH-CAELLAGH, fee Hy-Leagh.

MAGH-CIERNAN, fee Brefine.

MAGH-COITEOGHAN, fee Hy-Falgia.

MAGH-COITLAN, fee Hy-Falgia and Hy-Leag.

MAGH-CRU, or the *field of murder*, a place in Conaught. Towards the clofe of the early ages, the ancient Irifh nobility diftinguifhed under the name of Milefians, by the flattery of the bards and other circumftances carried themfelves with great haughtinefs towards the plebeians, not confidering them of the fame race, violating the chaftity of their wives and daughters with impunity, and triumphing over their lives and properties according to their wills. The people had long groaned under this tyranny of their chiefs without the power of redrefs, as the arms were entirely lodged in the hands of the Milefians, the lower orders not being allowed to bear any other weapons than flings and ftaves. However about the beginning of the firft century, Caibre called by hiftorians *Cin Cait* or chief of the Scots, a herdfman in Conaught, having attained fome authority among his brethern from the quantity of his poffeffions, was determined to attempt the deliverance of the people; but as force could not be employed, recourfe was had to ftratagem. For this purpofe Caibre invited the principal chiefs to a grand entertainment at Magh-Cru on condition that they came unarmed, this term being affented to, the plebeians during the feftival, fell upon the defencelefs nobles and put them to death, fparing neither age or fex. Such a maffacre fpread univerfal confternation throughout the ifland, and numbers of the Milefians fled to Britain and Gaul, whilft others took refuge in unfrequented woods, leaving their raths or caftles to the infurgents who ufurped the government of the feveral diftricts for near fifty years, but at length by the mediation of the Druids, who were in the intereft of the Milefian race, an accommodation took place, on condition of the plebeian order receiving feveral privileges, and a fecurity being given for their lives and poffeffions, and thofe who had obtained any confiderable property in herds were entitled in fome meafure to the rank of Milefians. So that from this period we may date the commencement of the emancipation of the old Irifh plebeian race [*].

MAGH-CUILAN, fee Dalnaruidhe.

MAGH-DUINE, or the field or plain of the people, celebrated from a battle fought there, between Lachtna the brother of Brien Borumh againft O'Floinn, about the year 953 [†].

MAGH-DUNEL, fee Dalnaruidhe.

MAGH-EAN, or the plain on the water; a plain between the river Erne and the bay of Donegall. See alfo Deaffii.

MAGH-FEMIN, derived from Magh-Bhoemoin, or the plain or field of the wet plain for cattle; comprehending all the boggy country round Cafhel, wherein the herds belonging to the kings of Cafhel were generally kept.

[*] Keating. Leabhuir Lecan.
[†] Collect. No. 4. p. 468.

MAGH-GAUROLL, fee Brefine.

MAGH-GENUISGE, fee Dalaradia and Damnii.

MAGH-GUIUR, fee Fermanagh.

MAGH-INIS, fee Dal-dichu.

MAGH-LABHIA, or the plain of the watery diftrict; being all the level country in the county of Dublin circumfcribed by the river Liffey.

MAGH-LEANA, or the plain of the level country; an ancient diftrict comprehending the greater part of the King's County, particularly that part denominated Hy-Allain, Hy-Fallia and Hy-Damfeigh. See Hy-Fallia, Hy-Allain and Cromla.

MAGH-NA-FEINE, fee Fearmuighe.

MAGH-NAY, or Magh-Neo, derived from *Magb-Noadb*, that is, the inhabited plain or country, comprehending the prefent county of Rofcommon, being the firft fettlement of the Belgic tribes in Conaught, and in which, the royal city of Croghan ftood. See Atha.

MAGH-RA-NALL. fee Conmacne.

MAGH-NEIRCE, fee Fearmuighe.

MAGH-RIADA, or the tribe of the plain or Savannah, or rather the inhabited plain, from *Magb* a plain or open in a wood, and *Riada* a tribe or vaffals of a king or chief, figuratively the demefne of a chief; The prefent heath of Maryborough in the Queen's County, the original demefne of the O'Mores, chiefs of Laoighois or Leix; in which was fought a memorable battle between the people of Munfter and thofe of Leinfter, under the command of Laoighois Cean Mordha about the middle of the third century; the bones of the flain being found at this day a few inches below the

surface of the ground on the borders of the heath *.
See Maiftean *.

MAGH-SGIATH, fee Lifmore.

MAGH-SLANE, Slane on the river Boyne
county of Meath †.　See Ferta fir feic.

MAGH-SLEUGHT, or Moy-Sleucht, that is
the plain of the hoft or facrifice; a place fituated
near Fenagh in the barony of Mohil, and county
of Leitrim, celebrated in the ancient Irifh poems
for being the place where Tigernmas firft introduced the worfhip of *Crom* or Fate, the principal deity
of the Cambric Britons, which, fome few years before the birth of Chrift, was by their Druids introduced into Ireland.　This circumftance however fo
difpleafed the ancient Hibernian Druids, the worfhippers of Beal, that Tigernmas and his followers
are faid to have been deftroyed by lightning ‡.

MAGH-TUREY, or Moy-Turey, derived from
Magh-Tora, or the high plain.　There were two
places under this name, the northern and fouthern;
The fouthern Magh-Turey was in the county of
Galway, not far from Lough-Mafk, and is celebrated in the Irifh poems for being the fcene of
action between the Belgian and Danan or Caledonian Septs, about eighty or one hundred years
before the chriftian æra, in which the former were
intirely defeated.
The northern Magh-Turey was fituated near Lough
Arrow in the county of Rofcommon, fo denominated from Tura an high hill or rock, being furrounded on all fides by mountains.　It is celebrated
for being the fcene of action between the Belgians
and Fomorians on one fide, and the Danans on

---

* Keatiug.　　† Annales Annon. 149.
‡ Q'Conor's Differt. p. 92.　McCurtin.

the other, some few years before the birth of Christ; in which the Belgians were again defeated *.

MAISTEAN, from *Naasteaghan*, pronounced *Naistean*, that is the place of the assembly of the elders, the place where the states of south Leinster met, it is the same as Carmen, which see. Here a battle was fought about the middle of the third century between the people of Munster and those of Leinster under the command of *Laoigheis Caen More*, chief of Leix in the Queen's County. *Laoigheis* according to Keating defeated the Munster army from the top of Maistean to *Athtrodain* now Athy in the county of Kildare; and pursued them into Leix, when the battle was renewed on the plains of *Magh-Riada* now the heath of Maryborough, where *Laoigheis* obtained a second victory and drove the fugitives into their native country †.

MAYO, corrupted from *Magh iii*, or the place or field on the water; an ancient city and university founded about the sixth century for the education of such of the Saxon youths as were converted to the christian faith. It was situated a little to the south of Lough Con, in the county of Mayo, and is to this day frequently called Mayo of the Saxons ‡, being celebrated for giving education to Alfred the great, king of England §.

MEDINO, see Miadhanagh.

MEDIOLANUM, an ancient city or district in the county of Meath, thought to be either Trim or Kells. The word appears to be derived from *Madh by lanioü*, or the district of the great plain of

* O'Conor's Dissert. p. 166. 167.   † Keating's Hist.
‡ Bedæ, lib. 4. cap. 4.   § O'Conor's Dissert,

the waters; and is moſt probably, the preſent county of Weſtmeath, calledʹ in former times *Hy Magb locblin*, or the diſtrict of the plain on the water; the ancient chiefs of which were the O'Maclaghlins kings of Meath, they were frequently elected monarchs of Ireland during the tenth and eleventh centuries; ſome of the Maclaghlins were in poſſeſſion of their ancient patrimony at the commencement of the laſt century. This diſtrict alſo in the early ages was denominated *Colman*, from *Coilleman*, or the woody country, whence the inhabitants obtained the name of *Clan-Colman* or the children of the woody country.

MENAPIA, an ancient city mentioned by Ptolemy, and was the capital of the Menapii; now Wicklow, the Euolenum of Probus.

MENAPII, an ancient diſtrict on the eaſtern coaſts of Ireland, mentioned by Ptolemy. *Menapii* is evidently derived from the old Britiſh *Mene ui poü*, that is, the narrow diſtrict or country; comprehending that part of the preſent county of Wicklow between the mountains andʹ the ſea, called by the Iriſh writers *Coulan*, or the narrow encloſed country. See Coulan.

MIADHANAGH, written ſometimes *Medino* and *Meteno*, that is the principal or honourable country, the preſent county of Meath. This diſtrict was the moſt ancient ſettlement of the Belgians in Ireland, in conſequence of which, the inhabitants were eſteemed the eldeſt and moſt honourable tribe. From which ſeniority their chieftains were elected monarchs of all the Belgæ; a dignity that was continued in the Hy nFaillian line without interruption until the arrival of the Caledonian colonies under the name of Tuath de Danan, when Connor

mor chieftain of thefe people, obtained or rather
ufurped the monarchial throne, obliging *Eoghach
Bhealach*, or *Eochy Failloch*, with feveral of his people to crofs the Shannon and eftablifh themfelves
in the prefent county of Rofcommon, where Crothar
founded the palace 'of Atha or Croghan. A circumftance which brought on a long and bloody
war between the Belgian and Caledonian races,
which was not finally terminated until the clofe of
the fourth century, when the Belgian line was
reftored in the perfon of O'Niall the great, and continued until Brian Boromh ufurped the monarchial
dignity by depofing Malachy O'Malachlin, about
the year 1001.

MILEDH, a people mentioned frequently in
the ancient Irifh poems and afferted by the more
modern antiquaries to have been Milefians, a fuppofed people from Spain, defcended from the ancient Carthaginians, who under the conduct of Heber
and Heremon, fons of Milefius, a prince of that
country, about the fourteenth century before Chrift,
arrived in fixty fhips on the coafts of Ireland, and
eftablifhed a numerous colony therein. Though
Irifh hiftories and chronicles of the latter ages are
very circumftantial on this fubject, yet the more
ancient fpeak but imperfectly concerning it. The
truth is, the whole ftory appears to have originated from fome affertions in the ancient druidic hif-
toric poems, about the beginning of the eighth
century. In thefe works, part of which is preferved, in the Leabhuir Leacan, frequent mention is made of *Miledh fliocht Fene* and *Miledh Efpaine*, as ancient inhabitants of Ireland. The old
pagan Irifh language, had in a great meafure become obfolete in the eighth century, and a num-

ber of expreffions in the ancient poems were in that period not understood. *Miledb* or *mBealadb Fene*, therefore by the christian clergy of the middle ages, were interpreted Milefius the Phœnician, as it has some refemblance to Milefius the Phœnician who fettled on the weftern coast of Spain about the fourteenth century before the christian æra. The word *Miledb* is evidently derived from *mBealedb*, that is, the worfhipper or defcendant of Beal, figuratively a nobleman or Druid; *Fene*, as we have obferved under that word, is a learned or wife perfon, whenc *Miledb Fene* fignifies a learned nobleman or Druid; and *Miledb Slioght Fene* is the learned noble race. In the fame manner, Miledh Eufpainne, the fon of Golam, under whofe conduct the Iberians fettled in the fouth of Ireland, is fuppofed to fignify Milefius the Spaniard; but *Eafpainne*, *Efpaine* or *Hefpin* in the old Celtic tongue fignified any naked, barren or dry place; and frequently a barren rocky or mountainous country; Whence *Miledb Efpainne Mac Golam*, fignifies the nobleman from the barren mountainous country of the Caël. From this confideration it is evident, that the Milefians who have made fo confiderable a figure in the Irifh annals during the latter ages were Britifh colonists, who under the conduct of their druids and chiefs, fled from the terror of the Roman arms, at the commencement of the first century. As to the three fons of Milefius, fo much fpoken of, they were no other than the different colonies of the Caël inhabiting the feveral parts of the ifland, fo denominated from their fituation, as Heremon the weftern country, Heber or the moft weftern country, &c. From the word Efpainne being annexed to fome of the emigrants it is probable they came from the mountains of Wales, in the western coaſt of Britain [*]. See Bolgæ, Heremonii, Fene, Scoiteigh and Hy-Failgia.

MILVIGR, of the ſame ſignification as Miledh.

MIS-SLIABH, or mountains of the Moon, from *Mi, Mios* or *Mis* the moon, and Sliabh a mountain. There are two mountains under this denomination, one in the county of Antrim where St. Patrick kept the ſwine of his maſter Milco; the other in the county of Kerry near Tralee bay, where according to Keating *Eadbna Dearg*, a king of munſter, lies buried who died of the plague a ſhort time after he had erected the firſt mint for the coinage of money at Airgiod Rofs. Theſe mountains are called *Mis*, probably from an adoration paid to the moon thereon, by the pagan inhabitants [†].

MOAN, ſignifies a bog or wet plain.

MODONUS, derived from *Mogh Dun uïſe*, or the river of the mountainous country, an ancient river mentioned by Ptolemy and thought by Camden to be the river Slany, in the county of Wicklow, as it riſes in the mountains; though Baxter endeavours to derive it from the old Britiſh *Modon uiſc*, or the deep river, a quality which certainly does not belong to the Slany unleſs it be in conſequence of its courſe lying through deep and dark vallies.

MOGH, Magh, Mabh or Moghum, from *mOgh* or *mOghum*, that is wiſdom or fruitfulneſs, whence Magh a plain or place capable of producing the

---

[*] O'Conor's Diſſert. Baxter's Gloſſ. Keating. McCurtin.
[†] Keating. Life of St. Patrick, and Vallancey's Eſſay on the Celtic language.

vegetable productions of the earth. In the old Irish and Celtic mythology the chief of the Genii who presided over the various productions of nature, and signified the genial influence of the sun or that universal vivifying spirit which exists throughout the universe, being supposed to nourish and bring forth the animal and vegetable productions of the earth. This divinity received several names according to the different departments it was supposed to occupy; when considered as the active principle of nature, it was denominated *Mogh* or wisdom, being the same as the Greek Minerva or Pallas; when the earth or mother of nature, it was denominated by the Irish *Tlacht* and *Eadhna*, by the Britons *Andate*, by the Greeks *Ceres*, *Cybele* and *Vesta*, by the Persians *Astarte*, by the Egyptians *Isis*, by the Italians *Ops*, by the Samothracians *Cotis*, and by the Saxons *Eostar*. When presiding over the forests and chief of the *Fiodh Rhebe*, it was denominated by the Irish *Mabh*, by the Greeks *Diana*, and by the Romans *Pan*. When considered as the genius of Plenty, it was called by the Irish *Satarn* or *Satharan*, being the Saturn of the Greeks and Romans, and when taken for the influence of the solar rays, it was denominated by the Irish *Mortinne* or the great or good fire, being the Mercury of the Greeks and Romans. See Tlachgo, Mogh-adair, Mabh, Saturn, Eadhna and Mortinne [*].

MOGH-ADAIR, or Magh-adair, that is the sanctuary of the wise divinity of the tombs, being temples or sanctuaries dedicated to *Mogh* or *Sodorn* and the manes of heroes. They were situated

---

[*] Vallancey's essay on the Celtic language. Jurieu's critical history of the church, vol. 2d.

either on plains or hills, but moft-generally on fruitful places in the centre of woods, and were differently conftructed. Some confifted of circular areas
furrounded with upright anomalous ftones; in the
centre of which was placed an altar, whereon facrifices were offered, as is evident from the remains
of feveral ftill vifible in different parts of Ireland,
particularly near Bruff in the county of Limerick,
New Grange in the county of Meath, and Slidery
Ford in the county of Down. In other places they
confifted of circular rows of upright ftones inclofing
an altar and accompanied by a conical mound of
earth or ftone, the whole circumfcribed by a rampart and ditch, as is feen at this day at Skirk in the
Queen's County. All thefe fanctuaries were cemeteries and fepulchres, the dead being interred under
the mound, altar and upright ftones; as is
evident by human bones or urns being conftantly
found under fuch as have been opened.

The facrifices performed in thefe fanctuaries were
at the time of the Bealtinnes, on the eve of war
and return from victory. The victims were in
general deer, oxen and captives taken in war; the
ceremonies ufed here being the fame as thofe obferved at the feftivals of Ufneach, Tailtean and
Tlachgo in honour of the fun, moon and univerfal
nature. It was here as on the top of the Cairns and
Tumuli that thofe flept who confulted the manes
of their anceftors who were fuppofed to inform
them either by dreams or vifions of circumftances
relative to the future events of their life. Here
alfo reforted the Druids whofe bufinefs was to
divine by dreams and vifions of the night, the
ghofts of the departed being fuppofed to vifit the

places of their interment, and inform their defcendants of the tranfactions of ages yet to come.
Whence is derived the notion of Spectres and Apparitions fo prevalent among the lower orders of
the people at this day *.

MOI-LENA, or the plain or open country on
the bay or gulph of the fea; fituated in the diftrict of Inis Owen near Lough Foyle.

MOIN-NA-INSEIGH, or the iflands of the bog,
called by Cambrenfis *Inchinemeo*, or the divine Iflands,
fituated about three miles from Rofcrea, in the
county of Tipperary. In this place, formerly in
the bofom of a large wood, a monaftery of Colidei, was founded in the tenth century; the ruins
of which confifting of the priory church and two
other churches are ftill vifible.

MOIN-MOR, or the great bog, all that marfhy
ground near the prefent city of Cork; being part
of the ancient Corcaluighe and celebrated from
being the field of battle between Mortogh O'Brien
king of Thomond and Dermod Mac Carthy,
king of Defmond in 1151, when Mortogh was
flain with the principal Dalcaffian nobility †.

MOMA, fee Muma.

MOMONII, the ancient inhabitants of the prefent province of Munfter. The word appears to
be derived from the old Celtic or Britifh words *Moi*
a region and *Mam* maternal, whence *Mouman* or
Momon a maternal or aboriginal country. This part

---

* Mc. Curtin's Ant. Jurieu's critical hift. ofthe church,
vol. 2. Collectanea, No. 5. Vallancey's Effay on the
Celtic language.
† Collect. No. 4. p. 580.

of Ireland being principally inhabited by the *Nemethæ* who retired from the Bolgæ on their settlement in *Heremonia*, the prefent Leinfter, about three hundred and fifty years before Chrift; we find in all the ancient Irifh hiftories the fouthern parts of the ifland denominated *Mumban* or the country of the Aborigines, and the inhabitants in confequence thereof called Mumhanii or Momonii, that is the Inhabitants of the country of the Aborigines *. See Nemethæ, Bolgæ and Iberii.

MOR, the fea, or any large extenfive piece of water. See Virgivium mare.

MOR-BHERGUS, fee Virgivium mare.

MOR-WERIDH, or *Mor Güerydh*, in the old Britifh fignifies the weftern or Irifh fea; at prefent denominated St. George's channel †.

MOY, fee Magh.

MUDHORN, or high land, the prefent barony of Mourne in the fouth of the county of Down; Here St. Jarlath the fecond bifhop of Ardmagh was born.

MULLABHOGHAGH, or the promontory on the water, or river of iflands; the prefent Miffen Head; the Auftrinum of Ptolemy, which fee.

MUMA, or Moma, from the old Celtic, *Mam moii*, or the place or fanctuary of the great mother; a cave celebrated for Druidic myftic rites, facred to mother Ops, or Aonach, in which the chiefs of the Bolgæ met on any emergency, to confult the manes of their heroes. It was moft probably the Drum-

---

* Baxter's Gloff. Brit. Keating.
† Baxter's Gloff.

Druid of the Irish writers; situated at Croghan, between Elphin and Abby Boyle.

MUMHAN, the moft ancient name of the province of Munfter; derived from the old Celtic *Mamman*, or the country of the great mother. All the Celtic tribes, in general, denominated themfelves not from their chieftains, as commonly fuppofed, but either from their fituation, or object of religion. The principal objects of adoration amongft them, were firft, Fate, or Providence, under the names of *Crom*, *Crim*, or *Crum*. Secondly, the fun or elementary fire, confidered as the active principle of nature, under the names *Baal*, *Beal* and *Bol*, or *Heul*, *Ull* and *Oll*. Thirdly, The earth or univerfal nature, confidered as the paffive principle, or great mother; under the feveral names of *Mamman*, *Ama*, *Anum*, *Anagh*, *Aonagh*, *Ops* and *Sibbol*. Thofe who confidered Fate as their object of adoration, denominated themfelves *Crombrii*, or *Crimbrii*, as thofe who inhabited the weftern coafts of Belgium. And thofe, as the aboriginal Britons, who confidered the fun as the principle, denominated themfelves Bolgæ, Bealadh and Ulladh; whilft thofe who thought the earth moft worthy of efteem, denominated themfelves Mamanagh, or Mamonii, that is, children of the earth, or great mother. The moft ancient inhabitants of the fouth of Ireland, derived their origin from the ancient Silures, who inhabited the fouthern coafts of Britain, and tho' of the Belgian faith, principally adored *Maman*, or the great mother; whence they in particular, diftinguifhed themfelves by the name of Momonii; and on their arrival in Ireland gave their divifion the name of Moma, or Mumhan; a name which is ftill retained in the prefent name of Munfter, comprehending the counties of Waterford, Cork, Limerick, Tipperary, Kerry and Clare; divided, during the latter ages, into *Defmond*, or fouth Munfter; *Ormond* or eaft Munfter; and *Thomond*, or north Munfter *. See Bolgæ, Miledh, Defmond and Thomond.

MURI, a celebrated Druidic academy in the north of Ireland, at or near Ardmagh.

MUR-OLLAVAIN, or the fchool of the learned high prieft; a celebrated academy of the arch-druid held at Taragh; erected about the time of the eftablifhment of the convention, and which gave rife to thofe of Eamania, Cruachain and Carmen.

MUSGRUIDHE, now the barony of Mufgry in the county of Cork, in which is fituated the Muffiry mountains, near Macroomp, on which Mahon, the brother of Brien Boromh, was flain, at the place called *Leácht Mhaghthambna*, or Mahon's Grave, about the year 976.

N.

NASS, or the place of the elders; now Naas in the county of Kildare, where the ftates of Leinfter affembled during the fixth, feventh and eighth centuries after the Naafteighan of Carmen had been anathematized by the chriftian clergy.

* Baxter's Gloff. O'Conor's Differt. Whitaker's Manchefter.

NAGUATÆ, derived from *na Gae taegh*, or the habitation on the sea; an ancient district in the west of Ireland mentioned by Ptolemy, and corruptly written in some of his copies *Nagnatæ*, it was called by the old Irish *Sliogbt Gae*, or the race on the sea; the present county of Sligo.

NEM, divine or excellent; the poetic name of the river Blackwater.

NEMETHÆ, pronounced *Momæ* or *Nomæ*, from the old Celtic *Mou* or *Nou* a country, and *Mam* or *Mae* maternal, whence Momæ or Nomæ original people; the aboriginal inhabitants of Ireland according to the most ancient poems and histories. They appear to be the same as the Partholanii and are said to be antecedent to the Bolgæ being some of the aboriginal clans of Britain who transmigrated to this island before the arts of civil life had made any considerable progress in the western parts of Europe; for according to the Irish bards they subsisted entirely by the chace and on the spontaneous productions of the earth. In their time the *Fomboraice* or Punic traders arrived on the coast of this island about five hundred years before the christian æra under the conduct of Midacritus; a circumstance which in some measure ascertains the period in which Ireland first obtained its inhabitants. For allowing two hundred years from the arrival of the *Nemethæ* to that of the *Fomboraice*, seven hundred years before Christ will be had for the first arrival of the Celtic tribes on the Hibernian coasts. On the arrival of the Bolgæ in Leinster, the ancient *Heremonia*, numbers of the Nemethæ retired into the southern parts, which to this day bears their name in the present province of Munfter *. See Bolgæ, Momonii, Partholanii and Fomhoraicc.

NOTIUM PROMONTORIUM, the ancient name of a promontory in the fouth of Ireland, mentioned by Ptolemy, and thought by Camden to be Beer Head; but moft probably it was Miffen Head, at the entrance of Dúnmanus Bay. Notium is derived from *Nodui,* or the fortrefs on the water; being a rath or caftle of fome of the Irifh chiefs erected for the greater convenience of traffic with foreign merchants; it is the *Auftrinum* of Richard.

O.

O, fee Hy.

OBOCA, the ancient name of a river or bay in the eaft of Ireland, mentioned by Ptolemy, thought by Camden and Richard of Cirencefter to be Arklow river. Oboca is evidently derived from the old Britifh *Aviicb,* or the opening of the water; it moft probably therefore was the bay of Dublin; as the foreign merchants, from whom Ptolemy received his account of thefe iflands, feldom vifited fuch obfcure rivers, as that of Arklow.

OFFALLY, fee Hy Falgia.

OIGH-MAGH, that is the plain or refidence of the champion or chief; now Omagh in the county of Tyrone, one of the ancient raths or caftles of the old chiefs of that country.

* Keating, O'Flaherty, Baxter's Gloff. Brit. Plin. l. 7. c. 56. Herodt. p. 254.

OILEACH, a rath or palace of the O'Neals, three miles from Derry, the same as *Aileach*; which fee.

ORGIEL, Oriel and Uriel, derived from *Oir Caël*, or the eastern Caël; an ancient extensive district comprehending the present counties of Louth, Monaghan and Ardmagh, governed by its proper king, subject in some respects to the supreme monarch. The sovereignty of this district was generally invested in the family of the O'Carrols, hereditary chieftains of Hy Cairol.

OIRTHER, or the eastern country; a district in the south of the county of Ardmagh, it was also denominated *Hy An-lan*, or the district on the river, the hereditary chiefs of which were the Hy Anlan corruptly O'Hanlon; some of whom were in possession of their ancient patrimony at the commencement of the last century.

OLNEGMACHT, or Alnecmacht, that is, the habitation of the chief tribe of the *Belgæ* or *Bolgæ*, the ancient name of Conaught; comprehending the present counties of Roscommon, Galway, Sligo and Mayo. This province probably obtained this Denomination on the retreat of the Bolgæ from the Tuath de Danans, or Caledonian tribes, on their arrival in Ulster, about the commencement of the first century prior to the Christian æra. It was also called Conmachne or Conmacne cuilt olla, that is the chief race, from a Sept of that name inhabiting the present county of Roscommon; the hereditary chiefs of which were, for several ages, kings of Conaught, to whom were tributary the ancient tribes of *Slioght Gae, Gaemanda,, Morift, Galeng, Conmacne cuilt ola* with their subordinate diftricts. The government of the Olnegmachts was founded by Eoghy Fealogh or Crothar, on his fettlement at Croghan, about the time of Auguftus Cæfar. See Conmacne Cuilt ola, Atha and Crog-han.

ORMOND, fee Ara.

OSRAIGII, derived from *Uys raigagh*, or the kingdom between the water, the prefent Offory, called alfo *Hy Pau drüig*, or the diftrict of the coun-try between the rivers; this diftrict originally en-tending through the whole country between the rivers Nore and Suire; being bounded on the north and eaft by the Nore, and on the weft and fouth by the Suire. The hereditary chiefs of which were denominated *Giolla-Padruic*, or the chief of the country between the rivers; called alfo Mac Gilla Padruic, thefe princes make a confiderable figure in the ancient Irifh hiftory; and one in par-ticular diftinguifhed himfelf in the fervice of his country againft the Englifh on their firft invafion. In an early period they were difpoffeffed of part of their patrimony by the kings of Cafhel; and the fouthern parts were occupied by the Butlers and other Englifh adventurers; but the northern re-mained to the original proprietors; who on their connection with the Englifh took or changed their name to Fitz Patrick, whofe defcendants, to this day, enjoy a large landed property in the domini-ons of their anceftors, with the title of Earl of Upper Offory. Offory is at prefent part in Leinfter and part in Munfter, being fituated in the counties of Kilkenny, Tipperary and the Queen's county. During the middle ages it fometimes was tributary to the king's of Munfter and Leinfter alternately, as circumftances admitted, but the chieftains conftantly derived their origin from the Heremonian race, and not from the Heberian.

OVERNIA, fee Eiroin.

P.

PARTHOLANI, the ancient inhabitants of Ireland, mentioned by the bards, and faid to have been colonies prior to the arrival of the Bolgæ. All knowledge of thefe people are loft, as well as that of the Nemethæ. They probably were fome of the aboriginal Britons, and arrived in this ifland about the time of the Nemethæ, that is, in the beginning of the fixth century, prior to the Chriftian æra. Partholani feem to be derived from *Bhoerüys lan-ui*, or herdfmen from beyond the great water; they being perhaps, the firft colony which introduced cattle into this country.

PHENEACHUS, or the learned code; the code of laws enacted by the convention of Taragh, and written on tables of wood, much celebrated in Irifh poems.

PHÆNICIANS, the inhabitants of Phænice, the ancient Canaan; who in an early period eftablifhed colonies on the eaftern coafts of Spain, (the ancient Iferia). and at Carthage; and about 600 years before the Chriftian æra, obtained poffeffion of the weftern coafts of Spain. The later writers on the antiquities of Ireland, have fuppofed, from feveral expreffions in the ancient poems and traditions, that confiderable colonies of thefe people in a very early period fettled themfelves in this ifland. The circumftances which have led the learned into this opinion, is the word *Phene* or *Fene*, being frequently found in the compositions of the ancient bards, and which have been supposed to signify the Phœnicians. Phene, we have shewn under that word, imports a learned or noble person, and can have no relation to either the Phœnicians or Carthaginians. These people, were indeed, frequently denominated *Pæni* and *Phænices*, by the Greeks and Romans, though they constantly distinguished themselves by the name of *Canaich*, or merchants; the ancient Irish therefore must either have spoken of them under the denomination of Canaith, merchants, or *Fomboraicc* seamen or rovers; and Fomhoraicc they are actually called in the old traditions. Though there is the greatest probability that the Punic traders during their commerce with Britain, frequently visited this island, yet we are intirely ignorant in respect of the colonies established, or the improvements introduced into the country by such an intercourse. At the period the Carthaginians discovered the islands of Britain, the arts of civil life had made considerable progress among the Phœnicians and their colonies, on the coasts of Spain and Africa; especially in architecture, astronomy and letters; if therefore any colonies had been established in Ireland, we may suppose some remains of their buildings would have been visible at this day; but in the counties of Clare and Kerry, where, according to the ancient poems, the Fomhoraicc mostly frequented, no vestiges of any monument of antiquity that can with any degree of propriety be attributed to the Phœnicians, are to be discovered; whence we may reasonably suppose, these ancient merchants only occasionally visited the coasts of

Ireland, and traded with the barbarous natives, for fifh, fkins and fuch other articles of commerce, as the ifland then produced; whilft Britain, on account of its valuable mines of tin, remained the principal place of rendezvous, and where fome fmall factories probably were eftablifhed, for the convenience of trade. This trade, however, was abolifhed, about the clofe of the fecond Punic war, on the deftruction of Carthage, and the conqueft of Spain by the Romans, but was at length reftored by the Maffylians, who carried on a confiderable commerce with the Britifh ifles, until the arrival of the Belgæ under the conduct of Divitiacus, about 100 years before the Chriftian æra, when on the conqueft of Cornwall by thofe people, the ancient Silures, with the foreign merchants eftablifhed among them, were obliged to quit their native country, fome fled acrofs the Severn into South Wales, whilft others took refuge in the fouthern and weftern parts of Ireland, and were diftinguifhed by the Irifh bards by the names of Heberii, Dergtenii, &c. See Heberii, Fomhoraicc, Breoghan and Dergtenii.

PHENU, or the learned race; a people mentioned by the ancient bards, and by them faid to be the people who introduced letters into this country. They were evidently the Druids, who engroffed all knowledge amongft the ancient inhabitants of thefe iflands, and who retired in great numbers into Ireland, from Britain, foon after the arrival of the Romans *.

PHENIUSA-FARSA, fee Feniufa-Farfa,
PORTLARGI, fee Cuanleargi.

* O'Conor's Differt,

R.

RABIUS, fee Rhebius.

RACHLIN, fee Riccina.

RACHREA, fee Riccina.

RAITH, fee Rath.

RAPHOE, fee Rath-both.

RATH, Raith and Rha, a caftle or fortrefs of the ancient Irifh chiefs; confifting of an area, furrounded by a ditch and a rampart of earth, in which were erected palaces and other buildings; it fignifies alfo, any habitation.

RATH-ASCULL, fee Coalan.

RATH-BOTH, or the Rath or village of cottages, from *Rath*, a fortrefs, fenced place, or village, and Both or Boith a cottage; fituated near Lough Swilly, in the county of Donegall, and is the prefent town of Raphoe. Here a bifhoprick was founded by St. Eunan, about the middle of the fixth century, and a cathedral was erected on the ruins of the church of St. Eunan, in the eleventh. Patrick Magonail, bifhop of Raphoe, built three epifcopal houfes In 1360; and bifhop Pooley, by will, bequeathed £.200, for repairing the cathedral; which money was applied by his fucceffor. They fhew ftill the bed of St. Eunan, and within thefe few years, a round tower was ftanding on a hill in which the bifhops of Raphoe kept their ftudies. A celebrated crofs, famous for the performance of miracles, ftood in the cathedral, but was about the year 1438, removed to Ardmagh, by bifhop O'Galchor *.

* Harris's Ware, vol. 1.

RATH-INBHER, or the fortreſs at the mouth of the river. A caſtle of the chiefs of Croich Coulan, at the mouth of Bray river. Here Saint Patrick was refuſed admiſſion by the Pagan inhabitants on his arrival to convert them to the chriſtian faith *.

RATH-KELTAIR, or Rath-Coilletar, that is, the fortreſs of the woody country. It was the caſtle and principal reſidence of the chiefs of the Ulleigh or Ulidii, and was ſituated near Downpatrick, in the barony of Lecale, and county of Down, in the ancient diſtrict of Dal-Dichu. The ditches and ramparts of this ancient fortreſs are remaining to this day, and occupy near two acres of ground. It was probably erected by the chiefs of the Ulleigh on their firſt eſtabliſhment in this country, ſome few years before the birth of Chriſt. On the arrival of St. Patrick, this rath was inhabited by Keltair mac Duach, chieftain of this diſtrict, who granted a place for the building of a church on a hill called Dun, and from which Down has obtained its preſent name. The church of Down was made a biſhoprick by St. Cailan, about 499. See Dunum, Dal Dichu, Dal Riada, and Damnij †.

RATH-LEAN, or the fortreſs on the water; the caſtle and reſidence of the ancient chieftains of Ibhe-Eachach ‡.

RATH-LURE, ſee Ardſrath.

---

* Harris's Ware, vol. 1. p. 12.
† Harris's Ware, vol. 1. p. 193. and Hiſt. Co. Down.
‡ Collect. No. 4. p. 569.

RATH-MOR-MUIGHE-LINE, or the great rath or fortrefs near the water ; the royal feat of the kings of Dalnaruidhe, in the county of Antrim, fituated on the river Ban, and was probably the Rhoboghdiu of Richard of Cirencefter, and the prefent Coleraine ‖.

RATH-NA NURLAN, or the fortrefs of the clay or boggy country ; a caftle of a dynaft on the plains of Cafhel, where Lorcan halted on his vifit to Cormac, king and archbifhop of Cafhel ‡.

REGIA, or the royal refidence ; an ancient city in the north of Ireland, mentioned by Ptolemy; it was evidently the prefent Clogher, the rath or palace of the ancient kings of Ergall, before which, St. Patrick directed Macartin to build a monaftery, which afterwards became a bifhoprick.

REGIA ALTERA, or the high habitation of the king ; an ancient city in the fouth of Ireland, mentioned by Ptolemy, and feems to be the fame as Brughrigh, capital of Cairbre-Aobhdha ; fee Brughrigh.

RELIG NA RIOGH, or the refting place of the kings. The fepulchre of the ancient kings of Conmacne Cuilt Ola, near Croghan. It confifts of a circular area of about two hundred feet in diameter, furrounded with a ftone ditch greatly defaced. Several tranfverfe ditches are within the area ; alfo heaps of coarfe ftones piled upon each other, fpecifying the graves of the interred perfons. From the conftruction of this cemetery, it appears

‖ Collect. No. 4. p. 522. ‡ Ibid No. 4. p. 453.

to have been erected in the latter ages of paganiſm, about the cloſe of the firſt century *.

RHEBA, or the royal habitation; an ancient city mentioned by Ptolemy; ſituated according to Richard of Cirenceſter, ſouth of Lough Erne. It was the rath of the Magh Guires, ancient chieftains of the county of Fermanagh, the Erdinii of Ptolemy.

RHEBAN, from *Righ ban*, or the habitation of the king. A rath or caſtle belonging to the O'Mordhas, chieftains of *Eli ui Mordha*; ſituated on the river Barrow near Athy. The ruins of the rath are ſtill viſible, though much defaced; near which are alſo remaining the ruins of a caſtle built in the reign of King John, by Richard de St. Michael, created Baron of Rheban by Marſhal earl of Pembroke, lord palatine of Leinſter †.

RHEBIUS, a lake mentioned by Richard of Cirenceſter, and called by Ptolemy Rabius or Rabios; derived evidently from *Ro abb iu*, that is, the great water of the river; the preſent Lough Erne.

RHOBOGDÆ PROMONTORIUM, or the promontory of the race on the water, mentioned by Ptolemy; now Fair Head in the county of Antrim.

RHOBOGDIJ, a people who inhabited the north of Ireland, in the county of Antrim; mentioned by Ptolemy; Rhobogdij is evidently derived from the old Britiſh *Rhobb üog düi*, or the race on the water of the ſea, the *Dalnaruidhe* of the Iriſh writers ‡.

---

* O'Conor's Diſſert. p. 129. † Ware.
‡ Baxter's Gloſſ.

RHOBOGDIU, an ancient city, mentioned by Richard; the capital of the Rhobogdij, situated on the river Ban, the same as Rathmormuighe line, and Culraithen, which see.

RICCINA, an island on the northern coasts of the county of Antrim, mentioned by Ptolemy, and called by Antoninus Riduna, and by others Reglina; the Rachrea and Rachlin of the Latin writers; all which words are derived from *Rich*, *Rach*, *Ridh*, *Rudh*, *Riada*, and *Reuda*, a tribe or habitation; and *ean* or *lean*, water; whence the habitation in the water; the present isle of Rachlin.

RIDUNA, see Riccina.

ROSS AILITHRI, that is, the place of pilgrimage, of the water or sea; situated on the sea coast of the county of Cork, celebrated in ancient times for a monastery, bishoprick, and a famous school, founded by St. Fachnan in the beginning of the sixth century. This school was much resorted to during the middle ages. The bishoprick of Ross was united to that of Cork in 1586[*].

ROSCLOGHER, from *Ar osciou clogher*, that is, the stone building on the water; situated in the county of Leitrim on Lough-melve[†].

ROSSCREA, derived from *Ross*, a place on or near the water, and *crea*, earth, clay, or mud; whence *Rosscrea*, a place on the muddy water; figuratively any place near a stagnated pool or lake. In this place, situated in the county of Tipperary, a church and bishoprick were founded by St. Cronan, about the year 620. But in the twelfth

---

[*] Harris's Ware, vol. 1, p. 583.   [†] Harris's Ware.

century united to Killaloe. Some remains of the ancient cathedral of Rofcrea may ftill be feen in the prefent parifh church, particularly the weftern door, executed in the beautiful antique ftile of the ninth century; alfo a round tower of nearly the fame date.

RUDHBHEITHEACH, or the diftrict for cattle; a place eminent for breeding cattle in Conaught, deftroyed in 1133, by Conor O'Brien †.

RUDRICCII, from *Reuda*, a tribe, and *Riccii*, or *Ricol*, royal or noble, whence *Reudaricol* or *Rudriccii*, the noble or royal tribe; the ancient inhabitants of the prefent county of Monaghan, and the fame as *Mneghin*; which fee.

RUFINA, derived from *Ruadh eanagh*, or the habitation of the race on the water; an ancient city mentioned by Richard of Cirencefter, and capital of Ibernia; the *Infovenach* of the Irifh, and Uverni of Ptolemy. It is not certain where this port or city was fituated; but it appears either to have been the prefent town of Bantry or Kinmare.

S.

SACRUM PROMONTORIUM, a cape in the fouth of Ireland, mentioned by Ptolemy; at prefent denominated Carnfore Point, in the county of Wexford.

SAMOR ABHAN, or the river on the great fea; the river Erne, which falls into the bay of Donegal.

† Collect. No. 4. p. 566.

SATARN, from *fat*, fullnefs, and *aran*, bread
corn ; in the old Celtic mythology the genius who
prefided over the productions of nature, being the
genial influence of the folar rays and the univerfal
fpirit who enlightens the feveral parts of the univerfe. This fpirit was fuppofed to be conftantly
moving through the earth, fructifying the vegetable and animal productions, and enlightening the
minds of men ; for which reafon, the ancient
Gauls, Britons and Irifh arofe during the night to
offer prayers and fupplications to this active divinity, whom they frequently denominated *Mar-tinne*,
or the great or good fire, and *Mogh Rhehe*, or the
divinity of wifdom, being the Mercury and Saturn
of the Romans, and Minerva of the Greeks.
The time at which thefe nocturnal devotions were
performed, was at the crowing of the cock, that
bird being fuppofed to be the harbinger of day or
Aurora, as Aurora was fuppofed to be that of the
fun, or Jupiter among the Romans, and by them
denominated Mercury. The cock being thus confecrated to Saturn, or the generative principle of
nature, was facrificed to him at the time of the vernal and autumnal equinox ; a cuftom retained in
fome meafure by the country people in feveral parts
of Ireland to this day, who on St. Martin's eve
kill a cock in honour of that faint, he being the patron faint of the hufbandmen and millers, as Satarn
was of bread corn and plenty, amongft the old pagans. The other facrifices offered to Satarn were
made in conjunction with the fun and earth, or Beal
and Tlacht, on the Tlachgo and Bealtinnes, which
fee. There are fome drudic fables relative to this
divinity ftill remaining ; particularly that mentrion-

ed by Demetrius in Plutarch, who fays, being fent by the emperor to furvey the weftern coafts of Britain, the people told him that in a certain ifland *the giant Briareus held Saturn bound in the chains of fleep, attended by a number of genii.* The ifland here fpoken of is undoubtedly the Ifle of Man, where the ftory is told by the inhabitants at this day with little variation, and the part of the ifland where Saturn is fuppofed to be confined, is denominated Sodor. The fable has a threefold fignification, viz. divine, moral and hiftorical. Briareus fignifies peace, calmnefs, and gentle and falubrious air, Satarn or Sodor fignifies plenty; whence the moral fenfe of the fable is, that plenty is produced by peace and a falubrious air; or that the god of plenty will refide among thofe people who induftrioufly cultivate the arts of peace. The hiftorical interpretation relates to Noah's cultivating the earth after the univerfal deluge, *Briareus* in the ancient Celtic tongue is of the fame fignification as *Noah* in Hebrew, both importing peace and calmnefs; and the genii are the various productions of nature, which were produced in great plenty in the days of Noah, when the world was quiet and undifturbed by the jarring paffions of the human race *.

SCOITEIGH, fee Coiteigh.

SCOTII, or Scotts, the general name of the ancient Irifh amongft foreigners during the middle ages. The words Scot or Scotii, Scyt, and Cithæ, by which the ancient inhabitants of Ireland were diftinguifhed by foreign writers from the beginning of the fecond, to the clofe of the eighth century,

---

* Cæfar. Com. Plutarch. Jurieu's Critical Hiftory of the Church, vol. II.

feem to have originated from two fources; the one external and the other internal. The internal was derived from . *Coit,* a woody country, whence Scoiteigh, a race of woodlanders, or thofe who inhabit a woody country, called by the ancient Britons *Yfgwydbwyr* or *Scoit:ür,* whence the *Scotia* of the Latins. The external originated from the piratical depredations committed by the Irifh on the coafts of Britain during the third, fourth, fifth and fixth centuries, in fmall boats, conftructed of the trunks of trees and denominated *Coiti,* or *Cots,* a name yet retained for thofe fmall flat-bottomed boats ufed on the rivers in feveral parts of Ireland, whence *Scoiteigh,* the navigators of fuch veffels. From this circumftance, all fmall boats during the middle ages among the Latins obtained the name of *Scutariæ,* and their navigators *Scutarii* and *Scotii*; even foldiers raifed in Britain to oppofe the inroads of the Scots or Irifh were frequently denominated *Scutarii,* whence *Scutarii,* a general name for efquires and officers of the army during the tenth and eleventh centuries. From the unfettled mode of life which thefe *Scoiteigh* led, they were alfo called Scuitagh or Scythæ, that is, wanderers; whence Scoiteigh or Scotii, and Scuitagh or Scythæ were by the Latin writers of the middle ages ufed as fynonimous terms, and frequently confounded one with the other. Thus the Hibernian Scots have been afferted to derive their origin from the ancient inhabitants of Scandinavia, who obtained the name of Scythæ from their pyratical and maritime expeditions *.

* Dufrefne's Gloff. tom 3, Baxter's Gloff.

SCYTHÆ, fee Scotii.

SEINNON, fee Sena.

SEIN CULBIN, or the bay in the corner; the bay in which the Fir Bolgæ landed under the conduct of Larthon; it is not certain where this bay is, though probably on the fouthern coafts.

SENA, or the bay; a bay or river mentioned by Ptolemy, thought to be the river Shannon, called by the Irifh *Seinnon*, or the place of bays.

SENA DESERTA, Defert iflands at the mouth of the Sena, or Shannon, mentioned by Richard of Cirencefter; but as no fuch iflands exift, it is moft probable they were the prefent Blafques ifles off Dingle.

SINUS AUSOBA, the bay of Galway; fo called by Richard, it is the *Aufoba* of Ptolemy, which fee.

SINUS MAGNUS, or the great bay; the bay of Donegal, fo called by Richard of Cirencefter.

SIOL MUIRIDH, or the race near the river, comprehending the eaftern part of Connaght on the Shannon, deftroyed in 1095 by Mortogh mor O'Brien *.

SLAING, or *Slain*, from *Ifc lân*, the open water; the ancient name of the bay of Dundrum.

SLAING, from *Slioght aen*, that is, the race or inhabitants on the water, now Slain on the river Boyne in the county of Eaft Meath. This diftrict was the original fettlement of the Fir Bolgæ or Belgians, who tranfmigrated from Britain about 350 years before Chrift, under the conduct of *Learmon* or *Slaing*; they are afferted by the ancient bards to

---

* Colleƈt. No. 4, p. 551.

have tranfmigrated from the bay of *Cluba* in Inis Ona, now the bay of Cardigan in Wales, called by Ptolemy *Canganii Sinus*; and to have landed at Inbher Colpa, or the bay of Culbin, now the bay of Drogheda in the county of Meath, from whence they in procefs of time eftablifhed colonies throughout the prefent province of Leinfter, denominated by them *Heremon*, or weftern country. In this diftrict are ftill remaining the tombs of the original chiefs of this race, at prefent known by the mounts or tumuli of New Grange, and which, in after ages became places of Druidic facrifice in honour of *Tlacht*, or the earth. See Ferta fir feic, Heremonii, Bolgæ, Tlachgo, & Scotii *.)

SLANY, fee Modonus.

SLEGACH, fee Sligo.

SLEIBHTE CARMEN, the Wicklow mountains. See Firthuathal.

SLEIBHTE-COULAN, or the mountains of the diftrict of Coulan; the prefent Wicklow mountains.

SLEIBHTE MISS, There was two mountains in Ireland under this name. One three or four miles fouth of Tralee in the county of Kerry, and the other in the diftrict of Dalaradia, and the county of Antrim, on which Saint Patrick kept the fwine of his mafter Milco.

SLEIBTEAGH, or the houfe near the mountains. An ancient church and bifhoprick founded by St. Fiech in the fifth century, and afterwards tranflated to Leighlin. The only remains of this ancient bifhoprick are the ruins of a fmall church

* Keating. M'Curtin's Ant.

and two ftone croffes, apparently of the ninth century; it is now called Sletty and is fituated in the barony of Sleibhmarraghagh in the Queen's county, on the river Barrow, about a mile north of Carlow.

SLIABH CAOIN, or principal mountain, now called Sliabh Riach; between the barony of Fermoy and County of Limerick, faid by the annals of Innisfall to be the place where Maolmuadh and his brothers waited for Mahon, king of Munfter, and brother of Brien Boromh, to put him to death. See Mufgruidhe *.

SLICHNEY, fee Sligo.

SLIOCHT-EUGACH-MAC-ITHAY, fee Lugadii.

SLIOGHT-BREOGHAIN, fee Breoghain and Lugadii.

SLIOGHT-GAE, fee Naguatæ.

SULCHOID, from *Sulchath*, or the place of battle; fituated not far from Limerick, being a plain nearly furrounded by mountains, and frequently mentioned in different periods of Irifh hiftory, as a noted poft for the encampment of armies; in particular, celebrated for the victory obtained over the Danes by Mahon, king of Munfter in 968 †.

T.

TAILTEAN, derived from *Tille* a return or revolution, and *Teaghan* an affembly or place of worfhip, whence *Tilleteaghan* pronounced Tailtean;

* Collect. No. 4.   † Ibid. p. 479.

a place in the county of Meath, where the Druids facrificed in honour of the marriage of the fun and moon and heaven and earth, on the firft of Auguft, being the fifth revolution of the moon from the vernal equinox. At this time the ftates affembled, and young people were given in marriage according to the cuftom of the eaftern nations; Games were alfo inftituted refembling the olympic games of the Greeks, and held fifteen days before and fifteen days after the firft of Auguft. The poets have fabled thefe games were inftituted in honour of *Tailte* daughter of *Magh mor* by *Lughaid lam fadba,* a king of Ireland; but *Tille Magh mor* is the revolution of the great divinity, and *Lughaid lam fadba Rè* fignifies the time of puberty of the good planet the moon, whence this feftival was frequently denominated *Lughaid naoiftean* or the matrimonial affembly *.

TARAGH, fee Teamor and Bruighen da Darg.

TEABHTHA, or the habitation of the tribe, an ancient name of Weftmeath †.

TEACH NAOI DROMA RAITHE, or the houfe of the elder at the rath of the cave or hollow mount; the regal houfe of the kings of Meath deftroyed by Brien Boromh in 995, the fame as Bruighen da Darg which fee ‡.

TEACHTUATHAIL, fee Eiroin.

TEAMOR, from *Teagh-mor,* or the great houfe, and *Teagh-mor-ragh,* · or the great houfe of the king. The palace of the kings of Meath, and monarchs of Ireland, much celebrated in the ancient Irifh

---

* Keating. Vallancey's effay on the Celtic language, p. 19, 18, 136 & 142.

† Colleét. No 4. p. 542.   ‡ Colleét. No. 4. p. 518.

hiſtory, the place where it was erected is now called Taragh, and was the ſame as *Bruigben da darg*. In its neighbourhood is the hill or Naaſteighan, whereon the ſtates aſſembled for ſeveral ages; that is from the beginning of the firſt to the middle of the ſixth century. From which period we hear no more of the general convention of the ſtates, but each province was governed by their own local ordinances. See Bruighen da darg, and Laberus.

TEFFIA, ſee Angalia.

THOMOND, ſee Mumhan.

THYHAN, ſee Conalla.

TIPRAIC, ſee Clonemacnoiſe.

TIR-CONAL, that is, the land òr country of Connal. The word litterally ſignifies the country of the chief tribe, and comprehended the preſent county of Donegal.

TIRHYN FAIL,⎫
TIRONE,   ⎬ ſee Hy-Failge,
TIRONELD,   ⎭

TIR-MALGAID, or the land on the great ſea, an ancient diſtrict, comprehending the barony of Tirawley in the county of Mayo, the ſame as Gamanradii which ſee, as alſo Auterij.

TLACHGO, to go round, whence in the ancient Iriſh *Tlacbt* ſignifies the earth, by reaſon of its revolution round its axis; the word alſo was applied to ſignify the univerſe or nature in general. Alſo a place in the county of Eaſtmeath where the Druids, in time of Paganiſm, ſacrificed on the tombs of their ancient heroes to the earth or univerſal nature on the eve of the firſt of November, called in commemoration of this feſtival, *Oidcbe*

Shambna. According to Keating this facrifice was inftituted by *Thuathal Teachtmor,* and taken from the province of Munfter; But this is evidently a fiction of the poets; *Mbumban* fignifies, as we have obferved under that word, a paternal country, and here imports *magna parens,* that is the great mother or univerfal nature, being the fame as the Egyptian *Ifis,* the Italian *Ops,* the Greek *Cybele* and *Vefta,* the Syrian *Aftarte,* and the Britifh *Andate.* This feftival, on which were facrificed deer and fwine, was called *Tlachgo,* to go round, by reafon of the rotundity of the earth's; whence the dances ufed at this folemnity by the votaries encircling the fanctuary with lighted torches were called *Tlachiga,* yet retained in fome meafure by the country people, which dances were the origin of the modern French cotillons, the word *Cotillon* in the old Gallic dialect of the Celtic tongue is of the fame fignification as *Tlachgo* in Irifh. The fanctuary here fpoken of, in the county of Eaftmeath, is ftill remaining, being the Tumulus at New Grange near Drogheda, as is evident from a number of infcriptions found therein and explained in a former number of this work. The ftates being affembled on the eve of the firft of November, all criminals were tried by the Druids on the firft of May at Ufneach, and fuch as were found guilty of crimes worthy of death were facrificed and burnt between two fires of Beal, lighted in honour of the object of adoration on the fummit of the mount *.

* Keating. Collectanea, No. 5 and 7. Vallancey's effay on the Celtic language. Baxter's gloff. Brit. Juricu's critical hiftory of the church, vol. 2d.

TLACHGO-BAN, or Cairn-Ban, that is the white Cairn or temple of Vesta near Newry in the county of Down, being one hundred and eighty yards in circumference and ten in altitude. Another on the summit of Sliabh Croabh, on the top of which are twenty two smaller Cairns from five, four and three feet high. Also one at Warringston in the same county which was opened in 1614, discovering a dome, in the centre of which, under a tabernacle, was placed an handsome urn of a brown colour containing burnt bones†.

TRIM, see Druim.

TRUIM, see Druim.

TUATH MUMHAM, see Dalcas.

TUATH DE DOINAN, or the northern people; the ancient inhabitants of Ireland, asserted by the antiquaries to have been a colony from Britain, posterior to the settlement of the Firbolgæ. They undoubtedly were Caledonians, who transmigrated either from the Mull of Galloway or Cantire, about the commencement of the first century before the Christian æra. The ancient Irish bards appear ignorant of the leaders of the first colony of the Caledonians or Danans, as they call them ; but speak fully of the second, which arrived some few years before Christ. These people generally distinguished themselves by the name of *Ulleigh*, from *Ull*, or the sun, which in their dialect of the Celtic, was the same as Beal, whence *Ullagh*, the worshippers of Ull, and their country Ulladh or Ullin ; names, which to this day, distinguish the north province of this island in the language of the natives. On the arrival of the first of these Cale-

† Harris's hist. county of Down.

donian colonies under the conduct of *Olioll Aron*, or the captain of the great worshippers of Ull, about 110 years before Christ, the ancient Belgian inhabitants retired across the Shannon, and laid the first foundation of the Conaught government, which was fully established by Eochy Failloch, in the time of Augustus Cæsar.

TUATHAL, see Firtuathal and Glendaloch.

U.

UA-CAONNUIL GABHRA, see Conal Gabhra.

V.

VAIN, see Fane.

VALENTIA INSULA, derived from *Bel ins üi*, or the island of the cape in the water; the present island of Valentia, at the entrance of Dingle Bay.

VALLIS SCYTHICA, see Vergivium mare.

VELLABORI, derived from *Bell abh eri*, that is the inhabitants of the cape on the western water; an ancient people mentioned by Ptolemy, who inhabited the peninsula between the bays of Dingle and Tralee, in the county of Kerry, called by the Irish *Hy Dingle*, or the district of the peninsula.

VENDERIUS, derived from the old British Uind e Riü, or head of the river; a river or bay mentioned by Ptolemy, and thought by Camden to be the bay of Carrickfergus; but Richard calls it Viderius, and thinks it to be the bay of Strangford.

VENISNIA INSULA; derived from *Ven üis nü*, or the country in the water off the cape; an island near the north cape mentioned by Richard of Cirencefter, and made by him to be Tory ifle; but it was more probably the north ifle of Arran, being oppofite to the cape Vennicnium of Ptolemy.

VENICNII, the people inhabiting the country near the Vennicnium cape, mentioned by Ptolemy; comprehending the weftern coafts of the county of Donegall, the ancient *Ergall* of the Irifh writers.

VENNICNIUM Promontorium, a cape in the north weft of Ireland in the county of Donegall, at the entrance of Donegall bay; mentioned by Ptolemy. *Vennicnium* feems to be a corruption from the old Britifh *Ven üic nüi*, that is the cape of the Œftuary or bay.

UI, fee Hy.

VIDUA, from the ancient Britifh *Ui dov*, or the deep river, a river or bay mentioned by Ptolemy, and thought by Richard and Ware, to be Lough Swilly.

VERGIVIUM-MARE, derived from *Ibher giübbüi*, or the moft weftern water, that part of the Atlantic Ocean on the fouthern coafts of Ireland, called by the Irifh *Mor Bhergus*, or the fea of the moft weftern water, and by Gildas Vallis Scythica.

ULLAD, the ancient name of the province of Ulfter, the word is evidently derived from *Thuath all adh* that is the northern divifion of the *Oll* or Bolgæ pronounced Ullagh; *Ullad* or *Ullagh* originally comprehended all the prefent province of Ulfter, but was afterwards confined to the prefent county of Down; however it is to this day retained in the name of *Ulster* or the northern country, whence we find in the ancient poems and chronicles, the inhabitants of this district denominated *Tuath de Danans* or northern people *. See under the words Bolgæ, and Tuath de Doinans.

UMALIA, derived from *Hy mal gaë* or the district on the great sea, comprehending the present barony of Morisk in the county of Mayo, and half the barony of Rofs in the county of Galway, the chiefs of which were the O'Maly's †, some of whom are in poffeffion of part of their ancient patrimony this day.

VODIE, from the ancient British *Uydhieu iii*, or the woodlanders on the water; an ancient district mentioned by Ptolemy, and called by the Irish writers *Dergtenii* and Corcaluighe, which see.

VOLUNTII, derived from *Ull an teigh* or the inhabitants of the county of *Ull*; an ancient people mentioned by Ptolemy, and called by the Irish writers *Ullagh*, being the prefent county of Down. See Ullad.

UPPER-CONELLO, fee Conal Gabhra.

URIEL, fee Orgiel,

USNEACH, from *aïs* fire, and *neach* divine or wonderful, whence the divine fire. A mountain in the county of Weft Meath, on which fires were kindled by the Druids on the firft of May in honour of Beal or the fun. This was the grand Bealtinne of the northern parts of Leinfter, where the ftates affembled and held judgment on all crimi-

---

* Keating. O'Conor's Differt. Collectanea, No. 8. Introd.

† Harrris Ware, v. 1. p. 17. O'Conor's Ortelius.

nals worthy of death, and such as were found guilty, were burnt between two fires of Beal. Children and cattle also were purified on this day by passing them between the fires *.

UTERNII, from *Ubh ernii*, or most western people; a people mentioned by Ptolemy who inhabited the south parts of the county of Kerry and western parts of the county of Cork; the *Ibernij* of Richard of Cirencester.

UVERNI, an ancient city or port, mentioned by Ptolemy; the capital of the Uternii, the Rusnæ of Richard, which see.

Y.

YDHERDAN, see Eiroin.

* Keating. Vallancey's Essay on the Celtic language, p. 138. Jurieu's critical history of the church, vol 2d.

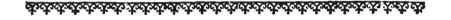

SOME ●

OBSERVATIONS

ON

IRISH ANTIQUITIES;

WITH A

PARTICULAR APPLICATION OF THEM

TO THE

SHIP TEMPLE NEAR DUNDALK. ●

ADDRESSED

To THOMAS POWNAL, Esq; F.S.A. LOND.

BY

EDWARD LEDWICH, L.L.B.

VICAR OF AGHABOE IN THE QUEEN'S COUNTY,

SOCIET. ANTIQ. HIB. & SCOT. SOC.

SOME

OBSERVATIONS

ADDRESSED TO

THOMAS POWNAL, Esq;

S I R,

THE trouble you have taken, in illuſtrating ſome obſcure parts of our antiquities, in the Archæologia; and your * late addreſs to our ſociety (communicated through a reſpectable member) containing ingenious conjectures on our *Ship Temple*, are marks of polite attention to the objects of our inſtitution, and meet, as they juſtly deſerve, our reſpect and gratitude.

It is from ſuch a friendly intercourſe and communication of ſentiments, that light will be derived on the darkeſt ſubjects: the bounds of ſcience extended, and the ends of literary aſſociations fully anſwered.

* Collectanea de Reb. Hiber. No. X. page 199.

Profound in every branch of antiquarian knowledge, and poffeffed of that maturity of judgment which can fafely fteer between the dangerous and narrow paffage that divides fiction from reality, your letter fupplies fome valuable hints towards a rational elucidation of our antiquities; from thefe I fhall take the liberty of deducing a few obfervations, and applying them to the *Ship Temple* near *Dundalk*.

In the examination of our antient monuments, you have pointed out two lines of inveftigation: the one referring to the commerce of the Phœnicians and Carthaginians here; the other to the inhabitancy of the Victs, who in early times, came from the fhores of northern Europe and the Baltic to Ireland. However candour and a deference to fome learned names might induce you to ftate thefe two modes of enquiry, yet you clearly faw which claimed the preference: your judgment decided in favour of the latter—" as moft " confonant to your own opinion."——As that opinion, in a great meafure coincides with mine; and as you have omitted the details neceffary to fupport it, I fhall beg leave, in fome fort, to fupply that deficiency, and offer, with great defference, fuch arguments as occur to me.

I. When antiquity became the mark of nobility among nations, it naturally produced pretenfions fimilar to thofe recorded of the * Egyptians and antelunar † Arcadians: when antiquity failed, refpect was fought for in nobility of defcent, and the Romans

---

* Herod. lib. 2.
† Orta prior Lunâ, de fe fi creditur ipfi,
    A magno tellus Arcade nomen habet.
                      Ovid. Faft. lib. 1.

found it in their beloved Æneas and his heroic Trojans, the French in their Francus, the Britons in their Brute, and the Northerns in their Odin and his Afæ.

From Virgil we learn how fashionable it was in the Augustan age to advance and embellish such fictitious origins: even profe-writers caught the contagion, and the grave Strabo (though perhaps it has not been adverted to) indulged his * fancy in such pleasing delusions; particularly in his account of Tartessus and Lisbon. The works of those elegant classic writers, at all times very popular books, tinctured the studies of national historians, and producen those figments, which, in most countries, have vanished before the sunshine of reason, history and criticism, but are still pertinaciously supported by some of our antiquaries.

Had any people adopted those mythological tales, without reserve, as true history, it had been some apology for our conduct : But the contrary is true : Livy and Saluft speak of the Roman traditions with doubt, and † Dionysius Hal. positively finds inhabitants in Italy prior to the Trojans. Neither has Strabo passed without ‡ censure. Even John Major and Hector Boece, fabulous as they are, have explicitly declared, that the story of Gadelus, and his pere-

---

* In the fourth book of his Geography, and other places. Tacitus also should not be omitted. His ———— habitus corporum varii : rutilæ comæ, magni artus, colorati vultus, &c. are more philosophic, but uncertain and fallacious. Vit. Agricolæ.

† Antiq. Rom. initio.

‡ By Lipfius ; Brodæi Mifcell. apud J. Grut. tom. 2. Reimann. Geograph. Homer, pag. 266.

N 2   grinations

grinations in Egypt and Greece were formed according to the cuſtom of other nations, and that the Scots might not yield to them the palm of antiquity.

II. Very different has been the conduct of our hiſtorians and antiquaries: inſtead of viewing the tales of bards and ſenachies as the ſports of imagination, and hiſtoric romances, they have ſtrained every nerve to reduce them to * chronological order and certainty; or render them † coincident with acknowledged hiſtoric events. Both ſchemes, proving ‡ too much, have diſappointed the expectations of the public, and at the ſame time demonſtrated, that every attempt of this kind is hopeleſs.

Still we are § preſſed with the Hiſpanian origination of the Iriſh, as the ſource from whence ſprung our letters, learning and religion. The Spaniards muſt be very inſenſible not to feel the infinite obligations they are under to the Iriſh, ‖ who have made " their anceſtors, of all the Scythian or Celtic na- " tions, the moſt martial and free, the moſt huma- " nized by letters, and the moſt converſant with the " Egyptians, Phœnicians and Grecians." The fabulous ¶ chronicles of Spain indeed vouch theſe things, and we may perhaps be allowed to doubt their authority; but where is the learned infidel hardy enough to withſtand the evidence of the Le-

---

* As O Flaherty in his Ogygia.

† As Mr. O'Conor in his Diſſertations.

‡ Stillingfleet's Britiſh Churches, Preface.

§ Mr. O'Conor's Letter in Collectanea, No. X. p. 211. and ſeq.

‖ Mr. O'Conor's Diſſ. p. 10.

¶ Univerſal Hiſtory, vol. 17. book 4. ſec. 3. edit. 8vo.

abhar

abhar Gabhala, the Pfalter of Cafhel, and the books of Balimote and Glendaloch * confirming thofe chronicles? Yet fuch is the lamentable perverfenefs of human nature, or the unpardonable inattention of hiftorians, that after all the treafures of eaftern wifdom thus liberally poured upon thofe Hiberians by fo many nations, the Roman writers reprefent them as not fuperiour to their neighbours in govern-ment, laws, learning or religion; they mention no traces of long civility, or oriental refinement among them.

III. Sinking under their own imbecility, and the fuperincumbent arguments of Mr. Whitaker and Mr. Macpherfon, our traditions were about to be configned to eternal oblivion, when they were un-expectedly releafed from impending fate, by a dif-covery of the affinity between the Hebrew and Cel-tic languages. This was eagerly caught at by the defenders of the old fyftem and brought as an irre-fragable proof of eaftern defcent. The connection between the Celtic, Hebrew and Phœnician was no new idea: to omit many others who have fpoken of it, † Mr. Ralph has declared :—" that the Phœni-" cian and Britifh were radically the fame, being no " other than dialects of the Celtic, many words as " well as cuftoms being common to both: there " are fo many proofs of this fact, that it would be " as ridiculous to deny it, as it would be to believe, " that thofe words were coined by the Britons, or " for them, after the Roman invafion."

* Mr. O'Conor's Letter, fupra.
† Hiftory of England, vol. 3. p. 1373, & feq.

Our

Our worthy member, Colonel Vallancey, with
that patriotic warmth which fuccefsfully carries him
through the moft laborious inveftigations, gave a
more copious * range to his examination of thofe
ancient tongues, and difcovered an almoft perfect
identity among them. This identity carried fo im-
pofing an appearance, as at † one time to make him
fay :—" that the Fom'oraig Afraic', or African pi-
" rates fo often mentioned in the antient hiftory of
" this country, were no other than the Phœnicians
" and Carthaginians."

What motive, it may be afked, could induce a
mercantile people to attempt the conqueft of a remote
ifle, unfurnifhed with natural products of value, without mines, manufactures or arts? Such Quixotifm
feldom enters the character of antient or modern traders. Colonel Vallancey muft have confidered better of this matter, and been convinced, that the
Irifh traditions were not defenfible on the ground
he had chofen, as he has omitted in the *fecond*
edition of his grammar the preceding quotation in
the *firft*. I fhall not infift on the abfurdity and im-
probability of a few rude and ignorant mariners occafionally vifiting this ifle (for that is the utmoft that
can be fuppofed.) Communicating the more refined
religion, language and learning of their countrymen:
this is fuch a phenomenon as never did, or can
occur.

If then there is any weight in the reafons offered
under the foregoing heads, the orientalifm difcover-

---

* In his different numbers in the Collectanea, and his Celtic Grammar.

† In the firft edition of his Iberno-Celtic Grammar,
preface.

ed

ed in the Celtic, in our antient religion, cuftoms and manners muft be referred to another origin, for confonantly with reafon and hiftory they never can be deduced from Spain or the Phœnicians. So that you, fir, had juft grounds for rejecting this line of inveftigation in explaining and clearing up our antiquities; The one, which you approve of, has infinitely a more rational foundation, and under the difcuffion of your able pen feems to approach to certainty. This ifle was primævally colonized from Britain, and occafionally admitted large bodies of Victs and other northern rovers. The teftimony of Bede and Florilegus brought by * Colonel Vallancey, allowing it all the weight he could wifh, will not fupercede other authorities and arguments proving the irruption of thefe Northerns at other times, and the general fpirit of enterprize which formed fo effential a part of their character.

But we fhall be afked, whether, even granting this northern colonization, the eaftern complexion of the Celtic and many of our ufages can thereby be fatisfactorily refolved? To this in general it may be anfwered, that we have not documents of thofe people fufficiently precife or numerous to determine the point. Befides, I, for my part, muft think, although in the Eaft they lodge corn in † mattamores as the Irifh did in the Souterreins; though the Orientals fet up heaps of ftones as memorials; ufed parti-coloured garments, and querns, and made cakes, fpotted

---

* Remarks on Governor Pownal's Letter. Collectanea. No. X. fupra.

† Harmer's Obfervations, vol. 1. p. 246.—253. vol. 2. p. 452.

with

with the feeds of poppy, coriander and faffron, like our baran breac; I say though the Eafterns and Irifh agree in thefe and many other customs, yet t'... appears no neceflity from hence to make the one derivative from the other; for in both they arose from the famenefs and monotony of the human intellect, roufed by fimilar objects to fenfation and reflection. In my humble opinion, it is exceedingly degrading to one part of mankind to fay they could have no kind of knowledge without imitating that of another: it is no lefs than depriving the former of rationality, and making them perfect apes;

Simia quam fimilis turpiffima beftia nobis.

How eafily fuch idle whimfies are formed, take the following extemporaneous inftance. Some of the inhabitants of the new-difcovered iflands, mentioned by Captain Cooke, ufe crucifixes; the hunter after origins inftantly concludes, that Chriftianity muft at fome period have been planted among them, and to authenticate or make it probable he tumbles over his library; after a great deal of ufelefs labour, he is faved the mortification of utter difappointment by perhaps difcovering, that the Crofs is a * Chinefe letter and, both with them and the Egyptians, the fymbol of perfection and the note of the number ten. This gives a new turn to his inquiries. Thefe iflands are then made to receive their inhabitants from the Eaft of Afia, and with them a fymbolic religion: their languages are compared, and all the tortures of etymology applied to make them harmonize.

* Sæpiffime inter characteres Sinicos fignum crucis, quod non fecus apud Ægyptios, numerum denarium fignificat, eft perfectionis fymbolum. Spizel. de Literat. Chinen. p. 78.

Your

Your extensive reading will furnish numerous examples of such learned trifling, such catching at words and distant refemblances.

As the frame of our mental and corporeal faculties will admit but of certain determinate perceptions and energies, how difguifed foever by various modifications, fo the cuftoms and manners of men will be the fame in all countries, fubject to fimilar fhades of difference, from local circumftances and degrees of civility. If then this reafoning be juft, we are not to derive one people from another, becaufe both have the fame ufages; fuch ufages, I think, are to be afcribed to a common principle. However where one country is known to have colonized another, it feems fair to illuftrate the practices of both by each other: this, Sir, you have happily done in your letter to our fociety. What I fhall now take the liberty to obferve in addition to what you have delivered on our *Ship Temple*, will, if I miftake not, ftrengthen and confirm what has been advanced. I muft previoufly remark, that I have not feen, nor do I know what the Abbé de Tontenu has written on the paffage of Tacitus to which you allude.

That excellent and accomplifhed fcholar, Lord Kaims *, has well remarked, that the mind, agitated by certain paffions, is prone to beftow fenfibility upon things inanimate: and that the perfonification is often fo complete as to afford an actual conviction of life and intelligence. This is the genuine fource of the groffer idolatry, and of that adoration of wood and ftone which was fo general antecedent to chriftianity. The men, who firft trufted themfelves to the watery

* Elements of Criticifm, vol. 2. p. 146—150. edit. 8vo.

element

element in a frail veffel, muft have done it with trembling and fear, and earneftly implored the aid and protection of fupernatural powers. When they found they were delivered from danger, they afcribed it to their own piety : to keep this alive and to efta-blifh a more permanent fecurity, they introduced their gods into their boats, and placed their ftatues in the moft confpicuous part of them. The boat at length came to be confidered as the temple of the deity, and the object of religious veneration. Let us now fee whether facts will fupport this theory.

The Parafemon, the fign, or divinity under which every fhip failed is noted in the Acts of the Apoftles, and in many antient authors. Thus the veffel that carried Ovid to Pontus, was called the Helmet; be-caufe on its head or prow, it had one, and on its ftern or poop, the ftatue of Minerva ;

Eft mihi fitque precor, flavæ tutela Minervæ

Navis; & a picta caffide nomen habet.

Here the tutela or ftatue is accurately diftinguifhed from the nomen or helmet, the emblem of Minerva.

The * Patæcus of the Syrians was a nanus, or pigmy divinity, placed on the poop, like the Chinefe † Neoman, and the St. Anthony of the Portuguefe. But as it was thought indecent to expofe their gods to every viciffitude of weather without a covering, fuperftition fuggefted the propriety of a lararium, or chapel, and one was erected on the ‡ poop.

In the downward progrefs of idolatry, the next ftep was to confecrate the fhip or boat, and hold it up as

---

* Selden de Dis Syris, pag. 356.

† Addit. Beyer. in Selden. fupra. pag. 332.

‡ Turneb. Adverf. lib. 19, cap. 2.

an object of religious worſhip. Thus, in an antient calendar preſerved in * Gruter, among the feſtivals is the *ſhip* of *Iſis*, the *ſhip* of † *Hercules*, and the *Triëris* of ‡ *Ammon* were alſo ſacred.

As ſhips were now believed to be the temples of ſome gods, and partaking of their eſſence, they were judged to be no unſuitable cemeteries for the deceaſed, and accordingly the dead were laid in them. Antinous, as appears by a paſſage of § Epiphanius, was interred in a boat. One of the laws of the Daniſh prince, Frotho, is, ‖ that each general and officer ſhould be burned in a pile made of his ſhip. The Icelanders buried in a boat. Aſmund would not ſuffer his faithful ſervant to lie in the ſame ſkiff with him,

" ** The room within the boat is too narrow,

" A warrior ſhould have a better place ;

" For I can govern a boat myſelf."

At length the Northerns erected royal tombs or tumuli, of the ſize and figure of a †‡ great ſhip. Theſe tombs were afterwards temples, whither the people ‡‡ annually aſſembled, to offer ſacrifice for the proſperity of the nation. Ship-temples were then a part of the northern ſuperſtition, and this ſuperſtition, ariſing from diſordered paſſions, was not confined to any country or climate.

* Inſcript. pag. 138. † Arrian. lib. 2.

‡ Harpocrat. in Αμμωνίς. § Cuperi Harpoc. pag. 14.

‖ Centurionis vero vel Satrapæ corpus rogo, propria nave conſtructo, funerandum conſtituit. Sax. Gram. pag. 44.

** Iſland's Landnamabock, ſive Origin. Iſland.

†‡ Regios vero tumulos ad magnitudinem & figuram carinæ maximæ navis. Step. Step. ad Sax. Gram. pag. 91.

‡‡ Quotannis ſacra peragerent pro totius gentis incolumitate. Worm. Mon. Dan.

From

From what has now been produced, the paffage of Tacitus, which he himfelf was unable to explain, and which has puzzled his commentators, receives elucidation. " Part of the † Suevi, fays he, facrifice to Ifis, I have not been able to difcover the origin of this foreign worfhip, unlefs it is, that the image itfelf, which refembles a Liburnian boat, fhews that the religion was introduced from a diftant part." Tacitus was certainly informed that the Suevi worfhipped a boat; fuch idolatry exifted in the north in the earlieft ages: but he knew of no other people doing fo but the Egyptians, who adored Ifis under that form. Unable to account for the worfhip of Ifis in the wilds of Germany, he hazards a conjecture: this conjecture, is neither received or interpreted, with the caution and diffidence with which he delivers it, by his commentators: they affume it as a fact, and fet themfelves to account for it. How was this religion introduced, ‡ fays one? Why from Egypt, by the Pontus Euxinus, near which Sefoftris planted colonies. Another § critic finds Tacitus contradicting himfelf, having before declared, that the Germans adored no images; this boat he makes a military trophy fufpended in a fanctuary. Tacitus did not recollect the facred and wonderful fhip of Æneas,

---

† Pars Suevorum & Ifidi facrificat. Unde caufa & origo peregrino facro *parum comperi*, nifi quod fignum ipfum, in modum Liburnæ figuratum, docet advectam religionem. Germ. cap. 9.

‡ Unde vero advectam? Nempe ex Ægypto, ubi Ifis colebatur, per Euxinum Pontum. Huet. Demonf. Evang. pag. 146.

§ Pelloutier Hift. des Celtes, pag. 296, 297.

which

which Procopius * affures us, was preferved to his time without decay: this muft have been the effect of fome inherent divine quality, and confequently muft have been an object of religious refpect: fo much the account implies.

I always relinquifh traditions, efpecially when they carry marks of genuine antiquity, with great reluctance. The Faghas na heun Naoi, or work of one night, the name of the Dundalk Ship-temple, has a venerable obfcurity, fimilar to the || Fairy rocks in France, the Giants'-beds of thefe kingdoms, and the ftrata Gigantium of the Northerns. It is extremely agreeable to the notions of former times to afcribe fuch works to unknown fupernatural beings. In fuch cafes, the name and the thing feldom illuftrate each other.

I have detained you too long with this hafty, and I fear, incorrect epiftle. You have ftarted frefh game for our antiquaries, whofe inquiries will be directed after other Ship-temples, which, no doubt are to be found in different parts of this kingdom.

I have the honour to be,

S I R,

Your moft obedient and humble Servant,

Aghaboe,
Jan. 3d, 1783.

EDWARD LEDWICH.

---

* Ad hoc lignorum quæ dixi nullum aut putruit aut cariem oftendit, fed quafi modo fabricata effet navis ad noftram ætatem, (fixth cent.) quod & ipfum miraculi fpeciem habet, manet incorrupta. Lib. 4. pag. 476. Edit. Grotii.

|| Caylus, Facueil. tom. 6. pag. 363.

In the Prefs, and fpeedily will be Publifhed,

Collectanea de Rebus Hibernicis.

NUMBER XII.

CONTAINING,

I.

1. An Effay on the Irifh Feftival LA SÁMAN, the EE OWNA or Hallow Eve of the modern Irifh; proving it to be the fame as the Samon and Samael of the idolatrous Jews, &c; the Afuman of the Perfians, and the Summanus of the Romans.

2. ON the Gule of Auguft called LA TATH; Lammas Day, &c. with further Illuftrations on the Round Towers of Ireland, and their Ufe affigned.

3. DESCRIPTION of the Banqueting Hall of TARA, or TAMAR; with a Plan of the fame, from an ancient Irifh vellum MSS. fhewing the Difpofition of the King's Houfhold at Dinner; the Names of the feveral Officers, and the Meat ferved to them.

4. CONCLUSION. The ancient Hiftory of Ireland vindicated; Probability of a Colony from Scytho-Polis in Paleftine, being brought to Ireland by the Phœnicians. Of the Phœnian and Thebaian Dialects of the Irifh, or BEARLA FENI and BEARLA THEBIDH. Names of Dogs from the Hebrew and Arabick. Irifh Names of Linen, and the Utenfils ufed in that Manufacture, of Oriental Origin. The Scytho-Polians, famous for making fine Linens, &c. &c. &c.

5. A FRAGMENT of SANCHONIATHON, wrote in the old Chaldee or Phœnician tongue, collated with the Irifh, with a literal tranflation.

By COLONEL CHARLES VALLANCEY.

II.

OBSERVATIONS on the ANTIENT TOPOGRAPHY of Ireland, by CHARLES O'CONOR, ESQ.

Collectanea de Rebus Hibernicis.

NUMBER XII.

BY C. VALLANCEY, LL. D.

האיים שבים אוקינוס ברטנייא רבה וברטנייא זעירה

Insulas maris Oceani Britanniam magnam & Britanniam
parvam, id est, plane Albionem & Hiberniam.

> SELDEN. Judicium de X Scriptor. Anglicanis, ex Rabb. A. B.
> Chaija in Sphæra Mundi.

Verbum addo de HIBERNIA quam Phœnicibus non fuisse
ignotam.

> BOCHARTUS. Geogr. Sacra.

Παρ δ᾽ ἄρα νῆσον ἀμειὅσιν IEPNIΔA.

> ORPHEUS.

Illa ego sum Graiis olim glacialis Ierne
Dicta, et Jasoniæ puppis bene cognita Nautis.

> HADRIAN. JUNIUS.

Et sane si Tzetzes hosce intelligo, in litore Britanniæ Magnæ
volunt reperiri navigia illa animabus onusta, indeque illa
cum remigibus rapta, impetu unico, ad Hiberniam ad-
pelli, tunc Scotiam itidem vocitatam. Atque huc spectare
videtur illud Claudiani

Est locus, extremum qua pandit Gallia litus
Oceani prætentus aquis, quo fertur Ulysses
Sanguine libato populum movisse silentum.
Illic umbrarum tenui stridore volantum
Flebilis auditur questus, &c.

> SELDEN. Judic. de X Script. Angl. p. 1197.

DUBLIN:

PRINTED BY W. SPOTSWOOD,

PRINTER TO THE ANTIQUARIAN SOCIETY;

AND SOLD BY LUKE WHITE, DAME-STREET.

M DCC LXXXIII.

ADVERTISEMENT.

SOON will be publiſhed in a Number of this COL-
LECTANEA, An IRISH HISTORICAL LIBRARY,
containing an Alphabetical Catalogue of all the Manuſcripts and printed Books, that have been written or publiſhed on the Affairs of IRELAND, relating to the State,
Church, Law, Hiſtory, Antiquities, &c. &c, as could be
collected from publick and private Information, to the Year
1782——
  By the AUTHOR of this Number.

N. B. To the BINDER.

The plate of TARA-HALL, *to be inſerted between p.* 542 *and* 543.

And the NUMERAL-TABLES, *and* PLATE II. *between p.* 576
and 577.

TO THE

SOCIETY OF ANTIQUARIES

O F

L O N D O N,

THIS NUMBER OF THE

COLLECTANEA DE REBUS HIBERNICIS

I S   O F F E R E D,

WITH GREAT DEFERENCE,

B Y

THEIR MOST HUMBLE,

MOST OBEDIENT SERVANT,

CHARLES VALLANCEY.

DUBLIN,
June 1783.

QUI LEGIT HUMANITER
VIVAT VALEAT
FELICITER

PREFACE.

IF this trifling performance, shall fall into the hands of an Hebræist, the author expects censure, for referring the Hiberno-Scythic or Magogian Irish so often to the Arabian and Persian ‖ languages, when the Hebrew and Chaldee, lay so open, and with more affinity to the Irish in both letter and sense. The censure will be just; and in reply, the author begs leave to observe, that the Irish language not being allowed, or esteemed, by many, to be so pure and ancient, as has been asserted by the author, it was collated with the Arabian, which is allowed to be a jargon of the Phœnician, corrupted by Mahommed and his followers, (in order to censure, both the *Jewish and Christian Religion*,) and had then received many words from the ancient Northern dialects. And this is a principal reason that the modern Arabian is so improper to be collated with the sacred scriptures, and was probably the cause of the Introduction of the Hebrew points, although Buxtorf places their use some centuries earlier.

The Greek scholar may think, I have made free with his favourite language; but he must be told that,

‖ Ita tamen, ut facillime possit ostendi, illud ex orientali, id est, ex *Ebræo Veteri* derivatum este; possent hic sufficere documenta, quæ statim ex Persica Lingua exhibuimus, quia & *Persas Scythas* fuisse ostendimus. (Campeg. Vitring. Obs. Sacr. p. 84.)

the fource of the old Greek and of the old Irifh, fpring
from the fame fountain head, viz. the Phœnician, mixt
with the Pelafgian or Scythian, for Scuthæ was the
Greek name of the Pelafgi, fignifying *Northern Wanderers*, as will be explained in the conclufion from
Campegius Vitringa. The Pelafgi divided into two bodies under Magog and Gomer, the former feated
themfelves early in Affyria, at Bethfan [*], from thence
called Scytho-polis by the Greeks, of which we fhall treat
fully in the latter part of this work. From the vicinity of
the Pelafgians to the Phœnicians and Ægyptians, they
were foon noticed by thefe idolatrous nations, confe-
derated with them, and joined with them in their at-
tacks on the iflands of Elifha, and from thefe, the
Greek language was formed. Hence it is that the
learned Duret when he treats of the origin of the
Greek language, begins thus, *Des Grecs ou Pelaf-
ges* [†].

    " The Pelafgi, fay the authors of the univerfal
" hiftory [‡], muft be allowed to have been one of the
" moft ancient nations in the world, and as appears
" from their colonies, in the earlieft times, very nu-
" merous and powerful. With regard to their origin,

---

[*] Pelafgi pop. Græciæ in genere per varias regionies difperfi,
qui *Pelafgi*, quafi vagabundi tefte Strab. dicuntur a *Pelafgo* Jovis & Lariffæ filio dicti. qui primi in Latium litteras docuiffe feruntur Ovid. l. 2. de arte. (Ferrarii Lex.)

   Hac tibi non hominem, fed quercus crede Pelafgas.

   See *iocam*, & *bile-ioc* the oak and mifletoe in the conclufion.

   Scythopolis olim *Mathora* tefte Zon. to. 1. Ann. dicta, quæ &
Nyfæ tefte Plin. dicta eft à Scythis condita. nunc *Bethfan*
tefte *Breitenbachio*. (Ferarii Lex.)

  [†] Hiftoire de l'origine des langues de ceft Univerf.

  [‡] Tom. 16.

" the

" the learned are not agreed, fome make them the
" defcendants of Peleg, who have very probable ar-
" guments on their fide; others deduce them from
" the Canaanites and Phœnicians, and others fuppofe
" them to have been of a Celtic original §.   The E-
" trufcans or Tyrfenians were a branch of the Pelafgi,
" that migrated into Europe and the Lydian Pelafgi or
" Etrufcans, conducted by Tyrfenus to Italy, and the
" firft Pelafgi that inhabited Greece, were the fame
" people."

From thence it would follow (if I am right in the derivation of the Irifh) that the antient Irifh and the antient Etrufcan fhould have a great affinity. To this I anfwer, that no two languages have a greater, and that
if the learned Swinton, Maffeus, Gorius, &c. had
known the Magonian Irifh language, they would
have found lefs difficulty in explaining the old Etrufcan, as fhall be fhewn in fome future number of
this Collectanea.

Strabo upon the authority of Ephorus, who, he fays
had his from Hefiod, derives the origin and name
Pelafgi from one Pelafgus, founder of the kingdom of
Arcadia, and fo does Macrobius, which is the more apparent, as the former tells us in the fame place, that
it was upon Hefiod's authority, that Ephorus had derived the origin of the Pelafgi from Arcadia, as being
defcendants of Pelafgus, for Strabo had a few lines before, cited Ephorus, in the following words, " Eos
" (Pelafgos) originem ab Arcadibus ducentes, vitam mi-

§ Kelt implies a fixed people, it was a name the Scythians or
Pelafgi, gave thofe colonies that had refided long in a place.
See Effay on the Celtic language.

litarem

PREFACE.

" *litarem* delegiffe, (author eft Ephorus :)" to which he adds, that having induced many other people to obferve the fame *military inftitution*, they were all diftinguifhed by the one common name of Pelafgi. This explanation of the name Pelafgi, accords extremely well with the Magogian Irifh ; in which language, *afca* and *afcath* is a foldier, (in Arab. *afker*, an army) *pleafgam*, is to conquer, and *plafca* or *pal-afcai* is the leader of an army ; thus we fay, *pal-maire*, the governor of a fhip, i. e. the rudder of a fhip.

Now Pelafgus being only a title given to their leader, by themfelves, has ftill involved the origin of this hero in greater obfcurity. Sir I. NEWTON makes him one of the fubjects of the *paftor kings* of Egypt, made fugitives by Mifphragmuthofis; but the learned Fourmont (the elder) is pofitive, the Pelafgi were Philliftines, and in the following pages, we fhall prove they wereMagogian Scythians, long fettled in Paleftine, having produced many authorities of the ancients, that they flourifhed at Bethfan, afterwards named by the Greeks Scythopolis, from their dwelling in that City. Potter in his Grecian antiquities, fays, the Pelafgi were Tyrhenians born, and (fpeaking of the building of Athens) taught the Greeks the art of building houfes of lime and ftone, and from them, walls and caftles were called Τύρσιι. Is it poffible that Potter could be ignorant that the Hebrew and Chaldee טור *Tur*, was a circular building, a tower, from the origin of languages ? Obferve the ancient hiftory of the Irifh in this particular, " *African fea-champions* landed in " Ireland, conquered the country, introduced their " language, and taught the inhabitants to build with " lime and ftone," to build what?—*Round towers* undoubtedly, for no other buildings were erected in Ireland

land of lime and ftone, for many centuries afterwards: but thefe conquering Pelafgi, thefe ingenious
artifts, who routed the Greeks from Elifha and built
the city of Athens, were called Pelargi, fays Straho,
(and after him Potter) from πιλαργοι, Pelargi, ftorks,
δια την πλανην for their wandering: and they built fhips
called πιλαργο χρωτις νιυς, (apud Lycoph.) *naves ciconia-*
rum affimili colore tinctæ. What a jumble of nonfenfe!
Our Pelafgi named Athens, Pelargi, for the fame reafon that the ancient Irifh named the city of Waterford *Bel-lairge,* and the harbour *Port-lairge,* meaning
thereby a town built at the (*lairge* or) forks of the river; this city having been firft conftructed at the
forks of the rivers Suire and Barrow, as Athens was
at the forks of the Ifys and fome other river the name
I cannot learn. The Irifh built veffels of *bark* and
called them *leabar-naoi* and *coirteas-naoi,* and hence the
latin *Liburnicæ naves* or light fhips and the Greek
χρωτινιυς. The Greeks dedicated this famous city to
Minerva goddefs of wifdomand named it Αʼθηναι Athenæ
becaufe in the Pelafgian tongue, as in the Irifh, Aithne
is knowledge, wifdom, &c. and every ignorant peafant in Ireland, at this day, looks up to his miftrefs
as an Αʼθηνη i. e. a woman of fuperior knowledge. Cecrops (a Pelafgian) having compleated this city called
it αςυ, becaufe in his language (and in Irifh, *afti*) is a
dwelling, and fo conceited were the Greeks of being
able to live *above-ground,* they called themfelves αςοι
dwellers in houfes, hence Terence *an in aftu venit?* We
have no other word at this day in Ireland to enquire
if fuch a one is in his houfe or at home, but *b'fhuil an*
fear afti (aftee) is the man at home? This calls to my
mind, ar obfervation of the ingenious Mr. Holwell,
he fays, " the annals of the Gentoos, give teftimony
" of

" of Alexander's invasion, where he is recorded under
" the epithets of a mighty *robber* and *murderer*; but
" they make no mention of a Porus—the Greek and
" Latin construction and termination of *places and names*,
" *princes*, and *kingdoms* of Indostan, said to be conquer-
" ed by Alexander, bear not the least analogy, or idiom
" of the Gentoo language either ancient or modern."
(Hist. of Indostan V. 2, p. 2. 3.) We shall find Porus
when we collate the Irish and Hindostan languages.

Let us now pursue the universal history. " The name
Tusci given to the Etruscans, seems to be of a later
date and to have been given them by the Greeks. The
use of *frankincence*, that prevailed amongst the Tuscans
in after ages, probably suggested this appellation to
that people." (Univers. Hist.)

Now frankincence in the *Greek* language is, λίβανος
and λίβανωτόν.* The Latin *Thus* is from the Greek θύος απο
τυ θύων, i. e. *odorem faciendo*; but the Greek is from
the Irish, *Tùsca*, the name of camphire, *frankincence*,
and is the word now used for that perfume, burnt in
the office of the Mass. It is therefore very improbable, that the Greeks gave this name to the Etruscans
from so trifling a cause; but that the Etruscans named
themselves Tusac, which in the Irish implies a hero,
warrior, noble †. *Tusci*, a thure nomen deductum
non videri, quod *thuris* usus non sit antiquus: *Tusci*
an *Thusci* a Rege vox tracta. (J. Dempstri de Etruria Reg. Ch. 2.) but I take *Tusci* to mean sorcerers,
as well as *Tages*.

* St. Mathew Chap. 2. from the Hebrew *lebona*. See Mai-
mon, in Sanhed. c. 13.
† See Collectanea No. 10.

In

PREFACE.

In the derivation of the names of nations and people, it should be considered, by whom such name was given, by themselves or by foreigners, there is reason to think Tusci was the indigenous name.

Etruria was divided into twelve tribes, called in the Tuscan language *lucumones*, and each was governed by its own *lucumo* or prince, and over the whole was a presiding *lucumo* or king. As the Etruscans were a *warlike* nation, and spoke at first a language not very different from the Hebrew or Phœnician, the word *lucumo* might possibly have denoted a warrior or captain. The Hebrew לחם *lochem* or *luchem* has undoubtedly such a signification. (Univerf. Hist.)

With great submission to these learned authors, there is much difference in the appellations given to the *governors* and *governed*. Prince and people, king and subjects are very different words in all languages, but the Pelasgian Irish can shew their mistake.

לחם *lachim* in the Hebrew, does signify *war*, and *victuals :* but לח *lach* is a strong youth (fit for war.) In Chaldee *lacheda* valdè; in Samaritan fortè, and *lechi* fœtæ bovis, *lechem* esca, panis.

In Arabic, *lekab* familiæ princeps. *m. lachab* percussit gladio. *Lekab* a certain tribe of Arabia which in pagan times had never known captivity, nor a dependance on kings. (Richardson.)

From these oriental roots proceed the following Irish words, viz. *lucht, luchd* a tribe, *folucht fo-luchd* a prosperous tribe, *fliocl* posterity or descent, *fluchd* a free tribe; *luchd* answers the French *gens* and *laochd* gens des armes.

Luchd and *liachd* a multitude, the people *, *laoch* an

* In the Hindoftan language *look*, in the Gentoo *logue*.

active

active youth, a foldier, a champion : hence *laochra* militia, *laoch-mon* a general, a great warrior, *laoch-ceis* a princefs, a general's wife.

† *Laighn* or *laichn* a fword, fpear, javelin, *laghinlann* a blade, *lannfgine* the blade of a knife, *laighin-tir* the country of (broad) fwords : hence *laighnftir* i. e. Leinfter, a province in. Ireland, from the arms they ufed in combat, undè λαιμάω & λιχμάω incidit gladio, vel dentibus, qui inftar gladii (Caftellus).

Laga, praife, fame, renown; an appellative common to the Irifh princes, as, *Lugbaidb-laigha Mac mogha nuadhat.*

Liocais, power, fway.

Ligmbi, an appetite.

Laogh, meat, veal, a calf.

Lo-ligheach, a new milched cow, becaufe of the great quantity of milk fhe affords.

Luchmaire, abundance of food.

Luchairt, a chief's houfe, a palace.

Lugh, active, expert.

Luch, a prifoner taken in war.

Luighan, to cut, to hack, to rend to pieces.

Loghm-fiubhal, a Viaticum.

But feeing the Pelafgi or Tufci were remarkable for their fkill in augury, forcery, divination, &c. which

---

† The kind of fword, peculiar (in the firft ufe of it) to the province of Galian, introduced by the monarch Laura, the feaman, on his return from exile in Gaul, fometime before the chriftian æra. Of the Gauls who followed his fortune, and enabled him to mount the Irifh throne, O'Flaherty fays, *A laticufpidum armorum, quæ noftris infueta, exteri illi intulerant, vocabulo* LANCEA *lagenia appellationem exinde fortita eft.* Ogyg. p. 262.

art the Irish derived from them, I beg leave to submit to the reader another interpretation of *Lucomon.* I have elsewhere shewed that the name signifying king, prince, chief, did also imply prophet, augur, &c. so in the Pelasgian Irish *laoc* is a chief, a poet, a sorcerer: it is written laoc, laoic, luich, and liag, whence *liagh,* a physician, one who has the power of healing by charms. Hence the *leug* or *leice,* the famous chrystal which the priests kept to work charms by, and still used in the Highlands of Scotland. Hence also the bird called *Luic* or *Luic fairge,* (the marine sorcerer) which Mr. Banks and Mr. Penant have described. The man who lives on Staffa, (as I am informed, says Mr. Shaw in his Irish dictionary) says, that they hatch their eggs by sitting on the ground at the distance of six inches from them, and turning their faces towards them, continue to repeat *Gùr legug* day and night ! ! ! *Gùr luighe,* is the false or lying prophet; and this was the mariners name for this bird, whose approach to a ship at sea, is still supposed to foretell a storm.

And as *osce* in the Pelasgian Irish implies skilled in sorcery, and *tua,* a lord or chief, it is more probable that *Tusci* is derived from *Tuaosce,* and that the Osci their neighbours, owe their name also to this derivation. See hereafter what is said of OSSIAN.

" The Phœnicians and neighbouring nations, were
" much addicted to augury and divination, as may be
" collected from scriptures. It is no wonder, there-
" fore, that their descendants, the Etruscans, should
" have discovered the same disposition. Their wri-
" ters pretend, that TAGES, (whom some have taken

" for

" for a god, others for a man, but *Tully* scarce knows
" in what light to consider him,) was the inventor of
" every thing relating to augury and divination."
(Univ. Hist.)

I have collected fifty words in the Irish language
relating to *augury* and *divination**, every one of them
are oriental, expressing the mode of producing these
abominable arts: they are, in fact, the very identical
oriental words written in Irish characters, and amongst
them is *tagh*, divination, *tagh-airm*, divination by
numbers †, *tuag-cheird*, the art of divination, &c. &c.
To return to the Greek.

Doctor

---

* Thus *Ainius* was one of the persons under the Druids,
whose office it was to make celestial observations, so called, say
the Irish glossaries, from *Ain*, the sun's orbit, as before explained in *Bel-ain*, a year, and *ius* or *eos*, knowledge, but this
word is evidently from the Hebrew עָנִין & עָנֵן, cloud mon-
gers, diviners by observations made on clouds. עֲנָנָה sorceress,
the false church that consulted the clouds. Bates. Hence *Ai-*
nius in our modern dictionaries is explained by *sorcerer*. But
Anius in *Virgil* was king of *Delos* and priest of Apollo.

    Rex Anius, *Rex idem hominum, Phæbique sacerdos.*

† See *Airm* in the conclusion. The *Etruscans* say that *Tages*
was born of a clod of earth that a husbandman turned up, by
dipping the ploughshare deeper into the ground than usual.
He immediately taught the art of divination to this husbandman
and the rest of the Etruscans. The moral of this fable is, that
no profession in life requires a better knowledge of the prognos-
tications of the weather, or of the revolutions of the seasons than
husbandry or farming. Now *Tages* or *Teageas* in Irish, is husbandry. *Teaghasam*, to manage a farm, to follow husbandry.
In the *Sclavonian*, *tègh*, agriculture. *Tegh*, labour, husbandry.
From *tagh*, divination, is derived the proper Irish name *tague*,
or *teag*, or *tadhg*, i. e. a diviner. And in the old Pelasgian Irish
thosaic did certainly signify a sorcerer as well as a prince, hence

ceart-

PREFACE.

Doctor Parsons, fellow of the royal and antiquarian societies of London, in his *Remains of Japhet*, printed in 1767, has very masterly collected the opinions of the antient and modern authors on this subject. We shall trace the learned author through his work.

" * Too much cannot be offered to the reader, of the Pelasgi, because they will become principal evidences, for the truth of what we imagine to be the state of the case, with respect to the origin of the languages of Europe : and by proving that both Celts and Scythians were first Pelasgians, we shall be able to ascertain what is offered in a future chapter, that the Gomerians and Scythians or Magogians spoke the same language."

" The Phœnicians and Egyptians began very early to attempt sending colonies to neighbouring countries; and as they both sprung from the same ancestors, the sons of Ham, they must have had much the same œconomical dispositions to improve their commercial and other interests. Maritime countries seem to be the first object of their intentions; and where could they find any place so likely to answer their ends as the isles of Elisha or Greece, now inhabited by Pelasgians, the issue of Gomer, and many of the descendants of Magog."

" We are informed, by Strabo and Dion. Halic. that they sent colonies thither, and began to disturb the

---

eeart-thosaighe, forcery, witchcraft ; O'Brien's dictionary of the Irish : from the Hebrew *Charthumim*, compounded of *Chart* celare & *tuma* claudere , hence *ceirt* or *keirt* in Irish is the knave of cards, that is, the juggler or forcerer. All names fignifying diviners, likewise fignify chiefs, princes : thus in 2d ch. Daniel, we find the fons of the kings of Israel only, called up to Babylon to be instructed in the *Chaldea* art.

* Remains of Japhet, p. 100.

Pelas-

Pelafgians two generations or 60 years, before the wars of Troy: and from that time continued to intrude, by fucceffive numbers, till they had well nigh replaced the original inhabitants, and had fubdued the maritime parts. It was then they became a mixed people, confifting of Pelafgians, Phœnicians and Egyptians; and from that time the æra of the Greek tongue may be dated. All was Pelafgian before the incurfions of Phœnicians and Egyptians, and the gradual combinations of the languages of thefe with the Pelafgian begat the Greek, called afterwards the Helenian tongue, in complaifance to Deucalion's fon, who, at his arrival there, found this language forming; while the Pelafgians enjoyed their own, unchanged, in the other parts of Greece, Afia Minor, in the country of the Trojans, Scythia, and all the neighbouring iflands in the Mediterranean fea, and all over Thrace, "&c.

" It may from hence, be eafily feen, that the people of all thefe countries were the fame, defcended from Japhet, through Gomer, Magog, and his other fons, and fpoke the fame language wherefoever they dwelt, until the incurfion mentioned into Greece, which was in time, called Celtic, Gaulifh," &c.

I cannot agree with the Doctor that all was Pelafgian before the incurfions of the Phœnicians and Egyptians, but that all was Pelafgian after their incurfions. The Pelafgians, Canaanites, Phœnicians, Magogian Scythians, and fome who had dwelt in Egypt, formed this mixed body, called Pelafgi, headed by Cadmus. They are diftinguifhed in the facred writings by the name of Cadmonites. Canaan contained eleven fundry people, at leaft 2200 years before Chrift, (See Genef. x. v. 16, 17, 18.) and therefore Willet in his Hexapla, obferves, though the Canaanites did confift of fo many

fundry

sundry people, they certainly spoke all but one language;—and he adds, " the Magogians were not the ancestors of the Goths or Germans, but were Scythians."

The Jewish writers always esteemed the Etruscans and Pelasgians as a mixt people. *Rabbini communi consensu Etruriam* משך *(mesk) appellant* (De antiq. Etruriæ. Anonym.) *Mesk* in Hebrew, and *measc* in Irish, implies a mixt people; this confirms the Doctor's assertion of the junction of the Pelasgians, Phœnicians and Egyptians, but he brings the Magogians there too early.

The Magogian-Scythians were early blended with the Canaanites, and there lost all distinction of name; but they preserved it in their route to Tartary and China; it was this mixed body that descended to Elisha, Africa, Spain, Britain and Ireland, (and even to Gaul and Germany, till driven away by the Gomerites,) forming a language as different from that of Gomer, as Italian is from French.

That Cadmus was the leader of this mixed body, is very probable; for if we recollect, that Joshua was ordered to write the words of the Law, upon large stones on Mount Ebal, as soon as he had passed over Jordan, which he accordingly did, (Deut. 23, 7. Josh. 8, 30.) *literary writing*, must from thence be tolerably well known to the Canaanites, or Phœnicians, amongst whom the Magogian-Scythians had settled.

Hence it was that Cadmus, who was a Canaanite, or as Herodotus asserts, a Tyrian, (which is the same thing) might also learn the art of literary writing, since it was not till some years after the passage over Jordan that Joshua was able to dispossess the Canaanites, and drive them out of the land by a total overthrow of

their

their forces *at the waters of Merom, where the Lord delivered them into the hand of Israel, who smote them and chased them unto great Sidon.* (Josh. 11, 7, 8.) From which place, or from Tyre, it probably was that Cadmus with the rest of his defeated companions, took shipping and fled into Greece, and carried with them the art of literary writing. And hence it is, that the Phœnicians are said by Lucan to have been the inventors of literary writing.

Phœnices primi, famæ si credimus, ausi
Mansuram rudibus vocem signare figuris.

Luc. l. 3.

But Phœnices was a name given to this mixt body by the Greeks; the sacred writers knew no such people; they denominated them all Canaanites, and as I have shewn before Canaan did consist of eleven different families or nations. Cadmus may therefore have been a Magogian-Scythian, and still very properly be called a Canaanite, or Phœnician. I am inclined to think Cadmus was a Scythian, because his name is truly Pelasgian-Irish, signifying head, first, chief, lord, see Kead or Cead, first; Cad holy; Keadmus or Ceadmus, first of all, imprimis, in all the Irish dictionaries. In Hebrew it implies an *Orientalist*, but that could not have been a distinct name in the East.

For that the Cadmonites were one of these colonies which were dispossessed of their habitations by Joshua, is plain from hence, because they are particularly specified in the promise made by God to Abraham, when he made a covenant with him to give him the land of Canaan for a possession, saying, *Unto thy seed have I given this land, from the river of Egypt to the great river, the river Euphrates. The Kenites, and the Knezzites,*

and

and the CADMONITES, *and the Hittites.* (Gen. 15, 18, and 19.

Diodorus accordingly fays, that Cadmus, who was the head of this tribe, brought the art of literary writing from Phœnicia into Greece; wherefore thofe letters, fays he, are called Phœnician. Juft as the Irifh fay that Phœnius, the Scythian leader, who was a Fear-Saidh or Sidonian man, taught letters to their anceftors in Paleftine. And in another place Diodorus fays, that Cadmus came to Rhodes, and brought with him the Phœnician letters: where was found an ancient vafe with this infcription, " *that* RHODES *was* " *about to be deftroyed by Serpents:*" that is, by the Hevites, who were his countrymen, and accompanied Cadmus from Phœnicia into Greece; the word *Heva* in Hebrew fignifying a *Serpent.* This circumftance is alfo related in the Irifh hiftory of Gadelas. But, if we confider the whole ftory of Cadmus, (as related by the Grecian hiftorians,) whofe wife's name is faid to be Hermione, and that he raifed foldiers by fowing of *Serpent's* teeth, it will add a ftrong confirmation to this opinion, that Cadmus was one of thofe Phœnicians, who were driven out of Canaan by Jofhua, when he purfued them to great Sidon. For when Jofhua numbered the hofts which came out againft him to battle in the land of Canaan, he reckons up amongft them the *Hevite under Hermon.* And now let us but fuppofe that Cadmus, the head of the Cadmonites, was married to the daughter of his unfortunate neighbour and ally the king of *Hermon,* whofe fubjects were called Hevites, and who being driven from their country by Jofhua, were forced to fly into Greece, and there is an eafy folution of this mythological ftory of the Grecian

Cadmus

Cadmus. For as the denomination, or name, which was given to the daughter of the king of Hermon, might probably be Hermione, and as the word Hevite, which was the appellation of the fubjects of the king of Hermon, denotes in Hebrew, *one fprung from a Serpent*; fo the Grecians made ufe of the double fignification of this word to graft upon it their fable of Cadmus, (the hufband of Hermoine) having raifed foldiers by fowing of ferpents teeth. See origin of hieroglyphics and mythology (p. 71.) by the late bifhop of Clogher, to whofe writings I am indebted for this obfervation.

To this let us add, the obfervations of the authors of the univerfal hiftory. " We come now to Magog, the fecond fon of Japhet , with regard to whofe fettlement, the learned have many different and confufed notions. Jofephus, Jerom, and moft of the fathers, held them to be Scythians about mount Caucafus, which name Bochart fuppofes was made by the Greeks out of Gog-hafon, fignifying Gog's-fort in Chaldee, of which he imagines the language of the Colchi and Armenians to have been a dialect. But perhaps it is rather a wrong pronunciation of Cuh-Kaf, which in Perfian fignifies the mountain of Kaf, as the Arabs call it *. That this plantation adjoined upon thofe of Mefhech and Tubal, appears from Ezekiel's making *Gog*, king of *Magog*, to reign over the other two. The Arabs, who have borrowed the beft part of their religion from the Jews, are acquainted with *Gog* and *Magog*, whom they call *Yajuj* and *Majuj*, and make

* We fhall hereafter find *Cuh-Kais* in Perfian and Irifh, is the mountain of Iron oar, for which *Caucafas* was remarkable. Pococke tells us that *Kaf* was a fabulous mountain of the Arabs. (See Notæ in Carmen Tograi, p. 71.)

them

'P R E F A C E.

them not inhabitants of the mountain *Kaf* or *Caucasus*, but removed them at a great distance, to the farther end of Tartary, towards the north or north-east. (See D'Herbelot) *. We are inclined to think the parts above mentioned between the *Euxine and Caspian* seas, are most likely to be those in which Magog settled. However, we can by no means omit this occasion of taking notice of an error, into which many of the modern writers have fallen, who place Magog in Syria. Bochart's great judgment would not suffer him wholly to come into it: however, he supposes Magog himself gave his name to a town there. Dr. Wells more cautiously suggests, 'that the name was long after taken from the Scythians, when they made an excursion into Syria, and took the city, as Bethsan in Judea was also called after them Scythopolis. But, Mr. Shuckford fixes Magog himself there, with Gomer, Tubal, Togarmah and Meshech about him. What gave rise to this opinion is a passage in Pliny, where he observes that Bambyce, otherwise Hierapolis, is by the Syrians called Magog; but this proves to be a palpable mistake of the transcriber, who has written Magog instead of Mabog, as has been observed by Dr. Hyde, who wonders nobody had corrected that error in Pliny.''

New lights have been thrown on the history of Assyria since these authors compiled the universal history: we must therefore insist on the Magogian Scythians having been early masters of that country.

* This is confirmed by my collation of the Magonian-Irish with the Kalmuc-Mogul, Tartar, Chinese and Japonese languages—there cannot be a surer guide of the Magogian colonies, every where to be distinguished from those of Gomer.

C   *Des*

PREFACE.

Des espèces de Scythes errants, sortis du mont Caucase, commencent à se répandre dans les plaines de l'Assyrie. (Ordre des Eveneinens de l'Histoire d'Assyria dont on ne peut fixer la Chronologie. Paris 1780, written by the learned Gibelin.)

We are obliged now, says the author of the Universal History, to say something with reference to the descendants of Joktan; who, if they were not concerned in the *first dispersion*, seem to have begun their migration in Peleg's life-time; with regard to which patriarch, we shall only observe here, that it is not probable the Pelasgians of Greece and Italy derive their original from him, as some imagine (See Cumberl. on Sanchon.) but it rather appears from scripture, that both he and his posterity remained in Chaldæa, within the lot of their great ancestor Arphaxed, till Terah the father of Abraham left Ur of the Chaldees, to remove into the land of Canaan." We find then, that this land of Canaan was the receptacle of every nation of the east; and though these authors will not allow the Pelasgians of Greece to have migrated in the life-time of Peleg, they still confirm my conjecture, that the mixed body which did migrate at that period, were properly called *Mesk*, or mixed people, and that they denominated themselves *Pleasgi & Phaon-pleasgi*, which in Irish signifies heroes, conquerors.

If we trace the histories of the Phœnicians and Chaldæans to their origin, in the most antient authors, there appears great reason to believe they were a mixed people of Scythians, Canaanites and Pelasgians. The authors of the Universal History, tell us, that it is not determined, whence Phœnice or Phœnicia

borrowed

borrowed its name. Some deriving it from one Phœnix (probably the Irish Phænius) others from the Greek Phænix, signifying a palm or date, as if that tree remarkably abounded there. Bochart observes that Phœnicia was known to the Jews by the name of the land of Canaan, a name he would derive from Canaan, and that the Phœnicians ashamed of their ancestor, took other names on themselves, but Canaan contained eleven different heads of houses or nations : this appellation could not affect them all. Phœnicia was certainly known by the name of *Chna*, and as Bochart observes the Hebrew *Chananæi* implies merchants; so we must observe does the Irish *chanaidhe*, and this word is commonly used at this day to signify traffick. *Ceanaim*, to buy or sell. *Ceanai-naoith*, marine merchants, traders by sea, but *Ceann* or *Kann*, is a head, chief, lord. *Cann-oine*, great prophets or diviners; so also in the Irish language, *Paineadh* or *Phaini*, is strong, valiant, and *aice*, is a tribe or people. *Acadh*, *aca*, a country or region, and these compounded form *Phainaice* and *Phanaca*. Hence *Pheinne*, *Phanaidhe*, *Fianne* and *Feinne*, is the name given in the ancient writings, to the Irish troops. *Phaon* or *Faon*, is a conqueror. *Faonbhach*, a conquered people. *Fine-gal*, a hero. *Fuanadh*, a refiner of metals. *Punnaice*, marching, sojourning. *Banaigham* or *Panaicam*, to lay waste a country. *Buin-aire*, *puinire*, a foot soldier. *Pont*, proud, austere. *Banachadh*, *phanacha*, pillaging, plundering. *Ban*, *pan*, light, the sun; hence *Phan*, a king; whence *Faunus* rex Etruriæ circiter CL (Eusebius) and Dion. Halicarn. says, contigit eo tempore quo venit Evander, esse regem *aborige-*

C 2   *nem*

nem Faunum, pronepotem (ut aiunt) Martis, quem ut genium quendam five indigetem, & facrificiis atque carminibus colunt Romani. (Pronepos autem ad pro-avum refertur, quoniam relativa funt.)

But the ftrongeft argument to prove the Pelafgi and Phœnices were of the fame origin, is drawn from the Irifh word *Phaoin-bleagan* or *Faoin-bleafgan,* or *pleafgan,* which in my ancient gloffary is explained by *Kannfacht* or *Ceannfacht,* i. e. conqueft. In this compound it appears, that *pleag* and *pleafg* and *Ceannfacht* all imply heroes, conquerors, and comprehends all the derivation given to the Pelafgi, by the authors of the Univerfal Hiftory.

And that the Phœnicians were Scythians, or allied with the Scythopolians of Bethfan, I think is extremely probable, from the author of the Book of Maccabees, book 1, ch. 11, v. 39. Moreover there was one Tryphon (τρύφων that is, *Tar-uph-ain,* the great forcerer) that had been of Alexander's part before, who feeing that all the hoft murmured againft Demetrius, &c. &c. Ch. 12, v. 39. Now Tryphon went about to get the kingdom of Afia, and to kill Antiochus the king, that he might fet the crown on his own head; howbeit he was afraid that Jonathan would not fuffer him, and that he would fight againft him, wherefore he fought a way to take Jonathan, that he might kill him. So he removed and came to Bethfan, (i. e. Scythopolis.) Then Jonathan went out to meet him, with forty thoufand men, chofen for the battle, and came to Bethfan. Ch. 13. v. 31. Now Tryphon dealt deceitfully with the young king Antiochus, and flew him; and he reigned in his ftead, and crowned himfelf king of Afia, and brought a great

calamity

calamity upon the land. Ch. 15. v. 11. wherefore (Tryphon) being purfued by king Antiochus, he fled unto Dora, which lieth by the fea-fide. v. 13. Then encamped Antiochus againſt Dora having with him 120,000 men and 8,000 horſemen, v. 37. In the mean time fled Tryphon by ſhip unto Orthoſias, v. 39. —but as for the king himſelf, he purfued Tryphon.

It is evident by this hiſtory that the Scythians did at this time poſſeſs all that country from Scythopolis or Bethſan, to Dor on the coaſt of the Mediterranean, near to Tyre, and by the retreat of Tryphon to Orthoſias, one of the moſt conſiderable cities of Phœnicia north of Tripolis on the coaſt of the Mediterranean, it is clear, that the Scythopolians and Phœnicians, were one and the ſame people.

This Tryphon ſome authors ſuppoſe to have been Diodotus, born in Apamea in Syria, whom Joſephus ſays was killed in that city in the third year of the captivity of Demetrius.

By this account of Macabeus, we ſee the Scythopolians took exactly the ſame route, as the Cadmonites in the time of Joſhua, and the laſt retreat of all theſe people, was to Tyre aud Sidon and from thence to Greece.

I might here fill twenty pages at leaſt from various authors, to prove that the Pelaſgi were of Phœnician or Hebrew original. Squire in his enquiry into the origin of the Greek language, concludes thus, " Up-
" on the whole therefore, whether we conſult the
" hiſtory of the Pelaſgi themſelves, or thoſe few au-
" thentic remains of their language ſtill preſerved in
" the ſcattered monuments of antiquity ; or whether,
" in the laſt place, we examine the language ſpo-
" ken

" ken by their undoubted colonies the Italians, we
" have on every fide, *the ftrongeft and moft convincing*
" *arguments of the great affinity between the Pelafgic and*
" *Hebrew tongues.*" Mr. Squire publifhed this effay
in 1741; and in 1750 G. Piet. Francefco Agius de
Soldanis, publifhed two effays at Rome on the *Lingua
Punica* ufed at this day in Malta, with a view to explain the Etrufcan. *Ovvero nuovi documenti, li quali
poffono fervire di lume all' Antica lingua Etrufcà.* From
this author's fmall dictionary of *Punica Maltefe*, I have
fhewn a perfect correfpondence with the Pelafgian-
Irifh, in a pamphlet containing alfo a collation of the
Punic fpeech in Plautus collated with the Irifh language? this pamphlet has been re-printed in the 2d
volume of this Collectanea. To return to Dr.
Parfons.

Thucyd. fays, that the Pelafgians were a numerous
people, fpread far and near before the age of Hellen
the fon of Deucalion, and Strabo fays the fame:
Theffaly was firft called Palafgia fays *Steph. de Urb. &
Scholion Apollon*, that the Pelafgians were a barbarous
nation, who inhabited Theffaly and Argos; Hefychius fays, the Pelafgians are Theffalians and Homer
places this people in Theffaly *."

·" The teftimonies are innumerable that argue for
the univerfality and antiquity of the ancient Pelafgians,
not only in Greece, but in every country round them,
as well iflands as on the continent: that the Thraci-

---

* Achaia Græciæ regio, quam Ptolemæus Helladen quoque
nominat Achaia alia Peloponnefi quæ ab eodem Ptolomæo Propria cognominatur, Ionia, Jas & Olenus eadem vocatur à Dio-
doro, Ægialos à Paufania & Plinio. Incolas *Pelafgos Ægiales.*
(Ortelius.) Deucalion was a Scythian. (Bailly fur les Sciences,
p. 256.)

ans

ans were inhabitants in Greece, from the very beginning and the people which were called the Bifaltes, Creftones, Edones, and particularly the Pelafgians, were counted Tyrrhenians, fome of whom dwelt in the 'ifle of Lemnos, and in the territory of Athens; and as the three firft of thefe were Thracians, the Pelafgians, who were forced away by the Phœnicians from the maritime places, retired to them as to their own friends and relations *."

" But the Pelafgians returned in fome time, and regained a part of their ancient country, fettling themfelves in Peliponefus, according to Herodotus, and were then called Dorians, and the moft famous of the Lacedemonians, whom Pezron mentions as Celts. Strabo fays that a great part of Greece, efpecially Macedonia and Theffaly, was inhabited by the Barbari, particularly Thracians, Illyrians and Epirotians; and Herodotus fays, that the Macedonians were refufed admittance in the Olympic games, becaufe they were of the Barbari." Gomer & Magog non funt idem populus: Veteribus Magog funt Scythæ

---

* The Pelafgians were not forced away by the Phœnicians, but united with them; they were originally Scythians and fo I believe were the Phœnicians. We have the teftimony of Berofius that the Scythians were very early diftinguifhed for a lettered people. We have in another place fhewn, from the old Teftament, that Nomades did not imply, as the Greeks would have it, Wanderers, Paftors, &c. for Macabeus mentions them as fighting men. So alfo does Xenophon. Ἱππεῖς καὶ νομεῖς; (νομέας paftores,) tametfi Xenophon dixerit τὸς νομῆς. Ne mireris fi homo bellis affuetus, nec urbanus, aliquem e patriis vocibus adulterat: ideo non eft quod quis illum Atticæ linguæ judicem fumat.

Photii Bibl. Edit. Steph. p. 1590.

& Gomer

& Gomer Phryges vel Galatæ qui Phrygiam occupa-
runt ufque ad Halim fluvium. Bochart Geogr. Sacr.
Ch. 38th.

The author of the univerfal hiftory obferves, it is
not fo eafy to find a place for Dodanim, the youngeft
of the fons or rather of the defcendants of Javan;
except we admit the change of ד d into ר r (which
letters in Hebrew are fcarcely to be diftinguifhed) and
call him *Rodanim*, as the feptuagint have done, in
order to fettle him in the ifland of Rhodes; which perhaps is not a worfe fhift than to extract the name of
Doris and the *Dorians* in *Peloponefus* from *Dodanim*.

Epirus was firft peopled by Dodanim, fon of Javan,
fon of Japhet, at leaft by fome of his pofterity, as
Jofephus informs us. Eufebius fays that Dodanim
firft fettled in the ifland of Rhodes, and that fome of
his defcendants paffed over to the continent and fixed
their abode in Epirus, where they built a city, calling
it *Dodona*, from their progenitor *Dodanim*. If the
opinion of Eufebius be true, the Dodonæans were
originally Greeks, and not Barbarians as moft of the
antient have ftiled them. However, in procefs of
time feveral barbarous nations fettled among them:
and hence they are faid by Strabo to have fpoken promifcuoufly the language of the Greeks and Barbarians. The various nations we find mentioned by the
moft ancient writers, as inhabiting Epirus, before
they became one people, under the common name of
Epirots, are the Selli, Chaones, Moloffi, Dolapes, Pa-
ravæi, Orefti, Dryopes, Hellopes, Œnianes and
Pelafgi. But as to the origin of thefe different tribes,
there is a great difagreement among authors, whofe
various opinions it would be too tedious to relate.

" When

PREFACE.

" When the Greeks became a nation of fome power, though they firft were but inconfiderable (which
may be feen in Herodotus) they always were fo extremely partial to themfelves, that they took every
ftep in their power to diftinguifh themfelves as a fuperior people, and to difgrace the neighbouring nations,
who were all Pelafgians, though under different denominations. This appears ftrongly in Homer's catalogue of the allies of the Trojans, who were all
Pelafgians of feveral denominations. Thefe were
Dardanians, Theffalians, Thracians, Peonians,
Paphlagonians, Enefians, Myfians, Phrygians,
Meonians, Carians, &c. and fought for the Trojans, their ancient relations and fellow Pelafgians;
and their enemies were the new inhabitants of Greece,
a mixed people, who made war with them, not more
on account of the rape of Helen, than to get poffeffion
of the territories of Troy (which was fo well fituated
for commanding the paffage from Europe into Afia,
and claiming the dominion of the fea) and to confine
the Trojan fhips in the Pontus Euxinus."

" Thefe notices, from fo many ancient authors of
great credit with the learned, would perfuade us,
that the Greek tongue is a mixture of Pelafgian,
Phœnician and Egyptian languages: but if thefe were
not fufficient for our purpofe, we do not want many
others, as powerful anecdotes, to prove it in the fequel. However, we are joined in this opinion by
Pelloutier, an author of note and refpect, who, in
his firft volume, p. 80, rejoices that the learned
Fourmont, the elder, a man well qualified for judg-
ing of matters of this kind, is of the fame opinion,
from whom he quotes the following paffage, fpeaking

of

of a Greek lexicon compofed by him, " I feek, fays
" he, the origin of the Greek tongue in this work,
" that is, the Greek words, which are truly primi-
" tive, by which I reduce this language to *lefs* than
" 300 words, fome of which are of Thrace and other
" neighbouring people, and others of the Phœnicians,
" or, in general, of oriental tongues; all by an eafy
" derivation, and to be underftood by the whole
" world *.

Now, in order to prove that Homer could not be a
ftranger to the Pelafgian tongue, let us pay due attention to that prince of authors upon ancient matters, Diodorus Siculus. " I will clearly declare,
" (fays he,) all that the Libyan and Greek writers
" have delivered concerning him, particularly one
" Dionyfius, the author of a very ancient hiftory,
" who has treated of the tranfactions of that perfonage,
" as well as of the Amazons, Argonauts, wars of
" Troy, with various other things, and alfo of all
" that the ancient poets and hiftorians delivered con-
" cerning them : he writes, that Linus was the firft
" inventor of mufic in Greece : that Cadmus invented
" the Greek tongue, having brought thither letters
" from Phœnicia, which were therefore in general

---

* It is furprizing the Doctor fhould have overlooked Dun-
ckel, who compofed a *Lexicon Græco-Celtico*, quo Græcæ et
Germanicæ linguæ fimulque matris Scythicæ, vel Celticæ ejufque
filiarum, tum & plurimarum aliarum linguarum convenientia
oftenditur. A fpecimen of this learned work may be feen in the
Symbolæ Literariæ, pars I. Bremæ 1745, which contains 153
Greek words between B and ΒΑΦΗ of Pelafgian, Magogian
Scythian, or Phœnician original; for there is great probability
thefe dialects, were one and the fame, for the reafons quoted
from the facred writings.

" called

" called Phœnician letters, that he gave *names* to
" many things; but, becaufe the Pelafgians ufed
" them firft, they were called Pelafgian letters."
" Linus, therefore had defcribed the acts of that firft
" Bacchus (Dionyfius) in Pelafgian letters, and left
" other fables behind him : Orpheus ufed the fame
" letters, as did alfo Pronapides, HOMER'S *MASTER*,
" a moft ingenious phyfician. Moreover, Thymætes,
" grandfon of Laomedon, who was cotemporary
" with Orpheus, having travelled through many
" parts of the world, came to the moft weftern parts
" of Libya, as far as the ocean, even to Nyfa; and
" finding that this Bacchus was brought up in that
" city by the ancient inhabitants, and informing him-
" felf of all the tranfactions of the Nyfeans, he com-
" pofed his poem, which is called Phrygia, in the
" *ancient* language, and with the *old* letters."

From this paffage, the reader will certainly fuppofe,
at leaft, that Homer muft have been verfed in the
Pelafgian tongue and letters, fince his mafter ufed
them. It is confeffed too, that Linus and Orpheus
ufed the fame, as well as Thymætes; and, if
Homer ftudied under a mafter ufing the Pelafgian
letters and language, he knew no other himfelf, and
that his works were alfo compofed in the fame; for
none of the famous men, now mentioned, are faid,
by Diodorus, to have ufed any others; nor do I believe any others were in ufe among the moft ancient
poets, muficians, &c.

We muft once more interrupt the Doctor, for the
honour of his country. Diodorus fays, that
Λῖνος (Linus) omnium primus Græcorum Rhythmos &
melodiam invenerit. In Irifh *Laoi & Laoin* is rhyme,

and

and *Laine* is melody, mufick; *ceol-laoin* a paultry verfifyer, who fings and plays to his rhymes. As to Dionyfius, fee H. Stephen's Greek edition, folio, printed in 1559, lib. 3. p. 140. fpeaking of the birth place of the great Dionyfius. Διόνυσος was a name of Bacchus compounded of the Pelafgian or Irifh *Duine* a man and *uas* noble, well born; *Duine-uas* a chief, literally a head-man: hence *duine-uafal* the modern name of a gentleman, Sir, &c. Arab. *aful* of a noble family. *Afil* root, archtype, prototype, honour, &c. ΔΙΟΝΥΣΙΑ were folemnities in honour of Bacchus, fome times called Οργια, which words though fometimes applied to the myfteries of other gods, does more probably belong to thofe of Bacchus. At thefe Orgia the Greeks ran about the hills of Athens, deferts and other places, wagging their heads, and filling the air with hideous noifes and yelling, crying aloud Ευοϊ Βάχχι Ιὼ Βάχχι. In Irifh *Orgha* and *Orghaon* is a poetical lamentation. (See *Caon* in the conclufion.) *Becc dechne Ofaigh na Filand*, i. e. *Becc* was the laft *Ofaigh* or forcerer of orders of the File or orators, or hymn-compofers. (See File, Ollom, &c.) *Airgea* is an an action done out of refpect or regard, and *bac* is a breach, a violent attack, *bach* drunkennefs, *baccaire* a drunkard. *Bactrach* the name of an Irifh druid, faid to have difcovered to the monarch, from an eclipfe of the fun, the paffion of our Saviour, the very time it happened. *Beach* a magical circle. *Beic* an outcry, a yelling. *Beice* crying out through grief. *Heb: bachah* flevit, deflevit cum lamentatione & elevatione vocis. — Hence the Irifh proverb *Cia tufa bheiceas um an Righ,* who are you that dare to cry out to the king.

Gorius

PREFACE.

Gorius in his mufeum Etrufcum has the following paffage relating to Homer. " Jam ex adlatis a me in hoc mufeo Etrufco, illuftribus monumentis, fatis conftare arbitor, Tufcos perfpectam habuiffe Trajani belli hiftoriam. Et facile crediderim, Homerum, qui tefte Strabone, ut mox fuo loco oftendam, Etruriam peragravit, perluftravitque multa, que narrat in Iliade & in Odyffea, ab Etrufcis didiciffe. S. Bochartus, vir cum paucis comparandus, l. 1. c. 33. Geogr. facræ, adfirmat Homerum Italicas fabulas, quafcumque habet, non aliunde didiciffe quam ex relatione Phœnicum, quorum nonnulli naufragum Ulyffem circa Charybdim nave fua exceptum, in Cretam deduxiffe leguntur.— Sed quum alia multa præter fabulas, nobis offerant edita Tufcanica monumenta, quæ Iliade & Odyffeam exornant; haud negandum cenfeo, ex fide etiam Etrufcorum, multa Homerum in fuis carminibus inferuiffe.

It is worthy of obfervation, that the fiege of Troy has been written in Irifh in a very ancient dialect, and is efteemed by the Irifh bards, as the greateft performance of their Pelafgian or Magogian anceftors.

We now return to Dr. Parfons.

It is not improbable, alfo, that Homer's works never reached Greece, till Lycurgus, in his return from Afia, whither he went from Crete, collected and brought them with him. Sir Ifaac Newton in his fhort chronology, fays, Troy was taken 904 years before CHRIST; but it is thought to be about 46 years earlier, and by fome much longer; he alfo fays, Lycurgus brought them out of Afia 710 years before CHRIST, which was 240 years after its deftruction.

ſtruction. It is therefore, very probable, that the tranſlation was not made till ſome time after their arrival in Greece. And we find, according to Sir Iſaac, p. 59. that when Lycurgus was publiſhing his laws, being old, " Terpander a famous lyric poet, " began to flouriſh ; for he imitated Orpheus, and " Homer, and ſung Homer's verſes and his own, " and wrote the laws of Lycurgus in verſe, and was " victor in the Pythic games in the 26 Olympiad."— By which it may be ſuggeſted, that Terpander had never ſeen Homer's works before Lycurgus brought them into Greece, and admiring them, began to imitate them himſelf; and that very likely after the tranſlation, or perhaps, he might be the tranſlator*.

" From

---

* Signor Carlo Denina profeſſor of eloquence and belles-lettres in the univerſity of Turin, publiſhed his eſſay on the revolutions of literature, not many years ſince. In his obſervations on the literature of the Greeks, he ſays, that the origin of literature is ſo uncertain and obſcure, that we muſt conſider and revere HOMER as the father of it. Whether that divine poet borrowed from others, to us is unknown, but extraordinary it is, that in the courſe of ſo many ſucceeding ages, there was no poet in Greece worthy to be reckoned his ſecond; and it is amazing, that after Homer's two capital works, in which, beſides eſtabliſhing a perfect ſtandard of elocution, the ſeeds of univerſal knowledge are ſo liberally ſtrewed, ſo long a time ſhould elapſe before any piece, even of another kind, was produced worthy of the like eſtimation ; for, *true it is*, that nothing appeared for above three hundred years after Homer, that *deſerved* the notice of poſterity. But when the wiſe laws of Solon began to render Athens a well governed republic, and the victories of the Athenians had introduced plenty and an honourable eaſe into their city, then, and not till then, the ſeat of letters became in a manner confined to ATTICA.

PREFACE.

" From this difcovery of Diodorus concerning Homer's mafter, it is eafy to fee his reafon for beftowing great applaufe upon the Pelafgians. He faw his mafter Pronopides, teaching him knowledge, probably in their language and letters, and his love of learning infpired him with an high veneration for a people, of whom he was *one*, and through whom the moft fublime literature was conveyed to him, whofe tafte was fo exquifite, and the enjoyment of his refined knowledge fo great, that he was tranfported to exprefs his gratitude to his glorious predeceffors, in the work which immortalized himfelf."

" There is another argument, and not a trivial one, which induces me to think, that, if thefe old authors, mentioned by Diodorus ufed the Pelafgian letters, they muft have wrote in the language of the Pelafgians only ; and that is, that as they had but 17 letters, which were always fufficient, in every cafe, in their own language, they can hardly be faid to have wrote in Greek, which cannot be expreffed without additional letters, to the amount of 24 ; and it is plain, that 7 more were added to the 17 primary letters, as the alterations in the Pelafgi were going on ; for new powers were wanting, to exprefs the mutilations and additions that gradually were introduced into the old language, which, at length, grew into a new one. Diodorus very punctually diftinguifhes between the old and the new, where he mentions the poem Phrygia of the Pelafgian poet Thymætes on Dionyfius."

Now, if thefe fecondary letters be omitted in the Greek alphabet, the remaining 17 are the letters of

the

the Magogian, now the Irish or Scotish language, which remain invariable at this day.

I cannot here omit one very strong circumstance in the Doctor's favour, concerning the alphabet.

There is not a language in the western part of the globe, the Irish excepted, wherein F when pointed (or printed with an hiatus, thus fh) loses its sound, as it did with the Pelasgian Greeks. Dion. Halicarn. is the only author I have met with, that explains this *digamma*. I shall give the Latin translation of Frideric. Sylb.—"itaque cum Pelasgis fœdus feriunt, & partem agrorum suorum eis assignant circa sacrum lacum, quorum pleraque erant palustria, dicta nunc *prisco linguæ* more *Velia* (i. e. οὐηλια.) Solebant enim prisci Græci nominibus a vocali incipientibus præponere syllabam ου scriptam uno charactere, is erat similis r duplici (γαμμα διπλαῖς) ad rectam lineam duabus obliquis additis, ut, Fελεπη, Fάγαξ, Fοῖκος, Fασύη, & multa similia.

Now the Irish ḟ or F pointed, reads like the Greek ου, for example, ḟ ios or fhios is pronounced ου-*is*; but if F is to be restored to the sound of V, then bh or ḃ is affixed; as *filim*, to be, in all its inflexions is written *bhfbuilim*; ex. gr. *bhfbuil se* (will she) he is. But the most extraordinary circumstance is, that the contracted Irish character for the particle *fa* is the same as that used by the ancient Greeks for ου. (see plate 2d, fig. 2.) except a small perpendicular stroke over the top, which probably was lengthened and became the Greek Φ phi, at which time, perhaps was laid aside the Greek F (Fαῦ) which we find after E in the 8th table of Doctor

Bernard

Bernard, entitled alphabetum Græcum Cadmi, five Ionicum, ante Chr. 1500, averfis literis Phœnicum, e nummis Siculis (Æginenfibus) Bœotis, Atticis, aliifque. I have added another Irifh contracted character after *Fa*, which ftands for *Con*, as I find it in an ancient MSS under my eye. *Con*, fignifies fenfe, reafon ; *fa*, is a prepofite article, implying *in*, *upon*, *as*, *under*, whence *facon*, fometimes written *facain*, fignifies motive, caufe, the reafon why : it is fo ufed in the paffage before me, *facon rug an fear, con-dibar-tbar, dilin* ; that is, " the reafon or motive, that a " man beftows this gratuity called *dilin*." I have never met with this character in the middle of a word. We find it ufed before a confonant, and if I miftake not, the Greeks did the fame, though the Greek author here quoted, fays, it was only ufed before a vowel.

Walfingham in his Hypodigma afferts, that, " Egyptiis in Mari Rubro fubmerfis, illi qui fuperfuérunt expulerunt a fe quendam nobilem Scythicum, qui degebat apud eos, ne dominium fuper eos invaderet ; expulfus ille cum familia, pervenit ad Hifpaniam, ubi et habitavit annis multis, et progenies ipfius familiæ multæ multiplicata eft nimis ; & inde venerunt in HIBERNIAM."

That the Saxons had their letters and learning from Ireland is well attefted by good authority. Camden fays, the Saxons in that age, flocked hither, as to the great mart of learning ; and this is the reafon, why we find this fo often in our writers ; *fuch a one was fent over to* IRELAND *to be educated.* And this paſſage in the life of Sulgenus, who flouriſhed 600 years ago:

> Exemplo patrum commotus amore legendi
> Ivit ad Hibernos, ſophia mirabile claros.

But ſoon after, he ſays, " nor is it any wonder that Ireland, which for the moſt part is now rude and without the glory of polite literature, was ſo full of pious and great wits, in that age, &c. Now, he relates from Bede, that Egfrid, king of the Northumbrians, about the year 684, landed in Ireland and deſtroyed every thing in his way with fire and ſword, which, ſays he, put an end to all learning and religion. But twenty Iriſh hiſtorians of *that very time*, agree in ſaying, that Egfrid landed in Eaſtmeath, and committed hoſtilities for a few days, till the forces of the then prince were collected; and that he and his forces were then driven on board his ſhips, with a great loſs of men, and did not attempt it afterwards. And it is well known, that Ireland continued to be called the *Inſula Doctorum & Sanctorum*, many centuries after that ſkirmiſh.

Inſula Sacra was a very ancient name given to Ireland, as appears from Avienus Feſtus, who flouriſhed in the joint reigns of Gratian and Theodoſius, about the year 379, and in his pœem *de Oris Maritimis* has theſe words, INSULA SACRA, *& ſic inſulam dixere priſci; eamque late gens* HIBERNORUM *colit*. By *priſci* he muſt mean the ancients before his time. And with regard to the navigations of Himilco, he profeſſes that he himſelf had read them in the Punic annals.

> Hæc olim Himilco Pænus, Oceano ſuper
> Spectaſſe ſemel & probaſſe retulit;

Hæc

PREFACE.

Hæc nos ab imis Punicorum annalibus,
Prolato longo tempore edidimus tibi.

These things of old on western sea
Himilco says, he tried and saw;
From hidden Punic annals, we
Relate, what we from thence did draw.

Mr. Ledwich a worthy member of our *triumvirate society of Hibernian Antiquaries**, in his letter to gover-Pownal on the Ship-Temple worship, in Ireland, has observed (p. 434. No. 11.) " that an identity of lan-
" guage carried so imposing an appearance, as at one
" time to make me say, that the *Fomoraigh Afraic*, or
" African pirates so often mentioned in the antient
" history of Ireland, were no other than the Phœnici-
" ans and Carthaginians: but, that I must have con-

---

* Consisting at present of the Rev. Mr. Ledwich, vicar of Aghaboe in the Queen's County; Mr. Beauford, an ingenious private tutor of the same county; and the author of this number of the Collectanea. This society was once composed of the most respectable men in Ireland, for learning and fortune; it continued but two years, and in the third, it was discovered, that three *Guineas* per *annum*, was too great a subscription for gentlemen to bestow on researches into Irish antiquities. The *Amanuensis* continues to be paid by the author a salary of twenty guineas per annum, which he or some other shall enjoy, till he has finished the antiquities of Ireland. From the above members, must be excepted, the right hon. W. B. Conyngham, who in the midst of the real patriotic schemes, this gentleman steadily pursues for the good of his country, with equal steadiness follows the elucidation of the antiquities of it. He has employed three eminent draughtsmen to take plans and views of whatever is remarkable in Ireland; a set are now engraving by the celebrated Sandby, which will soon convince the Antiquaries of Europe, that Ireland produces a rich mine in that line of study, as yet unexplored, and worthy of their attention.

D 2   " sidered

PREFACE.

" fidered better of this matter, and been convinced,
" that the Irifh traditions were not defenfible on the
" ground I had chofen, as I have omitted in the fe-
" cond edition of my grammar, the preceding quo-
" tation in the firft." Never was the worthy member more miftaken : it is the line I have followed in
all my refearches fince that publication ; furely, our
worthy member does not read all the labours of our
learned fociety that are offered to the public, or he
might have feen, that in the tenth number
I was obliged to have recourfe to the Oriental languages for the terms of the law, the ftate and the church,
that occurred in that publication, for want of fufficient gloffaries in the Irifh language. The learned gentleman will call them African pirates, though I fhewed
the word *Fomorigh* implied marine chiefs, princes,
&c. The proper word for a pirate is *Foghluidhe fairge*
a fea robber ; the word pirate was not intended in that
place, by the Irifh hiftorians, but was foifted in by
O'Connor, the vile tranflator and interpolator of
Keating's hiftory *. When the ancient Irifh fitted
out

* The ancient Irifh Seanchas fay, that Gan, Geanan, Conuing and Faovar, were African generals who drove the Nemedians
out of Ireland. That they firft fettled at Toirinis, which was
called *Tor Conuing* or the tower of *Conuing*, from the tower he
built there : this is the firft round tower mentioned in Irifh hiftory. That on their firft landing, finding themfelves too weak to
cope with the Irifh, Morc retnrned to Africa and ftrengthened
himfelf with fixty fail of fhips, and a numerous army on board,
and landed again at Tor Conuing. Now in Irifh *Conuing* implies a foreign language. See the conclufion of the Preface.
An army of Carthaginians on board fixty fail of fhips, was not
an army of pirates, as our worthy member will have it, and we
fhall

out a marine expedition, the commander was named *Fo-muir* or *Arg* from *Aire* a chief and *go* the fea. *Naoi* is a fhip plur. *Naoith*; hence *Naoithoir* failors, *Argnaoithoir* royal failors on an expedition; but *Argnaothoir* is now corrupted to *Argnoir* and implies a pirate or plunderer, and *Argnaim* to rob or plunder; which was originally written *Aghnoir*, from *agh* a conflict; thus in the Arabic *Agharet*, laying wafte an enemies country, in Perfic *Arghand*, bold, warlike, intrepid.—— Thefe references to the oriental tongues are certainly needlefs, fince our worthy member has difcovered from Ralph the hiftorian, that *the language, manners, and cuftoms of the ancient Britains, and of the Phœnicians were exactly the fame.* (Letter to G. Pownal, p. 433.) Thus, the learned labours of Bochart, Vitringa, Rheland, Selden, Leibnitz, &c. &c. may now be fold for wafte paper! Pity it is, fo ufeful a difcovery had not been made when Dr. Davis was writing his Welfh dictionary: the doctor was a good orientalift, yet could not produce above 200 words that he thought had an affinity with the Hebrew *, and in this lift are

---

fhall hereafter fhew that this ifland did produce much more valuable commodities than Great Britain at that period: it had tin, lead and gold. It was no Quixotifm to conquer fuch an ifland: but fuppofing it only had fur, was not the natural happy foil and fcite of the ifland fufficient to invite a conqueft by a people parched up on the coaft of Africa, who had reafon to expect a good reception from their relations.

* The Phœnicians, or mixed body of Canaanites, including Magogian Scythians, were in poffeffion of Britain as well as Ireland, till expelled by the Gomerian Celts, as Mr. Lhwyd has obferved; but our worthy Member and Ralph are wrong in calling them Britains, meaning thereby the Cumerag or Gomerian Welfh.

fome

ſome, that reſemble the Otaheite dialect, as much as the Britiſh. Ex. gr.

WELSH.	LATIN.	HEBREW.	IRISH.
aros	manere	ſhera	ſioram
arwydd	ſignum	oth	athara, com'-athar
aſgen	noxa	nezek	nas, neaſg.
attuph	qᵈ non germinat	ſopheach	miophas, (ſophais quod germinat)§
bargen	contractus	macar (vendere)	raçam † margam.
beddrwd	ſepulchrum	keburah	cubhar, kaobhar
bwccled	clypeus	magen	mogan
celwydd	mendacium	candibutha	ceandibhir, (ceandachd veritas)
crevan	cranium	cadra	ceadros
cwymp	ruinæ	mappula	miadhmbal, milleadh
cyfarwys	munus	arucha	rogha, arioghnait
cyfrwy	ephippium	mercau	marc-ſadhall
cyntaf	primus	kadmai	Cadmus, Ceadamus
cyſgod	umbra	ſacak	ſcath, ſcathac
&c.	&c.	&c.	&c.

To theſe I have added the Iriſh words, to convince our worthy member, that he and *Ralph* are quite right in their aſſertion, and that the Pelaſgian or Magogian Iriſh has not the leaſt reſemblance to the He-

§ And this is the meaning of the Hebrew *ſopheach*, ſee Holloway.

† The Hebrew *macar* read from right to left; this is not uncommon in the old Iriſh, occaſioned by their uſe of the *bouſtrophedon*, of which I have ſpoken in the grammar. We find the Etruſcans did the ſame.

brew

brew: the Welsh words are not picked, but taken in their alphabetical order.

I hope the reader will not imagine that I mean to speak with contempt of the Welsh language; on the contrary, I hold the old Welsh in the highest esteem. The Gomerian dialect was originally the same as the Magogian or Irish, and by the mixture of the Gomerians with the Magogians in Britain, the first have certainly retained some words of the Magogian dialect, now become obselete in the latter. But the Gomerians by a series of time, and by their long journies from the north of Asia through Europe, to Britain, (not having mixt with the Assyrians, Phœnicians, &c. as the Magogians did,) had lost much of their primitive language, and considering the many revolutions of Britain since the arrival of the Gomerians, it is wonderful that they have preserved their language so well. It has undoubtedly suffered a greater corruption in the last 500 years, than it had undergone before, as that learned Welsh antiquary, Mr. Lhwyd, has fully set forth, in his *Archæologia Britannica*. And when I speak of the ancient Irish, I mean to include under that name, the Hibernians, the Erse or Highlanders of Scotland, and the Manx of the Isle of Man, together with the inhabitants of the Western Islands of Scotland. They were originally Trifodi, as the ancient Irish poets stiled them, that is, three people of one stock, soil or origin: they were the same colony of Magogian-Scythians, Phœnicians or Canaanites, and Cadmonites, who came from Tyre and Sidon to Greece, Africa, Spain, Britain and Ireland. And they possessed the two latter till driven from Britain by the Gomerian Celts from Gaul and Britain, and

now

now remain poſſeſſed of Ireland, Mann, and the Weſtern Iſlands and north of Scotland or Caledonia. It is of little moment to the learned world, if the Caledonians poſſeſſed their country, by the route of the main land, through Britain, as is very probable, or if they ſailed to it from the North of Ireland, or if ſome of the Iriſh took their route to Ireland from Caledonia. The two iſlands were their own, and poſſeſſed by them at the ſame time: the emigration from Britain, might have been by both channels, at different periods, in proportion as they loſt ground in Britain on the arrival of freſh bodies of Gomerian Celts from Gaul: and it is in vain to ſearch for this knowledge in ancient authors. Foreign men of letters will ſcarcely believe that a diſpute of this kind, ſhould make a breach between two people of the ſame original ſtock, ſpeaking at this day, the ſame language, and having the ſame manners and cuſtoms in common, and that this breach ſhould encreaſe in magnitude, in proportion as the world grows more enlighted.

It is evident that the Greeks knew little of Ireland or Caledonia, but as they had the accounts from ſailors; the old Pelaſgian writings being loſt. Diodorus Siculus who lived forty-five years before Chriſt, mentions Britains inhabiting the iſland called Iris (Eirinn) lib. 5. And Strabo who lived ſeventy years after him calls Ireland, Britiſh Ierna, (l. 1.) and his ancient abridger calls the Iriſh, the *Britains inhabiting Ierna*. Theſe authorities are ſufficient to ſhew that Britain and Ireland were comprehended by them, under one and the ſame people. Dion. Caſſius, who lived in the third century, knew leſs of the Caledonii;

donii; he fays, " Cæterum Britannorum duo fent
" prefertim genera. Caledonii & Mæatæ, nam cæ-
" terorum nomina ad hos ferè referuntur. Incolunt
" Mæatæ juxta eum murum qui infulam in duas
" partes dividit. Caledonii poft illos funt. Poffidunt
" utrique montes afperrimos, & fine aqua: itemque
" campos defertos, plenofque paludibus: quodque
" mænia non habent nec urbes, agros nullos colunt:
" de præda & venatione, fruâibufque arborum vi-
" vunt, nam pifces, quorum ibi maxima eft, & in-
" numerabilis copia, non guftant. Degunt in tento-
" riis nudi & fine calceis: utuntur communibus ux-
" oribus, liberofque omnes alunt. (Epitom. Dionif.
" Severi, 21.)

This account of the Caledonians is as far diftant
from truth, as that of all the modern Greek authors,
who have made the Irifh to be cannibals. Orpheus
and Homer were much better acquainted with the
fituation of thefe iflands, and the manners of the inhabitants. The claffical fcholar, whofe learning
does not extend beyond Greek, confines his knowledge of hiftory to the modern authors, and from
them draws a picture of the people; although the
moft impartial Greek writers have declared, that the
Greeks received their fables, mythology and great
part of their language from the Barbari, our modern
writers will not be at the trouble of acquiring the language of thofe *learned Barbarians*; yet that divine
philofopher Plato gives them this advice: " the
" Greeks have borrowed many words from the Bar-
" barians; therefore if any man would endeavour to
" adjuft the etymologies of thofe words with the
" Greek language, and not rather feek for them, in
" that

" that to which they *originally belong*, he muſt needs be at a loſs."

When Beroſus [the Chaldæan, who flouriſhed in the time of Ptolemy Philadelphus, declared from his peruſal of the Chaldæan and Scythian writings, that the *Scythians were a learned people, and the firſt in arts and ſciences after the flood*; he had no conception of theſe people being afterwards ſtiled *barbari* by the Greek and Roman writers : no more did Diodorus Siculus or Himerius think the Hyperboreans would have received the ſame character, when they were deſcribing Abaris the Hyperborean, and *Prieſt of Apollo*, as one of the wiſeſt men that ever had converſed with Pythagoras, of which hereafter.

May this addreſs to the Hibernians, Manx, and Caledonians, have the deſired effect, in uniting them in one ſociety for the recovery and illuſtration of their antiquities, and thereby open a new mine for the republic of letters.

Our worthy member next proceeds to an ironical joke, on *crucifixes* being diſcovered by captain Cooke amongſt ſome ſavage people, and the concluſions that may be drawn, by a fool, from ſuch a diſcovery; theſe obſervations do not merit a ſerious anſwer : a compliment was to be paid to governor Pownal, on his diſcovery of the Ship Temple in Ireland, and our worthy member was to eſtabliſh the fact ; his readers muſt allow, he has done it in a very *maſterly* and *ſatisfactory* manner. But, a *blow* on *Etymology* we little expected from that quarter : it was unmanly in a man, who enjoys ſuch extraordinary abilities, as to be able, to explain the moſt remote antiquities of a very ancient people, without underſtanding a word

of

of its language; it was unmanly, I fay, in fo learned
a man, to aim a blow on *Etymology*, at a weak member of the *fociety*, who after dedicating many years to
the ftudy of the Irifh language, in order to explore
the antiquities of the country, finds himfelf fuch a
dunce, as to be extremely unequal to the tafk, though
in comparing the language with the *oriental*, *all the tor-*
tures of Etymology are applied to make them harmonize. The
hiftory of the antiquities of *Kilkenny*, by my very learned
colleague, will ever bear record of his fuperior abilities
in this art*: But, if our worthy member fhould think

proper

---

* It is a very common error, (fays Lhwyd) to endeavour to
derive the radical words of our weftern European languages
from the Latin or Greek, or indeed to derive conftantly the
primitive of any one language, from *any particular tongue.*
Whatever nations were of one common *origin* with the Greeks
and Latins, muft have preferved their language much better
than them, and confequently a *great many* words of the language of the old Aborigines, the Ofci, the Læftrigones, the
Aufonians, Œnotrians, Umbrians, Sabines, &c. out of which
the Latin was formed, muft have been better preferved in the
Celtic than in the Roman language. (Comp. Vocab. p. 35.) Lingua
Etrufca, Phrygica, and Celtica, (fays the learned Stiernholm)
affines funt omnes; ex une fonte derivatæ. Nec Græca longè
diftat. Eandem linguæ Latinæ originem afferit etiam Cl. G.
J. Voffius, in præfatione ad tractatum, *de vitiis fermonis*, cujus
tamen affertionis immemor, in Lex. fuo Etymolog. bene multa
vocabula *infeliciter*, & invitâ Minervâ, trahit ex Græca, quæ
commodè & fine violentiâ duci potuerunt ex CELTICA.

The Celtic (adds Lhwyd) has been beft preferved by fuch of
their colonies as from fituation, have been leaft fubject to foreign
invafions. Such is Ireland.

I would afk this queftion, (fays Dr. Parfons) Why do the
greateft part of our moft modern writers, of all the academical

feminaries

proper to proceed in *ironical controverſy*, it is to be wiſhed, he will find ſome other channel and ſome other title, to convey his works to the eye of the public, than COLLECTANEA DE REBUS HIBERNICIS. Controverſy muſt be extremely diſagreeable to our readers; as long as the public think proper to indulge my bookſeller in purchaſing the COLLECTANEA, I ſhall proceed with the *antiquities* of *Ireland*; my labours are beſtowed to him, and the plates engraved at my expence, yet he cries out with the poet :

Quis legit hæc? Nemo, hercule nemo, vel duo, vel nemo.

To conclude; before our worthy member can drive me from my reſearches into *oriental* literature, for the explanation of Iriſh antiquities, he muſt prove

1ſt. That the language and cuſtoms of the ancient Welſh and of the Iriſh were the ſame: that it was uſual with people to name their country from its poſition on the globe, with reſpect to one given ſpot: that the *Eaſt and Weſt Indies* were ſo named by the ancient inhabitants of them. That *Eirin* (the ancient name of Ireland) is derived from the Welſh *Yverdon*: that אהרון *ieroun*, is not Hebrew for Weſtward, and עבר־נאה *Iber-nae*, is not Phœnician for *ultima habita-*

feminaries of Europe, when they are employed in ſuch reſearches as theſe, reſt contented with only what is delivered by the Greek authors? The anſwer is obvious. The education of the youth of all Europe conſiſts in the ſtudy of the Greek and Latin claſſics: and when they come to the higher links of this chain of learning, and are well verſed in thoſe two languages, the *ne plus* preſents itſelf, and their future reſearches and lucubrations ſoar no higher. (*Remains of Japhet*, p. 364.)

tio,

tio, and that the ancient inhabitants of Ireland had not the vernacular names of *Innis-ealga, Innis-fodbla*, &c. &c. for their own country.

2d. That the names of the feftivals, &c. &c. contained in this number are all to be found in the Welfh language.

3d. That the ancient names of the mountains and rivers of Ireland and Britain are to be found in the Welfh language; and that it was not ufual with colonifts to name the features of new difcovered countries, after thofe they refembled in their native country, or where they had long refided.

4th. That a mixed colony of Phœnicians, Pelafgians, &c. did not trade to the Britifh iflands: that they did not fettle on the weftern coaft of Africa, and from thence extend through the ftraights of Gibraltar to *Hberne*, חרנא, beyond which they had not one colony, and that the Phœnician *Hberne*, the Hebrew *Jeroun* (Weftward) and the Irifh *Jarnae* are derived from the Greek οἱηρια, and that Feftus Avienus is an author of no reputation with learned men.

5th. That the Hebrews and Phœnicians did not name the Eaft קדים *kadim*, i. e. the fore part; before you: the weft אחור *abor*, i. e. the back part; behind you: the fouth ימין *jamin*, i. e. the right hand: the north שמאל *fhemol*, i. e. the left hand; and that the IRISH do not name the eaft *oirtbar, keadmus, oir, oirfkeart*, i. e. before, in front: the weft *jorar, jar*, i. e. the back part, behind: the fouth *lamb-imbeadboin, imbeaoin, deas*, i. e. the right hand: the north *cleit, cleid, tuag, fumbail, fumbain, kite*, and every other word that can imply the left hand, and

fo

ſo of the reſt: that the Gomerian Celts or Welſh did the ſame, and that thoſe words are to be found in the Welſh language, and that the Magogian Iriſh, have not technical terms alſo, for theſe points, that are only to be found in the Hebrew and Chaldee languages, ſuch as *daram*, the meridian ſun, compoſed of *dar*, over head, and *am*, time, whence the דרום *darom* quod *meridiem* ſonat Phœnicibus, from which word Drymos δρυμὸς in Bœotia, quia auſtrale erat oppidum. (See Bochart, &c. &c.)

6th. That it is not neceſſary for a man to underſtand the language of a people, before he writes of their hiſtory and antiquities.*

Amongſt many inſtances I can produce of an oriental colony arriving in Ireland, take the following: A catterpillar appears in Ireland in autumn, which the peaſants call the *codbna* worm: it is written *codbna*, *coghna*, and *connough*, the *d* and *g* being ecliſped.

---

* The ſtudy of antiquities is divided into various branches; the firſt object which ſtrikes us, as the firſt in order and natural pre-eminence, is the LANGUAGE of a people; in tracing which, through the many changes, frequent opportunities occur of diſcovering the origin of important cuſtoms and inſtitutions, and the cauſes of their denomination, in the ſimple occupations and amuſements of rude uncultivated nature. *(Burgeſs on the ſtudy of antiquities.)* The extenſive influence of opinions and manners on language, and even of language on opinions has reached the moſt civilized and poliſhed ages. *(Harris's Hermes.)* —L'hiſtoire des colonies & de leur parcours ſur la ſurface de la terre tient de fort près a l'hiſtoire des langues. Le meilleur moyen de dècouvrir *l'origine d'une nation* eſt de ſuivre en remontant *les traces de ſa langue* comparée à celles des peuples avec qui la tradition des faits nous apprend que ce peuple a eu quelque rapport. *(Preſid. de Broſſes.)*

This

This catterpillar is faid to be the only poifonous animal in Ireland, and to effect cows and fwine only.
Goedartius in his book of infects calls it the elephant
catterpillar, from its ugly form and dark reddifh brown
colour. It is as big as a man's thumb and above three
inches long. The old Irifh, thought, the only remedies for cattle poifoned by this animal, was, to bore
a hole in a tree, fhut up the worm therein to ftarve
and die, and to make an infufion of the leaves and
bark, wherewith to drench the cattle; or, if a man
crufh the animal, and let the expreffed juice thereof dry
upon his hands, the water he firft wafhes in, ever after, given to the beaft to drink, cures it. This is the
very cure the fuperftitious Arabs ufe for the bite of a
poifonous worm, exactly anfwering the defcription of
our elephant catterpillar, and its Perfian name is
Khagynè. Dr. Molyneux made many experriments to
prove our catterpillar was not poifonous, and we have
of late heard no more of the *connough* worm. *(See
Phil. Tranf. No. 168.)* and *coghna*, now implies the
diforder that ufually affects horned cattle. The names
of a worm are *cnumb, cnuimbag, biafdag, peiftog, piaft,
ferogha*; and of a catterpillar, *burris, lufcuæch, duilm-
biol, ailfag, bolh*; how came the Irifh by the Perfian
Khagynè, which is the *real poifonous* worm? again, no
nation in the weftern world has fo many *fynonima* as
the Irifh, for *writing, books, comments* on books, &c. &c.
and fuch words as are not indigenous, from the materials they were obliged to make ufe of in this climate,
are adopted from the Hebrew, Arabian and Perfian
languages, and are not to be found in the Welfh.
(See *Scriobam* in the conclufion.) In one inftance,
the

the Irish language can explain the meaning of two words in the Hebrew, which have perplexed all commentators, and were very probably Pelafgian or Scythian words introduced by the Scythopolians into Paleftine: I mean קרי וכתיב or the *Keri* and *Ketib*, the names of the *marginal* notes of the bible, inferted by the Maforæ, or as fome rabbies will have it, by Ezras, while others abfurdly infift, that thofe of the Pentateuch were written by Mofes.

The Hebræift is well acquainted with the various opinions of the learned on this fubject; but for the explanation to fuch as are not, I fhall inftance two.

Buxtorf in his Clavis Maforæ, fays, קרא, *kara*, aut *keriah*, fcriptura facra biblia, alias *mekera* quafi lecturam dicas. In Mafora communiter pro tota fcriptura V. T. fumitur, quandoque pro parte majori & definita, à qua aliquis liber exemptus eft. כתיב, *ketib*, fcriptum participium formæ Chaldeicæ pro qua Hebræi dicunt *catob*.

Leufden de Mafora. Unde hæc voces derivantur? Et quid fignificant : *keri* fignificat lectum a *kara* vocavit & vox *ketib* five *catob* fignificat fcriptum.

Our Hibernian druids always wore a key *, like the law doctors of the Jews, to fhew they alone had the key of the fciences, that is, that they alone could communicate the knowledge of the doctrine they preached. The name of this key was *kire* or *cire*, (and *eo*, a peg or pin, being compounded with it, forms the

---

* The figure of this key refembled a Cross ; thofe of the Lacedæmonians and Egyptians were of the fame form. Our worthy member before mentioned may add this note to his ironical obfervations on the Chinefe and Otaheite crucifixes.

modern

modern *eo-cire*, the key of a lock.) A comment, correction, remark or explanation of a writing was named *kire ceo keatfa*, i. e. the key and explanation of the fenfe (of the author;) thefe words are certainly corrupted from the Chaldee *keri ou ketib*, (keri and ketib.) Hence Dr. Keating who had no knowledge of the Hebrew language, entitles his explanation of the fervice of the mafs *Eo-kire fcia n'Aifrionn*, the hiftorical *key* of the mafs.

The names of church feftivals in the Irifh chriftian kalendar, are thofe ufed formerly by the pagan Irifh, and are all of *oriental* origin: but that is not all; the celebration of many of them is ftill obferved as in the Eaftern countries, for example; the feaft of Pentecoft or Whit-Sunday, is named *cainingaos*, *caingaos*, and corruptedly *cingis*, not from *quinquagefimus*, as fome of the modern monks will have it, (for they had a more proper name to have given it in that cafe, in their own language, viz. *caogad aos*) but, fays arch-bifhop Cormac, (who lived in the tenth century, and was a learned man) from *canaing* *, i. e. *gaill bea, la*, i. e. foreign tongues, becaufe on this day the gift of tongues defcended upon the apoftles. Now the pentecoft of the Jews is a high feftival obferved by them in memory of the promul-

---

* In Syrian *kanang* communicatio, focietas; *kanadjg* lampas, codex, volumen. Chaldee *canagnan*, or *canaan* Mercurius. (Bochart.) Arab. *kanagharon* valida voce. *kenagnaton*, fonora vox; *kandin* lampas, lucerna; *kanang*, fervus vernaculus; *kanangin*, qui loquebantur lingua ad Arabicum vergente: and hence I believe the name of *Genghiz-Khan*, who obliged the Neftorian priefts to introduce a foreign language and letters, among the Mongul and Kalmuc Tartars.

gation of the law from mount Sinai, and alfo a giving thanks to God for the return of the *barveft*, and this feftival has three names in Hebrew, one of which is חג קציר, *chag katzir*, † folemnitas meffis, a day they obferve, *lacteis cibis, ut fcriblitis & libis vefcuntur, eó quòd lex, tum temporis ipfis data, alba inftar lactis fuerit.* (See Buxtorf. in Synag. c. 20 & Leufden's Philolog. Hebræo. p. 275.) The Irifh ftill keep this day as in times of paganifm with *lacteis cibis*, &c. and although it is not the feafon of harveft in this climate, yet according to the cuftom of their oriental-Scythopolian anceftors, the breakfaft on Whitfunday is always compofed of cake bread, and the white liquor drank with it, is made of hot water poured on *wheaten bran*, which they call *caingaos* (or kingeefh from the day) and this liquor is alfo frequently made in time of harveft for the workmen in the field. The name of *penteçoft* in Welfh is *Ydegved a deygæn, Y Sylguyn*; in Cornifh, *penkaft*; confequently the Irifh borrowed neither the name or the mode of celebration from either: but the Manks call it *kingeefh*, for their lan-

---

† *Caingaos*, the Pentecoft, properly, (fays arch-bifhop Cormac) *caining-ceafar*, i. e. the gift of tongues at the harveft feafon; *an coegatmadh laithi o Cuifc*, the 50th day from Eafter. (*Cormac's Gloffary*, MSS in my poffeffion.) Now *cafair* is a word at prefent for that brightnefs which iffues from rotten timber in a dark place, commonly called *teine ghelain*, & I am of opinion that *ceafair* in Cormac's compound *caining-ceafar* alludes to th *cloven tongues, like as fire*, as the Englifh verfion expreffes it, and not to the harveft, for in agriculture, *cafair* is the furrow made by the plough; it is certain, that after cutting the harveft, the furrows appear, but I cannot find any inftance, where this word implies harveft.

guage

guage is Irifh, and the bible and new teftament
lately printed in the Manx language, is good Irifh,
only fpelt as an Englifh-man would write Irifh, by the
found of the voice.

Mr. Walker thinks, that in " Adamnan's time,
" A. D. 665, the Britifh and Scots language was not
" widely different; as, fays he, it was originally the
" fame, though fince divided into the dialects of
" Bretoon, Cornifh, Welfh, Manx, Irifh and Gallic;
" and greatly altered by diftance of place and length
" of time; yet the natives of the fix countries can
" go *near* to underftand one another to·this day,
" without an interpreter." (*Archæol. Soc. Antiq. Lond.*
v. 1.)

This gentleman has committed a very great miftake. The Irifh, Erfe * and Manx are one dialect,
the

* Tri-fod, i. e. *Eire, Manann* agus *Alba*; i. e. tri foide do
beartai ac cac tir dip condenta enaicde dip tre druidheacht, i. e.
Tri-fod, i. e. three divifions, viz. Ireland, Manx and Scotland:
i. e. thefe countries were divided into three by an act of druidifm. (*Cormac's Gloffary.* Cormac was arch-bifhop of Cafhel
in the tenth century.) May not this be the origin of the three
legs on the Manx coin.

Adfuit & Faunus fignatos igne relinquens
Italiæ campos, trifidoque cacumine rupem.

Nonnus Dion. l. 13.
trifido is here written for *trifodo*, from the Pelafgian Irifh *fod*,
a divifion; *fod-alam*, to divide. (*See the Dictionary.*)

It is evident that the ancients looked on the inhabitants of
Ireland, Manx and Scotland (or Eiris) as one people, the Britons are not mentioned. When it was the fafhion for nations
to adopt *patron faints*, the Irifh took Patrick, the Scots or Erfe
fhould have taken Colum-Kill, but he was an Irifhman; and

though

the Welſh, Bretoon and Corniſh another, of the *ſame original language*, it is true ; but ſo disfigured by the three laſt, for want of that recourſe to the fountain head the Iriſh enjoyed ; that at this day, the Welſh differs from the Iriſh, as much as modern Greek does from the ancient Pelaſgian Greek ; and from experience, I know, that the Iriſh, Erſe and Manx can underſtand each other perfectly well, for they have the ſame language ; but they cannot underſtand, or be underſtood by, the Welſh, Bretoons, or Corniſh ; in ſhort, they not only ſpeak with another *idioma*, but their *ſyntax* differs very much. The Iriſh have always expreſſed their contempt of the Welſh language, by calling a Welſhman, *Brito-balbb*, a ſtut-

though Patrick was a Scotchman, yet Ireland having adopted him through gratitude for the trouble he was at, in completing their converſion from paganiſm, (for there were three or four chriſtian miſſionaries here before Patrick, and Gottfreid Eraſmus, profeſſor of Berlin, ſays St. James was in Ireland,) yet the Erſe who have always *idly contended* with the Iriſh, which country was firſt peopled, (not which is the *oldeſt* people, for they all allow they were originally one and the ſame) would not, it ſeems, take their country-man Patrick, but they ſought out which of the *ſaints* had converted their Pelaſgian anceſtors the Scythians, and finding *that* part of the world fell to ſaint Andrew's lot, they very properly took him for their *patron ſaint:* we muſt not be ſurprized to read of ſome bigotted Highlanders in the days of popery, having undertaken a pilgrimage to Achaia, where St. Andrew was crucified, as ſome of the Spaniſh or Mileſian Iriſh have heretofore done, to Spain, in honour of St. James, whoſe *reliques* the Spaniſh writers affirm were brought from Jeruſalem to Campoſtella in Gallicia ; or probably it may be made out, that thoſe of St. Andrew are depoſited in Scotland.

tering,

tering, ftammering Britain. That the *original Irifh*
did formerly inhabit Britain, is evident; but, as
that great Welfh antiquary Mr. Lhwyd obferves,
" it was probably before the Gomerians or anceftors
" of the Welfh; for, fays he, it is manifeft that the
" ancient inhabitants of Ireland confifted of *two na-*
" *tions*; the Guidhelians were Britons, and what
" Nennius and others, wrote many ages fince, is
" an *unqueftionable truth*, when they afferted the
" Scotifh nation came out of SPAIN; but the Irifh
" muft have been the inhabitants of Wales, when
" the many names of rivers and mountains through-
" out that country were given, for they are identi-
" cally Irifh and *not* Welfh; for inftance, the word
" *uifce* *, water, (among many others) whence fo
" many rivers in Britain are named, and having
" looked for it in vain in the old Loegrian Britifh,
" ftill retained in Cornwall, and Baffe-Bretagne; and
" reflecting, that it was impoffible, had it been *once* in
" the Britifh, that both *they* and *we* fhould lofe a word
" of fo common an ufe, and fo neceffary a fignifica-
" tion; I could find no room to doubt, that the
" Guidhelians or Irifh have formerly lived all over
" this kingdom, and that our anceftors forced them

---

* *Uifce*, uifg, or uifge, from the Hebrew הׁשקפ *hifkah*,
he made or he caufed to drink, or he gave to drink, to water,
to moiften. Pfal. 86, v. 9. thou fhalt make them (hifkah)
drink of the river of thy pleafures. שקפ drink, liquor. Ufcu-
dama, the ancient name of Adrianople in Thrace, according
to Ammianus; in Irifh, *uifce-daim*, the watry refidence; for
daim is a houfe or habitation. *See this word more fully explained
in the fubfequent pages.*

" to

" to Ireland *." And in a letter to Mr. Rowland, author of Mona Antiqua, Mr. Lhwyd further fays, " it feems to me, that the Irifh have in a great mea- " fure, kept up two languages, the ancient Britifh " and the old Spanifh, which a colony of them brought " from Spain; for, that there came a SPANISH " COLONY into Ireland, is *very manifeft*, from a " comparifon of the Irifh tongue with the modern " Spanifh, but efpecially with the Cantabrian or " Bafque, and this *fhould* engage us to have *more* " *regard* than we ufually have, for fuch of their hifto- " ties, as *we* call *fabulous.*"

This is not the obfervation of a curfory traveller, but of a learned Welfhman, who ftudied the lan- guage of the Irifh, collected their moft valuable ma- nufcripts, (great part of which have now returned to my hands by the generofity of Sir J. Sebright,) form- ed dictionaries of the Welfh, Cornifh, Bretoon and

---

* The Phœnicians mixed with Pelafgian or Magogian Irifh, traded to Britain and Ireland, from Elifha or Greece, and taught the Greeks the way to both thefe iflands. It has been thought that Caffiterides was a Greek name given to the Scilly iflands, fynonimous to the Phœnician *Bretanas,* but in the con- clufion of this work we fhall fhew, that *keas,* the modern Irifh word for iron or tin ore, was alfo of Phœnician and Pelafgian origin, and is at prefent, the Perfian and Arabian name for iron ore. Thefe mixed people did certainly fettle in England and Ireland, and probably about the fame period, yet the Irifh hiftory informs us, that when the firft Pelafgian colony came from Elifha under Partolan, he found Ireland inhabited by a people, governed by one Ciocal, and that they had been here 200 years, living by fifhing and fowling on the fea coafts—thefe may have been ancient Gauls or Celts.

Irifh

Irish languages, and after comparing them together, forms the above conclusion, contrary to the wish and sentiments of his Welsh countrymen. This put Baxter to work on a *Topographical Glossary* of Britain, and by admitting Irish words, which do not exist, or ever did exist in the Welsh, he too, has imposed on the world, at the expence of the Irish*.

But still, probably, some *twittering swallow* will say, this is not sufficient; stronger evidence must be produced, to prove that the Pelasgi of Bæotia were the Pelasgi who settled in Ireland; I have collected much to prove it, and from my common place books, here throw in as much as can possibly be crowded into a preface.

* Mr. Lhwyd's observations that the Irish did anciently inhabit Britain and Ireland, is confirmed by the ancient historians. Strabo calls Ireland, British Ierna, l. 1. p. 110. as his ancient abridger calls the Irish, the *Britons inhabiting* IERNA, l. 3.

Diodorus Siculus mentions the Britons inhabiting the Island called Iris, l. 5, p. 309, and arch bishop Usher did not gasconade when he said, that the Roman people could not any where be found so anciently mentioned as Iernis. (*Prim. Eccles. Brittan.* p. 724.) In fine, Aristotle confirms (in his Mirabil. Auscultat.) that the Phœnicians (that is, the mixed body of Pelasgi, Canaanites, &c. &c. of whom we have spoken) were the first who discovered Ireland, when they sailed from Britain. Ireland therefore, lying so conveniently for the Phœnicians or Pelasgi, and for the Grecians and Spaniards, who learned the way hither from the Pelasgi, it was always a place of great trade; for which reason, Tacitus says, *that its ports were better known for trade, and more frequented by merchants, than those of Britain;* melius aditus portusque, per commercia et negatiatores, cogniti. *Vita Agric.* c. 24.

Tem-

Temmices Bæotiæ populus antiquiſſimus de quo præter Strabonem, Nonnum & Stephanum; Lycophron in Caſſandra

" Arnes vetuſtæ ex ſtripe Temmicum duces."

And Scholiaſtes adds, Temmicum id eſt Bæotorum à monte τιμμίχυ; *tamik* and *tamauk* in Arabic, and *tamach* and *tuamach* in Iriſh, do all ſignify height, depth, but *tamaich* in Iriſh and *tamukeen* in Arabic implies inhabitants, dwellers in towns, from the Iriſh *tuam,* a city or town; and this name the Pelaſgi applied to themſelves, in contra-diſtinction to the original Greeks, who then lived in caves, tents, &c.

About the city of Thebes, were the following places, the names of which Bochart has proved were all of Phœnician origin, and we ſhall prove were alſo Pelaſgian Iriſh; for the colony which Bochart purſues in his works, was a mixed body of Phœnicians and Scythians.

Aſcra, id eſt שרה, *aſcera,* lucus ubi ſteriles ſunt arbores. *Heſych.* Α΄σκρα δρύς ἄκαρπος.

——miſerâ prope lucum Heliconis in Aſcra (Α΄σκρῆ) durâ hyeme, ac æſtate gravi, ſemperque moleſtiâ. *Aſcra* or *eaſcra* in Iriſh, is always applied to a ſterile tree or field, it is formed of *ſcra,* a green turf, any vegetating *green,* and with the negative *e* forms *eaſcra,* i. e. ſterile; hence the ford in the county of Galway called *Ath-eaſcra,* or the ford of the *decayed wood, eiſcir,* a ridge of barren or ſandy land.

Til-phuſius, quaſi תל פוש *tel-phus,* mons ferax; Iriſh, *tul-fàs,* a mountain abounding in paſture; and *tul-faſac,* a deſart wild mountain.

Thebes,

Thebes, Phœnicium nomen fuit תבץ *Thebes* a luto nomen ; המס *themis,* liquefactio ; etenim per eam fluunt amnes duo (Afophus & Ifmenus) qui agrum omnem urbi * fubjectum irrigant. (Dicæarch.) Irifh, *teibbe,* overflowing water, diftilling, oozing, (whence *teibbe,* a chymift, a phyfician,) *taomb,* bilge water of a fhip ; *tamb,* the ocean ; *tibram,* to fpring ; *tibir,* a well, of *tiobb,* fpringing, and *bir,* water.

Efeptem Thebarum portis *Oncæe* nomen habent ab *Oncâ,* id eft *Minervâ* juxta Phænices, cui aram eo loci confecraverat Cadmus ; אגב *agab* apud Syris eft movere bellum ; proinde pro *Onca* nonnulli ὄγγαν *Ongan* vel *Oggan* fcribunt. *Hefych.* ὄγγα, Ἀθηνᾶ ἐν Θηβαῖς ; Irifh, *ogh, agh,* war, battle ; *oig,* a hero ; but *oenac,* a protector, defender, a liberal, noble man ; *oineac,* mercy, liberality ; *oinic,* a harlot ; *anac, anca,* a watch, guard, protector †.

Dirce, a well near Thebes, fo called from its pellucid water ; Irifh, *dirac,* pellucid ; *lan-dirac,* moft pellucid ; hence lough *Dearc* or *Dearg* in the county of Donnegall, and in the river Shannon, &c.

---

* Urbs eft ad hyemandum valde incommoda proptu amnes & ventus, nive enim obruitur, & cænum habet plurimum. (*Dicæarchi Lib.* βίος Ελλάδος. p. 174.

† *Onca* is a Phœnician and Arabian word, and fignifies great or powerful. So Minerva was the ὄγκα, the great and powerful goddefs both of Thebes and Athens. (*Jackfon's Chronol. Antiq.)* *Oinceadh,* Irifh, to preferve ; *do thuitfeadh Cionfhaoladh la Conghal fan troid, muna Oinceadh Cruinnmhaol è,* i. e. Cionfaoladh would have fallen in battle, by Conghal, if Cruinnmhaol had not protected him. Hence the old city of *Anaoch-dun* in Mayo, formerly a bifhop's fee.

Epi-

Epigranea, fons a Phœnicibus פגרן *pigran* vel *phigrad,* dictus est ab erumpendo ; Arab. *phagara,* in quarta conjugatione, *fontem aperire* ; in quinta, *fontem erumpere,* significat ; articulo præfixo ex *pigran,* factum *Happigran,* unde Græcum Ἰπαικρήνη, tanquam ab equô deductâ voce, & Persio *fons caballinus,* hinc nata fabula de fonte e terra edito equi ungula percuffa. *Abagraine* and *abagrinn* are common names of fountains or springs in Ireland ; the first is explained by *ab,* water ; *graine,* fandy, gravelly at bottom ; the fecond by *grinn,* neat, clean, it alfo implies a beard, and is fometimes ufed to fignify a well overgrown with long grafs at the mouth. The Pelafgian Irifh will alfo ftrengthen Bochart's derivation ; for *faoghar* or *phaogra* is a bubbling well, and *faoghar-thucaill* is a whirl-pool, literally the *forcerers well : linn fo lán phaoghar,* a ftream full of froth or bubbles.

Aganippe est אגן אבן *agan-ibba,* ad verbum crater viroris ; id eft, viridis, quia fontis crater eft

Margine gramino patulos fuccinctus hiatus.

Agan, Heb. proprie eft Crater. *Aganippe* etiam *Enippe* dicta eft, id eft עין אבא *en-ibbe,* fons viroris. Vibius Sequefter qui perperam in montibus recenfet *Aganippe Bæotiæ ante Enippe dicta.* In Irifh *agan-iobba,* pure, clear water for drink : I think the Greek *agneia* and *agna,* caftus, purus, would have come nearer the truth. *Enippe* is the Irifh *ain-iobba* or *iopha,* a fountain fit for drink ; fo *tiobar,* a well, is often written *tipir* ; *aighan* in Irifh, is a crater, a cauldron, &c. but the word feems improperly applied to a well.

Gar-

Gargaphie, fons fuit Dianæ facer in opaciſſimo luco circa Platæas ad radices Cithæronis ; in eo fingitur *Actæon Dianam vidiſſe nudam*, *&* *Actæon laceratus eſt a canibus*. Phœnicium nomen גרגפא, *gargapha*, factum a verbo *garaph*, quod de torrente dicitur qui per præceps lapſus omnia avehit. Sic Judic. 5. 21. Torrens Kiſon (garaphan) avexit eas. *Garabb* in Arabic, and *garamb* and *garbb* in Iriſh, is a torrent ; *garbb-thonn*, a boiſterous ſea ; *garbb-ſhion*, a tempeſt ; *garbb-ambain*, contracted to *garmbain*, a rapid river, a rough ſtream ; hence *Garumna* the Celtic name of the river *Garônne* ; but *garg* in Iriſh, is cruel, ſevere ; hence *garg-ab*, the cruel fountain, and the Greek *gargaphie*.

In Arethuſa de qua pluribus cum ventum erit ad Siciliæ Arethuſam, ſola terminatio eſt Græca. Syris enim אריח, *arith*, eſt rivas. In Iriſh *arith* is water ; it is from the Phœnician *arith*, a lake ; hence the lough *Arith*, now called lough *Arrow* in the county of Sligo ; but I take *Arethuſa* to be from the Pelaſgian Iriſh *rith-as*, a flowing ſpring, as we write *rith-bhior*, a flowing fountain, from whence *river*.

In this manner we have made a tour through Pelaſgian Greece, never wanting help from the Pelaſgian Iriſh, to elucidate the topography of Bæotia, Attica, &c. and wherever the learned Bochartus has led his favourite Phœnicians we have followed him, ſtep by ſtep, with equal ſucceſs. We cannot quit this pleaſing ſubject without mentioning two ſtrong circumſtances of the Pelaſgian coloniſts when in Ireland. Firſt. The druids gave the name of Tailcan and

Tailgan

Tailgan * to St. Patrick at his arrival. Secondly, They had made the cave of Tir-uamh-oin or Tribhoin as remarkable in Ireland, as that of Trophonius in Bæotia; both were of Tuſcan or Pelaſgian origin.

Tailgean or Tailgin or Gin-naoma, a name ſuppoſed to have been given to St. Patrick, by the druids. O'Brien's Dict. †

Tali-

---

* In the life of St. Patrick, inſerted by the author of the *State of the Britiſh Church under the Romans,* we are told, the real name of our ſaint was *Mag-on*; that is *On-magh,* a ſorcerer of the magi or druids, and that pope *Cæleſtinus* changed it to *Phadruc,* i. e. *phaid* prophet *ruch* of the Holy Ghoſt. *Talgan* implies the angel or genius preſiding over ſorcerers.

† Nam quid Præneſtis dubias, O Cynthia, ſortes,
　　Quid petis Ææi mænia *Telegoni* ?
　　Cur te in Herculem deportant oppida Tibur?
　　　　　　　　　　　　　Propert. l. 2. Eleg. 23.

The Pelaſgi were well acquainted with the myſteries of the Cabiri, by means of the Egyptians, (ſays Banier) or by the prieſteſſes of Dodona. As for the Telechines, they were a ſort of wizards who travelled the country to tell fortunes, and to attract the admiration of the populace, who are always apt to admire what carries an air of marvellous. (*Banier's Mythology,* v. 2. p. 82.) As Circe lived much about the time of the Trojan war, 'tis credible enough that Ulyſſes arrived at her palace, and that he actually fell in love with her. This at leaſt is the ſentiment of thoſe who affirm that he had a ſon by her named Telegonus. The charms of this princeſs having made him neglectful of his own honour, as well as of his companions, they plunged themſelves into the pleaſures of a voluptuous court, which makes Homer ſay ſhe had transformed them into ſwine, and what he adds of Mercury's giving that prince an herb named *moly,* whereby he had evaded Circe's charms, &c. &c. perhaps *moly* is wild rue. (*Banier,* vol. 4. p. 298.) *Muil* is the Iriſh name of an herb, the druids gave as a charm; it is called *lus*

(herb)

Tailghean, 1. *Mileadb craibbtheac do dbia.* Ex. *trioca Tailgeann ag pfalm ghabbail,* i. e. Tailghean, is a religious champion devoted to God. Example, 30 *tailgeann,* finging pfalms. Vet. MSS. TAILGEAN, TALGAN, a holy name given by the druids to St. Patrick. Shaw's Irish Dictionary.

Bochart after proving that the Phœnicians colonized the ifland of Rhodes, obferves that the third name given to this ifland by Strabo is Telchinis, à *Telchinibus infulæ incolis,* and Strabo informs us, thefe *telchinas* were *fafcinatores* & *præftigiatores,* qui fulphure admixtam Stygis aquam inftillarent ad perdendum animalia & ftirpes. See Ovid. Metam. l. 7, fab. 11. Suidas calls them *mali dæmones,* aut homines invidi & *fafcinatores.* And Hefychius, *Telchines,* fafcinatores, incantatores, invidi, auf a tabe, aut a deliniendo dicti. Bochart derives the name from the Phœnician לחש, *lachas,* incantare, whence *talchis* erat incantator; *telchinibus Hefychius* fucceffiffe tradit *Ignetes*; and adds Bochart, *Ignetes* feu *Gnetes* iidem qui γνήσιοι feu ιθαγενις, id eft indigenæ.

This is a miftake of the learned Bochart, for in the Pelafgian Irish *tailgean* or *tailchin,* and *eagnaithe* are fynonimous words; *talgan* or *tail-nama* is an augur, (in Arabic *tala numa.*) The Irish *gan-naoma* is the Arabic *kaubin numa* or *ganan-numa,* a foothfayer. *

The

(herb) *na muil,* (of *mul.*) See *Lus na muil,* penny grafs. (*Shaw's Irish Dictionary.*) but in Munfter *Lus muil* is the Umbilica Veneris, or Venus's Navel-wort. See *gan* explained in the next note.

* O'Brien has twifted this word into *gin-naomhtha,* to make it imply a holy offspring: the original word is *gan* or *can,* and the

The Hibernian druids made nice diftinctions between the foothfayer, augur, forcerer and enchanter, according to the various arts they were fuppofed to poffefs, which are all now confufed by the dictionary writers and tranflated promifcuoufly. This ifland was remarkable for divination in pagan times, it was the ifland of Anius or Anan, from *ainius*, a prophet; it was called *torc* and *muic*, two words unfortunately fignifying a boar and a hog, therefore the ifland was fuppofed to abound in them, yet when you are upon Torc mountain, or *Sliabh na Muic*, the old inhabitants tell you thefe are druidical names; thus, in Arabic, *taurik* and *maukit* implies an enchanter, a forcerer. The Phœnician word correfponding to *talchin* was *tailchin* or *tailgean*, and the Irifh *tallbha* is

the *neimi, neimid*, which the modern writers will tranflate holy, had no more meaning than foothfayer, augur, &c. hence the Irifh *faor*, a noble, Arabic *fuhr*, a forcerer. Irifh *fal*, a prince, (*fail*, fate) from the Arabic *faul*, an augur; *dea*, a forcerer; Arabic *daa*, augur, &c. &c. fo *gal* in Irifh, a hero; Hebrew *gala*, to prophecy, preferved in the Irifh in the imperfonal *gallaftair*, they prophefied; whence *Galei* vates Siculi (Bochart) and Galleotæ interpretes portentorum in Sicilia appellebantur. (Cicero de Divin. l. 1.) Galleotæ is compounded of *gal* and *eata*, times, feafons; Arab. *heta*; whence we had *Tail-eata* or *ete*, an augur, or obferver of the times, and the Greeks θελϲτη, θελητη præftigiatorem, magum, of the Egyptians. (Spencer, vol. 1, p. 423.) The termination *gan* fometimes written *ganan*, as the hill of *Talganan* or *Dalganan*; i. e. the forcerers hill, in the Co. Wicklow, is formed of the Arabic *ganan* (genius) and is now the name of the angel the Mahometans addrefs to obtain a knowledge of future events. *Et creavit ganan* ex puro igne. Vide Surat. 15, 9. & Cl. Ode Comment de Angelis, Sect. 3.

the

the fame as the Arabic *thalebs* or *thalby*, * i. e. a forcerer ; hence it is evident, that the *Telch-inis* of Strabo
for the name of Rhodes, is the fame as the Irifh
Tailg-inis (or *inis* ifland, *tailg* of prophets;) *eagnaithe*
implies philofophers in Irifh, and included all ranks
of foothfayers; yet the firft may be compounded of
tail and the Irifh word *infce*, an omen.

The prophets, enchanters and foothfayers of ancient Ireland were known by the general name of
Da-danan †.   Before we proceed to thefe, we muft
look back into the heroic hiftory of Greece and Ireland.

The Arcadians challenged in particular the name
of Pelafgi, (i. e. Scythians) from their pretended
founder Pelafgus, who did get fuch footing in Peloponefus, that the whole peninfula was called Pelafgia.
Thefe Pelafgians fpread over Attica, Theffaly and
Epirus, and are fuppofed to have laid the foundation
of the Dodonian oracle.   *Univ. Hift.*

Here is the origin of our Irifh *Da-danan*, miftaken
by the Seanachies for an oriental colony; whereas the
words literally imply *Danain* prophets and augurers,
for the Danai were the Pelafgi as we learn from
Euripides :

Ægyptus as fame's loudeft voice relates
Launched his adventurous bark, and on the coaft
Of Argos landed with his fifty fons.
Danaus, the fire of fifty daughters, leaving
Thofe fruitful regions watered by the Nile

---

* See Dr. Shaw's Travels into Africa, p. 80.

† Arabic *Danai-è*, fcience, knowledge, magic art; *daa*,
forcery; Heb. עד, *dang*, knowledge.

Which

Which from the fwarthy Æthiops land, its ftreams
Replenifhes, oft as the Hyperion melts
Thick flakes of fnow congealed, when thro' the air
He guides his fervid chariot, came to Argos,
Dwelt in the Inachian city, and thro' Greece
Ordained *that thofe who erft were call'd* PELASGI,
Should by the name of DANAI *be diftinguifhed.*
(Euripides. Fragm. Archelaus. v. 4. p. 248 : Wodhill)

Dan in Irifh fignifies learning, fcience, *dana* in old
Perfic doctus (Rheland.) *Tuath* i. e. Tagh i. e. Cheridh i. e. Cheridh-Draoidheact. Vet. Glofs i. e. Tuath,
Tagh and Cheridh, is forcery, augury, druidical forcery *. *Da* is alfo the art of forcery and Dan is fate,
deftiny, Arab. *daa kirdun* to augur.

---

* Tuath is the plural of *Tua*, lord, chief, doctor. Tuath
fignifies an affembly of the ftates, a council. (See Preface to
Nº. X.) The county of Donegall was fo called from its being
the chief refidence of the *Don-na-gaill*, i. e. the chief or head of
the *gaill* or augurs : it was afterwards named *Tir-Oin* or the
country of the prophets, it was alfo called *Tir-Coin-eol* or Tyr-
connel, all which are fynonimous names. Every province in
Ireland had a diftrict allotted for the augurs, diviners, &c.
which was commonly the moft romantic fpot could be chofen.
Such was *Tuath-Gearg-ain*, in Co. of Clare, i. e. the diftrict of the
forcerers or prophets of deftiny ; *tuath-Faith-liag* in the county
of Waterford, i. e. the diftrict of the prophets altar, &c. &c.
but the great fchool of forcerers was the counties of Donegall and
Tyrone, no country furnifhed more augurs, diviners, foothfayers, &c. than Ireland, and Joceline very juftly obferves, in his
life of St. Patrick, Magorum etiam, & maleficiorum, atque
arufpicum turba tanta in finibus fingulis fuccreverat, quantum
nulla in aliqua terrarum regione biftoria narrat. (Vita Patricii
a Jocelino.)

Herodotus

Herodotus endeavours to explain the fabulous Greek account of the origin of the Dodonian oracle, and says it arose from a certain prieftefs of Thebes, carried off by Phœnician merchants and fold in Greece, who took up her refidence in the foreft of Dodona, where the Greeks found her, coming to gather acorns, their ancient food; that fhe erected a fmall chapel at the foot of an oak, in honour of Jupiter and this was the foundation of the oracle. Bochart goes back to the Greek fable and thinks he has found two words in the Phœnician and Arabian of a double meaning, one fignifying a pigeon the other a prieftefs. Abbé Sallier takes this fable to have been built upon the double meaning of the word πέλειαι which fignified pigeons in Attica, but in the dialect of Epirus, imported old women. The abbé has here got hold of a Pelafgian-Irifh word *phile* or *filea* an augurer in holy orders and fynonimous to *Dadanan*; (we have treated largely of the *Philea* in the fubfequent pages.) Servius, fays, the name of the old woman was Pelias, and that the oracle fpoke by a foft murmuring noife of a running fountain, at the foot of an oak. But abbé Banier has difcovered that a number of brafs kettles were fufpended near each other at this oracle, which being lafhed with a whip, clattered one againft another and fo pronounced the oracle, for fays he *Dodo* in Hebrew fignifies a kettle: though he allows the minifter of the oracle, was always concealed in the hollow of an oak, and there gave his refponfe *. The genius of this

French

---

* In Euftathius and Steph. Byzantinus, we meet with three different conjectures in regard to the derivation of the name

French writer in antiquity, is full as lively in invention as that of the ancient Greeks; Aristotle does certainly say that there were two pillars at Dodona, and upon one was a *bason* of brass, and upon the other a child holding a whip, with cords made of brass; which occasioned a noise when the wind drove them against the bason;" but here is no brass-kettle-bells in a range to clash against each other.   The poets tell us, that the ships of the Argonauts were made of Dodonian oak, wherefore they spoke upon the sea, and pronounced oracles.   We must not then be surprized at the wonderful feats of our Irish *Tuatha-Dadanan*, who could raise a fog at sea whenever they saw an enemy appearing, &c. &c.

Dodona, which they say owes its origin either to a daughter of Jupiter and Europa, or one of the nymphs, the daughter of Oceanus; or, lastly to a river in Epirus called Dodon : but as Mr. Potter observes, we find the Greek authors all differ both as to the etymology of the name and the scite of this oracle. In my humble opinion Homer and Hesiod have not only agreed that it was not in Greece, but in Ireland, or some island at least as far westward.

> Ζεῦ, ἄνα Δωδωναῖε, Πελασγικέ
> Pelasgian Jove, that *far from Greece,* resides
> In *cold* Dodona.
> > *Iliad, π'. v. 235.*

Hesiod, whose testimony Strabo makes use of, is yet more express.

> Δωδώνην φηγόν τι Πελασγῶν ἕδρανον ἧκεν.
> He to Dodona came, and the hallowed oak
> The seat of the Pelasgi.
> > *Hesiod and Strabo,* l. 7.

Consequently the oracle was founded by the Pelasgi and not by the Greeks, and the ancient Irish being a colony of the Pelasgi, the hallowed oak might have been in Ireland.

The

The authors of the Univerſal Hiſtory obſerve, that ſome writers ſay, this oracle of Dodona was founded by the Pelaſgians, who were the moſt ancient of all the nations that inhabited Greece; of this opinion is Strabo, being led hereunto by Homer, who beſtows upon the ſame Jupiter, the names of Dodonæus and Pelaſgicus. Strabo alſo ſays, there was a fabulous opinion, that the oracle of Dodona was tranſlated out of Pelaſgia, a country of Theſſaly, into Epirus, being accompanied by a great number of women, from whom the propheteſſes in after ages were deſcended, and that from them Jupiter received the appellation of Pelaſgicus. Here I muſt remark a paſſage in the works of biſhop Huet, which ſhews that learned man's opinion of the origin of the Pæni or Carthaginians, who we ſhall have occaſion to mention hereafter. In his hiſtory of the navigation of the ancients, ch. 22. the biſhop ſays, " the Carthaginians had been maſters of the ſea till the time of the firſt Punic war, by which power they had acquired part of Africa, Spain, Sicily, all Sardinia and its adjacent iſlands; they infeſted freely the coaſts of Italy upon the ſlighteſt pretences, and not any one diſputed with them the commerce of the Mediterranean ſea, which they peaceably divided with the Tyrrhenians, *a people of their own race*, and their allies. Now the Tyrrhenians were of Pelaſgian origin, as we have proved in another place; conſequently, they were all of that mixed body of Canaanites, Egyptians, and Magogian Scythians, under the general name of Phœnicians. I beg leave to refer the reader to my *Enquiry into the firſt Inhabitants of Ireland*, Collect. Vol. II. No. V.

Euſebius

Eufebius makes the Pelafgi cotemporaries with Solomon, (Chron. l. 2.) and Huet obferves, the Pelafgi were a very wandering people, and even when the Greeks did begin to fettle themfelves, thefe Pelafgi ftill remained unfixed, roving about both by fea and land ; and this roving life made them both expert in navigation and powerful. Now the Lydians and Pelafgi, who were fo famous for their navigations, having given the firft rife to the Tyrrhenians, we need not be furprized, if they likewife communicated to them a love for the fea.

The fable of the Tyrrhenian failors, which Bacchus metamorphofed into fea monfters and cited by Ovid, (lib. 3.) confirms the antiquity of the Tyrrhenians and fhews that in the firft ages they applied themfelves to navigation, even before the Pelafgi had eftablifhed themfelves in Italy, under that name. Dion. Halicarn. was therefore of opinion that the commerce of the Tyrrhenians perfected the Pelafgi in the naval art, which they would long have enjoyed, had not the Carthaginians deprived them of it. (*Dion.Hal.*l. 1.)

The Irifh hiftory informs us, that Partolan (a name contracted from *bar*, learned, and *talan*, a prophet, a foothfayer,) a Pelafgian-Scythian, who had lived long in Egypt, and having defcended to Elifha, and there killed his father and mother, in order to obtain the crown and hinder his elder brother of the fucceffion, failed from Greece with a colony and conquered Ireland, in which country he then found certain inhabitants (the Britifh Celts, i. e. Gomerian Scythians,) who had poffeffed the ifland 200 years, under the

govern-

government of Ciaciall *,) fifhing and fowling upon the coaft, but had not cultivated the country. Parto-lan died and his four fons divided the kingdom be-tween them, and in fome years after a peftilence car-ried off moft of the inhabitants. About this time Nemed, defcended of one of the fons of Partolan, named Adla, who was left behind in Greece, arrived in Ireland †; Nemed in Irifh, and Numad in Arabic, is a leader, a guide. With Nemed came many Tuatha Dadanan, and in his reign the Africans ar-rived : thefe Africans were the Phœni another tribe of the Pelafgi : it is not furprizing then, that our Irifh hiftorians obferve, that thefe Africans fpoke the fame language as the Irifh. They conquered the country and taught the inhabitants to build round towers, having firft landed at the ifland of Tor or Tor-inis called alfo

* *Ciacioll*, i. e. *Cia*, a man, *cioll*, mortal ; for our Pelaf-gians fuppofed themfelves *anchiall* immortal ; *an* is præpofite ne-gative, very common in the Irifh, and is probably true Pelaf-gian or Etrufcan, hence Homer Odyff. l. 8, v. 112.

Nauteufque, Prymneufque & Αγχιαλος & Eretmus.
This is the *Anchialum* of Martial, fpeaking to the Jew, whofe God was declared to be immortal,

Non credo ; jura verpe per *Anchiolum*,
a paffage that has employed all the learned commentators. See *Cia, Cioll, Ciall* in all the Irifh dictionaries. *Anchioll* is a com-mon expreffion with the old Irifh poets.

† Nor are there wanting fome, who out of Orpheus collect that Jafon with his Argonauts, either landed in Ireland, or paff-ed by the coaft. From whence Hadrianus Junius introduces him thus fpeaking to Ireland.

Illa ego fum Graiis olim glacialis Ierne
Dicta, & Jafoniæ puppis benè cognita Nautis.
Ware' Antiq.

Tor

Tor Conuing from the name of the Carthaginian general (Conuing) and here is the firſt account we have
of our round towers.   This iſland is on the coaſt of
Donegall, and it is ſaid the continent is ſo called from
theſe Carthaginians, viz. Dunna-gaill which implies
diviners, learned revealers, augurers, ſoothſayers,
but our Nemedian Tuatha Dadanan having been
ſeated alſo in that part of Ireland before their arrival,
I am of opinion, it was ſo called before Conuing landed.   We are informed that the Nemedians or Iriſh
perfectly underſtood the language of the Fomoraich
or Africans : this is no wonder, for the Carthaginians
were a colony of the ſame people, viz. Pelaſgians,
Phœnicians, and Egyptians. Our hiſtory further informs us, that the Nemedians not reliſhing the yoke
of the Carthaginians, deputed ſome Tuatha Dadanans to Thebes, Athens, &c. * (their old Pelaſgian
friends and kindred) for aid, but during this embaſſy,
Morc, a Carthaginian general, arrived with ſixty ſhips
and a numerous army. The Dadanan being coldly
received by the Pelaſgian Greeks, fearing they would
cauſe ſome commotion in the ſtate, treated them
ſo ill, that they levied ſome volunteers, ſeized on the

---

* From whence probably *Fomorc*, i. e. *Fo* a prince and *morc:*
The tranſlator of Keating always calls theſe Carthaginian heroes, pirates, miſtaking the name *Fomoraic*, *Fo* being a prince
and *moraic* marine, yet when the Seanachas apply the ſame word
to the Danes, he then tranſlates it leaders, heroes.—The old
name of the giants cauſeway in the north of Ireland is *Cloch na
Fomaraic* or the ſtone of the Carthaginians or ſea commanders,
not pirates, as Mr. Ledwich will have the word to imply.

Græcian

Græcian ſhips and returned to Ireland, by way of Scotland.

I cannot help thinking that Euripides was acquainted with this part of the Iriſh hiſtory; his old men (diviners) without a name, ſo often brought into his plays, and his ſtory of Jocaſta, in the Phœnician damſels, and ſeveral others, give great reaſon to believe that Ireland is often changed to Argos. Our Seanachas have carried the Tuatha Dadanan to Thebes during the ſiege, where they performed wonders, bringing the Greeks to life as often as ſlain in the ſiege, till one of them treacherouſly imparted a charm to the Aſſyrians to render their power invalid.

The Tuatha Dadanan were called *Oinin*, *Ainin* and *Ainius*, i. e. Soothſayers*. Arab. Aenund, enchant-

---

* *Ainius* a ſoothſayer, Shaw's Iriſh dictionary. *Marbh tre ainine*, killed by ſorcery, Vet. MSS. Anani עננ׳ occurs in the 7 ch. and 13 v. of Daniel in a very extraordinary manner. Montanus tranſlates it thus. " Videns fui in viſionibus noctis, & ecce cum (Anani) nubibus Cæli, tanquam filius hominis veniens erat: The Engliſh verſion,—I ſaw in the night viſions, and behold one like the ſon of man, came with the clouds of heaven. Rab. Sam. and other learned men declare this Anani, eſt iſte Rex Meſſias qui eſſet revelandus, de quo in MSS Chald. a Clar. viro S. Clerico. See Caſtellus.

The reader will recollect the explanation of Tailgan in the preceding pages and that *Tal*, *Talc* or *Tail* implies a diviner in the Iriſh language and in the Pelaſgian Greek; hence Delos or Telos the iſland of Apollo. Virgil informs us, Trojani belli tempore Deli regnabat, *Rex Anius*, *Rex idem hominum Phæbique ſaoerdos*. And Cynthus was Deli mons in quô Latona edidit Apollinem, from the Iriſh *Cinith* and the Hebrew הגניטה chanita, productio, generatio, emerſio in lucem, hence the Iriſh *Cine* a tribe, a family. *Cineath* an offspring.

ment,

ment, magick. Heb. עןן anan. gnanan. augur, ha-
riolator, ex nubibus futura bona vel mala prædicens.
Anan in Hebrew literally implies, he covered with a
cloud; our Irish Oinin were remarkable for having the
power of raifing a thick fog at their pleafure. Hence
Ireland was called *Inis Anan* or the Ifland of prophets.
Rabbi Jonathan obferves from Aruch that the Arabians
named a bird *taer* and *taer-aun* becaufe *taer* implied
augurium capere ex avibus, (in qua re olim erant pe-
riti) for the fame reafon our Irifh augurs named a bird
eon, *ean*, יענה *ione* in Hebrew, (fays Bates) is a bird
of fome kind, an owl. Bochart fays an oftrich.
Hence Οἰωνίζομαι auguror. Οἰωνιςής augur. Οἰωνὸς ‡ avis.
omen. May not the עןק oinak (fuppofed to be Phœnicians) a people whether Ifhmaelites or no, (fays
Bates) be thefe forcerers? They are fuppofed to be fo
named from their bulk it is faid: but they were apof-
tates or revolters from the true God, they were a people much dreaded by others it is certain, but probably
only for their magical art; be that as it may, the Irifh
have adopted the word, naming a giant *anach, fia-
nach.*

‡ But Hefychius explains Οἰωνὸς by Ὄφις of which hereafter,
when we fhall fpeak of *Aub*. From the Pelafgian Irifh *Oin* is formed
the Greek *oenomai*, (apud Eufebium) argumenta contra Oracula, ac contra ipfum Eufebium. *Onomacriti* Sortilegi, fraudes
circa Oracula, and from *dreac* an image, fpeĉtre, vifion, and
oin is formed the Greek δρἀκοιλα, miftaken by the Greeks for
Draconem; eum fuiffe (poetæ fcripfere) cui cuftodiam Tellus
Oraculi mandaffet—fed nullibi in S. S. veteris Teft. Pytho pro
Diabolo fumitur, fic nunquam Apollo inter Græcos, nedum
apud Delphos. (Van Dale de Oraculis.)

Our

Our *Da Danans* being fettled in the county of Done-gal, the country was called *Tir-oin* or the country of *Oin* and they were named *Treabb-oin* or *Treavoin*, the tribe of *Oin* or forcerers. It is faid they brought with them from Egypt to Greece and fo to Ireland a ftone called *Leaba-dèa* or the altar of deftiny, otherwife *Liag-fail* the ftone of fate, known alfo by the name of *Clocb na Cineambna,* properly *Kinana* *, on which the Irifh and Scottifh kings were wont to be crowned; now in Weftminfter Abbey (as Mr. Shaw fays. See *Lia fail* in his dictionary.)   *Fal* and *fail* † in Irifh is fate, deftiny.   Ireland was named *Inis-fail* & *Inis-anan* the ifland of fate, the ifland of foothfayers.   In Perfic *fal* is an omen, in Æthiop. *pbal,* in Arabic *faali* a footh-fayer, *faul-goo* an augur.   Ireland was likewife called *Inis-muic* from the Arabic *maukt* a foothfayer, it was in fhort the Dadanan oracle of the weftern world.

Our Dadanan foon eftablifhed one oracle in an ifland in Lough Dearc and another on Cruach Agalla‡.   That on the ifland was as famous as the

cave

---

* Arabice *Kaubin. Kundae,* a forcerer. *Kaubinon,* forcery.

† Hence the *Falach da Fionn* which Keating fays were open places where Fion Mac Cumhail ufed to kindle fires: the words literally imply Fionn's facrifice of *Fal-achta* or deftiny.   Fal in Irifh and Arabic is an omen and *akht* in Arabic and *acht* in Irifh is an augur, hence it is commonly joined with *Draoi* a Dould as *Draoi-acht,* witchcraft, druidifm—Arabic *akhtur guftun* to augur, *faul guften* and *daa kirdun,* the fame.

‡ Agalla was the ancient druidical name for an oracle, from *agalladh* to fpeak, pronounce, whence the Greek ΕΥΑΓΓΕΛΙΟΝ; the Irifh adopted a word of the fame import, viz. *foifgealach,* from *fos* divine knowledge and *agalach* an oracle, whence its

dimunitive

cave of Trophonius and was called *Uamb-Treibb-Oin*, the cave of the tribe of Oin ||. It afterwards received the name of *St. Patrick's purgatory*, and the Irish monks have framed a story of a certain knight named Oin, from whom they say this part of the country was called, who saw much more here than Pausanias did at the cave of Trophonius.

diminutive *sgeal* a narration, and *sgealach* a narrator. This oracle of *Cruach Agala* seems to have been more noticed than Patrick's purgatory according to Joceline. " In hujus igitur montis de *Cruachan Aigle*, cacumine jejunare, ac vigilare confuescunt plurimi, opinantes se postea nunquam intraturos portas inferni, quia hoc impetratum a Domino putant meritis & precibus S. Patricii. Referunt etiam nonnulli, qui pernoctarunt ibi, se tormenta gravissima fuisse passos, quibus se purgatos à peccatis putant. Unde & quidam illorum locum illum purgatorium S. Patricii vocant.

Colgan.

Fuit ergo Purgatorium S. Patricii notum & frequentatum tempore Jocelini, licet ipse satis frigide de eo loquatur, & perperam ipsum statuit in monte de *Cruachan Aigle* in *Connacia*; cum sit in stagno de *Loch-Gerg* Com. Dungallensis in Ultonia.

Colgan.

Loch-Gerg was the ancient name of Loch-Dearg, *Gerg* is a corruption of *gearrog*, fate, fortune, destiny. In another place Colgan quotes an ancient author, who calls it Loch-Chre, that is *Cheri* or the lake of the soothsayers ; a convincing proof it was known for its miracles before Patrick's arrival. *Cheri* I have shewn to be the Chaldee *Cheruri* (hariolari) and the Latin *Hariolus* is formed of the Irish *Cheri* or *Heri* and *eolas* art, knowledge, science, *Ariolus* from *Aire* which implies not only a chief but also a diviner and *eolas* knowledge.

|| That is, one of the tribe or *Treabh*, of *Oin*. See *Treabh-hoin* before. Observe also that our Irish knight Oin entered our cave through vain glory.

Matthew

Matthew Paris has preserved the origin of this cave which has been copied by Colgan, and collected and translated into English by the *Reverend Father Thomas Messingham*, professor of the Irish seminary in Paris, and printed in that city in 1718.

For the sake of our readers we wish the narration was shorter, but it is so connected throughout with the remote antiquities of this country and of Pelasgian Greece, we must trespass on the reader's patience at this time; we shall contract it as much as possible.

" Sir James Ware, observes of this den, cave, " oracle or purgatory, that some have ridiculously " imagined that Ulysses first formed it when he dis- " covered the shades below, and adds he, I am in- " clined to believe that Ulysses, as it is historically " related or poetically feigned by Homer, was in Ire- " land, one of the British islands, or in Britain itself. " This, Circe implies in her instructions to Ulysses, " (in Homer) in his voyage to Hell, when she tells " him what wind would be happy, and the utmost " western parts he was to steer to."

Certain I am that Homer was well acquainted with the maritime geography of Ireland, which he proba- bly learnt from his Pelasgian master, and he most probably from his countrymen, who had formerly co- lonized Ireland and held a communication with them. —And from thence we are able to explain the Etrus- can or Pelasgian antiquities by the help even of our common lexicons. Thus Scylla in the Etruscan an- tiquities is represented as a tall rock in the sea, sur- rounded by a groupe of syrens, the guardians of the sea shore. In Irish *Sceile* is a high rock splintered

from

from a mountain, and *Sceile-go* or *Sceilg* that is a marine Sceile, is the name of such a rock on the coast of Kerry, on which was the Σ̄ᾱĈητων ιδɩ or the oracle of the suire or syrens, and where now stand the ruins of an abbey, and near to it is the island of Lemnos. (See Smith's hist. of Kerry) Scull near Cape Clear is another, and many other rocks round the western coast bear the same name. *Charybdis* in Irish implies *Carb* a ship and *deis* to stop or impede, and such power was supposed by the Etruscans and ancient Irish poets to be given to the suire, which is the Etruscan and Irish name of the syrens and sea nymphs. To the southward of the Sceilg is the promontory of *Cean Tail*, or the head land of the sorcerers, now the old head of Kinsale, where are remarkable caves, that issue forth wonderful sounds on the dashing of the water into them.—To the southward of this is the promontory of Cuirce, Kirk, or Circe, now called Cork head, from whence the city of Cork in Irish is also named *Cuirce*, pronounced *Kirk*. Hence the learned Bochart observes, *At ex Æoliis insulis in terras caudæ draconis subjectas, putâ in ultimam Thulem.* Verily, the *ultima Thule* of the Pelasgians, and that was Ireland, as I have proved in a former number of this work. Now Æolus was *Rex Etruscorum* (ejus nepos Ulysses) habitat in insulis frequentius, unde Æolus ventorum Rex creditur. (Dempster de Etruria Regali.) Thus, *Luna* (in Etruria) which signifies a date tree, was remarkable for its wine, so in Irish *Cran-Leain* is the date tree, and the Irish name for Ale (the substitute for wine) is *Leann,* & *Lunn.* *Falisca* in Etruria was also famous for its grapes, and in

Irish

Irifh *falaifc* is a kind of heath with which they brew a bad ale, &c. &c. thefe were fubftitutes for the produce of the country our Pelafgian Irifh had quitted.

To fupport the antiquity of St. Patrick's purgatory Sir James Ware, Joannes Camertes, father Meffingham, &c. &c. quote the following lines of Claudian in Rufin. lib. 1.

> Eft locus extremum pandit quà Galliæ littus
> Oceani prætentus aquis, quò fertur Ulyffes
> Sanguine libato populum moviffe filentum.
> Illic umbrarum tenui ftridore volantum
> Flebilis auditur queftus, Simulacra coloni
> Pallida Dea profiluit, Phæbique egreffa ferenos
> Infecit radios, ululatuque æthera rupit
> Terrifico, fenfit ferale Britannica murmur,
> Et Senonum quatit arva fragor, revolutaque Tethys
> Subftitit & Rhenus projecta torpuit unda.

Thus tranflated by Father Meffingham,

> Weftward of Gaul there lies a famous Ifle
> Where mountains nod and magick fountains boil,]
> Here the Laertian hero, is faid to fpill
> The blood of bulls, fat victims kill
> And raife a filent race by artful fkill.
> Here rueful groans of flying fhades abound
> And whifpering noife from hollow rocks refound
> Pale ghofts to men afford a dreadful fight
> And death-like fpectres, feem to walk by night.

The druids named Ireland *Mucinis*, that is, fay fome, *inis* an ifland, *muc* hog; but *much* was one of the Irifh and Perfian names of the Aliem or great
God

God—hence Euripides makes Antigone say when referring to this island

> Is this the man
> Who vowed that he the captive Theban Dames
> In slavery plunged, would to Mucene lead,
> To Lerna where the god of ocean fixed
> His trident, whence its waters bear the name
> Of Amymone *.

The antiquity of this purgatory, being established,
and to have existed long before St. Patrick arrived,
we will now proceed to the monkish tale of Oin.

There was a certain cavalier called Oin † an Irish-
man, who had for many years served in king Stephen's
army, the IVth king of England after the conquest.
This man having obtained licence from the king,

---

* Lern is a remarkable lake in the north of Ireland, about
which the Dadanan forcerers dwelt : probably Lerna was originally written Ierna by Euripides. *Amhain* is Irish for a river
and *Am-amhain*, the sweet or lovely river or water. Amymone
is said by the Greeks to be the daughter of Danaus, beloved by
Neptune. Kil-larney lake, is another of the same derivation.

† Colgan has the following note on Oin. A quibusdam
Oenus, ab aliis Owen, ab aliis Annon, sed mendose vocatur.
Proprium ei nomen vel Eogan, id est Eugenius, vel Oengus
five Ængussius fuisse videtur, hæc enim nomina, illa minimè
Hibernis familiaria sunt. Tria. Thaumat.—Oinin or Annon
was certainly the name of the officiating augur at our Dadanann
cave, signifying the great prophet, or cloud monger.—Eogan,
i. e. *gan-eo* was the angel or genius, i. e. gan, presiding over
the manes, tombs, dens, or caves of the dead; *Eo* i. e. a tomb,
cave, or den—hence Eoghan was the name of the son of Niall,
who possessed this country.

came

came to the north of Ireland his native country, to visit his parents.—And when he had reflected on the wickedness of his life, went to a certain bishop and confessed his sins.—Oin then resolved to go into St. Patrick's purgatory. The bishop related to him how many had perished in that place, but Oin who never had feared danger, would not be dissuaded: the bishop advised him to take the habit of a canon regular, but Oin refused till he should have gone into the purgatory and returned. He then marched boldly through the cave, though alone, where he soon found himself involved in darkness. Soon after a glimmering light appeared, which led him to a hall, in which there was no more light than we experience in winter after sunset. This hall had *no walls*, but was supported by pillars and arches, he then saw an inclosure, into which having entered and sat down, fifteen men in white garments, (clad and shorn like monks) coming in, saluted him and instructed him how to proceed, when he should be hereafter tormented by demons in this cave. Oin being left alone, soon heard such a horrid noise, that if all the men and all the living creatures on earth, in sea and air, had bellowed together, they could not have equalled it; and immediately an innumerable multitude of demons in various frightful shapes saluted him, and welcomed him to their habitation: they then dragged him through a vast region, dark and obscure, where blew a burning wind, that pierced the body: from thence he was dragged towards the bounds of the earth, where the sun rises at mid-day *, and being come to the end

* Ortus & occasus solis miscentur in unum. Inde Læstrygones collegit Crates habitare—ut in Arato habetur.

of

of the world, they extended towards that part of the earth where the fun rifes at mid-night : here Oinin faw the firft torments of hell : men and women with fiery ferpents round their necks, others had vultures on their fhoulders, driving their bills into their breafts, and pulling out their hearts. From thence he was led to the penal field, where he faw both fexes faftened to the ground with red hot iron fpikes; from thence he was conveyed to another penal field, where he faw ftill more torture; from whence he was carried to an iron wheel, the fpokes and fellows of which were armed with iron crooks fet on fire, and on them hung men fixed; from thence they dragged him towards a certain houfe of an extraordinary breadth and the extremities out of fight: this was the houfe of ful-phurious baths, which were fo numerous and clofe, that no man could walk between them, here alfo he faw both men and women bathing in great agonies; when on a fudden they convey him to an exceeding high mountain, where he faw feveral with their toes bent, looking towards the north, and while he was wondering what they waited for, a whirlwind from the North rufhed upon, and blew Oin, devils and all, to the oppofite fide of the mountain, into a river of moft intolerable cold water: from thence he was dragged towards the fouth, where he faw a dreadful flame of fulphureous matter, rifing out of a deep pit, vomiting up men and fparks of fire; the demons in-formed him this was the entrance of hell, but a new legion of demons appeared and told him, that was not hell, but they would fhew him the way over a lofty bridge, the furface of which was fo flippery, no

man

man could fix his foot on it: the courageous Oin boldly ftepped on the bridge and found it neither flippery or rough, but as the demons dared not venture on it with him, they departed, and when he had got clear over, he efpied the Elyfian fields: here he difcovers a beautiful palace, from whence iffued a more fragrant fmell, than if all the earth had been turned to fpice: the gate excelled the brightnefs of the fun, from whence iffued an orderly proceffion compofed of arch-bifhops, bifhops, abbots, monks, priefts, &c. &c. clothed in the very facred apparel they were wont to wear when on earth; they embraced Oin and conducted him into the gate, when a concert of moft melodious mufic ftruck up. They then conducted him over all the pleafant places of this new world, where night doth never overfhade the land: fome wore crowns like kings; others carried golden palms in their hands. When he had fatisfied his eyes and ears, the bifhops comforted him, and affuring him their company increafed and decreafed daily, by fome coming to them from the penal places, while others were carried away to the heavenly paradife; they took him to the top of a high mountain, and requefted to know of him, what colour the fky over his head appeared to him to be of? Oin anfwered, that it appeared to be of the colour of gold in a fiery furnace: that, faid the venerable prelates, is the gate of paradife; by that gate we are daily fed from heaven, and you fhall tafte of the food: at this inftant, certain rays, like flames of fire covered the whole region, and fplitting into fmaller rays, fat upon the heads of every one in the land, and at laft on the brave chevalier Oin.

They then told him, he muſt quit this delightful food, and immediately return the way he came; the prelates conducted him to the gate of paradiſe and ſhut him out, from whence he returned through all the meanders he had travelled before, the demons not daring to behold him or ſpeak to him, till he came to the laſt hall; here he was adviſed to haſten to the mouth of the cave, and was informed that the ſun now began to riſe in his country, and if he was not ſoon at the gate of the cave by which he entered, the prior who kept the key, would look for him, and if he did not ſee him, would deſpair of his ſalvation, lock the door and return to his convent: however, Oin came in time, and was received with joy into the prior's arms.

Trophonius his cave.

Mr. Wodhull in his notes on Euripides, has the following note. Of this Trophonius and his cave, which is become proverbial, Nicophorus Gregoreas, in his Scholia upon Syneſias on Dreams, gives the following account. There was a certain man, named Trophonius, a ſeer by profeſſion; who, through vain glory, entering a cave, and there hiding himſelf, ended his life: but the cave, 'tis ſaid, utters oracles to thoſe who enter and aſk queſtions on any ſubject. The ſituation is thus deſcribed by Strabo in his Bœotica, p. 414. At Lebadea is the oracle of Jupiter Trophonius, with a paſſage into the bowels of the earth, which it is neceſſary for thoſe who conſult the oracle to deſcend; it is ſituated between Helicon and Chæronea near Coronea. This is alſo to be remarked, that there was one fountain there called Lethe, whoſe

waters

waters were to be drank by those who were descending, that they might forget all they had previously seen, and another they called Mnemosunè, a draught of which impressed on their memory all they were about to behold in those subterranean regions *. (From *Barnes.*)

ION.

* If ye before these portals have with fire
  Consumed the *salted cates*, and wish to know
  Aught from Apollo, to this altar come ;
  But enter not the temple's dread recess
  'Till sheep are sacrificed.   EURIPIDES.

Toto tempore quo morantur in ipsa insula (Purgatorii Patricii) puta per novem ipsos dies, jejunandum erit in pane & aqua, non quomodo libet, sed una refectione ex pane subcinerito; vel cocto in Craticula ; vel certè farina avenacea incocta, aqua verò lacustri, sed cocta vel saltem calefacta in cacabo, *citra salem.*—— Estque ea vis istius aquæ quamvis stagnantis, ut quatumvis ex ea te velis ingurgitare, nullum inde gravamen sentias, perinde ac si ex vena metallica fluerit, quod de aqua *Spadana*, ex fonticulo acido emanante perhibent, qui eam epotarunt; absque onere suo vel stomachi gravamine.

(*Colgan de modo & ritu Purgat. Patricii.*)

Chorus in ION.

On thee I call, O thou who in this fane
Art stationed : is it lawful to advance
Into the inmost sanctuary's recess
With our bare feet?

Sanctuary, ἄδυτον. Irish *eidid* or *eidit*, place of horror; *edel*, prayers said in the *eidit*, or cave of purgatory.

——Admissi à patre spirituali qui purgatorio præest, ex instituto cannonicorum, ad peregrinationem faciendam, exuunt se calceos & caligas & ecclesiam quæ sancto Patricio inscripta est, devoti *nudipedes* ingrediuntur, ibique factâ oratione, sacros obeunt circuitus, introrsum septies in ipso templo, & extrorsum totidem vicibus in coemiterio. (*Colgan, ibid.*)

Pausa-

Paufanias fays, Trophonius was the fon of Erginus king of the Minyæ, or according to fome of Apollo. He and his brother Agamedes were celebrated architects and conftructed an edifice in which Hyrcius lodged his treafures; having placed a ftone in the wall, fo that they could remove it when tney pleafed, they committed frequent robberies there undifcovered: but upon Agamedes being caught in a fnare, Trophonius cut off his brother's head, left he fhould difcover his accomplice: the murderer was foon after fwallowed up in the chafm of the earth.—This childifh ftory is a copy of what Herodotus relates fully of one of the kings of Egypt and two brothers who robbed his treafures by a like ftratagem: in fhort the Greeks knew not the origin of the word Trophonius, it was at that time concealed from them by their Pelafgian conquerors, and was better known in Pelafgian Ireland: indeed our modern monks have made out a much better derivation from the chevalier Oin. Paufanias gives no account of the life of Trophonius and only tells of his death, and that the cave of Agamedes was in the facred grove of Labadea.

But as Paufanias declares he had confulted this oracle and fubmitted to all its irkfome formalities, hear his own words.

" The oracle was upon a mountain, within an in
" clofure of white ftones, upon which were erected
" obelifks of brafs. In this inclofure was a cave of
" the figure of an oven cut out by art. The mouth
" narrow and the defcent by a fmall ladder. When
" they were got down, they found another fmall
" cave, the entrance to which was narrow: the fup
                                        " pliant

" pliant proftrated himfelf on the ground, carrying
" a certain compofition of honey in his hand, without
" which he is not admitted *.　He firft puts down
" his feet into the mouth of the cave, and inftantly
" his whole body is forcibly drawn in.　They who
" were admitted were favoured with revelations, but
" not all in the fame manner, fome had the know-
" ledge of futurity by vifion, others by an audible
" voice.　Having got their refponce; they came out
" of the cave, the fame way they went in, proftrate
" on the ground, and their feet foremoft.　Then the
" fuppliant was conducted to the chair of Mnemofynè,
" and being there fet down, was interpreted what he
" had feen or heard.　From that he was brought back
" quite ftupified and fenfelefs into the chapel of *good*
" *genius* †, till he fhould recover his fenfes : after
" which he was obliged to write down in a table book
" all that he had feen or heard, which the *priefts in-*
" *terpreted their own way* ‡.　There never had been
　　　　　　　　　　　　　　　　　　　　　　" but

* The reafon of this we fhall find prefently explained in the Irifh.

† Maximis miraculis & virtutibus totam infulam Hiberniæ convertit ad fidem.　Et non fine maximo labore, non folum propter obfiftentes magos, verum etiam ab agreftia ingenia, duraque ac pervicacia corda Hibernorum.—Cum Patricius etiam fic orationibus & jejuniis devotior fieret, apparuit ei Dominus Jefus Chriftus, dans ei Evangelii textum & baculum—& Dominus Sanctum fuum in locum defertum eduxit & *quandam foveam rotundam*, intrinfecus obfcurum, oftendit ei dicens &c. &c. &c.

‡ Non multò autem pofteà, vivente adhuc in carne ipfo S. Patricio, intrabant illud antrum plurimi zelo devotionis & pænitentiæ pro peccatis ibi peragendæ ftimulis commoti; qui reverfi
　　　　　　　　　　　　　　　　　　　　　　teftabantur

" but one man who entered Trophonius's cave with-
" out coming back again ; this was a fpy fent by De-
" metrius to fee if in that place there was any thing
" worth plundering. What I have written is not
" founded on hearfay ; I relate what I have feen hap-
" pen to others, and what happened to myfelf ; for,
" to be affured of the truth I went down into the cave
" and confulted the oracle. This oracle was not
" heard of in Bæotia till that country being diftreffed
" with a great drought, they had recourfe to Apollo
" at Delphos, to learn from that god, by what means
" they might put a ftop to the famine. The prieftefs
" anfwered, that they were to apply themfelves to
" Trophonius whom they would find in Labadea.
" The deputies obeyed, but not being able to find an
" oracle in that city, Saon the eldeft of them, fpied
" a fwarm of bees and obferved to what fide it turn-
" ed. He faw that thofe bees flew towards a cave ;
" followed them and then difcovered the oracle. They
" fay that Trophonius himfelf inftructed him in all
" the ceremonies of his worfhip, and after what man-
" ner he would be honoured and confulted. (Paufa-

teftabantur fe clarè confpexiffe multos in fide vacillantes, ibi
multis pænis affligi : quorum & revelationes curavit S. Patricius
confcribi & in eadem ecclefia confervari. (and a little before he
fays) Jam ingreffuros & aquâ luftrali afperfos in oftio fpeluncæ,
quafi in tranfitu ad alium orbem, & è via ad terminum properan-
tes in agonia pofitos, cernere eft gementes, fufpirentes—igno-
fcentes toti mundo quidquid in fe deliquiffent.—Thus Colgan :
but he had forgot there were feveral chriftian miffionaries here
before Phaid-ruic or Patrick (or the prophet of the Holy Ghoft.)
Gottfreid fays James the lefs was here.

" nias)

" nias) §.   From this circumftance (fays abbé Banier)
" I conclude that Saon was himfelf the founder of
" that oracle, which no doubt was inftituted on ac-
" count of the famine I have mentioned."

At the clofe of the tragedy of the Phœnician damfels, by Euripides, Œdipus, by an order of the oracle of Phœbus, is exiled to *Coloneus fane, where Neptune's altars rife*, which Euripides fays is in Athens.
Cualan or a country abounding in harbours, was a
name of Ireland, according to the ancient Irifh poets:
there is ftill extant a well known tune called Cualan,
compofed to an ancient fong in honour of Ireland.

Mr. Wodhall obferves that the word Κολωνος or Κολωνη
is made ufe of by Homer and other writers to fignify
a hill. H. Stephens in his Greek Thefaurus, adds,
that there was a famous place in the Athenian territories known by that name, which was facred to Neptune, and called ιππιος, on account of that god being
confidered as the inventor of horfemanfhip. Thucy-
dides mentions Pifander's holding a council at Coloneus and fpeaks of its diftance from Athens as ten

§ In the Irifh language *Sean* is a charm. *Seanam* to blefs,
to defend from the power of enchantments; and this ceremony
of the *Sean* was performed by our Dadanan before the fuppliant
entered the cave. Again, *Saith* and *Saithin* or *Sain* is a fwarm
of bees, *Sainit* is an old Irifh word for honey, in Arabic *Sen-
nut :* and *Seang* is a bottomlefs pit in Irifh, i. e. *fad a-fad*, an
unmeafurable diftance. The reader will recollect that all thefe
circumftances and the peftilence in Ireland at the time of the
Dadananai returning to Greece under Saom Breas, compofe a
ftring of uniformities with the Greek account. *So-oin* in Irifh
is the great prophet, or obferver of Times, a word that might
eafily be formed by a Greek poet into *Saon.*

ftadia,

ftadia, or about a mile and quarter. Sophocles fays, Œdipus died and was buried there, and that in his laft moments he folemnly forbad any one to approach his grave; but it appears from Homer, that the body of that unfortunate king was, after his death, depofited at Thebes with funeral honours, it being faid of Meciftus, father to Euryales, one of the combatants at the games with which Achilles celebrated the memory of Patroclus, *that he went to Thebes, and was victorious at the tomb of Oedipus.* Phœn. damfels, vol. 1. p. 243.

Œdipus may have been buried at Thebes, but as Ireland was known in ancient times by the name of Cualan, as I have fhewn before, it is probably this ifland was the place of his exile.

In Euripides we alfo find frequent mention of the cave of Macra; the fable fays, this cave was near the citadel of Athens, where Erectheus was flain by Neptune, and Creufa a daughter of that monarch was there ravifhed by Apollo. Ion fon of Apollo, prieft and foothfayer, is fuppofed to be fo named from ιων the participle of ειμαι " who went," becaufe his father was told the firft perfon he fhould meet coming out of the oracle, would be his fon. It is more probable that Ion was fo called from *Oin* or *Eoin* * a prophet, and hence Ιωαννης, and the Irifh

---

* " Ion was he called, becaufe he firft his happy father met." (Chorus in Ion.) " My abode is this whole temple of the god, when fleep feals up my fenfes." (Ion. Euripides.) " Is the fpot on which he died called Macra." Ibid. " For him he hath at laft forg'd the new name of Ion to denote that he went forth and met him." (Old man in Ion.)

Eoan

Eoan, John, the great prophet and forerunner of CHRIST: he was also called *Sean,* that is the blessed: he who can defend from the power of heathen enchantments, from *Sean* a charm. Perf. *Sen* holy. Arab. *Senet* a miracle, a mystery.

The Pelasgian anceftors of our Hibernian Dadanan had established many *Macra* amongst the Grecian islands * : the word seems to imply an oracle, from *ra* to speak and *macb* a prophecy, hence the Arabic *mauky* and *maukit,* a foothsayer. *Macb* in Irish signifies also, great, mighty, magnificent, and *mucb* is deus. There was Macra island in Attica; *Macras* Campus Cœle-Syriæ, (Strab.) whence *Muckrus* a peninsula in Kerry, under Torc mountain. (Arab. *Tauruk* a forcerer) *Macris,* insula Cariæ in mari Rhodienfi: *Macris* etiam ob ejus longitutidinem dicta est *Euboea Insula.* (Strab. Arabicè *Embyia* a prophet) *macra,* (Plin.) *macralla* (Ptol.) Fluv. *Italiæ Liguriæ* Terminus.

Thus did our Dadanan name the island in Lough Dearg, where the purgatory of St. Patrick stood, Macra; and the mountains on the south side, where

---

* Ye shadowy groves where sportive Pan is seen,
   Stupendous rocks whose pine-clad summits wave,
      Where oft near Macra's darksome cave,
   Light spectres, o'er the consecrated green,
      Agraulo's daughters lead the dance.
                                   (Chorus in Ion. Euripid.)

This does not agree with the description of the country near Athens, but it is a lively picture of the situation of our Irish Macra, and was as Ion had a little before observed of Eubæa, " *with the briny deep between.*"

once

once was the oracle *Carn-macra*, *Tearman-macra*, now called Magrath's country *. The town of Donegall was called *Macra-beg*, and it ftill retains the name. On thefe mountains was preferved the holy fire, hence *Makarin* is the Perfian name of a certain mountain, where a holy fire is fuppofed to be kindled by angels, on the firft night of *Ramazon*, and which burns the whole month. I take *ramazon* to be a corruption of the Arabic *rubmanè*, that is, an oracle: the laft is certainly the root of our Irifh *reambain*, an omen, prognoftication, compounded of *re* and *eambain*; for *eambain* is alfo an oracle; *eambainfe*, wifdom, knowledge in miracles, whence the oracle of *Eambain Mbaca*, near *Ard-magb*, fuppofed to be derived from the Lord knows what, by Keating, the monks, poets, and *modern* topographical writers. To correct all their blunders, will be a tafk indeed! but a tafk we muft foon fubmit to, for the honor of *ancient Ireland!*

We find that, our monks had the art of removing this wonderful cave, as they found it moft convenient to anfwer their juggling tricks. Purgatory (fays Richardfon) was firft fixed in the ifle near the fhore, but a caufeway being made from the land into

---

* מחר *machar*, Heb. Quod jam brevi futurum per *machaar* exprimit atque minatur: feu potius predicit, exprimit Saul, dico, per vocem *machaar* quod & diem craftinum (frequentius) & tempus aliud indefinitè futurum, fignificat. Hence the Irifh *maharach*, to-morrow; *machar*, *maghar*, a word, oracle, prediction; *Machara failt* now *Magharfelt*, a town in the north, that is, the oracle of the prophets. I take this to be the derivation of the family name of Magrath.

it,

it, which gave the people free and eafy accefs to it, it was ftopped up, and another opened in a lefs ifland, farther diftant from the fhore *.

This famous and very ancient cave, was broke up in 1497, as a fictitious thing, on St. Patrick's day, by the guardian of the *Minorites* of Donegall and fome other perfons, by the authority of pope Alexander VIth. (*Ware.*)

Round Lough Dearg are the following hills named from the antient language, viz:

Rughd Cruach, Irifh, *rugh,* rue, a charm; Arabic *rukè, raukè,* an enchanter, a fpell; Perfic, *rigan,* addicted to magic †.

---

* This ancient oracle was well known in Greece, France, Spain, and wherever the ancient Irifh had intercourfe. Rymer has recorded a mandamus of Richard II. in favour of a knight of Rhodes, coming to vifit our cave of Macra. "Rex univerfis, &c. Sciatis quod cum nobilis vir *Raymundus vicecomes de Perileux* & *de Rhodes chivaler,* &c. &c. &c. verfus terram Hiberniæ ad purgatorium St. Patricii ibidem videndum & vifitandum cum 20 hominibus & 30 equis————vobis mandamus quod eidem Raym. cum hominibus—non inferatis—feu ab aliis permittatis injuriam Sep. 6, Ann. 21 Rdi, 2di, 1397. Rymer, tom. 8. p. 14. & in tom. 6, p. 107, may be found another of Edward III. in favour of *Maletefta Ungarus de Arminio miles.*

† Hence *Loch-rugh-raidhe,* or the lake of the prophet's oracle, in the Co. Galway. In the life of St. Patrick we find *rechrach* the name of a druid, "tunc in illo concilio furrexit quidam, nomine *Recbrach,* ut occideret Patricium, defcenditque ignis de cœlo & illum magum coram omnibus combuffit. Hence *Ciar-rugh* now Kerry, &c. &c. Mr. Wodhull very properly tranflates ευθμεισι, enchantment, in the cyclops of Euripides; *Ruth* or *rugh-mais* in the Pelafgian Irifh, is the *myftery of enchantment,* an expreffion quite agreeable to the paffage in the tragedy.

Ne-

Neroagh-breac, Arab. *Neeruk*, a magician.

Croach Brioc. Arab. and Irish, *Brioɛl*, forcery.

Tagh Tagha; *Tagh*, a diviner. Arab. *Taghut*, a foothfayer.

Croghra Coghna, Arabicè *Kauhin Kunda*, a foothfayer.

Goo-lagh, the altar of *Goo*. Arab. *Goo*, augury; *Faulgoo* an augur.

Goo-endeh, a forcerer *.

Bally Mac Aubneamh, the town of the fons of Aubneamh. Arab. *Aufnuma*, foothfayer.

Sceirgearg or *Gearrog*, the rock of deftiny, whence the lake was called Lough Gearg.

One of the iflands is named *Stafubr*. Arab. *Subr.* magick, *Subrbaaz*, a magician. Hence the town of *Ardfbru*, once a bifhop's fee, in Donegall.

Another *Inis Tagafc*, of which before.

Near this place is a great mountain named *Peift*; Arab. *Peifheenè*, a foothfayer †.

Another named *Ghaendat*, Arab *Ghaendeh, Gooiendeh*, an augur, Chaldee גדין. *Gadin* ‡, magi, augures. Hence *Magh Geidne*, near the outlet of Lough Erne.

                         The

---

* Invenit autem virem peffimum nomine *Foilgo*. (Vita Patricii.)

† על הפײסית *ol he pijfyth*, Heb. præfeɛtus fortibus. Buxtorf de perfonis facris, in antiq. Hebræorum, p. 90. Here alfo we find על הקינים *ol he kinim*, præfeɛtus avibus, from whence the Arabic *kauhin* and our *kinni* or *kenny*, an augur. Hence probably the chief town in this diftriɛt was named *Lettir-kenny*, from *liota*, a book or record, and *kenni*, a prophet, or from *lithar*, a folemnity, a feftival.

‡ *Gadin* malè pro Hebræo בירם, *baidam*, id eft, *augurus*, *magi*, *baid*, *magus*, (Buxtorf) Quid eft במיר *betir*? id eft, *Aftrologi*, (Baal Aruch.) From thefe roots are derived the Irifh *baidh*, *paidh*, *phaith*, *faith*, *faig*, a prophet, forcerer, druid,

                                     and

The *Gooibarith* river, not far from hence, runs from Daabeen mountain, into the sea north of Naran. Arab. *Gha-eb*

and *beterlagh* or *peterlagh*, the name of the old testament, that is, the law of the prophets. I have before shewn, that by the word *bagh* the Irish druids meant, the divine word, religion : that *oidhe-bagh* or *oi-bagh* were the *oide* or teachers of the divine word, or tenets of the druidic religion, hence *boghas* in old Persic, sacerdos. (See Hyde Rel. Vet. p. 1344) the Greek εὐαγεις, and from *agh*, the divine law and *oi*, a teacher, the Greek ὑάγης, by which words Ammianus and Strabo signify *druids*. Our *bag* is from the old Persic *back* sanctus, *boghas*, sacerdos, whence the Sclavonic *bòg*, deus. Of these *oi-bagh* were selected a certain number (twelve) to preside over ecclesiastical courts in all matters of religion, and these were named *Aire-oi-bagh*, from *aire*, chiefs. The *Aire-faigh* presided over a court where complaints were heard against diviners, augurs, &c. From the Pelasgian *aireoibagh* was formed the Greek *Areoapagus*, a sovereign court at Athens, so famous for its justice, that the go ls are said to have submitted to its decrees. Here the accuser was placed on a stool called Γ^̔ϱις, that is, say the glossaries, *injury*, and the delinquents on that of αναιδεια, *impudence*, or according to Junius's correction, of αναιλια, *innocence*, (these were two goddesses, whose temples were erected in the Areopagus) Now *aobradh* or *avradh* was the Pelasgian-Irish name of the counsel or pleader for the crown ; the word implies to inform, to accuse, from *aei*, instruction, knowledge and *abram*, or *radh*, to speak, relate. *Aighnith* or *Ainith* were the pleaders or counsel for the prisoner ; but the Greeks had either lost all knowledge of the Pelasgian foundation of this court, or designedly turned it into fable, and Euripides tells us, *Areopagus* is derived from Αρης, Mars, and Παγος a hill, and that Mars was here tried for killing the son of Neptune. Varro treats the whole as a fable, and Potter adds, the time of its institution is uncertain. (See *Aire* explained in No. X, Preface, and *aineas*, a pleading, vol. I. p. 401, of this Collectanea.) Hence we find the court of Areopagus, is said by the Greeks to be as ancient

Gba-eb, an augur. *Neerunk*, a magician. *Arith* Phœnicè, water; and north of *Gooibarith* is the mountain Sliabh Snatcht or Snow mountain; and adjoining to this is the higheſt mountain in this part, called Ara-gil or Ara-gal, i. e. the oracle. Heb. *Beth-Kol*, which literally ſignifies the daughter of Voice, an eccho.

Phœn. *Gelaiot*, a prophet, Gr. ταλϛις. and cloſe to it, is the hill of Achtur. Arab. *akbtur*, to augur. *Akb-turgoo*, an augur. *Roſſas* or *Roſſes*; Perſic. *Raz*, myſtery, enchantment, Iriſh *Roſſach*.

If we travel to the adjoining country of *Ins-Oin*, or as it is falſely named, *Innis Owen*, (i. e the iſland of Owen) for it is not an iſland, but implies *Ins* the abode, ſettlement, ſociety, *Oin* of the prophets; here we find *Carriraugh*, or the city of the prophets. Arab. *Rukè*, *Raukè*, an enchanter.

cient as Cecrops the Pelaſgian, and founder of Athens. We alſo find another court inferior to this, called Ephetæ, inſtituted by Draco; this appears to be the Iriſh *oi-faith* or *aireoiſaith*, a court of augurs and diviners. Our Iriſh *druids*, *oibaghs* and *faighs*, were ſupported by a *deac-creas* or holy tythe, from every houſe or family, the Greek *Areopagites*, received a maintenance from the publick, which they called Κϱίας (Lyſias in Agorat.) Κϱός, Κϱίας. τινὲς δικεφαλὴ. Heſychius. Now in Iriſh *deac*, is a tenth or tythe, and *creas* or *creaſan* is holy, religious, pious, whence *Creas* in the modern Iriſh, is a ſhrine or relique, and implies the offering to ſuch relique. In Arabic, *Kyreſet* is the hoſt, the holy wafer, among the Arabian Chriſtians, (derived they ſay, from *kurz*, baked bread in cake) but *Kyriz*, in Arabic, is a *ſhrine*. *Cras*, in old Iriſh, alſo implies the body, head, one family, whence *deac-cras* is alſo derived by ſome commentators on the Brehon Laws, as a tythe from every houſe or family. *Carai*, *Caraidhe*, and *Caraghe*, implies alſo a tax, tribute, &c. derived from the Chaldee *Caraga*, Cenſus Capitalis. Arab. *carga* exaɔtio, *khuraj*, tributum. (No. x. Preface, p. 28.)

Buas

Buas now *Foile* the harbour of Derry. Arab. *Baiz,* a forcerer. *Faul,* an omen. *Rofcaune,* Perf. *Raz,* a myftery. *Kaubin Kundae,* foothfayer.

Defart-tagb-ony parifh. *Tagb-oin,* prophets, forcerers, in Irifh, Etrufcan and Arabic.

Imegow, Kinegow, villages. Arab. *Kaubingoo* an augur,
Carn-daagb, the altar of the prophets, Arab. *Keren-daa.*

Cafbel-godin, i. e. the ftone houfe of the augurs. Heb. *Gadin,* Magi.

Glan-tagber. Drum-Tagb. Tagb. Etrufcan *Tages.* Arab. Taghut, foothfayer.

Glan-goo or *gutb,* Arab. *goo,* forcerer, voice, oracle.
Glan-gobbeny. Ar. *gbaeb. goo-been,* a forcerer.

Malin. Perf. *Mal* a necromancer, *ain,* forcery.

Port-abbas or *n'abbas,* the harbour of the *aub-ofs,* forcerers, giants, near the giants caufeway.

Toolemoon. Arab. *Tala-numa,* augur.

Bin-gutbar or *goor,* the giants caufeway or oracle of the prophets. Arab. *been-goor,* a prophet, but perhaps *bin* here means a pointed tomb.

Kinugb. Kennie. Arab. *Kaubin. Kundae,* a foothfayer; hence this part of the kingdom was named *Tir-Kaubin-ol* or *Tirconaill,* i. e. the country of the Præfectus Sortibus.

Carn-falg, the altar of. Arab. *faulgoo,* augur.

Roufkie. Perf. *Raz,* fpell, charm, myftery. *Ke* forcery. Arab. *Rukfauz* diviner. Irifh *Roffacb* forcery.

Ramulin-caftle. Arab. *Remmal,* foothfayer. *Remalin,* divination.

Stran-tulla, the road of the, Arab. *Tarvil,* interpreter of dreams.

Rofbeeny,

Rofbeeny. Perf. *Raz.* Arab. *Razbeen, Roodebeen* augur; and one hundred names more, all fignifying the great fettlement of our Dadanian prophets. But I muft not omit that in the centre of this country, the cloud-capt mountain of ALT OSSOIN prefides, and around him is the whole fcenery of Offian and Fingall, which has been fo beautifully defcribed by Mr. Mac Pherfon, and to the northward of Lough Dearg are the mountains, caverns and lake of Finn or Fingall, i. e. of the Finn, the forcerer; and in the capital of the country ftood *De Raidh* or the oracle of God, now Derry. De Raidh, Raidhte no Ruidhte, Oraculum, Plunket's Lex. Hence the Dal ruite in the county of Antrim.

The word *Offian* has certainly caught the reader's eye. We have traced him to the fountain head, from whence iffued the anceftors of our Hibernian hero. The word is Chaldæan אשא *afa,* Senex, Sapiens. (Buxtorf.) *Oin,* in the fame language, is a forcerer or diviner, hence Afa-oin; Afoin or *Ofoin,* the father of diviners. In the next ftage, we find him the progenitor of the diviners amongft the Guebres or fire-worfhippers of the ancient Perfians. "Ils comptent les annèes du monde depuis Adam, qu'ils nomment comme nous: mais ils donnent d'autres noms à fes defcendans. Ils difent que lors qu'il fut parvena à fa 30 annèe, OUSHYN vint au monde, & ils reconnoiffent auffi pour un chef. (Voyages de C. Le Brun. T. 2. p. 389.) What! if we fhould hereafter find fome of Offian's heroes, amongft the defcendants of the Oufchyn of the Guebres!

This is the ζῶον Ἄφεινον of Berofus, the man which fprung from the Red Sea, i. e. *Apherin* benedictus,

Oin,

Oin, Propheta, which Goar tranflates *animal ratione deftitutum*, but as Abbé Bannier obferves, this is not agreeable to the idea the Chaldean author had of him, and *Aphrenon* is not a Greek word; (Mythology of the Ancients, vol. 1. book 2. c. 1.) it is a Chaldean, Perfic and Irifh word, implying benedictus. This *Aphrenon* is alfo called by Berofus, *Oanes*, and by Helladius, *Oes*. Photius, alfo tells us, he was named Oes and Oen. Hyginus fays that Euhannès, whofe name is a corruption of *Oanes*, came by fea into Chaldæa and there taught aftrology. This could be no other than the Perfian *Oufhyn*, or *Ainofs*, the father of the prophets, who failed up the Perfian gulph and landed in Chaldæa, for that country had no other ports, but what were on this fea. Hence, he was faid to be half fifh, half man; to retire to the fea (his fhip) every night; that he eat nothing; becaufe he took his meals on fhip-board; and fo of the reft. But the Medes and Perfians were Scythians; all ancient and modern authors agree in this point. Hence Abbè Bernier, is inclined to think, that the Gauri, or Guebres, the fire-worfhippers of Perfia, derived their doctrine from Ur or Our of Chaldæa, and that Zoroafter did not eftablifh Sabifm, but Magifm, which the learned Hyde affirms to be the eftablifhed religion of thofe Gauri, in the fouth of Perfia.

Hence, then the Pelafgian-Irifh *os*, *ofs*, high, fu-preme, learned, magician; *ofal* or *uafal*, noble. Arabic *az*, *azz*, moft glorious, venerable, holy. *Ofa*, a particular fociety of Mahommedans. *Az-az*, a fanctuary. *Afil*, noble. *Ofwi*, ecchoes, i. e. the voice of fprites. *Afhyakh*, doctors, dervifes, prelates. *Ofh-mouil*, the prophet

VOL. III. N°. XII.　　　H　　　Samuel.

Samuel. *Az-imet*, incantation, charms. *Azif*, demons.

Perfic. *azfb*, *ozfb*, fagacious, learned. *Oz-az-il* thofe angels placed neareft the throne of God. *Ofraf* i. e. *Of-arruf*, forcerers. (Irifh Of-airibh) hence *uezir* a vizir. *Ofman* the anceftor of the grand feignor. *Afb-mul* bad omens. *Ofbari* the name of a celebrated forcerer, diviner, or doctor, whofe difciples ftill exift under the name of Afharim.

From thefe roots, the Infula Offion of Homer, which probably was written O'σσαι and not O'σιὼϒ. Hence alfo the Greek O'σσία Vaticinatio. O'σσύομαι auguror. O'σά fanctitas, pietas, juftitia : the Latin Religi-ofus, Religi-onis.—From thence the Irifh, Pelafgian and Chaldæan, *Bal-oin-os* and the Greek 'Απολλωϒ◌·, and the contracted Etrufcan APVL, is our *Bal.*—So from our *neas* and the Hebrew *nabas*, is derived *barnaffus*, and from the Irifh *Ler*, *Lere*, pious, holy. *Larnaffos*, another Greek name for Parnaffus. Hence likewife Offa, a mountain in Theffaly the refidence of Oinin (forcerers) faid to be inhabited by Centaurs, that is in Irifh *Cean-tar-os*, the head or chief of the forcerers, a word miftaken by the Greeks for giants, monfters, like the Irifh *Aubbos*, *Obbos*, or *Abbos*, which was a forcerer of *Aub*, or *Obb*, but now tranflated by our monkifh Lexiconifts, a giant. From the Irifh *Iris* holy, pious, is the Ægyptian *Ofiris*: thus alfo *Ofeum* the locus Augurum in Agro Veienti, according to Feftus, and from the Irifh *Os* with the prefixed augmentative *fo*, is formed *Sos*, divine knowledge and the Phœnician Zas, Zeus, and the Greek ziός Jupiter, derived alfo from the Irifh *puit*, uter quafi *aub*, and *air* or *aire*, a diviner, hence *Sof-*

piter,

piter, *Sopiter*, foftened by the Etrufcans to *Jopiter*. *Sofus* an Egyptian god. *Sof-bal-os* forms *Sofipolis* a god of the Eleans, and from the Irifh *uam* a cave or den, *fal* fate, and *os*, is derived the Greek ὀμφαλὶς, the cella or antrum of the Delphic oracle, explained by the Greeks and Latins very falfely by the word *umbilicus*. (See Æfchylus in Eumenid.) Hence *Uamb-oin* the forcerers cave near Cork, now called the Ovens. Thus the Latin *Antrum* is from the Irifh *Ain-tar-uam*, that is the forcerers cave; and this is the derivation of Antrim a town and county in Ireland, as *ofs* and *ruidb* from the Arabic *ruide* a forcerer, forms *Off,uidb*, now Offory, in the centre of Ireland.

Hence every name that betokens king, prince, chief, puiffant, learned, or noble, alfo implies a diviner. Thus *Sar* in Syriac a prince, in Irifh *Saor*, Englifh Sir, in the Arabic is a magician, as *Sybr* magick. Perfic *alm Sybr* necromancy. *Sybr allal* poetry, i.e. lawful enchantment. *Sybr-fag* enchanting. In Irifh *Air*, *Aire*, *Aireac*, *Airigb*, is a chief, from *Ur* of Chaldea, whence *Aire* a forcerer; hence the Latin **Rex**, **Regis**: from the Irifh *treab* a tribe, *daire* of forcerers, is derived the Trobadours of Provence in France. (Ce furent ces Troubadours qui reveillent en France la goût des Sciences au XI Siecle. Furetiere.) Thus *Aire* is a poet, and a man of fcience, for all knowledge was once lodged in this body of Chuldea's, from *Ur* their origin in Chaldæa, hence the common name *Daire* in Ireland and Perfia, all derived from the Chaldæan *ur*, *eir* or הַרְדֹּר *eirir*, fcrutari and אָרְנַז *aregaz*, which in 1. Sam. 6. 8. means the Ark, but as Buxtorf obferves, eft & nomen proprium MAGI.

Thus the Irish *Uphas* forcery is from the Chaldæan
פתה taphas, apprehendere, comprehendere, of which
the Greeks have made *Tuphon* and *Tuphos*, &c. &c.

From *Oin*, or *Ain*, and *gas* (the Chaldee *gafur* in
Arabic *ghauzoo*, *jauzoo*) is formed the Irish proper
name *Oingas*, written fometimes *Angos*, *Aongos*,
Aongus, fignifying a forcerer, or divener. And here
I muft obferve, that *ge* and *ce* does alfo imply the
magick art, whence we find the name written likewife *Ainge*. And as the ancient tradition of *Stone-
henge*, in Saxon, *Stan-henge*, is allowed by the ancient
Britons to be the work of Irifhmen; and Mr. Lhwyd
proving to a demonftration that the Magogian Irifh,
inhabited Britain, until expelled by the Gomerian
Welfh, I am inclined to think that *Stan-henge* implies,
not the hanging ftones, as a very fenfible author
lately has interpreted the word, but the *ftan* or *tan*,
i. e. the territory, or Chaldæa of the forcerers, or if
ftan be Saxon, i. e. a ftone, then it is the ftone or
altar of the *Aonge* or forcerers; and that if any fuch
being did exift as Hengift, it was a corruption of
Aongus and fignified a forcerer. I am the more inclined to think this is the true derivation, as in the
oracle near Drogheda, defcribed by Governor Pownal,
I read the word *Aongus*, or forcerer, in the Irifh
Ogham, or forcerer's alphabet, infcribed on one of the
ftones. See Geafa druima Draoidheact, in Shaw and
O'Brien's Dictionary of the Irifh language.

This Oufhon, the great father of the prophets of
the Perfian Guebres, or fire worfhippers, is frequently mentioned by our Druids. There is a long and
beautiful poem written by them on the fubject of
FATE,

FATE, which we may probably give to the public, in a future number of this work. A few lines are here tranſlated.

Ruina SORS ſemper male aſcendentis eſt,
Coſroïs, alti Regis olim Perſiæ,
Late & potentis, aureis ſcriptum notis,
Lectum hoc tiaræ in nobilis faſtigio eſt :
Multi quid anni, vita quid longævaque,
Per mille tracta caſuum diſcrimina,
Iraſque mille, mille SORTIS fluctum ?
Caput Tiara inſigne calcabant pedes
Villiſſimorum FATA poſt mortalium
Regnumque nobis traditum a majoribus
Trademus ipſi poſt futureram in manus.
Naſcuntur illa lege SORTIS principes,
Naſcentur omnes qui FUTURI Principes.
Oleas vagari extra, una SORS eſt omnium.
Gratum tibi eſt quod, SORTIS eſt faſtidium.
SORS eſt timenda illi, nihil qui jam timet
&c. &c. &c.

Vis noſſe SORTIS ex SCYTHIS imaginem,
Veramque SORTI haud diſcolorem imaginem ?
Pede illa deſtituta eſt, penna ſunt manus :
Prendenda & aliis ergo, ne mox avolet,
Reditura nunquam, ſi favere jam velit,
Ridentis & præbere dulce ſuavum.
Legatione nobili quondam SCYTHAE
Juveni illa talis picta PELLAEO fuit.
&c. &c.

BUXHORNIUS.

But to return to the ſettlement of the Iriſh ſorcerers in the north of Ireland.

Malin.

Malin. from Malineach, i. e. *Firbolg,* forcerers, fprites.

Doach Ifle.⎫
Doach beg.⎭ Arab. *daa* an augur; *daukus* a bad omen.

Muc-aos, Mountain. *Muc,* holy. Arab. *azae* a fpell, charm.

Cruach-falla, the prophets hill. Ir. *fal* an omen. Arab. *fal* omen, *faule* a forcerer.

Rin-ard-alluch point, *rin* a ridge, *ard* high. Arab. *ablu'l'kè* an augur.

Bally-Naafh, Vill. Heb. *naafh* a prophet.

Dunaneduan, village, *dun* a town. Arab. *aenund* enchantment.

Clan-da-bhadlagh, parifh, *Clan* tribe, *da* of. Arab. *butleb* magician..

Phaban, parifh, *Dun Phanachy* church. Hebrew *phenanah,* a revealer, a forcerer

Tar-lachan, village. Irifh *Tar.* Arab. and Chaldee, *Tair* to augur, *leachan* altar.

· *Dun-aff,* church and village, *dun* a town. Arab. *af,* *afsoon,* magick.

Dun-uph, arrauf, foothfayer, i. e. *Aire-af* and *Aire-feahh.*

Crenan, mountains and barony. ·Chaldee and Arab. *Karan,* a rocky country. *Ain,* forcerer.

Having now feen that the north of Ireland, was the great feat of our Dadanan forcerers and ominators, let us only obferve the confufed accounts of the Greek writers of the fituation of the oracle of Dodona. Some will have it in Theffaly, fome in Epirus, others in Thefpratia, Chaonia, and Moloffia, and others fay that it was fo called from Dodonim the fon of Javan.

But

But Herodotus afcribes the origin of it to the Phœnicians, and trumps up a fabulous ftory of a rape; to this let us add the words of that eminent Pelafgian Greek writer, Homer, and I think we may conclude, he was not ignorant of its proper fituation *.

Parent of gods and men, Pelafgian Jove
King of Dodona, and its hallow'd grove;
King of Dodona, whofe *intemperate coaft*
Bleak winds infefts, and winter's *chilling froft*,
Round thy abode thy priefts with unwafh'd feet
Lie on the naked earth.

Does this fituation of Dodona, correfpond with the climate of Greece?

The Irifh hiftory further informs us, that when the Affyrians had defeated the Athenians in a pitched battle, our Dadananai fearing the revenge of the Affyrians, for the magick art they had practifed, in bringing the dead Athenians to life, as faft as they were flain, left Athens and failed to Lochlon, or Lochlun, where they were kindly received and were divided between four cities, viz. Falias, Gorias, Finnias and Mburias, and having ftaid here fome time, they failed for Ireland, but were blown to the north of Scotland, where they continued feven years and then returned to Ireland. That on their landing they burnt their fhips, and were oppofed by the Fir-

---

* Dodona, Dodoa, or Cæneum, — its true fituation not known.

(Geogr. antiqua of Dufrefnoy.)

N. B. Here we find our Irifh *Cinuch* or *Cinnie*, forcery.

bolgs,

bolgs, who fay the poets were likewife a colony from Egypt, but laft from Pelafgian Greece and were the defcendants of the fecond fon of Nemed, as the Dananai were of the third fon. An old author fays, *Tangatur firbolg an Eirin Ballaftar a tang flaithifc, is do conarcas in dorn cè righi ag fgribind,* MANE, TETHEL & PHAREAS. i. e. the Firbolg came to Ireland when Ballafter (Baalfhaffar) was king, he, who faw the magic hand writing the words *Mane, Tethel, Phareas,* and he proceeds, Cyrus fon of Darius, foon after, took Babylon. Now *Firbolg* fignifies augurs *, *fir* a

man

---

* The ingenious and unhappy Eugene Aram, had ftudied the Irifh language; in the fmall mifcellaneous tract publifhed at the end of his trial, he has the following obfervations. " The " Latin *Vir* is precifely the Irifh *fir* a man : the old Irifh called " a colony which fettled amongft them Fir-bolg. They were " Belgæ, a word latinifed from bolg, which indeed imports " the fame, *and is the fame with the Greek Pelafgi.*" The learned Millius derives the name Philiftæi and Palæftini from the Æthiopic *phalas* or *falas*, i. e. migravit, exulavit, ut quafi terra exulum vocetur, quia Philiftæi & Ifraelitæ eo commigrarunt ex Ægypto. (Differt. de Terra Canaan, p. 129.) This may be the origin of the Pelafgi alfo, and in Irifh *phalam* and *falbham* is to migrate, *falafge*, he who migrates. Aram fell into this miftake from the great affinity he acknowledges there is, between the Irifh, and the old Greek and Hebrew : and this author, adds, " In my Lexicon, I have fetched as much as poffible " from the Irifh, and induftrioufly omitted the Britifh, left it " fhould be thought, as I know it has been fometimes, that the " Romans left us the words that bear any relation to the Latin, " while this can never be objected to the Irifh, fince the Romans " never fet foot in Ireland." Another obfervation of Aram's is worthy of remark. " Wherever hiftory fails in accounting for " the extraction of any people, or where it is manifeftly mifta-

" ken,

man *balg* of letters, learning and erudition. (See Scriobam in conclusion.) *Fear-bolg*, i. e. *mailineacha*, or *mailachane*, vet. gloss. Mr. Shaw in his Gaulick lexicon, thus explains *mailachan*, viz. the young of sprites in Scotland called Browny, it is a good natured being and renders good offices to favourites.——Thus the Rev. Mr. Shaw.

Arab. *baligh*, reaching the highest perfection in learning. Persic *belagh*, any vocable implying excellence, as purity, virtue. *Belaghet*, eloquence, fluency of words. *Belegh* eloquent. (Richardson.)

In the Sclavonian dialect *blog* is an interpreter, a lexicon, &c.

But Castellus proves that the Chaldees had an order of priests named Bélga, ab hoc, ordo ille sacerdotalis, cujus observatores Belgitæ dicti: and the ancient Irish glossarists fully explain our Firbolg were in holy orders, viz. *Bolg-ceard*, i. e. *Neas*, that is, the profession of a Bolg is (Neas, that is) divination, in Hebrew *Naash*.

In another ancient gloss. I find, bolg or builg, explained by *druchd rùn*, that is, the mystery of the dead, or of raising up the dead, by which I understand, conversing with the Manes.

So that the Irish *fir-bolg* means no more than the Augurs or Druids the Dadanan left behind, when they journeyed to Pelasgian Greece, to improve

" ken, how can this extraction be more rationally inferred, and " determined, or that mistake rectified, *than from the analogy* " *of languages? And is not this alone sufficiently conclusive, if* " *nothing else was left?* (Aram's Essay towards a Lexicon on a a new plan.)

them-

themfelves in fome new doctrine then broached, and fuch mafters of the magick art were they now become, the poets tell us, that on their return, they threw a cloud over the *Firbolg* for three days and nights, till they had made good footing on the fhore. The meaning of the whole is, that the Druids not approving of the new doctrine brought in by the Dadananai oppofed them, and we are told, that in the fpace of twenty-feven years, they had two noted battles, one at *Magh Tuire-deas*, and another at *Magh Tuire Tuag*, that is, at the plains of the fouth tower, and of the north tower; but, at length they got the better of the *Firbolg*.

The tranflator and fabulous interpolator of Keating's Hiftory of Ireland, has brought our *Da dananai* from Greece to Denmark and Norway, and made them inftructors of the young Danes in the magick art. I have carefully perufed Keating in the original Irifh, and the antient poem on which he forms that part of his hiftory, where I find not a fyllable of Danes or Norwegians, but a plain defcription of Etrufca. We fhall give a few lines of the original poem.

Tuatha Dadanann na fead fuim. ait abhfuaradar foghluim.
Rangadar a fuidheact flan. an draoidheact andiaigh ealtan.
Iar bannul faidh fionn go faill. mic Neimidhe mhic Adhnamhoin
Dar mhac Baoth, Baothach beartach. fa laoch leothach luamth-
    feargach
Clanna Baothaigh beodha angoil. rangador fluagh niadh neart-
    mhoir
Iar fniomh iar ttuirfi thruim. lion aloingfe go Loch-Lun *.

                                          Ceithre

---

* Luna, Sive Λύη, licet Ptolomæus Λύηγ, και σελήης, άκρον. Lunam & Lunæ promontorium diftinguat, aut civitas Lunæ, ut
                                        Hæc

Ceithre cathracha clu cheart. ghabfad a reim go ro neart
Do chuirdis comhloin gan cheas. ar fhoghluim ar fhireolas.
Falias agus *Gorias* glan. *Finias*, *Mburias* na morghal
Do mhaoidhiomh madhmann amac. Anmanna na mòrchathrach.
Morfios agus *Earus-ard*. *Abhras* is *Semias* fiorgharag
Re *nGarmann* as luadh leafadh. Anmanna fuadh gac faoirleafa.
· *Morfios* file *Falias* fein.   *Earus anGoirias* maith ameim
Semias a *Mburias* diogne deas. *Abhras* file-fionn *Finias*
Ceithre haifgeadha leo anall. duaflibh *Tuatha Dadanann*.
Cloidhiomh, cloch, coire-cubhraidh. fleagh re hagaidh ard Curadh
Lia fail a *Falias* anall. do gheifcadh fa Righ *Eireann*
Cloidhiomh lamha lughaidh luidh a *Gorias* rogha rochruidh
A *Finias* tair fairrge abhfad. tugadh fleagh lughaidh nar lag
A *Mburias* maoin adhbhal oll, cobra-mor mhic an Taghdha.

habet Anaftafius Biblioth. in S. Eutychiano, prima ac præcipua
Etruriæ antiquæ civitas erat. Plin. l. 3. 6. 5.   Primum Etruria
oppidum Luna, portu nobile.   Infeliciffime Joan Anius Viterb.
comminifcitur Latine *Lunam* dici, Græce *Selenem*, Etrufco idiomate Cariaram; *Car* enim effe Urbem, & *iaram* fignificare
Lunam; quafi ergo idem fit ac fi dicas Urbem Lunæ.

Hence, Berofus, calls this city Cariara, quæ et Luna; I have
fhewn in a former number, that *an* in old Irifh, fignifies a planet,
and *lu*, fmall; and that the moon was named *Luan*, or the fmall
planet, in diftinction to the *Sam-an*, or fun. *Car* or *Cathar*, in
Irifh, is a city; and *Re*, *Rea* and *Rae* is the moon. The poet
moft judicioufly brings our *Dadanai* to Loch Luna, the chief
feat of the Etrufcan forcerers and augurs.

Hæc augurum etiam, ac arufpicum, portentorumque interpre-
tum fedes erat. (Dempfter, de Etruria Regali, l. 4. c. 20.)

> Hæc propter placuit Tufcos de more vetufto
> Acciri vates; quorum qui maximus ævo
> Aruns incoluit defertæ mænia Lunæ,
> Fulminis edoctus motus, venafque calentes
> Fibrarum, & motus errantis in aëre pennæ.
>
> (M. Lucan, lib. 1. Pharfal. v. 586.

The moon was probably the arms of this city, as we find
from Martial,

> Cafeus Etrufcæ fignatus imagine Lunæ.
>
> Martial.

T R A N S.

TRANSLATION.

The purport of the *Tua-Dadanans* journey, was in queſt of
       knowledge;
And to ſeek a proper place, where they ſhould improve in
       Druidiſm.
Theſe holy men ſoon ſailed to Greece. The ſons of *Nemed*, ſon of
       Adbnamon
Deſcendants of *Baoth*, from *Bœotia* ſprung. Thence, to the care
       of ſkilful pilots,
This Bœotian clan, like warlike heroes themſelves committed,
And after a dangerous voyage, the ſhips brought them to *Locb*
       Luan *.
Four cities of great fame, which bore great ſway,
Received our clan, in which they completed their ſtudies.
Spotleſs *Falias, Gorias*; majeſtick *Finias* and *Mburias*,
For ſieges famed: were the names of the four cities.
Morſios and *Earus-ard*; *Abbras*; and *Semias* well ſkilled in magick
Were the names of our Druids; they lived in the reign of *Garmann*
       the happy.
Morſios was made *File* † of *Falias*; *Earus* the poet in *Gorias* dwelt;
Samias dwelt at *Mburias*, but *Abbras* the *File-fionn* at *Finias*.
At the departure of our *Dadanai*, four gifts theſe cities gave them;
A *ſword*; a *ſtone*; a *cup*; a *ſpear*: this laſt for feeble champions.
The ſtone of *Lia-fail* ‡, which declares *Ierna*'s kings from *Falia*
       came.
The ſword by which they ſwear, at *Gorias* was obtained.

                              The

---

* This is called Denmark and Norway by Keating's tranſlator, becauſe the Iriſh named the Danes *Loch-lonnach*, derived as ſome ſay, from *Loch* the ſea, and *lonnughadh* to dwell. Others ſay, from *Loch* and *Lonn*, ſtrong, powerful; others from *loch*, a lake, and *lann*, full; as coming from a country, abounding in lakes. See O'Brien.

† *File.* See this word explained in the chapter deſcribing the hall of Tara. פלא phile unde *niphla*, Arcanum, myſterium, occultum.

‡ *Lia-fail*, or the ſtone of *Fal* or Deſtiny; the *Leaba-dea* of the Etruſcans, from whence the city of Labadea and Labdacus
                                king

The never-failing fpear §, *Abhras* received at *Finias*,
And *Mburias* granted the great helmet of *Tage*'s fons ‖.

Here is not a word of Denmark, or of teaching the young Danes the magick art, as the tranflator has foifted in. *Lochluna*, or the lake of *Luna*, ftood on the *Macra* in the Etrufcan territories, and was famous for its port. (Strabo, l. 1. Plin. Ptolom.)

Falias, is *Falefii* the capital of the *Falifci* in Etruria, (Sex. Pomp.) fuppofed to be fo named from the ancient *Pelafgi* or *Phelafgi*, and was a place of great antiquity. (Strab. l. 5.)

king of Etruria. The kings of Ireland were crowned on this ftone, and it is faid, it made a groaning noife when the right heir was not elected king; it is alfo faid to be now under the chair in Weftminfter Abby, in which our kings are crowned. See Lia Fail in O'B. and Sh. dictionaries.

§ This fpear was known by the name. of *Gai bulg*, or the forcerers fpear, which was fure to deftroy the enemy. See Keating's Hiftory of the Milefians.

‖ The great helmet of *Tage's* fons: the original is *Taghdha*, the *dh* being adventitious, and not founded, in order to make the fyllables long. *Tadhg* or *Tagh*, in Pelafgian-Irifh fignifies a poet, a prophet, a prince; it is a common name, now written *Teague;* in Perfic *Tagj*, a prince, a crown. The Irifh *Tagmhodh*, a poem, is alfo of the fame root with the modern Perfic *Cheghame*, an ode. The Perfian ftory of the helmet of the Perfian *Gian*, is of the fame original alfo: this was as famous in Scythian hiftory as that of Achilles, and was for ages preferved by the Perfians. Ce bouclier de *Gian* etait myfterieux, il eut fallu un poete comme Homere pour le decrire. Ce bouclier fervait, non contre les armes de la guerre, mais contre celles de la *Magie*. L'Aftronomie prefidait à fa compofition. (Lettres fur l'Atlantide, par Bailly, p. 146.) *Tages* was the great enchanter of the Etrufcans. See p. x. of this Preface.

The

Gorias was either *Gære*, named alfo *Cære* or *Gravifca*; the laft was built by the Pelafgi in Etruria, and the firft ftood in Tarquinia in Etruria. (Strab. l. 5.) Gravifca, Metrodorus apud Julium Solinum γορχίαν vocat. (Dempfter de Etr. Regali,) probably miftaken for γορχαν.

Fanias is *Fan*, or *Fanum Jovis* in Etruria: there was alfo a *Fanis* or *Colonia Julia-Faneftris*.

Mburias was *Perus* or *Perufia*, an inland city of Etruria, on the Tiber. The modern Irifh commonly write *m* before *b*.

The names of thefe Dadanan druids were *Morfios*, that is, great knowledge: *Earus* or *Eiris-ard*, that is chief chronologer; *Semias* that is diviner, or augurer; and *Abbras* the *File-fionn*, that is *Abbras* the orator, and martial philofopher or druid.

This character of *Abbras* perfectly agrees with the defcription of the *Hyperborean Abaris* of Diodorus and Himerius, called by Suidas a Scythian, not improperly, becaufe our *Abbras* was of Magogian-Scythian blood, though born of Pelafgian parents from Bœotia, then fettled in Ireland.

There are ftill ftronger reafons to think that this is the fame Abaris, the druid or prieft of Apollo mentioned by thefe Greek authors: firft, the Hyperborean ifland is faid to be north of Gaul, and oppofite to it: the fouth of Ireland may be faid to be oppofite part of Gaul, as well as Britain: this Hyperborean ifland is reprefented as a very temperate region, and figuratively faid to produce two harvefts a year; this defcription does not agree with any of the Britifh iflands, except Ireland, where there is a perpetual verdure

and

and vegetation, owing to the mildnefs of its climate, and the hot lime-ftone foil: it is well known, that when the roads in England are rendered impaffable by falls of fnow, there has been no figns of fnow in in Ireland, in the fame latitudes.——Secondly, the Hyperborean ifland was frequented of old, by the Greeks, and in friendfhip with them: this is confirmed by the antient hiftory of Ireland; they were not only in friendfhip with, but allied to the Pelafgi or antient Greeks.—Thirdly, our *Abbras* was *file-fionn*, or chief druid of the Dadanan expedition to Greece, and thence to Etruria in Italy, in queft of knowledge; probably, to ftudy a new fyftem of religion; they had been informed had fprung up in thofe parts.—The Hyperborean *Abaris* of Diodorus, took the fame route; he travelled over Greece, and from thence went to Italy, where he converfed with Pythagoras, with whom he ftaid a confiderable time, and contracted an intimate friendfhip. (Porphyrius in vita Pythagoræ, and Iamblicus l. 1. c. 28.) Our Abhras brought home a new fyftem of religion, which was ill relifhed, by the Firbolgs or forcerers he had left behind in Ireland: it was the caufe of a civil war, which continued twenty feven years, till at length the Firbolgs were difmayed and the new fyftem eftablifhed. I have fhewn in a former number of this Collectanea, (from an ancient Irifh MS) that our Irifh Druids taught the Metempfychofis or tranfmigration of fouls: but I do not think this was the fyftem brought over by Abhras. It is faid that Pythagoras introduced it into Italy, but I think it is evident our Irifh Druids drew this doctrine from the fame fountain head, that the Bramins did,

before

before their migration into India; and from thefe it is faid Pythagoras received his knowledge of it. It has been long a queftion with the ancients, and they are much divided in their opinions, *whether the* Druids *learnt their fymbolical, and enigmatical method of teaching, together with the doctrine of* tranfmigration *from* Pythagoras, *or that Philofopher had borrowed thefe particulars from the* Druids? (See Diog. Laert. in proem. Sect. 6.) I fhall have occafion to treat of this, in the collation of the Irifh language, with that of the Gentoos or Hindoftans.—Fourthly, The defcription given of the *Hyperborean Abaris*, by the orator Himerius, is very applicable to our Abhras. " They relate, fays he, *that* ABARIS *the fage, was by nation a* HYPERBOREAN; *became a* GRECIAN *in fpeech; and refembled a* SCYTHIAN *in his habit and appearance. Whenever he moved his tongue you would imagine him to be fome one out of the midft of the academy or very* LYCEUM. (Ex Oratione ad Urficium apud Photium in Biblioth. Cod. 243.) The word *abhras* or *abras* in the Irifh language fignifies eloquent, a ready and witty anfwer, and it is derived from the the noun *abairt* fpeech, articulation, learning, politenefs; whence the verb *abram* to fay, to fpeak, to converfe. Again, the drefs of Abaris defcribed by Himerius is that of the ancient Irifh, not of a Scythian. When, fays he, ABARIS *came to* ATHENS, *holding a bow, having a quiver hanging from his fhoulders* (the reader will be pleafed to recollect our *Abras* was called *file-fionn*, the warlike Druid or File) *his body wrapt up in a bracan or plad, girt about his loins with a gilded belt, and wearing trowzers reaching from the foles of his feet to his wafte.*

(ibid)

(ibid.) Now had he been from Scythia, we fhould certainly have found him in fkins or furs. And, the character given of Abaris by this fame Himerius, fhewed him qualified for the important bufinefs he went from Ireland to execute: *he was, fays he, affable and pleafant in converfation; in difpatching great affairs, fecret and induftrious; quick-fighted in prefent exigencies; in preventing future dangers, circumfpect; a fearcher after wifdom; defirous of friendfhip; trufting indeed little to fortune; having every thing trufted to him for his prudence.*

As to Ireland being the Hyperborean ifland, mentioned by Diodorus, I think nothing can be more plain: he particularly mentions the frequent ufe of the harp there; the worfhip of Apollo in circular temples; that the city and temple were always governed by Boreades, a family, fays he, defcended from Boreas; this indeed is of a complexion with his Hyperborean ifland being fo called, becaufe *fituated more northerly than the north wind.* (Lib. 2. p. 130. *Borradbach* is the name with the Irifh poets for a valiant chief; *borr*, is great, noble, fplendid; *borrchean*, I have fhewn to have been the name of the great God in Irifh and Kalmuc Mogul; I find it the fame in old Welfh, (See Pref. to fecond Edit. Irifh Gram.) the word is from the Arabic *bur*, a great, haughty man; *burban*, a prince: but the druids of Ireland, in their magifterial capacity were called *borradbas*, from *borr* and *adb*, the law human and divine. (See Collectanea, No. X.)

The Greeks were fo ignorant of the fituation of Ireland, for a feries of ages after they had driven out the Pelafgi, it is no wonder they fhould name Ireland the Hyperborean ifland. Even Strabo, fays in his fecond book, *the utmoft place of navigation, in our time, from Gaul towards the North, is faid to be Ireland, which being fituated beyond Britain, is, by reafon of the cold, with difficulty inhabited, fo that all beyond it is reckoned uninhabitable.* I therefore have no manner of doubt that our Abhras is the Abaris of Diodorus and Himerius, who left Etruria and refided feven years in Scotland, and from thence returned to Ireland; but what new fyftem of religion thefe Dadanai introduced, fhall be the fubject of another work.

I think I can in fome meafure account for the confufion that prevails amongft the Greek authors, relating to the fituation of Ireland and the ifles of Scotland; it is to be obferved, that the fea between the north of Ireland and Scotland, is called by the ancient Irifh *muir chroinn,* which I think means the brown or dun-coloured fea, owing probably to its rocky, weedy bottom. Now Orpheus who has faid much of Ireland, calls the north fea, *mare cronium, idem quod mare faturninum & oceanus feptentrionalis.* (Ferrarius.) Orpheus having learnt from the Britifh-Irifh that this fea was called *Cronium,* the Greeks fabricated the ftory of Chronos being enchanted in Ogygia, an ifland weft of Britain, and this was followed by Pliny, Plutarch, Solinus, &c. &c. and this ftory took its rife from the fuppofed power of our Dadanan druids, to raife a fog by their enchantments, at pleafure. Pytheas who was a naval commander of Marfeilles, calls this fea Mare Cronium alfo, and if we may believe Herodotus, Pytheas failed very far towards the north.

north. It is evident that the Greeks knew more of the globe in the time of Homer, than of Herodotus, who was posterior to Homer by at least 400 years. " I cannot help laughing, says Herodotus, at those " who pretend that the ocean flows round our conti- " nent; no proof can be given of it. I believe, (adds " he elsewhere) that Homer had taken what he deli- " vers about the ocean, from some work of antiquity; " but it was without comprehending any thing of the " matter, repeating what he had read, without well " understanding what he had read." (Herod. l. 4. & 2.) From whence could Homer receive this knowledge, but from his master, who we have shewn was a Pelasgian.

Monsieur Gouget has made the same observation; " The ignorance of the European Greeks in geogra- " phy, says he, was extreme in all respects, during " many ages. They do not even appear to have " known the discoveries made in more antient voya- " ges, which were not absolutely unknown to Homer: " I think I have shewn that some very sensible traces " of them existed in his poems." (*Orig. of Arts and Sciences, tom. 3, l. 3.*) In the time of the Peloponesian war, the Lacedæmonians transported their ships by land from one sea to another, and this expedient was common. (*Strab. l. 8.*) What idea can we form of their marine in that age, about 430 years before Christ, when compared with the Carthaginians, who, in the time of Ezekiel the prophet, (590 years before Christ) supplied Tyre with tin and lead from the British islands? (*Ezekiel, c. 27 & 28.*)

I am

I am fenfible that the general voice is here againft me; that it is a received opinion, that the ancient Irifh could only navigate the narrow feas, furrounding their ifland; and certainly I can produce no other authority for the navigations they frequently perform- ed to Spain, Greece, Italy and Africa, than Irifh MSS. I apprehend this opinion has been adopted too haftily, from the name of a fhip in Irifh, viz. *currocb*, Welfh, *curwg*, mentioned by Gildas, Polyd. Virgil, Joceline, &c. and explained by Sir James Ware, to be a fpe- cies of a fhip, *fuppofed* to be made of wicker, cover- ed with hides. Bullet has fallen into the fame mif- take. (See Mr. Pegge on a paffage of Gildas, Ar- chæol. vol. 5. p. 274.) But this gentleman has fhewn us, that *curuca* in Latin is the fame as *navis*. It is certain that the Irifh *currocb* of this day, for paffing fmall rivers, is made of wicker, covered with hides; fuch may be now found on the rivers Shannon, Boyne, &c. and fuch may have been ufed by the Britons. The word is formed of *coire*, that is, any hollow vef- fel, hence *coire* and *corracan*, a pot, a cauldron, a cart, &c. &c. Arabic *kaure*, a pot, *kur-kaure*, a cauldron; but *corracb* aud *corrcorr* in old Irifh figni- fied a fhip built of ftrong timbers and planks, and is the fame as the Arabic *kurkur* or *kurkoor*, a large fhip. (*Ricbardfon Arab. Lex. & Schindlerus.*)

The Irifh had many names for a fhip, according to the fpecies of building, which I fhall here fet down, with the correfponding *oriental* names; moft of thefe words are to be found in *Lbwyd's Archæol. Brit.* under the word *navis*, and it is to be noticed, that when this learned Welfh antiquary, found Irifh words to diftinguifh

guifh every fpecies of fhip, he could only produce three or four common general names for a fhip in the Welfh, Cornifh, or Amoric.

Irish Names for a Ship.

Irish.

Long. This word is common to the Welfh, but is not to be found in the Hebrew, Chaldee or Arabic ; it is alfo a fhip in the Chinefe language. *Long* batiment des Chinois : les *longs* font affez femblables a nos galeres. (*Voyage de Matelief. See alfo Furetiere's Dict.*) *Long* in Irifh is likewife a houfe or habitation ; *long-phort*, a palace, &c. Welfh *Llong*, a a fhip, a float, a bridge : *vlungo*, a fhip in the Congo language ; *ionge* in the Javanefe ; *lengier* in Turkifh, an oar. From the Irifh *long*, a fhip, is derived the Englifh long-boat, that is, the fhip's boat, and not from the form or figure of the boat ; fo alfo the Englifh cock-boat, or a fmall boat, from the Irifh *coca*, a fmall boat, derived from *coca* or *cocal*, a hufk or fhell of a nut, in Arabic *khufhk.*

Carb, a fhip ; Chaldee, *arb* ; Arabic, *gbraub* ; *carb* in Irifh is alfo a cart, a chariot ; Coptice *markab.*

Sud, fudaire, a fhip ; Chaldee, *zidaria* ; *me fbud*, a rower ; Welfh, *fuddas*, blubbers floating on the water ; Bafc. *ont-zit-zarra*, Coptice *nyfytity*, a fmall fhip.

Sudbbhan, a fhip ; Heb. and Chaldee, *fephina.*

IRISH.

Efs, *effis*, a fhip; Heb. *zi*; Arab. *ajooz*; Hindoftan, *fjebaas*; Bafc. *ont-zia*, *unt-zia*.

Libbearn, a fhip, a houfe; Chald. *leburna*, *lepba*, a fhip; Perfic, *leb*, a houfe.

Scib, a fhip, a boat; Arab. *mur-zaub*.

Naoi, a fhip; Heb. *ani*, *oni*. N. B. *Naoi* in Irifh is alfo the name of Noah: *naibb*, *naif*, is alfo to fwim, to float, in Hebrew *naab*.

Cuadar, *cuadas-barc*; Arab. *kaudis*, a fhip.

Cnabbia, *cnarra*, a fhip; Heb. & Chald. *gnab-bara*.

Eatbar, a fhip, pronounced ahar; Coptice, *bamara*, a fhip.

Artbrach; Arab. *gawruk*, a fhip.

Barc; Chaldee, *da beruth*; Heb. *baricbim*, a fhip.

Currcurr, *currach*; Arab. *kurkur*, a large fhip; Spanifh, *carraca*, a great fhip, (navio grande.*)

Leaftar,

---

* Thefe Currachs of hides and wattles were invented by the Pelafgians or Etrufcans, the anceftors of the Irifh. Etrufcorum inventum navis & illa ex corio & vimine, Britannorum ritu, feu Scotorum; ex abiete, ex alno: tutela; varia genera. *(Dempfter de Etruria Regali, l. 3. c. 80.)* And Ifidorus gives the invention of fhips to the Lydians, who were alfo Pelafgians. Lydii primam navem fabricaverunt, pelagique incerta petentes, pervium mare ufibus humanis fecerunt. *(Lib. 19. c. 1.)* and in his Gloffary, this author defcribes the Carb to be of the Currach kind. "Carabus, parva fcapha ex vimine & coris. *Feftus Avienus, lib. 1. Oræ maritimæ, p. 191.*

———————————— fed res ad miraculum Navigia junctis femper aptant pellibus, Corifque vaftum fæpe percurrunt falum.

Hæc

IRISH.

Leaſtar, a boat, a milking can, a veſſel; Welſh, *lheſter*, a ſhip.

These were again divided into the following claſſes.

Ramblong, longrambac, galeir, ſculong, longfada, ſudlong, a row galley ; Chaldee, *ſbat,* a rower.

Arglong, miopara, longcreicbe, creacblong, a pirate ſhip.

Argnaoitb, pirates; *naoitb,* ſailors, is the ſame as the Chaldee *Ainiutb,* 1 Kings, 9. v. 27. in Arabic *ark* is a mariner, and alſo *nawte.*

Hæc prima origo navis, quam aliqui ad Janum referunt, qui navigio in Italiam deveƈtus.

Aulus Gellius mentions the various ſpecies of ſhipping uſed by the Romans, and if I miſtake not, the Iriſh *long* is one. L. 10. c. 25. Gauli, Corbitæ, caudicæ, *longæ,* hippagines, cercuri, celoces vel ut Græci dicunt celetes, lembi, oriæ, lenunculi, aƈtuariæ quas Græci ἐπικώπες vocant vel ᾽ἐπιβέλιδας, profumiæ vel geſeoretæ vel horiolæ, ſtlatæ, pontones, atatiæ, hemidiæ, phaſeli, parones, myoparones, lintres, caupuli, camaræ, placidæ, cidarum, ratariæ, cataſcopium. Julius Pollux claſſes them under other names, as prætoria ſeu turrita, roſtratæ, teƈtæ, conſtratæ, liburnicæ; onerariæ, caudicæ, curſoriæ, cuſtodiaræ, ſpeculatoriæ, tabellariæ, exeres, ſchediæ, epibates. Some were named from the *tutela,* others from cities and places where they were made, as Naxiurges from the iſland Naxo, Gnidiurges from Gnidus, Corcyriæ & Pariæ, from iſlands of the ſame name. *See Wolfgangus Lazius, l. 6. Comm. R. Rom.*

The Etruſcans were alſo the inventors of the naves roſtratæ; antea ex prora tantum & puppi pugnabatur; roſtra addidit Piſeus, Tyrrheni anchoram, *(Plin. l. 7. c. 56.)* or rather as Foxianus obſerves, Roſtrum addidit Piſeus Tyrrhenus, uti & anchoram.

Tratblong,

IRISH.

Trathlong, comlong, muirnsgib, longambarc, coimeada, bratha, a coafter, a look out fhip, a guard fhip on the coaft.

Breaflong, nabbarcba, riogblong, long ard-cobblagbeora, long-adala, long ad-mor-ala, priomblong, ceann-long, an admiral's fhip, a flag fhip; Arab. *adawlè.*

Lón-long, ftór-long, longftorais, a ftore fhip.

Ceatharn-long, buidbeanlong, a tranfport.

Long cbeannaithe, longmuirine, a merchant fhip.

Iomchar-long, aftarlong, long-malcaireacbta, a light fhip for paffage, or for making voyages of difcovery.

Featblong, brathlong, longambarc, a fpy fhip.

Long brataidbe, long meirge, long luimneachda, a fignal fhip, a flag fhip.

Long cbogaidb, a great war fhip; Arab. *adawlè-wugha.*

Long dba-rambaidb, long deil-cbeaflaidb, a galley with two banks of rowers.

Rufgan, a fhip made of bark, (Shaw;) fuppofed to be derived from *rufg,* the bark of a tree, but *rus* is timber alfo; Perficè *rofbun.*

Fuireann-loinge, trufgar-loinge, corugbadh-loinge, the tackle of a fhip.

Long-bbraine, fgafur-loinge, the prow; *fkibirr,* the poope.

Irr, urlar, clar-loing, the deck.

Crann-feoil, the maft, (arbor navis) Heb. *crann,* arbor; Chaldee, *tran,* a maft.

Barrcbrann-feoil, the top-moft.

Forcbrann-feoil, the fore-maft.

Iarcbrann

IRISH.

Iarcbrann feoil, the mizen-maft.

Seol, a fail; Arab. *jell.*

Luingeis, carlaoc, cabblach, fadith, plod, a fleet of fhips; Heb. Rabb. *mefaditha.*

Cadall, a fea fight; Arab. *keid.*

Meillacboir, long-feoir, mairneolac, martbidbe, arg. naoidb, fairrigeoir, cablacan, a failor; Heb. *cbebel, malach, aniuth;* Arab. *mullawb, nawte, ark, faure,* a failor; Copticè, *natyjawi, natyty,* a failor.

Long, a fhip or houfe, being common to the Mago-gian Irifh and the Gomerian Welfh, and to be found in the Chinefe, and not in the He-brew, Chaldee or Arabic languages; I conclude, this word is of Scythian origin. The Perfic *lenker,* an anchor; *lunjè,* to roll from fide to fide, and *lei,* a veffel for do-meftic ufe, have fome affinity to our *long.*

Another proof of the ancient Irifh being fkilled in the art of navigation, I draw from a fragment of the Brehon laws in my poffeffion, where the payment or reward for the education of children, whilft under the care of the fofterers, is thus ftipulated, to be paid to the ollamhs or profeffors, diftinguifhing private tui-tion from that of a public fchool. The law fays, " if " youth are inftructed in the knowledge of cattle, " the payment fhall be, three eneaclann and a feventh; " if in hufbandry and farming, three eneaclann, and " three fevenths; if in *meliacbt,* i. e. *glais-aigneadb as-* " *fearr,* that is, fuperior navigation, or the beft kind of " fea knowledge, the payment fhall be five eneaclann, " and the fifth of an eanmaide; if in *glais-aignedb*

is

" *istaini,* i. e. the second or inferior navigation, two
" Eneaclann and a seventh, and this low payment is
" ordained becaufe, the pupils muft previoufly have
" been inftructed in letters, which is the loweft edu-
" cation of all."

The word *meliacht* is not to be found in the common dictionaries.—We have feen that *Meilachoir* is a
mariner, and in O'Brien and Shaw's dictionaries,
meilliach is tranflated the terraqueous globe. In
Chaldee and Hebrew מלח *melach* is a failor, (Nauta.
See Plantavit.) In Arabic *mullawh* is a failor, and
melabet the art of navigation, and our Irifh *meilacht*
being explained by two other words fignifying marine
knowledge: the fenfe of it cannot be miftaken.

Carte in his hiftory of England, obferves, that the
conformity of religious worfhip between the people of
Delos, and thofe of the Hyperborei, produced a very
early correfpondence between them; for they are
mentioned by Herodotus, fays he, as utterly unknown to the Scythians, (who had no intercourfe
with the Britifh ifles) but much fpoken of at Delos,
whither they ufed to fend, from time to time, *facred
prefents of their firft fruits, wrapped in bundles of wheat
ftraw; fuch as were made ufe of by the* Thracians *in their
facred rights and facrifices to Diana;* and, adds Carte,
" There is not a fact in all antiquity, that made a
" greater noife in the world, was more univerfally
" known, or is better attefted by the graveft and moft
" ancient authors among the Greeks, than this of the
" facred embaffies of the Hyperboreans to Delos; in
" *times preceding, by an interval of fome ages,* the voy-
" ages of the Carthaginians, to the north of the
" ftreights

" ſtreights of Gibraltar, to which poſſibly the reports
" about that people might give the occaſion."

This author having collected every thing that the
ancient Greek writers have ſaid of Abaris, concludes,
that he was of the Hebrides or weſtern iſlands of
Scotland *; this agrees very ill with the deſcription of
the Hyperborean iſland, as being about the ſize of
Sicilly. It is indeed worthy of notice that the Iriſh
bards have carried our Dadanans in their return from
Greece and Italy, to the north of Scotland; but the
embaſſy of our Dadanans to thoſe countries, the nature of the embaſſy, and the particular mention of
Abras as the chief, leaves no room to doubt, in my
humble opinion, that he was from Ireland. It is indeed a matter of little moment, if he was of Ireland,
Scotland or Manx, for as I have ſaid before, they
were one and the ſame people, of the ſame (Druidical)
religion, and governed by the ſame laws.

It is ſuppoſed that Diodorus Siculus, was acquainted with Ireland under the name of Iris Britanniæ:
this name agrees much better with the Hebrides, for
as Carte obſerves, all this tract of iſles termed
Hebrides, was of old called Heireis:—to which we
may add the name Erſe ſtill retained in Scotland for
the Iriſh dialect:—in fine, theſe coaſts were little

---

* But he allows at the ſame time, that the ancient Greeks,
knowing very little of the northern parts of the world, comprehended the inhabitants thereof under general names: ſuch
as uſed bows and arrows, and lived like Numades, being termed
Scythæ; and thoſe who lived further north than the particular
nations whoſe names they had heard of being all called Hyperborei.

known

known to their hiſtorians, and Ireland may as well be meant by the Hyperborean iſland, as the Hebrides, Orkneys, or even Britain. If my poſition is right, of the Iriſh having poſſeſſed Britain and Ireland and the adjacent ſmall iſlands, till confined to the north of Scotland, Ireland and Manx, by the Gomerian Celts or Britons, (as they are now called) it is of no ſignification which of theſe was called Hyperborean by the ancient Greek writers. The fragment of the poem here produced, deſcribing Abaris, and his journey, may have been formed in Britain, and by tradition have come down to the Iriſh poets.

The ſacred preſents ſent to Delos by the Hyperboreans, we are told, were uſually accompanied by two young virgins, attended by five men, having the like ſacred character *. The fragment before us, makes no mention of ſuch a ſuite ; but this was not an embaſſy of that nature : it was a voyage performed by our Dadanans in queſt of knowledge, and ſuch was the expedition of the Hyperborean Abaris of Diodorus, &c. Herodotus, ſays, " that the ſuite of this Hy-
" perborean embaſſy, having been ill treated by the
" Greeks, they took afterwards another method of
" ſending their ſacred preſents to the temples of
" Apollo and Diana, delivering them to the nation
" that lay neareſt to them on the continent of Europe,
" with a requeſt that they might be forwarded to their
" next neighbours : and thus, (ſays Herodotus) they
" were tranſmitted from one people to another,
" through the weſtern regions, till they came to the

---

* Olymp. Ode 3d and 8th.

" Adriatic,

" Adriatic, and being there put into the hands of the
" DODONEANS, the firft of the Greeks that received
" them, they were conveyed thence by the Melian
" bay, Eubæa, Caryftus, Andras, and Tenos, till
" at laft they arrived at Delos."

I do not think the ftates of Europe, in this polite
age, could have been more civil, in forwarding a
prefent from Ireland to the pope or to the king of
Naples: and if I may be allowed to criticife on
Herodotus, I will fay, he has founded this ftory on
the journey of our Irifh Dadanans. For can it be
fuppofed that if the Greeks had been accuftomed to
receive *facred prefents of firft fruits*, to be facrificed to
Apollo at Delos, for a feries of years, and carried
thither by Hyperborean Druids, that they could poffibly have been at a lofs for the real fituation of that
ifland. It appears repugnant to common fenfe, and
I look upon this ftory to be fabricated by the Greeks,
from the expeditions made by the Dadanans of Ireland
or Britain, to Greece and Etruria, as recorded in the
ancient hiftory of Ireland.

There is a very ftriking affinity between the language of the ancient Irifh and that of the ancient
Etrufcans, for example.

The Etrufcans, (fay the authors of the univerfal
hiftory,) had feveral deities peculiar to themfelves,
viz.

Nortia was a goddefs held in high veneration.
Cormac archbifhop of Cafhel in the tenth century,
tells us in his gloffary, that Neart, is Virtus in Latin,
inde Neart, vel Saoith, Dia eigfi, i. e. Neart and
Saoith were the names of the deity of wifdom, with
the

the heathen Irish. And in the same glossary we find *Neid, Neitb, Dia Catba le Geinte Gaoidbeai,* i. e. Neid or Neit was the deity presiding over war, with the heathen Irish, and *Neid* nomina propria hominum a *Fomoriis* introducita, i. e. Neid, a proper name, introduced by the Carthaginians. In another glossary, I find, *Natb, ainm coitceand dona uilibb aifdibb*; i. e. Nath, is a common or general name for all sciences. *Neid, ainm gaotbe gloine,* i. *eig fi, Neid* is pure wisdom. *Ne Naith,* i. *teine Faid,* i. e. *Ne Naitb,* implies the wisdom of a prophet. *Pain* i. *ainm dur an Uafal,* i. e. Pain, a name given to nobles.

Ain. i. *Troidbe Dia, no Taulac, no Fen, no Mulloch,* i. e. Ain, Taulac, Fen and Mulloch are the gods presiding over battles.

Tein. i. *Teinm.* i. *Tuigfi-quafi Bal-tein, vel tion. Tion.* i. *Tofacb,* i. e. Tein, Teinm and Tuigfi implies wisdom, whence *Bal-tein* the god of wisdom; or *Baltion* the chief Baal, as *tion* implies head, chief, beginning, so that wisdom, fire, æther, were synonimous words. I take the *Valentia* of the Etruscans, to be our *Bal-ainitb,* or god of battles, corrupted to *Valainit.* Passerus in his Lexicon *Ægyptio Hebraicum,* explains these deities in the following manner.

" *Neit* Nֲֽ֣ט. Unum ex Minerve nominibus apud
" Ægyptios, ut constat ex Platone in Timæo, Urbis
" (Sais) præses Dea, Ægyptiace quidem Neit; Græce
" autem, ut illorum fert opinio ΑΘΗΝΑ." Utrumque nomen ex Hebræo est, eandemque retinet significationem sermonis, seu eloquentiæ. Nam ΑΘֲֽ֣η antiquis Græcis, Tuscis vero TINA est a תגה Thana, quo

quo etiam eloqui, & docere fignificatur. NEIT
vero eft a גאם, unde *Neum* fermo, elocutio; unde
Græcis ONOMA, Latinis NOMEN.

Arabic *Tunk* the fun, *tunk-puruft*, a worfhipper of
the fun, *afrookb-tun*, to fire, *fookb-tun*, to kindle,
angeekb-tun, to inflame.

In Irifh *Tine* and *Teine*, implies fire, *teinam* is to
diffolve, to melt. It is certainly the root of the
Englifh *Tin*, i. e. Oar eafily fufed, and of *Tinder* :
in fome parts of England they fay *tin* the fire, that is
ftir it up, make it burn. תגר Thanar in Hebrew is
furnus. *Itbunar* in Irifh is hell. Our Druids worfhipped the fun under the name of *Bel-tine*, or Baal's
fire, and I cannot think Pafferus right, in deriving
the Etrufcan *Tina* from the Hebrew *Tbana* docere,
becaufe we find in the works of the very learned
Millius, that Peltinus was the original Hebrew name
of *Montis Garizim*, on which the idolatrous Jews had
an altar of the fun. " In Hebræorum monumentis,
hoc de monte פלטנות (Peltinus) referunt : id vero
nomen montis *Garizim* effe." Rabbi S. Japhe
Afkenafi obfervat. *Peltinaus eft mons Garizim, quem
Cutbæi Samaritani fanctuarii loco babebant.* Now as the
Jews turned their faces to Jerufalem, and the Mahommedans to Mecca, in time of devotion, fo did
the Samaritans to Peltinaus. Oramus autem ad Do-
minum, facie ad montem Peltinaus (Garizim) do-
mum Dei (verfa) vefperi & mane. And the Samaritans continued this mode of worfhip in the time of
our Saviour, as we find in John ch. 4. v. 20. Our
father's worfhipped in this mountain : and ye fay,
that in Jerufalem is the place where men ought to
worfhip.

worſhip. (See Millius de cauſis Odii. p. 431. alſo in Epiſtolis Samaritanis Cellarii, p. 4.) Samaritani autem jam a Joſua, in eo monte (Garizim) ſynagogam & templum extruſtum fuiſſe contendunt. (Millius) Et Joſua Rex arcem extruxit in monte, qui adjacet ſiniſtro lateri montis Bendeſti, quique vocatur Samaria: (chron. Samar.) Here again is our Druidical *Sam-ar*, or mountain of *Sam* the ſun; the *Baal-tine*, and although many learned men have derived Garizim from the Arabic *garaz* excidit, obſcidit, yet we find the Samaritan name converted into Hebrew letters was הר גרזים *bar garizim*, but the old Arabian name for the ſun was *Khur* or *gur* and *zybb*, which compounded form *gurzybb*, and I have no doubt but this was the ſignification of the Samaritan name, as we find *Sam* was for the ſun and for the true God, and is the word uſed in Geneſis, ch. 1. of the Samaritan bible for the Hebrew *Aleim*. And if I am not miſtaken the Iriſh *Grian* the ſun is formed of *Gritham* to ſcorch, to boil, to burn, and *tine* fire, as we find it ſometimes writen *Grithan*. *Gris* in Iriſh is alſo intenſe fire, the ſun, and *Gris-chill* is now the Iriſh word for the ſanctuary. (See all the common Iriſh lexicons.) Therefore the Samaritan and Hebrew *bar-Garizim*, and the Iriſh *ar-gris* are all ſynonimous to *Ar-Sam* or *Sam-ar*, to which if we add the word *tan* which in Hebrew, Samaritan, Arabic and Iriſh, implies a country, region, diſtrict, we have *Sam-ar-tan*, and the Latin *Samaritania*, i. e. the country of the hill of the ſun, or our Iriſh *Bel-tine* and Etruſcan *Vol-tina*, as written by the Latins.

                        To

To this we will add the following obfervations of the learned Monf. Bailly : Vous favez, Monf. que chez les Chinois, le mot *Tien*, par lequel ils defignent l'Etre fupreme, fignifie primitivement le *Ciel*, & que le nom de Dieu des *Siamois*, viz. *Som-mona-kodom*, fignifie en Perfan, ciel ancien, ou ciel eternal & incrèè. Le Perfan, comme l'Hebreu, ne met point de difference entre ces fignifications. (*Lettres a Monf. Voltaire fur les Sciences.*) Here again is the Irifh *Sam-man-cad*, or the holy *man* or *mon* of *Sam*, i. e. the *Bel-teine*. With great propriety then, does this learned man afk this queftion, " pourquoi les Indiens ont-ils dans la " plus grande veneration le Mont Pir-pen-jal, l'une " des Montagnes du Caucafe fur les frontiers du petit " Thibet ? ils y vont en pelerinage."—The reafon is evident ; it was the *Borb-ain-fuil*, or mountain of the fun's revolution, of the Magogian Scythians, the common anceftors of the Indians and of the Irifh.

NEPHTIN. Hoc nomine juxta toties citatum Plutarchum, intelligebant Ægyptii finem, veneram, & VICTORIAM, Irifh, *tein*, force, ftrength ; *ieann*, bold, powerful ; *teann*, a love embrace ; *teannam*, to embrace a woman ; *tanas*, dominion, government ; *naom-tein*, the god of power, ftrength, victory ; thus *naom-tonn*, the deity of the fea.

MALCANDER. Nomen regis Biblii apud Plutarchum, qui uxorem habuit ASTARTEM, apud quos Ifis hofpitio excepta eft. Id nomen notat regem hominum a מלך, malach, regnare : unde Melech, rex : Ander vero Græcis ΑΝΔΡΩΣ, homo, eft ab אדם, Adam, rubere ; unde homo, eo quod ex rubra argilla

gilla compactus fit. Thus the learned Pafferius Pifav-renfis.

Malc, is a king in the Irifh language; but we have feen that *mullac* and *ain* were the Irifh names of the god of battles, (or angel fuppofed to prefide over battles, for our druids allowed but one God, the true almighty and omnifcient *one*) and *dae, daer,* a man, perfon.

If we fucced as well on a future day, with the reft of the Ægyptian and Tufcan deities, I flatter myfelf my readers will allow, that we have taken proper ground to proceed in our approaches towards an inveftigation of the ancient hiftory of Ireland, and that all is not fable, though at prefent obfcured in poetical fiction.

VENUS. Dictio Græcis ignota. Paufanias tradit antiquis Græcis etiam fuiffe ignotum, fed ab Ægeo e Phœnicia & Cypro in Græciam tranflatum. Tufcis id nomen VENDRA fuit, ut conftat ex antiqua patera, redoletque originem Hebraicam; nam מטרה-בן, Ben-tara, filia maris; quippe *tara* notat *humiditatem,* unde Græcis ΤΑΡΑΣ Neptuni filius.

In Irifh *bean, ban,* or *bhan,* (van) is a woman, daughter, female; and *trea, treathan, teathra, teara,* or *deathra,* the fea or ocean; hence the Tufcan *vendra* and Irifh *Ban-deara,* Venus. *Ban-dru* or *drutb,* is a harlot, and by miftaking the fenfe of *dru* and *dra,* probably arifes the lafcivious fables of the Greek and Latin poets refpecting this goddefs.

No people were fo celebrated for the magic art, as the Etrufcans; their defcendants, the Pelafgian-Ma-gogian

gogian-Irifh excepted : From the Etrufcans, it was in part handed down to the Latins, and from the following hint in Statius, I think that the Romans believed in the Metempfychofis * as well as our Irifh druids, witnefs the following lines on augury.

Seu quia mutatæ noftraque ab origine verfis,
Corporibus fubiere notos.

STATIUS.

And Ammianus Marcellinus fpeaks of this art, in terms, I believe, too myfterious for our underftanding at this day. Elementorum omnium fpiritus, ut pote perennium corporum præfentiendi motu femper, & ubique vigens, ex his quæ per difciplinas varias affectamus, participiat nobifcum munera divinandi & fubftantiales poteftates ritu diverfa placatæ, velut ex perpetuis fontium venis vaticina mortalitati fupeditant verba. *(Lib. 21. initio.)*

This magic art was certainly practifed before the *law* was written, as we find in Deuteronomy, ch. 18, 10. it is exprefsly forbid, and the art is mentioned under a variety of names, which have been all adopted by the Magogian-Irifh, but not by the Gomerian-Welfh, and there cannot be a ftronger proof of a dif-

---

* That Pythagoras took the doctrine of the Metempfychofis from the Bramins, is not difputed ; yet future times erroneoufly ftiled it Pythagorean, an egregious miftake, which could proceed only from ignorance of its original.

(Holwell's Hindoftan, p. 26, v. 2.)

Pythagoras died 497 years before Chrift, aged 80, (Trufler) his name both in Arabic and Irifh, denotes the great forcerer, or diviner.

K 2
ference

ference of religion between the ancient inhabitants of both countries; yet it is furprifing, that more oriental names in this art did not abide with them, from the firft Phœnician-Pelafgian-Irifh colonies that fettled there, and who were to all appearance driven thence by the Gomerians.

The Irifh words correfponding to the Hebrew, are as follow.

HEBREW.	IRISH.
kafam,	geafam, to divine; geafuph, a witch, a forcerer.
ounan,	oinin, ainin or ainius, a forcerer.
nahhafh,	neas, a diviner, a noble.
cheber,	geabhar, a forcerer.

The name Coarba given by the druids to St. Patrick is not greatly different, and Baal Aruch obferves, that this was a Perfian name; Perfæ vocant facerdotes fuos חברין, Chabrrin. The Etrufcan Samothracia, is of Arabian origin, viz. *fimia*, natural magic, and *tauric*, an augur; the Irifh words are *fuamb tarragb*, fometimes written *fuambain*; hence *fbaiman* fignifies a magician, at Tobal and Mofco. (*LeBrun.*)

The Hebrew *iadagnani* or *iadanani* is derived from *iad.ing*, he knew; it here implies a forcerer, and compounded with the Irifh *dea* or *daa*, a diviner, (Arab. *daa*, a forcerer,) forms the Irifh *Deadanan*. The old Irifh wrote it alfo with the found of the Hebrew ע, dagne, i. e. diogne, i. e. dræoichgne, Vet. Glofs. that is, dagne is a fpecies of druidifm: we alfo find the Chaldee דע to fignify fcientia, cognitio,

fententia

fententia in 32 ch. Job, v. 10. and this in Irifh is
dan. Caftellus.

The verfe before mentioned runs thus :

Deut. 18. and 10. v. There fhall not be found among
you קסם קסמים, (kafam kafamim) any one that
ufeth divination ; סעונן, (me, ounan,) an obferver
of clouds ; מנחש, me nahhafh,) enchanter ; מכשף,
(me cafaf) a witch ; חבר חבר, (cheber cheber,)
a charmer ; שאל אוב, (fal aub,) a confulter of
Aub ; ידעני, (iadagnani) a knowing one.

Caftellus interprets ידעני, ariolus, fciolus, futu-
rium divinator ; in the Syriac, magus, veneficus ;
in the Samaritan, omnifciens, (de Deo dicitur ;) in
the Æthiop. prædixit : fo that there cannot remain a
doubt of the proper fignification of the Irifh *Dadanan.*
Befides thefe names, our Irifh druids adopted another,
taken by the holy prophets of God, viz. *Ceadruicht*
or *Cadruicht,* in imitation of the Hebrew קדש רוח,
kodefruach, which implies, the *infpiration of the Holy
Ghoft,* whereby the party was enabled to prophecy
without apparitions or vifions. (*See Godwin's Mofes
and Aaron.*)

I believe no people in the weftern world, except
the Pelafgian Irifh admitted the אוב, aub, a fpecies
of forcerers who were faid to be ἐγγαςρίμυθες, or ventriloquifts ; that is, qui claufo ore loquuntur, quia videntur ex ventre loqui. The learned Selden, Feffel,
Van Dale and many others have written on this fubject. The rabbi's explain *aub* by פיתים, which is
thought to be the Greek πυθων, but I believe the Hebrew *pithim* here implies the fame as *aub,* i. e. uter,
for in the Irifh language *abb* and *puit* do both imply

uter ;

uter; *abb* alfo means the entrails in general ; *abb-aftradh* is to growl * inwardly, as a dog ; the Englifh and Flemifh *growl* feem alfo to be derived from the Irifh *goor*, a foothfayer, and *ambuil* or *ool*, like, fimilis ; i. e. *goorool*; *abbac* is a tarrier, becaufe of the growling noife he makes in his purfuit of game. That the oriental *aub* were forcerers, the learned Millius has very clearly demonftrated ; that the Irifh *abb* were forcerers alfo, is evident from the common verb *abb-fuidhim*, to prophecy, where *faidh* a prophet, is compounded with *abb*. Thefe were at the head of the Irifh forcerers, and I fhall hereafter fhew that there was a prefiding *aub* at each tower, and that the firft name for Chriftian, a bifhop in the Irifh language, was *aobb-ill-toir*, or an *aub* of many towers, or places of worfhip, for *tòr* not only implies a tower, but every thing belonging to a church †. *Aobilltoir*, i. e. *deoradh de*, i. e. *fer coragh de*, i. e. *Efpoc*, that is, *aobilltoir*, is a holy prophet, a bifhop. (*Commentator on the Brehon laws.*) But *efpoc* or *efpuc* is the fame as *aub-*

---

* The learned Spencer obferves, that *aub* or *obb* muft be an Egyptian word, and he refers to the Etrufcan *obba*, vas ventricofus, which muft be derived from this *aub*. This author's obfervation perfectly correfponds with the Irifh, in which language *oibne*, *abne*, *uibni* is a pitcher or bellyed can, and the Britifh and Englifh *pitcher* is from the Irifh *puit-cuar* ; *cuar*, a can, or veffel, *puit*, (*uter*) belly. I cannot conceive that the Greek *python* when applied to interpret *aub*, has any connection with the Hebrew *pethen*, or Syriac *pithun*, a ferpent; as we find that *aub* and *puit* in the Pelafgian, did both imply *uter*, correfponding to the Greek explanation per ἐγγασείμυθον.

† Hence *toir-dealbhach*, a proper name, now written *turloch* ; it originally fignified a tower-forcerer ; fee *dealbha* or *tealbha*, forcery.

puc,

puc, for *es* is *uter* and *poc* or *puic* is a forcerer. See
Lhwyd at *uter*. Hence the many places in Ireland
named *puic, phuic*, and *puican* ; as *Glann-phuic*, the forcerer's glinn. When chriftianity was eftablifhed, all
thefe names were turned into ridicule ; thus *draoi*, a
druid, now implies a witch ; *puic*, a fairy ; *puicin*, an
impoftor ; *puicinighe dubba*, dealers in natural magic,
witches, &c. &c. again, *aub-altoir* is the name of the
facred ftone under the chalice, in the altar of our mafs
houfes, it implies the altar of *aub* ; *eabul* is certainly
a ftone in Arabic, but has the fame derivation of our
aubaltoir, which like many other terms admitted into
the Irifh church, cannot be derived from any other
language than the Hebrew, Chaldee or Arabian.
Thus 1 Sam. 28, 8. Saul demands of the woman of
Endor קסומי נא לי באוב, *divina mihi quæfo per Aub*,
and afterwards adds, *et* ASCENDERE *fac mihi, quem
dico tibi* ; it is then evident that the *aub* was to confult
the *manes*, or infernal angels. Rab. Bechai therefore
explains *aub* or *obb*, *fpecies magorum eft & pythom vocatur, mortuumve elicit*, and adds, tradunt magiftri,
Baal Aub ex brachiis & axillis eorum loqui, nam (mor-
tuus) furgens, fedet fub brachiis ejus & loquitur :
and Apuleius confirms, that this kind of divination
was practifed by the Egyptians. "Zachlas adeft
"Egyptius, propheta primarius, qui mecum jam du-
"dum grandi præmio pepigit, *reducere fpiritum*, cor-
"pufque illud poft liminio mortis animare." (*Lib.* 2.
Metamorph. p. 62.) Bochart and Le Moyne think
thefe magi predicted *ab obb*, i. e. ferpente ;

becaufe

becaufe Hefychius explains οἰωνὸς by ὄφις *, but thefe
words both return to the Chaldee *ounan*, and *obb* or
aub, implying a forcerer. We fhall have occafion to
treat largely of thefe forcerers when we come to the
Milefian hiftory of Ireland, where the poets have
played off the whole artillery of divination, and fhall
therefore drop this fubject at prefent.

Aub, obh, being the magician or forcerer of the
Irifh, who was fuppofed to be able to converfe with
the dead, and perform fuch extraordinary feats by
fpeaking from his belly, with his mouth clofed; fo alfo
he was fuppofed to be mafter of all learning: hence
we have *abb-ghitir*, the name of the alphabet, from
ghitir, writing; *abb-litir*, the alphabet, from *litir*,
reading, writing, engraving; fee *fcriobam* in the conclufion: and from the Hebrew or Egyptian *aub* or
obb, are derived the following: *abb-che*, a fcholar;
abbac, a fprite, (Arab. hebka;) *abb-antur*, good luck,
good omen; *abb-rann*, bad omen; *abb-ran*, dark,
i. e. *ran*, feafon of *abb*, fprites, (Greek Εὐφρὶνη, νὺξ,

---

* Φήμεω & κληδὼν, (omen) are of Magogian or Pelafgian-
Irifh original alfo, i. e. *phaith-man*; *phaith* or *faith* ominator;
cleidh, myfterium; *oine*, ominatoris. I am much inclined to
think that *Caledonia*, or north of Scotland, is derived from
Clidh-oin-ia, i. e. the country of the myfterious ominators, feeing our *Dadanqnqi* fettled there fo long; yet, I acknowledge,
the Irifh *cleid*, the north, is much againft me; and here it will
not be amifs to mention, that the Greek *euroclydon*, which has
fo long entertained the critics, appears to me, no more than the
Pelafgian Irifh *oir-o-cleid*, eaft from the north, or a north-north-
eaft wind, which fo much endangered St. Paul,—of the μλω, *man*,
we are yet to treat in our topography of Ireland.

Hefychius

Hefychius from Æfchylus;) *abb-eil*, calumniator; *di-abb-eil*, the devil, (Arab. ablis, iblis;) *abb-fuigbam*, to be aftonifhed; *abhfe*, a fprite; *abb-feoir*, the devil, a gafconader, adverfary; *abbta*, *ubbta*, *upta*, forcery, witchcraft; *obban*, *uabban*, fear, dread, forcery; *obbnacb*, terrible; *uabb*, fear, dread, horror, miracle, (Perficè *ujubè*, Arab. *aajib*, miracle, prodigy, wonders;) *ubb-gaoitb*, whirlwind, i. e. *gaoitb*, or wind of *ubb* or *aub*; *ubb-uifce*, a whirlpool or water of *Aub*.

As I am of no party, have no fyftem to fupport, but write for information, and have produced ancient and refpectable authority for every thing here offered, fupported by living evidence, *the language of the people*: I think it candid to mention one great objection that occurs to me, againft this attempt to elucidate the hiftory of Ireland: it is this; the Irifh chriftian writers of the early ages, pofitively affert, that our Hibernian druids, permitted no idol worfhip, no graven images; and what feems to confirm this affertion, is, that no images have ever been found in our bogs, among the various reliques of druidifm, which have been difcovered. They fay, that the unhewn ftones capped with gold and filver, to reprefent the fun and moon, furrounded with twelve others, to reprefent the angels prefiding over the feafons or months, or by nineteen others, to reprefent the *lunar cycle*, or by twenty-eight, to reprefent the *folar cycle*; were the only fpecies of idolatry to be found; and hitherto, experience and obfervation lead me to believe it, and this furround of ftones was called the *cill* or *kill*, from whence *cill* now implies a place of devotion, a church; but we meet with many Cill in Ireland, where no traces of a chriftian church are to
be

be found, confequently they receive their names from the druidical temples which once ftood in thofe places. The word *cill* is not from the Latin *cella* as fome have imagined, but from the Hebrew *chill :* inter montem templi & atrium mulierum, erat חיל, *chill,* five προτείχισμα, fpatium antemurale. (Relandus Antiq. facræ. p. 29.) Cineres hujus vaccæ collecti in tres partes dividebantur—una in חיל, *chill,* five antemurali fervabatur in memoriam exuftioni. (Idem, p. 109.) The circle of ftones was called *cir,* as I have often mentioned, hence *cir-goor* or *kirgaur* was the name of the circles built by the augurs, and are always diftinguifhed by this name from the *cabara. Cirgaur* was the ancient name of *Stone Henge* in England. *Cirgaur* exifts in many places in Ireland, particularly near lough Gaur in the County of Limerick. This word has been miftaken by Mr. Cooke for two Hebrew words, viz. כיר, *cir,* the chonca marina, or any round building, and גור, *gaur,* congregatio. (*Cooke's Enquiry,* p. 52.)

The fame obfervation has been made of the Gomerian Celts by the learned Adamus Bremenfis. " Deos " fuos neque templis includere, neque ulla hamani " oris fpecie affimilare, ex magnitudine & dignitate " celeftium arbitrati funt; lucos & nemora confecran- " tes, deorumque nominibus appellantes, fecretum " illud fola reverentia contemplabantur." (*Hift. Ecclef.* c. 6.) He then gives a drawing and defcription of a druidical altar in Germany, at a place called *Brut-kamp,* and obferves, *brut,* hariolari, licet; but modeftly expreffes his doubts of this explanation : this is the Irifh *briocl,* a forcerer; derived of the Hebrew ב *Ruach,*

בּ *Ruach*, to divine by the Holy Ghoſt, as before explained: how then does this agree with Cæſar's deſcription of the Germans *neque Druides habent, neque ſacrificiis ſtudent.* (Bell. Gall. lib. 6.)

The ancient Arabs had alſo the rude upright ſtone or pillar. Arabes Deum quidem colunt, qualem tatamen minime novi: ſtatua autem quam vidi, erat quadratus lapis. (Maximus Tyrius.) The modern Arabs ſtill pay great veneration to this ſtone. Sic hodieque Meccæ in Alcahaba, lapidem nigrum colunt Arabes, & ob reverentiam oſculantur. (Bochart.) The learned Spencer, fully proves, that theſe pillars were the Cham-manim or Hham-manim of the Ægyptians. Nam Scriptura Sacra de Cham-manim loquitur tanquam columnis aut ſtatuis excelſis, aut in altum elevatis, non tanquam ſimulacris in formam orbicularem fabrefactis. Sic itaque naturam & formam eorum explicandam cenſeo. Chammanim Symbola quædam erant, aut figura conica, vel pyramidali facta, quibus idololatræ veteres ad ſolis & ignis cultum utebantur. Nam Deus ille in quo ſolem colebant veteres, ab Ægyptiis Ammon, ab Africanis Hammon, ab aliis Omanus, dictus eſt.—Veriſimili itaque conjectura ducor ut ſentiam, idololatras antiquos ad radii ſolaris formam, & ignis (ſymboli ſolaris) figuram pyramidalem, ea plerunque compoſuiſſe.— Non temere dubitandum eſt, Ægyptios, Solem, Lunam & Sydera impenſe coluiſſe.

Spencer derives Chamman from חמה a word in the Hebrew and Ægyptian languages, ſignifying heat, and the ſun as the fountain of heat. (Spencer De Legibus Hebr. v. 1. c. 25.) The latter part of the
compound,

compound, viz. *man*, fignified the emblem, and fometimes god : from this word *man*, many of the hills and mountains in Ireland receive their name ; as Sliabh-na-man, Man-garton, Man-a-Bheil or Man-avulla, &c. &c. and on the tops of all thefe, the Chammamin are ftill to be found.

The fcripture feems to diftinguifh the worfhippers of Baal in the groves, as having no graven images. 2 kings, c. 21. 1. Manaffeh did after the abomination of the heathen whom the lord caft out.—He built up again the places, he reared up altars for Baal and made a grove and worfhipped all the hoft of heaven and ferved them—he built altars in the houfe of the lord—he built altars for all the hoft of heaven, in the two courts of the houfe of the lord, and he made his fon pafs through the fire, and obferved times and ufed enchantments and dealt with familiar fpirits and wizards, and he fet a graven image of the grove that he made in the houfe.

And in Leviticus we find a diftinction made between the graven image and the upright unwrought ftone. Ch. 26. 1. Ye fhall make no idols, nor graven image, neither rear you up a ftanding image (pillar) neither fhall ye fet up any image of ftone (Heb. a ftone picture) in your land, to bow down unto it.

2 Kings, 17. 29. Howbeit every nation made gods of their own ; and put them in high places, which the Samaritans had made every nation in the city wherein they dwelt.—V. 30. The men of Babylon made Succoth benoth,—the men of Cuth, made Nergal,—the men of Hamoth, made Afhima,—and the Avites made Nibboz, &c. &c. fo that we find thefe idolaters clearly

ly diftinguifhed from the grove worfhippers of Baal.
Again we find the Ægyptians very early mentioned
as having magicians. Gen. 41. 8 And Pharoah fent
and called for all the magicians of Egypt and the wife
men.—V. 45. Can we find fuch a one as this is, a
man in whom the fpirit of God is? And he gave him
to wife Afinath, the daughter of Potipherah, prieft of
ON.

"Egypt (fays Mr. Hutchinfon) had priefts and
"they had lands affigned them ; and 'tis likely they
"and the magicians were the fame, and I think the
"city of ON, mentioned early, was a place of wor-
"fhip dedicated to this power, and that they had tow-
"ers, as the tower of Syene and Naph, Pathros,
"Zoan, Sin, No, Auen, Phibefeth, Tohaphnehes;
"fome are proper names, and 'tis likely the reft were
"fuch. And they had images, poles, or pillars,
"upon the tops of the towers. And they had pillars
"which 'tis likely were fet up as memorials of fome
"pretended atchievements of their gods, before wri-
"ting was : whether they were only pillars, or they
"had each the enfign of the fun, or a globe with rays
"of light on the top, and fo were called images of
"the light and fun, I am not certain, and thefe gods
"were called Dungy Gods, by way of contempt."
Mr. Hutchinfon has here exactly pourtrayed the worfhip of our Hibernian Druids, who with a knowledge
of the true God, mixed an abominable worfhip of the
infernal angels, and as Erafmus and Olaus Wormius
obferve of the German Druids, gratâ quâdam cultus
viciffitudine, cibis fumptis, hymnos facros in honorem,
veri & fupremi numinis ceciniffe.

And

And Tacitus informs us, that the Swedes thought it unworthy of the celeftial gods, to be fhut up in temples, or to bear any human refemblance. "Cæterum nec cohiberi parietibus Deos, nec in ullam humani oris fpeciem affimilare ex magnitudine cœleftium arbitrantur." (De mor. Germ.)

2 Kings, 23. 5.—And the king, (Jofiah) commanded to bring forth out of the temple of the lord, all the veffels that were made for Baal and for the grove, and for all the hoft of heaven and he burnt them.—And he put down the idolatrous priefts, whom the kings of Judah had ordained to burn incenfe in the high places, in the cities of Judah and in the high places round about Jerufalem : them alfo that burned incenfe unto Baal, to the fun and to the moon and to the planets, (TWELVE SIGNS OR CONSTELLATIONS) and to all the hoft of heaven.

Deutr. 7. 5. Ye fhall deftroy their altars and break down their pillars, and cut down their groves, and burn their graven images with fire. V. 25. Thou fhalt not defire the filver nor gold that is upon them.

Our Dungy priefts, as Mr. Hutchefon calls them, (inftead of דעני Danani,) our priefts of On, in the country of Tir-Oin, had one On, Clogh *, or ftone pillar,

---

* _Onn_ is rendered in the Irifh Lexicons, a ftone, but it implies a ftone pillar dedicated to the fun. We find _On, Eon, Aon_ in the old gloffaries, explained by _Sam_, i. e. the fun. And _Ong_ is a fire, a hearth, from the fires conftantly kept burning in honour of Baal or the fun—and as the priefts of the fun, were admitted by unction, _Ongadh_ is to anoint, whence _ong_ has various meanings as, clean, clear, healing, curing, anointing, fire, ftone, hearth, forrow, grief, a figh, gain, profit,

pillar, remarkable for the quantity of gold, with which it was overlaid; this was called by way of eminence On-oir or Clogh-oir, and the place where this stood, is now a bishop's fee, known by the name of Clogher: this is the common tradition, but I think Clogh-oir is derived from *aire* forcery,—the ruachan-stone, *vulgo* rocking-stone, is described by Borlase; it was the prophetic stone or oracle.

Notwithstanding all these authorities drawn from the sacred writings, and the great uniformity and similitude that reigns in all the ancient Irish MSS. between the worship of the ancient Irish and that of the ancient Egyptians, Chaldæans and Phœnicians, I cannot prevail upon myself to think, that, our mixt colony of Pelafgian or Magogian Scythians, Phœnicians and Ægyptians, did emigrate to this country at fo remote a period; and yet it is certain that the most ancient idolaters built no temples, and like our Irish Druids, chose the tops of the highest hills and mountains for their altars and places of worship. Thus Herodotus tells us of the ancient Persians, that, " they had no images, neither did they build altars or temples; charging those with folly who did those

fit, &c. &c. Hence the temple of Onias near Memphis, built by permiffion of Ptolemy Philametor, which the Greeks called Ονιε ιερον and often Ονειον and the adjacent country ονιε χωρα and the metropolis known also by the name of Heliopolis, was changed to Ονιε μητροπολις and then it was ludicroufly faid the Jews had worfhipped there an afs τον ονον, but what is moft extraordinary, the Gnoftics, chriftians of Judea, in the firft ages the church, reprefented their god Sabaoth in the figure of an 'afs, and a monkifh ftory was foon trumped up of Zacharias having feen Sabaoth in his affanine form !!!

things:

things: but that when they went to facrifice to
Jupiter, they afcended the higheft parts of the mountains." Strabo obferves likewife of them, " that
they had neither images nor altars, but facrificed to
the gods upon fome high place."—Thus we find
Cyrus having had a dream which affured him his end
drew near, " facrificed," fays Xenophon " on the
fummit of a mountain, as is the cuftom in Perfia.
And the fame was likewife practifed by the inhabitants
of Pontus and Cappadocia. (Appian de Bello Mi-
thrid.)

They certainly learned this, and the planting their
places of worfhip with trees, of the old patriarchs,
who thought it an unfit thing to confine the infinity
of God's majefty, and therefore made choice of
mountains rather than other places, for the worfhipping of God, and to facrifice to him upon ; planting
them with trees, that the awfulnefs of the fhade
might contribute to the raifing their devotion, and
render them proper folemn places for the adoration of
the deity. But the gentiles, (modern when compared to the Irifh Druids) though they retained mountains and groves for their public worfhip, foon corrupted their opinions which firft brought them into
ufe. Having made the fun, moon and ftars, objects
of their worfhip, they had the fairer view of their
gods, and thought it was agreeable to their advanced
ftation to worfhip them on the higheft afcents, and
that their prayers and facrifices would be more avail-
ing in thofe places, than in valleys; for, being nearer
to their deities, they might in their opinion, be the
eafier heard and better obferved by them. Thus
Lucian

Lucian tells us, that they had in the porch of the temple at Hierapolis which " ftood on the knob of a hill,
Priapus's three hundred cubits high, into one of
which a man gets up twice a year, and dwells feven
days together in the top of the phallus, that he may
converfe with the gods above, and pray for the profperity of Syria; which prayers, fays he, are the better heard by the gods for his being near at hand."—
This was the opinion of Lucian, but the fact is, thefe
pillars or round towers, were made for celeftial obfervations, as thofe ftill ftanding in Ireland, were by
our Druids. Tacitus was of the opinion of Lucian;
fpeaking of fome very high mountains, he fays, that
they did "maxime Cælo appropinquare, precefque
mortalium a Deo nufquam proprius audire." This
led the more grofs idolaters to dedicate their mountains
to fome particular deity. "In the early dawn of fuperftition, fays Lucian, mankind was content to confecrate their groves, mountains and plants, to fome
particular god."—Hence it is that Æfchylus calls the
Lydian mountain Tmolus ἱερὸν Τμῶλον, and Philoftratus
tells us, that the Indians called the mountain Caucafus,
Θεῶν Ὄικος. But, we muft confider thefe accounts are
given us by grofs idolators, for Jamblicus tells us,
(Sect. 1. c. 17.) from the old books of the Ægyptians,
that they efteemed the fun, moon and ftars, only the
feats of fuch celeftial fpirits as take care of human affairs. And the Philofophers Pythagoras, Plato, &c.
who travelled into the Eaft in fearch of knowledge,
were not fo abfurd as to believe that the hoft of heaven were really and abfolutely gods, but taught at
their return, that they were the feats and refidence of

their gods. Therefore Zeno, when he afferts, that the fun, moon and ftars, are intelligent and wife, fiery fire, muft be underftood to mean, that thefe bodies, which he imagined to be compofed of fire, were informed and actuated by a wife intelligent being: wherefore Pofidonius fays of the Stoicks, that they thought a ftar to be a divine body. And Philo the Jew, who was a great Platonizer, calls the ftars, " divine images, and incorruptible and immortal fouls;" which muft be in regard of the fpirits which he fuppofed informed them: and Proclus calls the fun the king of intellectual fire; this makes Homer, fay " the fun from his lofty fphere all fees and hears." (Od. 12. v. 326.) Agreeable to this, Anaxagoras was condemned by the Athenians, and fined and banifhed, becaufe he held the fun to be nothing but a mere mafs of fire, and the moon a habitable earth; as if the denying them to be animated, was the fame thing as to deny them to be gods. Hence the Baal of the eaft and of Ireland, the fuppofed agent of the *Ti-mor*, became the Greek ℨꞷ́ꙅ, (from the Pelafgian Irifh *fos*, omnifcient) and the Roman Jupiter, that they made to inhabit the fun: a ftrong proof of what filly and abfurd hypothefes men are capable of erecting, when once they give way to vain fpeculations, and fcience falfely fo called, and what fools they become, when once they profefs themfelves wife! It would be happy for the world, fome modern chriftians were as free from cenfure, as the pagan Hibernian Druids were.

In low flat countries, they raifed artificial afcents for their altars: thefe carns are innumerable over Ireland, Scotland and England. Kircher is of opinion,

that

that this was the use of the Ægyptian pyramids: in confirmation of his opinion, he produces Abenephius an Arabian, who says, " the Ægyptian priests piled up huge stones in the figure of a cone, or lofty pyramid, and called them, the altars of their gods." And he affirms, that the Coptites likewise called them the pillars and altars of the gods.

When the Spaniards first came into Mexico, they found the same sort of places built for worship there. Gage describes them as their common temples; one of them, he says, " was a square mount of earth and stone, fifty fathom long every way, built upwards like to a pyramid of Egypt, saving that the top was not sharp, but plain and flat, and ten fathoms square; upon the west side were steps up to the top, that their priests might turn their backs to the sun, for their prayers were made towards the rising sun."

By the account Gemelli gives us of the Mexican pyramids at Teotiguacan, (which in that language, signifies, says he, *a place of gods*, or of *adoration*,) they like the Ægyptian, were erected both for sepulchres and the worship of their gods: the first he saw was that of the *Moon*, about fifty yards high. This Mexican word is literally Irish, *Ti-teag-uaghan*, the sepulchre of the house of the spirit (God.) See *Ti* explained in Xth Number collated with the Chinese.

All these examples are convincing proofs of the remote antiquity of the ancient inhabitants of Ireland, and I flatter myself, the learned will agree, that the ancient language of the Irish is worthy of preservation, and is of use in illustrating the sacred and profane authors.

The

The ingenious Eugene Aram derives all this fimi-litude of cuftoms, language, &c. between the Irifh and Britifh, from the Celtæ, whofe language he fays was the foundation of the Greek and Latin—" that Celtic which polifhed by Greece and refined by Rome, and which only, with dialectic difference, flowed from the lips of Virgil and thundered from the mouth of Homer."—I flatter myfelf to have thrown new lights on this curious fubject, and to have proved that the old language of thefe iflands, was originally Paleftine-Scythic: it was in fact the language of that people which Monfieur Bailly calls *l'ancien peuple perdu.* (Lettres fur les Sciences and Voltaire's obfervation on them.) And if I may be allowed the expreffion, I efteem the Irifh, Erfe and Manx to be thefe very ancient people, and therefore they may properly be called *l'ancien peuple perdu, retrouvèe.* Dans l'Hiftoire de l'Aftronomie ancienne, publiee l'annèe derniere, on a parlè d'un peuple dètruit & oubliè, qui a prècè-dè & èclaiiè les plus anciens peuples connus. On à dit que la lumiere des Sciences & la philofophie fem-blaient être defcendues du nord de l'Afie, ou du moins avoir brillè fous le parallele de 50 degrès, avant de s'etendre dans l'Inde & dans la Chaldèe. On n'a point eu l'intention d'avancer des paradoxes: on a dit fimplement ce que les faits ont indique. (Lettres fur les Sciences. Preface.)

In conformity to cuftom, I have hitherto adopted the term Hiberno-Celtic for the language of the an-cient Irifh; now the Scythians or Tartars, the pofte-rity of Gomer, were the real Celtæ of the Greeks and Romans, and the Irifh Seanachies never acknowledge
themfelves

themfelves to be the defcendants of Gomer, but of Magog: Doctor Parfons has made this obfervation; " It is very remarkable, fays he, that the earlieft Irifh records are as clofely conformable to fcripture, in the divifion of the world between the fons of Noah, as they are in other refpects; efpecially if it be confidered, that feveral of them were wrote long before revealed religion was received in Europe, and others compofed and handed down by the fileas and bards, many centuries before the birth of Chrift, and committed to writing in later times: and in fuch of them as I have feen, not much is faid of Gomer, but they derive the firft inhabitants that came into Ireland, and indeed every other colony that afterwards invaded it, from Magog, the father of the Scythians. (*Remains of Japhet*, p. 162.)

The doctor then concludes with faying, that the firft inhabitants of Ireland were Magogian Scythians, and the firft of Britain were Gomerians; yet in the fubfequent part of his work, he attempts to prove that the languages were the fame: they were fo, moft probably, whilft they remained together in Scythia, but I am convinced that neither the Irifh or the Welfh will allow that they are fo at this day, or have any appearance of having been the fame language, at any time fince their arrival in Europe. I flatter myfelf to have traced the caufe of this variation, by deriving the Irifh from that great body of Magogian Scythians who at one time over-run Paleftine and mixed with the Phœnicians and Ægyptians, and in the conclufion of this work, I propofe to draw ftronger proofs of my affertions from language.

It

It is certain that the Polytheiſm of the modern Greeks, or even of the modern Ægyptians or Phœnicians, never were introduced into the druidical religion of Ireland. The druids taught the worſhip of the true God; they believed in ſubordinate deities or angels preſiding over the actions of mankind; they believed in a future ſtate of happineſs and the immortality of the ſoul; but they knew nothing of Apollo, Jupiter, Mars, &c. &c. they paid a veneration to the ſun, moon and ſtars, as the agents of the true God; and theſe were called *Cabara*, the great ones; כביר in Hebrew and Arabic, (potens;) the ancient Ægyptians and Phœnicians did the ſame, and had their *Cabiri*, which Pluche thinks were Oſiris, Orus and Iſis. (*Euſebius de præpar. Evang. l.* 1. & *Plato in Cratylo,* & *Abbé Pluche.*) The Iriſh druids held a correſpondence with the Greeks after they had adopted Polytheiſm, yet they would never permit ſuch groſs idolatry into their worſhip: like the ancient Scythians their anceſtors, they were ſo tenacious of their own laws, cuſtoms and worſhip, that they puniſhed every perſon who made the leaſt attempt to follow thoſe of any other nation: this was the remark of Herodotus in his Melpom. Anacharſis, a famous Scythian philoſopher went to Athens to pay a viſit to Solon, and was greatly admired by the Greek law-giver, for his great learning and extenſive knowledge:—but, becauſe he affected the manners and cuſtoms of the Greeks, when Anacharſis was ever mentioned, the Scythians would anſwer they knew nothing of him."

"Now

" Now, fays Doctor Parfons, becaufe the Scythian philofophers taught the doctrine of a future ftate, fome authors imagined they had it from Pythagoras; but we may, without doing any violence to fuch hiftorians, reverfe this opinion, and affert that he was taught by the Gomerians or Scythian theologifts. Abaris was a very famous philofopher among the Scythians; he and Zamolxis wrote of a place of blifs after this life, and if we give credit to the words of Trajan, they believed they fhould live again. Thefe and many other Scythian philofophers mentioned in the Irifh records, who flourifhed feveral centuries before Pythagoras was thought of, had always correfpondence with the Gomerian fages, the druids, even from the time of Japhet; and it is certain, that the moft ancient nations had their knowledge of thefe matters from Noah and his iffue; the purer doctrines from that of Japhet and Shem, the more corrupt from that of Ham: fo that the Gomerian, Scythian or Magogian, and Chaldæan philofophers had originally the fame pure notions of the DEITY, and did not deviate in any wife, till idolatry and polytheifm had overtaken them, and caufed in many places, their divifion into different fects refpectively. But the affinity in the fyftems of the Scythians and Gomerians in their notions of the theogeny, lafted longer; for, when idolatry had overtaken them, the corruption affected them both alike, as they migrated weft and northweft upon the continent of Europe; but *the worfhip of* GOD *was untainted in* BRITAIN *and* IRELAND many ages after its adulteration elfewhere." (*Remains of Japhet, p.* 140.)

" Doctor

"Doctor Burnet makes no question but the druids
"were of the ancient race of wife men; not the Gre-
"cian, fays he, whom Pliny, after the oriental ex-
"preffion, calls the Magi of the Gauls;—in fhort it
"is not an eafy matter to point out the rife and firft
"ages of the druids."

Strabo fays, the Turditani or Bœtici who were the
wifeft of the Iberians, had commentaries of antiquity,
together with poems, and laws written in verfe, feveral thoufand years old. Doctor Parfons has proved
thefe Iberians were Magogian Scythians; again, fays
the Doctor, the Hetrurians of Italy, were a fet of
Philofophers, who, according to Diod. Sicul. applied
themfelves to the ftudy of nature, efpecially the phe-
nomena of the atmofphere, portents and prodigies;
befides which, they philofophifed concerning the origin and end of the world, and the time of its duration;
infomuch, that upon every unufual appearance in nature, they were always confulted, even by the ftate,
as well as individuals, and their decifion was held facred, and their advice followed: Who were the Hetrurians, but a race defcended from the firft PELASGI,
who went into Italy after the flood? And who were
the Pelafgi, but Gomerians and Magogians from the
ifles of Elifha and Iberia, which I have fufficiently
proved elfewhere? And in fine, who were thefe latter
"Hetrufcan philofophers, but a felect fect of ftudents
"taught by the druids, and in time diftinguifhed by
"the name *Hetrufci*; but not till after the Latin lan-
"guage was formed." (*Remains of Japhet*, p. 141.)

Milton, an author, who was as full of learning, as
he was void of illiberal prejudices, who was an enemy

to low fervility, or partial narrow fentiments, and not
at all addicted to credulity, tells us, " that learning
" and fciences were thought by the beft writers of an-
" tiquity, to have been flourifhing among us, and
" that the Pythagorean philofophy, and the wifdom
" of Perfia had their beginning from Britain; fo that
" the *druids* of the Gomerians, and the *fileas* of the
" Magogians, whether in thefe iflands or on the con-
" tinent, were the original fages of Europe in all the
" fciences from Japhet."

" The druids of the continent never committed
" their myfteries to writing, fays Doctor Parfons, but
" taught their pupils *memoriter:* whereas, thofe of
" Ireland and Scotland, wrote theirs, but in charact-
" ers different from the common mode of writing;
" but thefe were well underftood by the learned men,
" who were in great numbers, and had not only ge-
" nius, but an ardent inclination to make refearches
" into fcience; and therefore they were the more rea-
" dy to receive the light of the gofpel from Patrick, ef-
" pecially as great numbers continued diffentients,
" all along, from the fuperftitions of the druidical fyf-
" tem; and it was with a general confent, and the
" applaufe of the learned, that this apoftle committed
" to the flames two hundred tracts of the pagan myf-
" teries.' (*Remains of Japhet*, p. 144.)

Thofe great antiquaries, Lhwyd, Rowland and
Borlafe, make the fame obfervations refpecting the
Irifh druids committing their tenets to writing, whereas it was death for a druid of the Gomerian race, both
in England and Gaul. Can it then be fuppofed, that
the

the religious tenets of the Hibernian druids, and of the Welſh, were the ſame?

They differed alſo in another very material cir-cumſtance: thoſe of the Gomerian race had ſuch power and aſcendancy over the minds of the people, that even kings themſelves paid an implicit ſlaviſh obedience to their dictates; inſomuch, that their ar-mies were brave in battle, or abject enough to decline even the moſt advantageous proſpects of ſuccefs, ac-cording to the arbitrary prognoſticks of this ſet of re-ligious tyrants; and their deciſions became at laſt pe-remptory in civil, as well as in the affairs of reli-gion.

But this ſlaviſh conceſſion to the wills of the druids never prevailed in Ireland, notwithſtanding the gene-ral eſteem they were in with the vulgar, becauſe they had ſchools of philoſophy, and their princes were as well verſed in the nature of things as their prieſts, and therefore ſcience gave them liberty to think for them-ſelves. Their *fileas* ſupported this ſpirit in the gentry, and their *brehons* or judges ſuperintended in civil mat-ters; ſo that the druids had no power in the framing or adminſtration of the laws.

The learned Cooke in his enquiry into the patriar-chal and druidical religion, ſays, "Not to lay any "greater ſtreſs than needs, upon the evidence of the "affinity of words, with the Hebrew and Phœnician, the "multitude of altars and pillars, or temples ſet up in the "ancient patriarchal way of worſhip, throughout ENG-"LAND, IRELAND, SCOTLAND, and the ISLANDS, "form an argument concluſive, that an ORIENTAL "colony muſt have been very early introduced."

Sammes

Sammes in his history of Britain, brings the Phœnicians to Britain in the time of Joshua ; for, says he, they were driven up into a slender nook of earth, too narrow to contain so great and numerous a body, they disceded themselves into good shipping, to seek their fortunes in most parts of the world, of whose company Britain received a considerable share.

Carte, author of the general history of England, says, it was about 450 years before Christ, that these Phœnicians first discovered the British isles; and a trade to these parts was opened by the Carthaginians, who about the year of Rome 307, sent Hanno and Hamilcar, with each a fleet, to sail, the one south, the other northward from the Streights of Gibraltar, to discover the western coasts of the continent of Africa and Europe, and the islands that lay in the Atlantic ocean. (P. 41.)

Now Carthage was founded by the Tyrians 1259 years before Christ; is it probable that a nation so well skilled in navigation, would reside there 800 years without being acquainted with the Atlantic ocean? Bishop Huet asserts, that before the time of Joshua, some colonies of Phœnicians were settled on the coast of Africa ; for the expedition of the Phœnician Hercules into Africa, says he, was about 300 years before Jasan went to Colchis. And it is this Hercules that Sanchoniathon has mentioned under the name of Melecarthus, and therefore his voyage into Africa was preceding the time of Gideon, cotemporary with Sanchoniathon. So that before the time of Solomon, of Hyrom and of Homer, the Phœnicians had overrun the greatest part of the coast of the ancient world.

Be

Be it noted that the Phœnician word *Melecart*, in Irish signifies skilled in navigation. (See p. cxxii.)

M. l'Abbé de Fontenu has clearly proved that the Phœnicians had an established trade with Britain before the Trojan war, 1190 years before Christ, (*Mem. de Litterature*, tom. 7. p 126.) and that this commerce continued for many ages; that the Carthaginians afterwards took up this trade, and excluded all other nations from the knowledge of the situation of Britain, and quotes a passage from Strabo, where he relates that the captain of a Carthaginian vessel, seeing himself followed by a Roman fleet, chose to steer a false course, and land upon another coast, rather than shew the Romans the way to Britain; so jealous were the Carthaginians of enjoying the immense profits they got by the fine tin of the Britannic isles *.

Who then can doubt, says the Abbé, but that the ancient Britains, after that close correspondence with the Phœnicians and Carthagenians, for so many ages, had adopted, not only the manners and customs, but even the religion of the Phœnicians. For, this commerce could not have lasted during so great a space of time, if the Phœnicians had not great establishments in these islands, and the liberty of making a public profession of their religion. The Abbé then proceeds to shew, that the Saxons borrowed from the Britains the worship of Isis, a deity of the Phœnicians, which the Saxons, he thinks communicated to the Swedes, and here the Abbé quotes the follow-

* If the Carthaginians could alter their course at sea, at pleasure, they certainly had the use of the compass. See *Fan-iul* in the conclusion of this number.

ing

ing paffages of Tacitus, " fignum ipfum, Ifidis, in modum libernæ figuratum docet advectam religionem."—And alfo—"pars Suevorum & Ifidi facrificat" to prove that the Swedes reprefented Ifis in the form of a fhip. I am of opinion that Tacitus here confirms the Arkite worfhip, fo learnedly handled by my worthy friend Mr. Bryant, becaufe *Efs* and *Eis* in Irifh, or Magogian Scythic, and *ajooz* in Arabic, fignify a fhip: and Apuleius tells us, that the moft expreffive fymbol of Ifis, with the Ægyptians, was a veffel of water.

To this let us add that the ancients attributed the invention of navigation and the art of building fhips to Ifis and Ofiris, and affert, that the fhip in which Ofiris failed, was the firft long fhip that had been upon the fea, for which reafon the Ægyptian aftronomers placed this fhip in the celeftial conftellations: it is the fame, the Greeks afterwards named the conftellation of Argo; but Eifs-aire and Arg in Irifh are fynonimous names for a fea commander. Some authors obferve, that if Ifis had been known to the Pelafgians and other ancient Greek nations, Homer would certainly have mentioned this deity. To this I reply, that Homer has fubftituted Ceres for Ifis, and Diodorus Sic. and Herodotus affure us, that Ceres was the fame as Ifis; and in the Pelafgian Irifh, *Caras*, is a fhip of war, and confequently fynonimous to Eis, or Ifis; Caras a firft rate fhip, Shaw's Dictionary of the Irifh language. Now the words Eifs, or Efs and Caras, being peculiar to the Irifh and not to be found in Welfh, Cornifh or Armoric, to fignify a fhip, there can be no doubt of the words being Magogian-gogian-Scythian and that they were not introduced into the Gomerian Celtic, and confequently the Irifh and Welfh were different dialects.

It is therefore probable that the ancient Greeks and Romans adopted the Scythian word *Eifs*, a fhip, for the goddefs of marine affairs, and accordingly dedicated to her, pictures of wrecks at fea, as Juvenal obferves in his 12th fatyr; juft as the Spaniards and Portugueze do at this day to St. Anthony; and in time, this was fuppofed to be the Egyptian Ifis, Cybele or Kybele, the mother of the gods, Natura, &c. &c.

Plutarch and Apuleius introduce Ifis fpeaking thus, Rerum natura, parens fum omnium elementorum; and Macrobius fays, that Ifis was nothing elfe than the earth and nature : but Tacitus mifguided by the word Eifs, tells us that the Egyptian queen Ifis, penetrated into Suabia and taught the Germans to honour deities, to till the ground, and fow corn, and that in commemoration of the fhip that had brought the queen from Egypt, the Germans adored her under the figure of a fhip. The French antiquaries go fo far as to fay, that the arms of the city of Paris being a fhip, are derived alfo from the Egyptian Ifis, and that the name Paris, was a Greek word, and came from παρὰ Ἰσις, near the famous temple of Ifis, fince we muft fuppofe, fays Monfieur Danet, that a temple was dedicated to this goddefs, where the abbey of St. Germain now ftands. But in the infcription of the column dedicated by the ancient Greeks or Pelafgians, to the Egyptian Ifis, as related by Diodorus Sic. we find no record of her maritime expedition; it runs thus:

thus: "I am Iſis, queen of Egypt, inſtructed by Mercury; nobody can aboliſh what I have eſtabliſhed by my ordinances; I am the wife of Oſiris; I firſt invented the uſe of corn; I am the mother of king Horus; I ſhine in the dogſtar; by me the city of Bubaſti was founded, wherefore rejoice thou Egypt, rejoice, thou haſt brought me up and fed me." Now in the Pelaſgian Iriſh, the word *Natura* is expreſſed by *aos, ais, uis* and *tabach*; the laſt is from the Chaldee טבע, *taba*, natura;—Arab. *ſaba*;—Æthiop. *tabady*; whence in Iriſh and Arabic *teibe* is a phyſician, a ſtudent of nature: *aos* in the modern Iriſh is compounded as in *duthcas, dualdas, toiceas, bèas, nos, meineas*, all ſignifying *natura*, whence *aos-dana*, a magician; *leigh-eas*, a phyſician; *uis-arb*, death; that is, deprivation or ceſſation of nature: and as the Egyptian *Ceres* is derived from the Hebrew גרס, *gheres*, i. e. maturam ſpicam, ſo in the Iriſh, *caoras*, is ripe corn, fruit in cluſters, berries; and as the Egyptian *Cybele*, i. e. Deorum mater, is derived from the Hebrew חבל, *chebel*, i. e. parere, (as Paſſerius has ſhewn in his Lex. Egypt. Hebr.) ſo in the Pelaſgian Iriſh *chobaille*, is pregnancy; *cebil*, a midwife: in Arabic, *hhabila*, pregnant; *kebil*, or *kebilet*, a midwife, ſpecies, tribe, family, generation, progeny. Again,

The word *Re* in Iriſh ſignifies the moon, (in Hebrew *ireahh*) which joined with *aos* or *ais*, (the ſame as the Egyptian Iſis,) forms *aiſre*, which I believe is the אשרה, *aſhre*, of the bible; a word that, (as Bates obſerves, Crit. Hebr. p. 54.) has been falſely rendered into Engliſh, *groves*, for a grove could not grow in the houſe of the Lord, or under every green tree.

tree. Maachah made an image to Aſhre and Manaſ-
ſeh a graven image of it, and ſet it in the houſe of
the lord ; which he could not do to a grove. 1 K.
xiv. 23. They built them high places and pillars and
Aſhres, on every high hill and under every green
tree.—xvi. 12. He reared up an altar for Baal, and
Ahab made an Aſhre.—xviii. 19. The prophets of
Baal four hundred and fifty, and the prophets of
Aſhre four hundred.—xvii. 16. And they made an
Aſhire and worſhipped all the hoſt of heaven and ſerv-
ed Baal.—xxiii. 4. Bring forth out of the temple of
the lord, all the veſſels made for Baal and for Aſhre
and for all the hoſt of heaven.—6. And he brought
out the Aſhre from the houſe of the lord, and burnt
it, and ſtampt it to ſmall powder.—Therefore, ſays
Bates, it was covered with ſome metal, it appears to
have been the eaſcar, or rough ſtone, capped with
ſilver, uſed by the Iriſh druids to repreſent the moon,
as that of Baal or Sam, was capped with gold to repreſent the ſun,—hence the Greeks and Romans repreſented the Ægyptian Iſis, with a half moon, holding a ſphere with her right hand and a veſſel full of
fruit with her left. Bates imagines Samel mentioned
2 Chron. xxxiii. 7. to be the ſame as Iſis, but Samel,
I believe is the Sam or Baal (ſun) of the ancient Iriſh
and of the Aſſyrians ; Aſhre being always mentioned
with Baal, I conclude it was a repreſentation of the
moon, named in Iriſh *eaſc, eaſcar, eaſconn*, (the Eſ-
wara of the Indians, named alſo eſkendra) words very
ſimilar to *eaſcra* or *aſcra*, a decayed grove, derived
from the Hebrew אשרה Aſhera, i. e. lucus ubi ſteriles ſunt arbores, and hence the miſtake of the
Engliſh tranſlators.

We

We are told that the Ægyptians afcribed the over-flowings of the Nile, to the tears that Ifis fhed for the death of her hufband Ofiris : this appears to be ano-ther fable foifted in by the Greeks, for *eas*, *as*, and *eafar* in Irifh fignifies a cataract, a cafcade, an over-flowing of water after great rains or thaws, and moft probably fignified no more in the ancient Ægyptian. It is alfo worthy of notice that Suris or Syris was the Ægyptian name of the river Nile, a name adopted by the Irifh in the river Suir that runs by the city of Waterford.

.Syris. Nomen Nili apud Æthiopes. Dionyf. Perieg. de Nilo.

———Syris ab Æthiopibus vocatur.
Quanquam Plinius, lib. 5. c. 9. non toto ejus decurfui id nomen attribuat, fed parti tantum. Dubium in-terim an hoc nomen a calore Regionis, feu potius a navigatione factum fit; nam סיר Syr etiam, fluvia-tiles fcaphas fignificat, ut Exod. xvi. 3. (Pafferius)

Sur, is an original word, has paffed into moft languages of the world, (like the word *Sac*, a bag) Ex. gr. *Swi*, *Swr*, water, river, fea, Welfh—*Chura*, rain, *ufu*, water, *Sourga*, a great river, in Tartary—*Suero*, milky water, Spanifh—*Surgeon*, a rivulet, Old French—*Zut*, an inundation, *Suabb*, to fwim : *zupb*, to flow. Heb. and Chaldee—*Subb*, liquid, Syriac—*Zur*, a well, a ciftern, in the fame—*Suth*, liquor, Ethiop.—*Suts*, to wafh, *zui*, to fprinkle, Arab. —*Sur*, water, Old Perf.—*Sui*, a river, Perf.—*Sou*, wa-ter, Cophtic—*Tzou*, the fea, Armen.—*Soui*, *Oufou*, wa-ter, Kalmuc Mong—*Sou*, a river, Indian—*Su*, water, Chinefe—*Xu*, liquor, Japonefe—*Su*, water, Turkifh—*Sio*, the fea, a river, Swedifh—*Sior*, the fea, Iflandic—*Soo*, a lake, Finland—*Saiw*, a pond, Gothic—*Sea*, Englifh, &c. Hence the name Sirenes, Syrens or fea goddeffes, may have its origin; though others derive it from the Phœnician word *Sir*, to fing.

The paffages herein quoted, relating to the philofophical terms adopted by our Hiberno-Druids, are a proof that every fragment of Pagan antiquity contributes to the explanation of the facred fcriptures; fhews the origin of that fuperftition which prevailed amongft the moft ancient Greeks, and is an evidence of the truth of the Mofaic writings; we find all the moft remarkable ftories contained in them, difguifed in fuch a manner by the Heathens, as was neceffary for the reception and carrying on of idolatry. Let fuch as have too haftily fhewn a difrefpect for the writings of the old Teftament, ferioufly confider, if the want of a due veneration for them, has not proceeded from the want of underftanding them.

The like fuccefs attends the inveftigation of any ancient Greek words in the Pelafgian Irifh; for example Delphi, one of the moft ancient cities of Greece, was remarkable for its oracle; Æfchylus, Euripides, Pindar, and many others, call this city Ὀμφαλὶς, and Πυθὼ, Omphalos and Pythio, Python or Pythia. Pindar tells a ftory of two Eagles, fent by Jupiter, one eaft and the other weft; they met here and confequently this fpot was Ὀμφαλὸς τῆς γῆς,, the navel of the earth. Phurnutus derives the name from Ὀμφὴ, a divine voice. And Pytho is derived from Πυθιοται, to interrogate, to underftand. All thefe were cer-

tainly

tainly Pelafgian words, and are ftill preferved in the Irifh and not to be found in the Celtic or Welfh, viz. *Om-phaile* or *Om-faile*, is the cave or den of augury, or of fate :—*Dalbha* or *Dalphai*, is augury or forcery, and *Puith* is the fame as *Aub*, i. e. *uter*, and thefe were ventriloquifts, as we have defcribed already. Thefe facts fpeak for themfelves. It is alfo remakable that the Hyperboreans of the Greeks, (whom I have reafon to think, were the Magogian-Scythians or Irifh) gave the firft Προφηται (in Irifh *bro-phaith*) or prophets to this temple of the Delphi, as we are told by a very antient tradition preferved by Paufanias, and that they came from beyond the feas to fettle at Parnaffus. In another fragment of a Hymn compofed at Delphi by a woman named Beo, mention is made of three Hyperboreans, viz. Pagafis, Agyeus and Olen ; the firft performed the office of the prophet of Apollo, and declared the fenfe of the oracle in hexameter verfe. Olen is probably the fame as Ωλην Λυκιος of Paufanias, and was of the Ollam of Ireland, of whom we fhall treat in the fubfequent pages. Now, Bag-ois, Agh-ois and Ollam, were three names given to certain ranks of the Hibernian Druids, expounders of the bagh or holy word, of the Agh or holy law and the Ollam was a philofopher, or expounder of the law of Nature. See the defcription of the hall of Tara in this number.

Having thus cleared the moft ancient part of the hiftory of Ireland, of the fables in which it was enveloped, and fhewn from good authorities, that it is founded on facts ; I propofe in fome future number, to continue thefe obfervations to the arrival of the colony from Spain, under the conduct of Milefius.

M 2   Let

Let not the Irish historian be dismayed at the accounts of the Magogian Scythians, given by the authors of the universal history. They have copied Herodotus only, who in his first book and c. 103, says, that king Madyes, the Scythian, conquered the Medes under Cyaxares and that they were masters of Asia only twenty-eight years: Cyaxares reigned forty years and died five hundred and ninety four years before Christ.

We have much better authority for the great antiquity of the Magogian Scythians, being masters of Asia and part of Egypt. Justin in the beginning of his book, speaks of the Scythian king Tanais as cotemporary with Vexores king of Egypt, and in his second book, he says, that Asia was tributary to the Scythians fifteen hundred years, and that Ninus was the first who freed his country from that yoke.

Strabo l. 15. affirms that Idanthyrsus the Scythian, conquered all Asia and part of Egypt. Arrian, declares that the Parthians were a colony of Magogian Scythians who left their country under Jandysus who was king of Scythia in the time of Sesostris. To these let us add the authority of the learned Gebelin, who has lately published a history of Assyria, which I have quoted in the preceding pages. Monsieur Boivin has proved that Vexores and Sesostris were the same person, and Sesostris died fourteen hundred and sixteen years before Christ.

To the historian I leave the chronological part; in the course of twenty years residence in this country,

I have

I have known but one learned gentleman, acquainted with the ancient Irish dialect, and who is equal to the task; this gentleman has collected great materials for this defirable work; but alas! I fear his advanced years and domeftic embarraffments, will not permit him to arrange thefe materials for the eye of the public, and when death fhall throw the javelin at this gentleman with his right hand, he will fnap afunder the laft ftring of the Irifh harp with his left. If there is a fpark of real Milefian patriotifm left in this venerable ifland, this gentleman will fpeedily be enabled to end his days with eafe and happinefs, and to complete a work, which will reflect honour on himfelf and on his native country.

I muft now apologize to my readers for the awkward drefs in which this Preface appears; it is abftracted from an abundance of materials, collected with a view to form the Ancient Hiftory of Ireland. Fully convinced that no printer or bookfeller in Ireland would hazard the expence of the prefs on fuch a work, it is detailed in this manner for the perufal of the few, who are curious enough to purchafe the Collectanea: and whilft this Number has been at the prefs, it has been notified to me by the bookfeller, that finding he cannot difpofe of three hundred copies of the Collectanea, and that more than two hundred of each of the former numbers lie on his hands; if on the clofing of the third volume with this number, he fhall find no quicker fale, he muft decline the hazard of publication. Such is the low efteem our labours are held in, or fuch is the want of curiofity in the readers of Ireland.

P O S T-

POSTSCRIPT.

The following work came to hand after this preface was printed; it was presented to the library of Trinity College by the author, and we have made the following extracts from it for the satisfaction of our readers.

PARERGA

PARERGA HISTORICA.

JO. UPHAGEN.

1782.

GOMER, iidem certiſſime ac Cimmerii, nempe latiori illo ſignificatu, quo hæc gens, per Boſporum Thracium forte Europæ primum illata & ſolum ejuſdem Pontum tenens, poſt per occidentaliorem ſeptentrionem ſenſim diſperſa, etiam Gallos cunctos & Cimbras ſub ſe complectitur. Nec audiendus eſt Macpherſon, qui Caledonios a Germanis deducit.

Magog ob graviſſimas cauſas cum gente e ſe orta, ex Ezechiele notiſſima.

Gog, conjungi debet, ambæ per totum orientem in hunc diem, ſub nominibus, Yagui & Magui celeberrimæ, & tamen ipſi ſuæ poſteritati ſub iiſdem tam parum agnitæ, ut etiam pars cum reliquis Mahummedanis diris omnibus eaſdem devoveant. Eædem & antiquiſſimi vere ſunt Scythæ, ut Joſephus aliique eos vocant, non quidem Herodotei illi, attamen incolarum

vaſtiſſimæ

vaſtiſſimæ illius intra ac extra Imaum Scythiæ, haud
ſpernanda portio.

Primitus hi quid regiunculam Mogan, quæ a ficto
quodam Japheti filio Mogan, quod quidem traditionem de ſumma hujus nominis antiquitate involuit,
dicta traditur. *(Ottei, t. 1. p.* 290.) Moſique Chorenenſi Mucania vocatur, Mediæque tribuitur, videntur habitaſſe, uti illi alteri Gogarenum *(Strab. l.* 11.)
Moſis Chor. Gugariam, ubi nunc Karabagh eſt regio
ad auſtrum Araxis ob montium aſperitatem in via.
(Hanway.) Sed jam primis ſeculis haſce terras reliquerunt, novaſque in Scythia ſedes ceperunt, quibus
in Pſeudo-Zoroaſtreis Odsjeſtanæ nomen, a Gogitis
deſumptum, inhæret.

Hiſce melius colluſtrandis domeſticus gentis ſcriptor
ſatis auctoritatis adeſt, Abulghaſi Bayadur-Chanus,
qui licet ſuperiori demum vixerit ſæculo, tamen præter
traditionem gentilitiam apud principes majores ſuos
conſervatam, variaque alia domeſtica ſubſidia illiterati populi, quo præter tumulos in memoriam facti
alicujus congeſtos, & in primis antiqua patria pertinent carmina, qualia apud vicinos Baſkirios etiam in
uſu ſunt, apud exteras gentes, Perſas ſpeciatim, quæcunque ad propoſitum ſuum facerent, laudabili etiam
conquiſivit induſtria. De integritate vero ejus ipſe ille ingens hiatus optime teſtatur, qui antiquiſſima heorica tempora in hoc opere inſequitur, quam traditionis jacturam alius levioris fidei ſcriptor minima opera
ex ingenio reſarciviſſet. Haud audiendus ergo eſt
Viſdelou, dum Sinenſium narrationibus unice inſiſtens,
antiquiora illa his incognita plane rejicit. *(Bibl. Orient.*
v. 2.

v. 2. p. 287.) quasi notitiam hujus populi ullam Sinenses habere potuerint, antequam ipsorum finibus appropinquasset; quod primis demum post Christum natum seculis factum videtur.

Sistit autem nobilissimus auctor in genealogia sua Tatarorum primum gentis Patriarcham pro more e nomine fictum Turcam unice, eodem modo, ut se Mogol-Khanus, Tatar-Khanus, Kipzak aliique ibidem sistunt, pro veris hujus stemmatis auctoribus, tam Magog utriusque populi, quam Gog Oguziorum speciatim conditore, indebite substitum.

Javan; cui e 4 ex ipso ortis gentibus jungi debent. 1. ELISA & 2. DODANIM, cum optime simul tractabantur.

Haud nego, inter primarias antiqui orbis gentes, hoc capite recitatas, plures occurrere, a patriarcha suo sic dictas uti Gomer cum 3 ab ipso ortis populis, aliisque adhuc praeter Arphaxad, Chus & Canaan certissime huc referendos. Sed certe dimidia fere pars gentium harum aliunde nomen suum accepit, inque his etiam illi, de quibus nunc loquimur, Dodanim.

Equidem illam Graecorum, pro more omnibus fere gentibus consueto, fictam stemmatis sui genealogiam, nec flocci facio. Potius indicia Mosaica, quod humanam fontem, a Phoenicibus hausta, ulterius profequenda duco, quo facto fat perspicue videbimus, e populo Javan. f. Ionibus, praeter Achaeos, qui Mosaico aevo recentiores fuisse videntur, 2 praecipue majores exiisse populos, qui cum materna illa stirpe tribus potioribus in Graeca lingua dialectis post ortum dedere: nempe ELISA. f. Œoles, forte primitus circa

Elidem

Ēlidem sedentes, & DODANIM. s. Dores, asperiora illa montium juga, Thessaliam ab Epiro dirimentia, ab initio tenentes, ubi & Doris regio, ac Dodona antiquissima urbs, ab EGYPTIA colonia primum fundata, notæ sunt, quarum posterior forte Dorum appellationi primam dedit occasionem.

Scio quidem illam antiquiorum Græcorum in Pelasgos & Hellenes distribitionem, graves hic parere difficultates. Sed hæc forte, ut hic breviter prælibem, quæ infra aptiorem invenient locum, sic componi poterunt. Primo tempore Pelasgorum nomen barbaris quibusdam, tunc Græciæ illatis, proprium erat. Ast post confæderationem Dorum quorundam Hellene auctore, contra illos initam, a qua socii Hellenum nomen sibi sumebant; omnes reliqui Græci, huic fœderi haud consentientes, aut ab ipsis, aut quod magis mihi placet, a posteris demum, non convicii alicujus ergo, sed ut melius modo distinguerentur ab Hellenibus propriis, per oppositionem Pelasgicum nomen accipiebant, sic extensum ut ipsius Atticæ etiam cives omnium Græcorum politissimi, sub eodem comprehenderentur, qui tamen exceptis Saiticis quibusdam colonis, indubie Jones erant.

3. CHITTIMIM. Fieri potuit, ut horum quædam pars in Macedonia, Threiciis alias coloniis potissimum repleta, consederit. Sed tamen probabilior multo eorum est opinio, qui nationem hanc in Italiam transcisse, hujus Aborigines ex eadem ortos volunt, in qua CETII nomine satis appropinquantes, post Latini dicti, noti sunt.

4. THARSISH. Cum hoc antiquissimæ proprie PHOENICIAE coloniæ, in Bœtica ante ipsas Gades

conditæ

conditæ, nomen idemque Tarteſſus ſit, quod Moſis
ævo jam in proxime accolentes Turdetanos, forte &
in omnes univerſim Iberos, a Carthaginienſibus ob
tranſmarinum ſitum ſic primo dictos, tranſierat, hac
occaſione in origines totius gentis, ex qua Gallæci,
fabuloſis tamen additis circumſtantiis Græcam jam
olim ſibi aſſerebant originem (Juſtin.) inquiramus
paullo ulterius.

Videtur mihi autem hæc gens eadem fere e Græcia
in Hiſpaniam via proceſſiſſe, quam Leibnizius ipſi olim
ex conjectura ſagaciſſima præſcripſit.

Ante omnia vero, qui filus Ariadneus noſter erit,
attendi velim CANTABROS. s. BISCAIINOS hodi-
ernos, Iberorum propaginem, ſe ipſos OSCOS, Euſcal-
dunœ, vocare, ac Sertorium metropolin, quam Iberis
condebat, a gente Oſcam, nunc HVESCA, dixiſſe.
Nunc, age, pergamus.

An jam intra Græciæ fines, ut ſeperatus extiterint
populus; haud liquet. Videntur vero maritimo, &
quidem breviſſimo trajectu, inde in Italiam inferiorem
transfuſi antiquiſſimo jam ævo, ut etiam ideo Favorino
Aurunci & Sicani cum PELASGIS, i. e. populo
Chittim primi Italiam tenuiſſe dicantur. Siquidem ea,
quæ viri docti ad Feſtum in vocibus: Mæſius &
Oſcum, adnotarunt conſideres, haud nimis ſollicite
Oſcos ab Auſonibus aliiique hujus generis diſtingui
debere, mecum putabis, cum iidem vernacule Oſci
dicti, Græcis Auſones, Latinis vero plerumque, magis
adhuc deformato nomine, Aurunci dicti ſint, Volſcique
cum Sidicenis imo & ipſis Sabinis pro parte, eorun-
dem fuerint propago. Ab iiſdem populis Oſcorum
nomen alio adhuc modo in illud Opicorum, ob ſer-

pentum

pentum in ipforum terra multitudinem, deflectebatur.
Hic porro Rycquio Platonis locum quendam debeo,
unde ipfe quidem colligit, Opicos ejufdem cum Siculis originis fuiffe, fed Phænices additi, de Sicanis
potius Platonem loqui voluiffe docent, qui eam Siciliæ
partem, quæ Punis poftea ceffit, antiquitus tenebant,
nec Stephani locus aliud fuadet, cum Sicanorum &
Sicalorum facillima femper fuerit confufio. E.
Sicilia eofdem Ofcos porro in Africam proxime
diftantem tranfiiffe, Atlantumque gentem, cui Plato
notis locis Græcam adfcribit originem, cujufque cum
Aufonibus cognationis fictum alias genealogicum
fchema, obfcura quædam indicia continet, condidiffe
aio. (Rycq. de prim Ital.)

Ut nihil fublunarium rerum ftabile femper in eodem
manu ftatu, florentiffima etiam Atlantum conditio,
poft cladem demum ab Ægyptiis, ut videtur, acceptam,
a Phuteis barbaris irruentibus, qui antea circa Ægyptios
fe fines continuiffe videntur, ac tandem a Phœnicibus,
omnia hoc circum fibi fubjicientibus, everfa videtur.
Equidem notam ab Antæo Atlantum ifto ævo R. ac
Tingitanæ urbis conditore fabulam, qui in certamine
cum Hercule, quoties in terram prolabebatur, toties
ab hac fua matre novis recreatus viribus refurgebat,
nec antea vinci poterat, quam Hercules ipfi elevato
jugulum ad fuffocationem ufque compreffiffet, *fic mihi
explico*. Antæus hic damna a Phœnicibus advenis
perpeffa, a littore ad interiora regionis recedens, plus
una vice refarciebat, novifque civium fuorum copiis
inftructus, bellum reparabat, donec tandem undique
ab eis circumclufus, atque fuga prohibitus, cum tota
fuorum manu cæderetur.

Licet

Licet autem Phœnicii maxima huc copia advenerint, tamen omnibus illis perficiendis operibus quæ ipfis adfcribuntur, minime fufficere potuerunt. Sic enim CADMUS, i. e. Orientalis vir, five verius populus, præter illud nubibus vicinum, in Atlante M. pofitum oppidum, centum adhuc alia ibidem condidiffe dicitur ; fic Tyrii trecenta alia oppida in ulteriori Oceani Africano littore ftruxiffe perhibentur. Præterea etiam Maurorum genti, quæ iftud nomen a Gaditanis Phœniciis ob fitum accepiffe videtur, diverfa a vicinis Africanis, adfcribitur origo, modo ab Indis, modo rectius aliquantum a Græcis repetita. *(Strab. & Plut.)* Hinc recte concludi poffe auguror, cum nullum poftea Atlantum in hiftoria fuperfit veftigium, præter Atlaﾠtes illos barbaros, qui Herodoti ævo circa Atlantem M. fe continebant, nec tam Atlantum noftrorum pofteri, quam potius Phuteorum propago, a vicino monte nomen adepti videntur, integram Atlantum gentem poft devictionem fuam cum Phœniciis coloniis unum in populum coaluiffe, ac non folum oppidis illis innumeris implendis plurimum contuliffe, fed etiam toti Maurorum genti ortum dediffe cum Phœnicibus ALIISQUE CANANAEIS fugitivis fimul. Ob fimilitudinem cum ex adverfo fitis Iberis, lingua moribufque, forte evenit, quod ultimis Imperii Romani temporibus, Mauritania Tingitana Hifpaniæ accenfebatur, ut e Notitia utriufque Imperii videre licet. Eadem ut Maurorum, etiam Libyphænicum in Africa propria originem puto : nempe e colonis Phæniciis & Atlantibus, fub Lybyum appellatione minus recte ipfis adplicata, latitantibus. *(Aldrete Antiq. de Efpana.)*

Tempus

Tempus inſtat, ut ad hanc clariſſimam OSCORUM propaginem, Hiſpanos veteres accedam, qui ob deſerta horridiſſima a meridie, poſt repleta Africæ littora, ſat cito ex Atlantibus tranſiiſſe videntur. Hoc non ſolum ex Moſaico teſtimonio de gentis TARSHISH exiſtentia, ſed inde etiam concludo, quod præter ampliſſimum Iberorum populum, Aquitanos etiam condiderunt, qui Galliæ partes ad Rhodanum, Ligurumque fines, *ad Celtarum uſque irruptionem tenebant. (Strab. l. 3. Scylax.)* imo & in ipſam BRITANNIAM tranſierant, ubi Tacitus *(De V. Agr.)* SILURIBUS Hiſpanicam originem tribuit ; unde & hodie VASCONICAE. ſ. BISCAIINAE linguæ quædam cum HIBERNICO idiomate communia eſſe, nemini mirum videbitur.

Inſtitutum ideo OSCORUM iter, antequam Atlantes ab AEGYPTHS erudirentur, cenſeo. Iberorum enim cultura Phœniciis eſt adſcribenda, nec prius eſt effecta, quam poſtquam magna inter veteres colonos novoſque advenas præceſſerant bella. *(P. 55 & ſeq.)*

This author dates theſe tranſactions from the year of the world 1656 to 1826, and before Chriſt 2553. We have aſſigned our reaſons for thinking the Pelaſgi ſhould have been included *cum Phænicibus, aliiſque Cananæis fugitrvis.* The diſtinction he has made between the Gomerian and Magogian Scythians, is conformable to our idea and obſervations, and alſo the affinity between the Biſcayan and Iriſh dialect, which we have treated of at large in the preface to the laſt edition of the Iriſh Grammar ; and we make no doubt, if ancient MSS in the Biſcayan language could be found,

that

that we fhould find a greater affinity, than can be produced in Larramendi's dictionary of the modern dialect.

Ireland is not the only nation which has been left to tell its own hiftory. Palmyra and Balbec, two of the moft furprizing remains of ancient magnificence, have been neglected in hiftory. We feel, (fays the learned, ingenious and modeft Harmer) fomething of an incredulous anxiety about the accounts the facred writers have given us of the extent of the kingdom and of the fame of Ifrael in the days of David and Solomon, whereas we find few or no traces of this mighty power in prophane hiftory. The great kingdoms of the Seleucidæ and of the Ptolemies became part of the dominions of a fingle city, whofe name we in vain look for in hiftory. (Obferv. on feveral paffages in facred Hift.)

CON-

CONTENTS.

OF

ALLHALLOW EVE,

NAMED BY THE IRISH,

OIDHCHE SHAMHNA;

Of the LA SAMAN and MI SAMAN;
or, the Day and Month of SAMAN of
the ANCIENT IRISH:

Of the DEUS SUMMANUS of the
ANCIENT ROMANS:

Of the סמאל SAMAEL and שמעוני SA-
MAONI of the IDOLATROUS JEWS:

And of the ASUMAN of the ANCIENT
PERSIANS.

SAMHAIN, All Saints-Tyde, genit.
SAMHNA. OIDHCHE SHAMHNA, All Saints-
Eve. O'Brien's Irish Dictionary.

SAMHAIN, All Saints-Tyde. Shaw's Dictionary.

SAMHAIN, All Saints-Tyde. Lhwyd's Archæol. Britan. *

Vol. III. No. XII. O LA

* Samhain, says Lhwyd, from some modern glossarist, is
compounded of Samh, summer and fhuin the end: this is a
false derivation; Samhain could not then form Shamhna in
its inflexions, but Samha-fhuin or Saimh-fhuin: the glossarists
                                                        were

LA SAMHNA, Hallowmas-Day. Mac Donald's Galick and Englifh Vocabulary.

MI SAMAN, i. e. MI DU, i. e. NAOI MI, the Month of November. Vet. Glofs.

The MI SAMAN of the ancient Irifh fell on the month of November; it was alfo named MI DU or DUBH, that is, the month of mourning, being the feafon appointed by the Druids for the folemn interceffion of the quick, for the fouls of the dead, or thofe who had departed this life within the fpace of the year.

They taught the Pythagorean fyftem of the tranfmigration of fouls; and that *Samhan* or *Baal-Samhan* at this feafon called the fouls to judgment, which, according to their merits or demerits in the life paft, were affigned to re-enter the bodies of the human or brute fpecies, and to be happy or miferable during their next abode on this fublunary globe; hence *Samman* was named BALSAB, or Dominus mortis, for *Bal* is lord, and *Sab* death. But the punifhment of the wicked, they taught, might be alleviated, by charms and magic art, and by facrifices made by their friends to *Bal*, and prefents to the Druids for their interceffion.

The firft day of November was dedicated to the angel prefiding over fruits, feeds, &c. and

was

---

were ignorant of the meaning of the word. Lhwyd marks the word as taken from Keating; but this author does not attempt to explain the Etymon; he only fays, that the militia of Ireland went into winter quarters *o oidhche Shambna go Beilteine*; i. e. from All Hallow Eve till May Day. *Saman* was the firft month of the winter quarter, and not the laft of the fummer quarter:—Thus Cormac, in his gloffary, fays, the four great fires of the Druids, were in the beginning of February, May, Auguft, and November.

was therefore named LA MAS UBHAL, that is, the day of the apple fruit, and being pronounced LA-MASOOL, the Englifh have corrupted the name to LAMBSWOOL, a name they give to a compofition made on this eve, of roafted apples, fugar and ale. —This feftival of the fruit, was alfo of oriental origin, as will be explained hereafter.

The eve of *All-hallow*, is named in Irifh *Oidhche Shamhna*, i. e. the night or eve of *Saman*; by the afpiration of the confonants, it is pronounced EB OWNA; and the day following, was the great feftival of *Saman*, to whom facrifices of black fheep were offered for the fouls of the departed, and the Druids exhibited every fpecies of charms or natural magic the human mind could invent, to draw prefents from the people: The facrifice of the black fheep is recorded by Virgil.

Poft, ubi nona fuos aurora induxerat ortus,
Inferias Orphei lethæa papavera mittes,
Placatam Eurydicen vitulâ venerabere cæsâ
Et NIGRAM mactabis OVEM, lucumque revifes.

Georg. l. iv. 546.

This feftival lafted till the beginning of December, which was named MI NOLAGH (*b*) or the month of the NEW BORN, from the Hebrew נבלה *Nolah*, i. e. parire, to bring forth young; from whence the French word NOEL, and the Irifh NOLAGH, Chriftmas-day. This month was therefore a feftival of great rejoicing, as the preceding was of

O 2   mourning,

(*b*) The feftival of *Nolagh* finifhed on the firft day of the new year, or the commencement of the circle of *Sam* the fun, becaufe, the original of fpirit, heat, and light, are the prefervers of life; therefore, Macrobius, *the fun, the author of the race of my progenitors*, p. 255.

mourning, and this rejoicing continued till the laſt quarter of the moon in December, when the ceremony of cutting the holy misſletoe began, in preparation to the grand feſtival of preſenting it, on the firſt day of the new year.

The ancient Perſians named this month *Adur*, that is, fire. *Adur* was the angel preſiding over that element; in conſequence of which, on the 9th, his name day, the country blazed all around with flaming piles; whilſt the *Magi*, by the injunction of Zoroaſter, viſited, with great ſolemnity, all the temples of that element throughout the empire, which, upon this occaſion, were adorned and illuminated in a ſplendid manner. *Richardſon.*——It is very probable, that the Iriſh *Mi'du* is a corruption of *Adur*.——The Iriſh cuſtom of lighting up the houſes in the country on the 2d of November, certainly originates from the above ſolemnity of the Perſians; and in ſome places, the fire or *Beil-teine* is yet kept up.

The primitive Chriſtians could not have placed the feaſt of All-Souls more judiciouſly, than on the *La Saman*, or the 2d day of November; or, that of the Nativity of our Bleſſed Lord, at a more proper ſeaſon, than in the feaſt of Nollagh, or the new-born; but *Childermas*, or Innocents-day, a feaſt intended to mourn, in memory of the children of *Bethlehem*, murdered by order of *Herod*, was miſplaced in a month dedicated to joy for the new-born; and ſo late as the year 1645, we find, the primitive inſtitution of our Chriſtian fathers was forgotten, and the rejoicings of the new-born ſubſtituted in its ſtead; ſo hard are vulgar cuſtoms to be removed, as we find by the following authors.

Feſte

Feſte des Innocens. Rejouiſſance qui ſe cele-
broit la vielle et le jour de la fête des innocens, á
peu-pres comme la fete des foux, dans les cathe-
drales & les collegiales. *Naudè* dans la plainte
q'uil ecrivit a *Gaſcendi* l'an 1645 dit, qu'en certains
monaſteres de Provence on celebre la fête des innocens avec des ceremonies plus extravagantes,
que n'etoient autrefois les ſolennitez des *faux-
Dieux*. Furetiere.

Heretofore it was the cuſtom, to have dances in
the churches on this day, wherein were perſons
who repreſented biſhops, *(it ſhould have been Druids)* by way of deriſion, as ſome ſuggeſt, of the
epiſcopal dignity ; though others, with more probability, ſuppoſe it to be done in honour to the innocence of childhood. By a canon of the council of
Cognac, held in 1260, theſe were expreſsly forbid.
Chambers.

It has been the opinion of ſome learned men,
that the *Baal-Zebub* of the idolatrous Jews, was the
god of flies or locuſts, as the LXX have tranſlated
it Deum Μυιας, *muſcam*, or Μυιαγρὸς *muſcarum averrun-
cum*. *Baſnage* is ſingular in ſuppoſing this deity to
be Mars, or the god of battles and of arms, becauſe, ſays he, the Phœnicians might readily convert צבאות tſabath into זבוב Zebub; the Iriſh or
Iberno-Celtic retains both ; for *ſab* is death, and
alſo ſtrong, potent, valiant ; ſo in Hebrew, צבא
tſaba, *militia* ; in Arabic, *zab*, repelling by force ;
zabin, a life-guard-man, and *zaaf*, death : but our
Iberno-Druids retaining *Bal-ſab*, ſynonimous to
Saman, it is evident, *Baal-Zebub* is Dominus
mortis.

The

The LXX, fpeaking of this deity, name him ἀρχοντι δαιμόνων, Dæmonum Principi, which is the appellation given by the Jews to *Baal-Zebub*, or *Beel-Zebulo*, as in St. Matthew, ch. xii. v. 14, and St. Luke, ch. xi. v. 15, confequently, Baal-faman, Baal-Zebub, and Baal-Zebulo, are the fame.

No deity of the ancients correfponds fo well with our *Saman*, as *Pluto*, whom all the Heathens acknowledged as prince of hell, i. e. *Inferorum Præfes*, *Pluto* is alfo derived from the Iberno Celtic, *Blotac* or *Blutac*, a dweller under ground. So Beel-Zebub, in the gofpel, ΑΡΧΩΝ ΔΑΙΜΟΝΙΩΝ, is called, Dæmonum *Maniumque* Princeps: thus in the writings of the ancients, we frequently meet *Pluto* or *Serapis* defcribed as ΑΡΧΩΝ ΔΑΙΜΟΝΙΩΝ, fee Porphyrius, apud Eufebium, l. iv. præp. Evang. c. xxiii. and Clemens Alexandrinus ftiles him ΜΕΓΑΛΟ ΔΑΙΜΟΝΑ, i. e. *magnum illum Dæmonem*; thus in Æfchylus, *Pluto* and *Inferorum Rex*, is befeeched to command the *manes* of Darius to return

Γῆ τε καὶ Ἑρμῆ Βασιλεῦ τ᾽ ἐνέρων
Πέμψατ᾽ ἐνέρθεν ψυχὰν ἐς φάος.

Terraque & Merçuri & (tu) Rex Inferorum
Mittite ex inferis animam in lucem.——

Sophocles in his Oedip. ftiles him ΕΝΝΥΧΙΩΝ ΑΝΑΞ *Noctis tenebrarum Rex*. The Latins named him SUMMANUS, explained by Pliny, lib. ii. Hift. Nat. c. 52, to be *Summus Manium*: there is a remarkable infcription in Gruterus, fol. 1015, where this deity is mentioned with Pluto;

PLUTONI SUMMANO
ALIISQUE DIS STYGIIS.

Cicero makes particular mention of *Summanus*, but Ovid feems to be ignorant who he is. See

Faft.

Faſt. 6. 731. Thus Cicero, cum Summanus in faſtigio Jovis optimi maximi, qui tum fictilis, e cælo ictus eſſet, nec uſquam ejus ſimulacri caput inveniretur, Hauruſpices in Tiberim id depulſum eſſe dixerunt, idque inventum eſt in loco, qui eſt ab Hauruſpicibus demonſtratus. De divin. l. i. But this is a Druid's tale, and the ceremony of ſearching for the head in the Tiber, is ſtill preſerved in Ireland, on the feſtival of *Saman*, by dipping the head into a tub of water, to take up an apple in the mouth; and by the people of the weſtern iſles wading into the ſea, in ſearch of SHONY, on this feſtival.

This Pluto of the Greeks and Latins, is explained by the Rabbi's by בסד SAMMAEL, i. e. *Angelus improbus*. Angelus *Sammael* improbus princeps eſt omnium Diabolorum; and the like power is aſcribed by the Heathens to Pluto, whom the *Magi* and *Druids* ſtudied to reconcile to them: thus Porphyrius, hos (Dæmones) et maxime eorum Principem colunt, qui mala per MAGIAM perpetrant.

Rabbi Sim. Ben. Jachai, names theſe deities שמעוני Sammaoni, i. e. Dæmones, part 2, fol. 14, col. 1. A name evidently of the ſame origin of the Iriſh *Saman*, (b) and of the Perſic ASUMAN, an

angel

(c) The Hibernian Druids, underſtood by *Saman*, that being which had power from *Albeim* or God, over the ſoul, which they taught was immortal. This is the Hebrew *Shemab*, or ח. *Shemab*.

The Hibernian Druids had five names to expreſs the ſoul of man figuratively, and but one for the rational ſoul. Theſe five figurative expreſſions are literally the ſame as thoſe of the Jews, ſelected from the Holy Scriptures, and as they do

not

angel who prefides over the 27th day of every Perfian folar month, and is confidered the fame with

MORDAD,

not occur in any other Celtic language, they are here de-
ferving of notice, becaufe they explain our Druidical *La Saman:* they will be more fully difcuffed, when we come to
treat on ecclefiaftical fubjects.

The rational foul was called *anm,* i. e. the living fpirit ;
the life, from whence the Lat. *anima.*

The figurative expreffions were,

1. *Neobbas,* i. e. immortality, from *bàs,* mortality, death :
neo is a prefixed negative.

2. *Ruice,* i. e, air, fpirit, æther, life.

3. *Samban, Samal,* i. e. the likenefs of the great *Samb* or
Sun, which, they thought, was the likenefs of the *Albeim.*
Heat and light is the producer and preferver of life ; there-
fore, Sol was the god of nativity.

4. *Coidbcbe,* i. e. immortal, continual, for ever.

5. *Ceid, Caid,* i. e. the gift of god, the divine love of God
to man ; hence *Ceidfhamb,* or *Ceidamb,* is a name for the
month of May, from the folemnities of that feftival, to
Samb ; it was alfo named *Cad-am,* or the holy feafon ; and
Ceit-am or *Kit-am,* i. e. the affizes.

N. or *Ne,* in Hebrew, is a fervile letter ; when prefixed, it is paffive, or a noun. The ancient Irifh had no P,
they ufed always B, with an hiatus. *Nephefh,* becaufe it has
a vegetative power, whereby it occafions the growth of
man. *Humphreys in his Apologetics of Athenagoras.*

Manaffeh Ben Ifrael, from the *Berefbith Rabba,* informs
us, that the ancient Jews had five names for the foul
of man, viz ; 1. *Nephefh.* 2 *Ruach.* 3. *Nefhemah.* 4. *Kajab.*
5. *Jechida.* We will produce fome explanations of thefe
words, according to celebrated writers, referving the greater
part for another time, being foreign to the fubject of this
effay.

Nephefh, to breathe out, refpire, take breath, the animal
frame, the perfon in rational creatures ; and it is applied to
the vegetable life in plants, once in the bible ; but it is never the rational foul. Lev. xxi. 2. Neither fhall he (the
priest)

MORDAD, or ASRAEL, the angel of death. Richardſon Arab. Lex. vol. i. p. 117. *Murdad*, in
Perſic,

prieſt) go into any *(nepbeſheth muth)* dead body ; it is the vital
frame, whether alive or dead. Bates Crit. Heb.

Fás, in Iriſh, is to vegetate ; but *neofàs* will imply a dead
body, that can vegetate no longer.

Ethiop. *Nepheſh*. There are two ſouls in man ; the one,
which is the breath or ſpirit of life, (i. e. the rational ſoul)
proceeding from the mouth of God, the Creator, which relates not to the elementary nature of man, neither doth it
die ; the other, is the animal faculty, (that is the ſenſitive
life or ſoul) and this is compounded of the elements, and is
itſelf mortal. Job vii. 7. Remember, that *(ruch)* breath
is my life. xii. 10. In whoſe hand is the *nepheſh* of every
one that lives, and the breath of every fleſh of man. Caſtellus.

Nepheſh, as a verb, ſignifies to breathe; and, as a ſubſtan-
tive, an agent, a breather, a frame breathed in. Hutchinſon.

Neſhemah, ſo called, as having the intellectual faculty
which diſtinguiſhes man from all mute creatures : it is derived from *ſhamaim*, heavens, and, therefore, this name is never read in the Holy Scriptures, as given to beaſts, but to
man only. Humphreys' Apolog. of Athenagoras.

Neſhemah, breath, the animal that breathes ; but it is not
appropriated to the immortal ſoul ; it is called, God's blaſt
and breath, Pſ. xviii. 16, and 2 Sam. xxii. 16. at the *(neſhemah)* blaſt of *(ruch)* the breath of his noſtrils. Bates
Crit. Heb.

After I have ſhewed the nature of man, his ſtation, &c. I
muſt ſhew, that there is a neceſſity, and that it cannot be
otherwiſe, but that all the ideas we have of eſſence, or powers
of our own ſouls as other ſpirits, nay, even of God, muſt be
taken from thoſe in the *air* ; and, as *neſhemah* is taken from
the air, in the ſaid condition and action, *balitus*, *flatus*, which
is the true and real idea of the word, it is uſed here for a
being of an eſſence, not otherwiſe to be deſcribed, of a different nature, and diſtinct from the ſubſtance of *Adam* the
man, the creature that lives, and has his powers from the
element of the air. Hutchinſon's Introd. Moſes's Prin. p. 38.

By

Perfic, implies *giving death*; but he was also one of
the reputed guardians of trees, fruits, feeds, and
herbs. Ibid. p. 1568. But MURDAD was alfo the
ancient Perfic name of the month of *November*.
Quintus menfis in anno Gjol. (Julius) fed in anno
vet. *November*, i. e.. *Murdad*, vulgo *Mirdad* et
Amirdad, qui eft angelus qui præeft arboribus, fru-
gibus, ac feminibus et *Hyemali parti anni*, fed *Murdad feu Mordad*, q. d. *mortem dans*, fignificatur,
etiam *angelus mortis*. Hyde Relig. Vet. Pers.
p. 243. *Mordad* eft *Azrael*, qui motiones fedat &
animas a corporibus feperat, ut credunt Perfarum
Magi. Cazvinius.

Apud quofdam veteres Judæos בםאל *Sammael*, i. e.
venenum Dei, exponitur angelus mortis: is tamen
aliis eorum eft *Satanas*, feu Princeps diabolorum,
quem aiunt inequitaffe ferpentem antiquum et fe-
duxiffe Evam: nam *Sammael* exponitur *Afmodeus*
feu tentator, de quo aliàs dicitur *Sammael* eft *Princeps maximus qui in cælis*: huic tanquam Diei Judicii
advocato dant feu offerunt *munus* in die propitiatio-
nis,

By *Samb*, our Druids underftood the fun, the likenefs of
the *Albeim*, or God; hence our *Saman*; from this idea, *Sa-
mail* is a likenefs, an image, a vifion, fpectre, ghoft; hence
the Latin *Similis*.

I believe, the reader will allow, that our Hibernian Druids
could have argued well with our modern philofophers on
this fubject;—he will be pleafed to recollect, that I have
often afferted, and think I fhall hereafter prove, that the
Irifh Druids were not *idolaters*, had no graven images, and
received the light of the gofpel fooner than any other religi-
fect in the weftern world.

In the beginning of the Samaritan Pentateuch, we read,
in principio creavit *Afma* cœlum & terram.—*Shem* is frequently ufed by the modern Jews for *Aleim*, Deus.

nis, ne Judæos propter peccata accuſet. Hyde. Rel. Vet. Pers. p. 244. See more of this deity in Buxtorf.

The feaſt of *Murdad*, the angel of the ancient Perſians, who preſided over fruit, falling on the 1ſt of November, is evidently the ſame as our *La meas ubhull*; and from hence is derived the cuſtom of eating a great quantity of apples and nuts on this day; and the ceremony of the *La Saman*, or the following day, is blended with it, being both kept on the vigil of the latter.

I have not met the word *Murdad* in any ancient Iriſh MSS. but as this deity preſided over herbs, and our Druids were great botaniſts, it is not improbable that the Iriſh name for agrimony, (viz. *murdrad*) to which they attributed ſo many excellent virtues, may be a corruption of *murdad*, and ſo called by way of excellence.

The Phœnicians believed Pluto to be DEATH, as we find in Philo. Bybl. ap. Euſebium, l. i. c. x. p. 38. " nec multo poſt Μοτ filium ex Rhea genitum vita functum conſecret: but, μωθ is the Hebrew מות muth, and the Iriſh *muath*; thus the Iriſh ſay, *ata ſe dul a muath*, it is petrified, i. e. dead and gone.

Pluto was the modern name of *Sammaon* or Sammael: The general derivation of Pluto is from πλυτος, i. e. Riches,—dictus eſt Pluto, ſay the gloſſariſts, απο τυ πλυτυ, hoc eſt a divitiis,—quæ ex terræ eruuntur viſceribus: true; but we ſhall find the Greek πλυτυ to be of Iberno-Celtic origin: We will now trace the hiſtory of Pluto in a few words.

Pluto, the ſon of Saturn and Rhea, or Ops, was the youngeſt of the three Titan brothers, who

eſcaped

efcaped the cruelty of their father: Italy and Spain fell to his lot. Pluto retired to the extremity of Spain, and applied himfelf in carrying on the working of the gold and filver mines, with which that country once abounded, as we learn from Poffidonius, Avienus, and many others: they even defcribe its mountains and hills to have been all of gold and filver, efpecially thofe near Tarteffus. Ariftotle fays, that the firft Phœnicians who landed in Spain, found fo great a quantity of gold and filver, that they made their anchors of thofe precious metals; and the author of the book of Maccabees, l. i. c. viii. fpeaking of the Romans, fays, that by the conqueft of Spain, they made themfelves mafters of the mines of gold and filver.

This, doubtlefs, obliged Pluto, who before was named *Agefilaus*, and *Agefander*, (or the leader of men, &c.) *Dis*, &c. to fix his refidence about *Tarteffus*; he was fkilled in mining, and this made him pafs for the god of riches.

Blot, in Irifh, is a mine, a cave, or any fubterraneous place.

Blotac, is a miner or dweller in caves. Shaw's Dictionary, & Vet. Gloff.

P being mutable with B, formed the Irifh verb *plutadh*, to dig, to mine, to break in pieces: metal being early the ftandard of money, *blot*, *blat*, and *blath*, fignify price, value; and from gold and filver being eafily polifhed, we have the adjective *blothach*, as *cloch blotach*, a polifhed ftone. Hence the name of Pluto, and of the Greek πλυτο, riches; and from Tarteffus the Latin *Tartarus*, hell.

Pluto continually employed labourers in the mines, who were obliged to work far in the earth,

and

and, in a manner, as far as hell and the gloomy mansions of the *manes*, in search of hidden treasures; and thus Pliny describes them, *in sede maniumque opes quærimus, nos ad inferos agunt*, l. xxxii. c. i. hence he was said to dwell in the centre of the earth: add to this, that they who work in the mines of gold and silver, commonly die there; so was Pluto reckoned the king of the dead, and the very name he bore; viz. ADES, signified death, destruction; and from the Phœnician ED or AID, exitium; in the Iberno Celtic, EAD or EAG, death.

- The learned Millius, it is true, derives Pluto from the םלפמ miphlezet, mentioned in the 1. Kings, c. xv. v. xiii. the root of which is ףלפ, philets or phlets, i. e. *terrendo*, as most interpreters agree, but this word is better preserved in the Irish *pleisdam* or *phleisdam*, to slaughter, to butcher, to flay, from *phlesdar* or *fleisdar*, a butcher, anglicé, a *flesher*; but *miphlizet* is feminine, and has been well explained by the Rabbis, and even allowed by Millius to be the same as *Hecata*.

It does not appear from any Irish MSS. in what places the Druids offered sacrifices to *Saman*. We know, those of the *Ti-mor*, or great invisible spirit or *Baal*, were performed in *excelsis*, according to most ancient custom; and from history we learn, that the Greeks and Romans, in the worship of their infernal deities, dug little trenches or pits, which they made use of, instead of altars. Spencer, b. ii. c. xv. Fabricii Bibl. Antiq. c. ix.

Festus tells us, that when they sacrificed to their celestial gods, they did it *in ædificiis a terra exaltatis*, in buildings exalted high above the earth; when to their terrestial gods, *in terra*, upon the ground; but when to the infernal, *in terra afossa*, in holes or

pits

pits dug in the ground: and thus the fcholiaft on Euripides, in Phœnis, fays, that βωμ⦿ is an altar or building raifed with fteps to go up, upon which they offered facrifices to the gods, who had their dwelling above; and 'Εσχάϱα is a ditch or pit dug in fome *elevated* ground, of a certain figure, but without fteps, where they facrifice to the infernal deities.

Eafcar, or *Eifkir*, in Irifh, is a fmall hill, and many places retain this name from their fituation; we alfo frequently find fubterraneous buildings in Ireland, which are evidently of Druidical workmanfhip, fuch as that of New Grange near Drogheda, (d) which may probably have been the place of facrificing to *Samman*. This hint may lead our Hibernian antiquaries in fearch of the 'Εσχάϱα.

Rabbi Mofes Bar Nachman, in his notes on Deut. xii. 23. (e) thus defcribes this fuperftitious worfhip: " They gathered together blood for the devils, their idol gods, and then they came themfelves, and did eat of that blood with them, as being the devils guefts, and invited to eat at the table of the devils; and fo were joined in federal fociety with them: and by this kind of communion with devils, they were able to prophefy and foretel things to come. According to the opinion of this Rabbi, they thought their demons efteemed it fuch a favour and obligation to be treated in this manner, that they would, in the wild and open places

where

(d) See a defcription of this temple, by the learned Governor Pownal, vol. ii. Archæol. Soc. Ant. Lond. vol. ii.

(e) Only be fure that thou eat not the blood; for the blood is the life, and thou mayeft not eat the life with the flefh.

where they haunted, and which therefore were made choice of for the performance of thefe fuper-ftitious rites, appear vifibly to them, and foretel them any thing they had an inclination to know. Thus Horace defcribes Canidia and Sagana performing thefe rites:

Vidi egomet nigra fuccinctam vadere palla,
Canidiam, pedibus nudis, paffoque capillo,
Cum Sagana majore ululantem, fcalpere terram
Unguibus, et pallam divellere mordicus agnam
Cæperunt, cruor in foffam confufus, ut inde
Manes elicerent, animas refponfa daturas.

Sat. l. i. Sat. viii.

And thus we read in 1 Kings, c. xviii. v. 18. that Baal's prophets cried aloud, and cut themfelves after their manner, with knives and launcets, till the blood came.

The ceremony of facrificing to *Saman*, is thus defcribed in an ancient MSS. entitled, *Dun-feancas*, or the topography of Ireland, under the word *Magh-fleacht*, or the field of adoration, as the Irifh gloffarifts will have it; but I fhall hereafter fhew that it fignifies the worfhip of the great God.——" *Magh-*
" *fleacht*, fo called from an idol of the Irifh, named
" *Crom-Cruaith*, a ftone capped with gold, about
" which ftood *twelve other* rough ftones. Every
" people that conquered Ireland, (that is, every
" colony eftablifhed in Ireland) worfhipped this
" deity till the arrival of Patrick. They facrificed
" the firft born of every fpecies to this deity; and
" *Tighernmas Mc Follaigh*, king of Ireland, com-
" manded (*cucu*) facrifices to this deity, on the
" day of SAMAN, and that both men and women
" fhould worfhip him proftrated on the ground,
" till

" till they drew blood from their nofes, foreheads,
" knees, and elbows;. many died with the feverity
" of this worfhip, and hence it was called, *Magh-*
" *fleacht.*" Vet. MSS.

Cucu, a facrifice ; in Hebrew, *Chug,* the Pafchal
Lamb ; and agreeable to Mr. Hutchinfon's defcrip-
tion of the Hebrew *Chugul,* or worfhipping of God
as the Creator of the. univerfe, this ancient word
Crom-Cruaith, literally .implies, the temple of the
Cruth, i. e. Creator : This is the word ftill ufed for
the tranfubftantiation of the hoft in the mafs. -
Cromthear is a prieft ; *Crom* or *Chram,* in the Bohemian language, is a church or temple ; *Chrama,* or
Charma, in the Phœnician language, is *Anathema,*
execratio. Hence, fays Bochart, *Charma* or *Harma*
Bœotiæ locùs erat *Columnis feptus,* propter vatem
Amphiarum hiatu terræ ibi abforptum ira execrandus, ut fama fit neque aves illis columnis infediffe,
neque feras herbam attigiffe in intercolumnio illo
crefcentem. See *Cuirm afcaon, in the conclufion.*.

The. word *Crom,* has been .fo much miftaken by
the monkifh writers of the eleventh and twelfth
centuries, it deferves further. notice. In fome ancient MSS. I find *Crom* ufed as an attribute of
God : the fame word occurs in the fame fenfe in
Arabic. *Cruth* is a form, fhape ; and *Cruathoir* is
the. only word now ufed for God the *Creator* ; it is
probably the root of the .Latin word. *Cruaith* is the
genitive cafe, therefore, *Crom-Cruaith* implies, the
Lord of the Creation: it is fometimes written *Crom-
Cruach,* perhaps, fignifying the hard and difficult
devotion to be paid to *Crom,* as defcribed above ;
but .I rather believe, it is the fault of the tranfcriber.

The

The following extracts from oriental authors, will elucidate our Irish word *Crom :*

Heb. *Chrom.* (with an Heth.) optimates ; from whence *Heros.* Bates. Crit. Heb.

Arab. *Krim, Kerim,* one of the attributes of God ; a most religious man, a true believer. *Kiram,* venerable, noble. *Kerami,* most revered. *Kira-met,* a miracle, i. e. the work of God.

Perf. *Gawran,* worshippers of fire. *Keruger, Ke-ruter,* an attribute of God. Richardson.

And in Castellus, under ברם *Crom* or *Kerem,* are the following observations.

Chaldee. Synagoga. Nomen lapidis pretiosi, Locus publicus.

Syr. Nomen Idoli.

Samarit. Nomen Lapidis.

Æthiop. Annus.

Arab. Honorificatus fuit ; Veneratus fuit ; Vir credens & religioni addictus ; Munificentia Dei ; Maximus ; Majestate verendus thronus ; Venera-tio ; Gloria ; Signa a viris sanctis edita ; Nobilissi-mus ; Benedicta.

These sufficiently prove, that *Crom* was one of the attributes of the great God : hence, *cruim* signi-fies thunder ; *Crom-Leac,* the altar of the great God. *Magh* and *Mugh,* are Irish words, express-ing the attributes of God ; in Hebrew, *Magen,* No-men Dei, metaphorice vocatur ; i. e. Clypeus. Thus, also the Irish, *Borr-Ceann,* God ; in Hebrew, *Bore-ruach* ; i. e. Creator venti. Amos iv. 13.

On the OIDHCHE SHAMHNA, (Ee Owna) or Vi-gil of *Saman,* the peasants in Ireland assemble with sticks and clubs, (the emblems of laceration) going from house to house, collecting money, bread-cake, butter, cheefe, eggs, &c. &c. for the feaft, repeating verfes in honour of the folemnity, demanding preparations for the feftival, in the name of St. Columb Kill, defiring them, to lay afide the *fatted calf*, and to bring forth the *black fheep*. The good women are employed in making the griddle cake and candles; thefe *laft*, are fent from houfe to houfe in the vicinity, and are lighted up on the (Saman) next day, before *which* they pray, or are fuppofed to pray, for the *departed fouls* of the donor. Every houfe abounds in the beft viands they can afford: apples and nuts are devoured in abundance; the nut-fhells are burnt, and from the afhes, many ftrange things are foretold: cabbages are torn up by the root: hemp feed is fown by the maidens, and they believe, that if they look back, they will fee the apparition of the man intended for their future fpoufe; they hang a fmock before the fire, on the clofe of the feaft, and fit up all night, concealed in a corner of the room, convinced that his apparition will come down the chimney, and turn the fmock; they throw a ball of yarn out of the window, and wind it on the reel within, convinced, that if they repeat the Pater Nofter backwards, and look at the ball of yarn without, they will then alfo fee his *fith* or apparition: *(f)* they dip

for

(f) *Sith*, an apparition. *Sith-bhreog*, the fame; i. e. the apparition of the *breo* or fpirit, fire, æther, &c.—It is fometimes written *Sidh* & *Sigh*. ‏שד‎ Sheth, Heb. nates, podex, dæmon. Et hæc vox Judæis frequens eft in ore, nam fub fpecie amicæ falutationis obvios Chriftianos in Polonia & Germania, farcafticè & impiè compellant *Sheth wilkome*; i. e, *podex vel dæmon falve*. *Shedh* enim eft Dæmon. Hinc *Seth* vel *Set*, quafi thefis vel pofitio; *femen*; viz. pro *Abele* fubftitutum.
Bythner, Clav. Linguæ Sanctæ.

for apples in a tub of water, and endeavour to bring one up in the mouth; they fufpend a cord with a crofs-ftick, with apples at one point, and candles lighted at the other, and endeavour to catch the apple, while it is in a circular motion, in the mouth; thefe, and many other fuperftitious ceremonies, the remains of Druidifm, are obferved on this holiday, which will never be eradicated, while the name of *Saman* is permitted to remain.

The inhabitants of *Siant*, (one of the weftern iflands of Scotland) had an antient cuftom to facrifice to a fea-god, called SHONY, (Shamhna) at Allhallow tide, in the manner following: The inhabitants round the ifland, came to the church of St. Mulvay, having each man his provifion along with him; every family furnifhed a peck of malt, and this was brewed into ale; one of their number was picked out, to wade into the fea up to the middle, and, carrying a cup of ale in his hand, ftanding ftill, in that pofture, cried out with a loud voice, faying, *Shony, I give you this cup of ale, hoping, that you'll be fo kind, as to fend us plenty of fea ware, for enriching our ground the enfuing year:* and fo threw the cup of ale into the fea. This was performed at night time. At his return to land,

P 2
they

Sitb-bbreog, the fame as Sigb-brog, a fairy; hence *bean-fighe*, plural *mna-fighe*, women fairies; creduloufly fuppofed by the common people, to be fo affected to certain families, that they are heard to fing mournful lamentations about their houfes by night, whenever any of the family labours under a ficknefs, which is to end by death: but, *no families*, which are not of an *ancient and noble flock*, (of oriental extraction, he fhould have faid) are believed to be honoured with this fairy privilege. O'Brien's Dict. Hib.

they all went to church, where there was a candle burning upon the altar; and then standing silent for a little time, one of them gave a signal, at which the candle was put out, and immediately all went to the fields, where they spent the remainder of the night, in drinking, dancing, and singing. Martin's Western Islands, p. 28.

From this passage, it is evident, that SAMAN was esteemed the angel presiding over the fruits of the earth, and was the same as MURDAD of the antient Persians, as before explained.

According to Pythagoras, the number two was the most unlucky; for which reason, our Hibernian Druids fixed this solemnity on the 2d day of November, or the month of Saman; and, for the like reason, the Romans removed the feast of Summanus, to the second month of the year; viz. to February.

Of ALLHALLOW EVEN; vulgo, HALL E'EN, as also, NUTCRACK NIGHT.

From the Appendix to Brandt's Observations on Popular Antiquities. Newcastle upon Tyne. 1777. 8vo.

In the Antient Kalendar of the Church of Rome, so often cited, I find the following observation on the 1st of November:

Festum stultorum veterum huc translatum est.

The feast of fools is removed to this day.

Hallow E'en is the vigil of All Saints Day.

It is customary on this night, with young people in the North, to *dive* for apples, catch at them

when

when ftuck on at one end of a kind of hanging beam, at the other extremity of which, is fixed a lighted candle, and that with their mouths only, having their hands tied behind their backs; with many other fooleries.

Nuts and apples chiefly compofe the entertainment; and, from the cuftom of flinging the former into the fire, it has, doubtlefs, had its vulgar name of nut-crack night. The catching at the apple and candle, at leaft, puts one in mind of the ancient game of the quintain, which is now almoft forgotten, and of which a defcription may be found in Stowe's Survey of London.

Mr. Pennant, in his Tour in Scotland, tells us, that the young women there determine the figure and fize of their hufbands, by drawing cabbages on Allhallow Even, and, like the Englifh, fling nuts into the fire.

This laft cuftom, is beautifully defcribed by Gay, in his *Spell*.

Two hazel nuts I threw into the flame,
And to each nut I gave a fweetheart's name;
This, with the loudeft bounce, me fore amaz'd,
That in a flame of brighteft colour blaz'd;
As blaz'd the nut, fo may thy paffion grow.
&c. &c.

The Rev. Mr. Shaw, in his Hiftory of the Province of Moray, feems to confider the feftivity of this night, as a kind of *harveft-home* rejoicing: " A " folemnity was kept, fays he, on the eve of the " firft of November, as a thankfgiving for the fafe " ingathering of the produce of the fields. This, " I am told, but have not feen it, is obferved in
" *Buchan,*

" *Buchan*, and other countries, by having *Hallow*
" *Eve fires* kindled on some rising ground." (g)

He tells us, also, in that little fore-taste of his
work, with which he favoured the Public, in an
Appendix to Mr. Pennant's Tour, that " on Hal-
" low Even they have several superstitious cus-
" toms:" I wish he had given us particular descrip-
tions of them, for general accounts are exceedingly
unsatisfactory; curiosity is indeed tantalized, not re-
lieved or gratified by them. End of the Appendix
to Brandt.

The month of Nollagh, or *regeneration*, for so
the word implies, appears to be borrowed from the
Ægyptians: the great festival of the Druids, in this
month, was about the 25th of *December*, the day
fixed for the celebration of the birth of our Saviour.
I therefore offer the following observations to the
learned reader: The overflowing of the river *Ado-*
nis, and the retreating of the waters, were periodical:

(g) Cormac, Abp. of Cashel, in the tenth Century, in his
Irish Glossary, tells us, that, in his time, four great fires
were lighted up, on the four great festivals of the Druids; viz. in February, May, August, and November: the
Irish have dropt the fire of November, and substituted candles: the Welsh still retain the fire of November; but can
give no reason for the illumination, says the author of Letters from Snowden.—I believe, his enquiry into this solemnity, was not very deep, for the Welsh are, in general, well
acquainted with the ancient ceremonies of the Druids.
These festivals shall be explained in future publications, as
opportunity serves: they strengthen the affertion I have often
made, that the customs of the common people of Ireland,
and the MSS. still in being, afford more opportunities of explaining the tenets of the religion of the Druids, than those
of any other people in the world, the *Brachmans* excepted.

cal: the firft was fixed for the beginning of their mournings; fo did a very extraordinary circumftance, point out to them precifely, when to change the mourning, into the moft extravagant mirth and rejoicings. The Egyptians put a letter into a bafket made of bulrufhes, and with ceremonious incantations, delivered it to the river on its reflux, which carried it to the fea; and this letter, of its own accord, went to Byblis, about eighty leagues diftant, where the women, who knew the time of its approach, received it with the greateft reverence: this letter informed them, that *Adonis* was *regenerated*, or come to life again; their mourning was immediately turned into joy, and the whole city filled with revelling and licentioufnefs. We meet with this ftory in Lucian: " There was," fays he, " a man's head brought every year from Egypt " to Byblis, over the fea, in the fpace of feven " days, the winds carrying it with a divine gale, " that it turneth not to the one way, nor to the other, " but comes in a ftraight paffage directly to Byb- " lis; which, though it may feem miraculous, hap- " pens every year, and did the fame when I was " there."

This is the reafon, we fo often fee on old coins the *Dea Syria*, with a head in her hand: it is fuppofed, that Ifaiah (xviii. 2.) alludes to this, where he denounces *woe to them who fend ambaffadors by fea, even in veffels of bulrufhes upon the waters.* The word *Tfirim*, which we tranflate *ambaffadors*, fignifies idols; and Bochart, therefore, underftands it, of the head of *Ofiris*; which, he fays, they fent *by the power of the devil*, from Egypt to Byblis: The LXX tranflate it by ἐπιστολὰς βιβλίας, as if they were
letters

letters that were fent to Byblis: The Irifh antiquary could have informed them, that *os iris,* in their language, implies, *the holy or divine head.* This ftory is not unlike that publifhed not many years fince, in the life of St. Wenefrede, for the ufe of the pilgrims who vifited her well, and which the editor very gravely endeavours to perfuade us to believe: it is this; that fhe annually fent St. Beuno a curious embroidered waiftcoat, and, wrapping it in a woollen cloth, caft it into her well, from whence it paffed down the ftream into the river, then into the fea, and landed near the monaftery where St. *Beuno* dwelt, at *Clynnog,* near Carnarvon, many miles diftant.

I fhall conclude this fubject with a paffage from Porphyry, becaufe, it was the fentiment of our Hibernian Druids.

" We will facrifice," fays he, " but in a manner
" that is proper; bringing choice victims with the
" choiceft of our faculties; burning and offering
" to GOD, who, as a wife man obferved, is *above*
" *all, nothing fenfual:* for nothing is joined to mat-
" ter, which is noti mpure; and, therefore, incon-
" gruous to a nature, free from the contagion be-
" longing to matter: for which reafon, neither
" fpeech, which is produced by the voice, nor even
" internal or mental language, if it be infected with
" any diforder of the mind, is proper to be offered
" to GOD : but we worfhip GOD with an unfpot-
" ted filence, and the moft pure thoughts of his
" nature."

Thefe arguments were brought by the Heathens, to defend worfhipping the images of their Gods; and their Gods, for aught we know to the contrary,

were,

were, when on earth, though their posterity soon fell into idolatry, as *good saints*, that is, as acceptable to Almighty God, and perhaps more so, than St. Francis, Ignatius Loyola, and a great many other Enthusiasts, who make a considerable figure in the Romish Kalendar.

OF THE

GULE OF AUGUST;

OR,

LAMMAS DAY;

CALLED BY THE ANCIENT IRISH,

LA TAT AND LA LUGHNASA.

TO WHICH ARE ADDED,

FURTHER ILLUSTRATIONS

ON THE

ROUND TOWERS.

THERE cannot be a more pleasing study to
the Irish antiquary, than that of the ancient
Irish Kalendar; and, if a complete work of this
kind could be found, it would, doubtless, afford a
most curious enquiry, and lead to discover the ancient colonies that settled in this island.

The names of some of the ancient festivals, are
handed down to us by the mouths of the common
people; such as BEIL TINNE, or the month of
May; SAMAN, the month of November; NOLLAG,
of December; and LUGHNASA, of August: but the
greater

greater part, are only to be found in the perufal of the ancient MSS.

The name of TAT or TATH, carries us up to the moft remote period of antiquity; it is of oriental origin, and, in my opinion, eftablifhes the ancient Hiftory of Ireland, as given to us by their ancient Seannachies or Antiquaries; I mean, where they affert, that an eaftern colony fettled in this kingdom at a very early period, and introduced their language, rites, and cuftoms; becaufe, if thefe names had travelled from Gaul to Britain, and fo on to this ifland, it may be reafonably concluded, that we fhould find fome traces of them, in the hiftories or antiquities of thofe nations, particularly in that of the Britons, the Walfh having been moft ftudious in their refearches and explanations of Britifh antiquities: but, in the courfe of my reading, I have not been able to difcover any words, in the leaft fimilar to thofe of the Irifh, for this feftival.

LA TAT, the firft day of Auguft. Vet. Glofs.

LA TAITHE A' FOGHMHAIR, the Day, Tat, of harveft. Idem.

DIA TAITHE 'POGHAMHAIR, (h) the firft day of Auguft. Mr. Charles O'Conor, from the *Dinfbeanchus*, one of the moft ancient records of the Irifh.

LUGNAS,

(h) *Fogh*, in Irifh, implies, an abundance, a gathering, a harveft; hence, it is ufed, to exprefs a great feaft, an entertainment, &c. *Fog*, is an old Celtic word, ftill retained in Yorkfhire, and applied to the foil; they fay, fuch a field has a good or a bad *fog*.

Fog, (fogagium, Law Latin; gramen in forefta regis locatur pro *fogagie*. Leges foreft. Scotice) aftergrafs; grafs which grows in autumn, after the hay is mown. Johnfon.

LUGNAS, the month of August. O'Brien's Dictionary.

LA LUGHNASA, the first of August. Idem.

LUGNASD, Lammas Day. Shaw's Galic Dict.

LA LUANISTAIN, Lammas day, or 1st of August Mc. Donald's Galic Vocabulary.

Scaliger, in his Emendatióne Temporum, shews us, that תת Tot, or Thoth, was the first month of the Egyptians, which commenced on the kalends of August. We need go no farther for the derivation of the Irish TAT. He adds, also, that Albetinus asserts, that the Ægyptians named this month, likewise, LAGNAHIR, but that the Coptick, or Ægyptian words, were so falsely printed in this Author, little dependance was to be placed on the orthography; sed multa apud illum autorem depravatæ leguntur, sive interpretis inscitia, sive librariorum culpa, ut cum apud eum legitur ALKEPT pro ELKUPTI, &c. &c. from whence, we may conclude, that *Laghnahir*, and *Lughnasa*, have the same origin.

The Ægyptians, had also, a second *Neomenia*, in March, named TAT, hence, the distinction made by the Irish, by *Dia Taithe a foghamhair*, the Day, Tath, in harvest.

The month, TAT, in the Tabula Syro-Græcorum of Scaliger, is named LOUS; I therefore conclude, that Albetinus wrote *Laghnasir*, instead of *Laghnahir*, a word afterwards contracted by the Syro-Græcians to *Lous*.

The Irish glossarists, of the eleventh and twelfth centuries, derive the name from Lughaidh-lamhfada, or long-handed *Lughaidh*, a monarch of Ireland, who, they say, established *nasa*, or fairs or assemblies,

semblies, to be held annually at Talton, *(i)* on the first day of this month. It is certain, that this was a public day, or festival, in the moft remote times; and *Cormac* informs us, it was one of the four great fire-days of the Druids, as we have fhewn in the preceding pages.

Toth, or *Thoth*, is faid to be fo called by the Ægyptians, from a king *Thoth*; but it being the name of the firft month of the year, *Thoth* became the name of the *Epocha* of the fun's calculation. In Irifh,

Tat, i. e. tofach, a beginning. Vet. Glofs.

Tath, i. e. leomhan, a lion Idem. In this month, fays Scaliger, *Thoth* primus neceffario cæpit ab orbe *Caniculæ* (the dog ftar) fole in *leonem* tranfeunte, novilunio :———And here it will not be amifs to ob-ferve, that *mi madadh*, or the dog month, is ano-ther appellation in Irifh, for the month of Auguft, correfponding with the canicula, or dog ftar.

Teith, heat, warmth.

Tethin, i. e. Tithan, the fun. See all the Dic-tionaries.

Taithneadh, to thaw, melt, or fufe; hence, *Teine*, fire.

Taith, the courfe of the fun.

Various are the opinions of antiquaries, of the ori-gin of the name of Lammas Day.

LAMMAS, Calendiæ Sextiles feu Auguftæ, q. d. Miffa, (i. e. Dies Agnorum, tunc enim Agri exo-lefcunt

---

(i) *Tail-ton*, fignifies, the hill of augury : hence, the Druids named Patrick, *Tailgan*, that is, the great prophet. See O'Brien. The modern Irifh, have done what they could to ruin the an-cient language. In Arab. *tala-numa*, an augur. See the Preface.

lefcunt, & in ufu menfarum effe definunt. Vel ut ex *Somnero* monet ab Anglo-Sax: *hlaf-meffe*, q. d. Loaf-mafs, fortè quia eo die, apud Anglos, oblatio panum ex tritico novo fieri folebat. Skinner.

Lammas Day, the firft of Auguft, fo called, as fome will have it, becaufe lambs then grow out of feafon, as being too big;—others derive it from a Saxon word, fignifying *Loaf-mafs*; becaufe, on that day, our forefathers made an offering of bread, made with new wheat. On this day, the tenants who formerly held lands of the cathedral church of York, were bound by their tenure, to bring a *lamb* alive into the church at high mafs. Chambers.

Lammas Day, otherwife called, the *Gule* or *Yule* of Auguft, which may be a corruption of the Britifh *gwyl Awft*, fignifying the feftival of Auguft, or may come from *vin-*CULA, (Chains) that day being called, in Latin, Feftum S. Petri ad Vincula!!! Blount.

It is a ufage, in fome places, for tenants to be bound to bring in wheat of that year to their lord, on or before the *Gule* of Auguft. Ham. Refol. to fix Queries, p. 465.

In the preceding article, I have fhewn the derivation of *Lambfwool*; that it was the day on which the Druids celebrated the *la-mas ubhal*, or the day of oblation of the fruits of trees: So this day, (the Gule of Auguft) was dedicated to the facrifice of the fruits of the foil: LA-ITH-MAS was the day of oblation of grain; it is pronounced *La-ee-mas*, a word readily corrupted to Lammas: ITH, is all kinds of grain, particularly wheat; and *mas*, fruit of all kinds, particularly the acorn, whence maft.

CUL

CUL and GUL, in the Irifh, implies, a complete circle, a belt, a wheel, an anniverfary. CIR, implies, a bending, and fometimes a circle; but, in fpeaking of the mathematical circle, it is always compounded as CIRCUL, a circle.

Cul, i. e. *gul,* i. e. carbad, a wheel. Vet. Glofs.

Culbhaire, i. e. Saor deanmha carbaid, a wheelwright. Ibid.

Cul, a chariot, a waggon, or any wheel-carriage. *Do threig a chula,* his wheels failed. O'Brien.

Carbad, Coifte, a wheel. Lhwyd at Rota: N. B. Carbad and Coifte, now fignify a coach or chariot.

Cuidhal, or *Cual,* a fpinning wheel.

GWYL, a feftival. Welfh.

GWLEDD, Epulæ, Convivium. Davies' Welfh Dictionary.

Gwyl yr holl Sainct, the Gule of All Saints. Welfh Kalendar.

Gwl Awft, the Gule of Auguft. Idem.

Cùl, or Gul, fignifying a circle, a belt, &c. was a term properly adapted by the Celts, to exprefs an anniverfary, feftival, or the day in the fun's annual courfe, affigned to particular holy days. Thefe, and other feftivals which were governed by the *Neomenia,* were proclaimed to the people, a week or more, before the appearance of the moon; hence it was neceffary to calculate the motion of the heavenly bodies; and this was the bufinefs of our Druids: and, as they afcended the high hills, to have the firft obfervance of the new moon, fo, many hills and fteeples, or round towers, preferve the name to this day, fignifying their ufe; as *Cnocna Re, na-Re*, the Hill of the Moon, in the county of Sligo; Killrè, the Moon's Steeple, &c. &c.

We cannot explain this word CUL, without referring to the oriental tongues; and, in truth, the Celtic language, the Iberno-Celtic in particular, is fo united with the Hebrew, Arabic, and Perfic, it is impoffible to penetrate into the remote antiquities of the Celtic nations, without a competent knowledge of thofe languages; as will appear from the following words:

HEBREW.

גלה *gala*. This is a very general word, and has great variety of application: to roll in whatever manner; to roll down; roll together; roll back; roll round; to revolve as the earth in its diurnal and annual motion; and, as a heap of ftones rolled together. *Galath*, orbs; rings; rounds; things that would eafily turn round, *Vas rotunda*, round inftruments; to be rolled away, as when the folar light is by the motion of the earth rolled off our hemifphere. As a noun, it feems a general name for the great material heavens. As a mafs, circles, rings, or turning round on a centre. Derivations, *wheel, well*. The Saxon, *wealcan*, to roll; whence *welkin*, the heavens. Perhaps the Latin, volvo; whence revolvere. *While*, fpace, or revolution of time. Packhurft's Heb. Lex.

Gola, Cyclus, Cyclas. *Gol*, vas concavum & rotundum.

Gala, revelare, propheticum verbum: inde *Galei*, Vates Siculi: Bochart, Amos iii. 7. Surely, the
Lord

Lord God will do nothing, but *(gala)* he revealeth his secret unto his servants, the prophets :—Hence, the Irish verb, *galastair*, they revealed. It is also used as a noun, as, *cuirim ann ceill, ciall, cuill,* or, *geill,* i. e. I will reveal or declare.

Chalad, Hhalad, Sæculum ; hence *Baal-Chalda,* Dominus Sæculi, from whence Jupiter was called, Aldus and Aldemius : in this sense, also, the true God is called, *Melk Hhalim,* i. e. Rex Sæculi, vel Mundi.   Bochart.

The Canaanites had a temple to their God, *the Heavens,* called *Beth-chagule,* i. e. the temple of the circulator.   Josh. xv. 6, and xviii 19.   Marius calls it, *Beth-gul,* i. e. the house of revolution. Cocceius says, *chugg* signifies motion, and that in a circle :—Marius, that *gul* expresses the inward joy of the mind, by the outward gestures of the body : Cocceius, that *gul* denotes to exult, and the outward expression of joy, by dancing, jumping ; hence, the two words are joined in the Irish, to express a goat, a lamb, &c. viz. *caghal, coghla, cadhal,* a goat, a lamb.

The celebration of the Meccha festival, is called by the Arabians, *Chug* ; it signifies, also, *the year,* a bracelet, a ring :—in Irish, *cuig-me,* a bracelet or ring.

In Syriac, *chugal,* is a circuit, an eclipse, to turn round ; in Irish, *cuigeal,* is a spinning-wheel, *cuig,* a circle.   The Hebrews often joined these words together ; viz. *chug-gul* ; and then it expressed both motions, to roll in a circle or sphere ; as 1 Chron. xvi. 31.   Let the earth *chugul,* i. e. revolve.   *Cuig* is used singly by the Irish, to express the number *five*; that is, the tips of the fingers once counted round: *deic*, ten, is the contraction of *da-cuig*, or twice five, from which number, all nations begin a new count. *(i)*

" This

(*i*) From the explanation of the Irish glossarists of the word, *cuig*, five, to be synonimous with *cuar*, or *cuir*, a circle; *deic*, ten, i. e. two cuig, or circles, and *fighi*, twenty, to signify also a noose or twisting, the following conjecture arose, of the ancient method of reckoning or counting: I do suppose here, an ancient Irish merchant trafficking with a foreigner, ignorant of his language, and, according to ancient custom, seated on the ground; the natural way of making the latter sensible of any number up to five, is, by turning the palms of the hands towards the face, in which position, the tips of the fingers form a circle, *cuig*, or *cuar*; from whence the name: To signify this number at once, he would hold up his hand, and extend his fingers, which will then form so many V's, and hence, I suppose, this character did stand for five: He would count over the second hand, which he would name *di cuar*, or *di-cuag*, that is, two circles, which might be contracted to *deic*, ten; to signify this number to a foreigner, he might naturally cross his arms, and shew both hands, with fingers extended, and this could not be better represented, than by the character X, from which number, all nations begin anew. To express twice ten, he might *fighi*, or twist both hands about, running the fingers of one through another, and this number would be called, *fighean*, twenty, i. e. a twisting: From whence, *fighenti*, and the Latin viginti, the sign would be the X repeated, and so on to fifty, which might be by an X, and two twists, as the Irish expresses; viz. *deic agus da fighidh*, ten, and two twists; but in the position of sitting, the body being kept erect, and the thighs and legs closed and thrust out, would be represented by the character L, or, in a standing posture, the arm stretched out, would form a *gamma* Γ, a figure we find, in Fabricius, to have been insculped for L. For a hundred, he might point to the head, which, from its orbicular form, might be represented by O; the name of the head being *cean*, *cut*, or *ceat*, the Latins

named

" This attribute in a God," fays Hutchinfon, (Principia, p. 259.) " is to make fomething go " round in a circle. One of the fervices the hea- " thens paid to this attribute, was to dance or " move in circles: hence, the Arabians call brace- " lets and ear-rings, which were the reprefentations " of this power in the annual circle, by the part " of the word which expreffes it; and fo ufed the " fame word, *Chug*, for the year itfelf."—In Irifh, *Cuigme*, a bracelet; but *Cughtaidh*, or *Cuch-taid*, is the *Creator*, the *Former*, the *Maker*. " This, " continues our author, was a fervice required by " the law of God, to be performed at ftated times

Q 2

" or

named the character *centum*, and the Irifh *cead*. For ten hundred, or a thoufand, the X répeated, and the hand on the *mull*, or crown of the head, would be reprefented by O, and an X within the circle; and, from *mull*, the contraction *mil*, and the Latin *mille*, and the character M, which alfo refem- bles a man fitting, with his two legs drawn up: or this num- ber might be expreffed, by grafping a large lock of hair; i. e. a *milic*.

The Irifh, like their anceftors, the Scythopolians, have ever been remarkable for the making of Linen, a manufac- ture depending on the exact number of threads; it was ne- ceffary, therefore, they fhould count the threads of yarn when reeled: This reckoning thus goes on with the good woman and her reel: at every twenty, fhe made a *fcor* or notch on a ftick, hence *fcore*: every ten fcore, makes a *cut* or *centus*, i. e. *centum*; and every twelve cuts, makes a *cion mor* or *fkean*, or, as we call it, a fkain or hank: the reel is alfo named *cros tocais*, the X or crofs for reeling; and, if I miftake not, the Greek τυλι, is from an ancient word, τᾶς, implying, a *circle*, as well as *omne*; for the Greek πανσιληνῶ, plenilunis luna, is the fame as the Iberno-Celtic, *bann-luan*, from *bann*, a circle, belt, girt, or zone; and εκᾶτον, a hundred, is our *cut*, the head, &c. &c.

" or feasts, under these and other words, in
" Exod. v. 1. The Lamb, which was the repre-
" sentation of this power, and was to be eat at the
" passover, in Exod. xxiii. 18. is called *Chag*; it is
" so called, when it is made a sacrifice in this ser-
" vice, in Psal. cxviii. 27." In Irish, *Chag-al*, is a
goat, a lamb; and, in a very ancient Irish MS.
quoted in the preceding essay, *Cucu*, is the name of
the sacrifice ordered to be offered to Saman; and
in all the Lexicons, *cogh-bradh*, or *codh-bradh*, is a
sacrificing, an offering. This may be the reason,
that the primitive christians in Ireland, changed the
word *Paisc*, into *Caisg*, still adhering to the word
Chag, or *Chug*, the name of the Lamb offering; and
hence, probably, *Cag-aos*, lent season. *Cargus*, has
another derivation, as will be shewn hereafter.

I must remark in this place, that the Irish name,
Cloga, or *Clug*, for the round tower, may very readily be a contraction of the Hebrew *Cugul*; especially, as we find one name for a tower, to be *Caiceac*,
or *Cuiceac*. See more under the word *Caiceac*.

The corresponding Irish words, are, *coghar*, order, series. *Coghal*, a nut; *cuagan*, the round work
of a bird's nest (from *ean*, a bird); *cuachag*, a pail,
a bowl; *cuag-fholt*, curled hair; *cuag-ran*, a round
kernel in the flesh; *cuig-crich*, a bound, or land li-
mit; *caght*, or *cacht*, the world.

Nergal, the *Aleim* of the men of Cuth, 2 Kings
xvii. 30. from *ner*, light, and *gal*, to revolve: it
seems to denote, the *solar fire*, or *light*, considered,
as causing the *revolution* of the earth. Parkhurst.

The Rabbins say, the idol was represented in
the shape of a *cock*: Among the later *heathen*, we

find

find the *cock* was facred to *Apollo*, or the *Sun*; be-caufe, faith *Proclus*, he doth invite, as it were, his influence, and, with fongs, congratulates his rifing: or, as *Paufanias*, they fay this bird is facred to the fun, becaufe he proclaims his approaching return. So, *Heliodorus*, by a natural fenfation of the *fun's revolution* to us, *cocks* are incited to falute the God: And, perhaps, under the name, *Nergal*, they meant to worfhip the fun, not only for the *diurnal return* of his light upon the earth, but alfo, for its *annual revolution*. The emblem of the cock (in Irifh, *gal*, *caoile-ac*, or *galeac*) is proper, for he is frequently crowing both day and night, at the time of the year when the days begin to lengthen. Our Irifh word, *neirghe na greine*, i. e. the rifing of the fun, has a wonderful affinity with *Nergal*. *Shakfpeare* has re-marked,

> Some fay, that 'gainft that feafon comes
> Wherein our Saviour's birth is celebrated,
> The *bird of dawning* fingeth all night long.
>
> Hamlet.

And here it may not be amifs to take notice of the beautiful propriety with which a *cock* was made ufe of, to awaken St. Peter from his guilt, after he had denied our Lord. *Step. Morinus*, proves, the *Cuthites* were of *Cutha*, in Perfia, and that they wor-fhipped immediately the *fun*, or *fire*, as an em-blem; therefore, *Nergal* could not be an idol: for *magiifm*, or fire worfhip, and not *zabiifm*, or image worfhip, was, at that time, the religion of that country, (vide Prideaux's Connect.) as it was of the Druids of Ireland.

Gal,

Gal, revolvit, cumulus, acervus lapidum, juxta *gal,* i. e. acervum, radices ejus implacabantur, fequitur domus lapidum, *galim,* altaria—*me-gala* volumen, libros in cylendri morem, *gal-gal* quicquid in circulum volvitur.—Schindlerus.

Cheled, ævum, tempus, mundus quafi aliquid inftabile.

Chol, arena, vitrum quod fit ex pellucidis arenæ granulis. Chald. & Syr. *Chala* vitrum; from this root, is formed, the Irifh word *chloine,* or *gloine,* for glafs, i. e. *chala-thinne,* vitrified fand, or fand vitrified by fire, and the Hebrew *Glin,* vitrum.

Chalal, perforari, foffæ, cavernæ, tibia, fiftula quafi perforata, inftrumenta mufica: from this root, the Irifh, *chlairfi,* a harp, i. e. *chala-arfi,* the ancient inftrument of mufick.

Cacham, to be wife, have wifdom, all wifely.

Chak, a ftatute, a lawgiver.

CHALDAIC.

Gala, revelavit, manifeftus; *Geli,* the fame.

ARABIC and PERSIC;

FROM RICHARDSON AND SCHINDLERUS.

A. *Chalid,* tempus, feculum, ætas, perennis, *Khalud,* perennis.

Chalas, elevatio, cumulus, acervus.

Chalac, condidit, creavit.

Gal, revolvit.

Al-galala, cingulum. Schindlerus.

Ghellet, harveft, fruits, grain.

P. *Ghelle,*

P. *Ghelle,* flower : Irifh, *ceall.*

P. *Ghul-ghul,* proclamation.

A. *Kyl,* a caftle, fort, citadel : Irifh, kill, a church. *Kyl,* a chain, a band.

A. *Kyld,* a periodical return of the feafons.

A. *Kela,* a caftle.

A. *Kulel,* fcattered people affembled together.

P. *Kululè,* P. a wheel, a reel, a fphere.

P. *Kullè,* a tower, a fteeple, a belfrey.

A. *Kyllyet,* a cell, a vault.

P. *Kelivan,* an adorer of fire.

P. *Kalè,* a yarn reel : Irifh, cuidhal, or cual.

A. *Cacham,* philofophy. *Cachmoni,* a family name; i. e. a wife man, a teacher of wifdom; i. e. thofe fkilled in all the branches of the knowledge of nature. Hutchinfon, Icon, and Boaz, p. 10 :— hence, the Irifh, *ceac, ceacht,* or *kak,* inftruction, wifdom. *Cacht,* a holy day, a faft proclaimed by the wife men.

The Canaanites had a temple to their god, the *heavens,* by the attribute above-mentioned ; (Jos, xv. 6. and xviii. 19.) viz. *beth-hgule,* or *chegule,* that is, the temple of the *circulator : Marius* calls it, *beth-gul,* i. e. the houfe of *revolution.* Hutchinfon fays, they have omitted the firft half of the word, viz. *chug,* or *chuggu* ; that is, to be in motion, to dance in circles, to go round. *Cocceius* interprets *chug,* by motion, and that in a circle ; but *Marius,* fays, *gul,* expreffes the inward joy of the mind, by the outward gefture of the body ; and, *Cocceius* adds, it is the outward expreffion of joy, by dancing, jumping, &c. In Arabic, *Chug,* is the celebration of the *Meccha* feftival, the year, a

ring,

ring, a bracelet. In Syriac, *chugal*, a circuit, to turn round. One of the fervices paid to this attribute, by the heathens, was, to dance, or move in circles; *(k)* and, in this manner, our Irifh Druids, obferved the revolutions of the year, feftivals, &c. by dancing round our *round towers*; and, from the Syriac *chugal*, the word *clog* was formed, implying, any orbicular form, as, the *fkull*, a *round tower*, &c. *Cuighal*, a Spinning wheel; *cuig*, the number five, becaufe, once told round the tips of the fingers of one hand. *Cuagan*, the circular work of a bird's neft. *Cuach*, the cuckow, becaufe, of its periodical return. *Cuige agus uaidhe*, round and about. *Coig-crick*, a bound of a country;—hence, *coig*, and *cuig*, a province, and not from *cuig*, five, as our moderns think, for there were but four provinces in Ireland. *Cogh-bradh*, a facrificing, an offering. *Clo-gad*, or *Chugala*, a round town; hence, *cul-de-four* in French, a fpherical vault; and, in this form, are the roofs of our round towers: Latin *colum*, i. e. fafligium templi rotundum: Irifh *cul-teac*, an oven, a bake-houfe.

Galac, Gealac, and *Geal*, are Irifh names for the moon, from the above root, *gala*, to revolve; whence, *gil*, in Hebrew, a planet: (Thomafs. p. 338.) hence, many of our hills are named, *gil*, and *gal*, from the ufe made of them by the Druids,

for

(k) This was a fervice, required by the law of God, to be performed at ftated times, or feafts, under thefe and other words. The Lamb, which was the reprefentation of the paffover, and was to be eaten at that feftival, is called, *chag*, Ex. xxiii. 18. It is alfo fo called, when it is made a facrifice in this fervice. Pf. cxviii. 27. Hutchinfon.

for the difcovery of the *neomenia,* or new moon. The Earl of Tyrone's Park inclofes part of a very high hill, called *Gil-kak,* i. e. the proclaimer of the moon, from the Hebrew, *cachim,* fcire, revelare; hence, the oriental aftronomers call the feven fpheres of the planets *galgalim;* a little fphere *gil.* See Icon and Boaz. p. 43. And, hence, the Irifh word, *galac, gavilac,* and *caileac,* a cock, i. e. the herald.

In A R A B I C and P E R S I C.

Kulleh, a round tower; *kullehcheh, kaukh,* a turret; *fouruf, fourfut,* a turret; *Taumoor,* a tower; whence, our *Tamar,* or *Tara,* which had three towers. *Kulaufb,* a cock, a watchman; *heiaat, cheiaat,* aftronomy; *chookool,* an obfervator of the ftars; hence, our *cuil-ceach,* or *cheakkuil,* a round tower, i. e. an obfervatory.

Perf. *kal-ab* manfio quædam lunæ. *Kelanè,* a fire hearth; *kalender,* wandering monks; *kel-kis,* a boy's top whirling round; *gulé,* a cotton reel; *gullé,* a fwallow, from its periodical return; *Kuliché,* the body or difk of the fun or moon, rotundity, a round cake; *kelifa,* a church, a fynagogue; (hence, our *Kileefba,* the name of feveral old churches in Ireland there is a caftle, tower, church, and facred grove of oak, fo called, near St. Luke's Well, between Waterford and Knocktopher); *Kilu,* is alfo a Perfian word for a manifefto, a proclamation, a place where the Mahometans *watch* before prayer.

Heb. *He kul,* a temple. This is the root of our *Eacal,* and *Eaca-lios,* a church, and of the Latin and Greek

Greek ecclefia; but *Lios* is the Irifh termination, fignifying a houfe; for all ancient temples were in open places.—We muft alfo diftinguifh between *Eacal-lios* and *agal-lios*; both imply churches; but *Agall*, was originally an *Oracle*; whence, *Cruach Agall*, now mount *Aigle*, or *Cruach Patrick*. See Preface.

Perf. *Mc-Gele*, the chamber of audience; quia ibi omnia rerum arcana propalantur. (Thomaffinus).

Heb. *Chacam* חכם fcire, fapere, peritum effe. Perf. *Kak*, a mafter, a preceptor, hence, the Irifh, *ceac*, or *kak*, fcience, knowledge, grammar. *Uire-kakt*, the rudiments of grammar, from *uire*, or *aire*, a magician: Thus, the Irifh *Seanchies*, fay, that the name of *Partolan's* Druid, who firft came to Ireland from Ægypt and Greece, was named *Cacchair*: (for this word, fays Mc. Curtin, implies a fkilful man) Now *cach*, in Hebrew, is an inftructor, and חרור cheruri, is hariolari, to augure. (*l*)

Chaldee. *Tara* תורה, doctrina, lex vel Mofis vel totum verbum dei.

Hindoftan. *Pungol*, a revolution, anniverfary, New-Year's-Day; Irifh, *bangul*, a proclaimed revolution or anniverfary.

.IRISH.

(*l*) The Reader muft be fenfible, from the few examples here given, of the difficulty of explaining Irifh antiquities, without a knowledge of the oriental tongues :—If he does not bear this lighted flambeaux in his hands, he will ftumble every moment over the rubbifh thrown in the way by the monks and hiftorians of the eleventh and twelfth centuries, as too many pretended antiquaries of Ireland have done already, to the difgrace of our *Triumvirate Society* of *Hibernian Antiquaries*.

IRISH.

From the preceding oriental roots, are derived, the following Irish words :

Gull, or *gaill,* i, e. *carrtha cloche,* a stone column, or pillar, that is, one of the ancient round towers, (Cormac's Glofs. Vet.) *is aire is bearor gall* (says Cormac) *difuidiu fo bith ceata ro fuighidfeat in Eire,* i. e. they were so called, *gall,* by the colonists who settled first in Ireland *(m).* From the Hebrew, *gala* revelare, the ancient prophets of Ireland, were also

---

(m) Cormac says, these pillars, columns, or towers, were so named by the first settlers in Ireland. *Gall,* in the modern Irish, is a general name for foreigners, in particular the English, but here means a tower.; now גדל *gidal,* or *gadal,* in the Hebrew, is a tower. See Hutchinson, Icon and Boaz, p. 49. May this not be the root of the word *Gaodbal,* or *Gadal,* i. e. the Irish people ? And might not the name of *Gadelas,* their hero or leader, have been adopted from his being the leader of a people who built towers ? Thus *tor* or *tir,* in Hebrew, implies a fort, as being furrounded by a circle ; *Tir,* is also a pillar ; a pillar-like vapour : it is also the orbit of the stars ; hence, Homer uses the word τυρσα for the stars : Does not this name also point to the use of our *tir* or tower ? *Tur, tor,* in Hebrew, implies, *ordo,* intermixed with *tir,* a palace. *Tir,* in Chaldee, to divine ; from whence, the Irish *tirgire,* or *tairgire,* prophecy, divination ; a word compounded of *tir,* divination, and *cir,* a circle. Mr. Hutchinson translates *turim,* columns of light. Icon and Boaz, p. 60. All which names seem applicable to our round towers. *Carrtba,* a column or pillar, is certainly the same as the Hebrew *catharoth,* 2 Chron. the chapters on the heads of the columns ; for the Hebrew verb, *cathir,* is to furround : as a noun, it implies a crown : the word, says Packhurst, may properly be rendered a sphere or circle. In Persic, *diz-ghale* is a tower, from *diz,* an inclosed place, a castle, and *ghale,* a tower.

alſo called, *gaill*, whence, the country of *Dunagaill*. (See Preface).

Cual cunnaid, i. e. brèo; *do cum teineadh re haghaidh mairbh do luſgadh*, i. e. *Cul-cunnaid is a brèo*, or great fire, which (Cormac explains) was laid on the corps to burn it to aſhes: *cunnaid*, is fire wood; *brèo*, is a great fire; from the Hebrew and Arabic, *bera*, incendium res combuſta. As a proper name, *Tabera*, Num. ii. v. *3.* & vocatum eſt nomen illius *Tabera*, eo quod *bera* arſerat in eis ignis Domini. Schindlerus. Therefore, *Cual-cunnaid*, does alſo imply, a fire lighted up on the *Cual*, or anniverſary, as well as a funeral pile: and thus, O'Brien, at the word, *breo-chual*, a bonefire, a funeral pile; in Hebrew, *brekok*, pyra. Schindlerus.

Cuil-ceach, or *cùl-kak*, corruptè *claiceach*, a round tower; as *Cuilceac Cluana-umha*, the tower or ſteeple of Cloyne. O'Brien. This word, adds he, ſeems to be corrupted of *clog-theach*, that is, the bell-houſe. I have had occaſion before, to ſhew, that Dr. O'Brien, had very little knowledge of the roots of his mother tongue, for *clog*, is a contraction of *cugal*.

Cuill-kak, *(n)* is evidently the annunciator, inſtructor, or proclaimer of the feſtivals. See *cùl*, *gùl*,

---

(n) The princes of the *Tuatha-da Danans*; viz. *Eathoir*, *Ceathoir*, and *Teathoir*, ſays Keating, worſhipped *Cuill-Keaɐ-Grian*, and ſo were nick-named, *Mac Cuill, Mac Kaɐ, Mac Grian: cuill*, ſays he, is a log of wood; *keacht*, is a plough-ſhare; but *grian*, is the *ſun:*——how abſurd !—— *Cuill-kakt-Greine*, is moſt evidently the annunciation of the ſun's courſe, proclaimed at our *cuill-kak*, or round tower: But *cuilceach*, was not a name peculiar to the round towers, but to every high mountain aſſigned for theſe aſtronomical obſervations:

gùl, and *kak,* in the preceding lift of oriental and Irifh words. Hence, it is rather more than conjecture, that our Irifh round towers, which *Cormac* tells us, were built by the firft people who came to this ifland, were the buildings from whence the approaching feftivals were announced. Thefe feftivals, were generally governed by the motion of the heavenly bodies, and, particularly, by the *Neomenia*; was it not then necefſary, that the people fhould be warned of their approach? The Druids, we know, were well ſkilled in aftronomy, for the dark ages they lived in: It is alfo, probable, that a certain order of the church, were allocated to this office; the name of this order has not yet been difcovered; what! if they fhould have been the *cul-de,* or *cul-da,* i. e. the revolution-prophets, (for *da* is a foothfayer) or the obfervers of time, as they are called in the Bible; Ifa. ii. 6. viz. *ain*; in Irifh, *ain-as*; which alfo fignifies a foothfayer. It muft be allowed, that all hiftorians are dubious of the rife and name of this order; fome deriving it from *colidei,*

or

obfervations: hence, *Cuilceach,* a mountain fo called, in the County of Cavan, mentioned often by the famous Dean *Swift,* in his Letters to *Sheridan,* under the name of *Quilqua.*

Our Hibernian Druids, believing in the tranfmigration of fouls, named the body *culn, coln,* and *colna,* that is, the *cul,* or revolution, pipe, cafe, &c. of the *ana,* or *anal,* life, breath, fpirit; or of the *anm,* living life, breath, fpirit, foul; from whence, the Latin, *anima.* Synonimous to this, they named the body, *cirb, cuirb, cuirp,* i. e. the circle or cafe of *bi,* life; from whence, the Latin, *corpus.* A doctrine conformable to Pythagoras, is explicitly contained in the word *colna*; and the Rabbinical and Hutchinfonian philofophy, is comprehended in *cuirp.* The *Tuatha-da-Danan,* we have fhewn, in the Preface, fignified *Danian* or *Pelafgian* foothfayers.

or *cultores dei*, others denying that they were of the clerical order, and others making them the *chorrepifcopi* of Gaul and Germany. See *Ducange*, *Boethius*, *Buchannus*; and *Chulda*, the prophetefs. 2 Chron. ch. xxxiv. v. 22. *Ludolphus*, in his Comment on the Ethiopick Hiftory, gives a judicious account of the words we render charmer, foothfayer, &c. by tranflating them *gathering together a company*, i. e. *cùl*; and Mr. Richardfon, in his Arabic Dictionary, under the word *khelde*, refers for the explanation to the words *fulb* and *ajuz*: *fulb* fignifies crucifixion, burning, rude, right, real, patient of labour, dignity, modefty, chaftity. *Ajuz*, has no lefs than fixty different fignifications; among others, it implies, a traveller, heaven, the univerfe, the world, the fun, the temple of Mecca, a chriftian church or monaftery, hell, five particular days at the winter folftice, &c. &c. Many of thefe are very applicable to the Irifh word, *cul-de*; but Caftellus and Golius, in their Dictionary of the Perfic Language, explain *Kalyud* by Eventus, Res & Narratio, Belgicè Aventur, the very employment I have affigned to the Irifh *cul-de*.

Another name for the round towers, is *fibheit*, *fithbheit*, and *fithbhein*. See O'Brien and Shaw's Lexicons. In Hebrew, the word *zapha*, is an obferver, a looker-out, fpeculator fuper muro aut turre urbis confiitutus, ut annunciet & videat quis urbem ingrediatur. Schindlerus. *Mi-zapha*, an obfervatory, a place on high: *Zaphit*, the afpect or profpect, as Ifa. xxi. 5. watch in the *zaphit* or watch tower. Hutchinfon, Icon and Boaz, p. 39. In Arabic, *zefi*, is to go up on high; *fabyhat*, ftars, planets;

planets; *fabat*, a fcaffold; *fahur*, the moon; *fubat*, a gallery, piazzo, portico; and *febeb*, a track or quarter of the heavens.

In Hebrew, *fhith*, is to fhew, to point out, to fet, to appoint.

In Arab. *feteh*, divinator quidam, Golius; from whence the Irifh, *fithir*, a diviner, and the *feer* (or poffeffed of fecond fight) of Scotland; *fahyr*, in Arab. a learned magician; and thefe compounded, form foothfayer in Englifh. Arab. *feteh* columnia tabernaculi. Caftellus.

Satar, recto ordine conftituit, præfectus; infpector Rei.

Syr. *fit*, forum.

Sether, סתר or *fathar*, in Hebrew, a fecret, a hiding place, place of protection, fhelter; Pf. xviii. 12. He made darknefs his *(fathar)* fecret place; lxxxi. 8. I anfwered thee in the *(fathar)* fecret place of thunder. " Thefe and other texts, " (fays Bates, in Crit. Heb.) refer to the fiery cloud " in which God dwelt;" From whence the moft ancient name of God, in Irifh, (and probably the Druidical name handed down to us) is *Seathar*. See all the Lexicons. At *Sinai*, there were thunderings and lightenings, and a thick cloud upon the Mount: the mountain burnt with fire unto the midft of heaven, with darknefs, clouds, and thick darknefs; and the Lord fpake out of the midft of the fire. Exod. xix. 17. Deut. iv. This was the fecret place of thunder and of darknefs, David fpeaks of above; and hence, (fays Bates) we have the name and hiftory of Satan, the fon of Cælum and Terra. See Crit. Heb. pag. 402.

The

The Irish word, *Sith-bheit*, is literally, the *Beth*, or house of *Sith*; which may imply, the house of peace, of pointing out the seasons, or, the house of adoration. *Sith*, particularly, expresses every place established by the Druids in Ireland for devotion. *Sith-drum*, was the ancient name of *Casbel* or *Caisiol*, that is, the *Sith* upon a hill: the tower of *Caisil* is thus situated; *Caisiol*, implies also, a house built of lime and stone. *Sith*, is pronounced *See*, the *t* being aspirated: I think it bids fair to be the root of the Latin, *sedes*, and the English, *see*; i. e. the diocese of a bishop. Ainsworth, derives the word from the Greek, ἳ̈υ edes. *Sith-bhein*, in Irish, will imply the place of benediction, of pointing out, or proclamation, of the anniversary, or of the vigils, the evening place of prayer, and, lastly, *binn*, is also a bell, used by the Romish church in excommunication. Gur beanadh *binnèan* chiarain, air. Chron. Scot. ad An. 1043.

Caiceach, the last name I find for the round tower, is supposed by the glossarists, to be compounded of *cai*, a house, and *theac*, a house; this is tautology with a witness! The word may be compounded of *cai*, a house, and *ceac*, instruction, &c. but I rather think it should be written, *caig-theac*, or *caig-each*, i. e. the house of solemnity, or of the feasts or festivals. כn chag, in Hebrew, as we have already shewn, is a circle, festival, anniversary. Exod. x. 9. we have a *(chag)* festival day, xxiii. 18. nor shall the fat of my *(chag)* annual sacrifice, remain till morning. The Hebrew, *chag*, is the root of the Irish, *cagaus*, a name of lent. *Cargus*, i. e. *cag-aos*, the season of *Chag*. Vet. Gloss. *Cag*, is an old English word for fasting, or abstain-

ing

ing from meat or drink. *Cargus*, has another derivation.

In Arabic, *chag*, annus quod anniverſaria illa
ſunt ſacra. Caſtellus.

In Syriac, *chaga*, feſtus dies, ſolemnitas.

In Chaldee, *chagiga*, feſtivitas, apud Rabb. oblatio pacifica. Of theſe words, we ſhall treat largely
in a future Number, by which, it will appear, that
the Iriſh introduced oriental words ONLY into the
church, and which exiſt to this day.

Theſe towers were certainly belfries in after-
ages; and, probably, were not only obſervatories,
but belfries too, at the time of their conſtruction.
It is worthy of obſervation, that all feſtivals are
proclaimed in the eaſtern countries from the top of
the *miſgir*, or *diz-ghalè*, or round towers of the
moſque: bells might alſo have been uſed by our
Druids: the hand-bell is of a very ancient conſtruction; and the Latin name for a bell-ringer, viz.
tintinaculus, ſeems to be of Scythic origin; and,
alſo, *tintinabulum*, a bell. *Tein*, in Iriſh and Arabic, is noiſe, a ringing-noiſe: *tein-tein*, is doubled
in both languages, to expreſs the greater noiſe:
bualim, in Iriſh, is to ſtrike, which was the ancient
mode of ſounding the bell (o). *Cul*, as we have
ſhewn, is an anniverſary, a round tower, a ſteeple;
in Perſic, *kullè*: but *keol*, in Iriſh, is a muſical note,
muſick. I ſubmit theſe obſervations to the notice
of the Iriſh antiquary, and, flatter myſelf, they merit his reſearches.

Nor does it appear, that the modern names of
theſe towers, viz. *cloghad*, or *cloig-theac*, ſuppoſed to

ſignify

(o) Tot pariter pelves, tot tintinnabula dicas pulſari.
Juv. Sat. 6.

fignify a bell-houfe, are any inducement to think they are modern buildings. *Clog* is certainly a bell in Irifh, fo named, from *clog*, the *cranium* or fkull; in which form, our firft bells were made, and thofe at this day ufed in *clocks* are caft; but *clog*, the fkull, owes its name to its orbicular form, as we have fhewn before.

It is evident, that all our *cloghads* have not been belfreys: in many there are no marks of the wall having been broken within for hanging a bell; nor are they always annexed to churches. There are many in the fields, where no traces of the foundations of any other buildings can be difcovered round them. Had the primitive Chriftians of Ireland poffeffed the art of building thefe towers with lime and mortar, it is reafonable to think, they would have preferred building the churches of the fame durable materials; but we are pofitively told, that *Duleek*, or *Dam-liag* church, was the firft that was built with fuch materials; and was fo called, from *leac*, a ftone. Near to the church, is a Druidical monument, or *leac*, of enormous fize, to which, probably, it owes its name.

The fire of the Druids lighted on the *Cul*, or *Neomenia* of the four quarter months, was called *Tlachtgha*, or *Teine-tlachd-adh*, contracted from *Tallacht-adh*, or *ath*; it was, fays O'Brien, a fire kindled for fummoning all the Druids to meet on the ıft of November, to facrifice to their gods: they burned all the facrifice in that fire, nor was there any other fire to be kindled that night in Ireland: This is copied from Keating, an author who often miftook the Irifh MSS. We have fhewn the occafion,

fion of this fire on the *La-Saman*, in the preceding Effay.

Tlacdgha, or *Tallacht-ad*, was the fame as the Arabic, *Tehwil-awt*: *Tehwil*, a folemn oath made by the Pagan Arabians before a facred fire, called *awt*, or *hawt*. Richardfon. This fire was named by the Irifh, *ath*, *aodh*, *aoth*, and *idd*; and, in the Lapland language, *oth*. From *aoth*, or *ath*, the facred fire, and *nae*, an ifland, the Pelafgi named Mount Ætna; but *aoth*, is alfo a bell in Irifh: and here is another opening for our bell-ringing etymologifts. Several hills in Ireland bear the name of *Tlacdgha*; alluding to thefe fires, where no round tower is to be feen.

In Arabic, *Tela* and *Tulua*, is the new moon when juft appearing: this is another name favourable to my ideas, of thofe Irifh round towers, named *Tulla*, and not conftructed on a *tullach*, or hill: fuch a tower is in the county of Kilkenny, near Gowran, fituated in a low, plain country; and I have feen many others in like fituation.

Talak, in Arabic, is DIES DOGMATIS. *Taku* in Æthiop. ordo, feries, words pointing out the ufe of our towers: *Tallak*, in Arab. fervet Deus corpus, perfonam, vitam tuam. *Talak*, permiffus fuit facrificare, hilaritas, abfolutus. Caftellus.

Talak, in Arabic, fepulchri; in Irifh, *Tlacda*; a contraction in both languages, of *tul* tumulus, and *leacht* fepulchrum: *leach*, is alfo an oblation in Hebrew, Arabic, and Irifh. *Tiodhlacadh*, a gift, did originally fignify the fame as *Tlacdga*, i. e. a gift on the altar; from whence, *lac*, and *laac*, in old Saxon, is a facrifice; *lacan* offerre, facrificare. *Lochem* in Heb. non tam panem quam cibum fignificat; eft

generale

generale nomen. Buxtorf. In Exod. xxv. 30. it is *fbewn-bread* upon the altar. Num. xxviii. 2, my bread of the offering. *Lach*, in Heb, a ftone table: Ex. xxiv. 12, and Deut. ix. 9, tables of ftone; from *talak*, our *Tallaght*, or *Talla*, the palace of the archieopifcopal fee of Dublin, written by the pedantic monks, *Tamleacht*, i. e. fepulchrum mortuorum.

What facrifices our Druids offered at thefe *Cul*, or *Tlacht*, we are ignorant of, but very probably, they confifted of he-goats and fat heifers. *Cul-bhoc*, is an old Irifh name for a he-goat, and *col*, or *culach*, a fat heifer: *cul*, is a word, neither fignifying fex, gender, fpecies, or condition of body, and can only bear reference to the facrifice: *agh*, is an ox, bull, or cow, but *cul-agh*, a fat heifer. In Hebrew, *cùl*, is meat, a feaft; in Irifh, *colt*; but *chul-al*, in Arabic, exprefsly fignifies, *animal idoneum maclari in hoftiam*. Caftellus.

The name, *Cluan*; was, I believe, originally given to all thefe towers: it appears to be a contraction of *cùl-luan*; i. e. the return of the moon: *cluan*, certainly fignifies a lawn; *cluan*, fays O'Brien, is a name given to feveral of our bifhops fees, as *Cluan Umha*, now Cloyne; *Cluan Haidhneach*, Cluan Mac Nois, in Leinfter, &c.—We meet with many places in this kingdom, named *Cluan*; that are fituated on hills, confequently, they did not derive their names from a plain, or level country.

A plain, in Irifh, is exprefſed by machaire, magh, leirg, cathan, achadh, faitche, faithemeid, maighneas, raodh, reidhlein; and, *clogad*, can no more be derived from *Tlachdgà*, than *homo* from *Adam*.

Le Brun

Le Brun defcribes a tower, in Turkey, which the Turks name *kifs-kolæ*, i. e. the tower of the virgins :—in a few pages after, he fays, they call it *kfes-califi*, i e. the caftle of the virgins. He faw, alfo, the tower of the *patriarch Jacob*, near Bethlehem, but it was fo ruinous, he could form no idea of its magnitude : he gives a plate of the ruin, by which we may fee, it was then about twenty feet high, circular, and exactly refembling the ftate of many of our Irifh towers. The *kifs-kolæ* or virgin's tower, of the Turks, carries the air of oriental romance in the name : *cais-caili*, in Irifh, is, indeed, the virgin's tower, but I am inclined to think the name is a corruption of *cais-cuile*, or of *ceach-cuile*, i. e. the tower of proclamation of anniverfaries, &c. See Le Brun's Voyage de Levant. *Kifs*, in Arabic and Perfic, is holy, religious.

I muft now call in another very ancient language to my affiftance; I mean, the *Sclavonian*; becaufe, in the fequel of this fubject, there will be many references to it, as a language, which the learned Abbot Jablinfki has contended to be a dialect of the Phœnician.

S C L A V O N I C E.

Kolác kuha, a circle, fteeple, ring of people, multitude.

Kolacich, a fmall circle, cake : *Kolaç*, publick prizes.

Kolaç, a round pillar ; *Kòlar*, a mafter builder.

Kolafee, a reel, a wheel : *Kolenda*, ftrena, a new year's gift, the hymns fung on the eve of New-Year's Day, Chriftmas Day, &c.

Kolendati,

Kolendati, canere cantiunculum ante nativitatem Domini, &c. &c.

Kolje, a palace; *Kollifeo* Amphitheatrum; *kollo,* a wheel.

Kollo od fkakanja, Chorea, a circular dance.

Kollo na nebber, feptentrio, urfa major, Plauftrum.

Kollobar, a circle; *Kollo-voz miefe,* Sextilis, AUGUST; Irifh, *Cuile-mhos-mios;* *Kolocep, Calamotta,* the NEEDLE, compafs, loadftone.

KOLUDRIÇA, vel DUMNA; (Ital. monaca) Lat. moniales.

KOLUSETAR, a cloifter, monaftery, college, &c.

KAKO MISE, meo judicio.

Cekati, to look for, wait for,·expect.

Chiuchjenje, learning, fenfe, reafon.

Cloujek ueoma, rerum agendarum ufu illuftris.

The learned Monf. Count de Gebelin, in his *Allegories Orientales,* Paris 1773, is profufe on the Etymon of the word *gule* or *yule,* and indeed offers fuch proof, that we can no longer doubt of the true origin of this very remarkable word. *Jol,* fays he, pronounced *hiol, iul, jul, giul, hwoel, wheel, wiel, vol,* &c. is a primitive word, carrying with it a general idea of REVOLUTION and of WHEEL.

Jul-iom, fignifies, in Arabic, the *firft day of the year;* literally, the day of *revolution,* or of *return (p).* *Guil-ous,* in the Perfian tongue, is ANNIVERSARY; it is appropriated to that of a king's coronation *(q).* *Hiul,* in Danifh and Swedifh, wheel; *wiel,* in Fle-'mifh; *wheel,* in Englifh.

Well·en,

(p) This was alfo the day of *guil-am* of the Druids, when they prefented the *giul,* or *uile-ice,* i. e. mifsletoe, to the people. See Preface to the Irifh Grammar, 2d Edit.

(q) In Irifh, *cuil-aos,* an anniverfary.

Well-en, in German, fignifies, to turn ; *wel*, implies waves, which are continually coming and going : it is the French *houle*, the Latin *volvo*.

The *folſtices* being the times when the fun returns back again, have their name from that circumſtance ; hence, the Greek name, *tropics*, which fignifies return *(r)*.

It was the fame amongſt the Celts ; they gave the name *iul*, to the folſtices, and to the months which commence at the folſtices, which, in like manner, fignified return *(s)*.

Stiernhielm, ſkilled in all the languages and antiquities of the North, informs us, that the ancient inhabitants of Sweden, celebrated a feaſt, which they called *Iul*, in the winter folſtice, or Chriſtmas ; that this word means revolution, wheel : that the month of December is called *Iul-month*, the month of return ; and that the word is written, both *Hiule* and *Giule*.

The people of the county of Lincoln, in England, ſtill call a *log*, or ſtump, which they put on the fire on Chriſtmas-day, a *giule-block*, i. e. the block, or log of *iul* ; in Yorkſhire, it is termed, the gule clog.

We muſt not be furprifed, then, if our month of *July*, which follows the *ſummer folſtice*, has had its name from hence : 'tis true, the Romans tell us, this month took its name from Julius Cæfar, an etymon that fuited well with the flatteries they heaped on
their

(r) In Iriſh, *cùl*, is backwards ; *culam*, to return ; hence, *cuil*, a fly, from its circular motions in flying to and fro.

(s) With fubmiffion to Monf. Gebelin, I have never found it written *iul* but *cùl*, as *grian-cùl*, i. e. *grian-ſtad*, i. e. *grian-tas*, the Zodiac.

their emperors, though they had done nothing but altered the pronunciation of the word *iul*, to make it agree with *Julius*, probably pronounced by them as *Julus*, the same with Afcanius, the fon of Æneas, from whom he boafted his defcent; a name which afcended from thence, *even to the primitive languages of the eaft*.

The cafe had been the fame with the month following.

If thefe two months were fixed on, to bear the names of their firft and fecond Emperors, it was, principally, becaufe their names already refembled thofe of Julius and Auguftus.

They did it alfo, in imitation of the Ægyptians, who had given to thefe two months, the names of their two firft kings, *Mefor* and *Thot*.

As the month of Auguft was the firft in the Ægyptian year, the firft day of it was called, *gule*, which being latinized, makes *gula*: Our legendaries, furprifed at feeing this very word at the head of the month of Auguft, did not overlook, but converted it to their own purpofe. They made out of it the feaft of the daughter of the tribune, Quirinus, cured of fome diforder in her throat, (*gula*, being Latin for the throat) by kiffing the chains of St. Peter, whofe feaft is folemnized on this day. (*t*) Thus far Monf. Gebelin.

It is certain, that, in all the ancient languages, *gul*, implies feafting.

IRISH.

(*t*) In the ancient kalendars of the Romifh church, we find the fubfequent obfervations on the ıft of Auguft.

Catenæ coluntur ad Aram in Exquiliis
Ad vicum Cyprium juxta Titi thermas.

IRISH.

Gall, gull, a round tower, feafting, gluttony; *eir-cul,* a circle, hence, the Latin *Anguilla,* an eel, or twifting fifh.

Goile, the ftomach, an appetite for eating: Latin, *ingluvies.*

Gola, guala, gluttony, feafting, joy.

Gul, the eye, to fee; *gul, coel, cul,* augury, prefcience; hence, *galleotæ,* interpretes portentorum, in Sicilia appellebantur. Cicero de Divin. lib. i.

WELSH.

Gwledd, a feaft.

Gwledda, to make a feaft, to debauch onefelf; *guild,* drunk; (Erfe).

Gwiliad, a guard, a watch, a centinel; *gwilio,* to fee: this correfponds with my idea of the *cul dia,* who were to look out for the *Neomenia.*

Coel, augury, prefcience, news, faith.

BAS BRETAGNE.

Gwel, feaft, folemnity, joy.

Gul, fight; hence, the Latin, *gelafinus* nec pulchra eft facies cui Gelafinus abeft. Martial.

BASQUE, or BASCUENCE.

Eftar-goa, or *gola,* an appetite; Spanifh, *gula.*

Gueilzalac, an immoderate appetite.

Jaiz-aina, a feftival, or annual feaft; literally, annual days; this is the fame as *Dias-aina;* in Irifh, *di* and *ti,* being turned by the Bifcayans into *j,* as I have fhewn in the Preface to the Irifh Grammar, and

and is of the fame fignification, as the Irifh *bliain*, or the circle of *Belus* or the fun.

I fhall conclude with one more obfervation on the word *ule :* The Irifh word, *amhuil*, pronounced *ule*, or *ool*, is annexed to nouns, to form the explicative adjunctive particle, in Englifh, *ly*, as, *fear-amhuil*, or *farool*, manly.

Gean-amhuil, *ganool*, lovely.

Speirthamhuil, or *fpeirule*, fprightly.

So *bliadhan amhuil*, or *blianule*, an anniverfary, i. e. yearly; from whence may be derived, the Angelo Saxon *ule*, or a periodical return of a feftival : *amail*, *amhail*, in the Celtic, was of the fame force and meaning, as the Greek ἰμαλος, and Latin *fimilis*, and when fuffixed to nouns, betokened likenefs, aptnefs, fitnefs : it was originally pronounced with two fyllables, viz, *a-wail*, and was, probably, foon corrupted to *awl*, *ool*, *uly*; from whence, the Englifh *ly*. I judge, the ancient Irifh grammarians, were fenfible of this corruption; and, as *bh*, forms a ftronger *v*, or *w*, than *mh*, I perceive, they wrote *abhail*, inftead of *amhail*, and this forms the Englifh termination, *able*, *ble*. This not being regarded by all writers, the Irifh grammarians diftinguifhed fuch words as terminated in *able*, by a prepofite word, fignifying, *more apt*; I mean, the prepofite *fo*, (Arab. *zu*) which forms all fuch compounds in the Irifh, and is to be traced in the Greek and Latin, and, I believe, the origin not known. " Σ, fays Portroyal, is often added (pre-" fixed) to enforce the fenfe of a word, as φάω, σφάζω; " the Lacedemonians rejected it, (as a fuffix) as in " μῦσα, μῦᾶ : The Latins termed the afpirate in σ, as " ἱπὶρ, fuper ;" Irifh, *fo-bar*, from *bar*, upper ; ὁδὸς perfectus,

perfectus, Irifh, *fo-os*, more perfect than others; *ob-equa fugio*, from *fo* and *imi*, to go: *fuperbia*, from *fo* and *borb*, high, lofty; *fupremus*, from *fo* and *priom*, i. e. *primus*, &c. &c. *amhuil*, and *abhail*, formed the *ilis* and *bilis* of the Latins, as from *doceo, docilis; amabilis*, &c. it alfo forms the Englifh termination *le*, when the laft letter of the noun, if a confonant, is repeated, as from the Irifh, *leit*, half, *lithamhuil*, not half, a part; Englifh, little; fo riddle, middle, &c. &c. &c.

There are other names for the feafons, in Irifh, worthy of attention; fuch are *Abran*, *Abarann*, February; the laft month of the year; the firft month of *Earrac*, or the fpring; in Perfic, *bahar*, is the fpring, and the month of April; *bahari*, the fpring, from whence, the Irifh, *earrai*, the fpring; and *Aban*, is the month of February, in Hyde's *Menfum ordo antiquiffimus*, p. 190; in the next page, in Menfium ordo *Gjelalæi*, it is the month of October; and, likewife, in Mr. Richardfon's Lexicon:—This learned author's defcription of the Perfian feftivals in the month *Aban*, correfponds perfectly with thofe of the ancient Irifh *Abran*, or *Faoilidh*: " This " month, fays he, in old times, having been the " laft of the year, they annexed to it the five fup- " plementary days; on this occafion, they held a " continual feftival for eleven days, which began " on the 26th, and ended on the 1ft of the fubfe- " quent month: during this folemnity, amongft " other ceremonies, the MAGI ufed to place upon " the tops of high TOWERS, various kinds of rich " viands, upon which, it was fuppofed, the *Peris*, " and fpirits of their departed heroes, regaled them- " felves."

Ceatain,

Ceatain, is an ancient name of the month of May, so called, because, in that month, the Druids held their assizes or trials, and the persons condemned to be burned *idir dha teine Bheil*, between two fires of Baal, were first tried by the brehon, or judge, and suffered if the chief Druid confirmed the sentence: In Hebrew, *Sanhedrim Kettena*, was the name of one of their civil courts, and in Arabic, *kitt*, is the written decree of a judge.

These days were called by the Irish, *dubh laoi*, or days of mourning, from whence the *jubilee* of the Romish church, which had nothing (except a similarity of sound) to say to the *jubilee* of the Jews, or the blowing of the horn, or rather the act of blowing, as the word expresses, i. e. the *reverberation of the air*; that was a season of rejoicing and feasting, but our *dubh-laoi*, and the *jubilee* of the Romish church, is a time of fasting, alms, and prayers: the *d* and *t*, of the primitive language, was often turned to *j*, as *tiearna* into *jarna*, i. e. Lord. See Irish Grammar, Remarks on the Cantab. Dialect. See *Mi du* or *Dubh*, p. 1. of this Essay.

Faoilleach, Faoilidh, half of February and January; it signifies, the season of rejoicing and feasting; it was the Irish Carnival. *Mi duireadh*, or *Duireadh*, December, or half December, and January; it literally signifies the wet, dropping month, in the Irish language; but I am of opinion, these names are all oriental.

In Hyde's Religio Vet. Persarum, we find the following:

Anni Yezdegherdici 5 dies Appendices.

1st. *Apherin,*

1ſt. *Apherin*, i. e. *Benedictio, ſeu Salutatio, in initio Appendicum.*

2d. *Pherruch*, i. e. *Felicitas.*

3d. *Phiruz*, i. e. *Victoria.*

4th. *Ramiſht*, i. e. *Contentatio.*

5th. *Durud*, i. e. *Valedictio, in fine anni.*

Ramiſht eſt idem quod *Ramiſh*, ſeu *aramiſh*, i. e. contentatio, quies, uti quando ex cantu & muſica animus demulceri ſolet, ut exponitur in Libro Ph. Gj.

N. B. *Reim*, in Iriſh, is of the ſame ſignification, viz. evenneſs of temper.

Et tandem *Durud* eſt Valedictio totius anni, i. e. ejuſdem finis, nempe ſec. vim vocis *Durud* eſt apprecatio boni ; quæ ſi fit a Deo erga homines, tum nomine *Durud* ſubintelligenda eſt miſericordia : ſi ab Angelis erga homines, tum ſignificatur remiſſio, ſeu condonatio : ſi hominum erga ſeinvicem tum eſt precatio, ſeu apprecatio boni, quæ inter valedicendum adhiberi ſolet. Et *Durud* avium & beſtiarum eſt laudatio. Ita variè uſurpatur vox *Durud* uti & Arabum formula precatio ſeu benedictio Dei ſit ſuper illum.

N. B. In Iriſh, *druidheadh*, ſignifies diſſolved, abſolved, poured out, to operate upon; and this appears to be the root of the Latin *Druidas*, Welſh, *Drud*, a Druid, i. e. the Abſolver or Remitter of Sins ; ſo the Iriſh *Drui*, a Druid, moſt certainly is from the Perſic *duru*, a good and holy man : in the Menſes Gjelalæi, *Adur*, is November, fire (*u*).

The

(*u*) This word ſeems to allude to the Druidical fires of November, *Adur*, was the name of the angel ſuppoſed to preſide

The learned Hyde, does not explain the other three appendices, but it is evident, the Irish word *aifrin*, the Mass, is from the Persic *apherin*, benedictio.

Fearachas, is manhood; *earrac*, is the spring of the year, the *faoilidh*, or season of rejoicing, which corresponds with the Persic *Pherruch*, felicitas.

Firsi, is strength, power, courage, from the Persic *Phiruz*, Victoria.

✦✦✦✦✦ ✦✦✦✦ ✦✦✦✦ ✦✦✦✦

The ORIGIN of our *Culdea* merits a further Investigation than could be properly introduced in the foregoing Paragraph, where they are mentioned; the following Observations on ancient History, are offered to the Irish Antiquary:

The religion and boasted learning of the Babylonians, are so blended together, that we hardly know how to separate them into distinct heads; for the *Chaldeæs*, properly so called, were not only the priests, but also their learned men, whose whole science seems to have been subservient to the purposes of superstition and infatuation. These Chaldœes were, perhaps, more distinguished from the people than the clergy are from the laity with us; and were as much revered in their country as the Egyptian priests were in theirs; and are said to have enjoyed the same privileges. (Diod-Sicul. Bibl. l. ii.) They were wholly devoted to the business

prefide over fire, and this was, says Richardson, the first month of the Persian year, which commenced from high antiquity at the vernal equinox.

finefs of their fuperftitious religion; and pretended to prophecy, and to the gift of prediction, by the rules of *augury*, the *flight of birds*, and the *infpection of victims*; they explained dreams, and all the extraordinary phænomena of nature, as portending good or evil to men or nations; and were thought, by their inchantments and invocations, to affect mankind either with happinefs or mifery. Diod. Sicul.

Having, by their fituation, been early addicted to CELESTIAL OBSERVATIONS, they, inftead of conceiving, as they ought to have done, juft notions concerning the omnipotence of the Creator and Mover of the heavenly bodies, and of being confirmed in a due belief and practice of what had been handed by tradition down to men, by *Noah* and his fons, fell into the impious error of efteeming thefe bodies as gods, and the immediate governors of the world, in *fubordination*, however, to the Deity, who was invifible but by his works, and the effects of his power. (Diod. Sicul.) They concluded, then, that GOD had created the ftars, and great luminaries, to govern the world; that he had, accordingly, placed them on high, and fubftituted them his minifters; and that it was but juft and natural they fhould be praifed, honoured, and extolled; and that it was even the will of GOD they fhould be magnified, feared, and worfhipped, juft as a king defires his fervants fhould be refpected in honour of himfelf. (Maimonid. in more Nevoch). Perfuaded of this, they began to build *Sacella* to the ftars, to facrifice to them, to praife them, and to bow down before them; that, through their means, they might obtain the favour and good will of GOD;

so

fo that they efteemed them as mediators between GOD and man. (Maimonid.)

Such was the firft rife of idolatry, and the original of the *Sabian* doctrines, which, taking root among the *Chaldæes*, at laft fpread fo far, as to keep in darknefs, at one time, all the nations of the Eaft. (Univerf. Hift. Babylon).

Properly fpeaking, there was no fuch country as *Chaldæa*, nor no fuch people as *Chaldæans*, as a Nation : they are mentioned in the facred fcriptures, by the word *Chafdim*; the prophet Jeremiah, after predicting the deftruction of the Philiftines, to be effected by a mighty river overflowing from the North, particularly mentions the people of that river or nation, by the word *Sachaim* and *Chaf-dim*, that is, the *Scythians*, the men of *Chas* or wanderers; but the *Chafdim* had overrun *Affyria* and *Ægypt* long before this prophet's time, as is very evident from the facred and prophane writers. *Chaldæa* was a fmall territory fouth of Babylon, abounding with lakes and mountains, bordered by the *Euphrates* on the north and fouth, and by a great ridge of mountains on the weft, extending to the Perfian gulf: This fpot was allocated to the *Chaldæes*, as the north of Ireland was to their defcendants, the *Tua Dadanani*, of whom we have treated in the Preface. *Daniel*, who was perfectly acquainted with the *Chaldæes*, exprefsly calls them *Chafdim*, throughout his writing: not only fpeaking of them as a nation or people, but as forcerers and diviners; as in Daniel, chap. ii. viz. " The king commanded to call the magicians, " aftrologers, forcerers, and (*Chafdim*) Chaldœans"

Montanus

Montanus never tranſlates this word, *Chaldæi*, but *Chaſdi*.

The LXX ſometimes write χαλδαιοι, and ſometimes χαλδαιοι. Joſephus, Antiq. l. i. c. 7, tranſlates *Chaſdim* by *Chaldæans*; (w) he ſays, it is ſuppoſed, *Chaldæa* borrows its name from the *Chaldæans*, or *Chaſdim*.

Theſe *Chaldæes*, were *Magogian Scythians*, who remained in *Aſſyria*, and inſtructed the *Babyloniſh* prieſts in the art of *Chaldæa*, or of predicting the revolutions of the heavenly bodies.

Bochart proves, that the ancient Greek authors, gave the name of χαλδαιοι to many nations: for example, he ſays, *modò junguntur Tibarenis, ut cum ſupra Trapezuntem & Pharnaciam ponit Tibarenos & Chaldæos, id eſt, Chalybes*; addit (Strabo) *enim non multo poſt; qui autem nunc Chaldæi Chalybes olim vocabantur, eadem in Dionyſio legas, & Apollonio, & Plinio, & Valerio Flacco, & Ammiano Marcellino.* *Bochart* makes this obſervation in his chapter on *Tubal* and *Meſech*, (chap. 11. Phaleg) where he alſo mentions, that the *Syrians* and *Chaldæan* Interpreter, by the word *Meſech*, do always mean the *Pelaſgi* or *Tuſci*; "*quem avide ſequti Hebræi poſteriores, nomine Meſech* TUSCIAM, *id eſt Italiam, & Romanorum imperium intelligunt.*" I have ſhewn,

(w) Joſephus certainly borrowed the name from the Greek and Latin Authors: Strabo and Pliny mention the *Chaſdim* under the name of *Chaldæans*; I can find no ſuch word in the Sacred Scriptures, and Claud. de 6, Conſ. Honor. mentions them alſo;

> Pugna ſui Chaldæa magno, ſeu Carmina ritu
> Armavere Deos.

Hence, I believe, it is evident, that *Chaldæa*, as a country or a nation, was not known to the Hebrews.

in the Preface, that no name could be more proper for the *Pelasgi* than *Mesech*, which, in Hebrew, signifies a mixed people, the same as the Irish *Measc*. *Bochart* thinks the prophet Isaias ch. xviii. v. 2. names the Ægyptians *Meshech*, quia *gens tracta*, vel in longum extensa: but is it not more agreeable to the Sacred History, that they should be called a mixed people, as Jeremiah had foretold, that five cities in Ægypt should be possessed by, and speak the Cananitish language? Now, *Gog* is said to be, princeps capitis *Mesech* & *Tubal*, in *terra Magog:* And, as our learned author observes, *Mesech*, in Hebrew, does certainly imply dilatio, prorogatio, when speaking of time, but when connected with nations, people, &c. will signify peregrinatio. The *Chaldæi* were consequently in the land of *Magog*, as well as about *Babylon*, and it appears to be the general name for the calculators of time, soothsayers, &c. &c. and, from the *Magogian Scythians*, the name descended, with the *Pelasgi*, to Ireland, and formed the name *Culdea*.

Histoire d'Assyrie dont on ne peut fixer la chronologie. Des espèces de *Scythes* errants, sortis du mont *Caucase*, commencent à se repandre dans les plaines de l' *Assyrie*, recemment abadonèes par cette partie de l'Ocean, que, pour se faire entendre, il faut bien appeller *Mer Caspienne*. Les *Oans*, plutot civilisès que ces *Scythes*, parce qu'ils avaient un commerce plus direct avec les *Atlantes* de la Métropole, pènètrent, de leur coté, dans la *Chaldèe*, ils avaient, a leur tête, le hardi navigàteur *Oannes*, dont la Fable a fait un amphybie. (Hist. d'Assyrie. Paris. 1780).

We

We shall find, in a few pages, that this *Oannes*, *Omios*, or *Ainris*, was the founder of our *Dadanani*; and that *Colgan's*, Chevalier *Omin*, took his name from hence. In short, *Oannes* and *Chaldæa*, are fynonimous terms for prophet, foothfayer, aftronomier, in the Affyrian, and Magogian Irish language.

The *Babylonians* were famed for learning, particularly the *Chaldæans*, who were their priefts, philofophers, aftronomers, aftrologers, foothfayers, &c. and, in refpect of this pretended claim to learning and fupernatural knowledge, the *Chaldæes* are *quite diftinguifhed* from the *Babylonians*, and are faid to have inhabited a territory peculiar to themfelves, next to the *Arabians* and the *Perfian* Gulph. (Strab. l. 16.) They were divided into feveral fects, as the *Orcheni*, the *Borfipenni*, and known by other names of diftinction, borrowed either from particular places, where different doctrines on the fame points were held, or from particular perfons, who had doctrines peculiar to themfelves. *Oannes*, might have been the Ægyptian *Ifis*, or *Ofiris*, or both:—The *Greeks* were better acquainted with the *Egyptians* than with the *Babylonians*, and the *Egyptians* may have impofed on the *Greeks*, fo that nothing certain can be found in the Greek writers on this head. (Univ. Hift. Babyl.)

The *Chaldæes* taught, that the world was eternal; that it never had beginning, and never fhould have an end; they acknowledged a Divine Providence, and owned, that the motions of the heavens were not directed by chance, or performed fpontaneoufly, but by the guidance and direction of fuperior

perior

perior agents: They are univerſally allowed to
have been perfect aſtronomers, and to have made
ſuch progreſs therein, as to have not only diſcovered the exact motions of the heavenly bodies,
but alſo certain influences they have over things below; and to have thence been able to foretel what
was hidden in the womb of futurity.   (Diod. Sicul.
bibl. l. 2.) In ſhort, they were muſicians, poets, and
phyſicians.   Such was the learning of our _Hiber-
nian Druids_.   They were remarkable for the manufacture of fine linen, and for embroidering: In theſe
arts, the _Magogian Iriſh_ alſo excelled.

   But theſe _Chaldeans, Babylonians_, and _Egyptians_,
originally ſprung from the _Scythians_, (as we are informed by the author of the Hiſtoire d'Aſſyrie
Paris, 1780).—_Diodore, Herodote, & après eux Boſ-
ſüet & Rollin, ont cru la population de l'Ægypte
antérieure à celle de l'Aſſyrie ; ce qui les a engagés
à commencer leurs hiſtoires par celle des ſujets des
Pharaons : Plaignons ces hommes juſtement célèbres de
n'avoir pas été aſſez phyſiciens pour voir le néant de
leurs ſyſtèmes : aujour-d'hui que la théorie du globe eſt
mieux connue, nous ſavons que l'Ægypte inondée par le
Nil, n'a pu être habitée, que lorſqu'à force de patience
& de génie, on a fait un lit à ce fleuve, & prévenu par
des digues puiſſantes les ravages de ſes inondations pé-
riodiques._——Suivant ce principe je conçois comment des _Æthiopiens_, des _Syriens_, &c. fatigués dans
le ſecond age du monde par une population exceſ-
ſive, allerent s'établir dans les fanges du _Delta_,
qu'ils fertiliſèrent : mais des _Syriens_, ces _Æthio-
piens_, &c. &c. ſi prodigieuſement antérieurs aux
habitans des rivages du _Nil_ n'étaient pas eux-mê-
mes

mes des peuples *indigènes*: ils descendaient de la nation primitive du CAUCASE. Nous avons donc une foule d'Histoires à traiter, avant d'en venir à celle de cette *Ægypte, si orgueilleusement ignorante*; mais qui a fait croire *l'Europe* à son *antique sagesse*, grace à l'audace *d'Herodote*, à l'eloquence des *Bossuet*, & á la credulité des *Rollin*. (Tom. i. p. 22.)

N. B. *Geasad*, or *Ceasad*, in the ancient Irish, implies sorcery, divination: this might have been the root of the Hebrew *Chasim*. In the Chaldæe Lexicon, by Buxtorf, we find, *gazar* decidere, decernere, decretum, Prædestinatio, Fatus, decretum divinum: *Gazarin* Haruspices, quasi Sectores dicti. Præterea usurpant Hebræi etiam de decreto divino, quod homini, aut rebus humanis tanquam inevitabile impositum est: *item de influentia ex astris indeclinabili*: hence, the English words to guess, a star-gazer. I take the Chaldæe *gesher*, a bridge, to be of the same root, that is to say, the work of a sorcerer; as the Irish word *draochad*, a bridge, is derived from the Irish *draoch, druich,* magick, sorcery, Druidism.

D E S C R I P-

DESCRIPTION

OF THE

BANQUETING-HALL,

OF

TAMAR OR TARA;

WITH

A PLAN OF THE SAME,

FROM

AN ANTIENT IRISH MANUSCRIPT,

IN TRINITY COLLEGE, DUBLIN. (*a*)

THIS valuable fragment is in the collection lately presented to Trinity College by Sir John Sebright; it appears to be the fragment of a fragment; the writer takes notice, that the description

---

(*a*) This hall was appropriated to the king's houshold or domestics: The royal banqueting-hall, in which the monarch with his family, chief Druid, secretary, &c. dined, is described in the Translation of Keating's History of Ireland, p. 135. It is an interpolation of the translator, from the Psalter of Cashell, he says.—When that work falls into our hands, we will give it a place in our Collectanea. The liberties this translator has taken with Keating, give great room to suspect his authority.

Tamar

ſcription of the palace, and of the royal apartments, are wanting; and from ſome other work,
he gives a very ſhort account of them.

ORIGINAL.

Suidhiugh Tighi Teamhra, canlaſta indiu amail
bae la Con cead cath, agus Teach n Airt agus Cormac, agus Cairpri Liffeachair, agus Teach Cathair
moir agus Teach gach Righ ro fallnai Tamar co
Niall naoi ccleach airulaedan ſo tri, agus ro giall
hiu do ſo tri.

Samlaid bae Teach Laegaire Mac Niell iar cein
iſin ro ſiacht trian tigi Cormac, tri cead troighead
hitaig Laegaire, coecad imdhaigh ann; coecat ſir
in gach imdaigh, coecad airel eaſſib, XX ſir in
gach airiul, XXX cub: a airddi ſuas, VII tre diu
immon Raith, VII ndoirſi foraib, LLL comol na
timcholl fri ſin tſluagh, L Cornn claſach nordha, L
leaſtar finnruini forſin righraidh feiſin, LL nool inna
dabhaigh, V cub: a chaindelbrai, IIII torſi airedha
ſir, VII rannaire, VII ndailemhain ſir, in charpait
foraigthaig immo thenid ſo chuairt, In *Drui* in
Druith accommat, agus in chleaſamnaigh agus in
airſiti no Orfeaſal, na ma iſin tigh ſin. In tſluaigh
olceana iſin fortaigh imontech dia necht-air itir in
da muir, acht in ti do gairt o Laegaire do cum an
tighi ſin, &c. &c. &c. &c.

Suigiugh

Tamar or Tara, was alſo called *Aicbill*, or *Aikill*. In the
Preface of an ancient code of laws in my poſſeſſion, it is ſaid,
Loc den Liuburſa Aicill aireac Tamar, i. e. the place where this
book was written, is called *Aicill*, or noble Tamar. The
Græcian *Achilleon*, *Troia, Iliacus, Iliaca gens*, &c. have a won-
derful Affinity with our Iriſh names of the royal ſeat.

Suigiugh Tighi Teamhra la Cormac ria funn ba fain fon, IX cead traigheadh a Teach, VII indiu ind Rath immon Teach, LLL imdhaigh ann, LLL aireol eaiſſibh, LX fir in cach aireol, X cub; a tealla; tri IX cub; a fordleas, LLL Cornn com nol, XV cubail, XV dorus, mili no othard Cormac cach laei, cearn motha fearti-fuadh, aefdana, agus rinnola di or agus argut agus cairpthit, agus eochuc agus eairreadha in fin.

TRANSLATION.

The palace of Tamar, *(b)* was formerly the feat of *Conn,* of the hundred battles; it was the feat of *Art,* and of *Cairbre Liffeachar,* and of *Cathar Mor,* and of every king who ruled in *Tamar,* to the time of *Niall* of the nine towers, formed or conſtructed

on

(b) Tighi Teamhra, is the genitive of Teagh Tamar, or Teach Tamar; *teac,* in the modern Irish, implies a dwelling, but originally ſignified a houfe of ſtone, a royal palace; in Arabic, *Tekbt* is a royal refidence, and *Tak* an arched building; and this is the reafon it is commonly added to fuch names as exprefs a tower vaulted at the top; as *cleach-thear, tuill-ceactheach,* &c. See the preceding Eſſay. Of the names *Tara, Tarack,* and *Tamar,* I fhall treat at large in a future number of this work, wherein the feveral names of places in Ireland, which cannot be derived from the Irish language, will be ſhewn to have exifted in remote times in *Judea, Phœnicia,* &c. and moſt certainly to have been introduced by oriental colonifts; and fhall only notice here, that at the triennial affembly of the ſtates at Tamar, the chronicles and atchives of the whole kingdom were read and compared; and, that in Arabic and Perfic, *Taarick* implies Chronicon, Annales; whence the Greek and Latin *Archion, Archium.*

on three, for he had vowed to build three towers (c). Such was the palace of Laogaire Mc. Neill, which was but the third part of the palace of Cormac; for in Laogaire, his time, it was but three hundred feet square, contained fifty apartments, and fifty men in each, fifty barrack rooms or dormitories (d) for guards, and twenty men in each, and the height thirty cubits; seven *diu*, i. e. casts of a dart, the diameter of the *rath* surrounding the palace, and seven entrances; one hundred and fifty common drinking cups, fifty curious gilded drinking horns, fifty cups, curiously engraved for the use of nobles only, one hundred *ol* (e) (of Metheglin) daily served in the Vat, five cubits the height of the candlesticks, and four flambeaux in each.

Seven astrologers, seven historians, and but one Druid, one mimick, or comedian and professor of music: (f) No more were allowed in this palace:

one

(c) Arab. *Taamur*, a tower, a steeple, a belfry. Richardson.

(d) *Aireol*, is a bed, in all our Lexicons, but here signifies a bed-chamber: it is compounded of *ar*, high, and *eol*, which is certainly the same as the Hebrew עלּיה *oli*, an upper room, Psal. civ. 3. who layeth the beams of his *oli*, or of his chambers; hence, *moli*, in Hebrew, signifies steps, stairs.—The palace of *Tamar* was thirty cubits high; it certainly had an upper story.

(e) *Ol*, and *olas*, is a drink, but whether it here implies any liquid measure, I am not certain; a drink is no specific measure: *olaz*, in Hebrew, is to make merry: I do not recollect any measure of this name in the oriental dialects.

(f) *Aon Drui, aon druith*, one Druid, one comedian: here is a distinction worthy the notice of the Irish antiquary. In modern times, the word for a Druid is written many ways, as drabi, druith, draoith, &c. &c.

Airfiti,

one carriage or chariot only at a time within the court, to prevent confusion : a large body of troops were also within the walls.

In the reign of Cormac, the palace of Tamar was nine hundred feet square, the diameter of the surrounding

Airfiti, vel *Orfeafal*, the chief musician ; the first is composed of *aire*, a chief, and of *pheit* or *peit*, a musician, properly written, *peitil* or *feitil*. Mr. Shaw, in his Galic Dictionary, translates *fitbil*, a poetaster ; this is a mistake, he corrects it at *peit*. פתיל *phetil*, in Hebrew, is a twisted cord ; such were the strings (we call cat-gut) used by the Irish harpers, and by those of Wales to this day. From this word is derived *Phatara*, a city in Lycia, where Apollo had a temple and oracle : Apollo's priests were called *Phataræ*, (i. e. aire-phitt) hence, says Bates, in his Crit. Heb. an old word *patter*, applied to prayers. The Irish still retain this old word in *paidir*, signifying an oration or prayer ; but now, says O'Brien In his Irish Lexicon, emphatically applied to the Lord's Prayer: *paidirin*, the rosary or beads, literally, the *division* of prayers, from *phetil*, the Irish word *fidhlin*, i. e. a small harp or fiddle.

The explanation of Airfiti, by *Orfeafal*, by the Irish author, is well worthy of notice : Or, is found, from *o*, the ear, hence, the Latin *auris* : *feas*, or *fios*, is art, knowledge, science ; *fea-fal*, is the adjective, implying expert, knowing ; so that *or-feafel*, is expert or skilled in the harmony of sounds, a most proper name for a professor of music : In Arabic, *fexl* and *fe-zylet*, is science, art, learning, doctrine, superior excellence. The Latin name *Orpheus*, is derived from *Aire-feas*, chief or most skilled in all sciences. I suppose the word had been written *Orfeas* by some Etruscan author, and was mistaken by the old Romans for a master of sounds or music ; but *Orpheus* is allowed to be a most ancient learned author and excellent poet ; and Horace observes, that the meaning of his leading hills and woods a dance by the force of his music, implies no more, than that by his eloquence, (or *aire-feas*) he reduced a barbarous people to civility. *Aire* is often written *oire* ; thus *airfit* is to be found in most of the Irish Lexicons, under *oirfit* and *oirfid*.

rounding Rath, feven *diu* or cafts of a dart; it contained one hundred and fifty apartments, one hundred and fifty dormitories, or fleeping rooms for guards, and fixty men in each, the height was twenty-feven cubits, there were one hundred and fifty common drinking horns,. twelve porches, twelve doors, and one thoufand guefts daily, befides (Fearti Suadh) Princes, (*g*) orators (*h*) and men

(*g*) *Fearti fuadb*, the nominative fingular is *feart*, which, by the Irifh gloffarifts, is explained to imply any good or virtuous act: *Fearta feile*, an act of generofity: *Feart* is alfo a region, province, country; and *fuadb* is noble. Feart is a word of great antiquity, and occurs in the Bible but thrice; Efth. i. and 3, vi. and 9, and Dan. i. 3. *Phartim* is tranflated nobles; it is, fays Bates, in his Crit. Heb. put before the *princes of provinces*; a term ufed by the *Perfians* and *Chaldæans*, whofe language we have not enough of, to fay certainly what it means. This paffage in our Irifh MSS. fully explains the word *feart*, for *fuadb*, nobles, being joined with it, plainly indicates they were the *provincial princes*, who might occafionally lodge with *Cormac*, or the monarch of Ireland, on occafional vifits; hence, *Fvart Ullach*, a territory in the county of Meath, anciently belonging to the O'Dooleys, O'Brien. *Suad*, a noble, is the fame as the Arabic *Sadi*, Lord: the Heb. *Sadi*, all bountiful, an attribute of God. Gen. xvii. 1. I am *al fad*, i. e. the all bountiful God.

I have often afferted, that the *Iberno-Scythic*, or *Irifh* dialect of the *Scythic*, was of great ufe in explaining many paffages in the Bible, and moft ufeful in the ftudy of the hiftory and antiquities of all nations: the above paffage, is a proof of my affertion, and I am not fingular in this opinion. In the collection of papers publifhed at Edinburgh in 1738, added to an Effay on the Antiquities of Great Britain and Ireland, we find many minutes of a very learned fociety of gentlemen in Scotland, who underftood the *Irifh* or *Erfe* language well; they declare, that by the Irifh, they had been able to trace the *Latin* language to its fountains, to illuftrate the antiquities

men of ſcience, engravers of gold and ſilver, carvers, modellers, and nobles.

SUIGHIUGH TIGHI MIDHCHU-
ARTA AN SO,

Da imdai deac in fo hiçeachtar ada leithe & tri-
athartha in gach imdai, VI fir deac hi ceachtar ada
airetear & ochtur a rannairib & reachtaireib &
daileadhmnaibh in iarthar in tighe & dias hi ceachtar ada imdai iſin dorus, cead fir huili in ſin.

Da bae & da thinne (i) & da muice a proinn
rainneadh coecat for ceachtar in da bo, &c. leth do
leath & leth illeith naili, Bruidhean midcuarta ainm
in tighiſin.

On the oppoſite page of the original, is a plan of
the hall, and the ſcite of the tables, with the names
of the houſhold, and the joints or parts of the beaſt
allotted to each, according to their rank. The plan
is twice the ſize of the annexed plate, which, being too ſmall to have the names, &c. engraved
on it, we have made uſe of references.

TRAN-

ties of *Greece*, and the *Greek* language, in which the New
Teſtament was written, to follow the *Greek* language up to its
ſource ; and that the *Hebrew* and *Chaldæe* languages may
receive a great deal of illuſtration from the *Iriſh*; that it gave
great light to the languages of *America*, particularly of that
ſpoken about *Darien*, &c. &c.

(b) *Aoſdana*, orators, learned men ; from *aos* or *aoſad*, a
community ; in Arabic, *yzzet*, and *dana*, learned men : *dax*
alſo implies poetry ; in Perſic, *dana* is learned, (*doctus*) and in
Arabic, *deivani* is a perfect poet.

(i) *Teinid*, a ſheep : Arab. *Tinet* and *Timet*, a ſheep of a ſu-
perior kind, never allowed to go with the reſt, but milked
at home, and only killed in ſcarce ſeaſon by the poor.
(Richardſon).

TRANSLATION.

DESCRIPTION OF THE BANQUETING OR EATING HALL. (*k*)

Twelve stalls or divisions in each wing, (with tables) and passages round them; sixteen attendants on each side, eight to the astrologers, historians, and secretaries, in the rear of the hall, and two to each table at the door; one hundred guests in all; two oxen, two sheep, and two hogs, at each meal, (*l*) divided equally to each side. The name of the hall is BRUIDHEAN. (*m*)

AN

(*k*) *Midbcuarta*, i. e. *teach festa no eurme*, i. e. *Midbcuarta*, is a feasting or banqueting room. Vet. Gloss.

(*l*) See the Bruighs explained in the Brehon Laws, No. x. Preface, p. 34. In Arabic, *burj*, hospitality: In Perfic, *berkh*, feasting, *burkendam*, a carnival.

(*m*) *Proinn*, a meal at noon, a contraction of *bro*, meat, food, and *min*, noon. *Pbit* or *fit*, is a breakfast, a snack or short meal, from the Hebrew פת *pbet*, a morsel or mouthful: the Latin *prandium*, is supposed to be derived from the Greek ἄρτο and τᾶδος, i. e. *cibas-meridianus*; but the Iberno Scythic *proin-dia*, a meal in the day-time, appears to be the root of *prandium* and of τᾶδος. The chief meal of the ancient Irish, was at even; and in the annexed plan, we find the hall was lighted by torches and lamps. This meal was called *cuid*, which implies a meal, share, portion, entertainment, and also a supper. In Arabic, *kedd* and *kyd*, is a portion, part or share; *kedat*, a collection of meat and drink; but *kudas* is the Lord's Supper, with the Christian Arabs: the consecrated wafer is named by them *kyriffet*, from *kurz*, baked bread; of which in some future number.

AN OBSERVATION.

Fulucht na morrighra an so; blogh di feoil huim (n) & di fheoil fhonaithi & mir rimmiarfe & ni leagad anim & ba fonaith anom & ni ba loifethi an bruidhi & moale no bitis a triur for in mbir, do dechatar tri naoi cuici feomra do cuimgid indeoine & IX naifle inti & do bearad cach dib a aifil na laim can ateagdis caichi & condrictis cach dib for a ecoffa & no thocabtha combeag comard.

TRANSLATION.

The grandeur of the royal palace is here unnoticed; the quantities of meat and butter that was daily confumed there, furpaffes all defcription: there were twenty-feven kitchens, and nine cifterns for wafhing hands and feet, a ceremony not difpenfed with from the higheft to the loweft.

Before we proceed to the explanation of the annexed plate, it will be neceffary to mention the ranks of *file*, or philofophers and poets, as I find them in another part of the fame manufcript, entitled, *feacht gradh fileadh*, i. e. the feven degrees of *file*:

1ft. *Ollamhan* or *Ollamh*, 2d. *Anfruth*, 3d. *Cli*, 4th. *Cana*, 5th. *Dos*, 6th. *Macfuirmidh*, 7th. *Fochlocc*; Students of three claffes, viz. 1ft. *Taman*, 2d. *Drifiu*, 3d. *Oblaire*.

I have

(n) *Uim*, butter: Heb. *aimu*

I have not been able to tranflate all the feveral
joints and parts of the animal, with which each rank
of the houfhold were ferved, fuch as I could not
difcover, I have left in the original Irifh.

Martin, in his Defcription of the Weftern Ifles,
gives fome little defcription of the clafs of men we
are going to explain ; in p. 115. he fays, the orators
in their language, called *ifdane*, (aofdana) *(o)* were
in high efteem both in thefe iflands, and on the
continent, until within thefe forty years; they fat
always among the nobles and chief families; their
houfes and little villages were fanctuaries as well
as churches, and they took place before doctors of
phyfic. After the Druids were extinct, the orators
were brought in to preferve the genealogy of families, and to repeat the fame at every fucceffion of a
chief: they made alfo, epithalamiums and panegy-
rics on marriages, and births:—and at p. 109, he
fays, before money became current, the chieftains
in the Ifles, beftowed the cow's head, feet, and all
the entrails upon their dependants, fuch as the phyfician, orator, poet, bard, muficians, &c. and the
fame was divided thus: the fmith had the head, the
piper had the, &c. &c.—Mr. Martin probably
took this defcription from fome poor clan of the
Ifles ; in our fcheme, the fmith had allotted to him
moel, i. e. flefh without bones.

N. B. I am not yet able to diftinguifh the great
number of augurs, diviners and forcerers, mentioned in the following lift ; but hope, by the generofity of Sir John Sebright, foon to be able to explain

(o) **Dan**, in Arabic, an orator ; *dana*, Perfic, very learned.

plain their various claſſes, having met with a MSS. in his collection on the ſubject.

REFERENCES to the PLATE.

TABLE

1. *Marcaigh* no *Araidh*, cuinn doib & moer. Maſters of the horſe, the head and marrow to them.

2. *Citéare* & *Timpanaich*, muic forman doibh. Harpers and minſtrels, (ſome part of the hog, I know not which).

3. *Breitheamhain* lonchroichti doib. Brehons or judges. —— —— ——

4. *Suilitri* & *Taman*, (p) lonchroicht no primhekrochat doib. Heralds and tamans. —— ——— ——

5. *Ollamh file*, (q) loarce do; *anſruth*, cam cnaimh. Profeſſor of the file, the thigh to him; anſruth, crooked bones, (ſhins of beef).

6. *Bruigh*

(p) *Taman* : Taman is the latter part of the Hebrew compound *chartum*, a magician; *taman*, i. e. to hide; this expreſſes the dark doings practiſed by theſe conjurers in their caves, or in the adyta of the temples, with the obſcure ambiguity they uſed to return to their deluded clients; it implies purifications, luſtrations, &c. wherein they undertook to expiate crimes, and to avert evils and plagues, by crimes more black than any others, viz. by idolatrous rites and arts magic. (Holloway, Orig. Phyſ. and Theol. p. 223). In the *Carribean* dialect, *tamin* is a ſervitor to the prieſt.

(q) *Ollamh, Ollabh,* or *Ollapb,* we find the word thus written in the various MSS. *Allupb,* in Phœnician and Hebrew, is *doctor, magiſter, princeps, director*; in Perſic, *ulem,* a learned man; a doctor, in Arabic, *allam,* omniſcience; *alọn, ylm,* knowledge.

Pbela,

6. *Bruigh & aire trisiu*, laracc doib ;

The bruigh and chief of the Drisiu, student or File.

7. *Ogtairsaire*

Phela, in Hebrew, relates to any thing which is beyond common, as to knowledge, excellence, power. Our Irish *silea*, were philosophers, compósers of (*neimeadh*) odes, anthems, &c. they were also judges in spiritual causes under the Druid ; they were ominators ; hence, *sal* an omen.

In Hebrew, *philila* judicium, *tephilla* oratio : Chaldee, *precatorium, oratorium* : In Syriac, *phil* acutè, *phil-phel* subtiliter differuit, (de re aliqua, ut in scholis fieri solet). *Phile-phel* disputatio subtilis, acuta ; subtilitas; acumen in disputando & dijudicando : In Æthiop. *sal* omen, *sabal-sale* ominator. *Fale-sale tybab* (in Irish, *tobair sail*) fons sapientiæ, *Titulus Sti. Pauli* : Chaldee, *philea* interpretatio, sententia allegorica & parabolica : Syriac, *mephille* symphoniæ : Arab. *sali* elevatus, O quidam vir !—pretium divinationis : *saal*, a soothsayer ; *sebl*, excelling in any profession, especially poetry : Persic, *sal* an omen ; *silek*, the *Magi* ; a small number of the ancient Persians were so called, who adhered to the tenets of Zoroaster ; they fled from the Arabians, in the seventh century, to the Isle of Ormuz, and soon after took refuge at Surat and Guzurat, where their descendants still remain under the name of *Parsi*. (Richardson). This is the *Phallon* of the Greeks : according to Diod. Sicul. they derived this deity from Ægypt, and mistook his attributes for *ball* pudendum ; which *Bapt. Passerius* very properly corrects, and derives from the Hebrew *Phala*; from whence *niphla* arcanum, mysterium. (Lexic. Ægypt. Heb. p. 15. 84).

No word in the Irish has been more mistaken by the moderns, who have classed the *file* with the *bard* ; *file is neime uasal*, agus *eascop is neime an eclais* : the file and the bishop, are both *neime* or holy men, says the old glossarist ; and certainly our *file*, was the *philiu* or *ignicola Magus* of the old Persians. (See Hyde, p. 361). I am of opinion, the Greek φιλοσοφοσ is derived from this word *file*, compounded with *so-feas*, i. e. σοφία : *so* in the Hiberno Scythic, is a preposit, signifying aptness, goodness, excellence ; (Arabic, *zu*) and *feas* is science, art, &c. *so* forms many of the Greek and Latin com-

7. *Ogtarfaire macfaofma a tanaifi,* cam cnaimh doib ;

Young forcerers to fucceed as vacancies happen ; fhins to them.

8. *Faifhiri*

pounds, with the fame force of expreffion ; as Σφαξος, fuperbè ; Irifh, *fo-bor* vel *borb*. Σοφισμα, commentum ; Ir. *fo-fifeamb*. The oppofite to *fo*, in the Irifh, is *e* or *mi*; for example, *breith*, fenfe, judgment ; *fo-breith*, found in judgment, fober ; Lat. *fobrietas* ; Gr. σωφροσυνη : *ebreith*, out of his fenfes, drunk ; Lat *.ebrietas* ; Gr. μιθη.

The modern gloffarifts fay, *phile* or *file*, is derived from *balg*, a man of erudition ; whence, *bol*, a poet, art, fkill, eloquence ; *bolachd*, poetry : but this *bal* and *balg*, are evidently from the Syriac *bal* mens, animus, cogitatio ; Chaldee, *bul*, cor, animus ; *balab* confiliarii, from whence, βουλη confilium, and not from βη and λαω (video). Arabic, *belg*, eloquens : *Bilga*, was alfo the name of an order of priefts with the Chaldees ; ab hoc, ordo ille facerdotalis, cujus obfervatores *Belgitæ* dicti. (Caftell).

In Perfic, *Pulkenjik*, is a comic poet.

The *anfruth* was fo named from *fruth*, knowing, difcerning, and *an*, good, great. *Sruth*, in the modern Irifh, is a man in religious orders, though not yet promoted to holy orders. (See Bifhop O'Brien's Dict.) It was fometimes written *fuith* or *faoith*, which O'Brien tranflates, a tutor. The Irifh *bar*, when prefixed, being equal to *an*, *bar-fuith*, is certainly the root of the Greek Παρασιτος, who, as Potter obferves, was certainly a perfon in holy orders, and was allowed part of the facrifices, together with the prieft ; this is evident, from an Infcription on a pillar in the *Anaceum* ;

ΤΟΙΝ ΔΕ ΒΟΟΙΝ ΤΟΙΝ ΗΓΕΜΟΝΟΙΝ ΤΟΙΝ
ΕΞΑΙΡΟΥΜΕΝΟΙΝ ΤΟ ΜΕΝ ΤΡΙΤΟΝ ΜΕΡΟΣ ΕΙΣ
ΤΟΝ ΑΓΩΝΑ ΤΑ ΔΕ ΔΥΟ ΜΕΡΗ ΤΟ ΜΕΝ ΕΤΕΡΟΝ
ΤΩ ΙΕΡΕΙ ΤΟ ΔΕ ΤΟΙΣ ΠΑΡΑΣΙΤΟΙΣ.

Thu. fays, from σιτος frumentum, but *barfaoth* is an old word for a bifhop, and *bardhien* a mitre, in the Irifh language ; from the Druidical word here quoted.

8. *Faiſbiri (r)* & *comail*, colptha doib;
   Augurs and their diſſecters. ——   ——
9. *Ailtire ſaor & ſaor chrann*, & *raith-buinnithir*, hir
   croichti doib;
   Architect, carpenters and rath-builders. - :
10. *Carnaire* & *buinnire*, *(s)* midh-mir doib;
    The ſacrificing prieſt and his attendants. - :

11. *Rinnaire*

(r) *Phaſar* occurs but once in Hebrew, Eccleſ. viii. 1. but
often in Chaldee, in Daniel, to interpret: There are three
words, *pharas*, *phaſar*, and *pharat*, which have ſome affinity
in ſenſe, as hath *phatach* alſo; and it would be hard to ſay
that any of them, or if any, which of them, was not genuine
Hebrew. Bate's Crit. Heb.—N. B. All theſe words are
common in the Iriſh, ſignifying ſoothſayers, ſorcerers, prophets, and interpreters of dreams, as *faiſiri, foras, forat, fait-
beach, faithg*, &c. &c. Dr. Keating gives the title of *foras-
feaſa*, to his Hiſtory of the Antiquities of Ireland. *Foras-focal*, is an expoſitor or interpreter of words, an etymologicon.
The Arabic word *fariz*, is tranſlated by Mr. Richardſon, *distinct ſpeech*. *Foras* ſometimes implies a preface in Iriſh; that
is not the ſenſe of the word; it means an index; the Arabic
febris, is an index, a canon, a rule; and *foras*, in Iriſh, is
alſo *law*, foundation: the word here implies an interpreter of
dreams; and the ſorcerer, or he who divined by twigs,
ſticks, or arrows, was named *crannfaiſitboir*, from *crann*, a
ſtick or arrow; hence, *crannfaiſtine*, ſorcery.

   Comail, is a dwarf in Iriſh and Arabic; it alſo ſignifies *perfectus, perfecta ſacrificia*; and I believe here ſignifies thoſe employed in diſſecting, being claſſed with the *faiſbiri*, augurs or
interpreters.

   (s) The *Carnaire* was the principal *ſarcificulus* of the Druids, ſo called, ſay the gloſſariſts, from *carn* fleſh, and *aire* a
chief in ſcience; *carneach* is tranſlated a heathen prieſt, in our
modern Lexicons; they were both *ncimeadb*, and claſſed with
the *files*. The Rev. Dr. Clever, firſt chaplain to his Excel-
lency Lord Temple, has ſo very learnedly explained theſe
two words, in his notes on the *Decretum Lacedæmoniorum con-*

11. *Rinnaire* & *neafcoithri*, loatan doib.
Aftronomers and genealogifts, or diviners.

12. *Cairem-*

tra Timotheum, Edit. Oxon: 1777, p. 26. that with his permiffion, they are here inferted :—It muft be firft underftood, that
neimh, in the Irifh, implies law, poetry, fcience, and holinefs ;
and a gloffarift of the twelfth century, thus explains the
word *neimh* : *Cia neimeadh is uaifle ? File, an eaclais neimeadh
n'Eafcop*. i. e. who are fuperior, *neimhe ?* File, and neimeadh,
bifhop, are both *neimeadh* ; Hebrew, *neum* arcanum.

" Nomum ideo fic dictum fuiffe, conjicit Ariftoteles, quod,
" quum adhuc literas nefcirent homines, leges cantare con-
" fuefcebant, ut memoriæ eas perpetuæ mandarent ; & pro-
" inde cantilenas antiquitus vocari nomos ; neque multum ab
" hac conjectura abludit Ariftides Quinctilianus. Sed pro-
" fecto mirum omnino effet, fi vetufta adeo invaluerat vox
" νόμος, pro *lege*, eam nufquam in ifto fenfu apud Homerum re-
" periri ; cui νόμος acuitur, & denotat pafcuum : Cum quo
" quidem fenfu Nomi Etymon conjunctius effe videtur.

" Nomum primum hymnum fuiffe in *Apollinem* confcriptum
" plurimi teftantur auctores. Porro a Proclo traditum eft,
" *Apollinem* a nomo appellari Νόμιμον, lege Νόμιον. Eandem
" adftruunt fententiam Poetæ.

————— καὶ ἅγιον Ἀπόλλω-
ν' ἀνδράσι χάρμα φίλοις
ἄγχιστον ὀπάσσαι μῆλοι,
ἄγρια καὶ Νόμιον.

Pindar, Pyth. 7.

Κλαγὴ τ' ἀγριελαιος Ἀπόλλωνος Νομίοιο.

Theoc. in Idyll. 32.

Φοῖβον καὶ Νόμιον κικλήσκομεν, ἐξ ἔτι
κείνου,
Ἐξότ' ἐπ' Ἀμφρυσοῦ ζευγίτιδας ἔτρεφεν
ἵππους
Ἠιθέου ἐπ' ἔρωτι κεκαυμένος Ἀδμήτοιο.

Callim. Hymn. in Apoll.

" Eadem

12. *Cairemhain* & *tornoire-reamhur*, nimhda doib. Shoemakers and turners in coarfe wood.

13. *Cuiflin-*

" Eadem de caufa Pan etiam dicitur Νόμιος apud Schol.
" ad Ariftophan. Aves. 746.

Περί νόμυς ἱερὰς ἀναφαινε——

" Ἔστι Νόμιος ὁ θεὸς. Quocum facit illud Phornuti ; Νόμιος, παρὰ
" τὸ νέμω. Unde Nomum exiſtimo fuiſſe primo carmen, quod
" ἐν νομαῖς (in pafcuis) cantabant paſtores, Apollini dicatum,
" qui et ipſe olim paſtor Admeti oves pafcebat. Porro Car-
" niis, feriis itidem Apollini dicatis, folenne illud habebatur,
" ut νόμους, aut potius νομούς, concinerent Καρπίυς. Καρπίυς,
" etiam appellabatur Apollo, ἀπὸ τῶν κάρπων, ἥγυν προβάτων.
" Hefych.

" Sed nomi certe, utcunque de origine ejus ſtatuerint viri
" docti, duplex erat notio. Quarum altera defignabant mo-
" dum Muſicæ, cujus generis magnam fuiſſe copiam apud
" Græcos notiſſimum eſt. Plut. de Mus. Altera, *Poefeos*,
" quandam fpeciem, quam fupra aliquâ ex parte defcripfi-
" mus ; cujus quidem ea fuit conditio, quum ex Reipublicæ
" auctoritate *feſtis diebus* caneretur, ut non tantum materiam,
" fed et muſicæ numeros ex confuetudine præfcriptos haberet.
" Harmonia *Nomi* fuit continua, quippe cujus carmen erat
" hexametrum, atque adeo rhythmus graviſſimus."

Ὁ μέντοι νόμος, γράφεται μὲν εἰς Ἀπόλλωνα. *Nomos* quidem in
Apollinem confcriptus, a quo appellationem fumpſit. *Nomi-
mus* enim *Apollo*, qui ita appellatus eſt quod veteribus choros
conſtituentibus, & ad tibiam vel lyram *Nomon* canentibus,
Chryfathemis Cretenfis primus ſtola ufus infigni & accepta ci-
thara, *Apollinem* imitatus folus cecinerit *Nomon*, qui cum eo
genere vehementer probatus eſſet.

Eſt autem Dithyrambus incitatus & multum furoris cum
faltatione oſtendens, ut vehementiorefque affectus compara-
tus. *Nomos* contra per affectus & numeros leniores remitti-
tur, *compoſito gradu*, & *magnifico* incedens. Videtur autem
Dithyrambus in ruſticorum lufu & *hilaritate*, inter *pocula* re-
pertus eſſe. Photii Biblioth. p. 986. Edit. Stephani.

From this learned and accurate defcription of the Greek
Nomoi, we can readily difcover the reafon of the modern
Irifh

13. *Cuiſlinnaigh,* colptha doib.
    Pipers.

14. *Scolaighe,*

Iriſh making diſtinctions in the word *neamb* ; as *neamb-nuall,* or *naombran,* an anthem or hymn. O'Brien's Dict. *Neam-beadb,* a poem ; *neamb,* is heaven, bright, noble, holy ; *ne-ambidb,* divine ; *neamb-maiis,* the office of the Druidical prayer and adoration. In Perſic, *nemaz,* prayers, devotion ; *namutenabi,* divine ; all which are derived from the Hebrew ℵﬦﬠ *neam,* ſermo. elocutio.

In Iriſh, *kéarn, karn,* an altar ; *karn-duais,* the prize-laurel ; *karn* or *kearn-airrdbe,* a trophy ; *keirnine,* a ſmall harp ; *kearnacb,* a prieſt ; *kearnaire,* a ſacrificulus, before the eſtabliſhment of chriſtianity in Ireland ; i. e. a ſacrifice to *Karneios,* Apollo or the ſun, named by the Iriſh, *Crian* or *Grian,* from whence *Granneus Apollo.* In Arabic, *keren* the rays of the ſun, the upper limb of the ſun. (Richardſon). In Perſic, *giryan* a ſacrifice. Tartar and Scyth. *gbiun, gbiurn,* the ſun ; hence the Iriſh *goor,* light, *gorm,* warm, a firebrand : Perſ. *gurm,* hot : Arab. *jerm :* Iriſh, *garam,* to warm ; *gair-tbeas,* the glittering reflection of the ſun from the ſea ; *griam,* to ſcorch : Hebrew, *cor,* fornax.

N. B. The number of *aire,* in this liſt, is ſuprizing ; they were all diviners, augurs, and ſorcerers : *Aire,* a ſorcerer, and *eolas,* knowledge, form the Latin *airiolus* or *bariolus.* In Arabic, *aurif,* knowing ; *arrauf,* a ſoothſayer ; *aul,* art, ſcience. It is aſtoniſhing, that *Voſſius,* who was ſo good an Hæbreiſt, ſhould not have looked into the Arabic ; his Etymologicon Linguæ Latinæ. is a diſgrace to all his other works, and expoſes him to the cenſure of every ſchool-boy, the leaſt acquainted with the Arabic : in this example, he derives *bariolus* from *fariolus,* i. e. *bædus, fædus,* vel ab *balando* quia *ba-litu,* quia *balitu* ſoleat mortalem animam quaſi excludere, ut recipiat divinam : ſed primum malim : and this he borrows from *Scaliger.* Every word in Arabic and Iriſh, which implies arts, ſcience, knowledge, do alſo ſignify poetry, ſorcery, augury, &c. &c.——And as the learned Van Dale obſerves, apud Ethnicos ergo *fortes* erant varii generis, militares, politicæ, divinitoriæ, &c. &c. (De Oraculis, p. 289). So had our Iriſh monarch ſeveral claſſes of ſorcerers, which we expect to be able to explain in our next number.

14. *Scolaighe*, leafs croichte doib.
Royal fcholars. ———— ————

15. *Cearda, (t)* hircroichti doib.
Braziers, tinkers, &c. ———— ————

16. *Gobainn*, moel doib.
Smiths, meat without bones to them.

17. *Toathaith*, milgittain doib.
Augurs. I cannot diftinguifh if this word is *toathaith* or *tuathaith*, both imply augurs, forcerers, and diviners. See *Tuatha dadanann* in the Preface.

18. *Saercarpat*, milgittain doib.
Carriage makers and wheelrights. ———— ————

19. *Cleafamhnaigh*, colptha muic doib.
Kings jefters. ———— ————

20. *Cainte re muir*, nimdha doib.
Lecturers on navigation. ———— ————

21. *Dorfaire righadh*, dronn doib.
Royal porters or door-keepers, the chine to them.

22. *Fidhcheallaigh, (u)* colptha doib.
Chefs players. ———— ————

23. *Deoch-*

(t) *Ceard* fignifies any mechanic: Perficè *kerd*, he made; *ker*, a mechanic, art, commerce; *kar*, a trade; *Kerdagher*, God, i. e. Conditor—Lingua Indica, Gentoo, vel Indoftan; *ceirdeor*, a tradefman; *kertar, factor*, a mechanic. Hyde Rel. Vet. Perf. p. 134. Millius Ling. Indoft.

(u) *Fidcheallaigh* or *fitchilaigh*, chefs, a word corrupted from *fill-cluithiagh*, or chefs-players: *Fill* is the game at chefs, fometimes written *fithcill*, to diftinguifh it from *fall*, another game on the tables, which are called *taibble-file*: *Phil* is the Arabic name of chefs, from *phil*, the elephant, one of the principal figures on the table The ancient Irifh were expert at chefs, and at *taibb-liofg* or backgammon: In Perfic. *tawlè*

23. *Deochbhaire*, leafcroichti doib.

 Cup bearers; they were alfo called *bachlamhal*,
 from *bachla*, a cup: Perficè, *bekawul*, cup
 bearer to the king: Arab. *bukla*, a cup.

24. *Humaidid, (w)* and *Oinmite*, Hercroichti doib.

 Appraifer of viands, &c. and his tribe; *amaidd*,
 i. e. *amainn*, i. e. *oifigid*, an office. Vet. Glofs.

25. *Leighi & luamha, (x)* maol doib.

 Phyficians and inferior clergy, folid meat to
 them.

26. *Luamhaire, no luar-remuir, (y)* milgitain doib.

 Sea pilots.

27. *Crea-*

tawk is a kind of trick-track, backgammon, or draughts.
Richardfon.

 The Irifh had another game on the tables, called *falmer-
mor*, wherein there are three of a fide, and each throws the
dice by turns. The ruftics of Connaught play backgammon
to this day remarkably well; and it is no uncommon fight,
to fee tables cut out of a green fod, or on the furface of a
dry bog; the dice are made of wood or bones. Martyn, in
his Defcription of the Weftern Ifles, tells a ftory of
Sir N. Mc. Leod: being at play at *Falmer-mor*, the turn of
the game depending on his movement, he was at a lofs, till
his butler whifpered and told him the movement that won
the game; p. 320. I find the name of the elephant, in Irifh,
was alfo *fall*, as *fall fogblach na fear-foirne*, fall, the robber or
taker up of the *fear-foirne* or chefs men.

 (*w*) *Amad*, Heb. Chald. eftimavit pretium vel menfuram
alicujus rei. Caftellus, *Ormith* Chald. populares tribus.

 (*x*) *Luamb*, comprehended all the inferior ranks of clergy
under the Druid: After the eftablifhment of chriftianity,
luamb was the name adopted by the abbots and priors. We
read of *luamb Lis-moir*, the prior or abbot of Lifmore, &c. In
Arabic, *lubem* implies wife men, fage, excelling in virtue.

 (*y*) *Luar re muir*, in Perfic, *lur*, is the channel of a river,
harbour, &c. but the Irifh adjunctive, *re muir*, of the fea,
fufficiently explains this title.

27. *Creacaire,* cam cnamh, no, colptha muicci.
Carvers. ———   ———

28. *Fuirſeoire,* (*z*) colptha muic doib.
Maſters of the ceremonies: Maitres de hotel.

29. *Braigitoire re muir,* nimhdha doib.
Naval officers. ———   ———

30. *Druith righeadh,* drommona doib.
Royal mimicks or comedians. ———   ———

31. *Araid,* cam cnamh doib.
Bridle-makers. ———   ———
Moer, cuinnid doib.
Stewards. ———   ———

32. *Suithiri,* muicformuin doib.
Brewers. ———   ———

33. *Aireforgill,* lonchroichte doib.
See the titles of honour in No. X. of this Collectanea, Preface, page xxxii. where the ſeveral degrees of *aire,* are ſet down in order: the
word ſignifies chiefs, nobles, and diviners. ———

34. *Ruiri-rioghan,* & *ri-ruireac,* leaſcroichti doib.
The queen's knights, and king's champions.

35. *Aire-ard,* loarc doib.
The aire-ard, or chief augur. ———   ———

Cli,

(*z*) This word is to be found in the Iriſh Lexicons, at
fuiras, i. e. an entertainment: There is great reaſon to think
theſe people diſtributed the meat and drink at the funerals of
any of the royal family. The Hebrew word *pharaſi,* implies
to break, to divide, and as Mr. Bates properly obſerves, to
deal out. Iſa. lviii. 7. is it not *pharas,* (to deal, to divide)
thy bread to the hungry. Jer. xvi. 7. Neither ſhall men
pharaſi, (deal out) i. e. their bread to them, i. e. to comfort
the mourners; neither ſhall men give them the cup of con-
ſolation. The funeral feaſts were to cheer up the mourners,
a cuſtom ſtill kept up in Scotland: Bates Crit. Heb.—it is a
univerſal cuſtom ſtill in Ireland.

Cli, camen.. .. doib.

Third File. ⸺ ⸺

36. *Aire tuifi*, cam cnamh doib. — —

The tuife forcerer. ⸺ ⸺

Seancha, (a) loarc doib,

Antiquaries and genealogifts, the thigh or round of beef to them.

37. *Aire deafa & dos, & macfuirmi, & aire eachta,* colptha doib. Aire deafa, & dos, *(b)* are the fifth

---

(a) Seancha. This very common-word is peculiar to Ireland: The *Seanchas* were called antiquaries, becaufe they repeated or renewed what had been recorded of the hiftories and genealogies of the kings. In Hebrew, *fhen*, a renewer, from whence, *fhena*, a year, to repeat, change, alter ; l. *fhenim*, tongues, languages ; from thefe roots are derived, the Irifh *fain*, unequal, more than one ; *faine*, found ; *finne*, the elder in years ; *fian*, a voice ; *fian-meid*, an accent ; *fean*, old ; *feinn*, to fing ; *fean-gal*, wife ; *fean-mor*, a fermon ; *fainfios*, and *fean-fean*, etymology ; *fanas-anuidbe*, a gloffarift ; *fanas*, knowledge ; *fean*, old ; *feanach*, knowing, crafty, cunning ; hence it is the name of a fox : *fean*, myftery, a charm ; *feanam*, to defend from the power of enchantments ; *feanta*, *feanacht*, fo bleffed, from the power of charms ; from whence, *feanct*, holy, and the Latin *fanctus*, holy, a faint, i. e. one who has the power of defending from enchantments :— Arab. *fhenn*, a charm, a myftery, craft, trade, profeffion ; *fhenn*, old ; *fenat*, a charm : Perfic, *fen*, old.—N. B. The Irifh bards fay, that the river *Seinni*, was the fecond that burft out in Ireland, (for they pretend to affert the exact time of the breaking out of each fpring, lake, &c.) and was fo called, as being the oldeft of the moft confiderable ftreams, the firft being a trifling effort of nature.—Now, *Sheni* is the name of the fecond river in Genef. ii. 13. To *Seinni*, they added *ain*, water, fountain, and formed *Shannon*. Our antiquaries were alfo fatirifts, and often expelled for their invectives. Heb. *fheninib*, a biting word.

(b) Dos was alfo an order of the Druids ; they were the operators or executioners of a facrifice, from which is derived

fifth and fixth file, and *aire eachta*, all augurs and diviners: In fome copies, we
find *macfaofma*, which I take to be a corruption of the Hebrew *mecafaf*. Deut. xviii. 10.

38. *Fochlochir & aire deafa*, croichti doib.
The feventh file, and aire deafa or augur.

39. *Cuthcaire & cracoire no cornaire*, midh mire doib.
Huntfmen and horn-blowers. —— ——

40. *Ruthbugi & oblaire*, milgitain doib.
Old men, and oblaire or fophifters. ——

41. *Aire*

rived the Latin *facer-dos*, a prieft: in Heb. *dafs* ftrangulavit;
Arab. *das*; Perf. *dafb* coadjutor; in Arabic, *dafan*, dedicavit,
munus altaris; *defis*, roafted, toafted: In Perfic, *deftyar*, is a
coadjutor; (fuch was our *Dos* to the Druids) *dexfb-khym*, an
executioner: in Irifh, *deafam*, to roaft or bake. I am of
opinion, that the *aire deafa* was the chief of the *dos* or *das*,
and that they were both facrificers and augurs; though here
ranked with the *file*: Every order of the *file*, bore the fame
name in the order of the Druids; they were diftinguifhed by
the prefix *fagab*, in the clerical order, and in the laity, by the
fimple word, or by the prefix *an*; hence, *fag-airt*, Ir. a prieft,
and *facerdos* Lat. The Greek ΊΕΡΟΣ, facer, præftans, magnus, is from the Scythic *iris*, religion, law, faith; Perfic,
berai; which forms the Greek ΙΗΡΑ; but the root fignifies in
Irifh, a record or chronicle, an æra of the feftivals and ceremonies due to God. Ἰερθύς, facerdos, is probably the fame
as the Irifh *Iris-tus*, magnus in rebus religionis, or compounded of our Dos; from whence, the Greek Δόξα majeftas,
fplendor, gloria, dignitas, fententia, opinio, mens, Plat. Po-
nitur pro axiomate vel propofitione rata. Ariftot. Ἱεραμοιβοι
vates deorum, from the Scythic *iris*, religion, faith, and
maoibbm a theorem, a hard and difficult expreffion or word.
Ἱερός facer, divinus, auguftus, has the fame force of expreffion
as the Irifh *agb-ufad*, explained in No. X. of this Colle&.
Thus the Irifh *eafcoph*, a bifhop; in Arabic, *teffekuf*, created
a bifhop, is evidently the Irifh *tus-eafcop*. The further explanation of thefe words, is referred to the Ecclefiaftical
Hiftory of ancient Ireland.

41. *Aire eachta & cana,* cam cnamh doib.
Aire eachta, fourth file. ———   ———

42. *Muirigh & clasaigh re uuir,* nimhtha doib.
Admiral and chief navy officers. ———   ———

43. *Reamaire, (c)* mael doib.
Ambassadors or messengers, solid meat to them,

44. *Dalbhairi,*

(*c*) *Reamaire:* The word implies interpreters, prognosticators and travellers; I have therefore translated it ambassadors. In Hebrew, *barim* from *rimah,* which signifies to project, to cast, to deceive, and when applied to actions of the mind, to deceive, from whence projectors and deceivers are synonimous to this day. From the word *oram,* the epithet of the devil in the serpent who tempted Eve; hence *Hermes;* the prince of frauds, tricks and cunning; also the god of arts and sciences; likewise the interpreter or messenger of the gods: Εφμηνω to interpret.:—So (says Hutchinson) they applied the attributes this Hebrew word expresses to *Hermes,* and emblematically made him a head and wings to it; but he was not made for thinking; that is all imagination: they have confounded the attributes of one god with another, and the emblems, so that at last they knew little further of their god, than the image they saw, and talked and writ accordingly. Upon such blunders as this, the later languages, and consequently all the knowledge in them is founded. Confusion of Tongues, p. 92.
In Irish, *eirim* is an interpretation, a summary, index, but *reamaire* is a traveller, from *reim,* a step, a way, a road; hence, *Mercury* was the god of the travellers. *Reamam* is prognostication; *ream-lon,* a viaticum; *ream-rad,* a preface; *reim-ambuil,* bearing great sway, from the Hebrew *rim,* to exalt; *reaman,* from the beginning of all things, hence, Arab. *Rebman,* God: Perf. *Reaman* and *Raiman,* the Devil. The Irish *eirim-mianadh,* to interpret, i. e. to explain the *mian* or mind of one person to another, bids fair to be the root of the Greek εφμηνω. The stones set up in honour of *Hermes,* were called *margam: marg* in Irish, is commerce, hence, *margad*

44. *Dalbhairi*, mael doib.
   Sorcerers.

45. *Reachtaire*, *(d)* mael doib.
   Secretaries or fcribes.

C. C. C. C. *Coindeall*, candlefticks : Arabic, *kendil*, candle, lamp, chandelier : Chaldee, *kandil*,

D. *Dabac*, veffel with beer, to drink. *(e)*

L. *Lochrann*, a lamp fufpended by a chain next the door.

46. *Herlar*

margad, a market : *margoir* is a merchant ; quære, if this be not the derivation of his name *Mercurius?* The Scholiaft upon Appolonius fays, *Kadmilus* was a name of *Hermes* : from the Irifh *Cadmus primus*, and *eolas*, knowledge.

(d) Reachtaire, fcribes. See *Scriobam* in the conclufion. The Irifh words *raichtim*, *racam*, *fcribim*, *fcreabam*, to turn up the ground, to dig, are the roots of the Latin fcribo, Belgæ fchreiben, wroeten : Ang. Sax. a writan, to write, and probably of the Greek *γρτὸ*, the written decree or fentence of a judge. From thefe roots, proceed the Irifh *ratheoir*, *raightheoir*, a boor, a countryman, a plowman ; *reactaire*, a judge, a fcribe.

From the preceding fynonima, it appears evidently, that the ancient Irifh received all the names for writing, book, &c. &c. from the orientalifts ; and in my humble opinion, the word *du*, ink, is a ftrong confirmation of it. *Ink*, fays Skinner, a Belg. inck, inckt, enckt ; Fr. G. encre ; Ital. inchioftro ; hæc a Lat. & Gr. encauftum, atramentum autem confonis aliquantum vocibus fed diverfæ prorfus originis ; Hifp. *Tinta*, Teut. *Dinte*, *Dinten* appellatur, hæc a Lat. *Tincta* pro Tinctura. *Du* is fometimes written *dubb*, from whence the Perfic *dubir*, a writer, a fecretary.

(e) The drink of the ancient Irifh kings and nobles was *meadh*, *meith*, or *meithaclan*, i. e. *mead*, or what we now call *metheglin*, i. e. fermented *meith* or honey ; it was alfo named *mil-deoc*, or fweet drink.

That of the chiefs and of the houfhold, was *fuith*, or *fuithbruith*, i. e. beer ; called alfo, *cuirm* and *leann*.

That

46. *Herlar caich.*

Area for fpectators.

◄◄·►►◄◄·►►◄◄·►►◄◄·►►◄◄

That of the common people, was *chlaba*, or *baine-claba*, *meathar*, or *biotbràn*, and *cin-cis*, or *kin-keefh*: The laft is a fower liquor drawn from bran; I know not its derivation.

Meadh or *metheac*, was a very ancient liquor made of honey; it was ufed by the Ægyptians, their country abounding in bees, and not producing vines, as we are affured by Strabo, Ptolemy, Herodotus, and Mofes.

In Hebrew מתק *methak*, is pleafant, agreeable, fweet, correfponding to our Irifh *mil-deoc*. In the Brehon laws, I find great attention was paid to the property of bees, and to the making of *meath* and *futh*, or beer.

In Perfic, *mayè* is ferment, rennet; in Irifh, *meig*, whey, any ferous liquor; *mei*, wine; in Greek *methu*.

In Arabic, *mebran* is honey.

Cuirm, ftrong beer; Phænicè *chamar*, vinum; Gr. Κύρμι; Lat. *curmi*; (Welfh, *kwrw*), * *Sutb*, fometimes written *fuithir*, and *fuire*, beer: The word implies fermented liquor, but when joined with *bruith*, (brewed) denotes beer, or a decoction of *orn* or barley: It was in general named *futbb*. In Hebrew, *fetaf*, to fteep, to feeth; but *fhet* is drink; *fheti*, drinking, a drinking bout. Ecclef. x. 17. for ftrength, and not for (*fheti*) drunkenefs; hence, *mifhti*, in Hebrew, a drinking bout, an entertainment, a feaft; in Irifh, *meifti*, *meifce*, *mifga*. 1 Sam. xxv. 36. He held a feaft in his houfe, like the feaft of a king, and Nabal's heart was merry within him, for he was very (*meifhti*) drunken: Thus the convivium vini of Ahafuerus in Efther, is named *mifhti*.

In Perfic, *meft*, *meifti*, *meftanè*, *meigufar*, drunken.

In Arabic, *mufkir*, *mefkir*, *mufeken*, drunk; *mukbefhim*, very drunk; from whence, we fay, in Englifh, as drunk as *muc*.

Suth was alfo the liquor of the Egyptians; called by the Greeks ζύθο; by the Latins *zythum*. Dubium num vox ea ac res ipfa a *Gallis*, an *Ægyptiis*: Sed *Ægyptiis* affignat Plinius. Voffius.

Hoc

---

* Vinum in Lingua Hindoftanica eft, *an gurri ciraal*, i. e. red *gari*; in Irifh *cuirm caoral*, red cuirm or wine; Arab. and Perf. *chamar*.

Hoc (*zythum*) maximè utuntur Ægyptii. Hieronymus.

As in Hebrew, so in Irish, *futh* betokens strong drink and mirth; *bi go futha*, (be so merry) is the compliment at this day of every peasant, at his entering an alehouse.

Meathar or *meadar*, otherwise called *biothran*, implies a serous liquor, made of sweet milk, fermented some days with four milk; it is usually given to the harvest labourers in Munster. I have drank it often, and found it a pleasant and cooling drink, not unlike cyder. *Biothrân* certainly did once imply strong drink. In Arabic, *bita* is wine made of honey: *batt* signifies intoxicated: probably this is a corruption of the Irish *bac*, drink.

Chlaba, or *baine-chlota* thick, four milk: this is also a Hebrew word, חלב *chlab*, rich, fat, unctuous matter, whether of flesh, corn, wine, oil. &c. Bate's Crit. Heb. Gen. xlix. 12. teeth white with (*chlab*) milk: The word is often used in Heb. for milk. Gen. xviii. 8. He took butter and (*chlab*) milk, and the calf he had dressed and set before them. Jud. iv. 19. She opened a bottle of (*chlab*) milk, and gave him to drink. Prov. xxx. 33. The (*mits*) churning of (*chlaba*) milk, produceth (*hema*) butter: Here also we find the Irish *meatfacan*, fresh churned butter, meat, mead, or *migh*, *maigh*, a churn, and *eim*, *iom*, or *im*, i. e. butter; hence, the Arabic, *bemet*, a churn. *Baine*, the Irish word for milk, is certainly of Hebrew descent. חלבנה *chal-bani* is the Latin *galbanum*, a *milkish* distillation from the herb *fennel-giant*, in yellowish drops, and white within. *Gal* and *ban*, in Irish, imply white, and milk: The *galbanum* was one of the ingredients in the holy perfume which was burnt in the Holy of Holies, and which it was death to imitate. Exod. xxx. 34. from whence the Greek λίϐανϴ, frankincense.

There are many places in Ireland named *Galbani*, probably from the quantity of wild fennel growing there. In Persic, *binu* is thick milk, or rich milk; in Arabic, *le-ben*, new milk: Heb. *laban*, white.

Bita, in Arabic, as I have before observed, means *meath*, or wine made of honey, and *batt* is drunken. *Bita* and *bital*, in Irish, imply any inebriating liquor. *Ufca* is a distilled spirit: in Persic, *ufkefh* is a strong spirit made of hemp, says Richardson, and in general any strong drink; it is the Irish word *ufca* or *ufacht*, strength, power: *Ufca-bita* was the

ancient

ancient Irish name of this strong spirit, which has been mistaken for two words very similar in letter and sound, i. e. *uisce-beatha*, i. e. *aqua-vitæ*, and now called *usquebaugh*. *Uisce* is certainly water, but should be written *isce*: thus we say *uisce fiorath*, or contractedly, *uisce-fior*, i. e. spring water, or water fit for man's use. *Pharat*, in Hebrew, and *farat*, in Arabic, imply *aqua-dulcis*, sweet water; from whence, the Greeks formed *Euphrates*, a river remarkable for its good, sweet water; and with their usual tautology, added *eu* bené. *Bitàhl*, contractedly *bitàile*, is particularly applied by the Irish to rum; it is a very extraordinary word. The Cornish called America *Lollas*; and rum was named by them *dour tubm Lollas*, i. e. West India spirit; and *dour tubm Franc*, French spirit, i. e. brandy. Borlase's Diction. of the Cornish. In Irish, *dut tobban Lollas*, has the same signification as *bitahl*, i. e. the strong water of *Lol*; quære, from whence is derived the word *Lollas*, for America, or the West India Islands? The Welsh lay claim to the discovery of America, before Columbus it is true, but I am of opinion, Mr. Borlace has mistaken the word *Lollas*; that it does not signify America, but strong drink: *Lolloa*, in the Basque or Cantab. dialect, is drunkenness; from whence, the Latin *loluim*, the Italian *logiio*, the German *lolch*, *lulch*, the Flemish *lulch*, the Dalmatian *lyuuly*, all signifying drunken; but *lollas* is omitted in the Cornish dialect, when applied to brandy.

Lolium, *quasi* ✲✲✲ hoc est *adulterinum*, fit enim e corruptis tritici ac hordei seminibus.   Vossius.

I think the derivation of this word, must come from the Scythic language: In Irish, *lo* is water; *all* is strong; *lo-all* strong water; *lott* is a drunken bout, a potation: *Loth-ola* is pronounced *lola*, and will imply a compotation, tending to drunkenness; *lollac* is a giant, a strong man, from the Arabic *lala* a wolf, breaking bones, &c.

In Arabic, *lal* mulier quæ ebrietatem suam prodit cum vinum inebriat; *lala*, shaking, staggering as a drunken man.

✦▸◀◀ ✦▸◀◀ ✦▸◀◀ ✦▸◀◀

In the preceding pages, (514, 515) the word *diu* and *idiu* occurs, as the measurement of a certain space of ground, which is explained by the commentator, to signify the *cast*
of

of a dart; the same word occurs in several parts of the Brehon laws, as a land measurement, and is always explained in the same manner, viz. by *umcor fleafcaig*, the cast of a dart. This name, I apprehend, at length, signified a greater space, and was applied to a certain square measurement, like the English acre.

The Irish *idiu*, the cast of a dart, is certainly derived from the Hebrew and Chaldee ידה, *iadah*, jacere, projicere, jaculari, as in Jeremiah 50, v. 14. All ye that bend the bow, shoot at her, (that is, *idu*, jacite contra eam.) Hence the Hebrew *iad*, a hand; that is, the instrument whereby any thing is thrown, or cast forth. From this root are derived the following Irish words, viz. *iad, id*, the hand, a ring worn on the hand; *idna*, missive weapons; *diad, doid, miad, mad*, the hand; *idir*, a certain space; *idionnoir*, a protector, a guardian; *dideann*, a fort, sactuary, protection; *did-deanam*, to defend, to protect, *to take by the hand.*

The ancient Irish often wrote this word *indiu* and *indiugh*, (a cast of a dart or stone) making the letter *i* nasal; the Arabs do the same, as from *eed*, the hand; *andauktun*, to cast; *andauz faukhtun*, to cast; *andauze*, a cast; *neezeh andaukhtun*, to dart a javelin; and that this was also an Arabian measure is evident from the word *andauzeh*, which signifies both a cast and a measure.

I am of opinion, that the Irish *idiu*, a certain measure of land, is the root of the old British *hide or hyde*, e. g. a hide of land; and that this is one of the many words retained by the Britons not to be derived in the Welsh, which gave cause to that great Welsh antiquary Mr. Lhwyd, to say, that the ancient Irish had certainly been the primitive inhabitants of Britain, until expelled by the Gomerian Celts or Welsh.

Chamberlain observes, that the distribution of England into *hides* is very ancient: the *hide*, says he, denoted a measure or quantity of land, containing so much as could be yearly tilled with a single plough.

Beda calls the *hide* of land *familia*, and defines it to be so much as was sufficient for the ordinary maintenance of one family.

Crompton fays, a hide of land contained one hundred acres, he adds, that eight hides made a Knight's fee, others make it 120 acres. *(Jurifd. fol. 222.)*

Sir Edw. Coke notes, that a Knight's fee, a hide, a ploughland, a yard land, and an oxgang of land, do not contain any certain determinate number of acres.

Spelman fays, the word *hyd* is not derived from the A. S. *hyd* as Pollidore thinks, from a *cows hide*, but from the Saxon verb *hyden*, i. e. *tegere*, but this verb is certainly from the Magogian-Scythian or Irifh *idion* as before in *idionoir*, a defender, protector, guardian, &c.

Quantitas *Hydæ* in diffidio eft, (adds Spelman) Angliæ per *hydas* diftributio perantiqua eft : non *Aluredo*, licet infulam multifaria infignit divifione tribuenda. Occurrit enim *hydarum* mentio in L L. Regis *Inæ* (qui fupra 100 annos *Aluredum* præceffit) cap. 14. & hydarum nomine antiquius cognofcuntur 12 ille portiones, quæ 12 Jofephi Aramathiæ comitibus in Glaftonienfis monafterii territorio feruntur affignatæ.

From this word was alfo formed the Saxon *Hidagium*, a tribute collected from every *hide* of land. Thefe are alfo derived from the old Irifh *iod-agh*, and *iod-beirt*, an offering, a facrifice, a tribute, from *beirt*, a gift, and *iod*, a certain quantity of land; the word compounded is written *iodhbbeirt*, and pronounced *ioveirt*; this founds very much like the Arabic *ifra*, facrificing. See *iodhbairam*, in the Irifh dictionaries.

The *hidagius* is alfo evidently the old Irifh *iod-agh*, or tribute to the *agh*, or holy ufes; whence *bagius* fanctus, a Græ. ἅγιⓈ, fays Spelman. See *agh* explained in Collectanea, No. X. p. xv.

In like manner the Anglo Saxons adopted the Irifh druidical or ecclefiaftical divifion of Ireland, into *cir* or *kir*, which were circles of certain extent, round each *mon*, *man*, or *fammon*; the Saxons firft wrote this word *cire*, and afterwards *fchire*, forming the latter from the Saxon verb *fchiran*, to cut or divide, whence the Englifh *fhire*; the druidical *cir* ftill exifts in the *circles* of Germany.

N. B.

N. B. The word *reactaire*, which I have tranflated *fecretary* in the preceding pages, implies alfo, a fubftantial farmer ; it likewife fignifies a prince or judge, according to the following explanations in the lexicons, viz. *reactaire*, i. e. *cleireach*, a writing clerk, a fecretary ; *reactaire*, i. e. *righ no breitheamh*, a prince or judge ; *reactaire*, a farmer : and amongft the modern peafantry, this word fignifies a dairy-farmer ; one, who rents a great number of cows of the landlord, with a proportion of grazing ground, at a certain annual rent upon each head of cattle.

In the Arabic I find *raukaurees*, i. e. a writing-farmer, called alfo *zemeendar*, a man of confequence, who receives a temporary farm from the prince of a large diftrict, which he lets out in fubdivifions, and accounts for the revenue ; his jurifdiction and powers is very great. *(Richardfon's Arab. Dict. at the word* farmer.) This without doubt was the old Irifh *reactaire*.

OF

Plan of the common Eating Hall of TAMAR or TARAH *from an Ancient Manuscript*

OF THE

KISS of SALUTATION;

OF CURSES, &c.

THE kifs of falutation is univerfally practifed in Ireland, except in the metropolis: it is of Oriental origin, and at one time, was common to all polite nations. "Eft Perfis in more ofculare cognatos? maximè dixiffe Cyrum cum faltem & intervallo temporis allii alios videant, vel a fe invicem aliquo difcedant." *Cyrop. edit. Hutchinf. p.* 43.—"Tradit, ni fallor, Herodotus, Orientis morem fuiffe, ut æquales in occurfu invicem ofculum darent; qui inferiores effent, manum ejus, qui dignitate prætabat, ofcularentur, qui humillimi, fefe incurvarent." *Voffius in Maimonede de Idol. p.* 6.—"Nec vos negare poteftis, qui contra nos fcandala ponitis, dum aliqui veftrum & non intellectas proferunt lectiones: ut auferant etiam illud, quod inter omnes homines

folet

folet effe commune, falutationis videlicet officium.
Nam & vos ipfi aliqui in perfunctoria falutatione
ofcula folita denegatis." *Optatus*, l. 4.

The Latins made three diftinctions of kiffes, viz.
the *ofculum* between friends ; the *bafium* was a kifs
of refpect, and the *fuavium* between lovers: but
Tiberius in order to check the progrefs of vice a-
mongft the Romans, prohibited the kifs of falutation.
Pliny tells us, that men were allowed to kifs the
women near of kin. " Non licebat id fæminis
Romæ bibere. Cato, ideo propinquas fæminis ofculum dare ut fcirent an *temetum* olerent—hoc tum
nomen vino erat." Lib. 14. c. 13. " *Ofcula officio-
rum* fint, ut, cum peregere advenientes ofculamur,
bafia pudicorum affectuum, ut patris erga liberos,
fuavia libidinum vel amorum ; fed difcrimen id minimè obfervatur." *Voffius.* The French academi-
cians make the fame diftinction, " les peres & les
meres baifent leur enfans au *front*; les amis fe baifent à la *jouë*; les amans à la *bouche*; on baife la
main d'un Evêque à l'offrande ; la *robe* d'une prin-
ceffe, & la main d'un Seigneur à qui on rend la foi
& hommage." *Furetiere.*

The church at length made *ofculum* to imply
eulogia, benedictio. Hen. Imper. Pafchalis P. P.
fpeaks of the ofculum in ore, in fronte & oculis.

Hieron. & Greg. Tour. of the ofculum *genuum* &
manuum. Anaftafius of the ofculum *pedum* pontificis.
And Amalarius explains the ofculum *pacis* of the
church. " Ordo Romanus, cum dixerit *pax Domini fit femper vobifcum*, mittit in calicem de fancta.
———interim Archidiaconus *pacem* dat Epifcopo prio-
ri,

ri, qui & ultra dabit juxta se stanti, ac deinde per ordinem cæteri, atque populus osculantur se in vicem osculo Christi——observandum porro tertio die ante Paschatem die, quæ Cænæ Christi Domini dicimus, ab ejus modi osculis abstinuisse, ob mæstitiam Christi passionis, unde in Ordine Romano, dicat *agnus Dei absque osculo.* l. 3. c. 32.

The Jewish rabbi's and commentators are much divided about the kisses so often mentioned in S. S. In the Bereshit Rabba, sect. 70. the *neshik* or kiss is thus explained: " Omnis osculatio est *neshik* * *tephalut* (i. e. ad fatuitatem, i. e. fatua, stolida) exceptis tribus quæ sunt

Neshik Pherkim, osculum magnificentiæ & dignitatis.

Neshik Pherisuth, osculum seperationis vel discessus.

Neshik Koributh, osculum propinquitatis.

In Shemot-Rabba, the *te-phalut* is said to be osculum fatuum, lascivum, unde in Glossa explicatur per Pharuzuth, protervia, lascivia; unde suspicor (ait Buxtorf) Drusium in hac voce *te-phaluth* impegisse, & pro ea legisse *tepluth,* osculum precationum, deinde transfero *Neshik Pherakim* osculum compitorum vel biviorum." That is, what we call in Irish, *easgai braid.*

---

* *Neshik* in Hebrew implies a kiss, from the same verb, that is, to approach, to come close; in Irish *neasachd,* i. e. contiguity; *neasa,* next; *pòg-neasachd,* is a kiss pressed hard upon the lips.

Pleiffer

Pfeiffer in his Antiquitates Ebraicæ, makes no other diſtinction than the *oſcula licita & illicita* †.

That the moſt ancient Iriſh kiſſed the beard, according to oriental cuſtom, I think is evident from the following words;

IRISH. *Buſs*, a mouth, a kiſs.

Pus, the lip, a kiſs.

Phuſog, feuſog, a beard, compounded of *phus* and the Hebrew *zak* or *zakan*; for the proper name of a beard in Iriſh is *grinn, grean* or *ulcha*.

PERSIC. *Bus, buz*, the mouth, lips, a kiſs.

Fuſh, a beard; *anfuſh*, a great beard.

And Joab ſaid to Amaſa, art thou in health, my brother? And Joab took Amaſa by the beard (*zakan*) with the right hand to kiſs him. 2 Sam. 20. 9. Thevenot ſays, that among the Turks it is a great affront to take one by the beard, unleſs it be to kiſs him, in which caſe they often do it. (P. 1. p. 30.) Our Lord reproaches the Phariſee who invited him to eat bread (Luk. 7. v. 45.) that he had given him no kiſs, whereas the perſon he had been cenſuring in his heart, had not ceaſed kiſſing his feet, from her entrance into the houſe. It is viſible by the contraſt (ſays Harmer) that our Lord ſuppoſes, between the womans kiſſes and the compliment, he had reaſon to expect from the Phariſee, ſome other kiſs of ſalutation.

† The reader may conſult alſo Herenſhmid in Oſculologia, Kempius de oſculis, Salmuthus, &c. &c.

When

When beards became unfashionable, the Irish naturally kissed the cheek, or the lips, a custom that still remains amongst all people of equal rank.

The modern Irish have but one word to express a kiss, viz. *pòg*; those of the middle age had three, viz. *pòg, meam, falùt:* the first implies the kiss of salutation, given on the *poc, puc, pòg*, that is, the cheek; a word derived from the Syriac *pacca*, the maxilla or cheek bone; or from the Chaldee *pag*, the cheek, from whence *Betb-phage*, i. e. domus *buccæ*, the temple of the *cheek*, or of the *trumpet*, because the cheeks are puffed out in the action of blowing. See *Bernhardus* in sermone ad milites templi. Persicè *pej*, the cheek.

The *meam* of the Irish, was the *osculum lascivum* of the Jews (the Irish *suamb* or Latin *suavium* did not express the meaning of *meam*;) it was the obscene *memra* or *mumass* of the libidinous Arabians.

The *falutb* or *folutb* was the *osculum salutationis,* made by kissing the tips of the fingers to every person they met; from whence *lùt* now implies respect; *dean do lùt*, make your bow or courtesy. The common salutation of the man or woman of the house, to a person entering, is still made by *failte*, i. e. welcome, I salute you; *cuirim failte*, (i. e. *falùt*) I greet you. The Sclavonians like the Irish, use *pog* to kiss; to which they add the word *lips*, as *pog-liubgljnje*; but the salutation is expressed by *fala*, welcome,—*fala Boggu*, gratiæ sint Deo,—*faliti*, laudo. The Welsh have corrupted the word to *arfolli*, welcome.

The

The old French word for a kifs was *pocq*, and *poki*, to kifs; the Welfh fay *poccyn*, and the Cantabrians *pot*; but the Irifh word *failtbin*, fignifying an idle, foolifh, babbling, intermeddling fellow, explains the *ofculum phaluth* of the Jews.

The falutation of the Irifh at parting is *flàn leaſt* or *leat* *, i. e. peace and health be with you; this is evidently a corruption of the Hebrew שלום לך, *ſhalom lach*, the ordinary falutation of the Jews, and which is ufed by our Saviour, in the gofpel, to his difciples. The root in Hebrew is *ſhalam*, he was perfected, or made perfect; the Irifh *flan* has·the fame fignification; Punico-Maltefe, *ſliema*, i. e. falutazione. *(Dizion. Ital. e Pun.-Malt. dal Agius de Soldanis.)*

Sela is a word in the Irifh language, which I muſt here notice though out of place.

Sela, i. e. *foileodb*, i. e. *fiol*, i. e. *gac fortan*, that is, *ſela* or *foileob* or *fiol* exprefs every praife and thankf-giving that can be given by the creature to the Creator. *Vet. Glofs.*

Siol, gac fortain on tuinn Dhe, that is, *fiol* is every praife that can be poured forth to God; C. O'Conor, Efq; from ancient MSS.

Let us fee if the modern Hebrew lexicographers have explained this word better than our old Irifh gloffarifts.

---

* *Leachd* is the proper word, when implying to take in the hand, or about you, in poffeffion, as *beir leachd fin*, take that (thing) with you. לכך, *lacad* in Hebrew, fignifies the action of taking with the hand. *(Solom. Doylingii Obf. Sacr.)*

Lexicon

Lexicon to the fynagogue fervice. Anonym.

סלה Selah, " it hath been ufually by many looked
" upon and taken only for a note of Mufique, but
" I conceive there is more marrow in it: it may
" be derived from *falal* he lifted up, or exalted,
" and fo is a note of exaltation or lifting up the
" heart, foul, and mind, with the voice in the
" praifing of God——or it may be taken from
" *falab*, he did throw down, lay low and level,
" and then it will imply the deep humiliation of
" the heart."

PARKHURST.

Selab, " a word which occurs above feventy
" times in the pfalms and thrice in Habbakuk. I
" would interpret it after many learned men as a
" note requiring our particular attention, as a N. B.
" mind, attend to this. It literally fignifies ftrew
" or fpread it out, i. e. before the eyes of your
" mind that you may thoroughly confider it."

BATES.

Selab, " to tofs, to heave up, to caft down,
throw up and along. Pf. 68. 5. Sing unto God,
fing praifes unto his name, extol, rather throw up
(fcil.) the voice and hand to him, i. e. lift up or
fwell the voice to him and where Selah occurs, that
elevation in the voice and mufic fhould be ufed,
and perhaps thofe very words laft cited were then
fung. Pf. 3. 5. I cried unto the lord with my
voice and he heard me out of his holy hill Selah,
i. e. now add the exaltation, i. e. exalt him that
rideth on the heavens, and fo it would be equiva-
lent to Hallelujah, Prov. 4. 8. *Sel-felab* exalt her
(wifdom) very much and fhe fhall lift thee up."

So

So likewise in Irish *Siolam* is to throw about, to scatter, but it means to scatter with profit, i. e. to sow the ground with feed : and *Siol* fignifies feed, an iffue, a tribe, a clan, from *Shil* in Hebrew a fon*.—Many of the old clans had this word prefixed as *Siol-Malyre, Siol-Na-Macne,* &c. &c.—But *Seillon* is an old Irish word fignifying a bafe in mufic —a chorus, hence it is the name of the humble bee, from its noife ; and it is probable it was a Hebrew word now loft, fignifying a chorus, or the ftriking up of fome mufical inftruments.

The Irish have another falutation at parting of great antiquity and not to be explained without the affiftance of the oriental languages : it is this, *Slan leat gan bafc gan barn* †, i. e. health and happinefs to you without *bafc* or *barn.*

Bafc is barn ort, i. e. *bafc and barn* to you, is a great curfe. The words are obfolete in the Irish language ; they are not to be found in the modern lexicons and we muft refer to the oriental tongues.

In Hebrew *bazach* illufio, derifio, ludibrium ; *buz,* contemptio ; *bazab* defpicere.

In Syriac *baſſna* defpectio, contemptio, *baſa* contemnare.

In Arabic *baſkat,* malum & periculum, *baſkb* in adverfa incidit. *Al-baſky* ftultus, vecors. (Qui
Arabica

* See Hutchinfon on the word *Shilu,* where he explains it, the emblematical copulation ! ! ! Vol. 6. p. 210. 213.

† Sometimes they fay *Sith-leat* or *Si-leat,* i. e. peace be with you ; this is the Hebrew *Selati :* the burial fervice of the Jews is thus, " Let his foul be bound in the garden of Eden. Amen, Amen, Amen." " *Selati.*"

Arabica ignorat.)—*Barm* moleftiam & mærorem animi inde concepit, *bazab* vir depreffit fe, gibbus pectoris, timor.

In Perfic *buran* cutting, *beran-dakbten* to fcatter, *beran-gikbten* to extirpate, *berenj* torment, *berwend*, *perwend* a cut-throat, a murderer.

But the moft bitter curfe of the Irifh is *croidbe cradbta dbuit*, fignifying *the fluttering of the heart to you*. This conveys every idea of the Hebrew חרדת *chradat*, that is, to tremble or flutter as the heart in a fright, or through care and folicitude, or ground in an earthquake. (Bates Crit. Hebr.) In Irifh *Craiba Talmbain* is an earthquake. Thus in Exod. 19. 18. it is faid, the whole mountain (charad) quaked greatly, and in 1 Sam. 4. 13. his heart (chrad) was trembling for the ark of god, and in Hof. 11. 10. it is faid, the children fhall (chrad) from the Weft; they fhall (chrad) flutter as a bird from Egypt and as a pigeon from Affyria. The verfions (fays Bates) have none of them hit upon the fenfe of the paffage, but the vulgate.

The Jews ufed this word alfo to denote their fear and awful obedience to the Almighty, as *le-chradatb aleim* in trepidationem Dei (Caftellus) hence it is the Syrian name of the Crocodile, the fight of this devouring animal caufing the heart to flutter.

I flatter myfelf that I have by this time convineed the reader, that the language, manners, and cuftoms of the Irifh, differed from thofe of the Welfh Britons; and that if Ireland was peopled firft from Britain, as it moft probably was, the language brought into Ireland, was that of the

mixed

mixed body of Canaanites or Phœnicians, who had been masters of Gaul as well as Britain, till expelled by the Gomerian Celts.

Let the reader only compare the grammars of the Welsh and Irish languages, and he will find as great difference in the syntaxes, as between the Latin and Hebrew. Now this would not have happened, between a colony and its mother country, distant only a few hours sailing, (and between whom a correspondence was certainly kept up, insomuch that in later days, the princes of each country, intermarried;) again, the British antiquaries have all noted, that the tenets of the Druids of Ireland, were different from those of Britain, and that the former committed their doctrines to writing, which was forbid to the latter. See Rowland, Borlase, &c. And, that great master of the Celtic dialects, Mr. Lhwyd, observes, "That the Irish have preserved "their letters and orthography beyond all their "neighbouring nations, and do still continue the "same." (comparat. Etymology. T. 1. Obs. 8.) The fact is, that the Magogian Scythic (Irish) and the Gomerian Celtic (or Welsh) were both dialects of the Hebrew, and at first the same: the latter has been corrupted, by their running from the fountain head, and the Irish restored by Oriental connections.

I shall therefore take the liberty hereafter of omitting the word Celtic after Iberno and in future distinguish the Irish dialect by the name of Scythian, Magogian-Scythian, or Pelasgian-Irish.

CON-

CONCLUSION;

MISCELLANEOUS.

IN the preface to this number, I have attempted to prove, that the first inhabitants of Britain and Ireland, were a colony of Magogian-Scythians mixed with Phœnicians and Ægyptians, who first settled in the Greek islands under the name of Pelasgi. These Magogian-Scythians settled very early in Palestine at Bethsean, thence named by the Greeks Scythopolis. This city in the time of Joshua is said to have been in the possession of the Canaanites or Phœnicians (Ch. 16. v. 11, 12.) who were so strong that the children of Manassah could not drive them out: but it will be found that Bethsean was founded by the Scythians, consequently in the time of Joshua, Canaanite and Scythian were synonimous names. In the days of Jeremiah, the Magogian-Scythians are again described as the people who should overflow Palestine. Ch. 47. v. 2. that Prophet says, Behold the waters (nations) shall rise up out of the North, and shall be an overflowing flood, and shall overflow the land, and all that is therein. Accordingly we find the Scythians kept

poſſeſſion

poffeffion of Bethfean to the time of Jofephus, and from the holy fcriptures we can trace a communication between the Canaanites and Scythopolians from the time of Jofhua, 1400 years before Chrift. See Reland's Palaeftina, tom. 2.—Bocharti, Geogr. Sacra. Onomafticon of Brocardus, Hieronymus & Jofephus.

The city of Bethfan, was very early diftinguifhed for the manufacture of fine linen. In Midrafch Coheloth memorantur, fol. 92. 1. lina tenuia quæ veniunt Bethfane.—De linificio Scythopolis vide codicem Theodofiarum. leg. 8. (Relandius.)

Now as the Irifh and Scotch have ever been remarkable for this manufacture, if we fhall find the names of the materials, machinery, &c. belonging to this art, to be the fame in the Irifh language and in the Chaldee, Hebrew and Arabic, I believe the reader will allow, it will be a ftrong argument to prove that the Scythian anceftors of the Irifh, were defcended from the Scythopolians of Paleftine.

IRISH.

Lin,   Flax. This word is fuppofed by moft gloffarifts, to be of Celtic origin: it is a miftake, for it was the old Chaldee or Phœnician name of flax and cotton. Rabbi Simeon was named Pikul-lin, i. e. goffyparius, a vendendo goffypio dictus. Gloffa in Talmud Berach, fol. 282. but it is evident he was alfo the dreffer as well as the vender of cotton, for pakel or phakel in

Chaldee

IRISH.

Chaldee is decorticare, Corticem detrahere, from whence the Irish feical and feacal, a hackle for combing flax. לינט, lanut, Chaldee, linteum, ad abftergendum corpus poft lotionem, Græco λίντιον.

Lin is the diminutive of the Arabic liha, the bark or fibres of a tree; Cantab. lihod, flax, from whence alfo our lea-bar, bark of a tree, and the Latin liber, a book, becaufe made of bark, which we have mentioned in another place: lea-bar is corrupted in Englifh to barc, from the Irifh barc, a little book, i. e. lea-barc: thus we fay barc-lann, a library, inftead of leabarclann.

Canach, cadus, caonur, canur. Cotton. Chaldee, kina, a wild tree. Pliny l. 12. c. 11. Arabiæ arbures ex quibus veftes faciunt, Cynas vocant, folio palme fimili; Chaldee kidda, the cafia alba or the caftus.

Cotin. Cotton. Arab. cotin; khennur, any foft or withered plant.

Maogcairce. Baftard cotton. Chaldee, magg, Junci fpecies, karach glabare fe. Rabbini ad fructus transferunt, quando mature, tegumenta fua abjiciunt & quafi calvefcunt. Unde *mefbkarku* COTONIA MALA & forba, ex quo calvefcunt, fcil. matura funt & decimas dant. Maaferoth c. 1. Buxtorf 2129.

IRISH.

Maoigreann. Cotton. *Maoilairce*, fine cotton. Chald. mecha, hatcheled, beaten, prepared for fpinning or weaving.

Tobblinta, tolanta. Fine linen. Arab. thaub, linteum, pannus, veſtis; plur. athveb and thiab, cloth, linen, veſtments, hence the Engliſh web. The T being aſpirated in Iriſh, loſes its ſound, thus tholanta is pronounced holanta, which is probably the Engliſh word holland, i. e. fine linen, i. e. thaub, pannus, linta, linteus: the Dutch being remarkable for this manufacture, may perhaps have received their name from this word. Our tobh-linta ſeems rather from tob, good, in order, and linta, threads of lin; tob, in Hebrew, good, in order, ſeries: hence the Iriſh tobir, i. e. tob-bir, a well of ſpring water; Heb. tob-bir, good water.

Anur, anurt. Narrow coarſe linen, made chiefly in Munſter for meal-bags and peaſants ſhirts: it is alſo called bandlamh and contractedly bandal, becauſe always made of the breadth of a certain meaſure named bandlamh; Perſ. nerd, a ſmall ſack for meal; newerd, a weavers beam: Arab. aner, thread, yarn, fila coagmentata: Chald. nart, a little ſack; Æthiop. animo, a web.

Bandl-amb. A cubit, the length of the meaſure ſpoken of above; Chaldee and Perſ. bandl,

a mea-

IRISH.

a measure; Heb. Ch. and Syr. amh, a
cubit, i. e. the arm from the elbow downwards. -(Bates Crit. Heb.) quanta est a
brachicis flexu, seu prominentia exteriori
usque ad medio digiti summitatem.
(Schindl.) hence lam, in Irish, the arm from
the elbow to the tip of the finger, it now
implies the hand; Arab. said, a cubit;
al-said, the great cubit, probably forms
our Irish slad or slat, i. e. a yard, the
breadth of our finer linens.

Seol, beart, anurt-seol. A weavers loom; Chaldee
azela, a weaver; azali, a ball of yarn:
Arab. sels, thread; silk, thread in warp;
hanut, a loom; berdi, the cotton of Pa-
pyrus; bett, a web in the loom: Persic
berdu, a beam; berdi, weavers reeds;
bart-aften, to weave, to spin, to twist;
Æthiop. ana-mo, a web.

Tocaras, tochrais, tasculac. A reel, from To and
cras; Heb. tuh, to weave; Arab. teslik,
reeling yarn; tuzulzul, a reel; tuzleek
kirdun, to reel yarn: Pers. terist, a weavers beam.

Crois tbecrais. A reel. Pers. chere; chuhreha
dook, a reel.

Geabb, geamb. The boll of flax, from whence
giobal, canvas; Heb. gibhol, was bolled;
LXX. ωμνωτζι, was feeding; the Hebrew is compounded of ghabab, to be
round or bunched, and halah, to ascend,

X 4   and

IRISH.

and so expresses in the whole, to protube-
rate, as flax does, into boll or pod. (Holloway.) hence the Irish coc-hull, to pod;
gabhail, to bind; gabhla, shot out, as
branches of trees; gablugadh, propaga-
tion, genealogy, from lugd, people;
giobal, coarse, knobby linen, i. e. canvas.

*Faith, faiths, faich, figh, fithg, fuith, fuan, clo, ce-lo,
keat, kealt, lin, keirt, oige, breig, keadac, dil-
lait,* cloth, linen cloth, (pannus Lat.) *

Faiths, expresly means linen cloth; fuithis, a linen
rag.; Heb. phesheth, flax, from phush, to
luxuriate, spread, or extend itself; the
name expresses the lusty increase of this
flouring herb. (Holloway.) T. phachat,
cloth, sewed, (Schindl.) In Irish, fàs,
(fawsh) is vegetation, and the combing of
flax or hemp is called cnap-fas, or knobby
flax, of this the Irish make a coarse cloth
called cnap-fàsh, for winnowinsh sheets,
&c. Heb. phatil, filum, panniculus contortus; Chaldee phitaga, findon, linteum,

* From the threads being numbered by scores to form the
required breadth of the cloth; the weaver, when he extends
the warp, at every score makes a figh, that is, a knot wove
round them, hence fighed, to weave, to twist and also the
number 20, written fighid or fighean, from whence the Latin viginti. When the peasants reel their yarn, it is usual with
the ignorant, to make a scor or notch on a stick at every
twenty rounds, and hence the English score, q. d. Skinner,
lignum incidere.

phatal

IRISH.

phatal duplicavit torquendo—funiculus duplicatus & contortus, fascia ex filis implexus contorta; begir, pannus; phekiah, glomus; phekaris, linum, vestis carni proxima; Syr. phatea, textura; phetach, tibicinæ textrinæ, vestis discolor; phatal torsit; Æthiop. fatal, fila contorsit; fatale, filum; gebyratfatyle, pannus; age, gossypium, linteum; Arab. fatal torsit; aifa, cloth, whence Ma-afir, the name of a country remarkable for a kind of linen cloth; fekh, interwoven; fekhet, a garment of one piece worn on holidays at Mecca; fitil, spinning; kitin, cloth; chait, thread; man-dil, cloth; kafyh, thick cloth; leh-leh, cloth of small thread; Perf. kir-bafè, fine linen or cotton; kertè, a linen shift; kar-gir, coarse cloth; Phænicè cau, thread; oigin and orgin, a weaver; Chinese, pi, phic, nomen clavis, (i. e. literæ) pannorum & telarum panni. (Fourmont. Clavis Sinenf.)

From these oriental words are formed, *Fith-doir, fighi-doir, oigbras, cafathoir, tocafor, cioſl, breabadoir, urachar*, a weaver; Chaldee kouva, kui, phikaguith, weavers, glomi; gerad, (ﬠﬢﬤ) kirus, shetah, a web; tishettin si texueris; Heb. arag, garrar, a weaver; koh, mekoh, linen, yarn; Phœn. orgin; Arab. cazis, caik, chaiq. harar; Perf. taziden, to weave.

Sna,

IRISH.

Sna, snath, gibnim, feisag, thread; Chaldee, nim, thread; Æthiop. sana, thread, sana-sale a chain, gybira a web, a loom, geby-rat fatyle, a web of linen cloth; Syriac, feshl, thread; Arab. sirra, thread, twisting, kiyab, the woof; snatir, thread, du al-snatir, rete cui gossypium intexatur.

Cnaib, canaib. Hemp; Arab. kunib, kunou, abik.

Gasda, sli, slin, srac. The slay or comb; Chald. salla, siriak, kirus; (see seol;) Arab. angauz, keshk.

Srac.   Is the Chaldee kirus reversed, i. e. surik.

Oigbreas. A web; Chaldee, kirus textura.

Oig, oigan, eig. A web; Phœnician, orgin, a weaver.

Tantboir, uinnioc, toir-tain. The woof; Heb. tora; Arab. ner; Perf. neir.

Slabbra, slabb-ara, toiche. The warp, (stamen.) Heb. shliab, set in order, equally distant one from another.

Dluth.   ⎫   ⎧Chald. M. ticha, kirus, the web.
Tochar.   ⎬ Warp. ⎨Perf. kunagh, arish.
Tocharas. ⎭   ⎩Phœnician, cau, fine thread.

Sniol, tiorsi, tiosi. The shuttle. A. shemlelet, swift as a weaver's shuttle; shimal, a fragment of cloth, a reaper's handful; turist, a shuttle; P. shurmal, to and fro. P. desè, a weaver's clew; also, two slender pieces of wood belonging to a weaver's loom; destè, a weaver's loom.

Gor, gor-muin. The beam, (jugum.) Heb. m-gor; Persic. kargah; Chald. garedith.

N. B.

IRISH.

> N. B. *Muin* is the floe tree or blackthorn, of which the beam is made.

Caimis. A linen fhirt; Arab. kemys, hence the French chemife.

Some remarkable NAMES of ANIMALS.

Sealc, feilg, &c. A hunting dog; fealgaire, a hunter, a fowler, falconer, &c. &c. Arab. faluki, a hunting dog, fo called from Saluk, a city of Arabia Felix, from whence alfo the Arabians had the al-druh, a coat of mail. (Bochart. Canum vitia et virtutes.) in Irifh, dreach, a coat of mail; dreachda, a troop fo armed.

> Partolan fixed his refidence at Inis Samer, fay the Irifh poets; here he killed his greyhound named Samer, from whence the ifland was fo called, (Keating, &c.) Arabic, fem & fem fem, is a greyhound, a hunting dog; confequently the root of the Irifh famer.

Gibne. A greyhound, becaufe of the circular form of his back, when fpringing on his game; Heb. gibban; Lat. gibbofus.

Nearaid. A hunting place; ftocked with wild boars; Perf. nariden, to hunt.

Madadh, cu, gadhar-greach, fagh, cich, cuib, gione, luan, colidh. Are the general names for dogs in the Irifh language; Arab. fugmaudeh, dogs; the gadar-grec, was probably

brought

brought from Gadara, a city of Paleſtine, long in the hands of the Greeks; Arab. hatar, a dog; al-kalati, Arab. Canis eſt parvo corpore, membris contractis, ab Hebræo kalat, quod ſignificat membra habere contracta, (Boch.) this is the exact deſcription of our Iriſh colid, a name always given to a little cabbin cur; ſunt et qui Zagari appellent, (Bochart) ſag, is a general name in Iriſh for a bitch, probably from the Heb. ſaga, to multiply; Arab. ſug, a dog; (plural ſug-maudeh, Richardſon.) In Hebrew, caleb is a dog; Alcamus derives the Arabic calib a dog from celib, a rabie furorem et delirium, from foaming at the mouth like a mad dog; we have already ſhewn the Iriſh chlaba, milk, to be the ſame in Hebrew, having the teeth white with chlab, Geneſis;—this explains the Hebrew caleb, a dog; the Iriſh maſdith or maſdi, a lap dog, (Arab. mauſtè) is ſtrangely metamorphoſed into the Engliſh maſtiff; the Iriſh cu and cuib is from the Arabic chupeh a lap-dog, (according to Richardſon.)

Buacal ſealgarieac. The hunting horn, Arab. booka ſhukkar; buacail bo is commonly explained by the Iriſh gloſſariſts, to be the herdſman's horn; but I think it is the Arabian book-boorè, or muſical horn, and the Ir. a'rc or adharc, a horn is certainly the Arab. rawk.

Caor.

IRISH.

Caor.   A fheep; Heb. car, a lamb; Ir. ceat, a flock; Arab. kut.

Ceis, keis, kaois. A fow, (Suf.) Hebrew chafir, a fow, ab oculi anguftia; Irifh, cais occulus, the eye; Arab. kaas and chifron, a hog.

     Nulli in Judæa fues, nulli fubulci; Gadara, ubi porcorum duo millia, Græca fuit urbs, non Judaica, fus, chazir dicitur, quia teres et rotundus, (Bochart.) Irifh, cafar, round, curled, frizzled; thefe agree with Bochart: but the more proper derivation feems to be from cafadh to bend, to wriggle about, a motion natural to the fwine; cafair is a glimmering light, which anfwers to the Jewifh interpreter's explanation.

Neas.   A weazle; Perf. nughchè, a weazle, nefhi, a hedge-hog; Arab. nifa-nis, a female marmofet.

Neimithigh. Ants eggs, igh eggs; Arab. hemat, an ant.

Nimb.   A ferpent; Arab. naim and naemut. N. B. there are no ferpents or fnakes in Ireland.

Aiream. To number, airi one, airis many, numeration, ex. gr. airifne na bliadhana fa truim do banbha broinigh, i. e. numbering of days fits heavy on breeding women. Under the word numerus, Plunket in his MSS. dictionary of the Irifh language, has the following words: " aiream, amfir- " dhutiarfa, andan, accant-cas, achmhang, " beann, coimde, comardod, com-freag-

radh,

" radh, cefól, diorna, ead, eagar, eagar-
" ord, eifb, forlion, gleas, lon, macn'uimir,
" macionran, meann, meit, meid, martha,
" mac-iomad-lion, mac-iomad-morân, ord-
" maith, ord-deas, rim, riom, riom-fcollad-
" arann, rann-femh, fuim, fuid, tamas,
" tocire." In Shawe's dictionary of the
Irifh, under the word *number*, we find,
" uimir, nuimhir, ionran," and under the
word to numerate, " meafam, cuntam,"
and in all the dictionaries we find cead,
an chead, to fignify primus; and ceadamus
imprimis; to which I fhall add fome words
in general ufe, in Munfter, fignifying to
count, or reckon, viz. córrigam, meafam,
and aireagnadh, i. e. air, number, and
eagna knowledge, from whence the Englifh
reckon.

SCHINDLER, under Numerus.

HEBREW and CHALDEE.

cafas,	facus, facan,
chefebon,	faphar, pl. mefapharim,
cefil, alfo the name of a planet,	tacan, tacaneth,
	tacona, numerus, arith-
Hhara LXX ⟨⟩, unus,	metica, aftrologia,
abhar, unus,	pharat,
efhebon,	taban,
mecas, micefa,	ah, unus,
mena, mana,	chad, unus,
metacaneth,	achad, primus.
e-tachana, aftrologia, nu-	
merus,	

Numerus,

Numerus, Arabic, fhumaur, hiffaub, hufb, add, adud, ydaud, taadaud, ta-addud, adeed, adeedut, yddut, hifsè, hufbaun, bool, mur, murreb, fufnut, al-hhor, gumla, macani, mudde, menah; one by one, erim, eekè eekè, numeratio, add, rukum, nuwaud, muhaufibut, deen, hufboun; urum, figns, ciphers, the tips of the fingers.

Ancient Perfic. Arafi, numerum five quantitatem generatim appellant. (Rheland de vet lingua Perf.) Modern Perfic, fhumar, number, fhuamur-den, to number; Arab. bè hiffaub, without number, innumerable; in Irifh airim-eifbe.

There can be no doubt but that the Irifh cefòl is from the Hebrew cefil; the Ir. ead from the Arab. add; the Ir. tocire from the Chaldee tacan, &c. &c. and that the Irifh airimeifbe, innumerable, was the real Scythic word and its meaning, which Herodotus explains by ari, i. e. unum et mafpus, i. e. oculus. No name could fuit the Scythians better than innumerable, and hence, John in the Revelations, ch. 20. v. 8. compares the defcendants of Gog and Magog in the four quarters of the world, to the fand of the fea.

It has been fhewn under the word Cuig, that the Irifh gloffarifts explain that word to fignify the number five, and alfo a circle; from whence I conjectured, the ancient Irifh made their aiream, or numeration, by the fingers of each hand. In Arabic, we find urem the tips of the fingers, erim one by one, which is the exact meaning of the Irifh aiream, to numerate, and in the catalogue of Hebrew, Chaldee and Arabic words for numerus,

we

we find very many fimilar to the Irifh words preceding. Airi a number, makes airith in the plural, and meith or meidh to reckon, forms the Greek Ἀριθμητικὸς; and airith and meafadh forms Ἀρίθμησις, numeratio. The Irifh nim, facere, facio and aire numeratio, forms the Latin numero. Cib or Cip, the hand, and air number, forms ciphair or cipher. Johnfon and Chambers derive cipher from the Hebrew fephar, number, enumeration, but the Hebrew fephar, comes from feph, rotundity; from whence it fignifies a bowl, and is the root of the Irifh fpeir, a fphere. Seph is alfo a wheel, whirlwind. Ifa. v. 28,—" their wheels like a whirlwind." Sephir, implies a number, whether by memorial, monument, book, letter or voice. (Bates Crit. Heb.)

The Hebrew ח which ftands for 5, implies the wide or circular opening of the mouth, and expreffes the ejaculation O! as, שמם ח O ye heavens! The Greek πωλι, five, is from the Hebrew אפן pen, a wheel; פנה pene is alfo to turn about, to revert, &c. The Æolian πιμπι, five, derives from πιμφις, bulla, gutta, quia rotunda. The Irifh cuig, (five) from חג chag or chug, in Hebrew a circle. But what demonftrates the explanation of my Irifh gloffarift, is, that the character to exprefs 5 in the Indian and Arabic numerals, is O, which is the character of a cypher, formed fays Chambers, thus O.

It is alfo remarkable, that in the Irifh, mair is a finger, formed of am and air, ufed in numeration, fang a finger, and air numeration, forms finger; ad in Irifh numeration, and al great, forms adal a finger;

figh

figh in Irifh is a form, fhape, manner, painting, a refemblance, and air numeration, form figure.

The ancients certainly had various methods of expreffing numbers by the fingers, as we find by the following authors : Plin. lib. 34. N. Hift. " præterea Janus Geminus a Rege Numa dicatus, " qui pacis bellique argumento colitur, *digitis ita* " *figuratis,* ut trecentorum fexaginta quinque di- " erum nota, per fignificationem anni, temporis & " ævi, fe Deum indicaret."—Quintilian, l. 11. c. 3. " Alii igitur *digitis complicatis* numeri, alii conftrictis " fignificabantur."—Mart. Felix Capella, de nuptiis —" in digitos calculumque diftribuit," and lib. 7. " digiti vero virginis recufantes & quadam incom- " prehenfæ fcaturignis nobilitate vermiculati, quæ " mox ingraffa, feptingentos, & decem, & feptem " numeros, complicatis in eos digitis, Jovem fa- " lutabunda fubrexit."——Sidon Apollinar, l. 9. " Epift. 9. " Chryfippus digitis propter numerorum " indicia conftrictis, Euclides propter menfurarum " fpatia laxatis."——Tertullian, Apologet. c. 90. " Cum digitorum fupputatoriis gefticulis affiden- " dum eft."—C. Plin. junior, l. 2. Ep. 20. " com- " ponit vultum, intendit oculos, movet labra, *agitat* " *digitos,* computat nihil."—Seneca, Ep. 88, " nu- " merare docet me Arithmetica, avaritiæ accom- " modare digitos." P. Ovid, l. 1, Faft. " feu quia " tot digiti, per quos numerare folemus."—Plautus, Milite, Act 2, Sc. 2.

" Ecce autem avortit nixus læva, in femore habet manum, " Dextera digitis rationem computat, feriens femur."

L. Apulejus,

L. Apulejus, l. 2, Apolog. "Si triginta annos pro decem dixisses, posses computationis gestu errasse, "quos circulare debueras, digitos aperuisse; cum "vero quadraginta, quæ facilius ceteris porrecta "palma significantur, ea quadraginta in dimidio "auges, non potes digitorum gestu errasse, nisi "forte triginta annorum Pudentillam ratus, binos "cujusque anni consules numerasti."——Refertur Orontis, Artaxerxes regis generi honore spoliati dictum. "Principum amicos videri similes com- "putantium digitis, nam Arithmeticorum digiti, "qui modo decem millia, modo unitatem repræ- "fentant."——Nicarchus an ancient Greek poet, in Antholog. l. 1. c. 9. Ep. 5:

"Quæ secla vidit cervo plura, quæ manu siniftra "Senium numerare iterum incæpit."

And the venerable Bede mentions this method of enumeration in his time. "Cum dicis unum, minimum in læva digitum inflectens, in medium palmæ figes; cum duo, secundum a minimo flexum ibidem pones; cum tria, tertium similiter inflectes; cum quatuor, eundem minimum levabis; cum quinque, secundum similiter a minimo eriges; cum sex, tertium elevabis, medio in medium palmum defixo; cum septem minimum super palmæ radicem ceteris levatis impones; cum octo, medium; cum novem, impudicum e regione compones; cum decem, unguem indicis in medio pollicis ortu figes; cum viginti, summitatem impudici inter nodos in- dicis & pollicis arcte figes; cum triginta, ungues indicis & pollicis blande conjunges; cum quadra- ginta, interiora pollicis lateri applicabis; cum qui- quaginta, pollicem ad palmum inclinabis, &c."

I de

I do not recollect to have met with any author, that points out the time, or cause, of the Romans adopting the letters for ciphers. Chambers tells us, " they were originally seven in number, C. D. I. L. M. V. X. which are all formed by describing a circle, and drawing two lines through it, crossing each other at right angles, in the centre." if they had been formed from this figure C 100, would have been a D reversed, thus ꟼ, and I, one, would have been a cross +, and how he could make out M, I cannot perceive: in Hebrew ם Mem. stands for 40, and M in Greek for 10 thousand; it is evident, they did not borrow from either of these.

Monsieur Furetiere explains the Roman numerals much better, " The Romans," says he, " originally hah but five figures to express numbers, which served instead of ciphers. I. signified one. V 5. X 10. L 50. C 100. They had no idea of numbers exceeding a hundred thousand. The C or mark for 100, was always turned towards the I. Thus CIↃ made 1000 *, and IↃ 500. When a stroke or bar was drawn over these cyphers, they then expressed so many thousand, thus V̄ was 5000, &c. Many learned men differ in opinion of the use of this bar or stroke.—The origin of the Roman Cipher, is from the method of counting with the fingers; thus for the four first, the four fingers represented that number IIII. and for five, the V was

* In the Gothick, M stood for 40 as in the Hebrew; R for 100 and X for 600.

adopted,

adopted, as reprefenting the middle fingers clofed, and the index and thumb only extended. As to the X it is a double V, one of which is reverfed; hence the progreffion is always made by one to V, and from V to X. A hundred was marked by a capital C." (—but why with C Monfieur F—? it is, becaufe C is the firft letter in the Scythian word *Ceann*, i. e. the head. See p. 476.) Since the firft inftitution of the Roman numerals, two more have been added, formed, either by breaking the firft, or by the convenience of the fcribes. They have made D ftand for IƆ, i. e. 500, and M for CIƆ or 1000, becaufe the laft bears much refemblance to the Gothick M, fo that at prefent, there are feven Roman ciphers. The Hebrews and the Greeks never ufed any other ciphers than letters of the alphabet.—As to the Arabic ciphers, they run on thus 1, 2, 3, 4, 5, 6, 7, 8, 9, to which they added a Zero o which ftands for nothing, without another figure joined with it, therefore the firft nine are called fignificative figures.

Monfieur Le Moine profeffor at Leyden, thinks the word *Zero* is Arabic, and corrupted from *fiffra*. Others derive it from the Hebrew *ezor*, which fignifies a girt or belt, becaufe it reprefents that figure. (See *Chiffre*, *Zero*, in Furetiere.)

We need only caft our eyes on the ancient Indian character in the annexed plate, (plate 2.) to be fatisfied that o or the circle of the tips of the fingers, counted once in this form, according to our Irifh gloffarifts expreffes 5, and the fecond hand being counted in the fame manner, was expreffed

preffed by o o, contracted into . o, called by the
Irifh *deigh*, *deich* and *deib*, i. e. ten, i. e. *da-cuig*,
two circles.

The learned Court de Gebelin derives the Greek
dactylos, Latin *digitus*, and French *doigt*, a finger,
index, &c. and its corruption *dix*, from the Celtic
deic, *deig*, ten, becaufe there are ten fingers on the
two hands; and hence, fays he, dextèritè, ad-
drefsè dans les doigts: adroit qui eft habile à em-
ployer fes doigts. From *dek* a finger, the Greeks
made *deikò* to point out, and the Latins *indico*,
&c. &c.

The ancient Irifh had numerical characters of
two kinds, one refembling the Roman, except
the X, which was formed of two Cˢ. thus ɔC or
ɔ C or ℔ and this was alfo their *Cor-fo-cafan* or
Bouftraphedon mark, as much as to fay, turn back,
or begin a new reckoning, as all nations do from
ten: the other character was Arabic, refembling
thofe of Jo. de facro Bofco, in the annexed plate,
and exactly the fame as thofe given in Dr. Bernard's plate of the Hifpaniorum ex Arab. A. D.
1000. We have added, for the fatisfaction of our
readers thofe of Planudes, thofe of the ancient and
modern Indian, the Arabian, and the ancient
Saxon.

Of the origin and antiquity of the arithmetical
figures, we cannot find a better account than that
given by profeffor Ward Phil. Tranf. No. 439.
Moft writers, fays he, who have treated of the
rife of figures, have thought that they came firft from
the Perfians or Indians to the Arabians, and from

them to the Moors, and fo to the Spaniards, from whom the other Europeans received them. This was the opinion of J. Gerard Voffius, John Greaves, Bifhop Beverige, Dr. Wallis and many others. And the Arabians themfelves own they had them from the Indians as both Dr. Wallis and Greaves have fhewn from their writers.

But If. Voffius thought the ancient Greeks and Romans were acquainted with thefe figures, and that the Arabians took them from the Greeks, and the Indians from the Arabians! For the proof of this he refers to Tyro and Seneca's notes, and the treatife of Boethius de Geometria. But as to the notes of Tyro and Seneca, they feem to have no affinity with thefe figures, either in the number or nature of them; for they are not limited to nine, but are many times that number, and all different in form. Nor are they fimple figns of numbers, but complex characters of feveral letters of thofe numeral words which they ftand for in the Roman language like our fhort hands*.

D. Huetius imagined the Arabian figures were only the letters of the Greek alphabet, corrupted and altered by ignorant librarians. And he thinks it probable, that the Indians had them from the Greeks, and the Arabian writers may not have known it—but we find the Greeks ufed only letters of the alphabet.

J. Scaliger, G. Voffius and Mabillon thought that thefe figures were not ufed long before 1300.

Wallis

---

* See Gent. Magazine, vol. 18. p. 6, 7.

Wallis has offered some arguments to prove, that Gerbertus, a monk, who was afterwards advanced to the papal see, and took the name of Sylvester II. had before the year 1000 learned the art of arithmetic, as now practised, with the use of nine characters only (whatsoever their form then was) from the Saracens in Spain, which he afterwards carried into France. These characters, however, were known for a long time after, only to such artists, and principally used by them in astronomical calculations; the Roman numerals being still retained in common use to express smaller numbers. Nor has he given us the figures used by any of those writers, before Joannes de Sacro Bosco, who died in the year 1256, and Maximus Planudes who flourished after him. Mr. Cope (in the same Transact.) exhibits the Indian and ancient Saxon arithmetical figures; he and Wallis then enquired at what time they were introduced into England. And they inform us, that the English had them from Spain, whither they were brought by the Moors, who had them from the Arabians and the Arabians from the Indians; and that they were first brought into England about the year 1130.

If the Irish had borrowed their figures from the English, they certainly would have copied them, but we find them perfectly to correspond with Dr. Bernard's table of the Hispaniorum ex Arabico.

The numeral letters of the ancient Irish are very like those of the Palmyrians given by Swinton in the Philos. Tr. v. 48. and engraved also in

Y 2   Bernard's

Bernard's tables. M. Furetiere obferves that in the Roman numerals the C or mark for 100 was always turned towards the I. The Phœnician numerals for 100 was I⊃I. See Bernard's tab. The Palmy-renian numerals for 20 was ⊃, that of the Irifh two C's viz. ⊃C or ⊃ C. See plate 2d.

Dr. Shaw, in his travels through Arabia, ob-ferves, that, " not even the firft operations, in " either numeral arithmetick or algebra, are now " known to one perfon in twenty thoufand, not-" withftanding their forefathers, if we may judge " from the name *, feem to have been the invent-" ors of the one, as they have given to all Europe " the characters of the other. However the mer-" chants, befides being frequently very dextrous in " the addition and fubftraction of large fums by " memory, have a fingular method of numeration, " by putting their hands into each others fleeve, " and there, touching one another with this or that " finger, or with fuch a particular joint of it (each " of them denoting a determined fum or number) " will tranfact affairs of the greateft value, without " fpeaking to one another, or letting the ftanders " by into the fecret. Yet ftill of a much more ex-" traordinary nature, (provided we could be equally " affured of the truth of it,) is the knowledge, " which the Thaleb of this country are fuppofed to " have in numbers; they pretend to fuch a pow-" erful infight into the nature and quality of them,

---

* Jabar eft reductio partium ad totum, feu fractionum ad integritatem, et hinc Algebra nomen habet.

" that

" that by differently joining and combining them,
" they can bring to light a variety of secrets."

Thefe Taleb were well known in Ireland: I shall have occasion to speak of them in another work. *Talbba* or *Dalbba* in modern Irish is a forcerer, and I think I have met with the very amulet, these Taleb difposed of in Arabia, to break the force of charms, which has been miftaken by the Irish for a circular Ogham alphabet.

The names of the numerals in Irish, Dr. Parfons thinks were the root of the Latin, Greek, and all European numerals; he thinks the Welsh *pedwar* and the Greek *Teffares* are derived from the Irish *Ceatbar*: it is certain, that Voffius, is equally abfurd in deriving τίσσαρα from πίτορα, but Scaliger says the ancient Greeks, had κάτυρον pro ἡ ἔτερον. But why says the doctor, should the Greeks be driven to such a shift as to say ἡ ἔτερον after treis? as if we should say, one, two, three, and another, for four, and then come to a simple name for five. He then proceeds to twenty called by the Irish *figbid*, and says it is found spelt variously as *ficbid*, *vicbid*, *vigbent*, *figbind*. And here, he endeavours to derive the Greek ἴκοσι from *figbi*, with much the same fucceſs as Voffius in deriving the Latin *viginti* from ἴκοσι.

I have never met with the letter *v* in the Irish, with the force of V, the *bb* was always fubſtituted for it: or the number 20, written *figbind*: the Latin *viginti*, I think, expreſses the *figb*, or twiſting of the hands or 20 as before explained, to be the quintus or fifth part of a hundred, and fo the

tens

tens run on, triginta, quadraginta, &c. up to centum a hundred, (the Irish ceantra:) thus 500 is quingenti, i. e. quinque—ceantra.

References to PLAT. II.

A. Ancient Indian figures—Gent. Mag. 1749.
B. Modern Indian do.—from Tav. l. 1. c. 1.
C. Arabian do.—from MSS.
D. Figures of John De Sacro Bosco,—from Dr. Wallis, which are the same with those of Roger Bacon's calendar in the Cotton library, except, the 2d which he has like 7.
E. Figures of M. Planudes,—from Dr. Wallis.
F. Spanish figures of the year 1000, from Dr. Moreton's tables.
G. Irish figures from MSS.
H. Arabian, Persian and Indian figures of the year 800, from Moreton's tables.
I. K. Numer. Indorum e Græco, A. D. 716, from Moreton's T.
L. Numerorum Notæ ex Sidonio—Phœnicibus, from Moreton.
M. Numero—Palmyren. ab Swinton.
N. Irish Numerals from MSS.

NAMES

PLATE II.

Numerical Charactures from various Authors collated with the Irish.

Ref.	A	B	C	D	E	F	G	H	I	K
1	1	9	1	1	1	1	1	1	l	d
2	v	z	v	z	µ	z.7	2	µ	2	u
3	w	ε	w	3	µ	3	3	w	3	2.
4	←	y	←	2	←	2	2	µ	8	2
5	08	y	0	G	∫	∫.G	4	∫8	2	C
6	7	3	G	6	4	6	6	4	3	5
7	V	9	v	^	v	1	1	v	9	3
8	V	z	^	8	^	8	8	1	2	u
9	9	c	9	9	9	9	9	9	3	2
10	0	9	1.	10	10	10	10	1.10	10	0.

L (1) 1. (9) ||||||||| (10) — p p (19) ||||||||| —
(20) N N 2 2. (90) — N N N N. (100) 1 2 1.
(900) 1 2 |||||||||

M 1. 11. 111. 1111 (5) y. 1 y. 11 y. 111 y. 1111 y.
(10) b. 2. (11) 1 2. (20) 2. 3. (30) 2 3.
(40) 3 3. (50) 2 3 3. (100) 2 1. 2 1. (500) 2 y.
(1000) 2 2 1

Fig. 2	Gr.	Ir.	Facon

Irish.

N 1. 2. 3. 4. 5. 5. 6. 7. 8. 10.
1. 11. 111. 1111. y. r. 1r. 11r. 111r. X.

20.   40.40   50   50   70   80   90
XX.   0. y.   1.   4   r   r   r

100   200   300   400   500   900   1000
c.K.h   M   b.e   3.p.   X   m

PONIAN.	ÆTHIOPIAN.
1. Ici.	1. Ahadu.
2. Ni.	2. Kyly. (Ir. Keile a couple.)
3. San.	3. Sylyfy.
4. Xi.	4. Rybyng.
5. Go.	5. Hamyfy *.
6. Rocu.	6. Sydis.
7. Xici.	7. Sybyng.
8. Faci.	8. Symini.
9. cu.	9. Tyfyng.
0. Giu	10. Afyry.
.0.	20. Afyra.
)0.	100. Myty.

(left margin, partly cut off: ah, il, en, ric, th, Bu)

New Guinea	Tika	Roa
Javan		Lo-R
Malay	S-atou	Dua
Ill. of Madagascar		Rua
Ill. of Mallicolo	Tikai	E-ry
Ill. of Tanna	Ridi	Ka-rc
New Caledonia	Wagi-aing	Wa-r
New Zeland	Tabai	Rua
Ill. of Savu	Une	Lhua
Malabar	Oona	Rund
Telenga	Oocate	Rund

1 Auniq. Oóuin

5.) 2 Oueców. Occo

3 Ououà. Oroa

4 Acourabamè. Ouirabama. Aocobai memè

5 Atonéignt. Oétonai

6 Tewyne yeclyckene

7 Tage yeclyckene

8 Terrewan yeclyckene

9 Tagine yeclyckene

10 Yemeralé mépatoen. Oyabatonè

20 Opoumè. Poupoubatoret

40 Opopoumè

N. Monfieur Biet, pretends that the Galibis
be had no numeration above 4; that to exprefs 5,
ues, they fhew one hand : 10, both hands; 20 the
five hands and feet: yet he fays oupoumè exprefes
aebi ses 20: and opopoumè 40, which word figni-
s of fies twice the hands and feet. Father Pelle-
ere prat and others have found regular words for
— the numerals, which we have here felected.
(See Dict. Galibi, par Monf. D. L. S.)

ENGA's on the coaft of COROMANDELL.

r Gebelin, that in all thefe languages the word
, for the initials L, R, N, may be efteemed the
ct, *Rima* the arm, *E-Rima* the hand: *Apou-Ri-*
vords derive from the Oriental *Rom, Rim,* ele-
h is in the arm : the arm, in the ancient word

of the propriety of our Irifh gloffarifts obferva-
or all thefe words here given exprefling
for example *lamb* is a hand from whence

N

V

Swe

1st. Nukhuft. Awul. (fem. oola) Awuleen.
  muKudduma.—Arab. Budatan. Fibude
2d. Duwum.—Ar. Saunè. Akhur. ukhra.
3d. Siwum.—A. Saulis. Saulifut.
4th. Chuhaurum. Chaurum.—Ar. Raubia
5th. Punjum.—Ar. Khamis.
6th. Shuſhum.—Ar. Sudis.
7th. Huftum. Huftumè.—Ar. Sauba.
8th. Huſhtum.—Ar. Saumin.
9th. Nuhum.—Ar. Tafia.
10th. Duhum. Duhumè.—Ar. Auſhir.

wa°
e
ra
m
k

tta
o
o
ugu
hun

VI

omin

Da

Feiluw
Dufura
Tefraw
Tſchau
Pantfc
Tſcha
Satuw
Athuw
Nawa
Dufva

(primus) is fuppofed to be derived from προ ante, ie compound of the Irifh *bro* and *tus :* and διοτερος id *traith* order, feries.

ius) in the lingua Sacra Graentham feu Kirendum to be from the fame root as the Irifh *bro* firft, il, order, feries, or *tamas* numerus.

Dachnici, appears to be the Irifh flai, princeps ihan.

ring the Indian names of the numerals in the eader will allow, that there is a much greater lee, Perfian and Irifh, than with the Greek.

Atbar-nimb, a viper, i. e. the twifting nim; Arab. naim, naemut, a viper. The Irifh athar, to bind, to twine, is from the Heb. athar, circumcingere, hence the Irifh atar, a bonnet, a hat; Heb. atara, from whence tiara. (See Nim, a ferpent.)

Ambas, a foldier, a hero; Hebrew amaz, fortis fuit; Arab. amazir, a brave, undaunted man, (Irifh amhafir) hence the Irifh amhafan, a centinel, a guard: quære, is not this the origin of the Greek fable of the Amazons, faid to be women of Scythia, who dwelt near Tanais, a word the Greeks have derived from *a* and μάζα, i. e. non mamma, without paps. Strabo denies that there ever were any Amazons. Pliny and Mela make mention of thofe of Scythia.

Ambra, ambrag, noble, great, good; Perf. amrugh, noble; Arab. amera, umera, princes, nobles.

Ana, Continuance of fair weather. (O'Brien and Shaw.) Arab. ain, continuance of bad weather—rain with little interruption for feveral days. (Richardfon.)

Amba, a plebean; Arab. ammet.

Ambaon, plurality, twins; Arab. ummani, plurality of kindred.

Aireac, a learned man; magus, a chief, a forcerer; Chaldee, arche. Chaldæus reddit Kiriath Sepher, i. e. urbs literarum, Kiriath arche, Græce πολιν γραμμάτων. (Bochart.)

Barann,

IRISH,

Barann, a royal ftandard; Perf. perend.

Bunaitbim, to build; bunafear, a builder, an architect; Arab. bani, a builder; Perf. benafer, an architect; bunyadker, a builder.

Bi, bith, life, fpirit, foul; Ægyptice, bai, the foul, from bith the Latin vita.

Beth, a houfe, city or dwelling; Heb. beth, Bethfena, the ancient name of Scythopolis in Paleftine,—Saine, a diftrict of Ireland fo called,—Dun-faine, a town in Meath; dun, beth, and baille, in Irifh imply towns, cities, villages; in Arabic dun, beth, belad, a city; balid, an inhabitant; in Irifh, bhfhuil fe ambaile, is he at home; i. e. does he inhabit here.

Boga, a bog, a marfh, a fwamp; Arab, bawgha.

Baile, a clan, a tribe, a town; Ar. balid,—bulud, a permanent fettlement, a city; Etrufcan, vol, vola.

Ball, a ftain, a fpot; Heb. bal, he fpotted, mixed, ftained.

Barrachas, men of great fway, fuperiors, foldiers; bairach, compagnie de Janiffaires, compofée de 60, ou de 100 hommes. Voyage de Kleeman. Berich, Heb. a foldier.

Cruitboir, a harper; Arab, cuthaira, a harp; Heb. kothrus.

Bean-do-bath, a fyren, i. e. a woman of the fea; Arab, benatu' l'behr, fyrens, alfo dolphins,

Cliab,

IRISH.

Cliab, a bafket, a cleeve: Heb. calab, Amos, 8. 1. a calab of fummer fruits.

Caoine, cine, (keena) and *ciche.* The IRISH CRY, or lamentation for the dead, according to certain loud and mournful notes and verfes, wherein the pedigree, land property, generofity and good actions of the deceafed perfon and of his anceftors, are diligently and harmonioufly recounted, in order to excite pity and compaffion in the hearers, and to make them fenfible of their great lofs in the death of the perfon whom they lament. This is the Hebrew cina, or kina, קִינָה i. e. lamentation, crying with clapping of hands; (planctus ploratus) 2d Sam. 1. v. 17. Sephir Cinoth, i. e. liber lamentationum (Jeremiæ.) Chaldee, cina, to deprefs, to grieve, to humble one's felf. Perfic, khunya, melody, fong; Arab. khenin, crying through the nofe; khan, a finger, a cryer, an invoker; Chinefe, kien, clavis rerum in abyffum corruentium; doloris, &c. &c.

The Irifh are remarkable for this brutifh cuftom, as it is called, of crying over their dead, for making coftly burials, with great feafts, in fo much, that the quantity to be eaten and drank at funerals was regulated by the Brehon laws, according to the rank of the deceafed.

This cuftom the Magogian Irifh brought with them from the eaft; as foon as any of the ancient

Jews

Jews departed this life, the corps was wafhed and perfumed, wrapped in a fhroud, and laid in a coffin. In the mean time, people from all parts, that is, as well thofe of the fame city or town, as adjacent places, came to condole with and comfort the relations of the deceafed; and as the multitude was very great in the houfe of the deceafed, where great lamentations were made, as likewife in the ftreets, through which the corps was carried to the grave, and that in both places, people were very fplendidly treated and feafted, and minftrels attended with inftruments of mufic, fo the expences thereof often amounted to fuch an excefs, that many of them were thereby impoverifhed; infomuch, that feveral not being able to undergo fuch vaft charges, abfented themfelves from the city, under fome fpecious pretence or other, for fear of expofing their credit. Thefe *cina* or lamentations together with the multitudes of people attending the corpfe to the grave, were efteemed of fo great moment amongft them, that they accounted thofe accurfed, who were deprived of either of them; this we learn not only from their tradition, but from feveral texts of fcripture; for inftance, in the 22d chapter of Jeremiah, that prophet, fpeaking of that infamous king Jehoiakim, declares from the mouth of God, that at his funeral there fhould be heard no fad cries and lamentations of his brothers and fifters, nor of the reft of the people: and in the 5th ch. of Maccabees, it is faid, that the ungodly Jafon was not mourned for. (Buxtorf. Synag. Jud. & Muret's funeral rites.)

The

The cina of the Irish is performed, while the corpse is carrying from the house to the grave; the lamentation in the house is called tòradh-bas or tòradh. Toir, is a burying ground, that is, the place of lamentation; it is derived from the Chaldee taradh, affligere, lachrymantes; Syr. torathwa, ululatio, whence the Irish toireamh, an elegy; Arab. terjim, a monument to the dead; tyrrek, a christian burial ground; tarikhi, an epitaph, an elegy: Chaldee, bas, ægrotare; Heb. baas, putruit, fætuit; Arab. baad, wuz, wuz-wuz, fooz, death.

St. Mark uses the term Θορύβος, (which signifies, a tumultuous body of people, a turbulent, violent meeting,) to express the state of things in the house of Jairus, when his daughter was dead. Ch. 5. v. 38. The Greek word taken in this sense, surely does not correspond with the idea of mourning and weeping of the relations of the deceased. St. Mark says, Jesus being come to the house of the ruler of the synagogue, and seeing (θορύβον translated) the tumult, and them that wept and wailed greatly; and when he was come in, he saith unto them, why make ye this ado and weep? (why make ye this θορύβεισθε και κλαιετε.) I cannot avoid thinking this Greek word is used here for the Hebrew or Irish torath-bais, especially if we consider that Jesus was here addressing a Jew, the ruler of the synagogue.

The assembling together of multitudes to the place where persons have lately expired, and bewailing them in a noisy manner, is a custom still retained in the east, and seems to be considered as

an

an honour done to the deceased, says Harmer in his observations on several passages of scripture. This ingenious and learned author had seen a MSS. of Sir J. Chardin's, from whence he gives the following passage. Sir J. quotes Gen. 45. v. 2. "*And he wept aloud, and the Ægyptians and the house of Pharaoh heard.*" "This is exactly the genius of the people of Asia, especially of the women; their sentiments of joy or of grief are properly transports; and their transports are ungoverned, excessive, and truly outrageous. When any one returns from a long journey or dies, his family burst into cries, that may be heard twenty doors off; and this is renewed at different times, and continues many days, according to the vigour of the passion, especially, as these cries are long in the case of death, and frightful, for their mourning is downright despair, and an image of hell. I was lodged in 1676, at Ispahan, near the royal square: the mistress of the next house to mine, died at that time. The moment she expired, all the family, to the number of 25 or 30 people, set up such a furious cry that I was quite startled, and was above two hours before I could recover myself, for it was in the middle of the night. These cries continue a long time, then cease all at once; they begin again as suddenly, at day break and in concert. It is this suddenness which is so terrifying, together with a greater shrillness and loudness than one would easily imagine: this enraged kind of mourning, if I may call it so, continued 40 days, not equally violent, but with diminution from day to day; the longest

and

and most violent acts were, when they washed the body, when they perfumed it, when they carried it out to be interred, and at making the inventory, and when they divided the effects: you are not to suppose that those that were ready to split their throats with crying out, wept as much ; the greatest part of them did not shed a tear through the whole tragedy." (Chardin's MSS.)

This is the exact description of an Irish wake and funeral, and if an Englishman should happen to be circumstanced in one of the great towns of Ireland, as Sir I. was at Ispahan, I believe he would likewise say it was an *image of bell*, and if he was a Greek scholar, he might possibly call it a *δοξ ιℶος*, if he happened to hear the Irish talk of their toradh-bais.

The making a kind of funeral feasts was also a method of honouring the dead, used anciently in the east, and is continued down to these times. The references of commentators have been, (adds Harmer) in common to the Greek and Roman usages, but as it must be more pleasing to learn eastern customs of this kind, I will set down what Sir I. Chardin has given us an account of in one of his MSS, and the rather as some particulars are new to me. " The oriental christians still made banquets of this kind, (speaking of the ancient Jewish feasts of mourning, mentioned Jer. 16. v. 6. 7. and elsewhere) by a custom derived from the Jews, and I have been many times present at them among the Armenians of Persia. The 7th verse speaks of those provisions which are wont to be sent to the house of the deceased, and of those healths that are

drank

drank to the furvivors of the family; wifhing that the dead may have been the victim for the fins of the family. The fame with refpect to eating, is practifed amongft the Moors, where we find the word comforting made ufe of, we are to underftand it, as fignifying the performing thofe offices." In like manner he explains the bread of men mentioned Eezk. 24. v. 17. as fignifying the bread of others; the bread fent to mourners; the bread that neighbours, relations, and friends fent to the funeral. (Harmer v. 2. p. 138.)

The Perfians, Scythians and Tartars are faid to leave the bones of the dead fcattered in the fields, yet they appear to have reckoned nothing more facred than the burying of the dead. Herodotus in his fourth book, tells us, that Darius fon of Hyftafpes, no being able to bring them to battle, becaufe of their rapid flight, fent one of his principal officers to them, to know when they would ftand a battle, to which they anfwered, *we have no towns to defend, but when you advance as far as the graves of our fathers, your mafter fhall be witnefs with what courage and refolution we can fight*; with which anfwer, Valerius Max. obferves (l. 5.) they for ever cleared themfelves of that foul blot of monftrous barbarity, which was before thought to be fo natural to them, fince a more pious reply could not have been made by the moft civilized people in the world. This paffage in Herodotus, fays Muret, proves that they did bury their dead.

I fhall fay nothing of the funerals of the Greeks; they were the moft whimfical people in the world in their funerals and mournings: but I cannot pafs over the opinion of that polifhed, civilized Greek,
that

that ſtoic philoſopher Chryſippus, born at Solas, who approved of ſome barbarous nations, that eat the fleſh of their fathers and mothers and beſt friends, and ſays it was one of the greateſt demonſtrations of piety, to give their relations a burial in their own bellies. And what ſhall we ſay to Homer? he has very particularly ſet down the honours that were done to Patroclus. Achilles having ordered the army to be ranged in battle round about the wood-pile, only cauſed twelve young Trojan gentlemen to have their heads cut off, beſides a vaſt number of oxen, horſes, dogs, &c. &c. &c. which were butchered and thrown confuſedly on the corps of his friend, and laſt of all he himſelf having cut off his hair, caſt it into the flames, and at this ſignal the army ſet up the *Pilli-lilli-lu*; but the Greeks were a poliſhed and learned people, and the Iriſh are barbarians, for crying over their deceaſed relations, and for viſiting annually their *aicre-eo*, or patrimonial *eo* or burying place, for ſuch was the ancient name, now turned to *acrerua*; and this was the Ægyptian name, which gave birth to the Acheruſian lake, acroſs which, the inhabitants of Memphis paſſed to what is called the *plain of mummies*, and this firſt gave origin to the Grecian fiction of Charon's ferry boat, the Elyſian fields, the infernal judges, and that long ſtring of nonſenſe, ſo poetically wrought up by them.

IRISH.

Oobh-ail, a place encloſed with ſtones, but not co
　　vered over head. (O'Brien.) The Phœnicians
　　and Hebrews called the three ſtones placed in
　　the centre of the great circle of ſtones, (like
　　　　　　　　　　　　　　　　　　　　our

IRISH.

our druidical monuments) Kobhe. See
Cooke's enquiry into druidical temples, p. 31.
al, in Irish, is a stone, therefore cobh-ail, is
the stone Kobhe of the Phœnicians.

Cobb, a cove or harbour; Heb. chaph, maris por-
tum.

Cotba, cotban, a cough, a difficulty of breathing;
coto, the swelling in the neck of the Indians
on the borders of the Cordeliers: a name probably given by the Spaniards.   Q.?

Cutban, cuan, a harbour; Phœnice, cothon; Heb.
chuz.

Crabba, devotion, religion; Heb. craa, genu
flexit, craiath, curvationem; corab, the inward thought; to bring an offering to the
Lord.

Ceirt, an apple, the apple tree.

Κετρίον, τὸ Ἰνδικὸν μῆλον. Hesychius.

Rhelandius, de Vet. Lingua Indica. Non Indi-
cum sed Medicum erat illud quod Citreum dicitur
sive Persicum. *Citreum & ipsum Persicum malum est*,
scribit Macrobius Saturn. l. 3. At unde nomen
Citrei? Fortè ex Persico Zert, Zort, flavus, color
Citrinas. Sed κίτριον & citrus Afracana alia arbor
est, & longe diversa ab Citrone Persica. There is
something very extraordinary in the name of an
apple, in all ancient languages. Ceirt or keirt implies magic, sorcery, in Irish, as ceirt-thosaice, ce-
ird-draoicheact; Chartim magician in Hebrew,
the Chartim were religious, says Bates, but of
what particular sort does not appear. Ubhall or
uphall,

uphall, another Irish name for an apple, is of the same root as upha or uphtha, a witch; tar-upha in Irish is the teraphim of the Jews; so likewise the Hebrew tapuach, an apple, the root is puach, which in Irish is an evil demon, a buck goat, a satyr. Now piyuk in old Persic is copulation, matrimony, &c. and we find the natives of Canaan had a temple to their god, under the attribute of Beth-Tapuach. Jos. 15. 53. Mr. Hutchinson thinks this word puach expresses all the action of the spirit, in supplying fire, &c. if that be the sense, the word should have been phuach; the Arabians have certainly so written it, viz. tuffah, an apple; tuffahu' l'jinn, the demons apple, i. e. the mandragora, or mandrake; tuffahi-mahi, the moon apple, i. e. the citron, orange, or lemon, but tapuach in Chaldee and Arabic implies chamomile, mandrake, the herb Aaron, or wake robin, the golden apple, &c. Hutchinson in his trinity of the Gentiles, says, " This was that species of a fruit which our first parents, by persuasion of the devil, through the serpent, eat, and was ever after among the heathens sacred; among the later heathens, to several of their gods and goddesses, as were many other species of trees and fruits. I cannot think Mr. Hutchinson has hit upon the right meaning of Beth tapuach, for as he very properly observes, where you find the Jews forge a number of stories about any word, you may be sure there is something of moment contained in it, which they endeavour to hide.

Irish.

Cuinde, a can; cuinneog, a fmall churn.

Κόνδυ ποτήριον Βαρβαρικὸν, Κύμβιον. Hefychius.

Relandius de veteri lingua Indica; Vox.
condou; Perf. hodie faccum frumentarium
notat, & kindi notat cantharum fed condy
genus vafis, feu pateræ, qua vinum libabant
Perfæ; cadah poculum majus e quo vinum
bibitur. Hibernicè cuadh.

Cuire, a foldier; cuirithi, foldiers, the royal guards;
Heb. cori, guards, patrolus, 2 K. 11. 4. hence
the Irifh ceann-cuire, an officer of diftinction;
cuirailte, a meeting of the ftates—thefe were
the kerethites of Solomon; Arab. kourilte, a
meeting of the ftates.

Caor, a fire brand; caoras, lightening, a thunder
bolt; Heb. charas, the folar fire. He hath
commanded חרם (charas) the folar fire, and
it arifes not. Job. 9. 7. חרה, charah, he
burned, he was kindled; Arab. kurkaura,
thunder, lightning; Perfic, cheragh, to blaze,
a candle, a glaring light.

Cuirm-afcaoin, excommunication. Shaw's Irifh
Dictionary. This lexiconift thinks cuirm here
is from the verb cuiram, to put, to fend, &c.
this is a miftake; the druids of Ireland had
three kinds of excommunication, viz. cuirm-
afcaon, cuirm-nid, & cuirm-fuimide; afcaoin,
is a curfe or malediction and was the greateft
excommunication; nid, implies manflaugh-
ter, and fuimide, want of refpect to the
church; חרם, cherem, in Hebrew is, devo-
tum,

IRISH.

tum, anathema, hence the charma Bæotiæ locus execrandus in quo abforptus Amphiarus. See Bochart. Geo. Sacr. 473. In Chaldee cheram, res devota, anathema. Cherama, res devota facerdotum. Charem, excommunicatio. Maimonides diftinguifhes the different kinds of excommunication of the Jews by Cheram, Niddui and Shammata, under Shammata, Voffius and Buxtorf note, fic volunt Judæi, illud Anathema Maranatha, cujus Apoftolus Paulus meminit, effe idem cum hoc Shammata.

Coi, *coice*, a mountain; Arab. cou.

Ceafla, *keafla*, iron ore; keafas, the fame; hence Mount Caucafus; Perfæ quo nomine Caucafum appellant? cou caf, i. e. ultimi litera in S mutata, coucas. (Reiland.) The Scythians named it cafim: fee Ifodor. Origin. l. 14. c. 8. Satis norim quanto opere mutaverint nomina barbara Græci & qui ipfis eruditionem fuam debent, Romani; quare & in voce Caucafi eandem mihi rationem obfervandam exiftimo. (Reland. de Vet. Ling. Perfic. p. 155.) A fragment of hiftory informs us, that the original founders of a Tartarian, Mungalian, and Scythian nation, called kajan and dokos, got, by a particular fate, among the Cuhiftanian and Caucafian mountains, which before were uninhabited, and after their fojourning there, for about 450 years, being become fo very numerous, that they were forced to look

Z 2 out

IRISH.

out for a larger tract of land, they were at a
lofs how to find out a way to pafs the mountains; when a blackfmith, pointing out to
them a place abounding in rich iron ore, ad-
vifed them to make great fires there, by which
means the ore melted, and opened them a
broad paffage out of thefe mountains. In commemoration of which famous march, the Mun-
gols celebrate an annual feaft and ceremony,
which they call coike-gaura, (in Irifh, gour,
is a blackfmith,) in this ceremony, they heat
a piece of iron red hot, on which the Chan or
Khan ftrikes one blow with a hammer, and all
the perfons of rank do the fame.   Here is the
foundation of the fable of Prometheus's being
faftened to Mount Caucafus, and his deliverance from thence by Vulcan.   The gou or
fmith was always a perfon much refpected by
the Scythians, Perfians, Irifh, &c.   See
Strahlenburg, p. 417.   Herbelot. Hift. Gen.
des Tartares, p. 74.

There are iron mines in Armenia named El-ku-
fas, and kufas means any thing made of that iron,
as a fpear, fword, &c. (Richardfon.) Keafas
and kafla in Irifh, is iron ore, fo alfo keis is a fpear,
a fword, &c. kaifli, polifhed iron; kafar, the iron
head of a hammer; kaf-gearam, to hew or cut
down with a kas.   The modern Tartars add tag to
the name of every mountain as Imaus-tag; in Irifh
teidhg, is a mountain.

                                            Gou,

IRISH.

Gou, gabb, a blackfmith, a farrier; Perfic, gao, the famous blackfmith of Ifpahan who defeated the ufurper Zohak. N. B. There cannot be a more expreffive word in the Irifh than fahac (faithac) for a ufurper, i. e. one who thrufts himfelf into the place of another by force of arms; Sclavonicè, koblar, a farrier.

Duan, a poem, canto, rhyme; duan-mordha, an epic poem; duan-tachd, poetry, verfification; duanaighe, a rhymer; Arab. divan, a compleat feries of odes or other poems by one author, running through the whole alphabet; Gaffani, Saouthi, Zemremi, &c. among the Arabians, and Hafez, Giami, &c. among the Perfians compleated divans. (Richardfon.) divanè, Arab. a perfect poet.

Duan-aireac, duan-arteach, a fenator; duangaois, Police; Arab. divan, a royal court, a tribunal of juftice, revenue, &c. a council of ftate, a fenate, a divan: the Afiaticks fay, that Solomon (fon of David) had a divan, in which he judged not only men, but likewife peris and genii, or demons, over whom he exercifed a defpotic authority.

Duadb, a village; duam and daim, a city; whence Tuam, the name of many noted towns and villages in Ireland; Perfic, dih, a town or village. The ancient name of Adrianople in Thrace was Ufcu-dama, according to Ammianus, i. e. in Irifh uifce-daimh, or the watry refidence, town or city; the Irifh uifce or

uifke

IRISH.

uiſke is from the Heb. הׁשְקָה, iſka, he gave to drink, or cauſed to drink; Chaldee iſhaki, to ſoak in water; ſhakia, adaquatio; ma-ſheki, aqua.

Dar, *dair*, *darac*, an oak, i. e. the temple of the druids; *dear*, *dar*, a houſe, i. e. a temple, hence Killdare and many other dar and derrys in Ireland; Arab. daraz, an oak; deir, a mo-naſtry, a chriſtian church; deir-magon, a tem-ple of the magi. No word in the Iriſh language has been more miſtaken by our modern topo-graphers than dair and derry; thus alſo meas is ſaid to be the acorn, or any other fruit: in Arabic, mezz, is a pomegranate; mazu, an acorn, fruit in general; but it originally implied the ſacred fruit, that is, the acorn of the druids, and the pomegranate of the Aſia-tics.

Damb, learning.

Damboide, a man of great learning, a ſchoolmaſter, from oide, a teacher damhta, a ſtudent; aice, a ſociety; aice-damhta, an academi-cian; daimheach, a ſchoolfellow.

DAIMHIATH, a powerful clan; daimh, connec-tion, conſanguinity; ta daimh agam leis, I have a regard for him, I live in ſocial friendſhip with him; Perſic dem, ſociety, from dem, breath, as breathing together, (Richardſon.) Quære if not rather from the Scythic daimh, blood, connection, conſangui-nity; Arab. DAWIYET, the order of the KNIGHTS TEMPLARS.

Corracb,

Corrach, a low fenny piece of ground; Arab. kerker, level, foft ground; Irifh, carcar, a large fhift formerly fwathed round the women's body; Arab. kerker, a woman's fhift.

Dubhar, a word; dubhart cad, a holy pious prayer; Heb. dabar, a word; Quære—is not the Irifh dubhart cad rather the fame as the Hebrew dabarim chadim of Genef. 11 and 1. and the whole was of one mode of prayer, worfhip or rites, as Mr. Hutchinfon has explained it.

Dia Taith, the deity Tath. (Vet. Gloff. Hibern.) Theuth & Menas, utrumque acceptum ab Ægyptiis, a quibus in Diis maxime colitur Theuth, tanquam artium, & fcientiarum repertor, & in hominibus Menas, quem omnium hominum primum in Ægypto regnaffe afferunt. (Herodot. Diodor.)——poft mortuos femideos primus regnavit Mines. (Africanus ex Manethone.) Irifh, menn, i. e. follus, firft born, anceftry, ftock, origin. (See Taith, p. 469.)

Duruth, *droth*, a carpenter. (Vet. Glofs.) druthloireachd, any kind of carpenters work. Perfic durudger, a carpenter.

Di an ceacht, *di an ceach*, i. e. Deus Salutis; ainm fuithe leighis Eireann, Di an na cumhacta; ceacht, i. e. cumhacta. (Vet. Gloff.) that is caech or ceacht is the deity fuppofed by the phyficians of Ireland, to prefide over health; deus falutis; ceacht is ftrength, vigour, power, and has the fame fignification as cumhachta.

IRISH.

hacta. כה cach, in the Hebrew occurs only
as a noun, and is conftrued ftrength, ability;
the inward ability or vigour. (Bates.)

Dagh-da, i. e. dagh-dè. The god Dagh; thus
defcribed in an antient Irifh gloffary, dia foin-
eamhail agna gentib è, ar do adhradais Tuatha
Dedanann do, ar ba dia talmhan doibh è ar
mhead a cumhacta, that is, dag the god of
profperity of the Heathen Irifh, worfhipped
by the Tuatha Dadanann; he was the god
of the earth, and fuppofed to have great
power.

דג Dagh, in Hebrew is to be fruitful, to multiply,
or increafe, and it is fpoke of people, fifh and corn,
hence דג dag, a fifh, from their great increafe, דגן
corn of any fort. Dagon, i. e. fertility; the name
of the Philiftine idol, by which they attributed all
their plenty and increafe from the earth and fea,
to their god, the heavens. Horace defcribes this
deity, in form of a woman and a fifh, " definit in
" pifcem muliet formofa fuperne."—Jud. 16. 23.
" The lords of the Philiftines gathered together to
" offer a great facrifice to Dagon, their god."
1 Sam. 5. 4. he is defcribed as an image of human
form. It is certain that the Irifh druids had no
fuch image, and by Dagh, meant no more than
the angel prefiding over the produce of the fea and
land. Yet the word feems to refer to the power
of Belus, as doigh or daigh fire, dagham to warm,
to finge, to burn. Dagh good, profperous; it is
written dagh and deagh, and enters into a multitude

tude of compounds. Deaghd, deachd, divinity, god-head. Doig-liag, the touchſtone, loadſtone, or magnet, which probably was ſuppoſed to receive its virtue from Dagh, the deity of the earth ; ſee Faniul. Dagon being repreſented as a deity, in the form of half fiſh, half man, there is great reaſon to think the latter part of the name, viz. On, is that deity mentioned by Helladius Beſantinus, recorded from his writings by Photius, Bibl. p. 1594. " Narrat verum quendam *Oen* in rubro mari viſum, habentem cætera membra piſcis, caput & pedes & manus hominis, & oſtendiſſe Aſtronomiam & litteras. Quidam dicunt illum natum eſſe è primo parente Ω″ε, & teſtari nomen, hominem autem omnino eſſe, piſcem vero videri, quod piſcis pelle indueretur." Now the ocean being expreſſed in Iriſh by the words, aighen, an, ain, &c. the compound Daghan or Daghon, would imply the deity preſiding over land and ſea, and moſt probably formed the Ægyptian Dagon. And, as in old Arabic, dakaa ſignifies earth ; and there is reaſon to believe, taga in antient Etruſcan did the ſame, I believe dagh in old Iriſh was terra ; Plunket in his Iriſh dictionary writes it duthaig, from whence duthaghan, duthan, a nation ; duthcaghas, duthcas, the place of one's birth ; Duthaidh, duthaigh, a land, a country ;—but, the Iriſh word du, (the former part of this compound) is land, country, region ; conſequently taig, or daig, is the ſame as the Arabic dakaa, and Hebrew dag, land, earth, &c.

Dagon,

IRISH.

Dagon, frumentum, unde Dagon dictus Azotiorum
     deus. Σιτων illum vocat Philo. Bibl. & fal-
     luntur Hebræi qui apifcibus dictum volunt;
     itaque nomen a forma non habuit fed ab in-
     ventione frugum.   (Bochart in Hieroz)

Diud, doid, diut, doit, i. e. mann-draoic, i. e. diud,
     or doit, is burnt wheat, or an inebriating grain.

Doit. A grain of inebriating quality, that grows a-
     mongft corn. (Shaw. Lex. Inebriation, miofg,)
     draoic, to inebriate, cuiram air an draoic.—
     (Shaw's Lexicon.)

Diut-cearn, i. e. fuitche cearn, i. e. the ember carn.
     (Cormac. Gloff.)

Dio-lanlas, i. e. diud-lanas, fornication.   (O'Brien.)

Diud-an. Giddy, intoxicated.   (Shaw.)

Druth, i. e. druc, i. e. meir-dreac, i. e. diraoth ifidhe,
     i. e. alofgadh ba dior di air fit aoth no teinne.
     (Gloff. Cormac,) i. e. druc eft meretrix & fic
     vocata eft, quia pudendum ejus aduftum fecit
     in cineribus.

Druictor. A fornicator.

    The word *diud*, is one of many in the Hiberno-
Scythic dialect, which may tend to explain fome
Hebrew words in the Holy Scriptures. I mean
not any part relating to the *word of God*, as given
by Mofes and the Prophets : that, does not ftand
in need of any other language, if ftudied in the plain
drefs, it was left to us: or of any romantic fyftem
of philofophy, built on the vifionary dreams of our
modern philofophers. But, I mean, of fuch parts
as treat of the obfcene and abominable ceremonies
                             of

of the idolatrous Jews, Ægyptians, and Phœnicians, which have been kept alive, with the later Heathens in this remote corner of the world.

The *diute* or *doite*, is a grain that is sometimes found growing amongst the wheat in Ireland, and I have been told by the peasants, if they mix the meal of this grain, in any considerable quantity, with wheat meal, that, cakes made of this composition, inebriates them, has the effect of cantharides, and throws them into a long sleep; in short, that they are for a while quite mad.

Mann-draoic. i. e. mandragora, codhlatan, colbha, codhl-luib, i. e. luib cuiraid codladh trom ar duine antan do nithear lamhnasagadh no crearadh, i. e. mann-draoic, whose Latin name is mandragora, is called codhlatan (sleepy,) colbha (love,) codh-luib, the sleepy plant, because it throws a man into a most heavy sleep, post coitum, vel post illecibras. (Plunket's Lexic. Hib.)

Codalian. Mandrake. (Shaw.)

Doddedig wenn. The women's herb, doddedig. Davis's Walsh dictionary.

In the 30th chapter of Genesis, v. 14. we are told, Reuben went in the days of *wheat harvest*, and found duda in the fields, and brought them unto his mother Leah. Then Rachael said to Leah, give me I pray thee of thy son's dudaim. And she said unto her, it is a small matter that thou hast taken my husband! and would thou take away my son's dudaim also? And Rachael said, therefore he shall lie with thee to-night for thy son's dudaim.

And

And Jacob came out of the field in the evening, and Leah went out to meet him, and said, thou muſt come in unto me, for ſurely I have hired thee with my ſon's dudaim. And he lay with her that night. And God hearkened unto Leah, and ſhe conceived.

The Hebrew dudaim is rendered in Arabic tuffahu'l'jinn, that is, the apple of the genii or demon. But, as Mr. Hutchinſon obſerves in his Trinity of the Gentiles, p. 308. Tuffa, in Arabic, not only ſignifies an apple, but alſo chamomile, the apricot, the herb aaron, or wake robin, the peach, the golden apple, the apple of the mandrake. In Hebrew, taphuahh is an apple, the root is phuahh, whence the Iriſh uphall, ubhall an apple, and tuphtha, uphtha a forcerer, diviner, &c. as explained in the preface.

Ezek. ch. 23. v. 3. Et fornicatæ ſunt in Ægypto in pueritiis ſuis fornicatæ ſunt ibi compreſſa ſunt dudaim earum & ibi contuderunt dudi virginitatis earum. V. 21. Et viſitaſti ſcelus pueritiarum tuarum in comprimendo ab Ægypto dudi tua, propterea dudi pueritiarum tuarum,—i. e. recordata es fœditatis adolaſcentiæ tuæ, quando compreſſerunt in Ægypto dudi tua. (Montanus.)

This abominable cuſtom was a feſtival in the Hiberno-druidic calendar, and was obſerved on the eve of the full moon of September, in which month is placed our ember week. In the ſouth of Ireland, this cuſtom is ſtill retained. On the firſt day of ember-week, the young men and maids of each village aſſemble on a green, with bundles of wheat,

peas,

peas, beans, or whatever they can plunder from the adjacent farmers; but beans and peas are preferred. The grain is burnt, or rather scorched in the flames of the straw, and when reduced to embers, it is picked out by the men; then, each young gallant by turns, hides one grain in the embers, crying out, *striolam, strailim, thógas mo graine,* i. e. I'll tear you to pieces if you find my grain; his maiden lover seeks, and great is her chagrin if she does not find it; on producing it, she is saluted by the company with shouts; her lover lays her first on her back, and draws her by the heels through the hot embers, then turning her on her face, repeats the ceremony, until her nudities are much scorched; this is called posadh-min, or the meal wedding. When all the maids have gone through this ceremony, they sit down and devour the roasted wheat, with which they are sometimes inebriated; but by this ceremony the maids are sure to fix the duda, or love of her future spouse.

The Portuguese observe this festival, by assembling the youth of both sexes over the embers of burnt chesnuts, particularly on All Saints Eve; they name these meetings magusta, a word probably borrowed from the Spanish, mauger de gùsto, a lady of pleasure; or of the old Irish muc giusa, the smoke and ashes of stalks. Meir-gusa, implies the harlot's delight. Gusta is also an obscene term of reproach between women, as, a gusta caligh! Darg, or drag, signifies coiens, as darg boin, i. e. go ndearna bo dhair, give the cow to the bull; see dairt in O'Brien's Lex. The Africans couple the

male

male and female dates together, at a certain feafon, and this operation Dr. Shaw fays, is called dhukar, which we may render fecundating.

דודא duda. Some kind of fruit which Rachael was fond of. LXX mandrakes. Could they but tell us what a mandrake is, we might be the wifer for the tranflation; they were a fruit which had materials, out of which fruit-bafkets were made. (Bates Crit. Heb.) Very good bafkets were made of ftraw! Of the fweet-fcented duda we fhall fpeak hereafter.

דד dud. To thruft or pufh forward; dudaim, the breafts of a woman; hence dudim loves; pleafures of love; duda a bafket; dudaim mandrakes; LXX μηλον μανδραγορα, the apple or fruit of the mandrake; (Parkhurft Heb. Lex.) The Greek melon is very properly explained by Mr. P. for maathla matha or maola matha, (in Ir.) is the frumentum of grain, particularly of darac or acorns, which were the food of the firft ages, and the glans Iberica of Spain, long remained a delicacy, and were ferved up in the nature of a defert. They are faid to breed headachs, and ventofifities, hence the Irifh verb maolagh, to be heavy, dull, and ftupid. In Arab. milgh, a fool.

דודאים dudaim. Mandrakes, an herb in Paleftine, diftinguifhed into male and female, bearing a berry of the bignefs of an hazle nut; that of the male being of an ochre colour, like the yolk of an egg; that of the female, like the white. Its root is *faid* to bear fome refemblance to the human form; and in particular to have fmall nipples like a mans. Whence Pythagoras called it ανθρωπομορφος, humani-
forma.

forma. It is of a moft fragrant fmell, good againft inflamation in the eyes, and caufes fleep and forgetfulnefs. Venus was called from it, Mandragoritis. What ufe Rachael wanted to make of Reuben's mandrakes, does not appear from the text. But, after all, though this herb and root was antiently fo celebrated for carnal ufes, among the Heathens, and was reclaimed for fpiritual emblems to believers, (Cant. 7. 13.) they are but little, if at all known, or taken notice of by the moderns. (Holloway, Orig. Phyf. & Theol.) This author has here defcribed our druidical berry of the Miffletoe plant, and the effect of our diud, henbane.

Dida was the god of love of the antient Ruffians, according to Neftor. Dida & Lel, i. e. Cupidon. Ces deux divinitès etoient en fi grande veneration chez les ancins Ruffes, qu'aujourd'hui 'encore, leurs noms fe trouvent dans les chanfons, fur-tout dans celles que l'on chante dans les feftins de nôces. (Hift. de la Ruffie, par M. Lomonoffow.)

Dreac, in the Irifh is an image or likenefs, hence man-dreac, the image of man, has been confounded for our mann-draic or drunken wheat, and this miftake has given rife to all the impofitions of the mandrake plant and its root.

The Chaldee tranflation has 'beruch pro dudaim, i. e. mandragora. Quidam violas explicant. Gerfon explicat **Affraunen**, & סיגלי figili, Sandhedrin. (Buxtorf.)

The Chaldee beruch correfponds with our braic malt or fcorched grain. The German Affraunen implies cineribus incantare, and the figili (violas)

of

of the Sandhedrin, is the same word as our seagal, which signifies rye, or any coarse grain like the doit or diud. The Teutonic word for the Mandragora, is mandragora-kruyt, i. e. baked mandragora. From what authority Buxtorf explains segoli to signify violets, does not appear. Schindlerus says, segol est botrus in Chald. hence segolin mandragoræ, i. e. botris similes; botrus is a bunch or cluster, and such is a sheaf of wheat, or an ear of corn. But Schindlerus explains this word otherways in the Hebrew, viz. proprium, singulare: res charta: PECULIUM; see Ainsworth's explanation of this last word segil, a reserve; what one keeps for one's self. (Bates, &c. Crit. Heb.)

The Algerines and Tunisians use a food named dweeda, much the same as vermizelli; bagreah, differs not much from our pancakes, it is fried in a pan named tajan. (Shaw's Travels.) Here is the Irish duid; the bairghean or thin cake the teasan or taosan, an old name for a griddle. The chich pea, when parched, is in great repute, and in that state is called leb-bebby. In Persic libas is love, a spouse, a bedfellow. In Irish leabe is a bed; laobh partial through love, laibhin leven, libh a dowry with a wife. All these words compared with the foregoing, seem to agree with this explanation of the Hebrew duda.

The balsam tree doth no longer subsist in Syria, and the musa which some authors have supposed to be the dudaim or mandrakes of the scriptures, is equally wanting; neither could it, I presume, ever grow wild and uncultivated, as the dudaim must

be

be fuppofed to have done. What the Chriftian inhabitants of Jerufalem take at prefent for that fruit, are the pods of the jelathon, a leguminous plant, that is peculiar to the corn fields, and by the many defcriptions I had of it, (for it was too early when I was in the Holy Land to fee it) fhould be a fpecies of the winged pea. It is certain that the bloom of all or moft of the leguminous plants yields a grateful fmell; a quality which the fcriptures attribute to the plant we are looking after. The whole fcene of vegetables, and the foil which fupports them, hath not the differences of variety from England, that we might expect in two fuch diftant climates. (Shaw's Travels in Syria, p. 369.) The vulgar Irifh name of this feftival is falac-pit, i. e. pudendum falacitatum, and is probably the die magni falpitium difertum of Catullus, which has fo much puzzled Voffius. Salaputiûm, *xíxss.* (Ainfworth.) i. e. pudendum. Suid. genitale.

The mandrakes or duda, in Cant. 7. v. 13. faid to give their fmell, are certainly different from Reuben's duda. The fweet fmelling duda is fuppofed by Rab. Jarchi to be violets or jeffamine; Junius, Tremellius and Pifcator call it the lovely flower. Ludolphus fays it is the mauz or mufa of the Arabians, which produces many heads to one ftem, from whence its name dudaim, i. e. many fruits to one lover or mother, the ftem.

In the bogs of Ireland grows a very large flower, refembling the garden rocket; its leaves, or rather puftules, are white, it is never feen blown altogether, the young fhoots, ftill being thrown out at the head, as the lower bloſſoms decay ; it has a fragrant ſmell, and is ſometimes as thick as a man's wriſt, it is called dúd ; our botaniſts ſay, from dud, ragged ; I think it anſwers Pliny's deſcription of the white Mandragora. (See his chapter de appetentia Veneris.)

Dudaim non ſunt Mandragora, ſed plane aliud. (Bochart.) Mandragoræ & Dodaim non idem ſunt. (ibid. in Hieroz.)

IRISH.

Fan-eol, finn-iul, iul, the magnetic needle, or mariners compaſs, called alſo béas-maire, or muir-béas, i. e. the ſea index ; béas-ſéola, the ſailing index ; luaim-béas, the pilots index ; beas-loingſeora, the ſeamens index ; beás-naoitheac, the ſailors guide, finnell, and corruptedly 'nealai ; finaiſe-draoid-heacht, i. e. the druidical fin, or the finaiſe of witchcraft, and ſometimes eol and iul, by which name it is now known in the Highlands of Scotland, in Manx and Ireland : the ancient Iriſh named it alſo badhbhſéola, i. e. the north-ſailor.   The name béas-ſéola is undoubtedly the etymon of the French bouſſole and Italian boſſola, which Furetiere derives from buxula, a little box ; but the box is a modern invention ; the ancients encloſed the needle in a reed of ſtraw, and laid it on the ſurface of a veſſel of water, ſlung in the ſhip, (as occaſion required) by which the needle kept floating, turned to the poles ; this muſt have been early

diſcovered

discovered, for a common needle will do the same without being enclosed; beas-naoitheac is also the Greek πύξο ναυτικη. Many learned authors have asserted, that the Phœnicians had the use of the needle : they say it is mentioned no less than six times in the S. S. under the word pheninim, supposed to be derived from phenith, to be turned towards any thing, to turn the face. Now the Irish word feannam and feancadh have the same signification, viz. to turn and twist about, to turn towards you, from whence fianisi and fiani, a witness brought face to face. They say the magnet is described by adamh, ruddy, in Irish, damh, sanguine colour; fionda, cæruleous ; da, is colour, hence fionn, red, from whence fionn, wine ; Lat. vinum.

Its power, they say, is described by Job in meshek, i. e. attraction ; Irish, maiseach, measach, mealsach. Mr. Cooke thus translates this remarkable passage in Job, ch. 28. v. 18. *Meshek checamab mepeninim*, the attraction of wisdom is beyond magnets. Now ceacht, in Irish, is wisdom, but ceacta-cama is the North pole, and *me* in Hebrew is both active and passive when prefixed, signifying *by* which, or *on* which it is done ; therefore the passage may be, *the attraction of the North pole on the magnetic needle.* From fan or phen the Irish form fean-laoc, a mariner, i. e. laoc, a champion of the *fan.* This word is generally used for invaders, and I believe the *fion-laoc-geinte* and *fion-geinte*, which

A a 2   has

has been tranflated Danes, Norwegians, &c. means no more than nautical invaders.

The Perfian name of the compafs is kebleh-nama, i. e. the book or index of the fhip; and ahen-kufh, thefe may be expreffed in Irifh, by cabla-neimeadh, the fhip's director, 'and aithne-cuis, fecret knowledge, or aighein-cas, the leader of the ocean.

The Sclavonian name is kolo-cep.

The Spanifh bruxula, is explained by Laramendi, by adivinar, to divine; this is evidently from the Irifh brioc, forcery, and iul, the needle; the Cantabrians name it, it-faforata, which in Irifh implies the magical dart or feather. Mercury was the Roman deity of commerce, he was alfo named Æolus. Lucian tells us, he had robbed Neptune of his trident, which feems to point to the word eol and the needle. Ulyffes landed on the ifle of Æolus, who prefented him with a zephyrus put up in a he-goat fkin; his companions thinking it to be fome hidden gold, opened the fkin while Ulyffes was afleep, and the wind drove him back to the ifland from whence he came; it is more probable they broke his nautical compafs. (See the 8th Odyff. throughout.) Again Al-kinous the Phæacian, had great fkill in maritime affairs, and his fon Hælius or Euryalus was a *princeps nautarum*. Hermes was alfo called Kadmilus, in Irifh keadam primus, imprimis-eol, the needle.

The golden or brafs cup, which is faid by many ancient authors to have been given to Hercules by Apollo or Nereus and Oceanus, and with which he failed over the ocean, can mean nothing but

but the mariners compass, to the knowledge of which he had at least attained; though I should rather imagine him to have been the inventor of it, by the name Lapis Heraclius, given to the magnet. (Cooke's Enquiry, p. 21.) Hercules, or Arcules seems derived from the Irish or Pelasgian-Scythic arc or arg commander, and iul the magnet, or aireac, magick, skill, and iul, the magnet: the Herculean stone was so named, says Plato and Euripides, because it commands iron, which subdues every thing else.

It appears that what was called the image of Jupiter Hammon (whose Libyan temple, according to Herodotus, took its rise from Phœnicia) was nothing more than a compass box, which was carried about by the priests, when the oracle was consulted, in a *golden ship*. (Cooke's Enquiry; Herwart de Magnete.)

It is probable, that the famous golden fleece was nothing else; whence the ship of Phrixus (who is Apher or Aphricus, and the same with Jupiter Hammon, which carried it, is said to have been sensible and possessed of the gift of speech; so also the ship Argos which fetched it from Colchis.

To these testimonies I shall subjoin that of the great Homer, who speaking of the Phæacians, and their extraordinary skill in maritime affairs and encouragement of every branch of nautical science, makes Alcinous (or Eol-ceanus, one who knew the use of the *eol* or *iul*, as his name declares in Pelasgian-Irish) gives to the shipping of his island the same common character with Argos and the

ship

ſhip of Phrixus in the following lines, which have puzzled all the commentators; and which either have no meaning at all, or plainly evince the uſe of the compaſs amongſt that ſea-faring people. (Cooke's Enquiry.)

τιτυσκόμ{μα} Φρεσὶ ῆις,
Ὁυ γαρ Φαιήκιοσι κυβερητῆρες ἔασιν,
Ουδιτι πηδάλι ἰςι τάτ᾽ ἄλλαι ῆις ἔχχσιν᾽
᾽Αλλ᾽ αὐταὶ ἴσασι νοήμαλα κỳ Φρίνας ἀνδρῶν,
Καỳ πάνλων ἴσασι πόλιας κỳ πίονας ἀργὺς
᾽Ανθρώπων, κỳ λαῖτμα τάχιϑ᾽ ἁλὸς ικπιρόωσι
᾽Ήρι κỳ νεφίλη κικαλυμμῥμαί.

(Odyſſ. l. 8.)

No pilot's aid Phæacian veſſels need,
Themſelves *inſtinct with ſenſe* ſecurely ſpeed;
Endu'd with wondrous ſkill, untaught they ſhare
The purpoſe and the will of thoſe they bear;
To fertile realms, and diſtant climates go,
And, where each realm and city lies, they know;
Swiftly they fly, and thro' the pathleſs ſea,
Tho' wrapt in clouds and darkneſs, find their way.

I muſt here leave the reader to his own conjecture, and ſhall only obſerve, that the uſe of the magnetic needle has been ſo long known to the Chineſe, that they have no records or notion of its origin.

I R I S H.
Fit, a breakfaſt after long faſting; Arabic, fetyr, the feſtival of breaking the faſt after the Mahommedan lent. (Richardſon.)

Iʒcam

IRISH.

Iocam, to heal; hence ioc, mifsletoe or mifsledine, the holy plant of the Druids, which commonly grows on the oak : it was called all-ioc, the holy ioc, and uile-ioc, all heal. Hence the Greek name ἰξὸς Æol. βισκὸς and the Latin vifcum, and the Englifh oak, from the tree bearing the ioc. An. Sax. aac, æc ; Run. eik, Belg. eycke ; Teuton. eiche, the oak, which Skinner derives from οἶκος domus. From cuir or cuira in Irifh a tree, and ioc, is formed the Latin quercus, and from the Irifh bhile a tree, if I miftake not, the Greek φίλαξ, (δρῦς, Hefych.) Voffius derives quercus from κιρχαλίος quod valet durus, afper ; thefe appear to be all from the Irifh ioc, which at length implied the oak, a tree facred to the ceremonies and rites of the druids. From fios or feas knowledge, art, fcience, charm, and iocas healing, is formed the Greek φύσική and the Latin phyfica, fcientia, as φύσις natura is from feas and fas ; fee Ollam, in the preceding pages at Tara.

Kifb, Kis, Cis, a dry meafure, ufually made of wattles ; it is at prefent ufed for a meafure of turf or peat.

Nakki, Naggin, Noggin, a meafure for liquids. The noggin contains a quart Englifh meafure, the naggin a quarter of a pint : it is now the meafure of a dram or glafs of fpirits, containing a gill Englifh meafure.

No words in the Hebrew language have puzzled commentators more than the nakki and the koſhi, in the plural keſhoth and menakkioth.

Koſhoth or *Keſhoth*, ſome veſſels, ſays Bates, in the temple, very poſſibly the patera or goblet,—Nakki, menakki, the bowl the libation was emptied out of.—The Keſhi I ſuppoſe was the ſame as the menaki—(Crit. Hib.)—But the learned Reland in his Hieroſolym. does not agree to this explanation, "tunc enim non menſæ ſed altaris Keſhuth, videntur dici debuiſſe. Vaſa erant altaris exterioris.—Et profecto conjecturis locus eſt, quoniam incerta eſt vocis utriuſque ſignificatio *." In the Chaldee Kis lignum, Kiaſa menſura aridorum. Arab. Kaſa, Kais menſura quædam. There is nothing more evident from Reland's deſcription of the uſe of theſe meaſures, than that the Keſhi was a pannier to hold the bread, and the nakki a meaſure for the frankincenſe. Of theſe more in their proper place, when treating of the weights and meaſures of the aucient Iriſh.

Luch, a new born infant, a dwarf, a pigmy. Bean luchna, or bean leona, a midwife; Obſtetrix, (Plunket's Ir. Dict.) Arabic luka, a child—hence the lucina of the Latins and lana of the Etruſcans, the goddeſs who preſided over child-bearing. From luch is formed the Iriſh

* This author obſerves in another place of the ſame book *Hebraca radices multa incognita.*

luchd

IRISH.

luchd, people, offspring, generation. Heb.
Lek. Hindoft. lugh.

Luchd, merchandize, cargo or lading of a fhip.
Luchdeifs, failors, merchants, the crew of a
fhip.—I take Luchdeifs to be the derivation of
Luteci, the ancient people of France, whofe
capital was Paris; this people were named
Nautæ Parifiaci, as appears by an infcription
written in the reign of Tiberius, difcovered at
Paris in 1710. See Efs, a fhip. Preface,
p. 118. and the learned Gebeline. (Allegor.
Orient. p. 165.) See alfo the fhip Ifis, the
arms of Paris, (preface.)

Laban, clay, mire, dirt, a brick. Labanach a la-
bourer, a ruftick, from his working in the
mire.—Perf. Liban a fellow-labourer, a flave.
Hebrew laben a brick, fuppofed to be derived
from laban, white, from becoming white, by
drying them before they are burnt.—Arab.
libn, a brick—confequently the Hebrew interpreters are miftaken in the explanation of
laben.

Lith-laith, feftivals, the days of lith.

Lith, a feftival. Exam. *is ainim dna airmid na Criosde*
LITH-LAITHE *agus latha follambanta naoimh
Patraicc ifeadhchimh Kal. April.* i. e. Lith is
the name the chriftians give to their reckoning
of the lith-laith, or days of folemnity; faint
Patrick fixed them on the kalends of April.
Vet. Gloff.

Lith-laith, 1. Nollag agus Caifg, i. e. Lith days
are chriftmas and eafter. The fingular is lai
a day,

IRISH.

    a day, and forms part of the Greek compound
τα-λαι pridem.

Litheas, folemnity, pomp. (Shaw) Litheamail
    folemnity. O'Brien. לטיהם Lateihem.
    (which we render their enchantments; LXX
    φαρμακίαι) magic feats performed on festivals
    with facrifices, herbs, minerals, &c. It is
    compounded of lahat, flame, fire. The word
    implies that fome ingredients were burnt in
    facrifices, or that they made ufe of fome
    things inftrumentally, as emblems of the
    light and as having fome lucid parts, and
    powers communicated to them by the light.
    This Hebrew name for the magicians of
    Egypt and their enchantments expreffes much
    of their offices and operations (Holloway Orig.
    v. 1. p. 229.)

Mith, *lea*; *Mithbae*, 1. *Greine*, that is, Mith, and
    Lea, and Mithbae are fynonimous names for
    Grian, the SUN. (Vet. Gloff.) Mithrio,
    Mithrufc. 1. lofga greine, that is, Mithrio and
    Mithrufc are names for the heat or fcorching
    of the fun: for its qualities, (Vet. Gloff.)
    In religious matters, the ancient Irifh named
    the fun Samh, and Bal; the ancient Perfians
    Mihr, which is the true pronunciation of the
    Irifh Mithrio, the T being eclipfed.

    Originem vocis mithra quod attinet, videtur illa
effe Perfica vox Mihr SOLEM notans, quam vocem
Græci pronunciarunt ita ut genius linguæ ferebat,
id eft, quum literam æquivalentem Perficæ *he* non
                        haberent,

haberent, exprimentes eam per ⊖ (Reland de Vet. Ling. Perf.) Jof. Scaliger and Ger. Voffius think mithra is derived from the Perfic mihter, major, præftantior, & fimpliciter Dominus; Selden is of the fame opinion, and quotes a Latin infcription DOMINO SOLI, &c. &c.

The Perfian mihter, Dominus, is the Irifh Machtair, from macht, power, ftrength, whence the Englifh might, and is a word foreign to mith, and mithrio. The words bae and rio compounded with mith in the ancient Irifh, form baeɲio, which lead me to think that πίɲɲα in the verfes of Lycophron fignifies the fun, as many authors have imagined, but Reland denies.

Σκιά καλύψει πίρραν, ἀμϐλύτων σίλας.

Reland would here read Μίρραν and derive it from mir; but Perra is a Coptick word for the fun, as may be feen in Potter's edition of Lycop. and moft probably compounded of the Pelafgian-Irifh bario.

In Spon we find infcriptions SOLI INVICTO MITHRÆ. SANCTISSIMO SOLI, &c. yet neither the Perfians or the heathen Irifh worfhipped Mith as God; they thought his exifting effence was there. Mithræ apud Perfas cultum, non effet adorationem divinam non obftantibus eis quæ Græci & Latini in hujus contrarium dicunt. (Hyde Relig. Vet. Perf.) The Perfians had other names for the fun, as Liu, Lab, Ruz, Ruzafken, Hazartaba.—At in Religionis negotio Sol præcipue appellatur Mihr.

(Hyde.)

(Hyde.)—In the Arabic the fun is named fhems, afitaub, mihr, khoor, khur, khurfheed, khawur, jawneh, zeer, tunk, hooz, iluhut, gaw, nei-ur, bei-za, &c. &c. from gaw and rio, probably was formed the Irifh grian, by adding an, a planet, viz gaw-rio-an : from the Perfic liu, the Arabic iluhut, or the Pelafgian-Irifh lea, certainly was formed the Greek ꙇ‌λιϙ and the Welfh Haul.

I R I S H.

Macallai, maccallai, an echo, i. e. the fon of a voice. The Hebrew name is Bath Kol the daughter of a voice. Between Malachy and John the Baptift, there ftood up no prophet, but only they were inftructed per filiam vocis, which they termed ‫בת קיל‬ bath Kol, and this was the reafon why thofe difciples faid, (Acts 19. 2.) We have not fo much as heard whether there be an Holy Ghoft.

The words in Hebrew and in Irifh which imply an echo, do alfo fignify an oracle. Thus Bath Kol in Heb. Berath Kola in Chaldee, both imply filia vocis, & oraculum. (See Shindlerus' Lex.) The Urim & Thummim was one of the four great oracles, from whence the Pelafgian-Scythian-Irifh formed Uire or Aire a prophet, Tua a diviner. From the Chaldee Berath (if it does mean a daughter, as all the commentators agree, for it is an extraordinary explanation) the Irifh formed Breith-cal, an oracle; by breith we mean a judge, a decree. —From the Hebrew Nebo-ah or oracle (in fecundo templo) the Irifh formed Neabh-raidhte, the latter compound

compound being of the fame fenfe as Kol a voice.
From Ruach-he Kodefh, the Hebrew of fpiritus
fanctus, they formed Kedruicht, Ruchte, Ruidhte,
an oracle, &c. &c.

I**R**I**SH**.

Meir, Meirdreac, a harlot. Heb. Meur, a harlot.
    Heb. drak, the oppofition of providence to
    wicked meafures—hence the Latin Meretrix.

Mbeic, bheic, (Wak) bravo! ufed at the end of a
    verfe of a fong; hence the fong Paddy
    Whack. Arab. Weika, bravo! well done;
    encore.

Mac, a fon—Caribean imakou. Sclavon. mac.
    The Irifh have all the Hebrew words for a fon,
    viz. nin, manon, fhilo, bar, and ben, but
    this word mac is applied in the fame manner
    as the Hebrew zacar a male child, becaufe,
    fay the Cabbalifts, the word fignifies memory,
    which is as much as to fay, *the memory of the
    father is preferved in the fon*; according to that
    fpeech of Abfolom, *I have no fon to keep my
    name in remembrance.* Mac in the old Irifh
    implies a remembrance, hence mactaim in the
    modern, to ponder, to weigh the memory:
    In Hebrew imecha to approve on recollection.
    M. mecha excellent. Æthiop. machaz Juvenes.
    Machak peperit. Syr. machan fraternitas.
    Arab. machan brevis homo & agilis. In Irifh
    macan a youth, a ftripling; mogh, moghal
    a man. Arab. makyl, a man, makhyz
    bringing forth; mac a calf; muhket youth;
    mekdum a boy; mekhdum an infant. So
                                        likewife

IRISH.

likewife in Irifh, in length of time, the word macaim fignified to bear or carry a child, to fondle, and a boy was diftinguifhed by ma-camh-ballaich, and a girl by macamh-mna; but the original fignification was from *ma*, the memory, and hence macoimh, maccar, a ftranger, one you do not remember, (Arab. mekkar) mac-memna, imagination ; mac-leabar, a book, i. e. an affiftance to memory, but at prefent ufed to fignify a copy of a book, as if, the fon of a book.

From the Hebrew, zacar, is derived the Irifh feicir or feikir, to remain, to reft in one place as a fettled family, and the oppofite feichràn or feakaràn, a wanderer, a ftroller, whofe name and country are not known.

Mas, meas, fruit in general; meafal, a baftard; meas, a fofter child ; meas, means procreation in general, hence that Hebrew proverb, " there is no herb in the earth, which hath not a mazal (ftar) in the firmament anfwering to it, and ftriking it, faying, grow and increafe." The Jews therefore called the planet Jupiter, mazal, whofe influence they thought of great efficacy and force in generation, hence the modern Jews pay their compliments to a new married pair, by writing the words, mazal tob, on their cards, which is to fay, good and fpeedy procreation to you. See Stukius de conviv. l. 2. c. 3.

Nainn,

IRISH.

Nainn, naing. A mother. Perfic. Vet. Nane, mater. (Reland.)

Scriobam. To write, to fcratch, or engrave, the antient method of writing was on thin boards, or the bark of a tree polifhed; hence leabar bark, alfo implies a book; from thefe Pelafgian-Irifh words is derived the Latin fcribo and liber; the participle is fcriobt, hence feanfcriobt or fcriot an antient writing, and this is the meaning of the Shanfcrite, characters of the Gentoos in Hindoftan; and from the Irifh feachd a ftylus, is derived the German fchreebfeder and belg. Schrii fuedu a pen. Liogam, lichtam, is alfo to engrave or cut in, and hence I believe leigam to read; Latin lego; Hindoftan me lechte, I read; probably from reading fuch engraving.

Dealbam. To write, to draw, to engrave; hence dealbhoir a forcerer, dealbh an image; diolam to write, to number, is like the Hebrew fephir, which fignifies a book, a fcribe, an account, numeration, &c.

Racam. To dig, to rake, to fcratch, to write; hence react-aire, or chief fcribes, in the domeftics of the kings of Ireland; fee the hall of Tarah in the preceding pages.

Grambam, grabbam, grapbam. To fcratch, to dig, to write; hence the Greek grapho, and grammar.

Ceartaim, creataim. To cut, to write; participle ceart, crat; hence coirt, the bark of a tree, a book; and the Latin charta, paper; Arab. kytt, chat,

IRISH.

chat, litera fcripta, chatat fcripfit; Hebrew
chrath, literas infculpfit, ftylo fcribere.

Gai, ngdair, ngtair, gitair. A writing from the preceding *.

Rocam, to wroll up; hence ruka a fheet of paper,
becaufe on the invention of parchment, they
rolled up the writing; hence rochail a winding
fheet; and probably the Englifh rocolo a cloak;
ruka alfo implies a letter in Irifh, that is,
writing folded up. Arabic rekk a parchment
book, rukim kurdin to write. The Cantabrians
have preferved the word fcribatzen, to write.

It is to be obferved that the fame words in Irifh
and in Arabic, which imply a man of letters or of
learning, or of having obtained the art of writing,
do alfo imply a forcerer, a prophet, a noble; for example: in Arabic, fuhr is a diviner, poetry; fuhir,
a poet; the Irifh faor has the fame fignification.
Arabic airooz poetry, aire a poet. Irifh aire a poet,
a chief, a forcerer. Arabic deewanè a poet. Irifh
dàn, a poem. Arabic noois a writer. Irifh nàs a
noble, a prophet. Arabic numik faukhtun, khutt
numooden, numnumeh kirdun, to write. Irifh neim
a noble, neim a poem, &c. &c. Obferve alfo, that
the Arabic kirdun is the Irifh cuirid, to make, to do.
And that the Irifh names of pens, ink, &c. are all

---

* The *ng* in the old Irifh is called n-gdieal or a nafal *g*;
it is a foft pronunciation of the Hebrew y, which fometimes
founds full, as in gnath, gnae, &c. It appears to have been
the digamma of the Pelafgian Greeks in the middle of
words; as, ἄγχω ango, ἄγγελ☉ Angelus, &c. γνόφۤ nubos.

Chaldee,

Chaldee, or Arabian words.—Thus in the defcription of Tara, we find reachtaire a fcribe; this word is compounded of the Arabic raukim, one who practices the art of writing, and aire or aroof a chief, a forcerer. Thus, all thefe again return to the Chaldee nimas; Greek ᴎᴍꙮ lex, jus, ftatutum; to the Arabic nemu, magnificatio; namu, arcanum; Heb. nimus Lex. Jus. Syr. Legalitas. Arabic nimas, Arcani participem fecit, exploravit. Nema feleƈtior pars populi. So alfo our Irifh mais, maithis druidifm, is from the Chaldee mifat. Greek ᴍꙏꙶᴋᴀ Arab. miftoor, resfacræ. So alfo our faor, faothar, fuidhir, a noble, a man of letters. Chaldee fithar. Arab. furrdar, arcanum. Ras, rae, a noble; raƈtaire, a writer, a noble; Chaldee raz, fecretum, arcanum; Irifh uafal; Arab. afool a noble, a learned man; Irifh eac, aireeac, a noble; Arab. eek, &c. &c. &c. Arab. khutt a writer; kutkhuda a chief; peifhenè a forcerer; peifh a chief; ain a forcerer; ain a chief; Arab. tunha a fecret; Irifh tanas dominion. In fhort, every word betokening a knowledge of arts and fciences, in all the Oriental dialeƈts, and in the Irifh, do alfo imply a nobleman, a chief, one above the common people, &c. &c. &c. Of thefe are formed the following compounds: fgribhean chirine, feilire chirine, graibh hieronoma, a manufcript.

Iʀɪsʜ.

Sed and *feod.* A word that frequently occurs in the ancient Brehon Laws of Ireland, for the payment or reward of labour, &c. In the preface to the Tenth Number of the Collectanea, p. 56, I have faid, that I fufpeƈted *fed*

IRISH.

to have been a piece of money; in perusing Hottingeri, Differt. de Nummis Orientalium, p. 94. I find שהד fhahad, was a coin or piece of money with the Hebrews, Syrians, Carthaginians and Chaldæans. And I believe the *afs* of the Irish, another piece of money mentioned in my preface, before mentioned at p. 57, to be the same as the Syrian אסר affar, nummis minutus Syris. Argenteus fuit, tantum pendens, quantum pendunt quatuor grana hordei. (Hotting. p. 105.)

Sruth. Clergy, minifters, (an order of the Druids.) fee all the Irish lexicons. Heb. fhirith and fhiruth, miniftry, fervice, to wait or attend upon. (Gr. ΣΟΤΗΡ.) Exod. 28. 43.—" they " fhall be upon Aaron, and upon his fons, " when they come in unto the tabernacle of " the congregation, or when they come near " unto the altar to (fhiruth) minifter in the " holy place," as the perfonal fervants of God. Num. 4. 12. The inftruments of (fhiruth) miniftry, wherewith they (fhiruth) minifter in the fanctuary. Jer. 15. 11. " the Lord " faid it fhall be well with thy (fhiruth) rem- " nant ;" there is nothing for remnant in this paffage, or is it fenfe. Jeremiah complains, that he was fent to oppofe all mankind, without any good to himfelf or them, being curfed by all ; but God tells him he would fupport him againft all oppofition, and his (fhiruth) miniftry fhould turn out to good,

both

IRISH.

both to himſelf and to others. Read the whole chapter. (See Bates's Crit. Heb.) Again, at Exod. 24. 13. Moſes roſe up, and his (ſhiruth) miniſter Joſhua.

Sar. The fiſh called mullet; quæ nunc Tyrus dicitur, olim Sarra vocabatur, a piſce quodam qui illic abundat, quem lingua Punica ſar appellant. (Servius.)

Scan-cas. The law.—Sanna Phœnicibus idem fuit quod Arabibus Sunna, i. e. Lex, doctrina, jus canonicum. (Boch.) ſee the Xth number of this Collectanea, preface.

Sliab. A mountain; Heb. ſhelab, prominentia; Syr. ſhelab, a vale between two mountains; in this ſenſe the Iriſh ſliabh is often uſed.

Torc, 1. *tigbearna.* A lord, prince, (Vet. Gloſſ.) Torcim, regem Perſice ſignificat, ſi fides Joan. Antioch. Malalæ—quod me ignorare fateor. (Relandus de Vet. Ling. Perſ.)

Goimb. Vexation, affliction, hate, malice, a grudge; this is a very extraordinary word in the Iriſh it implies alſo a tribe which you pity and hate, as goimhar; for which reaſon it is ſometimes written for gudhb, to ſignify a battle, a fight; the latter is the Hebrew גד and גדד gad and gadadh to aſſault, to attack, ſo is goimh the Hebrew גוים goim, the Gentiles, that is, all nations but that of the Jews.—And, as Pool explains the word in the 11th ch. of the Acts, homines incircumciſi, quos Judæi goim vocant. (Synopſ. Crit. vol. 4.)

Theſe

These words and a thousand others could be produced from the Irish language, that were not admitted into the British or Welsh. They had no such word as nim for a serpent; naidir and neidir were corrupted from the Irish nathair, i. e. the twisting reptile. A pig or sow was named by the Welsh huk, mokyn, turk, kynar; in Irish muc, torc, &c. but they never admitted ceis into the British language. There are many words in common with both nations, because originally they spoke one language, the Scythian; but, if the Irish had not received the aid and refinement of some oriental colony, why does the syntax of the two languages differ so much, as not to be understood, the one by the other people? and yet there was always a strong and natural connexion between them, many princes of Ireland having intermarried with the Welsh; and many were received into this country, when they were persecuted by the Romans and Saxons, In the County of Waterford is a settlement named Bally Commrag.

The multitude of oriental words to be found in the Irish language, can be no other ways accounted for, than by confirming the Irish history; that an oriental colony was established in Ireland. They may have been the Scythopolians, or Magogian-Scythians mixed with the Phœnicians. Let us now suppose them from Scythopolis. In the neighbourhood of this colony we find the following cities:

Tebetz. Vicus nomine ⲟ̄ⲗⲁ̄ⲥ in finibus Neapolis abeuntibus Scythopolin in tertio & decimo lapide. (Euseb. & Jud. ch. 9. v. 50.)

Tabbat.

Tabbat. Urbs in Menaſſe. (Jud. 7. 22.)

Thebes. Vicus diſtans Neapoli 13 miliaribus Scythopolin verſus. (Euſeb. in Onomaſtico.)

Phella, Pella. Urbem Decapolis & aquis divitem
eſſe.—Diruta eſt a Judæis quod incolæ recu-
ſarent ritus Judaicos recipere. Ant. 13. 23.
lib. 2. de bell. c. 19. jungit Geraſa, Phellam
& Scythopolin. Chriſtiani omnes divinitus
moniti eo fugerant ex urbe Hieroſolymitana
paulo ante obſidium. (Euſ. l. 3. c. 5.)

Phanea, Paneas. Φανια, eadem quæ Cæſarea Philippi,
quæ Phœnices urbs eſt, quam Paneada appellant. (Sozom. Hiſt. v. 21.) Cæſareæ Phillippi
quam Phœnices Paneda vocant. (Euſ. Hiſt.
7. 16.) Nomen habet urbs quod Gentes
PANIS ſimulacrum ibi poſuerint. Sed Joſephus a monte Paneo * (Reland Palæſt.—)
Belinas etiam ſcripſiſſe videtur, P; enim literam
Arabes non habent. (Scherif Ibn-Idris.)—In
vertice ejus montis inſigne templum (Hie-
oronym.) non ibi eſſet Templum, ſed montem
uti ſacrum in honore eſſet Gentibus. (Euſeb.)
This is the Iriſh Mon and Beilteine.

The Scythopolians by ſituation, by trade, and by
other ſocial intercourſes, muſt have had great

---

* In Iriſh ben, bin, a high mountain, or rather the pinnacle of a conical formed mountain, as Binborb, the proud
pinnacle, a mountain in the County of Tyrone; in Welſh
Pen, as Pen-man-mawr, i. e. the pinnacle of the great Mon;
but phan or fan, in Iriſh, is the ſun; whence I ſuſpect this
mountain in Paleſtine was ſo called, the ſame as the Peltine
of the Aſſyrians and Belteine of the Iriſh.

com-

communication with thefe neighbouring cities inhabited by Hebrews, Phœnicians, Syrians, and probably by Ægyptians; and in this intercourfe, muft
have adopted much of the Phœnician, Hebrew and
Syrian dialects.

Accordingly we find the Hiberno-Scythians have
time immemorial, diftinguifhed three dialects, ufed
by them in fpeech, which have been erroneoufly
thought to have been foreign to their native tongue,
called Scuit-bearla, or Scythian dialect, and fometimes gnath-bhearla, that is, the vulgar dialect, or
mother tongue.

The foreign dialects they name;

Barla Pheine or Feine.
Barla File or Phila.
Barla Teibid.

Like the Arabs, having no character, originally, to
exprefs Ph, * they ufed the letter F, as the Arabs
write Farfi for Parfi, a Parthian or Perfian.

Bearla Teibidb was a mixt Irifh, ufed by the phyficians, fays Dr. O'Brien in his dictionary. It is
certain, that tebid in Irifh is a phyfician, fo is tubèat
in Arabic, and tabieb in the Hindoftan or Gentoo
dialect, from the old Arabic word tuba, (natura.)
But the Irifh have many other names for a phyfician,
and why not name this dialect after fome of thefe
compounds, as well as from teibid ; viz. Fifioca †
a phyfician, from fis art, fcience, and iocam to heal,
this is the Arabic hakeem a phyfician; leagham

---

* See the Irifh Grammar, Obfervations on P.

† Fifioce, i. e. fis, the knowledge of Ioce, healing. I have
before fhewn in this number, the power of the word fis, in
fophos, philofophos.

is

is to heal, and leagh a phyfician ; yet we never meet with bearla-ioca or bearla-leagha ; fo alfo freapaire is a phyfician, from freapa medicine, and aire a chief; this is the Chaldee repa, repua, medecina; repui fanatio; but we never hear of any Irifh diale& called bearla-freapaire : confequently thefe diftinc- tions of dialeéts have another meaning, than that the Irifh lexicographers have given them.

Taibid in Irifh fignifies a fquib in fpeech, ac- cording to Shaw.

Teibidh, pedantic. Teibim to overcome by ar- gument; but this is derived from taiba in Chaldee, Vox, diétio, apud grammaticos Rabbinorum, (ac- cording to Buxtorf.) Elias explains taiba to be vox fcripta.

Thefe dialeéts then of the ancient Irifh, appear to have been fo named from the cities of Tebetz, Tabbat, or Thebes, Phella, and Phanea, which were contigu- ous to the fettlement of their anceftors in Paleftine.

The Irifh bearla or barla fpeech, is fuppofed by O'Brien, to be derived from beul the mouth, and radh fpeech; (a blunder with a witnefs!) the word is certainly corrupted from barol, compounded of bar fenfe, reafon, learning, and ol to pronounce, fay, declare.

Heb. Chaldee and Perfic, bar, barè, fenfible, pious, good, and ale to declare or pronounce ; and from the Hebrew bal, fpirit, air, foul, thought, we have the Irifh balradh fpeech, phrafe, idioma.

From the Irifh bearla or barola, are derived the French words, parole, paroler, parler ; fpeech, to fpeak; and from the Irifh abra fpeech, is formed another verb labradh to fpeak, from whence the Spanifh palabra.

Gnadh,

Gnadh, gnad and nad are the fame words, implying nature, therefore the gnath bearla was the
natural dialect of the Magogian Scythians, the anceftors of the Irifh ; Arabic nihaud, nature; Welfh
gnawd ufual, common ; Welfh gnaws. Dr. Davies
demands, if this is the root of naws, a word now
ufed to fignify nature ? Il paroit q'oui, (fays Bullet
in his Celtic dictionary) & que ce mot eft formè
de Geni. De geni on aura fait gnaws, enfuite naws.
De gnaws, gni, le Latins ont fait leur gnatos, & de
naws, leur nafcor, natos.

In like manner the Carthaginians had two dialects
of fpeech, the Sicilians four, and the Etrufcans three.
" Poeni, Punice & Lybice locuti funt, ut Bochartus
" oftendit; idque confirmat Virgilius, qui Tyrios
" bilingues memorat.   Siciliam quoque, quod na
" tiones diverfi idiomatis eum tenuerint, fuiffe qua
" drilinguem accepimus. Ex eo autem, quod Vir
" gilius, Mantuam Etrufcorum coloniam laudans,
" dixerit : *gentem illi triplicem, populos fub gente qua-*
" *ternos, ipfamque caput fuiffe populorum* ; conjicit
" Dempfterus, triplicem fuiffe veterem Etruriam—
" in quibus unius linguæ plures dialecti, ut fufpi-
" cor, in ufu fuere & adhuc funt. (Gori, Muf.
Etrufc. prolegom. p. 54.)

T H E

THE ANTIENT

ETRUSCAN LANGUAGE,

COLLATED WITH THE

I R I S H.

SPECIMEN.

To attempt an explication of the language of the antient Etruſcans, Tuſcans or Etrurians, is a bold undertaking, conſidering the various opinions of the learned, concerning the origin of this very antient people. But as my very learned friend, Governor Pownal, obſerves, in his treatiſe on the ſtudy of antiquities: " There is, as it were, a golden chain de-
" ſcending from heaven, by which all things are linked
" together in a general ſyſtem ; and that man has
" powers to trace back the links of this chain, up
" to the primary principles of this ſyſtem ; and
" that the ſtudy of antiquities ſhould be purſued in
" this ſpirit of philoſophy, and the knowledge
" acquired thereby, applied as the commentary of
hiſtory.

" hiftory. That without the aid of antiquarian
" labour, without regard to the communities and
" growing ftates of the antient world, we may read
" and learn a great deal, but fhall know very little;
" we fhall continue reading about a creature, that
" we do not underftand the nature or conftitution
" of, and fhall neither conceive the fprings, the
" means, nor the ends of its actions."

The loofe and fcattered obfervations we have
thrown out from time to time, on the laws, religion
and cuftoms of the antient Irifh, (never before brought
to light,) we hope will be confidered, as the materials
only of an edifice that may hereafter be conftructed
on this ingenious and learned author's plan;—un-
connected as thefe parts appear, they are ftill parts
of the whole, and will be of fervice to the workman
that fhall undertake the conftruction of the fabrick.

The authors of the Univerfal Hiftory have paid
very great attention to that part concerning the
Etrufcans; they fay, that the Etrufcan language
muft have been the fame or nearly fo, with the
Hebrew and Phœnician. On the contrary, Dionyf.
Halicarnaf. declares, " nec cum ulla alia gente eam
" lingua aut moribus convenire computum eft."
And Bochart concludes, " Tufcum faltem fermonem
" à Phœnicia vel Punico fuiffe diffimillimum con-
" ftat." Dempfter, who has treated largely on the
Etrufcan antiquities, pofitively affirms, their language had no affinity with the Greek or Latin,
whilft Pafferus declares it was totally Greek.—
Sufpicio totam quoque linguam Etrufcorum ex
Græca quæ adhuc cruda & inculta effet, proceffiffe;

nam

nam vix enim ex omnibus fcriptoribus vicinas
Phrygias voces fuperftites habemus, quæ diligenter
collectæ, nihil fere cum Etrufcis commune habent;
—multo plures remanent nobis ex vetere Ægyptia,
quæ tamen nihil omnino præeftant ad finem hunc
affequendum.—That the Etrufcan differed from the
Phrygian is certain; for the Phrygian was Gomeriari,
but the Etrufcan I think Magogian-Scythian, mixed
with the Phœnician under the name of Pelafgian;
" and the firft Pelafgian fettlements in Etruria,"(fay
the authors of the Univerfal Hiftory) " from what
" we have advanced, could not have been *many*
" *centuries after the deluge, and very few after the*
" *difperfion*; and at that time, the languages, or
" rather dialects of the Ægyptians, Affyrians,
" Babylonians, Syrians, Arabs, &c. muft have ap-
" proached extremely near to the Hebrew and
" Phœnician, which the learned allow to have been
" almoft the fame."—" Bourguet and Gori, have
" adopted a wrong hypothefis in their learned en-
" quiries, by fuppofing the antient Etrufcan lan-
" guage to have been but little different from the
" Greek; which certainly runs counter to what has
" been advanced by Dionyf. Halic. and Herodotus;
" thefe noble hiftorians, whofe authority will cer-
" tainly bear down all that oppofe them, muft
" convince every fober and rational enquirer, that
" the Greek and Etrufcan tongues were vaftly dif-
" ferent.—Bochart deftroys his own authority by
" palpably contradicting himfelf, and the Etrufcan
" words he produces, as entirely remote from the
" languages of the Eaft, have been proved agreeable
" to thofe languages, by Mr. Swinton.

" The

" The Etruſcan inſcriptions approach nearer to
" the oriental languages, in proportion to their an-
" tiquity ; ſome of them conſiſt chiefly of words,
" apparently deducible from theſe languages, and
" therefore were the produce of the earlier ages.
" Others indicate a lower period, by the Greek
" words incorporated in them ; and laſtly, others
" demonſtrate an age, not preceding the 6th cen-
" tury of Rome, by ſeveral infallible criterions, as
" will very clearly appear to every ſagacious ex-
" aminer of them.—However the Etruſcan alpha-
" bet was uſed in ſome parts of Italy, and the
" Etruſcan language ſpoken, till at leaſt, verynear
" the Auguſtan age. This we learn from the ex-
" preſs teſtimony of Gellius and Strabo, and from
" two Samnite medals, whoſe Etruſcan legends
" have been lately explained, by a learned Italian
" author.

" That the moſt antient Greek tongue ap-
" proached much nearer the Etruſcan language
" than thoſe dialects of it uſed by even the oldeſt
" Greek claſſics, appears from the obſolete radices
" of that tongue ; if the Etruſcan reſembled any
" of the Greek dialects, it muſt have been the
" Æolic ;—now, that the antient and later Æolic
" dialects were evidently different, has been evinced
" by Salmaſius, and yet the laſt diſcovers a con-
" ſiderable affinity with the Hebrew and Phœnician.
" Suppoſing therefore, the old Etruſcan language
" to have been related to the Greek, as Bourguet
" and father Gori contend, every rational critic will
" underſtand this of the firſt dialects that prevailed

" in

" in Greece, which if admitted, will exactly coin-
" cide with what we have advanced; but will by
" no means hold true of the Greek tongue, current
" in the claffic times, at leaft not fo ftrongly as the
" former.—If therefore, the learned men above
" mentioned, mean only that the Etrufcan language
" agrees with that firft fpoken in Greece, we rea-
" dily fubfcribe to their opinion ; but, if they are
" to be underftood of the later, or Hellenical Greek,
" we muft beg leave to differ from them."

It is furprizing that the authors of the Univerfal
Hiftory, take no notice of Pafferus, who has explained above one hundred words and infcriptions
in the Etrufcan language, by the Greek ; fee his
Diff. de Hellenifmo Etrufcorum & de Nummis
Etrufcis Pæftanorum, in the fecond volume of the
Symbolae Litterariæ; this author replies to Dempfter
in thefe words, " ipfa dubietas, cum qua maximus
" ille philofophus procedere videtur, quamquam &
" Græcarum Religionum, & patriæ linguæ peri-
" tiffimus, clare oftendit quantum hæ res occultæ
" haberentur, & ut ipfos Græcorum fapientiffimos
" laterent."

I have not yet feen Swinton's works on this fubject,
but from the perufal of Bochart, Gori, Pafferus and
Dempfter, it is evident to me, that the ancient
Etrufcan words given by them, have a ftrong affinity with the ancient Irifh, and that doctor Parfons
had great reafon to affert that the Greek was formed from the Pelafgian, which according to the authors here quoted, was an oriental dialect: the reader will judge of my opinion by the following fpe-
cimens.

Æfar,

ETRUSCAN.

Æſar, Deus; Hibernica, eaſar, i. e. creator; Arab. ezid, deus; ijra kirdun, creare, facere.

Mantus, diſpater; Hib. man-tus, deus ſummus; man, deus, tus, primus; Perſ. mana, ac-man, sjamana, nomina Dei apud vet. Per ſias, (Reland) & ;man dominus. Steuchus Eugubinus ex Theodoreto ſcribit Samaritinos Deum appellare Meniame.

Arimi, ſimiæ; Hib. airiſam, imitare; Perſ. aher-man, arimani, malus genius; Syris harim, ſimus.

Arſe vorſe, averte ignem; Hib. arraiſe foirſea, a-verte occam; adagium eſt apud Hibernos, ſed arraiſe ùrſo, averte ignem; item, cur ais ùrſo.

Falantum, cœlum; Hib. felan, flaitheamhnas, ru-agh; Arab. fuluk, eflak-rukea.

Capuæ, cui curvi ſunt pedum pollices; Ir. cap, ſe-nex decripitus, incurvus; Arab. kupooſh, curvus.

Iduare, dividere; Hib. eidirim; Arab. juda kir-dun.

Baltheus, cingulum; Hib. balt, a ball, i. e. circulus, rotundus.

Nepos, abliguritor; Hib. neam-bos, neam-aiſe; Ar. na-oon.

Hiſter, ludio; Hib. aiſtior, aiſtighoir; Arab. hu-zaut.

Laniſta, carnifex; Hib. lann-eis; Arab. laena-bu-daien.

Lucumo, rex; vide Præfat. p. 8.

Taſies,

ETRUSCAN.

Taties,
Luceres, } nomen tribus; Hib. taith-leac, luch-
Rhamnes, } taire, reim.

Mantissa, additamentum; Hib. man-taos, man-
taosga; Arab. muftanauk; Scaliger fic dici
vult quafi manu-tenfa eo quod manu porri-
gitur.

Natinare, factiones effe; Hib. ni-teann, nithear-te-
ann.

Neptun, deus maris; Hib. neamh-tonn, i. e. neamh,
deus, fub-deus & ton, mare.

Tiberis, fluvius; Hib. tiobar, fons; is, aqua, tioba-
ris, fluvius fontium, aqua dulcis.

Vadimon, Ianus vertumnus; Hib. faidhmon fubdeus
prophetarum apud veteres Ibernicos, (Vet.
Gloff.) & Fadheaman princeps fcientiarum,
fonat.

Vidua, a viro valde divifa; Hib. fidh-ua, i. e.
fadhbh.

Vola, oppidum aut Arx, ut Volaterræ, Volcæ, Vo-
lumnia; Hib. baile, vaile; Ar. balid, bi-
lud.

Volcanus, deus; Hib. bal-ceann, idem & bor-ceann.
(Vide Irifh Gram. Preface.)

Ificia, farcimen ex pice quadam; Hib. af-ioca, fuccus
vifcofus arbufculæ vifcæ (Mifsletoe.)

Polimina, tefticuli porcini; Hib. ball minnan, tefticuli caprimi.

Longana, farcimen longius quam duo hila, Hib. long-
ionar, hilla.

Næniæ, farcimen; Hib. inionar, nionar, hillula:
omafum.

Africia,

ETRUSCAN.

Africia, farcimen ex fanguine hircino: Hib. fraochan, farcimen ex fanguine cervi : omafum cervi.

Gratilla, pars hoftiæ ; Hib. greatlach, exta, vifcera.

Andas, boreas, feptentrio ; Hib. deas, aufter, i. e. dexter, & andeas, neamdeas, boreas, quia finifter.

Druna, principatus ; Hib. druinae.

Damnus, equus ; Hib. damh, equus, bos.

Agalletor, puer; Hib. giolla, giollathar, puer, mafculinus.

Byrrhus, cantharus, bure fermone vernaculo ; Hib. buare.

Sibiter, *anfihiter*, Jupiter—ΣΩΤΗΡ, fervator ; Jovem hoc attributo fervatoris cumulatum fuiffe, oftendit fæpe Paufanias, (Pafferius) Hibern. Seathar, Deus. Heb. שיאטר Shiator, Dominus. Arab. Satyh, Deus. Hibern. An-feathar, Deus maximus ; fee Sruth.

In this manner, and with equal fuccefs, I have formed a comparative vocabulary of all the Etrufcan words to be found in the authors before-mentioned, which may probably appear in fome future number of this work. And although inconvenient to prolong this publication, I cannot omit a few words more of the Etrufcan, becaufe they fhew that the antient druids of Ireland, and thofe of Etruria, agreed in one remarkable cuftom.

Nerfia, narcia, nortia, nurcia, vel nurtia; Dea Vulfinienfium dicitur, tam varia eft librorum fides ut notat Pamelius. Vetus Scholiaft. Juven. Sat.

Sat. 10. fortunam vult intelligi quæ apud
Nyrtiam colitur, unde fuit Sejanus. Errat
fane, nam ut verum fit, Nurtiam effe Fortunam, illud tamen ineptum apud Nyrtiam coli
—nullus enim locus, quod fciam in Tufcia
eo nomine. (Dempfter, de Etrur. Regal.)

The antient Irifh named the laft day of the year
nurith, a word explained in the old gloffarifts, by
nua-arith, that is, a new reckoning; it is commonly
written nuridh, and nurith. Nuridh, fays Mr.
Shaw, (in his Irifh dictionary) is the fame as nuarith, that is, *laft year*. I find it alfo named nua-iris,
that is, the new æra, which was probably written
nurfia by fome Greek or Roman author. The Irifh
have a proverb ftill in ufe, viz. gur mharamaod
flàn anuarith, or, anuairis, that is, may we be alive
and well at the next day of nuarith.—This day
clofed the druidical feftival of Nollag, defcribed
p. 464; it concluded by driving a nail into a fhield,
fufpended in each arch-druid's houfe, to denote the
number of years of each cycle. This was undoubtedly the cuftom of the Etrufcans, as defcribed
by Livy in his 1 Decad. l. 7. "Vulfiniis quoque
"clavos indices numeri annorum fixos in templo *
NOR-

* Prima Deorum templa fuere luci : aræ erectæ in montibus,
quos prifca religio Diis facravit ; hinc plures in Etruria ad
hoc tempus nomina antiquæ fuperftitionis fervant, ut mons
Jovis, Mons Summanus, Mons Cereris : ut fileam de his, quos
longa fæculorum ferie ignarum vulgus idiomate fuo corrupit,
Diifque dedicatos fuiffe manifefte adparet. Sacra Diis facta
fub arboribus, quas ipfis quoque Diis Etrufcorum Religio
facravit, clare adnotat Plinius : Vetuftior autem urbe in

NORTIAE Etrufcæ Deæ comparere; diligens talium monumentorum auctor Cincius affirmat."—Feftus Pomp: defcribes the fame ceremony, l. 3. " Clavis annalis appellabatur, qui figebatur in pa-" rietibus facrarum ædium per annos fingulos, ut " per eos numerus colligeretur annorum."

It is evident alfo, that the old Arabians had the word nuairis, to fignify a new æra or reckoning, from the Arabic now-rooz, ftill in ufe, to fignify the new year, becaufe rooz does not exprefs the word year, but arij is an epoch.

Camillus. Mercury; (Macrobius & Servius.) The Phœnicians are fuppofed to fignify Mercury by Chadmel, a name in Irifh, implying firft of princes.—Caomal in Irifh is the beloved; but camleir is the caduceus; it now implies a crooked ftick.

Nanus. The Etrufcan name of Ulyffes; (Ifaicus in Lycophron. p. 185.) Irifh, Naine, valour, prowefs, chivalry;—it is the name of an antient and noble family in the province of Ulfter in Ireland; the large territory of Cineal Naena, was the antient eftate of the O'Naines, or O'Naonas, from whom it derived its name. Monf. O'Neny, (as he now fpells the name) of Bruffels, Count of the Roman Empire, is the defcendant of this family. (O'Brien's Dict. at Naona.)

Vaticano ilex, in qua titulus aereis litteris Etrufcis: religione arborem jam tum dignam fuiffe, fignificat. (Gori de Ædif. Public. Etruf. p. 51.) See Nortia, Preface, p. 125. & Saman, p. 443.

Laus.

ETRUSCAN.

Larts. A tomb, a monument to the dead; Irish liart, i. e. lia a stone, irt death; lothort, i. e. lohort, i. e. feart, a tomb. (Vet. Gloff. Hib.) These words have been miftaken by Gori, Dempfter, &c. to fignify Diis Manibus, becaufe they are the leading words on the Etrufcan monuments.

Lupu. A tomb, a grave; Ir. luiba, leaba; hence the name of leaba graine, leaba dermod, given to thofe antient monuments, found in feveral parts of Ireland, defcribed in a former number of this work.

Terbyos. Τ.Θέμ, an oracle, (Plutatch) Irish tadhas, tathas, tathnhas, whence the Greek themis.

Clan. Children, fons, tribes; (filii, nati; Gori,) Ir. clann, children, pofterity, tribe, clan or family, a breed or generation. Several of the territories of Ireland begin with this word Clann, diftinguifhed by the family names of the tribes that inhabited them, as Clanbreafail, Clancolmain, &c. The word is a corruption of coic a child, and Ian perfect, coiclan, i. e. clan; Arabic kauk a child.

Fanum. A temple, a place of worfhip; Ir. fan, as Fan Lobuis, the church of St. Lobus, in the county of Corke, &c. the word is derived from the old word fan or phan, the fun, the facred fire; hence fan-leac, a druidical altar, the fame as Crom-leac; (fee O'Brien and Shaw at Fán.)

Fanu.

ETRUSCAN.

Fanu. A fepulchre; Ir. fadhbhan, (favàn) a tumulus, a mole hill, a tomb.

Lar, lares, lartes. Arnobius acknowledges thefe
words of Etrufcan origin; quafi Lauras dictos
a vicis, the god or gods who preferved both
houfe and lands, and prefided over cities and
private houfes; it fignifies alfo the chimney,
fire-fide, a dwelling houfe, with the modern
Latins.—Gori does not approve of this derivation, and thinks they are derived from the
Perfic art, a hero.—Bullet thinks, that as *lar*
in the Celtic implied a chimney, or fire-fide,
fo does feu (a fire) fignify a family or houfe
in French, and hence the gods Lares, that is,
domeftic gods, which they placed over their
chimney-pieces. In old Irifh, lar is the
ground floor of a houfe, the ground, land,
a family; but lere is omnipotent, puiffant;
whence it became a family name, now written
O'Leary; in Perfic ler, ler-ler, omnipotence,
a name of God; Arab. Leh, God. The
Etrufcan Lartes is compounded of the Irifh
Lere, Omnipotent, and Art, God, hence the
Lares were guardian angels of the Romans.
Voffius rightly obferves, that lar was an
Etrufcan name for prince, ruler, nam lar
Hetrufca vox eft, & principem fignificat, ut
docuit Scaliger ad Propertium; hence, in the
modern Irifh, lere is religion, devotion, and
fometimes written leor, as leor-gniomh, and
leor-dhoilgeas, fatisfaction, and contrition in

pen-

pennance. Ex. neartaidh me a Thiarna chum mo cheanna d'faifidin mailleria leor-dhoilgeas, i. e. ftrengthen me O Lord, to confefs my crimes with devout contrition! The Irifh now write lar, lathar, the *th* is not founded, but lengthens the fyllable, as làr; this liberty of the Irifh poets of the twelfth century, has hurt the language much; fee Lere and La-thar, in all the modern Irifh dictionaries.

Lar, *Iofdamh*. Teagh comhnaighe arigh: agus Patruin airighe gach tighe do reir Paganai. Lar, a houfe, a family, a dwelling, and the patron or guardian angel of each houfe, according to the Heathens. (Plunket's Irifh Dictionary, MS.)

The Etrufcans were remarkable for medicinal waters; 'fo were the antient Irifh and Scots.—Laudant celebres fcriptores Dionyf. Hal. Strabo, Varro, & alii in Etruria, medicatas faluberrimas aquas. (Gori de Ædificiis Etrufc.)

An hoc præftas hero, fili Diogenis,
Quod illi ex utre aquam mittis? an hoc te
Jactas?—at hoc pacto utilior te Tufcus Aquilex.
(Varro in Quinquatribus.)

Aquælicium dicitur, quum aqua pluvialis remediis quibufdam elicitur: ut quondam, fi creditur, manali lapide in urbem ducto. (Feftus.)

Aquilex, with the modern Latins, implies, he that conveyeth water by pipes, or findeth a fpring, a water bailiff.

Manalis,

ETRUSCAN.

Manalis ; That which belongeth to ghofts, or
to the gods below, that out of which water always floweth. Manalem lapidem, putabant effe
oftium orci ; The door of hell, by which the fouls
were thought to afcend to this world.

Now Aiche-leigheas in old Irifh, is a water-doc
tor, he that healeth by Aiche or Oiche, medicinal
water—and Aiche-leicc or the water ftone, was
a certain ftone, the Hibernian forcerers ufed to
throw into water, to give it a medicinal virtue; it
was alfo called menal or meanadhal-leicc, the ftone
of fate or deftiny.—Leicc, a large cryftal of a figure
fomewhat oval, which priefts kept to work charms
by. Water poured upon it at this day, is given to
cattle againft difeafes; thefe ftones are now preferved for the fame purpofes, by the oldeft and moft
fuperftitious in the Highlands of Scotland. (Shaw's
Irifh Dict. at Leicc.)

Quære, did not Feftus and Varro miftake the
fenfe of the Etrufcan Aquilex, and Manalis lapis ?

Plikamnam or *Phlikamnam*.   An infcription on a vafe
or urn—Gori thinks it fignifies, vas fuffitus—
In Irifh plic or phlic is an urn or vafe ; (Plunket) phlicmheas a meafure for liquids—fic-
neamh or phlicneamh, a facred urn, or vafe
for facred ufes—flichmeadh, any meafure for
liquids (Shawe and O'Br.)

Ian. Ianus ; Pater, Tufeorum deus omnium primus ;
Irifh Ionn, Iehovah, dominus, the Almighty God ; this word has been admitted
in

ETRUSCAN.

in the same sense by the Gomerian Welsh. In the Basque or Cantab : Ioun, Iauna, God, Lord. In the Sclavonic Iunak a hero (Ir. Aonach) Ionn the head, the upper part. (Shaw.) this word is often written aon by the modern Irish, ao and io having the same sound. If I mistake not, the Irish name of Wednesday, viz. cad-aon, or, dia cadiononn, the day of holy Ionn, was so named from the worship to the omnipotent God, assigned on that day. Ianus primus coronarum inventor fuit. (Draco Corcyræus) ; Ionn was the same as Baal or Belus with the Heathen Irish, and this accounts for Ianus being esteemed the same as Apollo by the Romans. (See Macrobius Sat. 1. 9.) "Some undertake, says " he, to prove Ianus to be the Sun, and that " he is represented double, as being master of " both gates of Heaven, because he opens " the day when he rises, and shuts it when " he sets. His statues are marked on the " right hand with the number 300, and on " the left with 65, to signify the measure of " the year. Cicero says in his third book of " Etymologies, that Cornificius, calls him " not IANUS but Eanus. In the antient " poems of the Salii, he is stiled the God of " Gods. He is drawn with a key and a rod. " He has 12 altars one for each month of the " year. Marcus Messala consul, & augur 55 " years, begins his discourse upon Ianus " thus

" thus. He who forms and governs all,
" united together the nature of water and
" earth, which by their gravity always tend,
" downward, to that of the fire and fpirit,
" which by their lightnefs mount nimbly up-
" wards, and thefe he has confined to the
" Heavens ; and to thefe Heavens he has
" annexed fuch an attractive force as unites
" and binds together different natures and
" qualities." This paffage from Macrobius
is good authority for the Scythian deity IONN
being the fame as the Etrufcan IANUS, or
EANUS, which was his name and not
JANVS.

As IANVS was the pater deorum of the Irifh and
of the Etrufcans, fo was Anu, the mater deorum
Hibernenfium (Vet. Glofs. Hib.) She was called
Anu, Ana, and Anaine. On a plate of Gori's,
where the figure is fuppofed to reprefent Pomona,
I read in the Etrufcan Infcription IA....VI OILAI
which I take to be IANVI CEILE, and this would
fignify in Irifh the wife of Ianus, and probably was
the Ancharia of the Etrufcans and the Anna perenna
of the Romans—by which name they probably
meant, mater deorum, in the original language of the
Etrufcans.

ETRUSCAN.

Orthium, an ode, a hymn. The title given by Gori
to the ancient Etrufcan infcriptions called
the Eugubine tables.—Hujus tabulæ Etrufcæ interpretationi tituli feci orthium, carmen
lamentabile, quia in tabula Pelafgica, quam
interpretatus

interpretatus eſt V. C. Bourguettius, nuncupatur orthium vers. 26, 36, 46, quod hujus carminis numeri quam altiſſima & intentiſſima voce ferentur; ὀρθιον enium græci dicunt, quod arduum eſt, & quam altiſſima voce elevatum—poſſunt etiam, ut recte fecit Bourguettius, inſcribi litaniae, quia preces ad Jovem cum ejulatu & lamentis altiſſima voce prolatis continent.—(Gori Muſeum Etrus. Proleg. p. 53. tom. 1.)

The Greek orthion is certainly explained by Suidas and Plutarch by ſublata and intenta voce; and the ὀρθια of Homer is undoubtedly the ſame as the Iriſh Ortha, a poem, a collect, a prayer, an oration, a charm, a prophecy, whence Orthia in Greek ſignifies vaticinor, to prophecy; (Heſych.) but as O'Brien obſerves, it ſhould be written Artha when taken in the laſt ſenſe.—Ortha, i. e. eile (Vet. Gloſſ. Hib.) Now eile in the modern lexicons, is explained by prayer, oration; but it was a publick oration or prayer to the deity, compoſed by the Phille or Druid; (ſee p. 523) and is the ſame as the Arabic ilahè, ilahe-ut, a hymn; in which language or, implies an oration rythmically compoſed, whence the Iriſh oràn a ſong but, or, in the Arabic alſo ſignifies a ſupplication made with humility, (Richardſon) and expreſſes the Iriſh laodhan a ſacred oration in verſe, (made with humility) from whence the Greek λιτανεια and the Latin litania, (litany) i. e. ſupplicatio: thus the Arabic dua, a prayer to Heaven, is turned by the Iriſh into duan, and now ſignifies a poem, canto, rhyme; in Perſic divan;

divan; a word which originally signified an oration in verse made to the deity, and this oration or prayer was made with (adh or odh i. e.) singing and musick, whence adh, and odh in Irish, and ada in Arabic and Persic, express eloquence, oration, song, musick, notes; this word the Irish compound with ra or radh speech (as adhradh,) to express worship, prayer to God; hence the latin ode, oda, an ode, a song; odeum a music room, adoro to worship, &c. In like manner if I am not mistaken the Irish crom, adoration, or the act of singing the ortha, (from whence cromchear a priest, a prophet) formed the Latin carmen, an ode, a prophecy; and the Bohemian chram, a temple, a place of worship; and from the Irish cuirm, excommunication, (Heb. cherem) the Latin carmen signified also, sentence or condemnation to punishment. (See Cuirm ascaon.) With great reason therefore the learned Gori concludes his prolegomena on the Etruscan and Pelasgian tables, with these words; "Ex his tabulis "tum Etruscis tum Pelasgicis observare etiam non "fine voluptate possumus, Latinae linguae incunabu- "la, quae non solum Graecae linguae, verum etiam "Pelasgicae and Etruscae ortum suum & augmen- "tum maxime debet, adeo ut horum quoque "indiomatum dialectus censeri debeat."

To this let us add his observations in the first dissertation of his second volume, and those of Dempster in the additions to his second vol. and compare what has been said in the preface to this essay with the short specimen here given, and the ancient history of the Irish, and there cannot in my humble

humble opinion remain a doubt, but that the ancient
Irish and the ancient Pelasgians, and Etruscans
were one and the same people. "Ab alia nations
" ortum habere (Etrusci) non potuisse, quam ab
" Ægyptiis—porro non mirandum, autores de his
" Ægyptiorum in hac Italiæ partem migratione
" verba non feciffe, nam vetuftiffimis temporibus
" ut plurimum facta populorum literis non com-
" mendabantur, vel deperditæ erant antiquiffimæ
" hiftoriæ. Ut autem conciliemus noftram hanc
" opinionem cum illa fcriptorum, qui paffim Etruf-
" cos a Lydiis ortos tradunt. contingere potuit,
" quod profugi illi ex Ægypto primum confederint
" in locis proximioribus Afiæ, & præfertim Lydiæ ;
" & poftea, irruentibus aliunde populis, pulfi in
" Italiam advenerint. Et Plutarchus in Romulo
" tradit, populos illos in Lydiam ex alia regione ad-
" veniffe ; & licet dicat, Pelafgos fuiffe ex Theffalia
" profectos ; attamem exploratum eft, fcriptores,
" cum eos latuerint antiquiffimæ gentium migrati-
" ones, eas tribuiffe fæpe fæpius recentioribus
" Pelafgis, quorum gefta magis nota erant, qui a
" Theffalia pulfi, vagi per varias regiones circumie-
" runt." (Additam. Dempfteri de Etruria Regali.)

Poft Aborigines diverfis temporibus in Italiam
trajecerunt Siculi, Umbri, Ligures & Aufones five
Aurunci, quos aliqui ante Aborigines adveniffe exif-
timant. Hos Scythicæ originis, ab Aufone Atlan-
tis filio ductos in Italiam, atque effe Homeri Laef-
trigonas—Pelafgorum prima fedes fuit Phœnicia,—
quod vero Tyrrheni ac Pelafgi ejufdem generis effent,
teftantur etiam plures veteres auctores, quorum
loca

loca adfert Bochartus—pro Barbaris habiti funt a
Græcis Pelafgi & Etrufci; Barbari etiam habiti
antiquiffimi Hifpani qui perinde ac Etrufci, a
Phænicibus artes & litteraturam didicere, ut videre
eft in eorum veterrimis numismatis, atque in edito
alphabeto, eorum litteræ eædem fere funt ac
Etrufcæ. Turdetani Hifpanorum doctiffimi, ut
tradit Strabo, & ut fama ejus tempeftate ferebat, a
fex annorum millibus, grammaticam & vetuftiffima
literis infcripta monumenta, quin & poemata,
legefque metris conditas, habuere.—Multa tamen
quæ Bochartus Phænicibus tribuit, vereor ne
etiam Etrufcis tribuenda fint.

SECOND

SECOND LETTER

To Colonel VALLANCEY,

ON THE

HEATHEN STATE,

A N D

ANTIENT TOPOGRAPHY

O F

I R E L A N D.

By CHARLES O'CONOR, Esq.

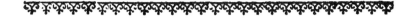

To Colonel VALLANCEY.

S I R,

YOUR reception of an essay of mine, on the antient inhabitants of *Ireland* in the times of heathenism, encourages me to request your further attention to some additional observations on the same subject. Your own learned researches give me a claim to this indulgence; as you are not so diffident of the authorities I made use of, as some writers of *your* native country, who have obtained great and merited celebrity in the republic of letters. The learned Mr. *Whitaker* of *Manchester*, in particular, has pronounced those authorities, groundless; and it is odd enough, but true, that he has preferred the bare assertions of an obscure monk of the fourteenth century, and even the novel of OSSIAN, to all our domestic documents, relative to the times which preceded Christianity in this island. Some learned men of our own country have adopted this judgment, and as they have published it, with additional objections of their own, in the *Collectanea*, I shall, with your indulgence, meet them on the same ground, and endeavour to prove (from their internal evidence alone) the competency of our
domestic

domeſtic documents in affording ſome uſeful information, which we ſhould otherwiſe never obtain.
The diſcuſſion of this matter between us, will at
leaſt, involve one advantage, which is ſeldom
gained from controverſy; the Truth muſt be ſoon
diſcovered; as in an age when criticiſm is under
philoſophic direction, it will take no long time to
decide, whether the Pagans of *Ireland* had a local
literature and civilization, improved by time in their
long repoſe from foreign interruption; or whether
they had been the rudeſt, as they were the moſt
ſequeſtered barbarians in *Europe*. Deciſion, for the
latter alternative, muſt doubtleſs be diſgraceful to
our predeceſſors; but Truth though a barren one,
is preferable to Error, founded on the inventions,
and ſupported by the claims, of domeſtic vanity.

This deciſion is not yet made, and the evidences
for a better, will I am confident, prevail, when
genius and ability unite, for collecting and examining thoſe evidences: I pretend only to exhibit
ſome, and ſome I have produced in my former
Diſſertations, wherein I confeſs that I have fallen
into ſome miſtakes, which on the peruſal of old
manuſcripts, put into my hands by yourſelf and
other friends, I have retracted. They are miſtakes,
however, neither conſiderable in number, nor
weighty in importance. I was not miſtaken as to
the *principal facts*; I ſay the principal facts, for
doubtleſs in the examination of the mythological,
and poetical matter which envelopes the earlieſt accounts of nations, we may miſtake. Thus it is,
and thus it has proved, in our more critical re-

searches, relative to the remoter periods of hiſtory, in every other *European* country, even the moſt en-lightened. It is enough, if we can diſcover ſome leading and uſeful truths, ſtripped of their falſe ornaments; and our ſucceſs on the preſent ſubject will be the more complete, if ſome facts diſcoverable in our earlieſt traditions, can be found to corre-ſpond with thoſe of the learned and diſtant nations of *Europe*, who held no intercourſe of literature or any other commercial engagements, with the an-tient inhabitants of this iſland.

Among thoſe learned nations, I allude to the *Grecians* in particular. The correſpondence between ſome of their oldeſt traditions, and ſome preſerved in *Ireland* among the people we denominate *Mileſians*, ſhews demonſtrably, that the two nations, had ori-ginally the ſame oriental maſters. It proves the early importation of the elements of arts and literature into our Britannic iſles; the Phœnicians have cer-tainly traded with thoſe iſles, and for the ſecurity of their commerce, have, very probably, made ſome ſettlements in each.

The elements of arts, once imported into remote and detached countries, may be obliterated, and no trace left of them in the courſe of revolutions and conqueſts; and from a civilized ſtate, nations may relapſe into their original ſavage life. No ſuch revolution took place in *Ireland*, from the æra of its ſubjection to a colony from the continent, to its limited ſubmiſſion to an Engliſh monarch, in the twelfth century. In a free and unconquered ſtate, they have not loſt the uſe of the elements imported by their Spanish or Celtiberian anceftors. In fome inftances, we find that they made fome progrefs in legiflation and arts, and we difcover, that in fome they made confiderable improvements.

What fuch a nation could have effected, in a long exclufion from any fcientific intercourfe with *Greece* and *Rome*, prefents an object of curiofity; and to take our enquiry from a high principle, the refearch may be rewarded with fome interefting information. You, Sir, have led the way, and have exhibited lights which invite others to enter into it. To know man as a focial being under focial or civil compacts, he fhould be tried by facts, and not eftimated by any refined theory. To add to our ftock of knowledge concerning him, he muft be viewed diftinctly, on every ftage of action; and judged by the influence of local religion, of manners, and of climate, on the action itfelf.

You need not be informed Sir, that very little can be learned, concerning the old inhabitants of this ifland from *Greek* writers, who thought very flightly about them, and who in general meafured the degree of their barbarifm, by the degree of their remotenefs from *Grecian* communication. The *Romans* alfo, who never fet foot in the country, have been much in the fame way of thinking, and both thofe enlightened nations, the former in particular, muft have received moft of their information from fea-faring men, who trafficked here, or occafionally touched on our coafts. Such informers, are generally the leaft to be depended on; they certainly muft know little or nothing of the internal ftate of the country. The Irifh were only known to the

Romans,

Romans, by the battles fought between them in *Britain.*

In this incompetency of foreign testimonies, the antient state of *Ireland* must be as little known, as that of any other northern country, if no credit be due to the documents still preserved in the old language of its inhabitants: and indeed much labour has, of late, been employed, to represent these remains, as the impositions of mercenary bards, on the pride and credulity of barbarous chieftains. It is however very remarkable, that *this sentence before trial*, did not produce its proper effect, in imposing silence on a subject, represented to be of all others, the most unproductive.—Far from it.—To fill up the great void made in time, and that by themselves, imagination, (a powerful instrument in the hands of such writers) was set to work, and soon found materials; the crude tales on *Fin Mac Cumbal*, and other Irish warriors, were picked up, and cast into a new and pleasing form. The principal intention was well answered, and next *to that*, those tales were to serve as the best ground we have, for *Scotish* history. *Oisin*, Fin's (not * Fingal's) son is made the historian. But it is well known, that these tales were at all times taken for what they are, mere amusements for the vulgar, recited in various shapes to this day, among them. They represent

---

* This name of *Fingal* was not known in the highlands of *Scotland*, till introduced by Mr. *Mac Pherson*. He was known there as here, by his proper name, of *Fin Mac Cumbal*, or *Mac Cool*, as we pronounce it. See an account of this *Fin* in the History of *Scotland*, by *Hector Boethius.*

D d 2

Oisin,

Oisin, (not Ossian) the son of *Fin*, as a poet as well as a hero, and some poems fathered on him, I have seen, but the language and matter, shew them to be modern compositions, destitute of taste and elegant invention. The more modern inventor has done *Oisin* more justice; but doubtless, any historical fabric, reared on this foundation cannot stand; and yet such was the immediate effect of this novel of Ossian, that it was thought a foundation of some solidity. Historical hypotheses varied, and in their nature, variable, were erected on it, and it afforded some diversion, to see each edifice demolished, by a new successor in this art of building.

From these theorists in history, and those who give them credit, our appeal to the fragments left us by the old natives, will not be deemed unreasonable. They are abstracts from the larger works which escaped the *Norman* combustions, which raged in *Ireland* through the latter part of the eighth century. In no country has literature suffered a greater destruction; it made a change in the minds of the generality, and on the repulsion of the northern Barbarians, some only, of our great men sat down to collect as much as possible of our historical wreck. Cormac, king and arch-bishop of *Casbel*, began a compilation at *Casbel* in the ninth century, and he complains of the neglect of his countrymen at the time, relative to the history of their ancestors: *Imprudens gens Scotorum,* (says he) *rerum suarum obliviscens; acta eorum quasi inaudita sunt.* The rebuke had its effect. The example of that good prince set other compilers to work, and the check given to the common heathen enemy, afforded leisure

and

and patronage for the undertaking.   Pity it is, that
they confined themfelves to epitomes, or that the
larger works they had before them, are moftly loft:
but to the labours of thefe epitomizers we owe the
prefervation of our earlieft traditions; the Scytho-
Celtic or *Celtiberian* origin of the antient *Scots*, and
their intercourfes with the orientals before their arrival in *Ireland.*—The poets, our firft hiftorians,
have it is true, mixed thefe truths with the heroic
and marvellous, but this was originally the practice
(as I have hinted already) in every *European* country.

On the arrival of the *Scots* in Ireland, arts were
yet in their infancy, through all the regions of the
weft.   It was only in a long courfe of time, that
local fcience was improved, and that laws were
framed and promulgated in this ifland.   Thefe improvements were the work of the Fileas, into whofe
order, as well as that of the Druids, fome of our
greateft princes have entered themfelves, and who
in the midft of the fierceft domeftic hoftilities, enjoyed profound repofe for ftudy.   Their improvements were doubtlefs gradual.   Some good lights
are thrown on particular periods and revolutions,
antecedently to the firft century of our vulgar æra,
when laws were firft committed to writing under
the patronage of *Concovar Mac Neffa*, king of Ulfter.
The epitomizers of the ninth century, have rendered
us this fervice: in other refpects, they exhibit but
little critical knowledge.   Little credit is due to the
catalogue of proper names they give us of Irifh
monarchs before the return of *Tuathal* the acceptable, from his exile in *North Britain*; years of reigns
and

and genealogies ill-regiſtered exhibit for the greater part, but a mere technical ſucceſſion, framed without regard to true chronology, or the ſtate of things in *Europe* before the time of *Cyrus* the great, and even for ſome time after. Theſe kings lived in almoſt a perpetual ſtate of warfare ; and our epitomizers, make no diſtinction between *legitimate* monarchs and *intruders*, who reigned only by their own party, and not by a national or legal election. The ſtate of civil government under monarchs who alternately killed one another in battle, muſt doubtleſs be very defective.

This ſtate of things had a period, and national calamities having arrived at the extreme, during the two deſtructive wars of the *Belgians*, with their *Mileſian taſkmaſters*, a great reform became the conſequence, on the elevation of *Tuathal the Acceptable* to the throne of Teamor, A. D. 130. The *Belgians* (in hatred denominated Attacots) were ſubdued, but reſtored to the privileges of freemen and to power alſo, particularly in the provinces of *Leinſter* and *Conaught*. A new conſtitution, in the order of hereditary ſucceſſion in a ſingle royal family was eſtabliſhed. Reigns of monarchs ; the temporary oppoſition to their adminiſtration, the ſtruggles of factions to ſet aſide the *Tuathalian* conſtitution are accurately recorded, and we meet with a lineal ſucceſſion from father to ſon, of ten monarchs the ableſt that ever reigned in Pagan Ireland. They flouriſhed during the three ages which preceded the converſion of the nation to chriſtianity. Their hiſtory proves the uſe and improvement of arts and letters among them in a high degree, and it can be

averred

averred without the hazard of a miftake, that among all the northern heathen nations of *Europe*, the old inhabitants of *Ireland* are fingular in tranfmitting good memorials of themfelves in their own language, long before the introduction of *Greek* and *Roman* literature among them.

In my former letter to you, fir, I have given fome proofs, that the uninterrupted tradition of the antient *Scuit* or *Scots*, afferting their origin from the *Scytho-Celts* of *Spain*, is well founded. They did not arrive originally from *Britain*, as has been lately advanced on mere conjecture, or equally precarious authority: They fpoke the *Celtic language*, in the form it bore among the *Celtes* or *Scytho·Celts* of *Spain*. In time, they improved it, 'till it became an harmonious, copious and vigorous tongue, and continued ftationary, in its fyntax, after arriving at its claffical ftandard. It could not arrive at this perfection certainly, without the gradual cultivation of it, by letters. It is as different in fyntax from the *Gomaraeg* of our neighbours the *Welfh*, as the modern *Englifh*, is from the *high Dutch* of *Germany* ; and indeed as different as any two tongues, defcended from the fame primævel fource, can be. What but a defcent from different *Celtic* ftocks, could produce fo little kindred of conftruction, in the tongues of the *Britons* and *Scots ?* Imagination prolific in ftarting objections, muft in the inftance before us labour in vain : for you, fir, have foreclofed everydoubt on the fubject. Through your learned refearches, we difcover a great number of oriental terms in the *Irifh* that cannot be found in the *Welfh*, and you demonftrate that thofe oriental words were

were learned on the continent, and imported from it, by a colony of ftrangers, who made a lafting and final fettlement in *Ireland*.

You have fhewn that the antient *Scytbians*, the moft roving people on earth, have wandered into the weft, and mixed with the *Celtes* of *Spain*, whofe language and manners were originally little different from their own. There, thefe *Scytbo-Celtes* were vifited, and inftructed by the *Phænicians*, and their *Cartbaginian* pofterity. Thus inftructed, a party among them, either too crowded at home, or opprefled by power, or impelled by fome other caufe, migrated into *Ireland*; hither they imported a particular dialect called the *Phænian*, in the explanation of which you have made a good progrefs : Hither they brought the elements of fymbolical writing, and letters in a number of fixteen cyphers, fuch as prevailed even in *Greece* before the additional alphabetical cyphers were invented. Such veftiges with the new lights you have caft upon them, from the oriental tongues, are fuperior in authenticity to the moft antient infcriptions.

Some traditions of the antient *Scots*, relative to their *Celtiberian* original, but omitted in my former letter, may properly have a place in this : The *Braga* and *Medobriga*, the *Hiberi* and *Herminii* of Spain, gave an origin, undoubtedly, to the *Breagh*, *Midbe-Breagb*, the *Hiberi* and *Heremonii* of Ireland. The *Finey-Breagb* of *Meatb*, called alfo *Clan-Breogbain*, we latinize *Brigantes*, and they were doubtlefs of the fame Celtic ftock with the other roving *Brigantes* of *Europe*.

The

The *Hiberi* and *Heremonii*, were the principal royal families of *Ireland*. The former who had their chief settlements in the south, held a correspondence with their parent country, of which we have an illustrating instance at the close of the second century; *Eogan* the great, king of *Munster*, exiled from his country by the *Heremonii*, took refuge under a *Spanish* prince of *Gallicia*, who received him with great sympathy. The *Irish Hiberian*, insinuated himself so much into the favour of the *Spanish* prince, that he shortly obtained the latter's sister in marriage, and after some time, he obtained also, a number of *Spanish* forces, at whose head he invaded *Ireland*, and regained not only his former government, but obliged the then reigning monarch of *Ireland*, to surrender up to him the dominion of half the island.

This revolution, one of the best authenticated in the history of the *antient Scots*, is well worthy of attention. It draws the earlier times into a contract with the middle ages, and it proves that the *Celtic* of *Ireland*, was still intelligible in the kingdom of *Gallicia*.* If the *Milesian Irish* were not descended from a *Spanish* stock, is it credible, that any tribe among them, would apply for succour, to a foreign

* After what has been advanced, on the *Spanish* extraction of the *antient Scots*, it will be vain to assert, that the evidences which depose for the fact, are not to be credited, unless incontestible proofs are produced to shew their incompetency.—In vain will it be, to oppose to those evidences, the contradictory hypotheses of Mr. *Mac Pherson*, and Mr. *Whitaker*.—See the Rev. Mr. *Ledwich*'s letter to Governor *Pownall*, Collectanea, No. 11. Pag. 432. 433.

and

and remote people, who muft be ftrangers to them, and to their language ?

The expedition of the *Scuit* or *Scots* from the Continent, to Ireland, cannot be afcertained with chronological exactnefs. We are however certain, that it took place, before the feveral dialects of the *primæval Celtic*, were transformed into tongues of different conftruction, like thofe of *Ireland* and *Wales*. From other ftrong marks in our earlieft reports, that migration muft come about, fome ages before the chriftian æra. On their arrival, thefe new comers, though conquerors, were greatly inferior in number to the natives, who were of *Britifh extraction*. It took a long time before their pofterity multiplied into numbers fufficient, for attempting any fettlement in a foreign land, efpecially in a country not very inviting, from its inferiority to their own, in fertility. In the third century, and not fooner, they obtained the fettlement of a colony in the coarfeft part of *North-Britain*, under *Carbry Riada*, the fon of *Conary*, 2d, whofe chronology (when monarch of Ireland) is well fet forth by Primate *Ufher*. The motives to that firft fettlement of the *Scots* in Britain, it may not be improper to mention here.

About the year 256 *Cormac o Cuinn*, the moft celebrated of our heathen monarchs, had his authority renounced to, by the *Ultonians*, the conftant enemies of his family. After defeating thofe rebels in feveral engagements, their remains fled for fhelter into the ifles and continent of North Britain. Supplied with an excellent militia, difciplined under the famous *Fin Mac Cumbal*, his commander in chief, and

and his fon-in-law, *Cormac*, followed his rebellious
fubjects into the places of their retreat. The terror
of his power brought matters to a fpeedy iffue. By
confent or force, he obtained from the *Picts*, a fettlement in *Kentire* and *Argyle* for his father's nephew *Carbry Riada* abovementioned; Thro' that
colonization (under his kinfman) he left no foreign
afylum open for his *Ultonian* enemies, whofe power
in *Ulster* he alfo curtailed, by ftripping them of the
territory now called the county of Antrim, with
fome contiguous diftricts well marked by *Ufher*.
That territory as well as the other in *North-Britain*, had the name of *Dalriada*, from *Carbry Riada*
their firft vaffal fovereign under the *Irifh Monarch*,
who vefted him with authority. Thus commenced
the power of the antient *Scots in Britain*, in the third
century, where it encreafed by degrees, till they obtained, finally, the fovereignty of nearly the whole
kingdom of *North-Britain*, as limited at the prefent
time.

To this firft fettlement of the *Scots* in *Britain*
under *Carbry Riada*, *Bede* bears teftimony. No fact
in the annals of *Ireland*, in the moft profperous
ftate of its monarchy, bears ftronger fignatures of
authenticity. But this fact has been contradicted
lately by two writers, of the name of Mac Pherfon,
who to the authority of the antients, have oppofed
their own: Yet the philofophic hiftorian, the profound thinker, and fine writer, * *Mr. Gibbon*, con-
feffes that he has on the prefent fubject, adopted
thofe gentlemen as *his guides* preferably to all our
Irifh documents, and to the venerable *Saxon* hifto-

* Hiftory of the Roman Empire, Dub. edit. vol. 4. p. 262.

rian.

rian. The preference is indeed amazing, efpecially from a writer, who in other refpects, is far
from being too credulous. His refigning himfelf
to fuch guides is not more extraordinary, than it
is unphilofophical.

From the teftimonies produced in this, and my
former letter, addreffed to yourfelf, Sir, I have, I
truft, given incontrovertible proofs of the true origin
of the antient *Scots*, and of their early initiation into
fome arts of the orientals. I have, I hope, fhewn
that this people, on their poffeffing themfelves of
this remote ifland, have not loft therein the ufe of
the elements of knowledge, imported by their anceftors from a country where thofe elements were
taught; but that they made improvements, fuch as
a fequeftered and undifturbed nation, might in favourable conjectures, accomplifh, and in fact, did
accomplifh.—Until you took it in hand, this fubject
has been little attended to, or it was rather wholly
neglected. The learned of our country, in general,
ftrangers to our antient literature, and to the language which preferves it, cannot be brought to believe that we had any civilization or literature, till the
introduction of *both*, by the firft preachers of the
gofpel. You and I know feveral learned men,
who are of this way of thinking. They reafon
from a precarious principle of analogy; for finding
little memory left of things which paffed in *Britain*
before its invafion by the *Romans*, they infer that we
muft be ftill lefs informed, relative to affairs in
Ireland; the argument is not conclufive. *Britain*,
a fine country near the continent, being frequently
expofed to revolutions from invading ftrangers,
the

the civil œconomy of the indigenous inhabitants
was foon diffolved, in the eftablifhments made by
new comers ; as thefe in time, gave way to other
eftablifhments, made by frefh invaders. Finally,
the *Romans* effaced the memory of all preceding
tranfactions, among tribes they denominated rude
and unhofpitable Barbarians, and had they poffeffed
themfelves of *Ireland,* we may be affured, that we
fhould know as little of its preceding ftate, as we
now know of that of *South Britain,* before their
conqueft of it.

When *Cæfar* invaded *Britain, Ireland* was peopled
by *Scots, Belgians, Domnonians, Danans* and *Galenians.*
The *Romans* comprehended *all,* under the name of
Hiberni, of whom they knew little or nothing. In
the following reign of *Auguftus, Propertius* mentions
the *Scuta-Brigantes,* which *Scaliger* has corrected
into *Scoto-Brigantes,* but each reading is good : the
Clan-Breogain, and *Kinea-Scuit,* that is the *Brigantes*
and *Scots,* (defcended from the fame ftock) were
then the dominant people in *Ireland* ; but it was only
in the third century, that the general name of *Scoti*
became familiar to the *Romans,* and fubftituted to
that of *Hiberni.* From the time that *Agricola* governed in *Britain,* to the arrival of the *Saxons* in
the fifth century, the *Scots,* in frequent alliances
with their neighbours, the *Cruthneans* or *Picts,* have
often made incurfions into the *Roman province.*
Through a period of more than three hundred
years, they frequently meafured their arms, with
the greateft people in the world, and in thus fig-
nalizing themfelves abroad, they certainly muft be
powerful at home. They were divided, it is true,

by

by domeſtic factions; but they were occaſionally brought to ſuſpend their internal quarrels, and to unite, not to defend themſelves, but to invade others; it is a proof that they were governed by monarchs of great ability and influence. Thus, the annals that have been hitherto preſerved, repreſent them through the reigns of the twelve monarchs of the *Tuathalian* line, who reigned before the reception of the goſpel; and doubtleſs, no ſucceſs of political wiſdom can be more difficult, than to repreſs internal animoſities, and reſtore concord among a divided people, in countries eſpecially, where, through defects in the civil conſtitution, freedom too often degenerates into licentiouſneſs.

Thus, Sir, have I given in this, and a former letter, the outlines of Iriſh hiſtory in its Pagan ſtate; in theſe deſultory notices I pretend to no more.— From the arrival of the *Scuit* or *Scots*, to the *Eamanian æra*, our accounts are ſo blended with poetic inventions, during the infancy of literature, that moſt of the reports contained therein are uncertain.— From the erection of the houſe of *Eamania*, ſix generations before Chriſt, we have more light thrown on affairs; but ſtill the genealogies of princes and their ſucceſſion, have been ill regiſtered. It is only on the concluſion of the civil wars between the *Mileſians* and *Belgians*, and the elevation of *Tuathal the acceptable*, to the throne of Teamor, that exactneſs in moſt of our dates and facts took place.

Thus, Sir, you ſee that I have received almoſt all my information about the earlier times, from our own domeſtic documents: foreign writers could

afford

afford me but little, as they knew but little, and
even that from hearfay, and precarious evidence.
When the monuments I perufed, are brought under
critical examination by *critical ability*, I think, that
an edifying part of *European hiſtory*, will at length
appear. The conventions of *Teamor*, of *Tlachta*,
and of *Taltion*, will exhibit a people who enjoyed a
peculiar and ufeful, local civilization, and who
availed themfelves of the advantages attending the
fine arts of poetry and mufic; arts which cultivated
uninteruptedly in this iſland, through a long fuc-
ceſſion of ages, infer a perfection, which muſt have
a vaſt influence on the human mind, and human
conduct. A philofophic genius, one of our monarchs of the third century, laboured for the
eſtabliſhment of natural religion in his kingdom,
and quarrelled with the Druids: he likewife endeavoured in his idea of legiſlation, to balance the
regal, the ariſtocratic and popular diviſions of power, into a fyſtem of good government, and he had
fome fucceſs; but it was not laſting; things fell
but too foon into their former diforder. Through
want of authority to enforce, or of talents to recommend, or perhaps without a wiſh to perfect
what the wifdom of one prince had planned;
Cormac's legiſlation did not operate long with vigour. The Oligarchs of *Ireland*, with their fubordinate factions, prevailed againſt it, and perhaps,
fuch a balanced *civil conſtitution* as *Cormac* intended,
cannot remain in vigour long, in any country. It
muſt be fufpended, or have but a faint operation
among a turbulent people, always in arms, and
too often governed more by hoſtile animofities,

than

than by laws. It was too frequently the case in *Ireland*, and in any kingdom thus circumstanced, several barbarous habits and customs are unavoidable. If in some instances this kingdom suffered from barbarous customs, the same reproach may be made *at this day*, to several nations of *Europe*, who boast so much of being enlightened: In a word, the civil evils of *Ireland* were owing to defects in the civil constitution; they were evils which led to anarchy, and ended in it.

Thus, sir, to the testimonies I have produced in my *former* letter to you, on the origin and local civilization of the antient *Scots* in their pagan state, I have in the *present*, subjoined some further elucidations; and many more relative to the three ages antecedent to the reception of the gospel might be produced. When we descend to the christian times, a more edifying subject will present itself. Throguh the sixth, seventh, and the greater part of the eighth century, when a cloud of Gothic darkness was spread over the western continent, this island became a centre, wherein the rays of true knowledge have been collected. Hither, students from most parts of christendom have resorted, and found an hospitable retreat. In the districts called *Termous*, the study of the sciences, was free from invasion or interruption, (as happened in the colleges of the Fileas in pagan times,) and this security remained inviolate, even in the most cruel exertions of civil warfare. It proves how much our civil vices, have been compensated by great virtues. The fact is glorious, and stands singular in the History of Nations.

You

You see, sir, that in this, as in my former essays on our insular antiquities, I pretend only to outlines, in hope, that genius and ability may be induced to work upon them, and give us an instructive picture of the singular manners and arts of a people long sequestered, in a sequestered island. It may be said that the subject has novelty in a considerable degree to recommend it, as we must confess, that the antient state of Ireland, heathen and christian, has not hitherto been exhibited with the advantages required for rendering history edifying: The materials for ours, have been long dispersed* thro' several countries : Few have had access to them, and fewer understood the language in which they are written : Unfortunately also, some native writers, wanting critical discernment to select the valuable from the useless, in the fragments they perused, have rather produced a disgust to examine, than any curiosity to investigate, whatever may be found profitable in our authentic documents. Such of the latter as fell into my hands, (and for some of the best I am indebted to you, sir) I have, I hope, made some good use of. I have surely gone on better grounds than some living hypotheses writers, who rather diverted than instructed us, in confuting one another.

I made little account of what the Fileas and Bards have left us on the first discoverers of this

---

* Many of these materials have been lately recovered, and are to be deposited in our own library of Trinity College, thro' the indulgence of a very worthy gentleman, Sir John Sebright, Bart. Trinity College is also enriched with a very considerable collection of our best Irish annals.

ifland. Like the other European nations in the earlieft times, the firft inhabitants of this country, led the favage life of herdfmen and rovers, who in a foreft ifland, had great plenty of game, and other means of fubfiftance, from our fruitful lakes and fea coafts. In a more improved ftate of fociety, new tribes of *Belgians* and *Danans* arrived from South and North Britain. Thefe fucceffors are worthy of notice, as they had a form of civil government on the monarchical plan ; had bounded territories, and fixed habitations ; ultimately, a people denominated *Scuit* or *Scots*, invaded this ifland, and having more knowledge in arts, than the people they found before them, they foon became mafters, and continued in power, with little interruption, till the diffolution of their monarcly, A. D. 1022, on the deceafe of *Malachy*, 2d, the laft monarch of Ireland of the *Clan-Colman* line.

The Scots having thus gained an eftablifhment among the old natives, the fmaller among the greater number ; the former labouring to enlarge their power, and the latter to preferve their property, jealoufies arofe, and contentions ended often, in bloody conflicts ; a ftate of things very deftructive to internal improvements, but unavoidable in times, when liberty was deemed of little value, without property in land, and when ambition had no means of extending power, but by a violent invafion of land. Partial injuries produced a general infurrection in the firft century of our chriftian æra. A cruel civil war enfued ; the Belgians under the opprobious name of Attocots [ᴁᴄhᴀᴄhᴄuᴀᴄᴀ] feized on the government, fet up a monarch of their

own

own, and expelled the royal Hugonian family, who were obliged to take fhelter under their Cruthenian kindred in *North Britain.* Miferies brought to the extreme, produced a reform, and the *Scots* were reftored to power under *Tuathal* the acceptable about the 30th year of the fecond century ; of this great revolution I have made mention before, and I recur to it here, as an ufeful period for tracing the topography of Ireland, through the antecedent and fubfequent times.

Our antient topography may afford but a dry entertainment, to the generality of readers ; but no antiquary fhould overlook it, as its ufe is confiderable in cafting good lights on the chronology of revolutions, and of other partial events. Some names of places and diftricts before the arrival of the Scots in Ireland, are preferved to this day, but moft denominations have been loft, in new names impofed by thofe Scots, as they gradually ufurped upon the old inhabitants, and their ufurpations from the fecond century downwards, have been more and more numerous, till they poffeffed themfelves of nearly the whole landed property of the kingdom, before the middle of the fifth century.

From this inveftigation, it will appear, that fince the reform made in Eamania and the fucceffion of Hugony the great, fix generations before the chriftian æra, the Scots were a felf-civilized people : That from the fecond to the ninth century, they were a very powerful, and (as the Roman writers have confeffed,) a very martial nation, not an aggregate of woodland rovers, without fixed habitations, till the tenth century, as Mr. Beauford has re-

E e 2 prefented

prefented them. Indeed Mr. Beauford is alone in the reprefentation, and he fhall be fpoke to here-after, on the prefent fubject of our antient topography.

Of the pofterity of thofe we may well call the indigenous inhabitants of Ireland in their feveral tribes and cantonements, as they ftood in the fecond century, we have a very antient and curious fragment preferved in the compilations of Glendalogh and Lecan : a copy from the former I found in the book of Balimote, and it agrees exactly with the copy from Lecan, taken by the great antiquary Duald Mac Firbis, whofe book (in his own hand writing,) on this and other fubjects relating to our antiquities, is now in the poffeffion of the Earl of Roden, a nobleman whofe defcent from one of the moft antient families in Europe, is his fmalleft recommendation.

Of the afore-mentioned fragment, (correfpondent with the ftate of things in the fecond century) I here give you a copy; it will prove that in that age, this was a country thickly peopled.

LEINSTER, firft denominated the province of the Galenians.

This province had three divifions, parcelled a-mong the Figdii, the Focmonii, and the Atacdii.

The Figdii inhabited the Fortauth of Leinfter, and Hy-Falgy.

The Focmonii fettled in the other parts of Hy-Falgy, in the Fothart Dairbreach, in Almain, and in the old diftrict of the Martinei.

The

The Atacdii on the eaftern diftrict of the Liffey, and extending to the fea.

The tribe of Bracradii in Leinfter Deafgabar, that is, in Offory.

MUNSTER.

The Treternii were fettled in Moy-Breogan, afterwards called the Eoganacht of Cafhel.

The Seamonii, in the Defies of Munfter.

The Caratii in Hy-Liathan, and Hy-Macally.

The Bibragii in Corcolaige, or Munfter Carbry.

The Narbconii in Fermoy.

The Bantragii in the Munfter Hy-Echach.

The Martinei in Mufkry Mitaine, in Eaft Femin, in Liagtuaill, in Tir-Aoda, in Breogan and Hy-Carbry.

The old Ernai in Kerry and Luachar Degad.

The Morcii and Geblinii in Hy-Conall.

The Rudii in Corcomroe.

The Eamaneii in Ormond and Ely.

The Numorii or Umorii in Dal-cas, and the South Hy-Fiacra, (called Hy-Fiacra-Aine.)

The Cathbarrii in Corco-Muchad, Corco-bafkin, Corco-Duibne, Corcomroe, and Corco-laige in Ely.

The Ducnii in Mufkry, and the Ocnii in Hy-Conall.

The Fernmii in the Eoganacht of Ros-Arged and in Aran.

CONAGHT, firft called OLNEGMACHT.

The Catragii in Hy-Maney-South.

The Concobarnii and Numoril in Hy-Brune, and the Confines of Loch-Kimey.

The

The Senkenel in North Hy-Maney.

The Tresenii in the Conmacney from Balimoe to the ocean.

Another tribe of the Numorii or Umorii in Umhal.

The Domnonii in Keara, in Tirawly, and in the North Hy-Fiacra from the river Roba to Drumcliffe.

The Cruthenians, (or painted men) in Moy-Hai, extending from Loch-ke to Bruiol, and to the Shanon.

The Cregrai, in the Leyney of Conaght, particularly in the parts adjoining Loch Teket (now O'Gara's Lake) Ceran, and the Barnas (the Defile) of Tir-olioll, and thence to Moyturey.

U L S T E R.

The Facmonii, and Guarii in Ros-Goll and Iargoll in a district of Tirconall, extending from Easroe to Moy-Ketney.

The Ardusi in Tyrone; a part of the North-Hy-Niall from Sliaw-an-Carn to Lough-Foyle, and thence to the Barnas (the Defile or Strait) of Tir-Aadha, and thence to the river Banna.

The Cruthenians in Ulad and Moy-Cobha.

The Buanii and the Sallii in Dal-Arady.

The Nemlurgii in Orgiall, from Glin to Loch-Erne, and from the Banna to Loch-Feval, now Lough Foyle.

M E A T H.

The Ligmanii in the Galeng of East Meath.

The Treogai in West Meath.

The

The Mafragii in Moy-Slecht and Hy-Brune-Breffny, (this mifplaced, as Hy-Brune belonged to Conaght.)

The Arbri in Teffa.

The Glafradii about Loch Silen in the Carbry of Meath.

The Conragii about Sliaw-Breagh, and in Mogorn, in Hy-Segan, in Fera-Ros, in Fera-Arda, in Fera-Lorg, and in the two Cremthans.

The Lugnii were placed in Breagh, in Hy-Laogary, in Hy-Mac-Uais, in Ardgal, and the parts leading from the Delvins to Cluan-Erard.

On the firft view, Sir, you will no doubt, judge that the above topography, regarding an antient period of Irifh hiftory, with a retrofpect to the foregoing times (up to Hugony the Great) will require confiderable notes and illuftrations; were they prepared, it would not be reafonable to expect room for them in a letter, already (I fear) deduced to too great a length. You have here a bare lift only of moft of the tribes of Britifh extraction, who had feparate diftricts among the Scots in the fecond century. From that time, the former were lofing ground gradually, but yet with hard ftruggles for their poffeffions. Irritated by the memory of former injuries, and inflamed by recent hoftilities; the encroachments on one fide, and the refiftance on the other, rendered the deftruction of one or other of the parties inevitable. The Scots prevailed. Before the end of the third century, the Heberians of the race of Olioll Olom, reduced the whole province of Munfter under their jurifdiction. The

Here-

Heremonians feized on Conaght, and annihilated the power of the Belgians there, as well as in Meath, which extended from the Shanon to the fea. They alfo fubdued and occupied the far greater part of Ulfter, leaving Uladh, (now called the County of Down) to the Milefian Rudricians. In a word, the reduction of all the old tribes of the kingdom was complete before the middle of the fifth century. With the lofs of power, they loft all confequence; they lived in a ftate of obfcure freedom, and we hear no more of them to deferve particular notice in hiftory.

We fhould obferve on this fubject, that as new diftricts belonging to the Belgians, have been from time to time occupied by new mafters, new names have been impofed by the occupants, and the old denominations were at length forgot, in moft of thofe diftricts. The change to new names began before the firft century; the gradual impofition of them is of great ufe in chronology, and from the firft to the tenth century, a more accurate topography than that of Ireland cannot be made out, in any northern country of Europe.

A topography of Ireland, (correfpondent with the early ages,) having lately appeared in the XIth Number of the *Collectanea*, I muft draw upon your patience for attention, to a few obfervations on that performance.—The author goes on ground, never I am pofitive, trod before by any writer, antient or modern, and I am very confident he will be left alone in it, even by the followers of the *Monk of Cirencefter*. His very firft ftep on this ground, is indeed a ftumble. " Little or no knowledge (he
tells

" tells us) relative to this fubject, can be obtained
" from foreign, and not much from our domeftic
" writers."—Where then, and from what ftores,
has Mr. *Beauford* collected his informations? He
certainly is not barren on a fubject, which he has
declared barren. With a liberal hand he deals out
facts to us through a number of 172 pages; he
only forgot to authenticate the far greater number,
and his not attempting to authenticate any, would
furely be prefuming too much on the credulity of
the moft ignorant age.—This conduct in an Antiquarian is extraordinary, and cannot be more fo,
than his confidence in etymologies, when it appears
with certainty, that he has obtained but very fu-
perficial knowledge of the antient language of this
ifland.—To fuggeft that he had an intention to
miflead or traduce, would be unfair; and yet,
what apology can be interpofed in his favour,
where he charges our old writers with facts they
never advanced, and facts alfo the very reverfe of
which is found, and invariably found in their
writings?—It is a charge that admits of no juftifi-
cation, and the beft apology we can make for him
is, that he has pronounced with equal temerity and
decifivenefs, on works which he has never perufed!

With writers in print, he has not indeed taken
the fame liberty of making them fay, what they did
not, but he rejects moft of what they borrowed
from our domeftic documents, and in facts the
moft material. Let me trouble you with one inftance, among a hundred examples that could be
produced. Our old writers are unanimous in the
affertion,

affertion, that (prior to the chriftian era) a colony from *Spain* arrived in *Ireland*, conducted by the fons of *Golamb*, furnamed by the Bards *Milea Efpane*, that is, the *Spanifh foldier or hero*; they add further, that thefe foreign adventurers have reduced the old natives, under their power, and that * Heremon, one of Golamh's fons, was declared king of Ireland, and the firft monarch of the Scots race : There is nothing incredible in this account, as I have obferved before. ' The memory of fo great a revolution, in an undifturbed country for many ages, could be preferved by bare tradition, and it could not fail of being fo effectually, in an ifland where the inhabitants, or the principal men among them had the ufe of writing in alphabetic cyphers, as well as in fymbolical characters. But Mr. *Beauford* rejects this account, and he does fo, upon grounds, which are yet unknown to the public. I give you fome of his pofitions in the following order.

1. † The Bolgæ fettled firft in the county of Meath under the conduct of *Hugony*, or *Learmon*. —Where is the proof ?

2. The Bolgæ gave the name of Heremon to the province of Leinfter, and to themfelves that of Heremonii.—Where is the proof ?

---

* The words of a writer of the eighth century (Angus the Culdee) may not be improperly quoted here. Hibernia infula inter duos filios principales Militis, Heremon et Heber divifa eft.—Heremon feptentrionalem partem cum monarchia accepit.—Heremon autem, *primus de Scotis* omnem Hiberniam regnavit, &c.

† See Collectanea, p. 263.

3. From

3. From the chief of the tribe of Heremonii, all the fubfequent kings of Meath, and monarchs of Ireland, were obliged to derive their origin, to obtain the dignity.—No proof of this.

4. Heremon fignifies *a weftern country.*—By no torture of words or ductility of language, can this be proved, any more than *Heber* denoting the *moft weftern country.*—It is, in truth, one of thofe etymological vifions, of which old *Buchanan* complained in his time. *Ifto enim modo quodlibet ex quolibet licebit effingere.*

5. In the beginning of the fecond century, Heremon, the original feat of the Bolgæ, was divided into two diftinct provinces by *Tuathal Teachtmar,* under the denomination of Northern and Southern Heremon, &c.

I fhall not follow Mr. Beauford through 170 pages, in remarking on thefe capital pofitions, and the variety of *hitherto unheard of* facts, which he has eftablifhed on them. The tafk would be equally irkfome and fruitlefs; when he exhibits proofs for the authority of thofe facts, unincumbered with fanciful etymologies, he fhall be attended to: but I crave pardon for your attending to me fo long, and be affured, fir, that I am, with great truth,

Your very faithful, and

very obedient fervant,

March 20, 1783.

C. O'CONOR.

CURIO's

CURIO's
SECOND LETTER
T O
COLONEL VALLANCEY.

SIR,

ENCOURAGED by the favourable reception given to my firſt attempt on Iriſh Antiquities, and highly flattered by the Poſtſcript, I am induced to dedicate this ſecond little production on that ſubject to you; to you, ſir, who have laboured with ſo much advantage to this country, and ſo much honour to yourſelf, and rouſed up a deſire of reſearch on ſubjects ſo important, which have lain dormant for ages, and, but for you, would have been ſtill unſought.

On a tour, laſt ſummer, I paſſed through the county of Down, and having heard much of the antient city of Ardglaſs, I viſited it, and was greatly ſtruck with its ſituation and remains, a ſhort deſcription of which ſhall be the ſubject of the following pages.

If ſome abler perſon had the ſame opportunities that I have, the world would be much advantaged by their obſervations.

But no one can have a greater reſpect for Colonel Vallancey's labours than
His unknown, moſt obedient ſervant,
W. M.
J. G.

DESCRIPTION

DESCRIPTION of the Antient City of ARDGLASS.

THE town of Ardglafs is situated in the county of
Down, seven miles south east of Downpatrick; it
stands on a high promontary, surrounded on three
sides by the sea—on the north by its own harbour,
on the east by the Irish sea, and on the south by
the bay or harbour of Killough, which running
from south to north, at full tide, leaves but an
isthmus. Its name I take to be derived from the
two words, Ard—high, and Glafs—strong. It
at present exhibits a striking spectacle of its antient strength and importance, being composed of a
number of castles, a ruined church, and a few
houses; but what is most worthy the attention of a
curious traveller is, a long range of building (also
in the castle stile) called by the inhabitants, the
New Works, although they have no tradition for
what use or intent this great building was erected,
nor do I find that any person in our time has made
observations on it. The history of the county
Down mentions it slightly, but erroneously.

It is situated close to the harbour, on a rocky
shore, and washed by the sea on its north end and
the rear; its front is to the west; it extends 250
feet in length, in breadth only 24; the thickness of
the walls three feet; it has three towers in front
joined to it, one at each end, and one in the centre,
which shews the design uniform and elegant. It
has (as appears by the corbel-stones and places in
the walls where the timbers were lodged) been
divided

divided into 18 different apartments, and the same number above, with a stair-case in the centre. Each of the towers had three rooms, 10 feet square, with broad-flagged floors so contrived and lodged in the walls, that they supported each other without any timbers. Each apartment on the ground-floor had a small gothic door and a large square window, which plainly shews they were shops, or ware-rooms, occupied at some very early period of time by merchants who came by sea (from what country is left to conjecture) but it must have been in summer, and summer only, as their lodging-rooms were over each shop, and could not be habitable in winter, being so exposed to the sea and having no fire-places, as it is remarkable that in the whole building there were but two fire-places, designed by the Architect (but were by him stopped up again with flags) one in each gable. The rooms on the ground-floor have been seven feet high, the upper-rooms but six and an half, in each of which rooms is a small water-closet, the flue of which runs down through the wall and was washed at bottom by the sea; some of the flagged seats remain perfect: this was a piece of luxury our ancestors had no idea of, nor was it till the present century such indulgences came into use. Within 10 feet of the south tower of this building stands a square castle, 40 feet by 30: it consists of two stories, and from the fire-places and other marks, appears to have been the kitchen and dining-hall belonging to the merchants. It is called the Horn-Castle, from quantities of ox,

deer,

deer, and goats horns being found about it; which plainly difcovers its former ufe.

Near to this is another fmall caftle called, the Cow'd-Caftle, which I underftand to be the Cow-Caftle, in which were kept, or through it were driven the cows, which made the greateft part of our bartered commodities.

King's-Caftle is a large building, now in repair and inhabited; it ftands weft, and over the principal gate to the land fide.

Jordan's-Caftle ftands in the centre of the town, and appears to have been the citadel; it is a very elegant pile, and though it has ftood upwards of 150 years without a roof, not a ftone of it has failed; at the door is a fine fpring-well.

There are the remains of other caftles and gates, whofe names are loft. It is fome what remarkable, that no two of them are on the fame eftate, or the fame perfon's property, although all ftand on about fix acres of ground.

Searching about for infcriptions, or cut-ftone, I made no difcovery but of this one—a coat armorial, cut on a red free-ftone, and much injured by time; it now compofes part of the wall of a cow-houfe, and is placed upfide down:

 It appears to me to be the armorial bearing of the city of London, prior to the year 1381, in which year, being the fourth of Richard the fecond, the dagger was added (in the dexter chief canton) to the arms, in commemoration of the rebel Watt Tyler being flain by Sir William Wallworth, Mayor of London, with that weapon.

This

This may lead to a very probable conjecture, that a London trading company was eftablifhed at a very early period in the port of Ardglafs, and that the New Works was no other than their bazar, or hall, to which they reforted in fummer. —If this can be admitted, that company muft have place, in point of antiquity, to any now known.

I obferve, that fo late as the beginning of Charles the firft's reign, the duties of the port of Ardglafs were let to farm.

We propofe to furnifh our readers with an accurate Drawing of the plan and elevation of this curious building, in a future number of this work.

CPSIA information can be obtained at www.ICGtesting.com
Printed in the USA
BVOW08s1059180914

367402BV00018B/268/P